A GREEN
ESTATE

A GREEN ESTATE

Restoring Independence in Madagascar

Gillian Feeley-Harnik

Smithsonian Institution Press
Washington and London

Editor: Robin A. Gould
Production Editor: Kathryn Stafford
Designer: Janice Wheeler

Library of Congress Cataloging-in-Publication Data

Feeley-Harnik, Gillian, 1940-
 A Green Estate: Restoring Independence in Madagascar / Gillian Feeley-Harnik.
  p. cm.—(Smithsonian series in ethnographic inquiry)
 Includes bibliographical references and index.
 ISBN 0-87474-440-7   ISBN 1-56098-090-7 (pbk)
  1. Sakalava (Malagasy people)—Kings and rulers—Religious aspects.
2. Sakalava (Malagasy people)—Kinship. 3. Ancestor worship—Madagascar—History.   I. Title.   II. Series.
DT469.M277S355 1991
969.1—dc20   90-26394

Frontispiece: The *ampanjaka* Soazara, from a series of photographs at her *doany* in Analalava, probably around 1936, when the Malagasy nationalist Ralaimongo attempted to gain Sakalava support by restoring her to her father's *doany* at Antognibe, and her guardians enlisted the aid of French authorities in preventing what they saw as a highlander's attempt to kidnap her (Service Photo-Cinéma du Ministère de l'Information; TY 13, no. 19).

Poetry on dedication page is by Ben Belitt, "From the Firehouse (for Paul Feeley)," *Possessions: New and Selected Poems, 1938-1985*, p. 39. Boston, David R. Godine. Quoted with author's permission.

Wallace Stevens, "Anecdote of the Jar," quoted by permission of Alfred K. Knopf, Inc., and Faber and Faber, Ltd.

Other permissions are indicated in the Preface.

British Library Cataloguing-in-Publication Data available
Manufactured in the United States of America
10   9   8   7   6   5   4   3   2   1
00   99   98   97   96   95   94   93   92   91   90   89

∞The paper used in this publication meets the minimum requirements of the American National Standard for Performance of Paper for Printed Library Materials Z39.48-1984.

For permission to reproduce illustrations appearing in this book, please correspond directly with the owners of the works, as listed in the individual captions. The Smithsonian Institution Press does not retain reproduction rights for these illustrations or maintain a file of addresses for photo sources

For my parents
Paul Terence Feeley (1910-1966) and Helen Webster

Living between two fires and two falls . . .

and for
Alan, Vanessa, and Paul
who have lived and relived these experiences with me

Ny fitiavako anareo tsy mety simba

Smithsonian Series in Ethnographic Inquiry

Ivan Karp and William L. Merrill, Series Editors

Ethnography as fieldwork, analysis, and literary form is the distinguishing feature of modern anthropology. Guided by the assumption that anthropological theory and ethnography are inextricably linked, this series is devoted to exploring the ethnographic enterprise.

ADVISORY BOARD

Richard Bauman (Indiana University), Gerald Berreman (University of California, Berkeley), James Boon (Princeton University), Stephen Gudeman (University of Minnesota), Shirley Lindenbaum (New School for Social Research), George Marcus (Rice University), David Parkin (University of London), Roy Rappaport (University of Michigan), Renato Rosaldo (Stanford University), Annette Weiner (New York University), Norman Whitten (University of Illinois), and Eric Wolf (City University of New York).

Contents

Figures

Plates

Preface and Acknowledgments

This book is about the international division of labor as seen from the perspective of people living in northwestern Madagascar in the postcolonial period of the 1970s. *Zanaka misy vola tsy sahira,* "Children with money don't struggle," as one popular proverb puts it. But here, as in many other parts of the world, people struggle. Moving about constantly in an effort to make a living, they divide themselves, their families, their friends, and supporters among rural villages where they grow crops, provincial centers where they seek wage labor, and religious centers where they continue to serve the ancestors of the royal dynasty that once ruled this area.

The French conquered Madagascar in 1895, or, more accurately, subdued diverse Malagasy polities over a period of several years beginning in 1895. Madagascar achieved independence in 1960. Yet Sakalava royalty and French colonial officials were still powerfully present in the Analalava region in the 1970s—in people's consciousness of radical change, but also in their acute awareness of work left undone, especially royal services (like reconstructing the royal tomb) that were prohibited during the colonial and immediate postcolonial periods. Ancestral and historical figures continued to interact with the living in the same place with much of the same intensity, albeit in different forms. People in the area began rebuilding the royal tomb when I was living in the area, so I too have focused on why they continued working for royal ancestors in the face of conflicting demands on their labor. These demands have persisted since the early nineteenth century, when slavery was fundamental to the political economy of the region, to the postcolonial decade of the 1970s, when wage labor had become essential to existence. I have tried to clarify their choices as a way of clarifying those of people in comparable circumstances elsewhere. As yet another participant in their expanding network of labor relations, I have also tried to clarify my own.

Most of the research for this book was done in Madagascar over a period of two years and four months in 1971–1973. I was then a Ph.D. candidate in anthropology at New York University, supported by funding from the National Institute of Mental Health (Predoctoral Research Fellowship 1 FO1 MH 50378-01). Together with my husband Alan Harnik and my daughter Vanessa Rose Mosarafa Harnik, born in Madagascar, I lived for twenty months doing ethnographic research in the Analalava region of the northwest coast and three and a half months doing archival research at the Archives Nationales de Madagascar, the Service Photo-Cinéma du Ministère de l'Information, and the Bibliothèque de l'Université d'Antananarivo.

Later, in summer 1978, I did archival work at the Archives Nationales, Section Outre-mer, and the Service Historique de l'Armée in Paris, with a summer stipend from the National Endowment for the Humanities. In the summer of 1980, I conducted further archival research at the Centre des Archives d'Outre-mer at Aix-en-Provence, funded by a fellowship from the Bunting Institute of Radcliffe College. I was able to return to Madagascar for a month in the spring of 1981 and three months in the fall of 1989, supported by Grants-in-Aid from the Wenner-Gren Foundation for Anthropological Research. I began writing at The Institute for Advanced Study, Princeton, in 1983–1984. I am grateful to all these institutions for their support.

I am indebted to the anthropologist Audrey I. Richards, whose work epitomizes for me the qualities of empathy, scrupulousness, and concreteness that I have tried to achieve here. *Land, Labour and Diet in Northern Rhodesia,* originally published in 1939, was an economic study in the best sense, ranging beyond careful measurements of fields and foods to detailed explorations of the ideas and practices involved in growing, giving, and eating, grounded in vivid accounts of daily life portrayed through the words and images of local participant-observers. In aspiring to this ideal, I have followed many of Richards's own suggestions.[1]

I am fortunate in having been able to do graduate work with Thomas O. Beidelman. He brought to his students the same intense feeling for the food and fields with which people illuminate their lives, combined with a deep appreciation of life's abiding murkiness. I owe the inspiration to work in Madagascar to John Middleton, who also enabled me to stay a year longer than I had initially planned. Mme. Bodo Rakotosihanaka provided the indispensable foundation to further study by giving Alan and a comprehensive introduction to the intricacies of the Malagasy language in weekly lessons during the year before we first went to Madagascar. I am grateful to the Malagasy Government for granting me permission to do research in the Analalava region of the northwest coast.

Many friends and colleagues made us welcome in Madagascar in 1971–1973 and 1981 and when I returned in 1989. I would especially like to thank Roger and Saïda Andrianasolo, Skip Barbour, Sina Marie Georgine *mianakavy,* Tim and Suzanne Lind, Mahasoatra, Mahatsara, Maso i Hassany, Paul Ottino, P. Patrice, M. and Mme. Rakotofiringa, Victor and Yolaine Rakotomanga *mianakavy,* M. and Mme. Rakotosihanaka *mianakavy,* M. and Mme. Ramarojaona *mianakavy,* M. and Mme. Raveloson *mianakavy,* Silamo, Zary Binty Saidy Silamo, Tiandrazaña, and Pierre and Juliette Vérin. Jean-François Baré and Dominique Thomas-Fattier kindly invited us to stay with them when Vanessa was born. The family of M. and Mme. G. Pain in Antananarivo generously allowed me to read and photocopy André Dandouau's manuscripts on Madagascar.

M. Jean-Aimé Rakotoarisoa, Directeur du Musée d'Art et d'Archéologie, and M. Manassé Esoavelomandroso, head of the Département d'Histoire at the Université d'Antananarivo, have worked tirelessly to support archaeological, historical, and ethnographic scholarship on Madagascar, including my own. I am indebted to the Wenner-Gren Foundation for Anthropological Research, then under the leadership of Lita Osmundsen, for providing the auspicious circumstances in which we met. I have also learned from conversations with colleagues James Armstrong, Maurice Bloch, Karl Eggert, Fulgence Fanony, Noël Gueunier, Rick Huntington, Conrad Kottak, Michael Lambek, Rodney Needham, Françoise Raison-Jourde, Jean-François Rabedimy, Narivelo Rajaonarimanana, Suzy Ramamonjisoa, Aidan Southall, and Peter Wilson.

This book has benefited from the insights of those who read part or all of the manuscript at different stages: especially Thomas O. Beidelman, Gerald Berg, David W. Cohen, Jennifer Feeley, James W. Fernandez, Alan Harnik, Vanessa Harnik, Ivan Karp, Emily Martin, and Annette B. Weiner. I am grateful to fellow colleagues and students at The Johns Hopkins University for providing a stimulating and supportive place to work.

I thank the editors of *American Ethnologist* for permission to use material in revised form from my article on "The Political Economy of Death" (1984) in Chapter 3. Daniel Goodwin, Ivan Karp, and William Merrill welcomed me to the Smithsonian's Series on Ethnographic Inquiry. Robin Gould, Kathryn Stafford, and Ruth Spiegel provided invaluable editorial assistance on behalf of the Smithsonian Institution Press. I thank Dean Pendleton for her care in preparing the maps and diagrams for publication and Janice Wheeler for her work in designing the book.

I am most grateful to the *ampanjaka* Soazara for having accepted us in her *tanindrazaña*. I am deeply indebted to my foster kin, neighbors, and friends in the Analalava region for their patience and kindness. I have tried to repay some small part of that debt by conveying their viewpoints as accurately as I can, while respecting their reticence on what they would 'keep quiet' about, including personal names used in making direct references. Where they would protect the privacy of people or places by using terms like *raiano* (this/that one), or a wide range of locatives like *eo/ao, ery/any, an-tanana, antsabo*, I have changed the names of all the individuals and communities who figure in this account. The only exceptions are the names of ancestral and living royalty and of prominent national figures, which appear in local accounts of Malagasy history and contemporary life, and the names of long-standing regional centers like Analalava.

I have written this book mainly from the perspectives of specific individuals because a more generic account would distort the diversity of passionately held opinions on matters of common concern. It is precisely this counterpoint of word and deed that defines where people stand, or rather where they are currently going in what amounts to a ceaseless round of movement involving complex networks of social relations that are not restricted to any one locality. The varied and changing standpoints of the individuals who figure in this account should be clear from what follows. These include Alan, Vanessa, and myself. But to heed Malinowski's call to anthropologists to "ply the full searchlight of methodic sincerity, as they move among their facts [not] produce them before us out of complete obscurity," I conclude with more details on the research we did together.[2]

During the two years and four months we were first in Madagascar, we spent twenty months doing fieldwork in the Analalava region. We rented a house in Analalava, a town of about 5,700 people, one of the important gathering places for people in the region. We lived there most of the first year and a half, except for trips to the royal cemetery (hereafter, Mahabo) on the island of Nosy Lava, just off the coast; the royal capital (hereafter, Doany), several kilometers south of Analalava; the Doany Andriamisara in Mahajanga; the Northern Bemihisatra domain of Nosy Be; the Ambolobozo Peninsula-Maromandia-Antsohihy area shared between Bemihisatra and Bemazava royalty; and three trips to Antananarivo, one of them for Vanessa's birth, which coincided with the uprising of May 13, 1972, when Madagascar's first President, Philibert Tsiranana, was replaced by General Gabriel Ramanantsoa. In November 1972, Alan got infectious hepatitis. We did archival work in Antananarivo while he recuperated. In mid-January we returned to the Analalava region, where we lived until early November. During these months, we traveled almost continuously in the Analalava-Antognibe-Ambolobozo Peninsula area, by outrigger canoe and dhow, and on foot.

When we first arrived in Analalava, we stayed in a room of an empty Indian store-home, next to the *hotely,* or eating place, run by Laza Be, described in Chapter 5. Through Laza Be, we came to know a kinswoman—here called MamanDjoma—who lived in one of the southwestern quarters of the post where we eventually settled. In keeping with certain priorities to ties through men, she adopted Alan as her son, and I became her daughter-in-law. During the first few months of fieldwork, I spent most of my time with my foster kin and some other families I came to know well. Vanessa's birth on the day of the "May Revolt" marked a personal turning point as well. Where we had been addressed by respectful terms like *baba* (F, FB, FFBS . . .) or *angovavy* (FZ, FFBD . . .), *dady* (women of the second ascending generation) or *dadilahy* (men of the second ascending generation), we were now addressed more familiarly by teknonyms. I was invited for the first time to attend spirit possession meetings, which were the main occupation of women besides their household duties, farming, and trading. During the last several months in the Analalava region, I also spent increasing amounts of time with people involved in royal service at the Doany and the Mahabo, in Analalava and in the surrounding countryside, at ceremonies and in their villages. We stayed in ten villages besides Analalava, including the communities I call Andonaka and Tsinjorano, discussed mainly in Chapters 4 and 5. We also took photographs and used a tape recorder to record songs, stories and, toward the end of our stay, some commentaries on royal texts.

Thanks to the careful instruction of Mme. Bodo Rakotosihanaka during the year before we went to Madagascar, we were able to communicate well in standard Malagasy (mainly Merina) when we began research in the Analalava region. Like other anthropologists, I began writing notes mainly in my own words, using more and more local forms of speech as time went on. I tried to grasp how people expressed themselves as well as what they said and did. Their statements—in double quotes, with single quotes for a speaker's own reported speech—are not derived from tape recordings. They are faithful, in translation, to the wording of shorter statements and of critical phrases and transitions in longer statements, some of which is indicated in my transcriptions of the original Malagasy. They also document the sequence in which the speaker presented them. Lengthy, uninterrupted statements are not completely verbatim, in part because I was more likely to fall back on English as a short-hand in such contexts. The original English, French, and Malagasy wording of all these statements is in my field notes. I have used the eloquence of individuals in the Analalava region to speak for more widely held concerns and for my own. But it should be evident from what they say that they continue to speak for themselves. The nature of the cross-cultural encounters expressed in the very rendition of these statements is a major focus of the analysis that follows.

Shortly after we arrived in Analalava, Abdallah Be Maso, a Muslim trader, responded teasingly to my earnest account of our purposes by citing a Malagasy proverb: "If you want to find out what's under the bed, you have to bend down to look." Now I would answer all those who helped: *Zay manoro lala, mamindra aina*—Who shows the way gives life.

Orthography

I have followed the orthography adopted in Thomas-Fattier's (1982) study of the "sakalava dialect" in northwestern Madagascar with these exceptions, indicated below. The "sakalava dialect" is not universally spoken in the Analalava region, as reflected in some of the orthographic inconsistencies in the text.

1. The velar nasal /ṅ/ (Thomas-Fattier 1982:45) is indicated as ñ.
2. The palatal nasal /ñ/, commonly found before a final /i/ (ibid.:38–39), is indicated as gn.
3. The sibilant /s/, unvoiced in contrast to /z/ (ibid.:34–35) and unaspirated in contrast to /sh/, common in highland Madagascar, is indicated as s.
4. The voiced affricate /dz/ (ibid.:36–37) is indicated as j.
5. The vowels /u/ and /o/ (ibid.:48–50), pronounced [oo] and [ô] respectively, are indicated as o.

Singular and plural forms are indicated by the same term as they are in Malagasy.

Kinship terms of reference are indicated by Malagasy terms and by the following symbols: M = mother; F = father; D = daughter; S = son; Z = sister; B = brother; W = wife; H = husband. For example, MZSW = mother's sister's son's wife.

Interests in Ancestors

To understand how a dead man can reign we have
to go back to our principles of ritual. We insisted
again and again that the principal need not be a
man, or even a living being: it may be a stone, an
image, the corpse of a whale; it may even be, as
with our philosophers, an Idea.

A. M. Hocart, *Kings and Councillors*[1]

INTERESTS IN ANCESTORS

The people of Madagascar are famed for their interests in ancestors.
The single fact that anyone is likely to know about the island's inhabitants is that they rejoice in the exhumation and reburial of their
dead. Death is the principal theme of numerous scholarly monographs
and articles.[2] It figures prominently even in foreign newspaper accounts. Cowell's analysis of Malagasy affairs in the *New York Times*
(July 26, 1983), entitled "Dead are revered and living well in Madagascar," suggested that only the dead were so fortunate. The Baltimore *Sun* (November 22, 1984) made a similar claim a year or so
later: "In Madagascar, the deceased play important roles in their families' lives." Malagasy put it differently in 1971 when they asked me
almost as soon as I arrived in the remote region where I had chosen
to do fieldwork: 'Why do you want to live here? This place is dead!'
(Maty tanàna ty é!).

I first went to Madagascar to study the role of migration and re-
settlement in the organization of ethnically diverse communities.
French ethnographers and historians had documented what they considered the migratory propensities of the Malagasy people. "Everywhere and always we find movement!" as the prominent historian-

administrator Henri Deschamps put it. "It's custom! It's who we are!" Malagasy along the southeast coast are said to have responded.[3] I wanted to find out how Malagasy lived in the heterogeneous communities resulting from these migrations, focusing not only on the *ethnies* that were said to compose them, but on the relations between 'masters of the land' *(tompontany)* and 'strangers' *(vahiny)* that seemed to be the important distinctions to local people. I was also interested in the continuing role of royalty in the organization of this diversity.

Monarchies flourished in several parts of Madagascar during the precolonial period, encompassing various groups of conquered peoples as well as slaves from Madagascar and Africa. The French abolished the highland Merina monarchy when they conquered the island in 1895, while using members of other royal groups to govern some areas of the provinces through indirect rule. The Analalava region of the northwest coast was such an area. People there included migrants from all over the island who had come at different times for different purposes: the descendants of the Southern Bemihisatra branch of the Zafinimena (Grandchildren of Gold) or Maroseraña dynasty, which had once dominated the west coast, as well as descendants of their former followers and slaves. The domains of the 'Sakalava,' as they called themselves collectively, were founded in the course of migrations and conquests that lasted from the late sixteenth through the nineteenth century. By the early twentieth century, Sakalava—the term for one of the eighteen officially recognized ethnies—were not known for moving about like Tsimihety, Merina, or Betsileo, ethnies identified with remnants of other precolonial polities. On the contrary, French ethnographers since the turn of the century described the Sakalava as dying out in the face of more vigorous competitors for their land.

In the early 1970s, royal followers in the Analalava region were preparing to rebuild the royal tomb. It turned out to be a project with important temporal as well as spatial dimensions. They had been trying to rebuild the tomb for some fifty years, since the last royal burial in 1925. They finally succeeded in gaining permission to do the work during the 'commotion' *(rotaka)* of 1972, widely seen as a second independence movement toward 'Malgachization' nationwide. What was said to have taken eight years to accomplish in the precolonial period was to be completed in a year. Eventually it took six years, from 1972 to 1978. As a result of their interests, I, too, focused my attention on the reconstruction of the royal tomb, on why some local people should persist in working for ancestral royalty as well as their living kin, neighbors, and strangers. I conclude in this book that contemporary Malagasy preoccupations with ancestors, attributed to age-old tradition, are a relatively recent development. The realm of the dead has expanded primarily because, in a complex way involving many different kinds of 'corpses,' it has become the hidden abode of production. It is currently the principle place where still unresolved—perhaps unresolvable—struggles over labor and loyalty continue to be carried on, largely outside the law as any of the participants would define it. To introduce this account of the hidden abode of production, I will begin with the interval between death and succession in which ancestors are born and made.

INTERREGNUM

In considering how dead men could reign, the anthropologist A. M. Hocart questioned "naturalism" in scientific inquiry:

> No satisfactory explanation has been offered why man should worship the dead. It does not seem to be considered necessary to give a reason, because it is so 'natural'. We have refused, however, to admit the word 'natural' into our vocabulary: it is the opiate of historical science; it drugs the spirit of inquiry and prevents it from exerting itself in the search for causes. The use of the word 'natural' must count as a confession of failure.[4]

To understand how a dead man can reign, we need to inquire into the ideas and practices, the whales, stones, and images concerning life, growth, fertility, prosperity, and death in which ancestors are involved. I try here to convey how people in the Analalava region see ancestors embodied in their fleshly land and earthly flesh through labor. These connections between ancestry, land, and labor contribute to clarifying why Malagasy 'interests in ancestors,' to paraphrase Evans-Pritchard, are shared by others who are interested in the land and workers in which ancestors are grounded.[5]

It helps to recall that Hocart wondered how dead men could reign when he was trying to analyze interregna from a comparative perspective. Throughout the world, the dead rule mainly between the reigns of the living. Kantorowicz's study of "the king's two bodies" in Tudor and Stuart England and Giesey's studies of the use of effigies in the funerals of French Renaissance kings provide some of the best documented examples of this phenomenon.[6] In western Madagascar, as in Europe, there were periods between living rulers when relics played a critical role. But as we will see in Chapter 2, the interregna of Sakalava monarchy, from the early nineteenth century onwards, involved outsiders in contests for rule, thefts of relics, and curtailments of funerals that historians of dead men's reigns in Europe have not taken fully into account. These contests for rule continued through the colonial period into the justly termed neocolonial period that followed independence in Madagascar in 1960, as it did in other former French colonies around the same time. People in northwestern Madagascar have been preoccupied with ancestors over the past century and a half because they have not been allowed to bury their dead and reassert the leadership of living rulers who would bring this long interregnum to an end.

I have tried to write a correspondingly 'ancestral' account, appropriate to the space of such an interregnum, by interweaving what some tried to keep fixed with what others tried to change.[7] So I hope to convey both shared and disputed senses of time, place, and movement that diverse participants see or have sought to embody in Sakalava royal ancestors. This book begins with accounts of deaths and burials and ends with the reburials from which ancestors emerge. At the same time, it turns on several historical events, notably the death of the ampanjaka Tondroko at the height of colonial rule in 1925, an event which was still central to everyday life in the mid-1970s, when royal followers finally succeeded in reconstructing the royal tomb. This was a period when people throughout Madagascar were once again moving out from under French domination to make connections between the precolonial past and their future *(ho avy)* on their own terms.

WORK AND SERVICE

What is ruling and reigning all about? Despite their different calculations of the relationship between a single one and countless many, Malagasy would agree with European theorists in seeing control over scarce resources as a major factor. The scarcest resource for 'leaders/ bringers' *(mpitondra)* throughout Madagascar is followers, specifically workers. People in the Analalava region are matter-of-fact in answering questions about their interests in ancestors. Royal service is part of the obligations they owe to royalty as their servitors *(ampan-ompo),* who are akin to, but not quite the same as, royal slaves, in their single-minded devotion to royalty. Royal followers explain that they continue to serve the ancestors because the French and Malagasy governments refused them permission to carry out services when they were required in the past. They do many kinds of work. Now, as in the precolonial period of the monarchy, royal service *(fanompoana)* stands apart from the other kinds of work *(asa)*—engagé labor, corvée labor, work for kin, contract labor, wage labor, and so on. They serve many kinds of masters. Work is, as it was during the precolonial period, an expression of political loyalty, an expression of diverse, often conflicting kinds of loyalties: *Asa Fa Tsy Kabary,* "Work Not Talk," in the slogan of the ruling (until 1972) Parti Social Démocratique.

Witnessing what Sakalava followers in the Analalava region saw as an ongoing struggle to resolve problems rooted deeply in 'the time of the Malagasy' *(fahagasy)* or 'time of the ancestors' *(faharazana),* I have sought to expand the scope of this study of the reconstruction of the royal tomb in the 'period of independence' *(fahaleovan-tena)* to encompass the events of the 'French' or 'European time' *(fahafrantsay, fahavazaha)* that provided the immediate impetus to the reconstruction, but also the nineteenth-century encounters between Malagasy and French in western Madagascar from which their intimate enmity grew.

E. P. Thompson's analysis of the transition from agricultural to wage labor in *The Making of the English Working Class* provides one close analogy to changing labor relations in northwestern Madagascar from a comparative perspective.[8] Inspired by Thompson's work and by more recent research on the international division of labor, scholars like Cooper, Marks and Rathbone, Mintz, van Onselen, and Atkins studying the transition to wage labor outside Europe have drawn attention to the enduring coexistence of alternative forms.[9] Working in areas where slavery had once been essential to production, they question sharp distinctions between so-called slave labor, contract labor, and free labor, which are found, as in Mintz's account of the Caribbean, "in conjunction and interdependent."[10]

As the concept of free labor is related to the concept of an autonomous marketplace, so these scholars have sought to return the study of labor to its social context and in particular to examine ways in which some people continue to control the labor of others.[11] Europeans have benefited from the productions of Malagasy workers since the early sixteenth century. The real difference in colonial rule was here, as Cooper has noted in Africa, "the intervention of a European power in the production process itself."[12] Events in the Analalava region show how, in closer quarters, their intervening became an entwining. French colonists, strangers to Madagascar, used strangers like Indians and Chinese, to estrange Malagasy from one another. In so doing, they were drawn into prior social networks, in which Malagasy rulers, strangers from 'Araby' in the case of Sakalava monarchy, used strangers in the form of slaves to achieve comparable goals.

LAW

Legislation was a major factor in the reorganization of labor relations between natives and strangers during the colonial period, but it worked in unexpected ways. As in Europe, where laws governing vagrancy, drunkenness, and indebtedness were combined with taxation to keep workers in line, so too in Africa. Van Onselen and Johnstone emphasize that the use of physical force in mine recruitment ended by 1910 or diminished soon thereafter. Mine owners relied mainly on what Johnstone calls "extreme extra-economic compulsion," in the form of pass and compound systems to force peasants into mine contracts and keep them there. In the southern Rhodesian mines, where the work was locally known as *chibaro* (slavery, forced labor), laws were hardly more than a front. Social controls based on the design of compounds, rations, prostitution, credit, and other such means became the norm.[13]

The Malagasy case shows a similar reliance on extra-legal means of control. Each new struggle succeeded not in bringing people into compliance with colonial law, but in pushing them into some realm outside the law by anyone's definition. "Enemies of all constraints, independent, they withdraw the farthest possible before the slow eruption of immigrants from the North and from the East, more hard working and better adapted to the new times," so Delelée-Desloges, Administrateur en Chef des Colonies, summarizes the Sakalava after three decades of attempting to subordinate them to the French 'law of work' *(loi de travail)*.[14] The efforts of French colonial officials to control Malagasy labor through legislation led to the use of prison labor on local plantations. They also encouraged efforts to replicate these controls outside prisons by what amounted to other than legal means.

I argue that these were typically *spatial* means, in keeping with the distinctive feature of the Malagasy as well as the African situation: that labor rather than land was the scarce factor. Though these spatial strategies never developed into pass and compound systems like those of Southern Rhodesia and the Republic of South Africa, they may help to put such efforts at controlling workers in a broader comparative context. If in Europe the main issue was, in E. P. Thompson's view, "Time, work-discipline and industrial capitalism," and time has continued to dominate the literature, while space is ignored, here it is *space* and work-discipline.[15]

In Madagascar, this involved more than the choice of migration as the staple topic of French ethnographers and historians. The purpose of the studies by Decary and Castel in 1941 and Deschamps in 1959 was to derive policy from existing practice, rather than rely on "forced migration," which had proven to be ineffective anyway.[16] As policy, the "politics of habitation" included relocation schemes, labor contracts, and identity cards. But it also took more subtle forms requiring cooperation with local elites, more knowledge of local custom, and the growing conviction that Madagascar was, as the demographer Chevalier said at mid-century: "...a civilization of death. Let us go further. Superstitions or religious rites that so compromise the efficacy of the struggle against death are only the expression of a submission to death which is perhaps the most fundamental aspect of the civilisation of these people."[17]

French interests in ancestors developed out of their need for Malagasy labor, involving them in efforts to control people by capturing or exiling the living and dead royalty, to whom they were tied, using means analogous to the relic thefts and kidnappings of the precolonial period. Their efforts brought them into conflict with the efforts of local royalty and Malagasy nationalists who sought to use the same spatial strategies for the same purposes, with unanticipated results.

French influence did not diminish following independence in 1960. Former President Tsiranana used to joke that the French were the 'nineteenth *tribu*' of Madagascar. In fact their close involvement in Malagasy affairs was one of the main reasons for the overthrow of Tsiranana's administration, the subsequent nationalization of most aspects of Malagasy economic and political life, and eventually in 1975, the formation of a socialist government under the current President, Didier Ratsiraka.

I argue that the reconstruction of the royal tomb must be seen in the context of these ongoing spatial strategies for capturing workers. The reconstruction of this place in the 1970s was in its own way a reburial of colonial rule, an assertion of the value of alternative labor practices inseparable from demands for the reorganization of labor and loyalty nationwide.

THREE DOMESTICITIES

Thus far, we have considered the entwined interests in ancestors of Sakalava royalty and Europeans embroiled in persistent controversies about who governs whom and who enslaves or employs whom. To these must be added royal followers' interests in their own ancestors, at odds with these rival embodiments of generation and often with each other as well. Current social relations in the Analalava region seem on the surface to exemplify two broad trends associated elsewhere in the world with the transition from slavery or peasant farming to wage labor: the narrowing of extensive kin networks to focus on households made up of pairs of spouses and their children, combined with a growing number of female-headed households in towns. The commonalities point to similarities in European colonial and postcolonial policies and practices concerning political-economic "development." But they gloss over important local differences in apparently similar social forms, notably the long-time importance of 'friends,' especially spouses, and the cooperation, yet tension, in relations between brothers and sisters that is one of the primary factors in the residence of women in towns in northwestern Madagascar. These relationships in turn must be seen in the context of other kinds of social ties involving kinship and friendship that have been adopted by various 'strangers,' including Europeans *(Vazaha)*, with whom local people interact in growing crops, getting day labor, and serving royal ancestors. In fact, 'kin' *(havana)*, including 'ancestors' *(razana)* and their 'generations' *(taranaka)*, 'friends/spouses' *(namana)*, and 'guests/ strangers' *(vahiny)*, while central to social relations in this area, turn out to be highly ambiguous terms, with broad and changing ranges of potential meanings derived from diverse historical sources, open to continuous reinterpretation depending on circumstances.

In considering how people, localized in different parts of the Analalava region, have competed over a common pool of workers by manipulating notions about ancestors, siblings, strangers, friends, spouses, and the like, I have been inspired by Willie Lee Rose's analysis of "the three domesticities" represented by planters, slaves, and plantation communities in the decades immediately before the Civil War and the abolition of slavery in the American South.[18] Rose argues that the paradoxically intimate enmity of planters and slaves in the American South must be understood as the outcome of specific historical events. Relations between masters and slaves were unspeakably hard during the eighteenth century. Gradually, for various reasons, slaves came to be regarded as too dangerous for brutal methods of domination. The slave population mounted steeply in proportion to whites throughout the eighteenth century and by 1790 constituted nearly half the population. Slaves were more acculturated, and therefore better equipped to get around. Some became highly skilled. The rise of free blacks in proportion to slaves and the prolonged struggle of Haitian slaves as well as discoveries of local plans to revolt, greatly increased the sense of danger. Finally, the slave trade was suppressed, beginning with the law in 1726 forbidding importation of new slaves and requiring emancipation of those illegally acquired.

Rose argues that planters attempted to keep slave-owning profitable yet safe by tightening legal controls over slaves while treating them more humanely. Thus, laws constraining manumission were accompanied by greater attention to the domestic arrangements of slaves and to their religious education; by strong public opinion against selling a slave away from his or her family; and by efforts to assure that slaves were well fed and well clothed. The result was "three interlocking domesticities," in which a slaveholder presided over his "blood family," his slaves' families, and "the larger family of the plantation community."

While the contemporary rhetoric of "patriarchy" might have applied to the community as a whole, Rose sees the planter's family organized around women. Slaves' families represented "ironically, about as close an approximation to equality of the sexes as the nineteenth century provided."[19]

Rose notes that, despite the vast literature on the relations of any one of these groups with the others, it is still not clear how they developed in relation to one another, becoming inextricably entwined in complex, even contradictory ways. Planters attempted to maintain their control by "domesticating" a population they believed to be highly dangerous. Instead, masters, drivers, foremen, and slaves were forced to recognize, indeed to create among themselves, some family connections, while denying others, tailoring their benevolence and retributions accordingly.

While the new laws seemed to subordinate slaves more effectively to plantation authorities, masters sometimes sided with their "people" rather than their overseers. Some slaves became loyal to their masters' families, while others put off running away interminably, so as not to leave their own. Paradoxically, "complex interdependencies of the plantation 'family' became a most significant bulwark of slavery as a working system, even for slaves who wanted desperately to be free."[20]

The reassessment of black family structures, formerly labeled as pathological variants of relations among middle-class whites, and now seen as "strategies for survival," suggests the persistence of such contrastively defined interdependencies long after the legal abolition of slavery in the United States.[21] Taken together with Rose's work, they also suggest the fruitfulness of applying the relational perspective of the "three domesticities" to the transformation from slavery to wage labor in the Malagasy context.

The internationalization of working relations in the Analalava region during French colonial rule and Malagasy independence marginalized earlier, no less rivalrous, divisions of labor and loyalty based on kinship and friendship in rural communities and on slavery in royal centers, but it has not eradicated them. As a model of tangled relations among people who stress their separateness, Rose's "three domesticities" helps to get beyond the dualisms of kinship and contract, slavery and free labor, to the intimacy, interest, and force with which people work to transform their ties to one another.

GREEDY PLACES

In trying to grasp the nature of these social transformations, mediated through ambiguities about 'kin,' 'friends/spouses,' 'ancestors,' and 'strangers,' I have also adopted local spatial strategies of separation and attachment. Residence is too often the black box from which politics, understood as self-interest, is sprung like a fox in the chicken coop, to set solidary kin in motion. When we look more closely at the several places in and through which people live and move, we find that they are all defined by different kinds of paired relationships— 'friendships'—that are not only contrasted with one another, but competing with one another for partners. People in the Analalava region make distinctions between farming villages, settled by the ancestors, siblings and descendants of first settlers and then latecomers; the post of Analalava, settled by traders, merchants, and workers constantly searching for wage labor; and the Doany and the Mahabo, settled by rulers and their guardians, formerly masters and slaves, related through 'royal service.' All of these places derive from struggles for domination between 'masters of the land,' rooted in the land through ancestors, and 'strangers' who are not.

My purpose is to examine how people, in their comings, stayings, and goings, create living embodiments of ancestry out of their changing places, how they reconstruct themselves and others by such means as following, attracting, inverting, separating, redirecting, capturing, covering, and exposing. While some people-places, for example centers of ancestral royalty, attract by their renowned capacity to cleanse and cure, they also draw pilgrims close to royalty by fleecing them of their own kin through service modeled on the work of slaves, identified in this area as 'people without kin.' I say "fleecing them" because of the stealing that has characterized these efforts over many decades. The image also fits the ways participants make these working relations into the second skins of new corporate bodies, of which the special clothing and the 'dressing places' of royal centers are only the most outward signs. These dressing places outside royal ancestral places are replicated in virtually every house in the region, where a ruler's clothes await the moment when his or her spirit comes down on a living person's body, displacing his or her 'mind' (jery) in the process, but also recentering them among their kin and friends.

Coser notes that domestic imagery lies at the heart of "greedy institutions" throughout the world.[22] Apart from dead men reigning, the most salient inversions involved in these competing efforts to attract and capture workers involve gender. Outsiders tried to put down followers of Sakalava royalty by feminizing them, transforming them from 'children of men' to 'children of women.' People in the Analalava region have responded to the marginalization of their rulers by taking monarchy out of the hands of the 'brothers' who once ruled, and elevating 'sisters' in their places. These controversial struggles for control continue to be pursued in gendered imagery focusing on the current preponderance of single women at the post, and the work they do there to support themselves and their brothers' children. I argue that people work in all these places to ground or "naturalize" competing notions of growth and power, conveyed in gendered images of death and rebirth, by building them into the places where they live, which include not only royal tombs and the houses of their followers and former slaves, but also rural villages and provincial capitals. These "architectures of social change," to use Hayden's description of American utopian communities, work in turn on the bodies of their inhabitants who live and move about them, bringing new people out of ancestral forms.[23]

REMEMBERING

The paradox of these living memorials to rival theories of growth and prosperity, even the most apparently enduring like royal tombs, is precisely that they are created from fleeting events. As Giesey says about the royal funerals that bridged the interregna of the French Renaissance:

> Time and time again (more often than I have indicated in the text) I have emerged with the conviction that some crucial innovation in the ceremonial first occurred quite haphazardly, although a contemporary chronicler may have tried to give it some plausible explanation *ex post facto,* and later generations when reenacting it embellished it with clear-cut symbolism. That is to say, on the level of the events themselves, chance frequently reigned; but symbolic forms affected the thought about the events, especially when they were consciously repeated at later funerals. On one hand, therefore, I deem that much was random or accidental, but on the other hand I see the expression of a pattern of ideas closely related to intellectual convictions of the times. These ideas were dramatized in the ritual, and verbalized if at all only incidentally.[24]

People in the Analalava region imagine this paradox by making royal tombs out of wood, stones, and sand rather than cement and galvanized iron, like the people at other centers of ancestral royalty along the west coast with whom they contrast themselves. Much of their interest in rebuilding these fragile monuments lies in the lasting questions they provoke: about the royal sister whose very brother betrayed her to their enemies; about the French official faced with an infant successor to the monarchy he thought he had destroyed; about the people fainting and falling off the tops of tombs during services that should be finished in a day; about the value of different kinds of work and growth. Much may have seemed "accidental" in these circumstances, but it was not for want of trying otherwise. "Structures" and "events," the results of people's efforts to immobilize or transform, occur in the context of their efforts to understand, if only to destroy. In these cases, even where people responded in the moment, it was not simply by groping through as things happened (as much as one can retrace the twisted paths), but by observing, studying, learning, and responding in terms of what they learned about others.

In reconstructing the royal tomb, workers were not simply remembering royal ancestry by recreating it there. They were also recalling their current place in the international division of labor. I came to this realization indirectly, by observing the observer observed. My stated purpose in doing research in northwestern Madagascar was 'to study, learn from, Malagasy practices' *(mianatra fomba malagasy)*, to 'gather meanings' *(mangala dikany)*, 'to take away forgetting' *(mangala hadino)*, as people consistently explained the presence of myself and my family to others. My efforts were more than matched by those of local residents. Royal officials asked me to copy books expressly created to communicate the 'customs of royal service concerning the *menaty*' [the innermost fence around the royal tomb] to 'descendants forever' *(taranaka doria)*, 'in order that the service should not be done wrong in the future.' While echoing the warnings of their predecessors to earlier rulers—'Don't change the customs of your ancestors!' *(Aza manaovany fomba ny Razanareo)*—they were also asking me pointed questions: 'How do you make a living?' 'What is your work?' 'How much do you earn?' and 'Where does your money come from?'

Every time I find some current term or practice cited in historical sources like Mellis (1938), Poirier (1926), Dandouau (1911), or Guillain (1845), I wonder whether it stands as clear evidence of deep continuity, or as further evidence of a process, well documented in the propensities of local people to write ancestral accounts *(tantara)* and make studies *(fianarana)* of their own practices, based on the work of experts as well as on written books, their own as well as those of others. I see how my own work has already been incorporated into that process (for example, Ndremahefa and Feeley-Harnik 1975). In any case, there is no one true account, cribbed by one side or another and fed back to later observers and participants. These coexisting efforts to "penetrate souls," as French officials described their own efforts, are also sources from which the ancestors of this region have emerged.

THE ONE MOST IN EVIDENCE

Hocart comments that "a great many investigators never get beyond the first use of the word that happens to come their way."[25] Confronted by "the one most in evidence," they persist in translating the Melanesian *tamu* as "father", explaining what they learn later about fathers' brothers and fathers' fathers' sons as "kinship extensions." Paradoxically, given their aversion to historical and evolutionary analysis, this involves them in reconstructing history.

When Malagasy and French people said, 'This place is dead,' I understood them as referring to the economic decline of the region—in part, they were. Eventually, I came to see that their words covered a much more complex domain, including moral and social as well as narrow 'economic' concerns. Now I wonder if researchers also find it difficult to get beyond the first uses of words because they are dealing with the multilingualism characteristic of cross-cultural relations on a global scale. Words and deeds have many meanings, reflecting the range of contexts in which they occur. These include meanings that were developed in response to the presence of Europeans and meanings that include those of Europeans. Observers may be deaf to some of these meanings, not because they are absent from their semantic worlds, but precisely because they are so deeply rooted there that they take them completely for granted. Using Bakhtin's insights into language as "a living, socio-ideological concrete thing, as heteroglot opinion . . . for the individual consciousness, ly[ing] on the borderline between oneself and the other . . . half someone else's . . . exist[ing] in other people's mouths," I have tried here to get back to the first uses of words and deeds without forgetting what came later.[26]

"The one most in evidence" has another feature that I have felt more strongly, but found harder to convey. Many times in the Analalava region, especially in 1971–1973, I felt I was a ghost—besides myself, an image of all the Vazaha who had lived and worked there before me. Many encounters with people, especially first encounters, were surrounded by this ghostly aura, in which the significance of our words and actions had historical, ancestral reverberations. Recognizing myself as yet another participant in the heterogeneous crowd of people long involved in reconstructing the royal tomb, I have tried here to bring out the ghosts hidden in my own words and actions.

OUTLINE OF THE BOOK

Part I, The Death of Kings, is concerned with how people in northwestern Madagascar, themselves migrants to the area, came to be serving many masters who were also migrant strangers. I describe how Sakalava royal followers identify themselves and are identified by others in terms of connections to ancestors conceived in the form of trees. Sakalava royal history, paradigmatic of changing relations among kin and strangers, chronicles the struggles in which ancestors are kept, lost, and regained as they branch out over new land, and how efforts to keep or capture ancestors have led over generations to the multiplication of places to which Sakalava followers are connected by descent and by service.

In Part II, Three Domesticities, I outline how the ancestries of Sakalava followers and others in the Analalava region are currently transformed in working to create the diverse communities through which people now move: the rural settlements where they farm; the provincial capital of Analalava, formerly a military post, where they sell goods and get day labor; and the Doany and Mahabo, centers of living and ancestral royalty, surrounded by pens of guardians who were formerly slaves. I examine how such different communities are linked historically and currently by networks of exchanges, including work, that range from reciprocity to theft.

In Part III, A Green Estate, I examine the work needed to grow the ancestors from which the Sakalava monarchy is remade, in the context of competing demands for the labor and loyalty of royal followers characteristic of the postcolonial period. I focus on the reconstruction of the royal tomb, an event lasting several years, in which participants reburied colonial rule and regenerated royal ancestors by incorporating themselves, living workers, into the innermost fence surrounding and protecting their tomb. I argue that their efforts in northwestern Madagascar are part of ongoing efforts to reestablish independence—*fahaleovan-tena*—in Malagasy terms in Madagascar as a whole.

The Death of Kings

Ancestry, Land, and Labor

Raha naty tsisy veloño.
A dead thing has no life in it.

Sakalava saying, Analalava region

ESCHATOLOGIES

Many observers have commented on the apparent contradiction that Malagasy who are so interested in ancestors should not have elaborate ideologies about life after death.[1] People living in the Analalava region raise similar questions in explaining their own religious beliefs. MamanDjoma, born to Sakalava and Tsimihety parents, raised as a Muslim after her mother married a Comorian, and then married to a Comorian herself, explained Sakalava disinterest in terms of literacy:

MamanDjoma, hearing that we had visited the ampanjaka at her house to explain our research, said we should also pay our respects *(mikoezy)* at her office [where she is *sous-gouverneur*]. We should say we had come to ask for health and good fortune in her country, and give a little money as an offering. Then she would intercede for us with the royal ancestors. She continued in this vein, then said: "God *(Andriamanitra)* watches over everything—over what's here and now *(doniàny)* and what's beyond *(kiàma)*. Fire *(Motro)* is where the bad people go and burn—murderers, sorcerers—they burn, burn *(may, may)*! Heaven *(Pepòny)* is the beautiful place, like a beautiful house with cool breezes. Everything is clear, sweet-smelling. This is Muslim *(Silamo)* belief. The Sakalava say the Comorians lie. They say, 'A dead thing has no life in it' *(Raha naty tsisy veloño)*. But it is the Sakalava who are lying. The Silamo have books, histories. The

Sakalava have no books. The living ruler (ampanjaka) is their book. They pray *(mivavaka)* directly to her. They have nothing written down like the Silamo. They don't know how to pray. They don't know how to read. Comorians like myself, we have books. They don't have anything like that."[2]

Followers of Sakalava royalty in the Analalava region do write and keep books, as we shall see. These are not treatises on the afterlife, but "histories" *(tantara)* of the actions of royal ancestors during the times they were alive and descriptions of important events like the birth of the current ruler's first child, as well as instruction manuals for royal services *(fomba fanompoana)*. Although Malagasy have written books, using Arabic and then Roman script, for hundreds of years, these books show in their language and composition the marks of having originated in conflicts with other people having books, as reflected in MamanDjoma's comments.

Followers of Sakalava royalty do not speak about lives after death in ordinary conversation either, but they are very precise about the activities of ancestors among the living. There is no separate land of the ancestors. Ancestors exist among the living, in the land that sustains them, in trees, in their very bodies. Living, land, and ancestry are inseparable because either people live where their ancestors first settled the land, and thus are 'masters of the land' *(tompontany)*, or they live elsewhere as 'strangers' *(vahiny)*, dependent on the ancestors of others as well as their own. To live with ancestors is to be grounded in the land in which they are buried through work ranging from sowing rice to invoking the ancestors and presenting them with gifts. 'Not to know the place where [one's] ancestors are' *(Tsy mahay tany misy raza)* is to be 'lost to [one's] ancestors' *(very raza)*. To be lost to one's ancestors is to be enslaved, because one's work does not contribute to the growth of one's own ancestry, but to the growth of the ancestries of others.

Close associations between ancestry and land, memories and places, are found in many different parts of the world. Fox and Kuipers analyze the close correspondence between genealogies and place names in different parts of Southeast Asia. Basso has done similar research among the Western Apache in the southwestern United States. Kuechler's work on the *malangan* sculptures of New Ireland shows how memories of political-economic relations among regional groups are embodied in images exchanged especially during lengthy funerals.[3]

Europeans and Americans also have long-established ways of articulating the linear and integrative powers of memory in the spatial imagery of caves, houses, temples, theatres, castles, and, more recently storehouses that can be emptied and restocked.[4] These 'chronotopes,' as one might call them using Bakhtin's term, play a central role in European and American literature and other art forms comparable to the oral poetry and ceremonies more often analyzed by ethnographers.[5] The bodily experience of memory in European and American social life is more fully articulated in these aesthetic forms than in the scholarship on spatial kinds of mnemonic devices. Personal letters, in which Americans convey to one another their different, changing places, express these associations still more immediately, for example, this letter from my 'Cousin Walter,' whom people in the Analalava region would recognize as a *tompondrazana* or 'master of the ancestors' on my mother's side.

> We are here in Paris [Maine] most of the time until early October.
> We hope that one day you'll visit here. It is not like Harpswell, not
> being coastal. The house is all sorts of things to us—a second home,
> a place for family reunions, a museum of antiquities, and a memorial
> to my parents. I am conscious every day of my mother's touch.[6]

That felt connection between people and places is what I want most to convey about experiencing ancestors in the Analalava region. To begin, we have to return to people's differences as MamanDjoma expressed them.

KARAZANA: KINDS
People in the Analalava region define *karazana* or 'kinds' of people in terms of contrasts. This awareness of contrast encompasses many different aspects of daily life because people 'study customs' *(mianatra*

fomba) of others as a matter of course. A prisoner from southeast Madagascar, imprisoned in the penitentiary on Nosy Lava and paroled to the village of Tsinjorano, built his house out of flattened bamboo. Fellow residents then proceeded to 'study' his techniques, as they put it, then experiment on their own garden shelters and kitchens.[7] People who identified themselves as 'Sakalava' would comment about their respective practices: 'Silamo almost always cook with coconut fat, while Sakalava don't, because it makes them sick.' 'Hova [Merina] eat chicken heads; Sakalava here would never eat the head.' 'Silamo build fences around their houses. Sakalava don't do that because it smacks of greed.' 'Sakalava throw the building in which a person died out into the forest, then they set fire to it; Silamo, however, don't do that.' 'Incest causes incurable, incapacitating wounds. Close kin may not sleep together! Even children born of the same father but a different mother. However, it's allowed for Silamo and Hova. Even children born of one father and one mother may sleep together.'[8]

This awareness of difference is also expressed more formally, for example, in spirit possession meetings. Thus, the ancestral spirit of the current ruler's father, visiting a coastal village known to have many Silamo residents, asked for questions from the audience, noting that Silamo in the community might be puzzled about some features of Sakalava royal custom. Studying customs was part of maintaining differences, but, as this example illustrates, it was also a route to conversion. Like MamanDjoma, the medium was aware that Silamo, like Vazaha (Europeans), saw Islam as more prestigious than Sakalava practices; in fact, Vazaha would put Christianity at the top of the hierarchy. But she also knew that Silamo married Sakalava, Tsimihety, and other 'children of the land' *(zanatany)*, as locally born people were known. MamanDjoma was not only born and raised in such unions, but was herself a medium of Sakalava royal ancestors, as it later turned out.

Even while claiming that the Sakalava were dying out, French scholars documented their steady absorption of people from other ethnic groups who migrated west in search of land.[9] According to Deschamps's analysis of migratory movements within Madagascar published in 1959, at the end of the colonial period, Tsimihety did not begin to move west in great numbers until the second half of the nineteenth century, when they started to raid for cattle there. In the mid-1950s, they outnumbered Sakalava around Antsohihy, east of Analalava, by about twenty-three to one. They each numbered about 14,000 in the area around Analalava, but Deschamps noted that Tsimihety might actually be more numerous than they appeared because many of them declared themselves Sakalava, married Sakalava women and thus, in acquiring access to land, "peaceably conquered the country." These relationships in the Analalava region were one of his rare examples of 'ethnic fusion'. Antognibe in the southern part of the region presented "the impression of general ethnic interbreeding *(métissage); it was rare that one of the people whom we questioned—whether he declared himself Tsimihety, Sakalava or Makoa—would not have in his ancestry relatives from one of the other two peoples."*[10] Use of the Tsimihety dialect appeared to be on the increase, yet Sakalava customs—certain traditional ceremonies, tribute to royal families, certain prohibitions, spirit possession—were practiced by the members of mixed marriages. Even Comorians born in the Analalava area adopted Sakalava customs, although in the districts of Ambongo and Morondava south of Majunga, Comorian settlers have tended to "islamicize" the Sakalava as they have in Nosy Be to the north.[11]

When we first met, MamanDjoma presented herself as a Silamo. Later, after we had gotten to know each other better, she talked about her Tsimihety kin, beginning with those affiliated to the royalty known as Zafinifotsy. Still later, in 1981, she responded to my question about her ancestry with a question of her own:

"Do you know about eight ancestors *(valo razaña)*? Mine are: (1) Antandrona—Zafinifotsy. The Zafinifotsy are all Antandrona. (2) Zafindramahavita—Tsimihety. The ampanjaka founded that group, created it because they accomplished work *(mahavita asa)* for the ampanjaka. That's what its name means [Grandchildren of those who accomplish (work)]. (3) Silamo. (4) Antotolaña—that's still Tsimihety, but each to his own name. (5) Zafibilaza—Tsimihety. (6) Maromangy—Tsimihety. (7) Antimahoro—Sakalava-Silamo. (8) Sihanaka." [Which came from your mother and which from your father?] "These came from both father and mother. They revealed *(nambara)* all these names. I don't know which came from whom."

In 1970, the most recent national census for which there are published results, Sakalava numbering about 435,000 were one of the largest of then twenty officially recognized ethnies in Madagascar.[12] They are no more homogeneous than the people who had followed Sakalava royalty in the precolonial period or who had since collected around French, then Malagasy, centers of power. Through their 'eight ancestors,' people keep open the possibility of choosing other affiliations, a possibility sanctioned by the widespread emphasis on individual destinies *(anjara),* often expressed spatially in terms of 'many paths'. Sakalava are still most different from other 'kinds' of people in being 'servers of the royal ancestors' *(ampanompo),* yet many people who have settled where Sakalava royalty are buried have also come to recognize their presence in the land, if not always to the point of serving them in royal work. As people who identify themselves as 'Sakalava' continue to marry people with other ethnic affiliations, so the Sakalava royal ancestors in this place continue to incorporate strangers regardless of their origins, embellishing themselves with some of their exotic customs as well. To see how people can reorient themselves to the royal ancestors, even to the point of effacing their own, we need to go more deeply into the relationship between people and land embodied in ancestors.

SAKALAVA

Sakalava identify themselves and are identified by others in the Analalava region as 'servants of royalty' or followers of the Maroserana dynasty who founded the Sakalava monarchy in southwestern Madagascar in the late sixteenth century, then conquered their way northwards in subsequent centuries. In the north, the dynasty is known as Zafinimena, short for Zafimbolamena (Grandchildren of Gold), or simply as Volamena (Gold), to distinguish it from the Zafinifotsy, short for Zafimbolafotsy (Grandchildren of Silver), a junior line with no living rulers, who are identified with the inland Tsimihety or Antandrona. The Southern Bemihisatra branch of the Zafinimena in the Analalava region, founded in 1849, was the last Sakalava domain to be established before the French conquered the island, deposing and exiling local rulers or turning them into colonial functionaries. Like other Sakalava followers, the Southern Bemihisatra recognize the authority of both living and ancestral members of the dynasty. The living ruler *(ampanjaka be, ampanjaka manjaka)*—the woman who succeeded her father as an infant in 1925—has a royal compound *(doany)*, surrounded by guardians descended from former slaves, on the coast overlooking Narinda Bay about a day's walk south of Analalava. She rules by virtue of her Volamena ancestry, represented by regalia kept in the 'ancestors' house' at the Doany, the most important of which is a knife known as the *Vy Lava* (Long Iron) said to date back to the dynasty's founders.

The most important place associated with the royal ancestors *(razan' ny ampanjaka)* is the royal tomb *(mahabo)* of the ruler's immediate kin—her father, elder brother, grandfather, and great-grandfather— who were all, except the brother, her predecessors in office. The Mahabo is separated from the Doany by its location on the island of Nosy Lava, about seventeen kilometers off the coast from Analalava. The royal ancestors are surrounded not only by guardians descended from slaves, but also by their most important living mediums.

Like her father before her, the ampanjaka first served as a sous-gouverneur in the administration of the subprefecture based in Analalava, where she has a house and office. As sous-gouverneur, she was formally, according to the roster posted in the subprefecture, in charge of the Hall d'Information, and informally in charge of assuring the collection of taxes from royal followers. In the early 1970s, she was also head of the Croix Rouge and the Section Féminine of the ruling Parti Social Démocrate or P.S.D. party. After the government changed hands in 1972, the office of governeur was abolished. The *ampanjaka* became head of the *firaisana*, a position she held in 1989.[13] From the perspective of royal followers, the ampanjaka's chief duty is still to serve the royal ancestors buried in the land from which they seek their living.

TANINDRAZANA: ANCESTRAL LAND

How people see land in the Analalava region depends on whose ancestors they see in the land. The Southern Bemihisatra domain is the land around the water, the mouth of the Loza River, and the bay extending to the south, but more exactly, the land around the island of Nosy Lava on which the royal ancestors are buried. This includes the land along the coast and around Narinda Bay from the northern Ambolobozo Peninsula to the Sofia River south of Antognibe and eastward to the low range of volcanic mountains, about thirty kilometers inland, known as the Manasamody Plateau in its southern reaches, where it runs into National Route 6 (Fig. 1). This mountain range runs the length of the region, rising from almost sea level at Point Berangony in the north to a height of 410 meters around Anjiamangirana in the south. East of the mountain range is the fertile, well-watered, and more densely populated plain in which the towns of Maromandia, Befotaka, and Antsohihy are located. Beyond the plain, at about 150 kilometers inland, steep cliffs mark the beginning of the mountainous interior of the island.

Thick forests of deciduous trees, including sandalwood, teak, ebony, and rosewood, once covered this region. Most of them were cut down by lumbering companies established early in the colonial period. Patches of forest still exist in hilly, sparsely settled areas like the Manasamody Plateau, the Komadjara Peninsula, and parts of the Amboloboro Peninsula. Big shade trees like tamarinds and mangos mark the locations of villages. Otherwise, most of the region is covered with deeply rooted perennial grasses, some growing to three meters in height, including *Heteropogon contortus (danga), Hyparrhenia rufa* and *H.dissoluta (vero),* as well as dwarf fan palms *(satra be* and *satra mira—Hyphaene shatan, Hyphaene coriacea, Medemia nobilis)* used extensively in house building, but difficult to clear in preparing the ground for cultivation. A sandy laterite soil mixed with volcanic rock predominates, interspersed throughout the Komadjara Peninsula and the islands at the head of the bay with large outcrops of porous limestone from which *tany fotsy/malandy* (white earth), the most important

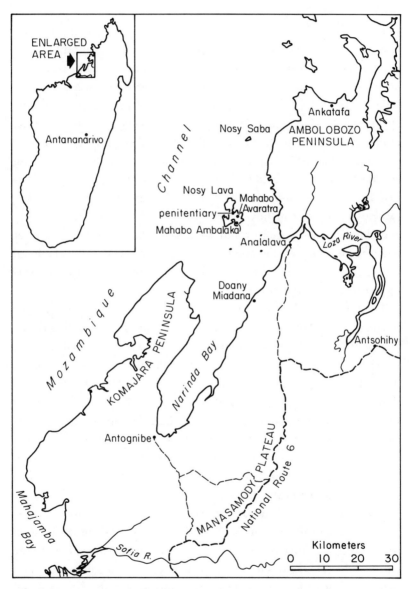

Figure 1. Map of the Analalava region.

medicine accompanying all blessings from the royal ancestors, is made.

The major concern for people living in the land around the water is water. The coastal plain in the shadow of the Manasamody Plateau is far drier than the inland plain. The rainy season *(asara)* comes on north-northwesterly "monsoon" winds, alternating with sea winds *(talio),* around October. The rains reach their peak with occasional cyclones in late December, January, and early February when daytime temperatures average in the 90s Fahrenheit, then taper off as it gets cooler in March and April. The dry season *(maintany),* beginning around May, is dominated by land winds intensified by the east-south-easterly trades *(varatraza),* which bring daytime temperatures to the low 70s Fahrenheit in July. There are occasional night rains in July and cloud-bursts in August and September, but steady rains do not begin again until October and November. The average annual rainfall ranges from 180 centimeters per year in the northern part of the area to 160 centimeters per year in the southern part.[14]

The Loza River is the main route to and from the interior via the inland town of Antsohihy, but it is too salty for use in irrigating fields. The only other navigable river in the area is the Anjango River, which separates the eastern and western parts of the Ambolobozo Peninsula. The Anjango, the Ovaribe River near Ovaribe and Ovarikely, the Ambohimenamaso River around Ambarijeby, the Antsangabe River in the southwestern Komajara Peninsula near Antognibe, and the Tsi-ribihina River near Mahadrodroka have water all year, thus enabling nearby farmers to grow dry season rice *(vary jeby)* as well as wet season rice *(vary asara).* The other smaller rivers and streams dwindle and sometimes vanish in the dry season.

The area is too dry to support lucrative cash crops like coffee, cloves, vanilla, ylang ylang, and sugar grown in the Nosy Be-Ambanja region to the north and tobacco, peanuts, and cotton grown in the Port Bergé and Mandritsara regions to the south. Cattle, coconut palms, and raffia palms in that order are the principle sources of cash. Some coastal dwellers do a small local trade in fish, but most people subsist on a mixed economy of horticulture (mainly rice, manioc, and maize), animal husbandry (cattle, goats, birds), fishing, hunting, gathering, small-scale commerce, occasionally "getting day labor."

The population in 1972 numbered about 48,000 people, averaging zero to five persons per square kilometer, making the Analalava region one of most sparsely populated areas of Madagascar. Most people live in the lowlands around the rivers and streams and along the coast. The rivers large enough to support second crops of rice during the dry season were the sites of the three major settlements: Analalava, Antognibe, and Ambarijeby, with populations of about 5,700, 1,500, and 1,000 in 1972–1973.[15] Analalava, then Antognibe, were the sites of the royal capitals that the Southern Bemihisatra Sakalava founded when they entered the region in 1849. French colonists transformed Analalava into their provincial capital and Antognibe into a cantonal capital when they entered the area in 1897. Later, in the 1920s, when they moved the head of the province to Majunga, Analalava became a prefectural capital. Still later in the 1960s, following independence when former President Tsiranana relocated the prefecture to Antsohihy near his birthplace, Analalava was a subprefectural capital. Since 1976, it has been the head of a *fivondronampokontany* (region) of the same name. Apart from the kinds of people already mentioned, local residents, especially in and around the administrative centers, also include several Muslim Indian families and individuals from Lebanon, Greece, France, and Taiwan, most of whom moved here during the colonial period and stayed on.

Followers of Sakalava royalty, who still see the land as centered on the water where their royalty are buried, recognize three 'kinds' of people living in the land around the water. Their first distinction is between the guardians (formerly slaves) surrounding living and dead royalty, known as Sambarivo (Every One a Thousand), and the rest of the population, known as Tsiaro, Bemihisatra, or Sakalava, regardless of whatever other ethnic affiliations they might claim. They make a second major distinction between people living in the Ambolobozo Peninsula north of the mid-line marked by the Loza River and the island of Nosy Lava and those living south of it around the bay. People from these areas participating in royal service are assimilated into the categories of Antavarabe and Tsimaniha, Sambarivo living north and south of royalty respectively.

A third major distinction is made between Antandrano, 'People living on the water', and Antantety (Antety, Antanety), 'People living on the land'. This distinction, shared by people living throughout the area, has broader analogues, not only in the Zafinimena and Zafinifotsy branches of royalty, mentioned above, but also in the official ethnies, Sakalava and Tsimihety, identified as coastal people and inlanders respectively. Thus, local people often compound the two, identifying themselves as 'Sakalava-Antandrano' or speaking of 'those Tsimihety, those uplanders' (ley Tsimihety, ley Antantety iregny). More often, the local ways of relating people to their places supplants the official terms altogether. The distinction between coastal people and inlanders has national parallels in the politically controversial distinction between côtiers and Merina, dating back to the precolonial expansion of the Merina monarchy, later entangled in French-English rivalries.[16] This distinction is also basic to Sakalava royal service, in which the local populace is reorganized around the royal ancestors buried in their midst, to which we now turn.

FANDEVENANA: BURIALS

As Fortes once observed about ancestry in Africa and Asia, "death by itself does not confer ancestorhood."[17] This is also the case in the Analalava region. People who identify themselves as "Sakalava" emphasize separation from the dead through burial and other means. They make these separations especially carefully in the case of royalty. The most important way that people separate themselves from the dead, besides putting them in the ground, is by silencing, as we shall see. To speak of specific deaths from direct experience is viewed as a form of sorcery because it suggests that the speaker wanted the dead person killed, even if he or she did not do it. Death is 'difficult' (sarotra) because of the terrible consequences of not achieving these hard prohibitions. But ancestry is more so, precisely because the work of bringing ancestors out of the dead requires the careful abrogation of prohibitions through which the difference is achieved, and thus the constant threat and even incipient experience of mortal illness.

When a person dies *(maty)*—the euphemism *vaha*, 'loosened, untied', is usually used in speaking of the death—the body is first prepared for burial by washing it. Women wash women; men wash men. The corpse is completely covered with a white cloth during this process. The washers' hands must also be wrapped in white cloth. As one woman insisted, 'The dead one cannot be seen at all, it *may* not be seen at all.' The washing is completed by pressing on the navel to expel the excrement from the body into a container through a hole cut into the bed.

Close kin do this work, with the exception of parents whose grief is too great. Once the corpse is clean, they put pieces of cotton soaked in cologne and sometimes camphor in all the orifices and 'places between' *(sefaka)*, and burn incense to cover the smell of decay.[18] They then dress the corpse, wrap it in cloth, and place it in a plain wooden coffin. While Silamo are prohibited from using anything but one piece of new white cotton cloth *(bafota malandy)*, non-Muslims may use all the good cloth they have available. Silamo must bury the corpse before sundown, but non-Muslims usually keep it in the house for a few days while mourners gather. Both cover the coffin with another piece of white cloth before carrying it to the cemetery.

The cemeteries throughout the area are outside, usually north, of the settlements of living people. Pregnant women, children, and royalty are not allowed to attend burials. Other prohibitions separating the dead from the living are made at the burial and afterwards. In contrast to Vazaha who, as Malaza of Andonaka put it, "don't know about placing—they bury the head in any direction," the body is buried with its head to the east and feet to the west, counter to the orientation of living people, for whom north is the place of honor in contrast to south.[19] The following abbreviated account of the burial of an elderly woman, head of one of the largest families in Analalava, exemplifies some features of this process:

Mme. T. died on a Thursday night at the age of 82. Her daughter said later that she died because she broke the prohibition forbidding a royal spirit to come in contact with death. Although she was possessed by two different spirits, she attended the funeral of one of her children, a sister's child. Her daughter emphasized that she had to go because of the closeness of the relationship. But when she returned, she fell sick herself, and after ailing for two years, she finally died, one of the spirits having killed her for the offense.

Widowed for six years, Mme. T. was buried by her children. The daughter and two sons, living in Analalava, arranged the details, and notified their siblings who joined in as they arrived over the next two days. Though a more distant kinswoman who worked as a nurse, they got some formaldehyde pills, dissolved them in water, and injected the liquid into the body to preserve it for the duration of the "watching over the corpse" *(miambigny faty)*. The corpse—dressed in white, including a piece of white lace to tie the jaws shut—was laid out on a bed, head to the east, covered from the waist down with a sheet. Netting had been stretched over the ends of the bed to keep off the flies, but the kin, who watched the body constantly during Friday and Saturday when it was on view, also used fans to keep them off the covering. Meanwhile, mourners gathered in the yard behind the house, cooking during the days, and singing to keep awake through the nights.

The coffin was made in advance by men who volunteered to 'receive that part of the work' *(mandray anjara)* because they knew carpentry. Then it was stored open under the bed, so mourners could keep an eye on it as well. The burial took place on Sunday afternoon, following a long procession, led by the coffin, born aloft by the grave-diggers, down the main street to the cemetery "At the Foot of the Bonara Trees" (Ambodibonara) at the top of the hill across the river marking the southern end of Analalava.[20] The grave *(fasina,* powerfully efficacious thing), oriented east-west, consisted of two rectangular holes in the ground—a 'big hole' *(hady be, lavaka be),* into the bottom of which a 'small hole' *(hady/lavaka kely),* exactly the size of the coffin, had been dug.

The grave-diggers, who had carried the coffin, lowered it into the little hole. Then one of them got the piece of red plastic on which it had rested on the bier, bunched it up and handed it down to the men in the hole, so it would be buried with the coffin too. Mme. T.'s female kin, who had begun to cry loudly as the coffin was lowered into the ground, fell quiet as the men covered it by laying several large flat stones across the top of the little hole. As one man explained afterwards: "Those are called *rangolahy* (tall/long, men/stones), big flat rocks, big! Sixty kilos, fifty kilos, thirty kilos at the very smallest. Need two people or three to lift them; one person couldn't do it."

When the little hole was completely covered, one of the men got a heavy hammer and cracked the remaining stones into small pieces, which the two men in the grave then fitted into the sides and cracks. Finally they mortared them together with mud made from the earth dug from the grave. While two of the men directed the work, two others made the mud and shoveled it in on top of the rocks, where they were directed to do so by the two men down in the hole. The men in the hole then picked up handfuls of the mud and threw them down so they penetrated between the rocks. Then they smoothed over the top. 'The mud is a substitute for cement' *(solon' ny ciment),* as several people said later.

Once the coffin was sealed in, the older of Mme. T.'s sons living in Analalava, who was serving as *tompon'havana* (master of kin) knelt at the northeast corner of the grave and began to invoke *(mijoro)* their ancestors. The rest of his siblings knelt behind him, while everyone else remained standing. He explained that 'we' *(atsika,* using the inclusive form) were here to accomplish ancestral custom *(fomban-drazaña)* for 'you ancestors' *(anareo razana).* He began asking for their blessings, but then broke down in tears and had to be helped away by one of his brothers. The official spokesman *(mpikabary),* who was not a kinsman, then took his place as planned. He had been chosen for his ability to speak eloquently. He began by emphasizing Mme. T.'s long life and the great numbers of her descendants: sixteen children *(zanaka),* of whom thirteen were still living; one hundred and nine grandchildren *(zafy);* and some twelve 'second-grandchildren' *(zafy faharoy).* Then he announced that people had brought gifts. The money they gave totaled 154,500 FMG, another indication of their great numbers (about 309), since the average gift is about 500 FMG. The speaker then thanked everyone for their participation, saying they could go now. The women and young girls dispersed, while the men and boys stayed to fill up the rest of the grave with the remaining earth, and cover the earth with the remaining stones. Later, it might be covered with a large slab of cement, stepped up as the hole had been stepped down.[21]

Men and women both said that men buried corpses because, as one man put it: "Only men have strength; women have no strength, women can't do the work" *(Lehilahy foña misy force, mañangy tsisy force. Mañangy tsy mahavita ny asa).* He then went on to explain that although the coffin is made in advance (but watched as closely as the corpse once it is done), the grave is dug, and the stones collected, only on the morning of the burial:

> "Before digging the ground, it's necessary to pour some alcohol out on the ground. It's necessary because the ground is being broken *(mamaky tany).* The grave is dug that morning; it can't be done

earlier for fear that during the night, someone might throw in medicines, to cut off descendants. Lead the still living into the pit, cut off descendants until there are none! Finished! *(Mitariky ley mbola velona anatin' ny lavaka, manapitra taranaka, fa tsisy! Fin!)* The coffin is covered like that, with rocks and cement, because there are no guardians. People in developing countries *(tanàna mandroso),* like the United States, have guardians. But here there are no guardians, and here people don't go to visit graves *(mamangy fasina)* unless there is another death. It's not customary."

"The grave-diggers volunteer to do the work. There is no salary, just alcohol. Together with people digging, there must be alcohol; it's needed to do the work. When there's a corpse, there must be alcohol. They are inseparable. *(Raha misy faty, tsy maintsy misy toaka. Tsy misaraka.)*"

The dead body is expected to keep decaying until it becomes bones *(taolana),* and finally dirt or mud *(fotaka).* Thus, when Maman-Mahasoa, the mother of a close friend in Analalava, was talking about kin she had and had not known in youth, she commented: "One we didn't see *(tsy hitanay),* the other was very old." Her sister-in-law asked about the one she didn't see: "Already mud?" *(Efa fotaka?),* and she answered, "There were still bones" *(Fa misy taolana).* This process can be hurried to induce forgetfulness. Another friend's sister had died in childbirth a few months earlier, and she was raising her sister's children, since the father was living with the woman whom she believed had killed her sister by cursing her. When the three-year-old boy asked yet again where his mother had gone, she said: "I told you already she's mud *(fa fôtaka izy).* I am your mother now."

Washing is the first act of mourners returning from a burial. Only after washing is it possible to reenter the house. Spirit-mediums, whose houses enshrine the belongings of royal ancestors tabooed from any contact with death, are especially careful about observing this prohibition (Plate 1).

In the precolonial period, the house in which the person died or where the body was prepared for burial, was burned after the burial. French authorities prohibited this practice in the first decade of colonial rule, leaving people with the alternative of living with death—that is,

Plate 1. Women from Analalava bathing in the sea after a funeral in 1973 (A. Harnik).

dying—or finding other ways of cleansing themselves of its filth.[22] Often, the house is abandoned, and either rented or sold to an outsider.[23] If this is impossible, then it is cleaned, like the body of a medium, using a special mixture of raw honey and water known as *ontso velo* (living water).

The dead are washed from living settlements and their corpses buried deep in the ground. They are also washed from the body, yet hidden deep inside there by prohibitions on speech. These prohibitions fall most heavily on spouses, but they also affect others, especially through the prohibition against uttering the names of the dead. Mourning customs *(fomba fisaonana)* impose an analogous kind of burial on the dead person's spouse. Spouses represent an ideal of intimacy and personal fulfillment unmatched by any other paired relationship, a point to which we will return in Chapters 4 and 5. This burial by wrapping, enclosure in the house, and silencing is achieved by 'holding fast to the lock' *(mitaña hidy)*, as the taboos on speaking or leaving the house are called.[24] Relatives receive visitors who 'bring tears' *(man-*

day ranomaso)—small gifts of money to defray the costs of coffee and cloth (*rakitra,* averaging $0.20–$1.00 in 1971–1973), often with a note naming the giver and the amount of the gift and apologizing that it is so small. This money can only be used to pay for expenses related to the burial. It is forbidden *(fady)* to use it for any other purpose. Spending this 'bad money' *(vola ratsy)* on anything else would lead to further deaths.

The widow or widower—in old clothes and unkempt hair—has to stay in the house without speaking to visitors. She or he can speak to very close kin of the same sex, but only in a very low, almost inaudible voice, with no eye contact. Close kin of the opposite sex may enter the house, but they can neither look at nor speak to the mourner, who may remain behind a curtain even inside the house. Greetings from outside have to be answered by clapping. In going outside to the *douche,* he or she must cover up completely, leaving only an opening for an eye to see the way. The spouse announces the end of mourning by dressing up in clean clothing, coming out of the house and speaking to people. Spouses are said to have observed these and other prohibitions for three months in the past. In the 1970s, they remained secluded for four or five weeks at most, women longer than men.

While formal mourning is limited in duration, people who identify themselves as kin are forbidden to speak about the dead person as if he or she were still living. This prohibition applies to any talk, but especially to the person's name. Somizy, one of my foster-sisters in Analalava, explained in response to my unwitting questions about her family names:

"I am afraid to say it [her dead father's name], it can't be done. [I would be] ashamed/disgraced [the condition of a person who has not observed the prohibitions entailed by respect]. You cannot utter the names of your parents after they are dead. They would punish you if you did. Your [Vazaha] family names are like those of the Hova [Merina] and the Tsimihety, and also the Comorians. All the children get their father's name as well as their own. When Sakalava die, they don't uncover/open *(mañokatra)* the body like the Hova and the Tsimihety. The Hova dig up the body again, if it died somewhere else, and take it back to its ancestral land *(tanindrazana)*. The Tsimihety do the same, burying men in rocks in the mountains *(lavabato)*, in different coffins from women. Sakalava just leave the body in the place where it died. Once buried—that's it, finished! *(Vaolevina—basy!)*."

Thus, I once overheard a man, renewing his *carte d'identité*, refuse to give his father's name to the Commissioner of Police, saying: "The name is gone/consumed *(Lany ny anarany)*." There is only one exception to the prohibition against speaking the names of the dead. As Saha Barimaso, a man in his fifties, said:

"Almost all Comorians bequeath names *(mandova anarany)* from grandparents to grandchildren, but Sakalava don't do that. The name is buried with the person. Even people who are not kin would not dare to say the name. They too would use words like 'that gentleman' or 'that lady' *(tompokolahy, tompokovavy)*. The names can only be spoken when invoking *(mijoro)* the ancestors."[25]

The stark brevity of their burial practices is one reason that royal followers describe themselves as "simple people," in contrast to their rulers. We will return to their invocations, but to put them in context, it is necessary to consider royal burials first.

FANOMPOANA MAFANA: HOT ROYAL SERVICE

A Sakalava saying from the colonial period states bluntly: 'Rulers don't return alive' *(Ampanjaka tsy ampody avelo)*.[26] As with commoners, most of the work of separation is accomplished in the burial and mourning that follows. The last royal burial in the Analalava area was held in 1925. We will consider contemporary French accounts of that burial in Chapters 3 and 7. Here I simply wish to summarize some parts of the earliest account of Sakalava royal burial practices in the Analalava region, published by André Dandouau in 1911. Most of the observations included here were confirmed in the general information that royal guardians and followers were willing to give me in the 1970s and the 1980s. I have used brackets to mark their additional comments and also to indicate what they never discussed.

André Dandouau wrote his account of Sakalava royal burials when he was stationed as head of the regional school in Analalava during the first decade of colonial rule.²⁷ His description of "traditional" Sakalava royal funerals probably came from the "royal children," one of whom was the current ruler's father, whom he taught in the Normal School for Native Teachers, including "a section for hostages," located in Analalava.²⁸ Dandouau noted that royal burials had lost their former grandeur. They were not so long, nor was the entire populace obliged to attend, bringing alcohol, rice, beef, and human sacrifices, since "the Sakalava kinglets exercise no more, thanks to our energetic action, than a purely nominal authority."²⁹

Dandouau begins his account by noting when a ruler's illness looked serious, he was described as "cool" *(manintsinintsy)* rather than "hot" *(mafana)* [a reversal of ordinary usage]. When death was imminent, he was moved out of the royal house *(zomba velo,* living house) [so the death would not pollute it]. The death was announced by saying, 'The land is broken' *(Folaka ny tany).* [Royal guardians in the 1970s echoed widespread opinion in saying that a person's death occurs when 'the breath of life is gone' *(ny rivotra ny aina lasa).* With royalty, this moment is expressed in the phrase, 'the clouds are gone' *(lasa zavona),* as seen in a mirror held up to the mouth.³⁰ Royal deaths are announced by saying *Mafana ny tany,* 'The land is hot,' referring to the heat still associated with illness and death. The phrase *Folaka ny tany* is also used, but *folaka* means 'filthy', not 'broken', in this context. A mother and daughter of Zafinifotsy royal ancestry explained this most clearly. They were describing the condition of people like themselves, or royal spirits, who have been polluted by contact with something forbidden to them. Only in response to my question did they mention royal death: "They are dirty *(maloto),* folaka! They must be washed, otherwise they will be angry." I asked, *"Folaka?"* "Disgustingly dirty, filthy, done dirt, struck with dirty things *(Vorery, makôta, mañano folaka, voa raha maloto).* Elsewhere it means 'broken,' like *vaky.* But here it means 'dirty, filthy'." I asked, *"Folaka ny tany?"* and they whispered in quick succession: "That is what people say when a ruler has died. Filthy ground, ground with a dead ruler in it" *(folan-tany, ley misy ampanjaka maty).*³¹]

According to Dandouau, the dead ruler was described as "keeled over" *(mihilaña)* [or as 'fallen down, decayed, gone to sleep' *(mirôtso)*]. Dandouau emphasizes how quickly royal subjects should gather and assume the dirty, disheveled state characteristic of mourning. [Mourners for royalty are also expected to 'bring tears' (*manday mahaitsapaly* in the royal vocabulary).] The doany or royal compound was renamed 'Does Not Heal' (Tsimahasenga). The ruler's officials began planning to move it to a new location, while others, known as 'Ancestor People' *(Razan'olo),* prepared the body for burial. [Razan'olo could be glossed as 'Peoples' Ancestors', as opposed to royal ancestors, or as 'People of Peoples' Ancestries'. As their name suggests, they stand ambiguously between living and dead people, and, as 'simple people,' inexplicably close to royalty.]

The royal burial is distinguished from all other forms of royal service as the 'hot service' *(fanompoana mafana).* The Ancestor People washed the body; tied the thumbs and big toes together and bound shut the mouth, filled with silver coins [or gold], using thin strips of a silk *(dalahany),* restricted to royalty, instead of raffia [or ordinary cloth] used in tying the mouths of commoners. They wrapped the body in silks known as *sobahia* and *daholy,* 6-10 meters long, then in a cowhide, which they sewed up, leaving an opening for the liquids of the decomposing body to run out. The liquids were caught in earthenware jugs placed underneath the wooden framework on which the body lay. The silk cloths and the cowhide were changed once a week for the next two months.[32]

Meanwhile a coffin was constructed from wood used only to make royal coffins. It had two parts: 'male' and 'female.' The male part was shaped like the steeply pitched roof of a house, with horns extending over the gable-ends, like a royal house. It was decorated with sculptures of lizards *(androngovato)* in silver with eyes of gold. The nonsculptured parts were decorated with silver five-franc pieces, often numbering more than one hundred. Dandouau does not describe the 'female' or bottom part of the coffin.

Once the corpse had been reduced to a skeleton, it was wrapped in a piece of silk *(dalahany)* and covered with jewelry, gold and silver coins, then wrapped in silks (sobahia and daholy), and put into the female part of the coffin. At dusk on the night of the burial, the male part was covered with silk to which the greatest possible number of little mirrors had been sewn, while the female part was covered with plain silk. The two parts of the coffin were dragged to the burial site on stretchers, to which the male part was attached by silver chains and the female part by twisted strips of silk. The female part of the coffin was put first into the grave: a long trench in the ground, lined with small stones and charcoal. The male part was put in on top of it. The hole was then filled with charcoal, gravel, and sand, in that order, and surrounded by rocks, because it was forbidden to allow the royal body to come in contact with dirt. Later, fine sand, called "white waves" *(riaka malandy)*, was laid around the perimeter of the tomb, between the two fences described in more detail below. No ground was allowed to show. 'That,' the Sakalava say, 'looks just like the seashore.'[33] [Dandouau mentions tasks assigned to specific categories of workers, which I have not included here. Royal guardians in the 1970s said that the Ancestor People were in charge of the 'hot service.' They never discussed the details involved in reducing a royal corpse to bone, creating royal coffins, or burying royal corpses. As they emphasized in many other contexts, details of royal service are known only to the 'masters of the work' *(tompon' ny asa)*, a point to which we will return in Chapter 6.]

The tombs of dead royalty in the Analalava region, as in most of the other royal domains along the northwest coast, are located not just outside the settlements of the living, but on islands. Royal regalia, perhaps including relics made from parts of the royal corpse, are kept inside the fenced royal compound at the Doany, but in a separate house—the 'royal ancestors' house' *(zomban-drazana)*—surrounded by a second fence, a high palisade of pointed stakes. The royal tomb is also surrounded by two fences: an outer fence made of live cuttings that gradually grow into a hedge and an inner palisade of *teza,* the hard cores of old hardwood trees, known as the *menaty* (red inside). The coffin-bearers, impelled by the royal spirit, break through the innermost fence to bury the corpse. The gap in the fence is covered temporarily with a cloth. The purpose of the menaty service *(fanompoana menaty)* following the burial, as described in Chapters 8 and 9, is to take down the old fence and build a new one big enough for the next corpse, cleaning the tomb in the process. The never spoken knowledge that death will recur, which the workers must build into the very structure of the tomb, is one major reason why royal funerals are considered especially 'difficult' *(sarotra)*.

The living ruler, surrounded by the 'People of the Living' *(Olo ny Manoro)*, as the guardians at the Doany are called, is prohibited from seeing or handling any of the personal possessions of her dead predecessors or the royal cemetery where they are buried. Photographs of her father were destroyed after he died.[34] Clothing, jewelry, and other personal effects are stored at the royal cemetery or inherited by the 'People of the Dead' *(Olo ny Mihilaña)*, the guardians of the Mahabo, who use them or give them to mediums. New living rulers neither resettle the doany of their predecessors nor turn them into shrines. They establish their own doany in new locations, although this was not immediately possible following the death of the current ruler's father in 1925, as we shall see.

Prohibitions against speaking the names of the dead are also imposed in the case of royalty. The practice of prohibiting the ruler's personal name, together with any other words resembling it, dates to the early nineteenth century if not before.[35] The prohibition applies to royal followers. Since it could be contested by a ruler's enemies—those who might well wish him dead—royal followers, like the kin and friends of deceased commoners, define themselves in part by observing such prohibitions. In contrast to commoners' ancestors, addressed generically as "Sir" *(Tompokolahy)* or "Madam" *(Tompokovavy)*, royalty receive individual praise names known as *fitahiaña* (blessings). These names, patterned after the term for a rich person—*ampañarivo,* 'one who has thousands' of everything—emphasize their countless followers, for example, "Noble One Who Nurtured Thousands" *(Ndramamahañarivo),* as the current ruler's father is known. Teknonyms, like "Soazara's Father" (BabanSoazara) for Ndramamahañarivo, are used in referring to or addressing the spirit in more informal circumstances, including spirit possession ceremonies.

FANGALA VORIKY: REMOVERS OF SORCERY

While the distinction between life-names and death-names is clear in principle, it too is 'difficult' in practice, as we learned by experience:

One day when we were in Tsinjorano, Bezara, the eldest son of the ampanjaka Maroaomby, the noble line there, showed us a piece of paper on which his ancestry was written.[36] It consisted of a list of the praise names of Zafinimena rulers in the form *X niteraka Y,* 'X bore Y,' ending in the praise names of the four ancestors buried in the local royal tomb, to which were added two names: another and finally his own. These were not in the form of praise names, and thinking he could say such names, we asked about the ampanjaka Maroaomby who had settled in Tsinjorano. He started to mention some other names, then got impatient with our writing them down, and said to his sister's son: "Write this down—X [male] bore Y, Y [male] bore Z, Z [male] bore A [male], then B [male]." Alan asked where the women were, and he stopped, saying he couldn't do this at all. "[They] would murder me *(mamono zaho)* if I talked about them, without alcohol or money. Alcohol, if not money, or otherwise money, like 100 FMG. Otherwise it can't be done. Saying the names of the ancestors may not be done. It is prohibited! They kill [those who break the prohibition]. 'Why are you talking about me?' *(Ino kabarinao zaho?)*, they would say." We all fell silent. Then his wife came along and started talking about something else.

This was not the first time we had been told about the practice of giving a token amount of alcohol, called *fangala voriky* (remover of sorcery), or a small amount of money. We had never known just what to do, never being sure whether such requests were essential to ancestral practice or simply part of relations with Vazaha like ourselves. We were also afraid that in giving money or alcohol we would be understood as trying to buy information knowingly or trying to get people drunk so they would give it unwittingly. The sensitivity of the issue came not only from tensions about 'profiting' *(manao profite)* on ancestral land, discussed further in Chapters 4 and 5, but also tensions about drinking. Many local people felt drinking was a scourge contributing to people's becoming lost to their ancestors. One guardian from the Doany even said about the Mahabo: "It's not the spirits who are talking, just the alcohol is talking *(barisa fo miteny)*." Nevertheless, we were instructed in *fangala voriky* again just a few days later, by MamanMahasoa's brother in Analalava, who came from a village not far from Malaza's village, Andonaka.

We said we wanted to go down and speak to Malaza in Andonaka about practices concerning the royal ancestors, and asked Mamoribe about how to do that. He said there was no special way. But then he said, "If you are talking about the ancestors—difficult things *(raha sarotra)*, not about royal services, or prohibitions, and such, but especially things concerning the royal ancestors—then . . . [pause] . . . There are some who don't, but

others will ask for some alcohol. To talk about difficult things like that is
to commit sorcery. The alcohol is called *fangala voriky* [remover of
sorcery]. You don't ask him whether he wants it—that should not be done
(tsy tokony hatao). But if you say, 'We'd like to learn about things like this,
like this, like this,' and he says, 'That's not possible,' then you can ask, 'Is
there anything that can be done to make it so these things can be spoken
about?' And he has to say 'Alcohol.'"

Gifts to the ancestors are essential to receive their blessings. The
critical point about giving a token amount of alcohol to the person
who serves as intermediary is that the alcohol creates a situation in
which people can talk to ancestors and about them without any sug-
gestion of intent to reach into their burial places in the ground or into
the silences of people in order to steal what kills. Silver coins are the
basis of all offerings to ancestors—one's own or those of royalty.
Fermented honey *(tô mainty),* called 'alcohol' *(toaka),* is the basis of
the celebrations honoring the royal ancestors at the beginning of each
new year. Saha Barimaso, one of the Father's mediums at the Mahabo,
echoed many guardians and royal followers in comparing the new
year's service at the Mahabo to the French new year's celebration,
which is also a big event in this area: "Tô mainty means *toaka mahintigny* [black liquor]. It's made in one month, then there is the taboo
month, when it becomes liquor. People make a kind of festival *(fety,*
from *fête).* They celebrate the arrival of *fanjava mitsaka* [the 'crossing-
over month'], the arrival of the new year. There are some who get
really drunk! The ampanjaka brings out the royal liquor!"

Royal followers celebrate their joyful reunion with the royal ancestors at the new year's service. But the toaka also expresses the difficulty
of talking about the unspeakable. Silence is what buries people, but
only talk can bring ancestors back out of the dead. People separate
themselves from the dead by burying them in the ground. They "don't
uncover ancestors" *(tsy manokatra razana),* as Somizy said in contrasting local practices with those of Tsimihety and Merina. But they cannot forget them either. Rather, they cannot lose them or become lost
to them; they cannot *not* look to find their hiddenness. To separate
from the dead is to live. To forget the dead is to die. But to recall

them in ancestors is to walk a most difficult path between the two, brushing against death for life.

Those who 'do not see there' *(tsy mijery any)* where their ancestors are buried, they are lost. Metaphors of 'not seeing,' especially not seeing or finding places, are the commonest ways of expressing the disregard, the lostness, that leads inexorably to sickness and death. Malaza in Andonaka put it most forcefully in speaking about the royal ancestors:

"No one knows anything or follows anything any more. This is why people get sick, why they go around half dead, killing each other. Makoveky came down here as an old man, asking about ancestral custom, just like you. He had become lost to his ancestors. I didn't dare to tell him about them. Another—one of Avoria's kin [an ampanjaka south of Antognibe]—came from Ankorefo. He was a sister's child who had gone to school, turned against ancestral custom, and gotten sick. I didn't tell him because they pray [as converts to Christianity]. A brother's son also got sick because he had forgotten ancestral custom. Slaves are people who are lost to their ancestors because they have been taken away from their kin. People who lose contact with their ancestors are like slaves, whatever their circumstances."

The sickness of ancestral anger afflicts one's whole being. As in spirit possession, when a royal spirit is thought to displace the medium's own mind, people can loose their minds *(very jery)* and become wandering or crazy *(mirendra, adala)*. Such wrong talking and doing alike is said to 'ruin the land' *(mandroba tany)* in which ancestors are embedded. Or, as the mother of Mamoribe in Analalava said about current affairs generally: "People have not paid proper respects to the land. The land is angry *(Meloko tany)*."

TSY MANOKATRA RAZANA: NOT UNCOVERING ANCESTORS

People in the Analalava region explain that they separate themselves from the dead be they royalty or simple people because everything about corpses is hot *(mafana)*, dirty *(maloto)*, rotten *(maimbo)*, bad smelling *(mantsigny)*, and deadly *(mahafaty)*. The spirits of dead people are jealous and vengeful, liable to cause more deaths among the living. But avoidance of the dead is also seen as a form of respect *(haja)* for the continued hiddenness of ancestors from whom living people grow. One does not suddenly become the other. Ancestors are made from remembering them. Remembering creates a difference between the deadliness of corpses and the fruitfulness of ancestors, which is not always evident in experience.

Like hiding the dead and forgetting them, the processes of finding ancestors by recalling and speaking to them are intensely visual and spatial as well as verbal. They are revealed in their burial grounds by opening, clearing, cleaning, and then seeing them in their mediums, in the regalia of the ancestors' house, and in the open enclosure of the tomb.[37] But they are also hidden again by reclosing, reburying, re-covering and resilencing these bodies and places.

Like forgetting the dead by prohibiting their names, the practice of invoking ancestors by saying those same names *(mijoro amin' ny razana)* also dates back to the 1840s if not earlier.[38] As MamanDjoma summarized it: "When Sakalava *mijoro,* they call on the ancestors and sprinkle water" *(Mijoro Sakalava—mikaiky razana, mitsipiky rano).* A white dish *(sahany,* from Swahili *sahani)*—Clean!, as people most often describe it—is used to hold the water. Fresh green leaves are added, and sometimes silver coins. The dish and coins are kept on the little shelf in the northeast corner of the house, which connects the different orientations of living people and ancestors.[39] Participants sit behind the dish and the elder man or woman who speaks for them, everyone facing east, men to the north, women and children to the south. The money, which is given to the speaker as part of the offerings, is called 'remover of the lock' *(fangala gadra/hidy),* because it enables him to speak to the ancestors. He is said to 'open the mouth of speech [like a door], and lay out speech [exposing its inside] *(mampibihaña kabary, mamavatra kabary).*' Once the speaker has invoked the ancestors' blessing, he or she takes the water in which the offering was made and sprinkles it back on the participants, after which everyone drinks it. People in the Analalava region call on their ancestors to present them with offerings, including sacrifices *(joro velo,* living *joro),* to inform them of major changes in the lives of their descendants and to beg for their blessings, to make and repay vows. Calling on the royal ancestors for their blessings is similar in form, but far greater in scale.

MANGATAKA HATSARAÑA: PLEADING FOR GOOD FORTUNE

Sakalava serve the royal ancestors by invoking them throughout the year, beginning with new year's services at the Doany and Mahabo. Participants compare these services, when the living ruler makes an offering to her ancestors and her followers make offerings of their own, to their own joro. The first and third months *(fanjava, volana,* 'moons') of the new year are the "invocation months" *(fanjava fijoroaña),* as Malaza of Andonaka once described them, because together, as a pair, they are times of new life.[40] Invocations are prohibited during the second month that separates these two, and during the last month of the year, which is also considered 'dead.' The moon must be 'bright' *(mazava),* waxing or full, that is, a 'living moon' *(fanjava velono).* To invoke the ancestors' presence during a 'red' *(mena),* 'rotten' *(motraka),* or 'dead' *(maty)* moon would be sorcery, that is, a clear attempt to kill them. Similarly, the names can only be spoken on 'good days' *(andro tsara)*—Friday, Saturday, and Monday. Invocations are prohibited on the 'bad days' *(andro ratsy)* when rulers in this area died.[41] Services begin in the morning, with the rising sun, concluding about mid-day. The afternoons are spent in 'play' *(soma),* activities without the prohibitions of work and service, especially dancing battles commemorating the victories of the Zafinimena over the Zafinifotsy, staged for the amusement of the spirits present in mediums.[42]

Taken all together, the invocations structure the entire lunar year, which unlike the local Muslim year, is calculated so that each event will recur at about the same time in the agricultural cycle. Preparations begin in the tenth month of the preceding year, toward the end of the rainy season. Around April, the guardians open the doors in the fences separating people from the royal ancestors and clean the courtyards surrounding the ancestors' house at the Doany and the tomb at the Mahabo in the 'dirt service' *(fanompoana kongo).*[43]

The clearing service is followed in the eleventh month by the 'mead service' *(fanompoaña tô mainty)*, when the guardians prepare a mixture of honey, water, and bark, which is left to ferment and darken—to become 'red,' as some people described it in contrast to the clear water of commoners' invocations—during the last 'dead' month of the year when the doors to the royal enclosures stay closed. Guardians resume their service in the first month of the new year, the 'crossing-over month' *(fanjava mitsaka)*, around July. The doors are re-opened, and the clearing service is repeated, after which the 'ancestors' (regalia) at the Doany and the 'ancestors' (tomb) at the Mahabo are washed, using the mead. The service concludes with a formal obeisance to the living ruler and the royal ancestors, attended by people from the surrounding countryside, during which they make their offerings, receive royal blessings, and drink the alcohol that remains. The guardians keep the doors closed the following month and reopen them again in the third month, when people can also pay their respects, make or fulfill vows, and listen to royal spirits speak through mediums on current events. Guardians continue to open and close the doors with much less ceremony during the remaining months of the year, when fewer pilgrims come there.

The overall purpose of the work, as guardians and pilgrims describe it, is to clean the ancestors of filth, the dirt done by killing and neglecting: to clear the ground, cut back the grass, and wash the regalia and the tomb, using the alcoholic mixture of honey and water known as 'blackness' *(tô mainty)*, which royal followers also compared to blood. As one of the female guardians at the Mahabo said: "We serve to gather up bad stuff, to gather up excrement, to gather up pee, to gather up filth, to gather up anger *(mangala raha ratsy, mangala tay, mangala amany, mangala vorery, mangala heloko)*, anger because the ancestors from Nosy Lava don't like things to be dirty."[44]

The times of the services, revolving around new years and living months, days, and parts of days, is built into the spaces of the Doany and Mahabo, centered on the living and ancestral bodies of royalty. The services always begin and end by unlocking and opening, closing and locking the doors implied in domestic invocations. In this case, the doors actually stand in the fences surrounding the royal ancestors. The prayer ground takes its name from its place 'At the Door' (Ambaravara), and the services as a whole are described in the same terms as 'opening the door' (mampibiaña varavara) and 'closing the door' (mampisôkatra varavara).

'We beg for a door' (Mangataka varavara) is one of the songs that pilgrims often sing in preparing to make offerings to the ancestors. When they 'receive a door' (mahazo varavara)—when the guardians open the door and set up the ancestors' drums at the entrance—they can speak to the royal ancestors through the 'supplicator' (ampangataka), the guardian whose special work is to say the names of the givers and convey their requests.

Being 'at the door' (ambaravara) of the royal ancestors' house at the Doany or the burial compound at the Mahabo is like being at the mouth of a spirit in a medium. Pilgrims pay their respects to the royal ancestors (mikoezy); they make vows (mañano vava); fulfill vows or otherwise explain their actions (mamantoko); beg pardon for their wrongs (mañato, mamonjy, malilo); and entreat the spirits' blessings (mangataka hatsaraña, radŷ, milamalama, mivalovalo). Here, as with domestic ancestors, speaking is inseparable from giving. People give money, cloth, and cattle, and they receive the spirits' blessings first in the mark of 'white earth' (tany fotsy/malandy), known as 'Great Remover' (Fañala Be) in the context of royalty, which the supplicator puts on their faces, and then in the 'blackness' of the mead.[45] They sing royal praise songs and dance to assuage the spirits' anger, and they receive the spirits' commentaries through mediums on current affairs. When the doors close, they all fall silent again.

The blessing in white clay—called tsontsoraka—marks a person who 'receives or accepts royalty' (mahazo ampanjaka).[46] As the 'Great Remover' of all forms of 'badness' (haratsiaña), it is thought to confer a 'clear or clean mind' (madio jery, mazava saina), undivided by reservations.[47] It also gives the petitioner the coloring of the cow with the black body and white face, known as 'luminous head,' required for royal sacrifices.

Relations with royal spirits in mediums are governed by the same taboos as relations with royalty at the Doany and Mahabo. But spirit-mediums are far more accessible, because they are settled throughout the region, in one's own kin and friends. The reciprocity that Sakalava anticipate when they invoke royalty is even more evident here. Such gatherings begin with the host's statement to the spirit—or spirits, because they are almost always accompanied by fellow spirits, their 'friends' *(namana)*—announcing the gifts that people have brought: money, cigarettes, matches, alcohol, rice, and cologne. The spirits respond by blessing everyone present. Gradually, in the course of the festivities, they return the cigarettes, alcohol, and cologne to thank their supporters for their songs and dances. By the end, all of the gifts are returned except the money and rice, which the mediums are expected to use for the spirits' clothes and other needs.

MAHABE AZY: MAKING THEM GREAT

In recognizing their ancestors—*seeing* them, reflecting on their significance, discerning the importance of practices with which they are identified—living people are said to "make them great" *(mahabe azy)*. The ancestors respond by blessing their descendants with fertility and prosperity. The growth of living people is the clearest sign of the greatness of ancestors who are hidden from view. Mamoribe's sister's daughter used the analogy of her own family to explain why she and her *zena hely,* his second wife, knew where the most important Zafinifotsy doany was, without knowing exactly who was buried there:

"In our house, Zama [her MB] and Zena [his senior wife] are the biggest. Since I and my brother and my mother's brother's children get out more, we are the better known. But the biggest are still Zama and Zena. The greatest rulers of the Zafinifotsy, the grandfathers of them all, are all at the doany at the mouth of the Loza. We don't know who they are. They might not appear by coming out on people [mediums]. Or they might come out on people very far from here. They have to say where they come from." [Why wouldn't they come out on people around here?] "Each to his own choice, each to his own pleasure *(samby am fidiny, samby am sitrapon'any)."*

MamanDjoma, who dissociated herself from her "Sakalava" and "Tsimihety" ancestries in describing herself as "Silamo," portrayed the reunion of living people with the dead in ancestors explicitly.

In 1973, MamanDjoma asked for copies of the photographs I had taken of her family. She said, "I want to put all the photos behind a piece of glass in a group. That way I could have all the ancestors *(razana)* grouped together in one place to show the grandchildren: 'This is your grandmother *(dady)*, no longer dady now, but razana.' Living people together with dry, together with wet *(Olombelono ndreky maiky ndreky lena)*. That means together with dead, together with living *(ndreky maty ndreky velono)*." I mentioned how some people were forbidden to look at photos of dead kin. She said, "Oh, no, not us." In 1981, her son, then living with his second wife, a Sambarivo from the Mahabo, had hung a photograph of his father across the northeast corner of the northern room of his house, which served as his salon. In 1989, MamanDjoma would have cut herself out of a photograph showing her with one of her in-laws who had died. But her former daughter-in-law, younger sister to the deceased woman, kept the picture, commenting, as did others, that few people still observed the old prohibitions concerning photographs of the dead.

From hidden roots—the dead buried in the ground—the living grow up and out over the surface of the land like a tree, which they work to nourish. The deeper the roots, the greater the tree. Ancestors *are* that fruitful union: expressed in explicitly sexual terms in royal funerals; as a union between husband and wife in the relationship between a spirit and its medium; and as a union between parent and child in relations among the living. Ancestors emerge in the birth of children.

The presence or absence of ancestors in living people is most apparent in their names. Parents usually call their babies and young children after animals around the house, like *Voalavo Kely* (Little Rat), *Amboaboa* (Little Dog), *Pisopiso* (Little Cat), or simply *Vahiny* (Stranger). Older people sometimes acquire nicknames referring to personal traits, like *Abdallah Petit* (Little Abdallah) or *Saha Droña* (Medium with the Missing Tooth). The proper names of adults express the good fortune that comes only from ancestors, for example, *Tsim-ijaly* (Does Not Suffer), *Mahatsara* (Beautifies), *Riziky* (Good Fortune), *Afisa* (Celebration), *Manambina* (Makes Fortunate). Sometimes these names are given at birth, itself a form of blessing, as reflected in names like *Nomenjanahary* (Godgiven), often given to babies born alive despite difficulties.[48] Parents may rename their children to commemorate later events when ancestors saved them from sure death. Masy (Powerfully Regenerative) explained how she got her name this way:

"My first name was Thérézy. When I was a month old, I was sleeping at night next to my mother. A visitor (vahiny) was staying in the house with us. During the night the visitor stole me and ran off with me. My mother awoke in the early morning because her breasts were so full of milk they hurt. She turned to feed me, and found me gone. My kin cried and lamented. They pleaded with the ancestors to bring about my return. Finally they got me back. In thanksgiving, they kept repeating: 'Powerfully regenerative are the ancestors' *(Masy ny raza, Masy ny raza, Masy ny raza)*, until Masy became my name."

Saha Barimaso (Medium with the Beautiful Eyes) said his real name is Tiandrazaña (Loved by Ancestors). At first he simply said that his parents had hired *(nikarama)* people to raise him; then, in response to my clear lack of understanding, he spelled out how his ancestors' love was revealed:

"They gave me to one. 'I can't do it!' the person said. Gave me to another. 'I can't do it!' Gave me to yet another. Finally my grandfather [MF] said, 'I'll take him,' and he gave me the name Tiandrazaña, which I still have now." [Why did your parents hire others to take care of you?] "Because I was born on a bad day for them *(andro ratsy amin'azy)*. So they gave me to other people. But I wouldn't die *(Zaho tsy mety naty)*. My father hired people and hired people. For three years I couldn't walk, just sick all the time. But I wouldn't die. Finally, my grandfather took me."

The harrowing encounters between the living and the dead from which ancestries grow are expressed even more directly in spirit-mediumship. Death is the focus of spirit-mediumship. Royal followers express the connection between the well-being of their rulers and the well-being of their ancestral land in terms like *mahasenga* (heals) for the body of the living ruler and *tsimahasenga* (does not heal) for the place where he or she dies. But they never murdered them to avert the disabilities of old age or lingering illnesses, which they interpret as the result of sorcery requiring different sorts of action. Even so, mediums do not show royal spirits in the prime of life; they embody them in the act of dying. The cause of every ruler's death is as well known as his or her death day. It is precisely that ominous weakness brought on by poison, the suicidal drinking from grief, the disastrous sea voyage, to which the medium's clothing, language, every gesture bear witness. As one medium put it, "that is what killed him, his other qualities merely kept him alive." When I once asked why even young rulers from Betsioko near Mahajanga, who are noted for their stylish dress, dancing, and conviviality, still have to be helped in sitting down and standing up, I was told: 'Because they have died *(nirôtso)*. They have felt many blows *(maro voa)!'*[49]

Mediums themselves die a little in becoming possessed. They let down their hair, as if in mourning, to receive the spirit. Their shaking bodies, draped with cloth, are stilled only by the spirit's entry. Then they have to be carried to their sitting places between the thighs of their followers. They portray the spirit in the peak of death, and after it leaves, they themselves have to be restored to life, especially by massaging the neck and shoulders, which have born the greatest burden.[50] In supporting ancestors on their heads, they themselves have experienced the affliction of death. Spirit possession begins in sickness, or rather, in dying, because the spirit who is not brought out from the body of its medium will finally kill it. Spirit-mediums, who have become adept at 'curing' *(mitaha)* death by going through this process, remake death into life by bringing the spirit out from where it is hidden in the body of a living person, and inducing it to speak, beginning with its name and place of origin.[51]

Praise songs that followers sing to honor the ancestors embodied in mediums during royal services celebrate the fruitful union between the dead and the living from which ancestors and descendants grow, imagined as a great branching mango tree—immense in stature, ever green, ever growing, and full of sweet-smelling fruits that can be eaten whether they are raw or ripe:

> *Ah Boanako Sarovola*
> *Tompoaiko tsy lany tavy Boanalahy é*
> *Fanompoako Sarovola Boanalahy é*
> *Fandrama miharo sira Boanako ô*
> *Ino koa ilainao Boanako ô*
> *Fanjakaña anao nahazo Boanalahy é*
> *Anao nahazo tsy nividy Boanako ô*
> *Nazonao am razanao Boanalahy é*
> *Anao tsy nividy tsy nanakalo Boanako ô*
> *Nazonao am razanao Boanalahy é*
> *Eeeeeeeeeeeeee, Eeeeeeeeeeeee Boanalahy*
> *Vololoña manga be Boanako ô*
> *Mena farany ambony Boanalahy é*
> *Mazoto mañano koezy andriaña Boanako ô*
> *Malaigny mañano dia ataony Boanalahy é*
> *Trongay magnindevo Trongay*
> *Trongay magnindevo Trongay*
> *Trongay magnindevo Trongay . . .*

Ah My Bwana 'Precious One'[52]
My master's fatness can never be consumed, Bwana-man é.[53]
My royal service 'Precious One,' Bwana-man é
Honey mixed with salt, My Bwana ô.
What more do you want, My Bwana ô?
You got the kingdom, Bwana-man é.
You got it, you did not buy it, My Bwana ô.[54]
You got it from your ancestors, Bwana-man é.
You did not buy or trade for it, My Bwana ô.
You got it from your ancestors, Bwana-man é.
Eeeeeeeeeeeeee, Eeeeeeeeeeeeee, Bwana-man é.
The new shoots of the great mango, My Bwana ô.
Red at the very top, Bwana-man é.[55]
The eager will assent to the royal ancestors, My Bwana ô.

The reluctant go their own way, Bwana-man é.[56]
Trongay enslaves, Trongay.[57]
Trongay enslaves, Trongay.
Trongay enslaves, Trongay . . .

Sakalava praise royalty by singing that hard-working people *mañano koezy* (do koezy), bow down, saying 'Koezy' in response to Bwana's every utterance. In recognizing royalty, they too will eat wealth— gifts known collectively as 'royal table scraps' *(mosarafa)*—and grow fat. The reluctant who go their own way—imagining that prosperity and fertility come from buying and trading, not from ancestors—will eventually starve. The praises suggest that rulers acquire followers not because they buy and sell people, which is how slavery is seen in this area, but because the royal ancestors satisfy every hunger. The contrast between slavery and devotion is sharply drawn in royal praise songs, perhaps because it is so often blurred in daily experience.

RAHA SAROTRA: DIFFICULT THINGS

Ancestors are 'difficult/precious things' because they emerge from confrontations with anger and death. They are heavy burdens, evident in the aching, ailing bodies of their mediums, and in the money, fear, and token drunkenness of their petitioners. These harrowing reunions between the living and the dead are essential to the continued recreation of ancestries *(firazaña)*, but their burdens and blessings are not evenly distributed.

Royal followers recognize several different ancestries associated with Sakalava monarchy. There are two royal groups: Zafinimena (Grandchildren of the Gold), members of the Maroseraña dynasty, and the Zafinifotsy (Grandchildren of the Silver).[58] The Zafinimena are senior to the Zafinifotsy, whose last living members are said to have drowned themselves in the Loza River north of Analalava during the early nineteenth century, rather than submit to Hova rule.[59] The Zafinimena include the living ruler *(ampanjaka be)* and nonruling royalty *(ampanjaka madiniky, anadoany)*, commoners *(vahoaka)*, and slaves *(andevo, Makoa, Masombiky,* or *olo mahintigny,* black people).[60]

According to the histories of the Zafinimena in the Analalava region, the current living ruler represents the twenty-seventh generation of the Maroserana dynasty in Madagascar and the fourth generation in the Analalava area. "Little ampanjaka" *(ampanjaka madiniky)* or "children of the doany" *(anadoany)* include Zafinimena from collateral, nonruling lines, as well as commoners who have been enobled in thanks for their special service to the monarchy.[61] The largest of the four groups of anadoany in the Analalava region are the Maroaomby of Tsinjorano, who—at least in Tsinjorano—represent their ancestry as grafted on to that of the Zafinimena. Explaining how the Maroaomby became ampanjaka, the eldest son of the ampanjaka Maroaomby in Tsinjorano said,

"When the ampanjaka was fighting enemies in the old days, we gave them support. When the enemies were dead, they gave us governing power *(fanjakaña)*. Those who help me, I give them government." [How are you related to the ampanjaka in the Analalava region?] "Every ampanjaka is akin to all the others *(Samby ampanjaka havana jiaby)*. There are some who aren't kin, however, but you say they are."

I do not know exactly how far back he reckoned his own ancestry because of the prohibitions mentioned earlier. Most people that I came to know well enough to ask them about their ancestries did not reckon them back further than the great-grandparents identified with their eight ancestors.

Slaves, including the special category of royal slaves known as Sambarivo, were distinguished in the colonial period as having neither ancestors nor descendants. They were slaves precisely because, having been taken far away, they were "lost, not knowing the land where their kin are" *(very, tsy mahay tany misy havana)*. Their ancestries were not grown or even grafted through work and service, they were cut by what royal followers themselves described as the sharp edge of force.[62] In 1971–1973 and 1981, some people who identified themselves as Makoa or Sambarivo said that they had kin in Africa or elsewhere in Madagascar, but they reckoned their ancestries mainly from grandparents through whom they had connections to other local people. The exception was one group of Sambarivo at the Mahabo, descendants of a noble family, enslaved for attempting to rival the royal line in the Analalava area.

Sakalava royal followers consider these ideas and practices concerning ancestors, the fruitful union between the living and the dead, to be critical to their 'kind' (karazana), differentiating them from other kinds in the Analalava region. As we have seen, they are most often imagined in terms of their spatial isolation: localized in tombs, people, trees, and other "difficult things," set apart by fences made from combinations of wood, stones, and prohibitions, and cultivated by guardians interested in seeing them bear fruit. I will argue that these places are not simply images of differences, but means of achieving them. In moving in and around the ground in which ancestry is articulated, people incorporate their understanding of such differences into their very bodies where their most forcefully immediate knowledge about their relationships to others lies. Drawing people into these places also serves to impose these ancestors on others.

The very hiddenness of the ancestors behind these barriers, the source of their fertile power, is central to the process by which some people's ancestors come to be recognized more fully than others. It is from the hiddenness of commoners' ancestors as well as the forced curtailment of slaves' ancestors that royal ancestors also grow, as revealed precisely in the fact that the powerfully generative hiddenness of royal ancestors is more fully, openly, elaborately recalled, and in being recalled, recreated in still more people.

The more visible hiddenness of royal ancestors compared to those of others is evident in the fact that when royal followers invoke their own ancestors, they call first on 'God' (Zanahary), then on the royal ancestors (Zanahary or ampanjaka fa lasa), and last of all their own ancestors. While they address their own ancestors using kin terms or generic titles like Tompokovavy (Madam) and Tompokolahy (Sir), they address royal ancestors with the praise names that distinguish them as historically unique individuals. Indeed, they 'bless' them in giving them such names, known literally as 'blessings' (fitahiaña). The practice of recalling ancestors is common to everyone, and some well-established kin groups have 'books of ancestors' *(bokindrazaña)*, listing their kin on their father's and mother's sides *(ampokondray, ampokondreny)*. But the praise names of royal ancestors are elaborated into histories *(tantara)*, written down in books that play a central role in legitimating their rights to rule over others.

Commoners bury their dead, do not revisit their graves, 'do not uncover ancestors,' and are prohibited from building fences even around themselves. While their dead gradually turn to mud, the bones of Sakalava rulers, forbidden to touch the ground, are continually remade. Sakalava rulers made relics from their dead in the precolonial period. During the nineteenth century, in circumstances discussed further in Chapter 2, they transformed their ancestral tombs into shrines, fencing them in both their places at the Doany and at the Mahabo.[63] The ampanjaka in the Analalava region also holds the Vy Lava knife, identified with the right to rule among the Bemihisatra branch of the Zafinimena dynasty. The royal ancestors in their several forms are never removed from their hiddenness. In fact, it was not wholly clear that there are ancestral relics in the ancestors' house at the Doany, a point to which we will return in Chapter 2. Nevertheless, their very hiddenness is cleaned and refurbished every year.

The royal ancestors in all their forms are most often called 'difficult/ precious things' *(raha sarotra)*, but their best known proper name is *Ny Mitahy*, 'Blessings', referring to their reputation as powerful 'medicines' *(aody)* protecting the land and people in which they live. In the precolonial period, their resting places were reputed as treasure houses, as indicated in Noël's account of Sakalava tombs in the heartland of the northern Sakalava domain of Boina, during the time when the last Sakalava domains were being established in the north:

> The Sakalava don't have cemeteries properly speaking, but family tombs sometimes quite close to one another. These tombs are ordinarily high up in inaccessible places like forests and the steepest rocks. The royal tombs are kinds of wooden mausoleums, decorated inside with magnificent draperies; they are generally thought to contain immense treasures, and if the inhabitants of Nosy Be are to be believed, that of Mrou-Vohai [Marovoay, near Mahajanga],

where five of the ancestors of Tsi-Oumeï-Kou [Tsiomeko, FFFM of
the current ruler of the Southern Bemihisatra] lie, would be one of
the richest in Madagascar. The royal graves ordinarily have only one
burial vault dug in advance; the tree trunk, which encloses the body
of the recently deceased prince, is put on top of that of his
predecessor in the tomb; and when the grave is full, it is sealed up,
and another is made for the future inhabitants of this gloomy
place.[64]

Royalty's greatest wealth is people. Commoners' ancestors do not
possess their descendants among the Sakalava royal followers, as they
are reputed to do among Tsimihety (Don't Cut), whose name is said
to derive from their refusal to cut their hair in mourning for royalty.
In contrast, the royal ancestors are embodied not only in their descendants, but may also possess the descendants of others—potentially
any other—by 'coming to rule' *(mianjaka)* over their bodies so intimately that their relationship is compared to marriage.

ADABARA TOKANA: SINGLE EYE IN THE BULL CONSTELLATION

Royalty, commoners, and slaves do not represent greater or lesser
versions of the same kinds of relations among ancestors and descendants. They are explicitly opposed. As local observers reiterated in
describing prerogatives forbidden to everyone but royalty: 'That's
what makes them rulers' *(mampanjaka azy)*. While royalty give people
the right to call themselves ampanjaka in thanks for their services,
there remains only one ruling or great ruler (ampanjaka manjaka,
ampanjaka be). While pairs are commonly idealized as 'complete' and
'true' in the face of conflict and deceit associated with the will to stand
alone, Sakalava rulers are uniquely complete in themselves. While
most of their followers are native-born 'children of the land' *(zanatany)*, they are strangers who came originally from Araby. A special
vocabulary, including a number of foreign words, must be used in
speaking about them, especially about their bodies, movements, and
immediate surroundings. Its whole purpose is, as Malaza stated, 'to

separate them from simple people' *(mañavaka azy am olo tsotra).* While most people marry out, rulers maintain their separateness by marrying endogamously, that is incestuously by the standards of their followers, though in practice they marry people of comparable economic standing like Silamo and Indians. Commoners and slaves can only be their concubines *(biby,* animals, or *ambala,* people in the pens). Birth, as well as death, is prohibited from the living ruler's compound. Royal relatives in the precolonial period were not snatched away, like slaves, but they were sent off to set up their own doany elsewhere, thus contributing to the gradual expansion of the monarchy northwards along the west coast. Royal infants are still born outside the doany and given to Sambarivo to nurse and raise. Royal kinship terminology puts them in the category of younger siblings to their royal parent, linguistically hiding the actual circumstances of their birth and transforming them into nonheirs and thus nonrivals who could not replace him or her *(misolo azy).* The current ruler's two daughters are allowed to live in a separate house in her compound in Analalava because the compound is not viewed as a doany. Yet whenever she travels, they are not permitted to stay there overnight.

The instrument responsible for the singleness of royalty, severing even ties to their own kin, is the long-handled knife known as the "Long Iron" (Vy Lava), identified with the royal ancestors and kept in the ancestors' house at the Doany. The knife's full name—The Long Iron Without Equal That Rules Alone *(Ny Vy Lava Tsy Roy Manjaka Tokana)*—echoes the fate *(anjara)* said to have been forged into its 'body' *(enge),* when it was made:

> *Adabara tokana—ankoay*
> *Mamba tsy roy an-drano*
> *Moasy tsy roy an-tanàna*
> *Tsisy bebe tsy izaho.*

> Single eye in the Bull Constellation—sea eagle
> Crocodile without equal in the water

Diviner without equal in the land
No one is greater if not I.[65]

The Vy Lava is the foremost embodiment of the *Mitahy* (Ancestral Blessing), as the royal ancestors at the Doany are known. It shows 'Ancestral Blessing' to be the source of royalty's greatest power, yet also its greatest weakness. As a sword of conquest, it accounts for Bemihisatra hegemony, and thus infinite numbers of followers. As a 'medicine of fewness' *(aody tsy maro)*, it has prevented the Bemihisatra from having many descendants of their own. The contradiction turns on the assumption that the deadliest enemies are not strangers but kin. Royal followers acknowledge the struggles of Sakalava rulers with Hova and French rivals in explaining their currently reduced circumstances, but they locate the most significant source of their living-dying in 'battles among kin' *(ady milongo)*. As Ndremahazo Jean-Pierre, a descendant of the Bemazava line of Sakalava rulers, explained:

"Although the Bemihisatra Sakalava rulers don't multiply, they don't die out either *(tsy miteraka maro, fa tsy matimaty koa)*. Just four of them have reigned here for at least one hundred years. They've not died out, but they've not multiplied either. They don't multiply because of the awful power of the Vy Lava, which extends even to the royal family. But if they gave birth to many, their descendants would fight among themselves for the ancestors and end up murdering one another. Ancestral blessing *(mitahy)* has many meanings."[66]

CONTRADICTIONS

I have begun this book in the middle by trying to convey the complex, often contradictory ideas and practices concerning ancestry, land, and labor, which are central to daily life in the Analalava region of north-western Madagascar.[67] Ancestors are separated from both the living and the dead by a variety of means, while remaining indispensable to daily existence. They exist in the names of their descendants, in dreams and spirit possession, and above all in the growth and decline of the communities of their descendants. Ancestors differentiate people who rule from those who follow and from slaves. People with ancestors thrive; people who lose or become lost to their ancestors dwindle and die.

Thus ancestry is essential to life, but people are not equally ancestral. Sakalava royalty, commoners, and slaves differ in having greater or lesser ancestors. In other respects, Sakalava royalty are absolutely contrasted with commoners and slaves as those who are singular are contrasted with those who are infinitely reproducible. These structural contradictions lie at the heart of the paradox that masters of the land are also servants of royalty, akin to slaves who have no ancestors by definition. They draw attention to the singularity of royalty compared to the reproducibility of 'simple people,' and to the role of force as well as devotion in the growth and decline of the monarchy centered on the royal ancestors.

People who forget their dead die. Those who have no forebears have no descendants. People who recall ancestors, find and see them, hear them and speak to them in the places and people where they are hidden—they thrive and multiply. But to thrive on these hidden roots is to reconnect with death. Ancestors are the greatest source of blessing, but they also kill.

"Death by itself does not confer ancestorhood," as Fortes pointed out, because not everyone who dies becomes an ancestor.[68] Ancestors, made from people who occupied authoritative positions in life, confirm their descendants in power, as many ethnographers and historians have shown.[69] The Sakalava case shows that ancestors are also unmade to turn other people into followers. Should we conclude that ideologies about ancestors are uniquely suited to oppression, that in their focus on the power of death, they facilitate the violent reformation of kin ties through slavelike labor, if not also killing? Yet followers of Sakalava royal ancestors have a keen sense of the frailty of ancestral power. Why? Is this too an ever-present possibility in any ideology based on certain death? Is it an ideology of death masking defeat, born out of their own particular history? Or is it an ideology from which new dominions might yet grow—new oppressors, new deaths for some, but new lives for others—as portrayed in spirit possession, where common mediums, though dying a little in the attempt, survive to master royalty?

Fortes's question still holds: "How does parental and lineage authority, as projected in ancestor worship, link up with political authority and its ritual symbolism and representation as in some African kingship?"[70] But what accounts for the continued force of these homely metaphors in circumstances where people are explicitly *not* related as kin, and where the monarchies themselves have been subsumed into larger, nominally republican or socialist forms of polities?

To answer such questions about the "authority of ancestors"—relevant to broader questions about the creation and subversion of absolutist forms of power—we need to incorporate the range of 'strangers' by which 'kin' are defined, recognizing that the authority of ancestors is not limited to the supposed kinship-based societies considered by earlier scholars. We must set these relations between ancestors and descendants, natives and strangers more firmly in changing historical and material conditions.[71] Finally, we need to follow through on the connections that participants themselves make between ancestors and their descendants, between death, sexuality, and fertility, that help to explain why, as Sakalava royal followers put it, 'dead things have no life in them,' but ancestors do. To see how people in northwestern Madagascar have gone at the work of growing, grafting, and cutting into one another's lives and deaths, distinguishing the singular from the infinitely reproducible, we will begin by examining how kings become queens.

Deadly Blessings

Mitahy—maro ny dikany amin'azy.
Ancestral blessing has many meanings.

Ndremahazo Jean-Pierre

DEATH AND SEXUALITY

Sakalava royal ancestors are commonly called 'difficult/precious things' *(raha sarotra)*, but their proper name at the Doany is *Ny Mitahy* (Blessing/Helping) or *Mitahy Razanandriana* (Blessing Royal Ancestors/Royal Ancestral Blessing).[1] The name evokes the mutual care from which ancestors and their descendants are thought to grow: royal ancestors bless their followers with fruitful lives, while their followers 'bless' royalty in giving them praise names *(fitahiaña,* blessing, helping) and in saving them from their enemies. As we have already seen, their worst enemies are their closest kin. So the Vy Lava, held by the living ruler, cuts both inward and outward, leaving Bemihisatra hegemony balanced precariously on a thin line of descendants, no more than one in each generation.

The mixed blessings of the Bemihisatra are magnified by contrast with the Bemazava from whom Ndremahazo Jean-Pierre is descended. The Bemazava branch of Sakalava royalty developed in opposition to the Bemihisatra branch during the late eighteenth century. Descendants of the two ancestries, as well as their followers, still define themselves and each other in terms of their opposed solutions to the contradiction between many kin and many followers. Bemazava recognize few of the Bemihisatra prohibitions associated with death, and none of their prohibitions concerning kin. Although they still distinguish themselves as 'royalty'—for example, by using praise names *(Ndria . . ., Ndre . . .)* that Bemihisatra forbid to living people—many have converted to Catholicism. Their cemeteries and villages, now concentrated in the Ambanja and Maromandia areas of the northwest coast, teem with the descendants of those who lost—they would say 'gave'—the Vy Lava to the Bemihisatra in the early nineteenth century.

'Ancestral Blessing has many meanings' not only in northwestern Madagascar, but elsewhere as well. Throughout Madagascar, *mitahy* refers above all to the beneficent actions of ancestors on their descendants, helping, caring, healing them often through 'medicines' *(ody)* in which they are embodied. Berg demonstrates the central role of ancestral *sampy* and *ody* in the "protector system" of the Merina monarchy during the nineteenth century.[2] Bloch analyzes the relationship between 'blessing' (mitahy) and violence in the context of circumcision rituals practiced by Merina commoners as well as royalty during the nineteenth and twentieth centuries.[3] Bloch argues that Merina ancestors, royal and common, are associated with men, and that ancestral blessing is achieved through violence directed against inferiors embodied in women.[4] There are data on historical and contemporary social relations in Imerina to support the close association between men and ancestors. But there are very little data on women, despite the fact that they weave the highly valued silk shrouds in which the most exalted ancestors are wrapped. They hold the corpses in Merina funeral rites because they are, as Bloch states in his study of Merina reburials, "the recognized vessels of kinship emotions." Yet in his view, they are finally "left holding the corpse" in Merina reburials, in the same way that they are left with the mortality of birth in Merina circumcision rituals. The regenerative blessing of the ancestors celebrated in Merina circumcisions and reburials is a male form of birth.[5]

In northwestern Madagascar, as elsewhere in Madagascar, the terms *razana, ampanjaka, andevo, mpanaraka*—ancestor, ruler, slave, follower—are not usually marked according to gender; when they are, both 'male' and 'female' *(-lahy, -vavy)* are used. Men are accorded priorities in relation to ancestors, but these are offset by priorities given to women. The very process of 'birth' *(miteraka)* is not inherently gendered. As we shall see, both men and women 'bear children' *(miteraka zanaka)*. The mutual growth of ancestors and their descendants is achieved through their union, as celebrated in the sexual imagery of burial rites and spirit possession ceremonies as well as in marriages. While the earliest Sakalava rulers are said to have been men, it is a curious fact that succession practices in western Madagascar, and in Imerina, changed radically during the early nineteenth century. Beginning among the Sakalava around 1790, and among the Merina in 1828, paramount rule shifted from men to women. The changing roles of men and women in the reproduction of singular rulers and their infinite numbers of followers, the vitality of ancestors and the deadness of corpses, are most clearly revealed in oral and written narratives about past generations called *tantara*. The tantara also show that the common concerns of Malagasy and their Euro-American ethnographers, which are evident in current scholarship, are rooted in their historical relations as well.

TANTARA: HISTORIES

In pronouncing praise names, royal followers invoke the ancestors' presence among the living. "To recount [the events of their lives] is to pray" *(mitantara—mivavaka),* as Laza Be put it. In recounting the tantara of the Southern Bemihisatra rulers, guardians and followers explain how they came to Madagascar in the first place, and then how they came north; for example "How the Ampanjaka First Came Here to Madagascar" *(Fanazavana Niantombohohany Voalohany Natongan' I Ampanjaka Teto Madagasikara);* or, "[The] Coming of the Ancestors of the Ampanjaka from Abroad" *(Naviany Razaniampanjaka Avy Tany Andafy).*

While talk about mitahy concerns the growth and decline of ancestries in general terms, the tantara are more circumstantial, reflecting the fact that they were composed, or at least recomposed and set down in writing, in the mid-twenties, during the legal dispute with French colonial authorities following the death of Ndramamahaña (Tondroko). Finally, after the intervention of an inspector from the Governor-General's office in Tananarive, the Southern Bemihisatra were allowed to install Ndramamahaña's infant daughter in his place, which she still occupies.[6] The tantara occasionally explain well-known prohibitions, like the prohibition against personal names following a ruler's death, suggesting that they were written for people unfamiliar with royal practices, as well as for royal followers.

One of the major purposes of the tantara was surely to substantiate the legitimacy of Soazara's succession in the eyes of the colonial administration, and later to substantiate the legitimacy of her first child, a daughter born in 1955. Another purpose, so I will argue here, was to justify her gender. The Southern Bemihisatra tantara and other historical sources indicate that gender, sexuality, and succession had been common concerns of Malagasy and French in western Madagascar since the early nineteenth century. While they agreed in using genealogies to substantiate legitimacy, their evaluations of gender were not only at cross-purposes, but based on entirely different lines of reasoning. In saying that mitahy has many meanings, Ndremahazo Jean-Pierre drew attention to the paradox that the royal ancestors, essential to the increase of the living, should also be responsible for their dwindling. Spoken tantara, documented by the French investigators Noël and Guillain during the 1840s, as well as the written tantara of the Southern Bemihisatra, recount in more detail how this dwindling resulted not only from battles among kin, but from wrongful, incestuous marriages. Noël and Guillain studied royal history for information about succession that would provide rules to guide the French in making their own appointments in the future. They interpreted the sovereignty of women as a sign of terminal barbarism, ultimately justifying colonial rule. According to the Southern Bemihisatra histories, an incestuous marriage between brother and sister led eventually to a shift in succession from 'children of men' to 'children of women,' represented by the brother and sister's child, Andriantsoly and Tsiomeko, who were rivals for power during the 1840s, when Noël and Guillain were making their inquiries. In recalling the same events, contemporary royal followers in the Analalava region champion the 'sister's child,' who is their current living ruler. But they also recount how the powerful expansion of the monarchy in the hands of men became a struggle to survive in the hands of women, following Andriantsoly's betrayal of his sister and his sister's children.

Guillain laid out his understanding of events for contemporary readers in his "General Map of the Western Part of Madagascar, 1843," a kind of chronotope (Plate 2). In exploring these regions now, I will use data from other Sakalava royal domains along the west coast to argue for connections that neither the Southern Bemihisatra nor the French make directly: that changes in living rulers from male to female, 'children of men' to 'children of women,' were inseparable from changes in ancestors from relics to tombs, and from a shift in the balance of power from royalty to commoners and slaves even before the French conquest at the turn of the century. We will begin with the association between male rulers and relics to which Southern Bemihisatra attribute the expansion of the Volamena dynasty.

MALE RULERS AND RELICS

Southern Bemihisatra histories chronicle the growth and expansion of the royal ancestors. They begin with the "two men descendants of Ibrahim" *(roalahy taranaka Ibrahim),* from Basiroly in Araby, portrayed as brothers who first established Sakalava rule in the south in the late sixteenth century. They continue through the generations of their descendants who moved ever-further north, ending with Soazara, the currently reigning ampanjaka of the Southern Bemihisatra in the Analalava region. Like ancestral invocations *(joro),* these histories are based on lists of ancestors' names. They are different from joro, and are more like accounts that royal spirits give when they possess their mediums, in the ways they elaborate on names. Like ancestral spirits, the tantara detail who gave birth to whom and who had no descendants, and they specify dates—the years of their reigns, and, for some recent rulers, the months and days.[7]

The *Fanazavana Niantombohany Voalohany Natongan' I Ampanjaka*

Plate 2. *Carte Générale de la Partie Occidentale de Madagascar*
1843, General Map of the Western Part of Madagascar, 1843
(CAOM c. 14, d. 28, reproduced in Guillain 1845).

Teto Madagasikara (How the Ampanjaka First Came Here to Madagascar) ends with such a list:

Ireto no Ampanjaka nanjaka (These are the Ampanjaka who ruled):

1. Andrianalimbe   *lahy* (male)
2. Marosiranana   *lahy* (male)
3. Andriamiandrivola
4. Andriamandimby
5. Andriamisara
6. Andriandahifotsy
7. Andriamandisoarivo
8. Andriamboniarivo
9. Andriamahatindriarivo
10. Andriamarofaly   *lahy* (male)
11. Andriamamelonarivo   *vavy* (female)
12. Andrianatolotrarivo
13. Tsimisarakarivo
14. Andriamamalikarivo
15. Andriamamitranarivo
16. Andriamanetriarivo
17. Andriamamahanarivo
18. Soazara *mpanjaka vavy manjaka amin'i izao ankehitri'izao Nanjaka nanomboka tamin' ny 2 Octobre 1925* (Soazara female ruler rules now. Ruling began on 2 October 1925)

The differences among the Southern Bemihisatra written histories will be discussed elsewhere. Although this list does not include the names of some early rulers appearing on other lists, it will suffice to guide the reader in the following discussion of issues common to all the histories.[8]

Andrianalimbe and Marosiranana sailed from Araby to southwestern Madagascar where they founded a kingdom at Trongay (possibly Tree Trunk) or Toliamaeva (Beautiful Place of Arrival) near the mouth of the Fiherenana River, near present-day Toliara (Fig. 2). Their descendants expanded out from Trongay to found new kingdoms to the

72

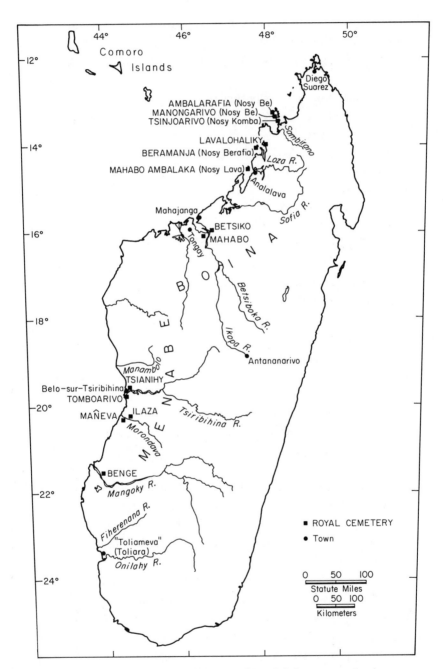

Figure 2. Royal cemeteries (mahabo) marking Sakalava expansion in western Madagascar.

south, east, and north during the 1600s. Andriamisara founded the first of the northerly kingdoms. His doany was located on the banks of the Saint-Vincent River in the Fiherenana region. When Andriamisara died, his only child—a son, Andriandahifotsy—moved up to the banks of the Mangoky River north of Fiherenana. His doany at Benge established the domain known as Menabe in contrast to Boina, the domain that Sakalava royalty later established in the north. His son, Andriamandisoarivo, and grandson, Andriamboniarivo, expanded the monarchy to encompass the entire area south of what is now Mahajanga on Bombetoka Bay.

The Southern Bemihisatra histories and one of the Sakalava manuscripts from the Mahajanga area attribute the conquests of living rulers to the royal ancestors embodied in relics called "grandparents" *(dady)*, like the ones located since the early colonial period in reliquaries (doany) at Belo-sur-Tsiribihina (where there is also a living ruler) and Mahajanga (where there is not).[9] Royal tombs are never mentioned. On the contrary, the fact that "the earth is filthy" or "the earth is hot" because a ruler has died, is the recurrent reason for moving the royal capital to a new location.

Travelers along the west coast during the seventeenth and eighteenth centuries commented on the importance of royal relics and their association with spirit possession. Père d'Azevedo, a Portuguese Jesuit who was one of the first missionaries to visit Madagascar, wrote concerning people around the Bay of Baly, south of Mahajanga, in 1617:

> they address their prayers and make offerings to the souls of their
> dead relatives, who are their idols and from whom they conserve
> preciously, like so many relics, the nails, hair, clothes, etc. They
> invoke these dead on every occasion, especially in difficult
> moments. . . . The devil enters often into the body of one of these
> savages and, claiming to be the soul of one of their recently deceased
> relatives, proclaims that, if such a person is sick, or if such a
> misfortune has happened, it is because one has forgotten him and
> one has not made him sacrifices.[10]

One hundred years later, in 1741, Dutch sailors on the *De Brack,* who had come to buy slaves in the neighboring Bombetoka Bay, reported that the local Sakalava "king" needed to consult ancestral relics before deciding to trade. They described the shrine filled with treasures, including "a great lacquered, gilded throne, all ornamented with sculpture," and reliquaries in gold and silver, ornamented with gold teeth "like those of a manatee." They also recorded the king's invocation to the spirits, asking if the visitors were free from evil intent and if their gifts too were "clean." This time, the ancestor's response, through "a broken-down old sorcerer," was positive.[11] Another century later, in 1854, at the royal capital of the ampanjaka Otsinjo on the Bay of Baly, the ancestors embodied in mediums told Otsinjo that the Jesuits who wanted to live in her domain should be put to the *tangena* poison ordeal, so the Jesuits stayed away.[12] The French sea captain, Guillain, describes relics stolen from the ampanjaka Vahiny on Betsiboka Bay at about the same time: "These relics consisted of certain parts of the bodies of Andriamandisoarivo and Andriamaha-tindriarivo, such as the nails, hair, and teeth, all preciously conserved. Possession of these relics is, in the eyes of the Sakalava, like the consecration of royalty, and the reigning king ought to be depository of them in order to be able to rally to him the whole population."[13]

Ancestral relics were still the focus of royal services among Sakalava south of Mahajanga during the early colonial period. Le Capitaine H. Rey, stationed in Menabe in 1912, echoes Guillain in observing that the power of Sakalava royalty "resides *exclusively*" (his emphasis) in possessing the royal relics; "a king without *dady* was a ruler without a sceptre; he had no authority." "Grandparents" *(dady)*, also called "difficult/precious things" *(raha sarotra)*, were thus the object of "inevitable and bloody wars" during the late nineteenth century.[14]

TRONGAY MAGNINDEVO: ROYALTY ENSLAVES

As we saw in Chapter 1, Southern Bemihisatra now praise the expansive powers of the royal ancestors by singing in their honor: *Trongay magnindevo,* "Trongay enslaves." Trongay was the name of the royal capital (doany) established by the two brothers at Toliameva; *Tongay* (or Tongaï), possibly Trongay, was also the name of Andriamandisoarivo's capital at Masselegem in Boina Bay, with which the northern domain of Boina is said to have been established.[15] As expressed in royal praise songs, Trongay—rulers embodied in their mobile, but always central place among people—enslave not by capturing people in warfare or buying them from slave traders, but by love (fitiavaña). People chose to settle around royalty. Yet traders' reports indicate that slave trading was fundamental to the growth of the monarchy and its northwards expansion during the seventeenth and eighteenth centuries.[16]

The traders were primarily Arabs, Portuguese, English, and Dutch. Their ships called at various western ports, but most of the trade was along the northwest coast. It began especially in the mid-1660s, when English ships began taking slaves to the New World, especially Barbados, and a few Dutch ships took slaves to the Cape of Good Hope. Despite their settlement at Fort Dauphin, on the southeast coast, since the 1640s, French trading in western Madagascar was still "negligible" at this time.[17]

In the early 1600s, the St. Augustine's Bay area (near Toliameva, where the two brothers from Araby were said to have landed in 1570), was characterized by "a barter economy based on the supplying of ships with provisions in exchange for copper and beads." There were occasional sales of slaves, but at "very low prices," compared to the Arab-controlled ports then active in the northwest.[18] Gradually, toward the end of the century, guns and then coins were introduced in exchange. According to Armstrong, who has done the major research in this area:

> The growth of this trade coincided with the Sakalava expansion . . .
> it may be inferred that the trade both benefited from and contributed
> to this expansion, through the provision of guns and powder to both
> the Sakalava (through Morondava) and to their opponents at St.
> Augustine's Bay. . . . The rise of the Sakalava kingdom in Menabe
> resulted in wars between the warriors of Lahefoutsy and those of the
> St. Augustine's chiefdoms, in which the latter were the losers. While
> this created opportunities on both sides for slave traders, the fact was
> that the winning Sakalava became a good source of slaves,

presumably many of them being prisoners of war. Conversely they offered a ready market for muskets, on a rough basis of one musket for one slave.[19]

Although English ships reported "good trading" at St. Augustine's Bay and at the mouth of the Morondava River during the 1670s and 1680s, the main slave-trading port during this time, for both Arabs and Europeans, was the island town of Massailly on Nosy Antsoheribory in Boina Bay, south of Bombetoka Bay.[20] Massailly is the Nova Mazalagem of the Portuguese Jesuit missionaries, mentioned earlier. The missionaries like Père d'Azevedo, who were there in 1613–1614 and 1616–1617, simply noted that "many captives" were taken. Later Portuguese travelers in 1663 and 1667 estimated the numbers at 3,000–4,000 and 3,000 a year. They came not only from the coast, but also from far inland, involving "Hova" (Merina) traders as well.[21]

On August 15, 1686, a Dutch ship reported that Magelagie (Massailly, Nova Mazalagem) was burned and deserted, as the result of a battle with the *Sacalave of lang oren* (Sakalava or long ears) from the mainland. By 1696, the Sakalava ruler Simanata (Andriantsimanatona) had moved the trade from the island to his capital on an elevated plain on the mainland.[22] Armstrong documents twenty-one more slaving voyages of Dutch East India Company traders along the northwest coast between 1700 and 1795. Filliot analyzes the increasing role of French slave traders to Mauritius and La Réunion during this same period.[23] Guillain notes that it was during the reign of the Sakalava queen Vahiny (circa 1780–1808) that Malagasy on the northwest coast began slaving expeditions against the Comores, and even as far as the East African coast, contributing to the great growth of her capital at Moudzangaï, near Mahajanga, on the north side of Bombetoka Bay.[24] The Arabs, who ruled Massailly before 1686, traded slaves to Europeans in exchange for some firearms, but mostly money in coins and novelties. The Sakalava rulers at Massailly after 1686 and at the other western ports, who used Arabs to do their trading for them, sought mainly firearms.[25]

Although slavery was critical to the expansion of the Sakalava monarchy, the historical and ethnographic accounts of the domains in Menabe and Boina do not say how it was practiced. Le Capitaine Rey, stationed in Menabe during the early colonial period, noted that slaves, regardless of origin, were known as *tsy raza*, "without ancestors."[26] Commoners also seem to have been subordinated by restricting the extent to which they could recognize their own ancestors.

> In the beginning, only royals and nobles had the right to have ancestors, the rest of the people didn't count. Then, as a result of services rendered to royalty by the people or to compensate for fealty, the kings ennobled a few Sakalava in giving them a title transmissible to their descendants who then had ancestors. From this institution dates the great families that were found on the west coast at the time of the conquest of Menabe [called] *olo misy raza, vahin'olo* [people with ancestors, people connected like vines]. The freed persons and slaves obviously had no ancestors, but the *mpanompo* [royal followers] kept their traditional ancestors.[27]

We will return to these matters later after looking more closely at some consequences of having kin.

ADY MILONGO: BATTLES AMONG KIN

Southern Bemihisatra tantara explain the expansion of the Zafimbolamena dynasty not in terms of battles among strangers to acquire prisoners of war they could exchange as slaves for guns; they describe them as 'battles among kin' *(ady milongo),* fought to gain control over ancestors in the form of relics, in which duplicity between siblings played a critical role. The importance of stealing ancestors in these battles among kin, turning siblings into enemies and captives into slaves, is confirmed by the involvement of others in the same tactics. As the Merina and then the French joined these battles, the ideology and practice of division seem to have changed from duplicity between brothers over moveable relics to a brother's deception of his sister, which led to the loss of the relics and the elaboration of royal tombs in their stead.

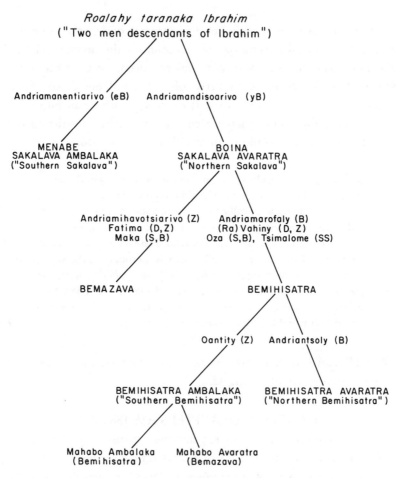

Roalahy taranaka Ibrahim
("Two men descendants of Ibrahim")

Andriamanentiarivo (eB)   Andriamandisoarivo (yB)

MENABE
SAKALAVA AMBALAKA
("Southern Sakalava")

BOINA
SAKALAVA AVARATRA
("Northern Sakalava")

Andriamihavotsiarivo (Z)   Andriamarofaly (B)
Fatima (D,Z)   (Ra)Vahiny (D, Z)
Maka (S,B)   Oza (S,B), Tsimalome (SS)

BEMAZAVA   BEMIHISATRA

Oantity (Z)   Andriantsoly (B)

BEMIHISATRA AMBALAKA   BEMIHISATRA AVARATRA
("Southern Bemihisatra")   ("Northern Bemihisatra")

Mahabo Ambalaka   Mahabo Avaratra
(Bemihisatra)   (Bemazava)

Figure 3. Divisions in two resulting from battles among royal kin *(ady milongo)*.

These divisions, already implicit in the "two men descendants of Ibrahim" *(roa lahy taranaka Ibrahim),* portrayed as two brothers, who first founded Trongay at Toliameva, are outlined in Figure 3.[28] No outside sources confirm or repudiate what the Southern Bemihisatra tantara present as the earliest example of duplicity among brothers, namely that the praise name of Andriamandisoarivo, Noble Who Deceived Thousands, commemorates how he duped his older brother,

Andriamanentiarivo, Noble Who Blessed Thousands (by anointing them with white clay), into giving him the ancestral relics that enabled him to found the domain of Boina, north of Mahajanga.[29] In contrast, various observers, notably the French consular agent Noël and French lieutenant commander Guillain, documented current opinion, including their own, on the struggles between the brother and sister, Andriantsoly and Oantity, in the 1830s and 1840s, which eventually led to the division between the Northern and Southern Bemihisatra, whom Southern Bemihisatra see as 'children of men' (Andriantsoly's descendants) and 'children of women' (Oantity's descendants). The very image of division as a pair of siblings, first brothers, then brother and sister, may be the product of these events in the 1830s and 1840s, put back to the origins of the dynasty. Nevertheless, all the participants see the succession around 1780 from Andriamarofaly to Andriamamelonarivo (Vahiny), distinguished as the first male-female pair in Southern Bemihisatra genealogies (see p. 71), as the turning point between the expansion of the dynasty embodied in living men and relics and its struggling decline embodied in women and tombs.

VAHINY: STRANGER

"Sakalava" tantara from the 1840s concerning Vahiny's succession to power around 1780, as documented in Noël (1842–1843) and Guillain (1845), are summarized in Figure 4.[30] Their perspectives on the earlier events, like those of the people to whom they spoke, were undoubtedly affected by contemporary controversies in which royal followers were then involved, the divisions between Bemihisatra rulers, Andriantsoly and Oantity's daughter (ZD) Tsiomeko, and between Tsiomeko and Tsimandroho, the male head of the rival branch known as Bemazava.[31] Whether or not Noël and Guillain spoke more to Andriantsoly's followers than to Tsiomeko's followers, as Noël's comments suggest, their bias toward Andriantsoly and against Tsiomeko is clear at other points in their accounts.[32] Guillain's praise is reserved mainly for Andriantsoly's Hova counterpart, Radama, and his greatest scorn for Tsiomeko's Hova counterpart, Ranavalona—"the coming of that woman to the throne of Imerina had the most lethal *(les plus*

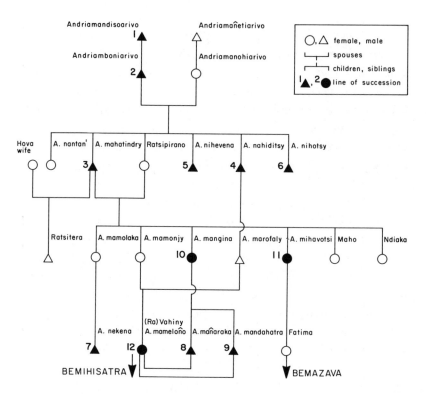

Figure 4. Genealogy of the transition from male to female rulers in the late
eighteenth century and the division between the Bemihisatra and
Bemazava, according to Guillain (1845).

funestes) consequences for the civilization of the country."[33] Later in
the 1880s, as we shall see, French officials represented themselves to
the Southern Bemihisatra as having dealt with Andriantsoly as the real
head of the Sakalava monarchy, not Tsiomeko.

Noël's and Guillain's accounts are more detailed than later ones,
perhaps because they were set down closer to the time the events
happened, but perhaps also because their European recorders found
the move from male to female rulers incomprehensible. As Noël puts
it:

> The admission of women to power among a people of the same
> origin as the Sakalava of Menabe would have remained for us a fact

entirely unexplained, if the intelligent minister of the king of Mayotte [Andriantsoly's minister] to whom we owe most of the information that we possess on Madagascar, had not given us some details on this subject.[34]

Guillain is more explicit about the reasons for his bewilderment:

> The principle of the absolute authority of the sovereign is the fundamental basis of order and power in barbaric societies, and the first Volamenas, in putting this character on their royal power, by this alone prepared for the superiority of the Sakalava over their neighbors. But the monarchial constitution, cornerstone of the edifice of their grandeur, had been later shaken by the rivalries between members of the royal family; and it was then profoundly modified by the admission of women to the throne, a truly lethal attack on the first law with chiefs as unruly as the Sakalava chiefs.[35]

According to both observers, male succession was so closely associated with endogamy that "in the absence of other kin, brothers had to marry their sisters, which took place, as will be seen for one of the sons of Andriamboniarivo."[36] This is why Andriamboniarivo's successor, Andriamahatindriarivo, married his youngest sister Ratsipirano (Asperged, Blessed). Even so, special precautions were taken to legitimate the union from which six daughters, including Vahiny, were eventually born. Guillain says: "Although such marriages were foreseen and authorized by Sakalava law, this one was preceded by a ceremony which consisted in asperging the woman, while reciting prayers to call happiness and fertility down on her, as if it were feared that a union so strange would draw on the new spouses the anger of the Supreme Being."[37]

Noël sees Andrianihevanarivo as the last male ruler in Boina because the brothers, Andriamanarakarivo and Andriamandahatrarivo, were the descendants of a female, not male member of the line: "In him ended that line of princes who continued by such good fortune the work of Andriandahifotsy." Guillain sees Andriamandahatrarivo as "the last male descendant of the Volamenas" because he was a man.[38]

They agree on the logic involved, using the same Malagasy terms and many of the same French expressions as well. Noël says:

> Paternity having always been considered dubious among the Sakalava, because of the extreme laxity of morals, the first king of the Zafimbolamena, Andriandahifotsy, decreed by his council that the princes and princesses of blood would ally in marriage only among themselves, and that if need be, the reigning prince would marry his own sister. That wise arrangement, still vital in Menabe, was poorly observed by the Volamena of Boina; and the Sakalava of that kingdom, in fear of being governed by princes foreign to the royal blood, established, according to their ideas about the uncertainty of paternity, that the children from the Volamena princes and women foreign to their family had less rights to the throne than those whom their Volamena mothers bore, however obscure the father of these might be, and to whichever sex they belonged besides, and that in consequence, women could rule. The children of princes are called *Tsy mahery n'fanjaka* [Not Strong for Ruling], weak as to the right to rule, and those of princesses, *mahery n'fanjaka* [strong for ruling], name with the opposite meaning. The children of the princes *Tsy mahery* are deprived of all rights to the throne; the children of the princesses *Tsy mahery* become, on the contrary, *mahery,* having solid rights.[39]

The brothers' mother was chosen as their replacement; then her younger sister who, suffering ill health, abdicated in favor of their older sister's daughter, Vahiny, a selection that Guillain explains as probably resulting from the important contacts Vahiny had made as the brothers' wife.[40]

Noël sees "physical purity" as the basis of Sakalava notions of "strength to rule." He pursues this topic by reporting on "Types and physical characteristics among the Northern Sakalava."[41] He contrasts Andriantsoly and his followers, with their "air of good fellowship and frankness," in whom "it is still possible to recognize the noble and regular countenance of the Arabs, their ancestors," to Tsiomeko and some of her followers. Their "blacker coloring, yellow eyes, large and dazed-looking, their deformed and protruding lips, create a physiognomy with an indefinable expression of foolishness and brutality" more like that of purchased slaves, "the type of negroes from Mozambique."[42]

Guillain's interests in purity are expressed in his discussions of marriage, endogamy being a practice that he and Noël also associated with Arabs who betrothed brothers' children. Vahiny, he was told, was the first Sakalava ruler to break the rule of endogamy by marrying out, the first who "went against the law of Andriamisara in allying herself with chiefs who were not of royal blood." Two of her four husbands were commoners, as were both wives of her son and successor, Oza.[43] Guillain acknowledges that Sakalava seem to have accepted Vahiny as their ruler, but goes on to argue that Fatima's son, Maka, head of the rival Bemazava branch of the dynasty, was Andriamahatindriarivo's proper heir, owing to his purer descent through women.[44]

Paradoxically, and inconsistently when it comes to Andriantsoly, Noël and Guillain extolled the purity of lines traced through women in order to support the positions of men. Both clearly supported the male rulers—Andriantsoly and Maka's son and successor Tsimandroho—who were contending for power with Vahiny's heir Tsiomeko at the time they were doing their research. Both were concerned to justify why France should have taken possession of Nosy Be and the adjacent mainland in 1841, and why they should eventually colonize Madagascar as a whole, by characterizing Sakalava as "weakened by internal struggles and softened by the reign of women," to use Guillain's words.[45]

Sakalava participants also seem to have had divided feelings about endogamy and exogamy, but these revolved not around racial purity, preserved through marriage, in European terms, but rather around the positions of children of men compared to children of women. While Maka's supporters argued for endogamy, like many contemporary Malagasy in central and southern parts of the island, the supporters of Vahiny and her descendants argued for exogamy, which is currently the norm among Malagasy living in northwestern Madagascar and the Comores.[46] Perhaps exogamy among royalty originated during Vahiny's time, or perhaps there was then, as there is now in the northwest, widespread ambivalence about the relative merits of unions with siblings or strangers. Whatever the case, the Southern Bemihisatra tantara speak for exogamy.

RUINOUS INCEST

Like Noël's and Guillain's accounts, Southern Bemihisatra tantara also describe the monarchy as "ruined" *(robaka)* following Andriamarofaly's reign, but they attribute this ruin neither to female rulers nor to their exogamous practices, but rather to an endogamous brother-sister marriage, now subject to the strictest prohibitions.

> Andriamahatindriarivo inherited the monarchy of his father Andriamboniarivo [and] ruled twelve years 1786–1797. Andriamarofaly his son inherited the monarchy of his father [and] ruled eight years 1797–1804. The monarchy was ruined then because a pregnant person was raised up, head erect, by people brother and sister, spouses. S/he gave birth to one:
>
> 1. Andriamamelonarivo   female
>
> This one too inherited the monarchy from her father [and] ruled twenty-five years 1804–1828. She bore Andriamandrangitriarivo, male, and Andriamandrangitriarivo too bore four:
>
> 1. Andriamanesiarivo   male
> 2. Andriamanorinarivo   female
> 3. Andrianatolotrarivo   female
> 4. Andriamanavakarivo   male[47]

The ambiguous phrase—"The monarchy was ruined then . . ."— does not appear to refer to Andriamahatindriarivo, as argued in the accounts from the 1840s.[48] Nevertheless, it could just as well refer to the marriages between Andriamarofaly and his mother's sister's daughter or Vahiny and her second or third husbands, where the partners were also related as "brother and sister, spouses" *(ampianadahy, ampivady)* (Figs. 4 and 5).

The outcome of these incestuously endogamous unions, from the perspective of Sakalava followers who supported Tsiomeko over Andriantsoly in the 1840s, and later for their descendants, was not stronger or physically purer unity, but rather greater division: between Andriantsoly's descendants, the Northern Bemihisatra who are chil-

85

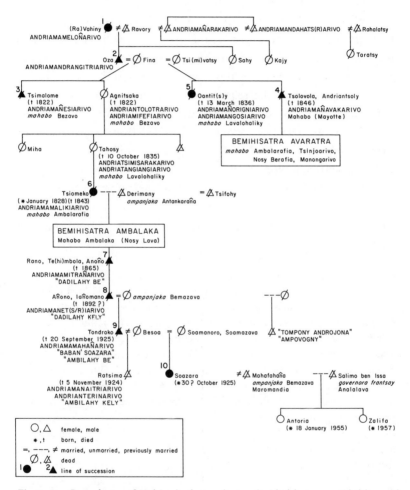

Figure 5. Genealogy of Vahiny's descendants, divided between Children of Men (Northern Bemihisatra) and Children of Women (Southern Bemihisatra), Guillain (1845) and Southern Bemihisatra sources (see notes 58 and 81).

dren of men, and his sister Oantity's descendants through her sister's daughter Tsiomeko, the Southern Bemihisatra, who are children of women. It took me some time to grasp that while the terms 'children of men' and 'children of women' usually distinguish the children of brothers and sisters born of the same mother, they may also refer to positions of superiority and inferiority persisting for generations, reckoned back to whenever the parties choose, in this case almost a century and a half, to the 1840s. The depth of these differences came out in discussions of local rulers in the Analalava area, like this conversation with Soatoly, a woman descended from guardians at the Mahabo who had left for Nosy Be. When she and her sisters got sick, and royal spirits in Nosy Be told them to return to their proper place, the sisters delegated Soatoly to go back as their representative.

I asked what 'children of women' *(zanaka vavy)* and 'children of men' *(zanaka lahy)* meant, as applied to Soazara and Riziky [an elderly woman in the northern Ambolobozo Peninsula, who was also recognized as an ampanjaka, though subordinate to Soazara]. Soatoly said, "They are children of children who are one stomach" [people also said 'one father, one mother']. [But how could Soazara be a *zanaka vavy* if she is the child of Ndramamahaña (her father who had been ampanjaka before her)?] "Because Ndramamahaña was a sister's child *(zanak' anabavy)*." [Then what is Soazara's relationship to Riziky?] "I don't know. Important people, like the *manantany* at the Doany, would know." [When I asked him, he said he didn't know.] "People at the Mahabo would know. It is hard to get Sakalava to talk about things like this. These are difficult/ precious things for Sakalava *(raha sarotra am Sakalava)*. To speak about them eats the mind, makes people crazy, wandering, mindless *(mihinana jery, mankadala, mirendra, very jery)*. If you ask people about these things, they will say, 'I don't know'." Then she told me how to ask.[49]

Many months later, Malaza at Andonaka gave one answer to the question in explaining his own origins:

Malaza said he's not a person from here. He also kept emphasizing that the eighteen ancestors of the ampanjaka Soazara, seventeen before her—came from abroad, from Arabia: "They are all from afar, like yourselves. The

Hova are also from abroad—Japan, China.[50] They are not natives
(zanatany). The Zafinifotsy [junior branch of Sakalava royalty] are natives.
They and the Hova don't get along. Hova really brawl *(mola)!*[51] They
came here and fought the Sakalava. Picked up knowledge from the English
and the French and conquered like the French [in trying to conquer the
whole island], not like the Sakalava. See how all the Sakalava have these
little domains, like Soazara's domain?"

"Ndramañavaka [Andriantsoly] fled from the Hova to the Comores.
What else to do, with little guns and spears, and the Hova with canons.
Soazara's kin are descended from his sister. He had twelve children. Riziky
is descended from one of his children. Avoria and Anatrona [ampanjaka in
the Antognibe area] are also descendants of his children. But Soazara is the
only one with the Vy Lava. It came from Ndramandisoarivo." He said
that Ndramañavaka's descendants are strewn up and down this coast. One
of them came up from the south and wanted to ask him questions, but he
refused because they have become Christians. "Can't tell with some, don't
know whether they go back and pray. Lots of ampanjaka pray. Can't tell
what they want" *(Tsy hay desiran'any)*.

The written histories of the Southern Bemihisatra list the descendants of the "two men descendants of Ibrahim," sometimes noting
whether they were male or female. When royal followers in the Analalava region talk about the recent ancestry of the Bemihisatra from
whom their ruler is descended, the critical distinctions are between
'children of men' and 'children of women,' and they always trace them
back to Andriantsoly and his sisters, on whose names they differ, as
they differ in the number and order of the intervening praise names.
People remember intervening praise names in ways that confirm the
prior designation of their own living ruler as a child of women. For
example, one royal official said he did not know the earlier connections—certain Sambarivo at the Doany would know those—but he
knew about how Riziky and Soazara were related: "Riziky's brother
was Soazara's grandfather: Ndramañavakarivo [Andriantsoly]. Soazara was a child of women *(zanaka mañangy)*." Having described Soazara as a child of women in contrast to living descendants of Andriantsoly, he then went on to trace her ancestry exclusively through
women, leaving aside even her 'father' (F), 'grandfather' (FF), and

'great-grandfather' (FFF) buried on Nosy Lava: "The grandmother who bore the mother of the father of Soazara was Andriamañorignarivo [Oantity]." From the Southern Bemihisatra perspective, Soazara is a sister's child, but she has the ancestors embodied in the Vy Lava. Andriantsoly's numerous children live all along the west coast, but like Andriantsoly, they have lost their ancestors. Andriantsoly lost his ancestors, when he abandoned his sister to their enemies.[52]

BROTHERS AND SISTERS AND THEIR CHILDREN

During Vahiny's reign, the Hova began to expand into western Madagascar, aided by competition between French and English rivals for their favor.[53] Andrianampoinimerina established relations with Vahiny through gift exchange beginning around 1800.[54] Hova troops invaded Menabe in 1808–1809, in 1820, and again in 1823, intervening where they could in succession battles among rival kin. Andrianampoinimerina's son and successor, Radama I, managed to establish a small number of garrisons in Menabe in 1823, but they were lost again in 1828. Menabe ceased to exist as a single political entity and collapsed into several more or less independent domains during this period, owing to recurrent battles over succession, but the Merina never succeeded in getting a strong foothold there.[55] Followers of Sakalava royal ancestors at Belo-sur-Tsiribihina during the *fitampoha,* or bathing of the relics, in 1958, said that Hova were able to fragment Menabe because some rulers remained loyal to ancestral custom, while others betrayed them, abandoning relics, even collaborating with Hova to conquer their brothers.[56] The similarities between the Sakalava dady enshrined at Belo-sur-Tsiribihina and nineteenth century engravings of Merina sampy, most of which were burned in 1869, may have resulted from the relic thefts involved in these battles.[57]

Andriantsoly (Noble Convert) became ampanjaka of the Northern Sakalava domain of Boina in 1822, after his elder brother Tsimalome died childless (Fig. 5). He converted to Islam then or shortly afterwards.[58] When Radama invaded Boina in May 1824, Andriantsoly, living at a doany south of Mahajanga surrounded by some 740 houses, fled to a nearby island where he was captured. The Hova established their own governor in Mahajanga and moved Andriantsoly to Ma-rovoay at the bottom of Bombetoka Bay. Guillain notes that the Hova who searched Andriantsoly's abandoned doany found relics in one of the rooms, but he does not say what happened to them. Observing that the deserted residence of the king showed the order and regularity that testifies to recent occupation, he says: "In the largest room thirty-six feet long by twenty feet wide, were placed the incontestable proofs of the royalty of the chief, preciously conserved in a kind of sar-cophagus surrounded by curtains of white cotton cloth."[59] Later reports show that the Hova kept the relics to control the local population.[60] Concerning the brothers' sisters, Guillain says only that Agnitsaka died of grief when Tsimalome died because he was "born of the same mother as herself and preferred by her for this reason over her other brothers and sisters."[61]

The Sakalava revolted in 1825. Radama sent new troops from An-tananarivo, while Andriantsoly, leaving his sister Oantity at Maro-voay, fled north to Mahajamba Bay, then Anorotsangana, and finally, in 1826, to Zanzibar, where he sought refuge with Arabs to whom he was related by a "blood tie" (fatidra) through his father.[62] Oantity, accompanied by Agnitsaka's daughter Tahosy whom she had adopted, followed Andriantsoly north, establishing a doany on Sahamalaza Bay where, in January 1828, Tahosy gave birth to a girl, Tsiomeko. Having learned of Radama's death in 1828, Andriantsoly returned to Ano-rotsangana to resume his position as ampanjaka. Oantity, Tahosy, and Tsiomeko headed north to join him there, but the Hova arrived before them, and Andriantsoly fled back to Zanzibar.[63]

Andriantsoly returned again in 1830. This time, according to Guil-lain's informants, his followers had tired of the influence of the Muslim traders who always surrounded him, and, "since no man of the royal family was with them, their choice fell naturally on Oantity." Guillain says that Oantity and her chief royal official (manantany) could not bring themselves to leave their land.[64] Andriantsoly left in mid-1832 for Mayotte, where he became the ruling sultan; ceded Mayotte to France on April 25, 1841, effective June 13, 1843; and died three years later.[65]

Tahosy died in 1835, just as the Hova—now governed by Radama's sister and first wife, Ranavalona—were renewing their campaign against them. Oantity designated Tahosy's daughter, Tsiomeko, then eight years old, as her successor. According to Guillain, Oantity was pregnant when Tahosy died. She gave birth to a boy who died three days later, and she herself died fifteen to twenty days after that, a few months after Tahosy, in 1836. Oantity was buried by the side of her sister's daughter, whom she had adopted as her own child, in a royal tomb (mahabo) at Lavalohaliky at the head of Sahamalaza Bay.[66]

Although Southern Bemihisatra now emphasize the close relationship of brothers and sisters, especially those of "one stomach," they do not mention the love unto death between Tsimalome and Agnitsaka. They focus on what they see as the brother Andriantsoly's betrayal of his sister Oantity.[67] Andriantsoly is remembered as Ndramañavakarivo, Noble Who Divided Thousands, by leaving Oantity, in sharp contrast to Tahosy—Tsimisarakarivo, Noble Who Did Not Separate From Thousands—whose steadfast loyalty to her mother's sister Oantity and their followers even in the most arduous of circumstances, is commemorated in their common tomb.[68] The low esteem in which Ndramañavaka continues to be held in the Analalava region is exemplified by the general disregard for his mediums, like Saha Ambary and Malaza's son, Faralahy, in the villages of Tsinjorano and Andonaka described in Chapter 4. Malaza implied that his son's possession by Ndramañavaka was simply an excuse to smoke marijuana, regarded as a Muslim practice.

"Ndramañavaka can't drink rum, because he eats marijuana (jamala). That is why he is so mean all the time. Haven't you seen my son in the fantsina [royal meeting place at the Doany]? Jamala makes people crazy so they just walk about all the time. Are there any in America?"

TSIOMEKO: I GIVE NOT

Guillain reports that Tsimisarakarivo's child—Tsiomeko (I Give Not)—acquired her name when she succeeded to Oantity's position as ampanjaka:

> The young queen was so named on the occasion of the following
> event: in a formal speech *[Kabar]* following the death of Oantity,
> Tsimandroho [son of the Bemazava ruler, Maka], who was plotting
> to succeed her, having wanted to seize the royal seat (a kind of block
> *[billot]* on which the sovereign sat in assemblies), the child
> immediately protested against this claim, uttering, with a tone of
> authority, these words: *Tsi ouméï kou,* I give not; and the Sakalava,
> delighted with this act of rebellion, named her from that moment
> *Tsiouméïkou.*[69]

Guillain himself saw the choice of "this weak child" as leaving political
decisions to intriguing counselors, while Noël saw "The Antiboina
[residents of Boina], abandoned to themselves [by Andriantsoly] and
governed by a child," as being at the mercy of the Hova.[70] Hova
troops did force Tsiomeko and her followers to withdraw to the island
of Nosy Be in 1839 where she established at least four doany in different locations.[71] In steps, beginning with an *acte de cession* on July
14, 1840, renewed on August 8, 1840, and concluding with *la prise de
possession* effective on March 5, 1841, Tsiomeko gave up Nosy Be and
the adjacent mainland to the French in exchange for their protection
from the Hova.[72] Shortly afterwards, she gave birth to a boy named
Rano (Water). Tsiomeko died in June 1843, at the age of 15, pregnant
with another child.[73]

Paul Charles Auguste Rang, a former capitaine de corvette, like
Guillain, and then commandant supérieur of what became "Nosy Be
et Dépendances" [including Mayotte] on August 29, 1893, described
to his superiors in 1844 how he had the baby, Tsiomeko's successor,
formally presented to him while he "pretended not to pay great attention":

> I then expressed my satisfaction to Tsimandroho and to Boba
> [Tsifohy's father and predecessor as Tsiomeko's *manantany*] for their
> conduct in recent matters [expeditions against Malagasy rebels]; I
> promised one of them a gun, and the second a saber, but I wanted
> them clearly to understand that having once merited and received an
> *arme d'honneur,* death alone could punish them for treason. I had
> myself presented with Tsiomeko's child, which is no longer referred

to that way. He was completely enveloped in shawls for fear of evil spells, but Tsifohy, his father, and Boba, his grandfather who is keeping him under his care and responsibility, hastened to undress him to show him to me better. I pretended not to pay great attention.[74]

After Tsiomeko's death, Andriantsoly's children—three born in Mayotte and the descendants of the third—reasserted control over Nosy Be and the adjacent mainland at Andriantsoly's insistence.[75] Gradually the rule of his living descendants became "openly Islamicized" in contrast to Tsiomeko's tomb at Ambalarafia in the middle of Nosy Be, which the Bemihisatra there still view as "purely Sakalava" *(Sakalava fo, Sakalava tsara be)*.[76] While Ndramañavakarivo separated thousands, Bemihisatra praise Tsiomeko as Ndramamalikiarivo, Noble Who Makes Thousands Return, an allusion to the reunion of Sakalava groups previously dispersed in Nosy Be, Androna, and Ankarana following Tsiomeko's treaty with the French in 1840. As Tsiomeko, who ceded royal lands to the French, was named "I Give Not," so too is she remembered as joining what was then lost.

The brutality of Ndramamalikiarivo's ancestral curse *(masiaka tigny)*, in contrast to the timorousness of the living Tsiomeko, which is also commemorated in the behavior of Ndramamalikiarivo's mediums,[77] may derive from this opposition between the two lines of descent from sister and brother. Ndramamalikiarivo's angry protection of ancestral custom distinguishes her in death from Andriantsoly's descendants who also cooperated with the French in allowing ancestral custom to become lost.[78] The ideological contrast between Andriantsoly's Islamic successors and Ndramamalikiarivo (Tsiomeko) in Nosy Be is reproduced in the relationship between the Northern Bemihisatra, as Andriantsoly's successors there became known, and Tsiomeko's descendants who went south to become the Southern Bemihisatra around Narinda Bay. This, at least, is how Southern Bemihisatra describe the difference, seeing themselves as keeping ancestors that Northern Bemihisatra have lost. The fact that the French, in their dealings with the Southern Bemihisatra during the latter half of the nineteenth century, represented the protectorate as

an agreement made with "their ancestor Andriantsoly," not Tsiomeko, may have contributed to this opposition.[79]

The separation between supporters of Andriantsoly and of Tsiomeko, who saw themselves in the 1970s as following children of men
and women respectively, was clearly forming in the decades following
Andriantsoly's abandonment of the relics in Mahajanga in 1824. What
finally precipitated the split was the French *ordonnance* of 1849 abol-
ishing slavery in their newly acquired Malagasy territories and award-
ing slave-owners a substantial indemnity. Sakalava officials kept the
money and when the slave-owners revolted, they took Rano and fled
south to the Analalava region.[80] Since Hova were still in the area, they
established Rano in a doany on the island of Nosy Lava at the head
of Narinda Bay.

Rano's descendants are indicated in Figure 5.[81] The succession of
fathers and sons ended in the colonial period with Ratsima's premature
death by poisoning; his father Tondroko's death from grief; and the
succession of Ratsima's infant sister Soazara to the position of ampanjaka, which she, with two daughters of her own, still occupies.

FROM RELICS TO TOMBS

From the perspective of Southern Bemihisatra, the main reason for
the extinction of the male rulers of the Maroseraña dynasty was the
ady milongo, battles among kin, sometimes fathers and sons, but usually brothers. The foremost solution to ady milongo was the formation
of new royal capitals (doany). Failed rivals founded their own domains
elsewhere, contributing to the expansion of the dynasty along the west
coast. The growing strength of the Hova closed these avenues. According to Southern Bemihisatra, they made the doany increasingly
untenable as a place from which to rule. Their memories of constant
flight and struggle are expressed in the songs called *kolondoy,* which
women sing in front of the doors to the ancestors' shrines during royal
services. For example:

> *Manohiala e e e e e*
> *Andriana e e e e e*

Ndria ampanjaka e e e e e
Ndria ampanjaka ndria . . .

They keep on going from forest to forest e e e e
Sovereign ones e e e e e
Sovereign ampanjaka e e e e e
Sovereign ampanjaka sovereign . . .

Laza Be, who served as one of the Ampanjaka's female attendants
(Marovavy), explained *manohiala* (connect forests) by saying:

"That's a great powerful song, a *kolondoy (antsa masina maventy, kolondoy
io)*. It commemorates the sufferings *(fijaliana)* of the ampanjaka Sakalava
when the Hova were pursuing them, and they had to run away, flee into
the forest, sleep in the forest, suffer, sorrow. Finally the Vazaha came, that
going from forest to forest was finished. The kolondoy are all histories
(tantara jiaby). They are praying *(mivavaka)* when they sing like that,
telling the histories of the ampanjaka. The Tsiaro [royal followers from the
general populace, in contrast to people with specific tasks, like Marovavy]
are the masters of those songs. . . . Those great difficult songs are sung
only by the Tsiaro."

These song-histories are confirmed by observers of the time. The
English sea captain and hydrographer Owen, who explored the Narinda and Mahajamba bays in 1824, found them both heavily populated. The Narinda Bay region had an especially large number of villages, whose inhabitants carried on even more trade than people
further south.[82] Between 1824 and 1842, when Guillain visited the
area, these villages had been destroyed or abandoned. Guillain found
just a few families, refugees from the Hova, temporarily established
on the northwest tip of the Maromany Peninsula west of the bay.
Commerce consisted only of occasional visits from Zanzibarian traders
looking for sandalwood.

When I asked Malaza where the Bemihisatra had located their doany
in the past, he named several places along the coast where they had
rested temporarily in the flight from the Hova. Then he said:

"The doany of Ndramañorigniarivo [Oantity]? They just fled from the Hova. Only the mahabo [royal cemetery] counts, there at Lavalohaliky. There is the mahabo. Her doany—the doany moved. They just fled, fled from the Hova!" *(Doany Ndramanorigniarivo? Nilefa fo aminy Hova, mahabo fo mikonty, ao Lavalohaliky, ao ny mahabo. Doanin'any—doany nandeha, nilefa fo, nilefa Hova!)*

What he did not mention was that the doany of Oantity and her successors were no longer founded on the relics known as 'Andriamisara four-men,' commemorated as founders of Boina, which Andriantsoly had lost to the Hova. The mahabo, or cemetery where the bodies were buried, may have developed as an alternative center not only because the doany was increasingly hard to secure, but also because the relics, from which "strength to rule" derived, were lost to their enemies. While Sakalava followers brought royal women into the doany as living rulers, I suggest that they maintained the strength of the royal ancestors, identified mainly with men, by burying them in high, fortified tombs that reproduced the doany in ancestral form, shifting the center of power from the doany to the mahabo in the process.

From the French point of view, sovereign women were a contradiction in terms. Whether Sakalava saw them in the same way is difficult to assess on the basis of available historical data. The tantara from the 1840s imply differences of opinion, analogous to those found in India and Europe, about whether ampanjaka, male or female, were 'owners' *(tompony)* of the royal ancestors, or whether royal ancestors 'possessed' *(mianjaka)* rulers, as they possessed others.[83] Female ampanjaka like Vahiny seem to have ruled in their own right.[84] Others were explicitly fronts for men. So Andrianantanarivo (Fig. 4) is said to have served her grandfather, Andriamandisoarivo, as head of the Muslim trading community in Mahajanga around 1780.[85]

In contrast, the transformation of ancestors from relics into tombs was a clearly radical act. According to Southern Bemihisatra tantara, the royal ancestors expanded north not only because they were conquering warriors, but also because they had to leave the 'hot,' 'filthy' places where their predecessors had died and were buried, taking only the relics with them. In contemporary practice, people still 'stand up' stones, trees, and other shrines for their ancestral spirits as ways of maintaining ties with ancestors while avoiding the tombs where they have buried their corpses.

Southern Bemihisatra continue to revere the royal ancestors embodied in the Vy Lava, but in building and rebuilding royal tombs, they have returned to just what they would ordinarily have shunned. Perhaps, having lost the ancestral relics at the same time as their male rulers, they were forced back on royal tombs, as the French thought they were forced back on women. Or perhaps they kept building and rebuilding tombs because they could not stop mourning their growing losses. Or perhaps, in trying to continue what others were trying to cut short, Oantity's followers did not simply acknowledge impossible contradictions, but embraced them as deliberate strategies for not giving what was being taken, hiding what was being shown, and finally elevating what was buried.

NOT GIVING WHAT IS TAKEN

Earlier Sakalava doany were established in conquering new lands. Later doany were established as Sakalava royalty and their followers were fleeing to protect themselves. The later doany seem to have been built to fortify living rulers behind palisades, possibly incorporating 'hedges' and 'pens' of followers, who were gradually transformed ideologically from 'slaves' into 'friends.'

Some data from the early 1800s indicate that the building materials of doany had ancestral qualities. When the Hova captured Andriantsoly, they moved him from Mahajanga to Marovoay at the base of Bombetoka Bay. Given a choice of where he wanted to live, he astonished the Hova by choosing a little hill between woods and a swamp. As Guillain points out, the location later helped him escape his captors. Meanwhile, "At the request of the Sakalava chief, a few jambs [perhaps door posts] from his dwelling at Mahitsapanzava were used, to which he and his family attached great value, as coming from houses in which their glorious ancestors had lived."[86] When Oantity fled north, she recreated her father Oza's doany by giving her own doany on Sahamalaza Bay the same name, Kapany.[87]

Noël notes that Tsiomeko wrote to the sultan of Muscat, requesting him to build stone forts along the coast to protect herself and her followers from the Hova, in exchange for "the sovereignty of Boina." Hova troops prevented the first fort from being built, forcing Tsiomeko and her followers to withdraw to the island of Nosy Be in 1839, first in the Ambanoro Bay, then at Mahatsinjo, not far from present-day Andavakotoko, near Hellville, then at Ampobilava, then at Antsoalañana (now Soalang).[88]

Guillain describes Tsiomeko, surrounded by *les débris* of the population of Boina, as imprisoned on the island of Nosy Be.[89] Sakalava undoubtedly thought of the island itself as helping to fortify her monarchy, even as Andriantsoly later used the island of Dzaoudzi. What their oral traditions do not explain is how their Sakalava rulers gathered and retained numerous followers under such embattled circumstances.

The efforts of royal officials to protect Oantity and her successors after Andriantsoly abandoned the doany at Mahajanga may have involved the reorganization of royal followers around the living ruler's compound. As we will see in discussing the current organization of Southern Bemihisatra centers, the ruler's compound at the Doany (the doany proper) is surrounded by 'pens' or groups of guardian-workers, formerly slaves. One of the pens, the Maromainty (Many Black Ones—*mainty* or black is another word for slave) are said to have served as police and body-guards during the precolonial period. Another group, the Voromahery (Falcons), said to have stayed behind when the Bemihisatra fled north, did similar work.[90] The pens are located according to the nature of their service, but in general southern pens work on the southern half of royal persons or things, and northern pens on the northern half.

Although Guillain does not describe the social organization of Sakalava capitals, I infer from other data that the use of 'pens' developed only in the Northern and Southern Bemihisatra domains founded during the early nineteenth century. They are not found in Menabe, south of Mahajanga, or among the Bemazava who split off from the Bemihisatra in the late eighteenth century. I suggest that this pattern of

holding royal slaves in 'pens' around royalty, into which royal followers were also incorporated, might have developed when the Bemihisatra began to be harried by the Hova.

The Bemihisatra might have been influenced in this by the organization of Hova military encampments. As Radama I schooled himself in features of English military organization to turn them to his
own account in his campaigns against the Sakalava,[91] so Sakalava
might have borrowed ideas from the Hova to use in defeating them.[92]
According to the description of a Hova military camp in Merina royal
traditions dating from the mid to late 1800s, the ruler was located
inside a rectangular wooden enclosure with the "idols" *(sampy)* inside
the doors in the middle of the east and west sides (Fig. 6).[93] "Palace
servants" *(tandapa)* surrounded the wooden enclosure; royal slaves
(tsiarondahy) surrounded the tandapa; "the people" surrounded the
tsiarondahy. Guards—men chosen from the people—bordered the
camp; specific military leaders and notables lodged at the four en-
trances to the camp. The people occupied specific places in relation
to the four "corners" of the royal compound, associated with the
cardinal directions, according to Hova principles of divination, the
Avaradrano in the northeast corner having been the first to join the
famed Andrianampoinimerina, Vahiny's contemporary, in unifying
Imerina.[94]

Judging by Guillain's account and later archaeological data, royal
followers in the Hova army were also incorporated into the structure
of their fort at Anorotsangana, built in 1837.[95] The fort, on high
ground overlooking the Sahamalaza Bay, near the various doany of
Andriantsoly, Oantity, and Tsiomeko, was surrounded by three palisades. Two were made of posts, 12–16 centimeters in diameter, from
the cores *(teza)* of old hardwood trees; the stone foundations of a third
are still standing. The palisades were reinforced by fortifications made
of people. A 'hedge' *(haie)* of some one hundred uniformed men lined
the narrow entrance into the center of the fort where the Hova governor and his principle officers awaited Guillain.[96] Guillain's visit in
1842 is a sharp reminder that the French, who had taken possession
of Nosy Be and the adjacent mainland in 1841, were trying to move

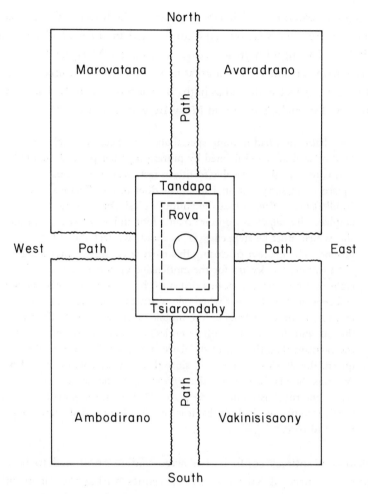

Figure 6. Outline of a Hova royal army camp, according to
Callet (1974, vol. 2, p. 444).

south at the same time the Merina were advancing north. The Sakalava
were caught between them for decades until the French conquest in
1895.

Noël describes Tsiomeko's doany, and those of Sakalava nobility
in Nosy Be during the same period, as differing from the houses of
their subjects only by their slightly larger size and the great care given

to their construction. In Menabe and Boina, the houses of important people "were very spacious and constructed in thick planks, fitted with difficulty but with great care by means of the Malagasy hatchet." Andriantsoly's residence had a great many connecting rooms, each 40 feet long by 25 feet wide and as high. By contrast, the only distinctive feature of Tsiomeko's doany in Nosy Be was its fence:

> That habitation had nothing special about it except its enclosure, a kind of wall in wood formed by putting together perfectly jointed beams to a height of twelve to fifteen feet, which encompass a square about sixty feet on a side. The door of the 'Enclosure of Gold' *(fefi-n'voulamena),* as the faithful of Tsi-Oumei-Kou emphatically call it, is no more than a foot and a half wide, and the sill, which must be stepped over, is about two feet above the ground. The manner of closing this narrow passage is interesting, but extremely awkward for the inoffensive visitor; it consists of eight or ten suspended beams that must be pushed hard from below and separated with effort when one wants to penetrate into the interior. In times of trouble, the mobile beams are solidly fixed to the sill, and the door then offers no less resistance to the efforts of the assailant than the rest of the fence. Besides the houses of the queen, the 'Enclosure of Gold,' since that is its accepted name, also contains the platform where that *princesse* gives her audiences and where the royal assemblies take place. That platform is made of thick, roughly worked planks; it is two feet high and sheltered only by a bad roof.[97]

Historical sources confirm that slave-trading continued to be an important source of Sakalava royal revenues during the nineteenth century.[98] Ranavalona's many expeditions against the Sakalava refuged on Nosy Be and neighboring islands to capture workers suggests that labor shortages were a problem for the Hova as well. There are few clues to how these laborers—purchased slaves, prisoners of war— were organized around Sakalava doany during this time. Guillain mentions a man who was "chief of the Sambarivo," but neither he nor Noël explains what Sambarivo were, nor how they related to other kinds of royal followers.[99] Noël mentions that Sakalava expressed opposition to their rulers by living as far away as possible from the court, where they might decide to choose another member of the royal family as ruler.[100] But neither he nor Guillain discusses how embattled rulers might have devised new spatial strategies to capture guardian-workers from the local populace and prevent them from walking away.

In contrast to Merina royal traditions, where Andrianampoinimer-ina's reorganization of labor is minutely described and justified, Southern Bemihisatra royal accounts are silent on these topics.[101] I infer from the current organization of Sambarivo in 'pens' around Sakalava rulers that they may have served not only as protective hedges around increasingly vulnerable royalty, but also as model colonies comparable to Hova garrisons, intended to attract more workers from surrounding populations.

The garrisons that Radama established in the northwest, within months of subduing the Sakalava there in 1824, were explicitly intended to protect Hova settlers from outside attack, but also incorporate local people into the new social order they represented. Guillain comments: "Radama wanted to make of them at once kinds of model colonies to which the indigenous people would be drawn and would habituate themselves little by little to living peaceably among the Hova, to searching for their well-being in agriculture and not in marauding; to recognizing, in a word, the advantages of a more civilized social state than their own."[102]

As we will see, current followers are recruited into royal service after the model of royal slaves, living and working north or south in the Doany and Mahabo, depending on the location in the region of their father's ancestral land *(tanindrazaña)*. Some data from the early nineteenth century suggests that even before the abolition of slavery in Nosy Be transformed relationships between rulers and their workers, there was an increasing emphasis on the friendship between rulers and their followers rather than a relationship governed by force. I have already noted how royalty rewarded supporters of the monarchy by giving them the right to call themselves ampanjaka and presumably other privileges. One ruler rewarded a devoted follower by giving him the position of manantany. They also formed blood tie *(fatidra)* relationships with their principal officials.[103] One small piece of evidence suggests that these relations of friendship widened as rulers grew more dependent on their followers for support. Tsiomeko moved her doany for the last time from a coastal location to a village in the center of Nosy Be. As a royal residence, the village was renamed Antsaolañana, "There where one goes of his own will," following Tsiomeko's announcement to her counselors that she did not oblige them to follow her.[104] Current Sakalava officials in the Analalava region now describe 'slaves' (andevo), the collective term for royal followers, in similar terms. They are 'not forced' (tsy samboringy); they are 'people who agree to serve the ruler' (olo mañeky manompo ny ampanjaka).

HIDING WHAT IS SHOWN

These transformations in living rulers, or recreations of royal ancestors in new living forms, were accompanied by transformations in ancestors created out of the dead. Purifications of ancestors (fandroana)— "shows" (fisehoana), as Hova settled in Mahajanga from 1828 onwards saw them by comparison to their own accession ceremonies—were hidden by taking them inside and restricting the kinds and numbers of participants.

Currently, royal followers in all the Sakalava domains along the west coast purify royal relics and regalia in fanjava mitsaka, the first month of the new year. South of Mahajanga, the "royal bath" (fitampoha) is a highly public ceremony, held every seven to ten years. At Belo-sur-Tsiribihina, for example, porter-guardians remove the individually named dady from the "royal house" (zomba), in which they are kept during the year, and carry them through crowds of pilgrims to the river mouth where they are washed in salt water.[105] According to Rabedimy, possession by royal spirits, which he sees as having originated in the Analalava region, occurs among Southern Sakalava only at royal burials (tsiritse) and on these occasions when the relics are washed.[106]

North of Mahajanga, among Bemihisatra in the Nosy Be and Analalava areas, royal followers purify the ancestors annually, while royal spirits possess people throughout the year. Southern Bemihisatra wash the ancestors in mead (tô mainty, blackness), made at the end of the preceding year. Participants drink what remains. The ceremony is conducted by pens of the guardians, formerly slaves, at the doany dedicated to the service of the ancestors there, together with officials in the administration of the living ruler. They bathe the ancestors inside the 'ancestors' house' at the doany. Current officials there emphasize that the 'difficult things'—nothing but the Vy Lava is individually named in this context—'don't move; there is no royal bath' *(tsy mifindra, tsisy fandroana)* among the Southern Bemihisatra the way there is among Sakalava to the south. Nor are the 'difficult things' publicly displayed at this or any other time. In fact, it is impossible to know whether the 'difficult things' include relics or not.

Followers of Sakalava ancestors seem to have begun hiding the showing of the relics during the Hova governorship of Mahajanga (1828–1895), after the Hova returned the relics to the doany there as a means of controlling local people. The Hova governor, Ramanetaka, moved the ceremony from outside to inside because he feared that large crowds of 15,000 to 20,000 armed Sakalava would seize the relics, thus ending Hova rule. Rakoto spoke to royal guardians at the doany in Mahajanga, when he attended a service there in 1938. He reports that the services held during the decades of Merina occupation were heavily guarded:

> All the streets of the town, except the one going to the Little Rova (= doany) are guarded on both sides by four rows of Hova soldiers armed to the teeth. All the doors of the fortress [the "Little Rova" with the relics, in contrast to the Hova governor's Rova],
> barricaded, have guards behind them; only the southern part of that construction facing the sea is not guarded, because it is in stone. Ten canons, four of them large, are directed on Mahabibo [the quarter where the doany was located] and ready to be used at the least act of rebellion.[107]

The Sakalava leaders began by pledging fidelity to the Hova monarchy in front of the governor. He gave them various kinds of cloth, rice, and cattle, and received "a lot of honey" in return. The Sakalava then proceeded to the doany together with five Hova officers, who accompanied them through the crowds, into the enclosure, down to the sea where the relics were washed, then back again. Each side suspected the other might try to steal the relics when they were outside the enclosure. So "at some ill-defined time . . . it was decided" that the bath would be held inside the ancestors' house at the doany, and the sea water was replaced by "a mixture of honey, castor oil, and water."[108]

In 1938, the doany had been moved from the quarter of Mahabibo to Miarinarivo on the outskirts of Mahajanga. Rifles were no longer shot off to celebrate the royal new year. The service itself took place inside the "big ancestors' house" (zomba be) to which the relics were brought from the smaller "forbidden ancestors' house" (zomba faly) where they were kept. The washing was done on the east side of a large cloth hung between the north and south walls, where only Sakalava nobility and their highest officials were allowed to go.[109]

In the Bemihisatra services north of Mahajanga, the ancestors have been removed still further from the public eye. In the Analalava region, the relic carrying, which is such an important part of bathing the royal ancestors at southern shrines, has been removed from the service altogether and transformed into one of the 'amusements' (soma) seen as the opposite of work or service, which take place in the afternoon after the service (fanompoaña) is over. Four dancers depicting two rulers and two followers dance out the battles between rival branches of Sakalava royalty that led to domination of the Zafinimena or Grandchildren of Gold over the Zafinifotsy, the Grandchildren of Silver (mirebiky). The two dancers playing the rulers are dressed in costumes said to represent the royal ancestors, except for a bundle of cloth tied to the back like a reliquary, which is said to be just an ornament. The rebiky dance is the only occasion besides spirit possession in which 'simple people' take on the attributes of royalty, and some participants do become possessed in the process.[110]

The service itself focuses on the washing, which is done inside the ancestors' house at the Doany and inside the burial compound at the Mahabo. Royal followers in the Analalava region may be motivated to keep the 'difficult things' hidden as a way of protecting them from seizure, as happened in their struggle with French authorities over the succession in 1925, and as they feared would happen at later times during the colonial period. Whether these include relics, as well as the Vy Lava knife, is not clear. According to the report of L'Inspecteur des Provinces Poirier, assigned as outside investigator in the struggle between the French and Sakalava over Ndramamahaña's (Tondroko's) successor in 1925, no relics were made from the body of Ndramamahaña in 1925 "because the Bemihisatra don't make the *dady* for the conservation of relics"; nor does his list of royal regalia, made after the seizure, include relics.[111] Southern Bemihisatra guardians told me that the French had not succeeded in getting all that was in the ancestors' house at the Doany, but they neither confirmed nor denied Poirier's claims.

Similar ambiguity surrounds the relic house at the doany of the Northern Bemihisatra in Nosy Be. Discussing the *tsyzoyzoy* at the Northern Bemihisatra doany of Ampasimena in 1972, which is the counterpart of the ancestors' house *(zomban'drazana)* at the Southern Bemihisatra doany, Baré comments: "The *tsyzoyzoy*, sometimes called *kizoyzoy* . . ., is only theoretically, in the case of the Northern Bemihisatra, a dwelling place of the royal relics. A consciously maintained ambiguity exists in that regard, so much the more easily since the greatest secret reigns as to the exact nature of the objects which are deposed there, which can be handled only by a very small number of dignitaries charged with religious duties."[112]

Followers of Sakalava royalty in the north have intensified the secrecy surrounding relics by putting the annual ceremonies for purifying the royal relics into the hands of specialists known as Ancestor People *(Razan'olo)*, assisted by Sambarivo. Southern Bemihisatra emphasize that they alone know the nature of their work. Ancestor People are not found in Sakalava domains south of Mahajanga, nor among the descendants of the Bemazava who split off from Vahiny's descendants in the early nineteenth century.[113]

Among Southern Bemihisatra, purifying the relics every year is secondary to the main work of the Ancestor People, which is to dry the corpse of a dead ruler by removing the liquefying flesh from the bones according to procedures they alone know. In other words, they work primarily on preparing the royal corpse for burial and later on reconstructing the innermost fence around the tomb. Their very prominence in the annual bath may derive from the increasing importance of the these new forms of ancestry and the tombs in which they are buried.

One last point might be made about the specialists who serve to embody Sakalava ancestors in relics and in tombs. The little information on Sakalava royal relics suggests that they were, at least partly, the work of craftsmen employed by wealthy rulers, jewelers, or goldsmiths who were skilled at putting together delicate coffers of wood and precious metals, adorned with rare cloth, beads, and stones. Royal tombs, at least among the Southern Bemihisatra, are more like fenced gardens, in keeping with the image of royalty as a huge overarching mango tree. Burying in the tomb is like cultivating land from which new ancestors will grow. The new goldsmiths of the "Grandchildren of Gold" are farmers.

ELEVATING WHAT IS BURIED

As the capitals of living rulers centered on reliquaries (doany) were built to reproduce those of ancestral predecessors, so royal cemeteries (mahabo) seem to have been modeled historically on the doany of living rulers. While ancestors in relics were shown hidden in their houses, ancestors in tombs, previously left behind in hidden locations, were shrouded in forests on hilltops and openly tended. Apart from the formulaic statements, like those in Sakalava tantara, indicating that rulers had to move north to get away from the 'hot,' 'filthy' ground where their ancestors had died, Southern Bemihisatra officials hardly talked about royal death and burial, past or present. A schoolteacher, descended from Bemazava royalty who had converted to Islam, was somewhat less constrained. Asked about royal burial practices in the past, he stated that there were no royal cemeteries in the south; relics were the only forms of the royal ancestors. After the relics had been removed, the rest of the body was taken away in the middle of the night by porters who were under oath never to return, so that its location was forever unknown. No one, not even his successor, knew where the body was located.

According to what Captain Rey learned from Sakalava followers in Menabe in 1912 (probably in the Belo-sur-Tsiribihina area), royal funerals lasted a long time because the body had to dry out completely before burying it. The dried corpse was then placed in "a beautiful coffin in sculpted wood (*tamango-lahy,* male coffin), then placed in a house (*valamasy,* sacred fence) constructed in *katrafay*" (a wood reputed for its hardness and durability). The ceremony concluded with "the transfer, in great pomp, of the remains, the relics [called dady, *rahasarotra*] . . . to the *jomba,* sacred house constructed in *mampandry* (wood that puts to sleep)." The relics, Rey goes on to emphasize, are the sole source of royal power.[114]

Jean-François Rabedimy, an ethnographer who did research in Menabe during the 1960s and 1970s, confirms that there are Sakalava royal tombs at Benge, Mañeva, Ilaza, Tomboarivo, and Tsianihy (see Fig. 2). They are distinguished in terms of their ancestral antiquity, Benge being the oldest and Tsianihy the most recent.[115] Nevertheless, they are not the focus of recurrent services honoring the royal ancestors. There are rites known as *tsiritse* (not dried out) at burial, and rites known as *lohavogny* (hidden head) to clean the tomb a year later; no other rites are held after that.[116]

Some evidence suggests that royal tombs might have become more important in the more northerly areas of Menabe in the course of the nineteenth century.[117] Royal cemeteries, called doany, also became important for Sakalava who remained in the Mahajanga area, after Andriantsoly fled north.[118] Bénévent's observations in 1897 are especially useful because they suggest that royal followers in this area might have developed the mahabo form of royal cemetery that later characterized Bemihisatra domains further north:

> Besides the veneration that they have for the shades of the four former kings, the Sakalava preserve religiously, in places called doany, the tombs of families of reigning kings. These tombs are

surrounded by wooden palisades forming a sacred enclosure. Upkeep
is confided to guardians who build their houses around the
enclosures; they cannot abandon their service under any pretext.
These doany are found at Kandrany, at Mahabo, at Trabonjy, at
Androtra, at Marololo and in many other villages. . . . Once a year,
there is a ceremony venerating the dead; each "doany" has a
particular day.[119]

Such published data as exist on the doany and mahabo of the Bemihisatra at Lavalohaliky, Choa, Ambalarafia, Nosy Lava, Tsinjoarivo,
and Manongarivo indicate that while the living ruler, identified with
the doany, moved from place to place, the mahabo came to embody
royal ancestors that could or should not be moved. In each case, the
tomb is surrounded by palisades, usually two, usually reinforced by
an outer ring of guardians who live at the tomb year-round.[120]

The tombs are not simply made and left; they are the object of
repeated ceremonies honoring the royal ancestors who are buried
there. These include ceremonies to cleanse the royal ancestors, carried
out in the first month of each year, at the same time as the ceremonies
honoring the royal regalia at the doany with which the mahabo is
paired. At some mahabo, they also include generational ceremonies
to repair the innermost fence around the tomb, broken down in the
course of burying a royal corpse.

Rano, the first of the Southern Bemihisatra ampanjaka to rule in
the Narinda Bay region, wrote to Commandant Dupuis at Hellville
in Nosy Be in the mid-1850s, asking for permission for "his people"
to "work on his mother's [Ndramamalikiarivo's (Tsiomeko's)] royal
tomb," saying "I have no father, I have no mother. It is you who are
all my kin." Assuring the Commandant that his people had not pil-
laged French ships and therefore owed the French no indemnity, he
requested permission from his "father" to return to Nosy Be, un-
molested, to see his mother's tomb and, with wood from the Commandant, to repair the surrounding fence.[121] He was probably referring to a *menaty* service, since Ndramamalikiarivo was the first to be
buried there (in 1843). No one else was buried there until one of
Andriantsoly's descendants died around 1886.[122] Rano's son and suc-

cessor, Añono, wrote letters to the French commandant at Nosy Be in 1883, making a similar request for permission to "fulfill their vows and do the customary ceremony at the Mahabo," as the commandant put it.[123]

Renel's description of a service to reconstruct the innermost fence *(menaty)* around a royal tomb, probably at the mahabo of Lavalohaliky in 1916–1917, gives an indication of the work involved, greater in scale even than the original burial:

> Another ceremony is celebrated to repair the interior palisade of the royal tombs. This rite is generally extended, and it can last for one or two years, because during all this time the people are obliged to furnish cattle and rice to nourish the royal following and the *mpanompo* or servers. When the *mpanjaka* orders the reconstruction, a camp is established in the forest according to certain rites. The felling and preparation of the posts, their transport to the village, are done ceremoniously, four men carrying a single post, and women accompanying them singing, while cooling them with their fans and giving them something to drink when they desire it. The work is done each month only around the full moon, six days before and six days after. It is interrupted when the moon gets meager, as the Malagasy say. Because one would then risk doing only meager work.[124]

The mahabo, intended to replicate the doany, seems in practice to have supplanted it among both Northern and Southern Bemihisatra. In both places, two doany have developed as living rulers withdrew from colonial and postcolonial authorities: a doany in town where the ampanjaka lives most of the time and a *doany be* (the main doany) in the countryside where the 'ancestors' house' is located. But even the doany be has dwindled in importance compared to the cemeteries where the ancestors are buried. At the Northern Bemihisatra doany be in the early 1970s, the 'ancestors' house' was the only building still intact; the rest had begun to fall apart, a point Malaza made several times.[125] In the Southern Bemihisatra domain at the same time, royal followers said that the doany be had been polluted by wild pigs about fifteen years earlier, and therefore needed to be moved to a new location. But instead of doing that, they reconstructed the innermost fence around the royal tomb in 1972–1978. The doany had yet to be moved in 1989.

IMAGINING THE IMPOSSIBLE

The funeral effigies of the French Renaissance royalty are among the best known examples of ancestral relics created to embody dynastic continuity, especially in the interregnum between the death of one ruler and the succession of his descendant. Since Giesey's pioneering study in 1960, scholars have related these changing images to other important ideas and practices concerning kingship and succession in France, such as the anointment of living rulers, the *lit de justice,* and the levée of Louis XIV.[126]

French ceremonial had its roots in English ideas and practices about "the king's two bodies."[127] Recently, Mayer has suggested that there were also structural and historical connections between succession ceremonies in Tudor England and those in the Hindu Princely States of central and western India during the first half of this century, before the States were incorporated into the Indian Union in 1948. In contrast to the English focus on such doctrines as "the king's two bodies," speculative thought about death and succession in Hindu Indian polities focused on thrones—cotton bolsters *(gaddi)* stuffed with deities.[128]

In Madagascar, as in many parts of Africa, there were not just two but many royal bodies, including living rulers, relics, tombs, and mediums.[129] Gender differences openly contributed to the variety of these forms. In fact, the major change in both the Sakalava and Merina monarchies of western and central Madagascar was the change from male to female ampanjaka around 1780–1828.

These different bodies of royalty developed in the course of conflicts over the people and other forms of wealth they embodied, complicated here, as in India, by the involvement of Europeans with their own assumptions about gender, power, continuity, and purity or legitimacy. The protean shapes clearly served to help people imagine amazing paradoxes like "the king is dead, long live the king," "monarchy never dies," or *ampanjaka tsy ampody avelo* (rulers don't return alive). Yet French participants balked at sovereignty in female form, which they saw as an impossible contradiction. We are accustomed to think of such paradoxes as transcending time and place. Yet here, partly because of the incomprehension of European participants, it is somewhat easier to discern the socially and historically specific roots of transcendent paradoxes. I have followed their changes here, as Malagasy participants present them, beginning with differences in living forms of ancestry, then going on to transformations in relics and tombs, which they entailed.

Tantara associated with the Northern Sakalava domain of Boina represent the Volamena or Zafinimena dynasty as originating in endogamy, associated with male rulers, and ending in exogamy, associated with bilateral succession, but mainly female rulers. Male rulers, once endogamous, came under suspicion for their adoption of foreign customs, like Islam, while female rulers—associated with strangeness, as exemplified in Vahiny (Stranger) who is remembered for marrying out—became emblems of loyalty to ancestral custom. As we shall see in Chapters 4 and 5 on social relations in the Analalava region, similar tensions exist between priorities given to children of men over children of women as 'masters of ancestors,' which coexist with equally strong emphases on indifferentiation and free choice. Whether the succession from male to female rulers depicted in oral and written tantara simply expresses these tensions, or whether they have deeper historical roots, is difficult to assess without further data on the domains of the seventeenth and eighteenth centuries when men are alleged to have ruled. In either case, the historical data concerning the decades since the 1840s suggest that Malagasy participants also began to see their own tensions about gender and power from the perspectives of those who were attempting to conquer them. Some backers of Andriantsoly and Maka may have welcomed French views supporting the priority of children of men over children of women in the formation of ancestries. But there were clearly others in those decades who reevaluated the strengths of women as rulers and conversely the weaknesses of brothers who abandoned their sisters and followers. Thus, while Guillain saw Vahiny's reign as a peak after which "the power of the Sakalava of Boina did no more than decrease," Sakalava followers commemorated her in the praise name Ndramameloñoarivo, "Noble Who Gave Birth to Thousands," legitimating the priority of children of women as represented by Agnitsaka, Tahosy, Oantity, Tsiomeko, and their descendants in the Analalava region, governed by the ampanjaka Soazara who now holds the Vy Lava. What the French saw ending in weakness, the Malagasy supporters of these women saw being reborn in a new form.

Guillain was told that Ndramameloñoarivo's praise name evoked memories of the peacefulness of her reign, in contrast to the incessant warfare of earlier times. Admiring the already ancestral Vahiny, Guillain took pains to emphasize that the peacefulness of her realm derived from a manlike strength, rather than a feminine clemency toward wrongdoers, as Noël had asserted.[130] Desires for peace were said to have motivated the choice of Oantity over her brother Andriantsoly.[131] The name of the current doany in the Analalava region is Miadàna (Go In Peace). Some say it celebrates the peacefulness of Soazara's reign resulting from strength, but others would attribute the apparent calm to the collaboration of a subordinate.

Impossibly sovereign females were indispensable to achieve the 'peace' necessary to regrow Sakalava monarchy, yet they were just one aspect of a larger process involving even more radical confrontations with the dead. I have suggested that the diminishing autonomy of living rulers, harried and eventually conquered by outsiders, gradually led Sakalava to shift their attention from the living rulers to ancestors, embodied in forms they could protect even when cornered. Royal relics, the paramount symbols of legitimate rule and the objects of the most important services honoring royalty in the south, were small, portable objects prone to theft. The doany-mahabo seems to have developed into its current form as a means of transforming the royal ancestors into something less portable or stealable by such powerful rivals as the Hova and later the French, probably after the Hova had indeed seized the relics that constituted the "root" of the Boina domain.

As Sakalava themselves were forced to retrench, so they may have brought the ancestors underground: in the hiddenness of annual ceremonies at the doany and in the development of royal tombs at the mahabo that "cannot be moved," as the Southern Bemihisatra emphasize. The transformation in the embodiments of royalty among the Sakalava, the meaning of their deadly blessings, cannot be separated from their larger circumstances: the gradual "death" of Sakalava monarchy in the context of changing relations with other polities.

In the following chapter, we will examine how these struggles over ancestral blessing intensified with the active intervention of French colonists in the organization of land, labor, and eventually ancestors, in the Analalava region. We will focus on the events surrounding the death of Tondroko, praised as Ndramamahaña, and the succession of his infant daughter Soazara, examining how the elevation of sister's children and tombs, in whom Sakalava ancestors are reborn, has contributed to the elevation of commoners and slaves as well.

La France Orientale et le Far-West Malgache

Aza manao Vazaha nahazo tany.
Don't act like a European who got land.

proverb from the Analalava region

FRONTIERS

When French emissaries of the Third Republic invaded Madagascar in 1895, turning it into a protectorate, and then a possession, they found themselves confronted with the same problems of recruiting and organizing scarce labor as the Sakalava and Merina rulers of the precolonial period. Early reports that Madagascar was heavily populated proved to be wrong. Reluctantly, colonial officials abolished slavery and turned to various forms of legislation concerning land, labor, and taxes to capture Malagasy workers. Colonial scholars produced an extensive literature characterizing the potential of different Malagasy groups as workers in terms of their propensities to move—to reproduce and migrate—or die. Deschamps's account of "le Far-West malgache" in the 1950s described not only the efforts of French pioneers to develop the land *(mettre la terre en valeur),* but also the natives' capacities to hide out. I have argued that Sakalava royal followers had already begun to hide out in their nineteenth-century encounters with French explorers and officials in Nosy Be et Dépendances. Here, I suggest that the reevaluation of women and sisters' children compared to men, which occurred during this time, facilitated the further reevaluation of commoners and slaves compared to living royalty. As colonial subjects, Sakalava followers hid out by hiding and protecting royal ancestors who embodied a different theory of prosperity, another organization of labor, which—as living rulers were killed, exiled, or made into functionaries—shifted into the hands of commoners and slaves.

When people in the Analalava region say, 'Don't act like a European who got land,' they mean don't take without returning. As one man explained:

"This refers to a person who borrows something, then refuses to give it back, but keeps it for himself. Like the Vazaha who came in here and measured land *(mandrefy tany)*, measured it out and instead of just using it like the Malagasy, took it, made huge concessions, and became rich people."

From the local point of view, the French who conquered, then colonized Madagascar in 1895, stole Malagasy land. They tried to seize the royal relics in the Analalava region when Soazara's father died. They tried to force people to work for them. Colonial officials began by legislating what royal followers regarded as illegal, expelling guardians of the royal ancestors from the cemetery on Nosy Lava in order to build a prison to house those who failed to observe the new laws; then using prison labor as civilian labor became unattainable. As they failed to enforce the law, they fell back on their understanding of ancestral custom, even as Sakalava hired French Communist lawyers to defend themselves.

French involvement in Sakalava monarchy intensified the shift from living rulers to royal ancestors that began during the precolonial period. The chief agents of this shift may once have been the rulers themselves, seeking to protect their several bodies from theft or attack by fortifying, feminizing, and infantilizing them. During the colonial period, when Sakalava rulers were removed from office or transformed into petty functionaries, "simple people" were the agents of transformation: former royal officials who found an infant to succeed their king in the 1920s and raised her to be a queen; ex-slaves who derive increasing financial and social benefits from their intimacy with

living and dead royalty; and commoners who account for the prolif-
eration of mediums of royal spirits since the turn of the century. The
result of popularizing royalty has been to pluralize rather than unify
political-economic power regionally as well as nationally.

LA FRANCE ORIENTALE

Guillain saw his *Documents on the History, Geography and Commerce of
Western Madagascar* as providing the framework in which French economic interests and, by implication, impending Franco-Malagasy relations of economic cooperation, were to be understood. He completed his "historical sketch" by describing the formal "act of taking
possession . . . consummated with the customary ceremonies" on
May 5, 1841.[1] Summarizing his account in French metaphors of space,
gender, death, and regeneration, he argued that Sakalava and Hova
efforts to conquer Madagascar were prototypes of what the French
themselves proposed. They revealed indigenous impulses to grow, as
well as indigenous impulses to colonize, but beyond a certain point
they were fatally affected by impulses to decline.

The vital strength of Sakalava and Hova royalty was epitomized in
their male rulers, especially the Hova king Radama who sought to
civilize the country along European lines. The impulses to decline were
revealed in the shift to female rulers beginning with Vahiny's reign
(1780–circa 1810) among the Sakalava and Ranavalona's reign (from
1828) among the Hova. Since then, Malagasy efforts to unify and
develop the country—Sakalava and Hova alike—had led to death; only
direct intervention could bring the country back to life.

> Let us say, after all, that this account does not appear to us to be
> completely without interest. It is always an absorbing sight to see a
> people, as weak as it may be, marching with courage toward the
> accomplishment of its destiny and struggling as a result with
> convulsive movements against the principle of death that it carries
> within its breast. . . . We have taken this Sakalava family from its
> cradle . . . across all the vicissitudes of its decline. . . . To prove that
> the acts of the Sakalava in the work of humanitarian development
> have not been completely null, it suffices to recall what they

accomplished or attempted for the political unity of Madagascar, more than half of which was subordinated to their sovereign authority. Therein lay their vitality; when they stopped in this path of progress to fall asleep in the shade of acquired glory, political death began.[2]

Guillain went on to say that the Hova monarchy, led by Andrianampoinimerina and his son Radama, then took up the task of political unification and economic development, just at the point when Sakalava were weakened by internal struggles and softened by the reign of women.

There was perhaps a moment when, thanks to the ambitious ardor and energetic intelligence of Andrianampoinimerina and his son, one could have believed that the Hova people, assimilating the elements of civilization that England brought them with calculated generosity, would go on to continue the work roughed out by the peoples of the West, and constitute a Malagasy empire, to the shame of France, which for nearly two centuries seemed dedicated to this glorious mission. But that hope is dead with Radama, and the reign of Ranavalona is a proof that, beyond a certain point, these Malagasy peoples can do nothing on their own, not even set the bounds of their own country. To expect henceforth something to come from mere contact with our civilization would be to hope for a resurrection from the union of a living person with a corpse.[3]

Guillain argued that to leave the Malagasy free was "to condemn them to die." They need "the direction of their 'elders in the human family'":

This active supremacy of the european race over the barbarous and savage races, here as everywhere, is more than a right: it is a duty that the former ought not let fall into oblivion.

Now, to whom of the civilized nations ought to fall this right and this duty of civilizing conquest over this country whose history we have just sketched? To whom, if not to France, who, two centuries ago, gave the whole island the name of *France orientale!*[4]

Guillain concluded his argument by extolling "the prize of such a possession," now wholly feminine in form:

> Who does not know that magnificent island, the queen of the Indian Ocean: the fertility of her soil, the variety of her products, her metallurgical riches, her vast and excellent ports, finally her wonderful geographical location, two steps from the african continent, not far from the great asian peninsula, between the two routes to India, China, and the western Ocean, between the Cape of Good Hope and the isthmus of the Suez?[5]

GIVING, TAKING, AND STEALING

Guillain's account makes it clear that transactions between the French and the Sakalava on the west coast were usually accompanied by gifts, intended to establish cordial relations between people but also to discourage stealing.[6] Sometimes the exchanges were formalized as pledges of blood relationship (fatidra).[7] The land and labor that the French acquired and the Malagasy relinquished during the later decades of the nineteenth century were assimilated to these social patterns of giving, taking, and stealing. In 1841, the Sakalava ruler Tsiomeko ceded the island of Nosy Be and adjacent mainland to the French in exchange for their military assistance against the Merina. In 1848, the French abolished slavery in their new territory, and instituted a system of engagé labor that would undermine the power of the Sakalava monarchy and provide sorely needed workers for their newly established sugar plantations in Nosy Be and the Mascarenes. They also made engagés of slaves in regions they did not yet control, for example, in the Analalava region in 1875, where they demanded 150 engagés from royal slaves in partial retribution for the alleged pillaging of a French ship.[8]

The French established a similar protectorate over Madagascar, following the conquest of 1895, ostensibly to safeguard existing claims. Within a week of General Joseph Galliéni's appointment as the first Governor-General of Madagascar in October 1896, two highly placed Merina officials were tried and executed on charges of rebellion. S. Ellis argues that Galliéni and his supporters fabricated the charges and supporting evidence to justify the move from protectorate to possession, thus consolidating French rule in Madagascar (Plate 3).[9]

The works of Cahuzac, published in 1900, and Decary, published in 1954, exemplify how contemporary and later colonial administrator-scholars interpreted the establishment of the protectorate in terms of legal battles over land rights. In the introduction to his book on Malagasy legal institutions, Cahuzac argues that the Malagasy did not recognize the rights of the French to the land on which their warehouses were located and therefore they wrongly broke treaties. Loath as they were to do it, the French eventually had to invade Madagascar to assert their legal rights.[10]

While making these points, he repeatedly emphasizes the naturally thieving and sly qualities of the Hova, and the general lack of recognition among the Malagasy as a whole of what they owe to others. Their very preoccupation with gifts, thefts, and sales indicates their venality and interest in money and thus their predisposition for development, however much they may claim to despise it.

Cahuzac laid out Malagasy [Hova] law so that here, as in other French colonies, the natives could be ruled according to their own customs. It is morally right and also politically necessary that the French and Malagasy act as full collaborators in the development of Madagascar. Hova methods of forced colonization during the nineteenth century provided a model for the design of French policies to reorganize land ownership through law, thus contributing to the country's economic growth.

Decary's purpose was also to argue that the conquest of Madagascar was a "taking of possession" according to law, not an act of theft. He notes that the international law required "to validate the acquisition of a territory by means of occupation consists in a real and effective taking of possession, manifest in acts of sovereignty of diverse nature." These were accomplished in various ways in the past, ranging from exploration and discovery, to trade, to establishment of comptoires, to taking possession of the comptoires, and finally "official colonisation, that is, the incorporation of these establishments under the direct action of the State," as laid out in Dislère's, *Traité de législation*

Plate 3. *Mademoiselle Galliéni et la reine Binao, 1903* (ORSTOM, *Types ethniques* III *[Sakalava du Nord]* E.C. no. 11). Owing to recurrent uprisings against French rule, Galliéni toured different portions of western Madagascar every year after becoming Governor-General in July 1897. He returned to Nosy Be several times, but so far I have found no photographs of him with the ampanjaka Binao, a descendant of Andriantsoly, who was the living ruler of the Northern Bemihisatra during this period.

coloniale.[11] Indirectly, Decary provides an important reminder of the extent to which functionaries conveyed their knowledge of such matters to their successors by word of mouth, rather than written documents. He concludes his chapter on "Transfers and Taking Possession" in the case of Nosy Be, by noting that he has never been able to find a copy of the critical act of July 14, 1840, either in the archives "that we have compulsively searched" *(que nous avons compulsées)* or in any history of colonization in Madagascar. He then goes on to suggest that the document may never have reached France. The letters from "the queen of the Sakalava and the sultan of Mayotte" were written in Arabic, and officials were still awaiting M. Noël back from Zanzibar to translate them in October 1843. Their heirs in Nosy Be in 1861 were already complaining of a lack of archives: "no plan of Nosy Be nor any kind of history of this locality, nor a map of Madagascar, nor a single treaty, nor a single one of the conventions that constitutes us as owners of the island and of its dependency Nosy Komba, and protectors of the points next to us." Twenty years later, in 1883, the Commandant of Nosy Be wrote to his superior: "I regret not being able to communicate to you the treaty by which the queen Tsiomeko ceded her rights on the northwest coast of Madagascar. This treaty does not exist in the archives of Nosy Be; it is even impossible to find the original in those of the Département de la Marine."[12]

While French officials attempted to find documents justifying colonization according to European law, and gradually expanded the controls they exercised through writing, Sakalava followers persisted in seeing their legal settlements in terms of theft. Indeed, the French occupation of territories in western Madagascar was often consolidated by confiscating ancestral relics. Bénévent, interpreter at the Résidence in Majunga, described the first of these in 1895 in discussing the religion of the Sakalava in Boina:

> Their true religion is that of the ancestors. These are of two kinds: the former kings and the Vazimbas [spirits associated with indigenous inhabitants]. The shades of the first four Sakalava kings

rest in Majunga. The natives have for these relics such a veneration that one could almost affirm that possession of these shades is equivalent to assuring the loyalty of nearly the whole country. Ramasombazaha, [the Merina] Governor-General of Boeni, was so well aware of this fact that he took care, in evacuating Majunga before the [French] bombardment of 1895, not to abandon this palladium. He took with him every object of the Sakalava cult, thus forcing the [Sakalava] queen of Boeni, Ramboatofa, to follow after him, bringing her subjects. Our troops were able to retrieve these relics only in Tananarive; they have been brought back to Majunga by General Metzinger, who has solemnly reinstalled them in their former place [at Trabonjy near Majunga in October 1895].[13] They are, at this very moment, guarded by Sakalava under the surveillance of local [French] authorities.[14]

The public report of the event in the *Journal officiel de Madagascar* of March 1902, declared the relics to be of "minimal importance." They were held merely for the sake of appearances until eventually it was decided that their return, as an act of magnanimity, would bring the Sakalava to the French side.[15] Nevertheless, the very month that Bénévent reported on the disposition of the Sakalava royal relics in Majunga, French authorities in Tananarive were carrying out what S. Ellis describes as "the greatest desecration which could be imagined [that] destroyed the Merina kingdom for ever."[16] Galliéni had officially abolished the monarchy and exiled Ranavalona III on February 27, 1897. That night she was escorted by Senegalese troops down to the port of Tamatave on the east coast and put aboard a ship for Réunion.[17] Galliéni then proceeded to move the corpses of the Merina kings, including the founder king Andrianampoinimerina, from Ambohimanga, the town where they were buried, to Tananarive twelve miles away.[Merina rebels, the *menalamba*, had tried to take Ambohimanga on the day of the Merina "royal bath" on November 20, 1896 and he feared they would try again.] On Sunday, March 14, 1897, exactly a year after the first major Merina uprising against the French, he had the bodies exhumed, "tak[ing] great care to observe the due rituals of royal burial." The bodies, followed by 30,000 mourners, were carted to Tananarive during the night. There the coffins were

opened, the contents were deposited in the Merina palace as the first
acquisitions of what was now to be a museum of Merina history; the
bodies were reburied nearby.[18] At the same time, Galliéni abolished
the Royal Bath, held at Ambohimanga on November 20 every year,
and proclaimed Bastille Day, July 14, as the major national holiday
of the year.[19]

A couple of years later, in January 1905, Demortière, Administrateur de la province de Tuléar, fearing *"une certaine effervescence"* on the
part of the Masikoro [Sakalava] in the southwestern district of Ambohibe, "withdrew" from their *chefs* the seven relics of their former
rulers. Like Bénévent, he explains the act in terms of the political
purpose of the relics: "Since possession of these relics gives the holder
great authority over those of his kind, I find it prudent to leave them
on deposit at the office of the district commander of Ambohibe until
the situation returns to normality."[20]

When Demortière wrote his note in November 1906, he claimed
that the Masikoro chiefs had completely forgotten about the relics,
and since "it would be scarcely *politique* to put them back in their
hands," he was sending them on to Tananarive.

LE FAR-WEST MALGACHE

In seizing ancestral relics, French authorities were attempting to extend
their political control from land to people by strategies they knew that
Merina rulers had used when they attempted to colonize western
Madagascar.[21] The common problem of Malagasy polities, centralized
or dispersed, was labor, but Malagasy spoke a common language of
ancestors, relics, and rulers by which to negotiate the competition for
workers. The most difficult and enduring problem for French administrators was also labor. As Cooper has observed, colonialism was
marked not by the emergence of Third World peoples on the world
scene, because they had long been involved in international trading
relations: "What was new, above all, under colonial rule was the intervention of a European power in the production process itself."[22]
The Malagasy case, from the French perspective, involved the imposition of radically different ideas and practices on a subject popu-

lation. In the words of Jacquier, a student of colonial law at the time: "the question of labor concerns the very basis of the organization of societies."[23]

Jacquier was one of several former members of the colonial army or administration in Madagascar who were writing theses on labor law during the first decade after the French conquest. As he explained in the first paragraph of his introduction: "Of the three elements necessary to the development of the colonies: land, capital, labor, it is certainly the latter that is, at the present time, the most difficult to get. The question of land regulations has received very satisfactory solutions in many colonies; in every case, it is very clear what solutions it involves and what progress can be made in this regard. For the question of labor, on the contrary, the more it is studied, the more it appears complicated and delicate."[24]

Although Jacquier spoke of French colonies, he might as well have referred to European colonies throughout Africa.[25] Indeed, his remark about the organization of societies was taken from Bernard's preliminary report on "Labor in the Colonies" to the Congrès Colonial International of 1900. As Jacquier went on to point out, most European colonies, and notably Madagascar, were "colonies of exploitation." They were too unhealthy for Europeans to settle there, so a limited number would handle the intellectual tasks of planning and administration, while using the natives for labor.[26]

Jacquier described the qualifications of the Malagasy people for this purpose, distinguishing them according to *tribu* (Plate 4). His remarks about "Sakalava" were echoed in later catalogues and in the reports of virtually every military and administrative official who served in the Analalava region:

> The Sakalava are warriors and nomads. They despise work on the land and are not attached to the soil. The cultivations that exist in the country—the minimum necessary for the population not to die of hunger—are abandoned to women as inferior work. They give themselves instead to cattle rearing, which corresponds better to their wandering habits. Not very intelligent, having no needs, they have remained very savage. If they are less apathetic than the

Plate 4. *Madagascar—Types Malgaches,* Madagascar—Malagasy Types
(postcard, blank, no date).

> populations of the East coast, they do not like work, and they
> exercise themselves especially in fighting and pillaging. Of an
> independent humor, they do not have that inborn respect for
> authority of the Hova and the Betsileo, which renders them so
> malleable. It goes without saying that they especially hate salaried
> work, that is, rule and constraint; it is very rare that they praise
> themselves as workers. From the economic point of view, the
> Sakalava people are not very interesting. . . . Besides, as with the
> Betsimisaraka, the population has little tendency to grow.[27]

Jacquier and his colleagues expressed wistful regret that their government could not retain slavery as a temporary solution to the labor
problem while other solutions were being sought. The lawyers ra-
tionalized their arguments by emphasizing the relative humaneness of
Malagasy slavery and the potentially disruptive effects of abolition on
the political, economic, and social order.[28] According to some Muslims in the Analalava region, many French planters continued to re-

cruit labor through slave traders, carrying out their transactions secretly in a famous cave on the coast. In principle, however,
emancipation was, in Jacquier's words, "complete and immediate. No
precautionary measure was taken, no transition arranged . . . a jump
into the unknown."[29]

Given the need to legitimate the conquest of Madagascar, perhaps
it is not surprising that the French who jumped into the unknown
were also armed with the law.[30] The history of Malagasy labor legislation during the colonial period is discussed in detail by the law
students André, Sabatier, Jacquier, and Cherrier;[31] by the geographer
Isnard;[32] by the ethnologist Kloosterboer;[33] and by the political sci-
entists Thompson and Adloff,[34] whose purpose is to explain the continuing stagnation, even decline of the Malagasy economy, despite
sudden population growth following independence.

By World War II, the French had enacted more labor laws to govern
the economy of Madagascar than existed in almost any other French
colony.[35] These laws failed to induce many Malagasy people to work
for Europeans. Every account of the situation suggests ways to supplement the growing numbers of ineffectual statutes. French law students argued that perhaps the real problem was not the regulation of
production, but consumption, an area in which Indian merchants
might play a critical role by awakening the desire to buy.[36] Jacquier
comments in 1904: "The Malagasy change themselves little by little;
their needs grow and it is thus that, by a slow evolution, work, in
which they still see only an insupportable constraint, will impose itself
on them like a law of nature."[37]

Galliéni assumed in 1908 that the best spur to native indolence was
the imposition of taxes, "at once utilitarian and morally edifying,"
but that solution was thought to have been pushed to its limit by
1930.[38] Cherrier, too, concluded that "all the laws have done little to
convince the Malagasy to work for Europeans." Indeed, Malagasy
had "a veritable horror" of labor contracts. By signing them, they
felt "a little like prisoners"; and not without reason, since some employers regarded contracts as "weapons against workers whom they
consider exploitable at will." He suggested that Europeans should be

required to treat their workers more humanely; even a few kind words would encourage workers to remain voluntarily in the service of gracious and kindly masters.[39] Forced labor, according to the decree of August 21, 1930, could only be used in the public interest and then only when it was impossible to find sufficient numbers of free laborers.[40] At mid-century, wage labor was still so scarce that most European plantations on the west coast, whether owned by individuals or companies, were worked by a system of sharecropping *(métayage)* that tended in practice to debt bondage.[41]

ENFORCING THE LAW

The recurrent problem for French observers and participants was law enforcement. Colonial officials in Madagascar enacted numerous labor laws, but they did not have enough magistrates and labor inspectors to enforce them.[42] Under these circumstances, the law itself entailed illegality. Malagasy people who observed colonial law jeopardized themselves in terms of their customary law; those who followed customary law risked breaking colonial law. The situation was further complicated by the fact that the French themselves, incapable of enforcing their own labor laws, when not deliberately disregarding them, adopted methods of inducing Malagasy to work that brought all parties outside the law as defined by any of them.[43]

To solve the problem of enforcement, the French turned to strategies of "indirect enforcement" on the model of the indirect rule with which they transformed military force into forms of coercion more suited to a civil administration with insufficient numbers of personnel.[44] Documents of the period usually refer to these strategies as *politique,* a term combining notions of pragmatic with partisan, possibly illicit behavior, which people in the Analalava region have since adopted to refer to double-dealing.[45] These policies had a decidedly equivocal character in practice. For example, *la politique des races,* the policy of giving every ethnic group its own leaders on an equal basis, which Galliéni had developed in Tonkin, was mainly an effort to undercut the power of the highland Merina while also serving to divide and rule in the provinces.[46] *La politique de l'habitat,* concerning the sanitation and safety of Malagasy houses and villages, also reorganized these structures in ways that would render their inhabitants more amenable to French administration and more receptive to French interests.[47] Resting on apparently long-standing cultural assumptions about the influence of spatial configurations on mental and social behavior,[48] the policy implicitly recognized that forms of habitation are related to ideas about proper relationships among inhabitants, and that changes in one will induce changes in the other.[49] Decary stated that the Malagasy "hut" was "surely, of all the factors of material life, that which presents the least tendencies to modifications or improvements," precisely because of its intimate association with the ancestors and ancestral traditions. As such, it constituted "a kind of break on the evolution which is carrying Madagascar along"[50] (Plate 5). Eventually in the Sakalava case, but I suspect more extensively in Madagascar as well, these strategies included what might be called *la politique de la mort*. The end result of the politics of death, as applied in the Analalava region, was the involvement of the French and the Malagasy in relations with one another, which had all the trappings of legality, but actually operated in a legal limbo.

This policy might have been developed and carried out intentionally. The clearly stated aim of the French was to destroy indigenous institutions and substitute their own, or at least to provide the conditions in which, as one French administrator put it, Sakalava monarchy would just "let itself die quietly."[51] Yet, it is probably more accurate to say that the policy developed inadvertently in the course of a long, slow, clumsy dialogue, replete with systemic misunderstanding.

The key problem on both sides was the "unknown" to which Jacquier referred.[52] Despite their efforts at cataloguing Malagasy people, the French did not know the Sakalava well enough to act as swiftly and efficiently as they might have. Perhaps they felt that such knowledge was impossible to acquire. Sabatier's opinion, expressed in 1903, was typical: "Between the mentality of a Sakalava and that of a European even of mediocre intelligence, there is not simply a difference but an abyss."[53] The Commandant du cercle, Capitaine Charbonnel,

MAJUNGA — Le Grand Baobab

Éditeur D. Boutoux, Imprimerie commerciale

observed at this time: "Certainly, penetrating the soul of the native, getting to the point that he accepts our domination without a second thought, is a long and difficult task. But it is completely inexact to claim that it is impossible to carry it out well. As a whole, the extremely mixed population of the area is very perfectible."[54]

Despite these ideas, contact between French officials and Sakalava royal followers was in fact extremely limited. Compagnon, the Chef de province d'Analalava, wrote to his superiors in 1907: "Lazy and apathetic the Sakalava is characterized by his failings: provided he is left quietly to cultivate his rice field, he searches to quarrel with no one. He is deeply indifferent to measures taken by the administration, even if these measures are not contrary to his habits. I had the occasion, a few days ago, to see a Sakalava who had never come to Analalava! For him the end of the world was Antognibe [the former capital]. The policy of non-assimilation has a bright future."[55]

French officials rarely knew the Malagasy language. They worked

←——————————————————————————————

Plate 5. *Majunga—Le Grand Baobab,* Majunga—The Great Baobab (postcard dated 1915, Editeur B. Boutoux, Imprimerie commerciale).
Correspondence on card:
Corps d'occupation de Madagascar
Mon cher Charles,
Dernier poste j'ai été envoyé à Majunga puis à Diégo—je ne sais ce que l'on va faire de moi—Peut être conduirai-je de rapatriés en France—Mille amitiés [signed]
P. Gallot 3e Malgaches Diégo Suarez
My dear Charles,
Latest post I have been sent to Majunga then to Diégo—I do not know what is going to be done with me—Perhaps I will take repatriates back to France—All good wishes. . .
address: Sous-intendant militaire C. Gallot, secteur 46 du front France.
stamped: Diégo-Suarez 31 Mai 15 Madagascar
The great baobab, overlooking the Mozambique Channel, was a landmark of precolonial Mahajanga reputed to be centuries old. The tree was incorporated into the structure of colonial Majunga as the center of the Square Poincaré, in front of the Résidence de Majunga, at the head of the main Avenue de France.

through interpreters, usually the Merina with whom the Sakalava were not yet on good terms.[56] The kind of misunderstanding that resulted is exemplified in the responses of French officials and Malagasy residents to the locust infestations and smallpox epidemics that ravaged the Analalava region in the first years of colonial rule and periodically thereafter. The French deplored the apathy of the Sakalava, their reluctance to plant second crops or to be vaccinated, while worrying about the effects of these disasters on the economic development of the region. The Sakalava, by contrast, explained them as punishments the French had inflicted on them for having resisted conquest.[57]

French administrators commented at the time that the Sakalava already seemed to be dying out, being too lazy, apathetic, or alcoholic even to reproduce themselves. As Compagnon put it: "This race is disappearing little by little and degenerating. The Sakalava produce no children, or almost none: the Tsimihety and the Makoa have more of them and absorb little by little the autochthonous race. It is not necessary to regret it."[58] Sakalava royal followers saw their demographic vulnerability in politico-religious terms as well. They identified themselves with the cattle herds, reduced by taxation, and thereby impoverishing the population and eroding the conceptual as well as material foundations of the monarchy.[59] They may have continued to reinterpret the Vy Lava from a sword of conquest, associated with the acquisition of infinite numbers of prisoners of war, to a "medicine of not-many-ness" (aody tsy maro) that prevents Southern Bemihisatra rulers from having numerous children, in relation to such events. It was during the colonial period that Amada (1878/1881–1968)—Andriantsoly's descendant and Binao's successor in Nosy Be—is said to have abandoned the Vy Lava, which the Northern Bemihisatra, like the Southern Bemihisatra, claimed to have held since the dynasty's beginnings.[60]

The French were sensitive to the association between religion and politics. One of the ways they maintained discreet surveillance over religious activities in which they were officially not involved was to require government permission for the construction of new buildings.

Thus, intermittently throughout the colonial period, they refused Muslims permission to build new mosques because they feared their influence on the Sakalava and their former slaves.

The Sakalava were thought to have no religion of their own. Camy, an army officer stationed in the Analalava region, reported in 1905: "They have neither religion nor beliefs. . . . It is only the culture of the tombs of their former kings, which exerts on them an authority as hard as it is savage."[61] Administrators at the end of the first decade of colonized rule emphasized the extent of their travels through the region, *kabarant* with the people, and thus their knowledge of the local "state of mind," an obligatory subject of discussion in every annual report.[62] As the Chef de province d'Analalava wrote to the Governor-General in 1908: "As for the sakalava, he is the perfect free thinker, who follows nothing at all, and on whom metaphysical ideas have no effect. Sorcerers suffice for him."[63] The provincial report for 1912 expresses a similar view, contrasting the complete absence of Sakalava philosophy with the prominence of "Muslim propaganda," which posed such obstacles to "our moral penetration and our economic actions": "We have had the good fortune in Madagascar to be confronted with natives having no religious dogma, no tradition that could serve as a basis for resistance to our activities. We find ourselves, as it were, before a blank slate . . ."[64]

KINGLETS AND QUEENS

It was, then, on the superficially familiar appearance of living *roitelets* and *reines*, *princes* and *princesses*, that French officers first concentrated their attention. Their approach followed "the politics of habitation" in that it depended largely on the spatial reorganization of people to reorganize their behavior and mental attitudes. But it came into contact with the spatial strategies of the Sakalava themselves.

According to Sakalava guardians at both the royal compound and the royal cemetery in the Analalava region, the Bemihisatra branch of the Volamena dynasty, located on the island of Nosy Be, split in two during the mid-nineteenth century owing to disputes about slavery. Rather than submit to the abolition of slavery ordered by the

French in 1848–1849, not long after they took possession of the island and adjacent mainland, some royal officials decided to leave the area.[65] In 1849, they seized the ampanjaka, Tsiomeko's young son Rano, and went south to the Analalava region, knowing that substantial numbers of his supporters would follow them, which they did.[66] The Southern Bemihisatra domain around Narinda Bay was the last Sakalava domain to be established before the French conquest.

Rano located his doany on the island of Nosy Lava to protect it from the Hova (see Figs. 1 and 5). In fact, he had two doany, as did all his successors in this area. According to Velondraza at the Mahabo:

"The ampanjaka Ndramamitrañarivo [the Great-Grandfather, Rano] lived at Amboanio [the main port on the northwestern part of the island, where the national penitentiary is now located]. But the doany, the real doany (doany marigny), was located at Ampasindava [on the southwest coast]. It was like it is now—the two places. Amboanio was the post (positra)—full of shops, merchants, Vazaha [Muslim traders]. The doany was at Ampasindava, away from all that."[67]

When Rano died around 1865, he was buried in a mahabo built in the southeastern part of the island, the orientation dedicated to the royal ancestors. His doany was abandoned. His son, Añono (Ndramanetsiarivo, the Grandfather), founded a new doany on the mainland. Some Southern Bemihisatra say that the new doany was founded at Antognibe, a coastal site in a rich rice-growing area at the bottom of Narinda Bay, interpreting this move as a sign of the increasing support of the local populace for the monarchy. Others say that the doany was founded first at Analalava. Although not as suited to rice-growing as Antognibe, it was already a well-established port for the Muslim traders who provided much of the royal revenue. Some people remember the land immediately north of the present market in Analalava as being Ndramanetsiarivo's former doany.[68]

According to Captain Toquenne, the soldat-colonisateur who occupied and then administered the area, beginning in May 1897, the Hova fought Añono at Analalava, and he then fled south to Antognibe at the base of the bay where the Hova had yet to reach when the French

campaign began in 1895.[69] Añono's doany at Antognibe was strateg-
ically located on the summit of a high hill looking north over the bay
because the Hova always attacked by land and sea at the same time,
as they had done with Andriantsoly at Anorotsangana.[70]

When Añono died around 1892, he was buried in the Mahabo on
Nosy Lava, and his doany was abandoned. The Bemihisatra tried to
reestablish themselves near the port of Analalava. The doany of Añono's young son Tondroko, born in 1890 according to Southern Bemihisatra tantara, was first founded at Andampy, a rich rice-growing
area about 7 kilometers south of Analalava, but almost immediately—
according to current accounts—they had to move further south, back
to Antognibe, to get away from the Hova.[71] Tondroko's doany at
Antognibe was founded on low ground, in the midst of rice fields,
about a kilometer away from his father's former compound on the
hill overlooking the bay. He had been living there four or five years
when Captain Toquenne occupied the area on September 30, 1897,
and established a military garrison on the hill where Añono's doany
had been. Malaza simply commented: "The Vazaha dared to do that;
no one else would live there." During the colonial period, the garrison
was transformed into a gendarmerie, with a radiotelephone trans-
mitter, which the Malagasy government continues to use.[72]

Like the Southern Bemihisatra, French officials saw the port of Analalava, where they established their Résidence, as being the most central place in the region. As Troupel, the Résident in Hellville, explained in a letter to Galliéni, then Résident Général de France à
Madagascar, suggesting that the seat of French authority in the northwest be moved from Nosy Be to Analalava:

> Analalava owes its importance to its geographic position, because
> this village commands, by water and land routes, all the routes in
> the region, whether for communicating rapidly with all the
> important points on the coast and in the interior, whether going to
> Majunga and Nossi-Be. It is situated equidistant from these two
> points and the "Mpanjaka" [the name of the Résidence boat, taken
> from the Sakalava title ampanjaka or 'mpanjaka] could stop there
> every month, without disturbing its schedule very much.[73]

In his first report for the government's *Journal officiel de Madagascar et dépendances,* written a few months after he actually settled in Analalava on May 14, 1897, Toquenne described the area from Narinda Bay to the Ampasindava Peninsula north of the Loza River as divided into two political territories: one south of the river and one north of it.[74] The southern territory, extending from the Loza River to Mahajamba Bay, was under the authority of Tondroko (then about twelve to fourteen years old), based at Antognibe. The northern one, extending from the Loza River to Radama Bay was governed by several indigenous "chefs" (also mpanjaka) "who had preserved a semi-independence," presumably from Tondroko. Sakalava followers now say that Tondroko was circumcised in one of the northern villages, and that he often made tours of the Ambolobozo Peninsula, during which he collected tribute.

Toquenne found the southern territory to be "substantially more populated" than the northern one, including some 15,000 inhabitants, the majority Sakalava, followed by numerous Makoa and a minority of Betsimisaraka, with Sihanaka south of Antognibe.[75] Guédès's estimate of 6,500 only a year later accords better with the 1906 census figure of 5,972 for the Antognibe sector, 750 of which were resident in Antognibe.[76]

Toquenne had not yet met Tondroko when he wrote his report of September 25, 1897. Tondroko's "prime minister" *(manantany)* had come from Antognibe to Analalava several times, but Tondroko had yet to present himself, nor had he answered any of Toquenne's letters. Nevertheless, Toquenne described Tondroko as the best known of the numerous indigenous chiefs to be found in the area, noting that "his popularity, which comes from his father, is, it seems, rather great in this area."[77] Presumably on the basis of his reputed popularity, Galliéni had already made Tondroko head of the Fourth Circumscription of the Province of the Antankarana and Sakalava of the Northwest Coast, with an annual salary of 1,200 F, in April 1897.[78]

In contrast to the "chiefs" in the northern part of the region, whose pretensions to authority were "much less" and who seemed to Toquenne to be more amenable to French influence, the young Tondroko was surrounded by a larger number of Muslim counselors who were decidedly hostile to the French.[79]

When Toquenne's superior, Troupel, first proposed to recentralize the French in northwestern Madagascar by moving the Résidence from Nosy Be to Analalava, he already hoped to induce Tondroko to re-establish his doany there too. Indeed, the power of the person was part of the power of the place for Troupel, Toquenne, and other French officials, just as it was for Tondroko and his followers: "The young king Tondroko must be persuaded to come to live at Doany [perhaps Andampy], where he used to live before. If that could be done, the importance of Analalava would be such that it would be possible to create one of the most important commercial and agricultural centers there, and the sale of land would bring, even that same year, a higher price."[80]

At first, Toquenne kept Tondroko under surveillance in Antognibe through the use of *dossiers politiques* and schooling financed by *bourses politiques*. To lessen the influence of his counselors and educate Tondroko in French ways, he entered Tondroko in "la section politique" of the École Normale d'Instituteurs Indigènes at Analalava, where the instructor "attended to him quite particularly."[81] By 1905, he was named a sous-gouverneur.[82] His duties were like those of other Malagasy leaders appointed to positions in the colonial administration: to keep order, collect taxes, and provide labor for public works and private enterprises.[83]

Toquenne commented on the fluid composition of Tondroko's court at Antognibe: "Although everything is relative, that court, even in a barbarous country, lacks prestige. Tondroko's counselors recognize it themselves and explain it by saying that their name, Sakalava, signifies, 'Who come and go in crossing the coastal rivers.' They are in fact very nomadic and, in Tondroko's entourage, changes of courtiers are frequent."[84]

By 1906, Toquenne's successor, Compagnon, was describing Tondroko as "a human wreck" *(une loque humaine)* whom the Sakalava obeyed only on rare occasions like ceremonies involving the royal tombs.[85] But just one year later, he was found guilty of fomenting a revolt, typifying for local administrators the way that the unpredictable behavior of the Sakalava could suddenly break the *sécurité absolue* of annual reports completed only weeks earlier.

Pont, serving as Chef de province par interim while Compagnon was in France, noted in his report of the incident that Tondroko was responding in part to the angry spirit of his father, speaking through the former royal slave who had been his wet nurse.[86] He argued that "the Sakalava or rather the Sakalava spirit still dominates the province. It is above all the spirit of independence, completely rebellious to direction. . . . Even if the local resident respects us, fears us, and appreciates current security, he feels for us absolutely no serious attachment. He still remains absolutely incapable of understanding the legitimacy of our action, of seeing our goals and appreciating the utility of the measures taken by our administration. He is still a child whose steps we must guide and sometimes correct."[87]

Yet Pont concluded that Tondroko's removal from the area went unnoticed because of marvelous reversals in the political and economic structure of the community, brought about by the French "law of work" *(la loi de travail)* that had paved the way for civilization:

> Now the majority of the population, composed of the liberated and newly-wealthy slaves of Sakalava royalty is no longer sufficiently favorable to Tondroko. Their former masters, who have not wanted to obey the laws concerning work, have gradually sold their goods, so they no longer possess anything, and by a just turn of fortune, have been reduced to putting themselves in the pay of their former slaves, who have become today's masters. The situation now favors us and the region has definitely entered on the path of civilization. With Tondroko's revocation and the recent death of the queen Salama to the north, the last vestiges of Sakalava royalty have disappeared from the province of Analalava.[88]

Tondroko was removed as sub-governor and relocated to a village 4 kilometers south of Analalava, which his followers renamed Manongarivo, "where thousands climb up [to the heights of royalty]," even though the French had permitted no more than a handful of his intimates to join him at the marshy, inland site. He was required to report to the Chef de province every Saturday; all other movements required a special *passeport*. During the First World War (1914–1918), he had to move into Analalava.[89] From a "complete free thinker" like other Sakalava, he became in the words of Chef de province Poirier's report for 1915: "a complete drunk, 37 years old, without thought, without malice, without will, occupied only by idleness; nevertheless he is venerated and revered by the Sakalava of the area. [He is] basically a good boy, but his weak character renders him irresolute and closed to our advice. Under surveillance, like his followers, he presents himself, flaccid, like an automaton, every week to the chef de province to confirm that he still lives and can do harm."[90]

TONDROKO'S DEATH

Tondroko died at Manongarivo on Sunday, September 20, 1925. Philibert, chief of what had shrunk to the district of Analalava, claimed that Tondroko died of alcoholism like his son the year before.[91] Current followers of the monarchy say that Tondroko died from rum, which he drank in grief after his son died from eating poisoned beef. As Saha Barimaso, one of the Father's leading mediums, explained:

"Sunday—that's the day he drank rum, La Girtan, one liter. He saw his son dead—rum, La Girtan, made in France, from there, a whole liter, killed him" (*Dimansy—io andro izy nigiaka rôm, La Girtan, litra araiky. Nahita zanakan'azy maty—rôm La Girtan, vita Frantsa, avy tany, jiaby litra araiky, nampihilaña azy*).

Europeans had established a monopoly on production and distribution of rum by 1901.[92] Local planters used gifts of rum as a means of controlling Sakalava workers, while official reports attributed the rapid depopulation of the country to the excessive consumption of cheap imports and homemade substitutes.[93]

Three of Tondroko's followers went to the Chef du district to announce the death that afternoon. As Philibert reports the encounter, he asked them: "'Then it's finished, you have no more mpanjaka?'

'Yes,' they responded, 'no more mpanjaka, that's the last one who's gone.'"[94] Backed by Chef de province Krotoff, Philibert granted them two months, extended to December 15, 1925 to hold the funeral services on Nosy Lava, in which "they delivered themselves of veritable acts of savagery on the remains of Tondroko."[95] The Sakalava won the extension through the efforts of a lawyer—M. Técher, the commercial agent in Analalava—whom they hired to argue their case.[96] Even so, the services were concluded "under administrative pressure" less than two months later on Monday, November 15, 1925.[97]

Shortly after Tondroko's death, Sakalava officials informed Philibert of the posthumous birth on October 30 of Tondroko's heir, whom they named Soazara, "Beautiful Destiny." She had been born to a Tsimihety woman from the canton of Antsohihy, southeast of Analalava.[98] Another woman, pregnant by Tondroko, was about to give birth. Philibert, supported by Chef de province Krotoff, refused to recognize the baby as heir, claiming that Tondroko had not had a wife in fixed residence for at least the last five years of his life. The woman had not been married to him by French law. He had been hopelessly alcoholic and syphilitic and could not possibly have fathered any children. The father of the child was probably Tondroko's "prime minister," related through marriage to the child's mother and head of the group claiming the child as heir.[99] Philibert also hoped to see an end to the monarchy altogether: "With Tondroko, deceased without heirs, Sakalava royalty is extinguished. . . . With him, the descendants of the Sakalava kings have disappeared."[100]

The Sakalava applied to the French the following February 8 for permission to remove the Vy Lava to a new location, Manongarivo having become Tsimahasenga (Place That Does Not Heal) after Tondroko's death. The location they had in mind was about 20 kilometers south of Analalava, very close to the present location of the doany chosen almost thirty years later.[101] The French again refused, ordering that the Vy Lava and other ritual equipment were to remain at Manongarivo until further notice. On May 11, 1926, they confiscated them "in the interests of public order" and brought them to Analalava, where they were stored in the Résidence, pending removal to the former Merina Palace, now an historical museum in Tananarive. Current guardians at the Doany say that the relics were never seized. They were hidden and later transported to Antognibe.[102]

The Southern Bemihisatra wrote to Amada, ampanjaka of the Northern Bemihisatra in Nosy Be, appealing for help in dealing with the French. Amada responded by asking the French whether Tondroko happened to have left among his goods "a sort of symbol or rod of leadership consisting of a little iron staff with, in one end, various ingredients," perhaps the Vy Lava, and whether the French happened to have confiscated it as he had heard.[103] It was soon apparent that Amada sought the Southern Bemihisatra domain for himself, while attempting to remain on good terms with the French authorities. The Southern Bemihisatra turned to raising money among Tondroko's subjects and Indian shopkeepers in Antognibe, with which they hired lawyers from Majunga to argue the case with the administration.[104]

French provincial authorities brought the case to court (the Tribunal indigène du 1er degré d'Analalava) by arresting five of the group together with a diviner who had developed a popular remedy against locusts, and charged them with perpetrating a "plot against the security of the State." The administration argued that the intimate association of the monarchy's supporters with the diviner's fraudulent activities indicated the existence of a "secret organization alongside the French administration," as serious an occurrence as Tondroko's revolt seventeen years earlier in 1908. The Southern Bemihisatra argued that their organization existed simply to procure the diviner's services in several villages, and that they had participated as notables not as officials of a subversive government.[105] While the French authorities regarded the diviner as a fraud, it is noteworthy that the Bemihisatra clearly regarded his divinatory powers and medicines as inseparable from his status as a royal spirit-medium.[106]

Owing to the intervention of an Inspecteur des colonies, sent from the Governor-General's office in Tananarive to investigate the situation, the provincial authorities were finally required to recognize the infant female, Soazara, as Tondroko's successor. They also had to return the Vy Lava and regalia, although Malaza said that they kept some gold and cloth. It seems likely that the Southern Bemihisatra used a tactic dating to the early 1800s, an element of their own politics of death. This strategy protected Sakalava royalty by withdrawing men to positions behind superficially powerless women, concealing the living while attending ever-more closely to the less accessible dead.

French authorities responded appropriately. They viewed the leadership of a baby girl as a religious issue having no political significance. The Inspecteur des colonies, Charles Poirier, began his report of 1926 by chaffing the provincial authorities for "seizing the relics," while countless thieves ran freely all over the region:

> While innumerable thieves, sportive gluttons, more greedy for grilled beef than manioc, help themselves to cattle feeding in the pastures of the Sofia River and trouble, shamelessly, the agrarian labors and pastoral existence of the Sakalava and Antandrona [Tsimihety] of Antognibe and Antsohihy, the provincial administration of Analalava devotes itself to the destruction of beliefs and rituals, the conservatism and traditionalism of the victims of theft, in prohibiting the Sakalava monarchy of the Southern Bemihisatra, in seizing the attributes and relics of the kingdom of Tondroko.[107]

Poirier went on to argue that the Sakalava monarchy, headed by a suckling babe "still at the animal stage of life," was nothing more than a kind of ancestor worship and that to suppress it was to give it an influence that it did not possess.[108] He closed his report with a mocking account of the return of "that black virgin, the young queen with a favorable destiny [her name], priestess of the clan" to her father's former royal capital at Antognibe for the presentation of her first tooth.[109]

Tondroko's chief administrator (manantany) had informed Poirier that "the Zafimbolamena dynasty of Nosy Lava-Antognibe is one of the purest in the coastal northwest."[110] The official's remark suggests that the Southern Bemihisatra had continued to recognize Antognibe as their true doany, even after Tondroko's removal to Manongarivo in 1908, just as his predecessors had lived in two places—one at the post and one "away from all that." Malaza later confirmed that, saying:

"The center of the monarchy is still in the south, around Antognibe. When Ndramamahaña moved up north to Manongarivo, he didn't bring people because the French had gotten the monarchy *(tsy nanday olo, satria nazon' ny fanjakaña ny Frantsay)."*

Whether or not the provincial authorities themselves recognized these distinctions, they refused to allow the infant Soazara to remain in Antognibe. As soon as the presentation was over, she was relocated to an old Muslim graveyard on the southern edge of Analalava (Plate 6).[111] Perhaps French officials were also unaware that living rulers

Plate 6. The ampanjaka Soazara, with female Sambarivo and Marovavy and male counselors inside the royal compound at Analalava around 1936, from the same series as the frontispiece (Service Photo—Cinéma du Ministère de l'Information; TY 13, no. 9).

were prohibited from contact with death in any form. Yet they must have known that she could not live where her father had died. That place, according to long-standing practice, had been rendered unin-habitable by his death. The Bemihisatra were already referring to Man-ongarivo as Tsimahasenga in a letter dated September 26, 1925, a few days after his death. Tsimahasenga means 'Place That Does Not Cure,' and since *mahasenga* is the name for the ruler's body in the royal vo-cabulary, it also means 'Not a Royal Body.' The same letter referred to Soazara's birthplace as 'place of the sweet palm wine' (Ankarafa-mamy), previously named 'place of the spoiled palm wine' (Ankara-faboka).[112] *Boka* also means false, counterfeit, having lost one's title, position, or honor, as in *'mpanjaka boka* (dethroned king).[113] As a noun, it means leper. People throughout the Analalava region see leprosy, once associated with banishment from the community, as a kind of living death.

The French missionaries, who received government permission to establish a leprosarium at Tsimahasenga a generation later, around 1946, were also unaware of the connections between lepers and de-throned or false rulers in Sakalava ideology. When they learned about it, they changed their approach. A priest stationed near Analalava in the early 1970s told me that he later named the Catholic leprosarium further north Mahasenga, 'Place that Cures,' to tell Sakalava that French Catholics did not abandon lepers to death. Without knowing the full significance of the royal cemetery, the French may have feared that the former residence of Tondroko, now Ndramamahana, would become a pilgrimage site for nationalistic Sakalava. Locating the lep-rosarium there, like locating the gendarmerie on the site of Ndra-manetsiarivo's (Añono) old doany at Antognibe, was one way to keep that from happening.

CEMETERIES AND PRISONS

Charles Poirier was a key figure in the growing recognition of local French administrators concerning the significance of the dead for the Sakalava. His detailed account of the incidents surrounding Tondro-ko's death and Soazara's succession even included letters written by

Malagasy participants to one another. His approach as Inspecteur des colonies emerged three years later, in 1929, when a highland Malagasy official filed a complaint against him for having entered his house without permission, searched his personal papers, and finally confiscated them together with valuable heirlooms. Poirier was relocated thereafter to Paris, although eventually he returned to live in Tananarive where he was working as a lawyer in the 1950s.[114]

Poirier was probably sent to look into the Sakalava case in 1926 because he had served in Analalava as Chef de province during the war (1914–1918). Poirier ordered Tondroko to live in Analalava and report to him weekly during these years. He also began the process in which the Mahabo on Nosy Lava was gradually supplanted by a national penitentiary, used for political prisoners as an institution of social control.

Almost as soon as they arrived in the area, French officials started building gendarmeries and penitentiaries, first to supplement and then to replace military force.[115] Late in the first decade, they decided to build a penitentiary on the island of Nosy Lava. The new penitentiary would house prisoners from all over Madagascar sentenced to periods of eight years or more. Work started on the prison in 1910. The annual report for that year mentions complaints on the part of laborers concerning working conditions.[116] The prison was completed in 1911; the first inmates arrived in October. Surveillance proved to be insufficient, and additional guards, mainly Muslims, had to be recruited locally, leading to certain abuses.[117] The same report suggests building a leprosarium on the island as well, to replace one in the Antognibe region that had recently been destroyed by a cyclone. Medical care at the prison would thus be cheaper, because the doctor in charge of the leprosarium could also deal with sick prisoners.[118]

The annual reports from 1910 through 1914 contain occasional references to the potential problems posed by having settlements of Sakalava on the island as well. But it seems likely that French administrators had no firm details concerning the significance of the Mahabo as a institution of social control in its own right until Poirier questioned Tondroko about it.

Poirier was motivated by yet another in a series of escapes organized with the help of Mahabo residents. This one was in December 1915, when 300 or more prisoners, in addition to the 412 already housed in the penitentiary, were expected to arrive. The new prisoners included some 200 members of the *Vy Vato Sakelika* (Iron Stone Branches), a Merina student organization accused of plotting to poison all of the Europeans in Madagascar.[119] The close association between prisoners and Mahabo residents was evident in the prison soap used throughout the village. Furthermore, residents of a neighboring village were found to have provided prisoners with metal to make counterfeit coins.

Poirier visited Tondroko on February 16–17, 1916. In his report, written the day he returned, on February 17, he advises that Tondroko, as an "article of veneration for the Sakalava" should be subject to continued surveillance. He also includes the first discussion in official reports of "the power of death" embodied in spirit-mediums and tombs. The residents of the Mahabo were moved, together with their cattle, to a coastal village on the Ambolobozo Peninsula north of Analalava on April 19. Poirier brought Tondroko there to visit them on May 7.[120]

It must be concluded that the politics of death succeeded only in killing off valuable labor or driving it underground in other ways. The prison, or "house of darkness" *(trano maizina),* as the Malagasy still call it, became a significant symbol of social control. Soazara herself—who was appointed *Gouverneur de 4e Classe* at age twenty-one in 1946,[121] and who joined the majority political party following independence in 1960—is remembered as threatening, "I'll lock you up! I'll lock you up!" *(Gadraoko! Gadraoko!),* rather than invoking the wrath of her royal ancestors. Yet the prison appears to have had no influence in redirecting the labor or loyalty of royal followers to the French. Administrative reports from the 1920s through the 1950s are filled with complaints that might have been written in 1897, when the French first introduced "the law of work." The head of a large construction firm in Majunga, with projects in several coastal locations including the Analalava region, made similar complaints in 1971:

"The Sakalava are very withdrawn. They don't like the Merina, they don't like the French, they don't like anything but their own way of doing things. They refuse to work, refuse to progress. They work only to get a bag of rice. They are dying out, that's it. They work for what they need at the moment, then stop. We had to hand out rice, a kilo a day, to get Sakalava to work. They wouldn't work for the money alone."

French settlers used presents to induce Sakalava to at least occasional day labor and *talatiers* ("Tuesday-ers") to get around the prohibition against work associated with the several royal death days.[122] Increasingly, they used the prisoners themselves. By the late 1920s the prisoners are described as the principal source of labor in the region, and that was still the case in the early 1970s and in 1981 and 1989.[123] Those Sakalava who did work on concessions during the colonial period were said to have stopped when independence was declared, causing many foreign owners in the Analalava region to sell to Malagasy functionaries who were in a position to employ prison labor. Local people themselves preferred to hire prisoners as water carriers, when they could afford to do so. As one woman put it in 1973, referring to the profits that women could make from selling prison-issue oil and soap they received from prisoners with whom they had liaisons, "Everyone knows—even in Majunga—prisoners support the women of Analalava" *(Olo jiaby mahay, ata Majunga—gadra fo mamelonteña ny mañangy Analalava).* The new administration in 1972 required merchants and other employers in the region to hire local "civilians," but prisoners continued to be used as laborers on concessions and on public works.

Meanwhile, the significance of the royal ancestors expanded, especially after spirit-mediums at the Mahabo, who lived around the royal tomb, were moved to the mainland, where these "people of the dead" were placed in closer contact with the rest of the population. Royal spirits began proliferating among the close relatives and acquaintances of the Mahabo guardians and then spread out into the surrounding countryside, where they have become important arbiters in local affairs, superceding the ancestors of family members.

The residents' petition to return to the royal cemetery on Nosy Lava, filed in 1926 as part of their suit against the administration in the matter of Soazara's succession, was refused "for many reasons: administrative, political, and economic." While Poirier claims that only one guardian was permitted to watch the tombs that remained there, current residents of the Mahabo say they won the case and were able to move back at the end of 1927.[124] The village of Mahabo on Nosy Lava reappears in census lists in 1956, just prior to independence.

The Mahabo residents also made repeated requests for permission to carry out the menaty service required to complete Tondroko's funeral by repairing the fence around the tomb that had been broken in the course of his burial. This would involve six to eight years of work if carried out properly. Unlike Sakalava groups to the north, who had permanently buried their royal dead in cement and tin, the Southern Bemihisatra planned to rebuild the royal tomb in wood, which would require them to rebury the royal ancestors in the future. They finally succeeded in 1972, after the uprising in which Madagascar's first president, Philibert Tsiranana, was replaced by General Gabriel Ramanantsoa as head of the national government.

Beginning with independence, Tsiranana, backed by the French government, had expanded the ranks of police and prison authorities to triple the size of the national army, mainly through the addition of coastal people like himself.[125] General Ramanantsoa was head of the national army, a stronghold of the Merina since the early nineteenth century. In the Analalava region, one of Tsiranana's close relatives became possessed by the spirit of the "Brother," while Tsiranana himself was widely rumored to be in the process of becoming possessed by the "Father" [Tondroko] himself.[126] General Ramanantsoa campaigned by urging the people not to listen to spirit-mediums. He won in that election, and responded to the support he had received around Analalava by granting the Southern Bemihisatra permission to rebuild the royal tomb.

PLURAL COMMUNITIES

French efforts to capture local labor failed in Madagascar as in other French colonies. Their legal, spatial, and ideological strategies led to the continued diversification of political power rather than to increased centralization at local, regional, and national levels. The preexisting polities, with and without ampanjaka, can be seen in terms of Horton's analysis of precolonial polities in West Africa—developing not in isolation, but as the common product of competing efforts at domination and decentralization.[127] From this systematic diversity, there emerged at least three different sources of political-economic power during the colonial period: the power of the gendarmerie, developed by the French in the course of the colonial period, and passed on to Philibert Tsiranana, the French choice as first President of the Independent Malagasy Republic; the power of the army later represented by the Merina General Gabriel Ramanantsoa; and the power of ancestors, especially royal ancestors, in different forms throughout the island.

Royal ancestors in the Analalava region also multiplied in the course of these events. From the time they first entered the Analalava region around 1848–1849, Southern Bemihisatra leaders seem to have tried to consolidate their hold on the people of the region by founding the first doany on the island of Nosy Lava where it was centrally located, but protected from Hova attacks. They tried to maintain this centrality in the next generation by establishing the new doany near Analalava, almost exactly opposite the southeast tip of Nosy Lava where they had just built the new mahabo. The prevailing southeast-northwest winds of the dry season, when the major royal services are held, still make the Analalava-Mahabo route one of the shortest ways to get back and forth from the island. By locating the doany near Analalava, they were able to keep the living ruler and the royal ancestors separate yet closely connected. In addition, because of the central location of Analalava and its already established role as the major port in the region, they would have been in a position to consolidate their support throughout the Ambolobozo Peninsula-Narinda Bay area, both north and south of the Loza River and inland. They would have had access to fertile rice fields, as well as maintaining the lucrative association with the Muslim traders on which the monarchy had long depended.

The Southern Bemihisatra strategy was confounded by the Hova army's continued harassment, then the French conquest and colonial rule. The colonial administration made every effort to suppress the

monarchy. They also reorganized the area after their own spatial design, making Analalava their own port and political center and Nosy
Lava their prison, in the process separating the Doany from the
Mahabo. In destroying the spatial relationship the Southern Bemihisatra had sought to establish in the area between the living ruler and
the royal ancestors, colonial rulers transformed the political-economic
and social relationships between them.

While the guardians of the royal ancestors were relocated north of
the Loza, the guardians of the living ruler—except for the small group
of followers permitted to surround Tondroko, then the infant Soazara,
under the eyes of colonial administrators—began to disperse throughout the south.[128] Customary services that would have brought the
doany and mahabo together were forbidden or severely restricted in
scale.

In the 1950s, not long after Soazara was appointed sous-gouverneur,
the Sakalava were granted permission to move the doany to a new
location about 20 kilometers south of Analalava, while Soazara continued to live in the royal compound at the post. Sakalava officials
now explain that the separation was necessary because French officials
were desecrating the ancestors' hallowed ground and preventing royal
followers from carrying out necessary services. Furthermore, the Vy
Lava, the source of the living ruler's power to rule alone, was preventing Soazara from having descendants. The doany had to be removed from the surveillance of French authorities in order for it to
continue to bear fruit for the next generation. The new doany was
overrun by wild pigs about fifteen years later in the 1960s, requiring
another move. At the time of the menaty service in the 1970s, Sakalava
followers were still debating the details of the move, probably involving a location about 20 kilometers further south along the bay.
The divisions that later emerged in the menaty service itself were one
expression of the complex tensions between the doany and the
mahabo. The doany had become associated primarily with the southern part of the region and the expression of support for the living
ruler, while the mahabo had become associated primarily with the

north and potential dissent—support of the royal ancestors, but not necessarily their currently living descendant.

These pluralities in national and regional relations were also reflected in the diversity of places in which royal followers in the Analalava region lived in the postcolonial period: the ancestral villages near their rice fields; the doany and the mahabo where they went to pay their respects to royal ancestors; and the "post" of Analalava, now the capital of the *fivondronam-pokontany,* where they still search for wage labor. To appreciate the work they put into rebuilding the royal ancestors' tomb in the mid-1970s, we need to see how the workers' own lives were divided among diverse communities still competing for their labor and loyalty.

Three Domesticities

C　H　A　P　T　E　R　　　4

Antsabo: At the Crops

*Samby mihina an-tanànany, samby an-tranony, samby
an-kibony.*
Each one eats in his own village, each in his own
house, each in his own stomach.

Soa at the Mahabo

SAMBY AM FIDINY: EACH TO HIS OWN CHOICE

Throughout the Analalava region, the people that we came to know
during the time of the menaty service strongly emphasized personal
choice in virtually every aspect of their lives. 'Each to his/her own
choice' *(samby am fidiny);* 'each to his/her own heart's pleasure' *(samby
am sitrapony);* 'each to his/her own winding way' *(samby an-kolakolatra)*
were the commonest explanations of behavior, whether people were
explaining why spirits possessed some humans, animals, or trees and
not others ('They are like people, they have different tastes') or why
they were doing one thing and not another.

This emphasis on choice derived in part from the belief that every
person has his or her own particular *anjara* or *vintana,* lot in life or
fate. Even descendants of the same ancestors might have divergent
fates *(tsy tokam-bintana).* Malaza from Andonaka explained anjara in
terms of food:

"People say *didy hena* [cuts of meat]. That means that all people have their
own lot, their own death. No one knows when another will die. You—
may what my mouth says be prevented from happening—you could die
before me."

Though a person's anjara derived from birth, he or she discovered it only in the course of living, in going outside the place where he or she was born, "searching [one's] lot in life"—*mitady anjara*—and 'seeing' *(mahita)* or 'getting' *(mangala)* it in the form of adventures, wealth, and especially 'friends' *(namana)*—paired relations in which one person might be fulfilled.

Thus, people identified themselves and others through places, ultimately the places where their ancestors were buried. Yet they were constantly moving about in trying to make a living, staying in one place no more than a couple of months at a time: out in their rice fields, in their natal villages, their spouses' villages, their children's villages, royal villages, in Analalava, or elsewhere in the northwest and beyond.

As people moved in the course of their changing relations with one another, so these collections of people moved and changed. As Raschid said, who showed us the way back to Analalava from Malaza's place in Andonaka, the maps are never accurate.

Walking from Andonaka back to Analalava, we stopped at the house of Bon Ali's son, who was living with his wife and child in a small cluster of houses outside Mahatsinjo. Raschid called his own place Mahatsinjo Vaovao, "New Mahatsinjo." Mahatsinjo has actually moved further east than it looks on the map. Raschid said that there were a lot of abandoned villages. "People around here move from place to place *[mifindra tany].* That is why the *carte* [he used the French word] is never accurate. It happens because a person dies. It doesn't matter if the person is really old, they still move. Just one death, and people say, 'This land is hot! This land is hot!' *(Mafana tany 'ty é! Mafana tany!).*"

Moving was often attributed to death. Raschid's own comments echoed the very words used in royal histories to explain the gradual northward migration of the Volamena dynasty, for example:

"So the government went north to Fiherena, because the ground was filthy with Andriandahifotsy, so his younger brother moved his dwelling place *(fonenana)* when the hot service [royal funeral] was completed."[1]

Yet deaths were seen to emerge from complex circumstances involving many shadowy lookalikes—hunger, sickness, anger, violence—such that dying was inseparable from the myriad ways that people tried to 'make themselves alive' *(mahavelon'tena)* or 'make their spouse alive' *(mamelom-bady)*, as they described their daily work. Like some 83 percent of Madagascar's population in the mid-seventies,[2] people in the Analalava region lived mainly by farming, but they could not live by farming alone. They moved around to trade and get wage labor. These movements among places of thriving and dying were inseparable from the creation of relationships in which people multiplied or became lost to their kin in leaving the places where their ancestors were buried in order to live 'at the cultivations' *(antsabo)* of others' ancestors, 'at the post' *(ampositra)*, or at the 'pens' *(vala)* surrounding living and ancestral royalty.

Local people identified these places with different kinds of work—'cultivation' *(mitsabo)*, 'working for people [for wages]' *(miasa amin' olo)*, and 'serving [royalty]' *(manompo)*—benefiting different 'masters' *(tompony)*. These masters included their own ancestors or those of their neighbors, merchants and government functionaries, and royalty. These separate places, oriented around different sources of power and prosperity, were linked by the competing efforts of masters to draw in and reorient local people to their own purposes. And they were linked by the locally migrant population who saw their competing efforts in contrastive terms. Ancestors and descendants, parents and children, siblings, spouses, masters, slaves, *patrons* and day laborers drew, in different ways, on broadly held views about the unique fates of individuals and the ways in which individuals find themselves completed or betrayed in paired companionship.

Farming is still the main way in which people 'make themselves living' *(mahavelon-tena)*. I will therefore begin this extended discussion of individuals and companions by examining working relations 'at the cultivations,' from which ancestors— people with ancestors and those without—emerge. After a few general remarks about farming settlements in the Analalava region, I will focus on what people in Andonaka in the south and Tsinjorano in the north have to say about working relations between 'ancestors' and 'generations,' 'masters of the land' and 'strangers.' In keeping with their own emphasis on individual choice, they see alternatives. These involve tensions between, for example, 'children of men' and 'children of women' born of brothers and sisters, or between siblings and spouses. Although these relations are commonly seen in contrastive terms, they are far from clearcut in practice. People recount their own 'histories' (tantara) of the choices involved in searching to decipher the significance of different acts of breaking and creating relations with others. These generational narratives take people beyond their cultivations to other places where they work. This chapter on Andonaka and Tsinjorano will suffice to lay out some of the alternatives, as people there see them, but we will need to move with them to appreciate how their efforts to cultivate ancestries relate to other, changing ways in which they 'make themselves living.'

TANINDRAZAÑA AND *ZANATANY:* ANCESTRAL LAND AND LAND'S CHILDREN

People born in the Analalava region—*zanatany*, 'land's children'—identified themselves and others through places where their ancestors were buried, their *tanindrazaña* or 'ancestral land.' As we shall see, this could be any number of places, depending on which of their grandparents or great-grandparents a person chooses to emphasize, though it was often a place associated with his or her father's ancestors. As kin multiplied and moved into adjacent regions, they carried these associations with them. Thus, generations *(taranaka)* spread out, forming 'networks' of people *(fehiny)*, tied to one another by what they had 'brought from the father' or 'brought from the mother' *(ndesigny am baba/mama).*[3] As zanatany described it, this growing and spreading was inseparable from dividing, as people connected by birth became separated into smaller 'groups' *(toko)*, when siblings split off to marry strangers and set up own hearths (*toko*, the three stones on which the pot is placed). Thus, when I asked AdanDezy's father whether the Ampanjaka Maroaomby were found only in Tsinjorano, he said:

"No, there are lots in A. [a village about a half-day's walk away]. They have many fehiny, having born many people." [Are they related?] "No, each to the land where he's settled *(samby am tany pitrahany)*."

"Each to the land where he's settled," but some people settle there before others. Descendants of the first ones to 'break open the land for planting' *(mamaky tany)* were recognized as *tompontany* or 'masters of the land,' in contrast to the *vahiny* or 'strangers' who followed after. The status of tompontany was marked by the presence of their ancestors' tombs. Tompontany held the best land, well-watered and close to the village, while strangers had to negotiate with them for what remained. But this changed over time, as land became divided among a couple's descendants, and they divided among themselves—retreating to their distant rice fields, moving to the villages of spouses or children, moving to the post, or out of the region.

Toko—households of tompontany and vahiny alike—marked their changing relations to one another by where they located their *tokotany*, 'portions of land' or house plots, identified ultimately with the toko or hearthstones. The ancestors' tombs were usually located just outside the village to the north. The descendants of the tompontany invariably lived in the northern half of the village itself. Sons usually settled south and southeast of their parents, while daughters were more likely to be living south and southwest, but this varied as we shall see. Later settlers, unless they married tompontany who had houses in the north, lived still further south.

In placing their houses in the cleared area—the *tanàna*, or village— settlers stated their priorities concerning ancestry, age, and gender. From these high, light, clearings, in which people cultivated their generations, they 'descended' *(nijotso)* to the surrounding area where the gardens and rice fields are located, which were described as being 'in the woods' *(anatiala)*, whether or not the surrounding area was actually lower or forested.[4] Similar assumptions about precedence were recalled in the structures of village houses and rice-field shelters and in everyday etiquette concerning where people could or could not sit, sleep, eat, and work.

In principle, these ideas about precedence gave priority to relations between generations traced from fathers to sons through 'children of men' *(zanakan' ny lahy)*, in which 'children of women' *(zanakan' ny vavy/mañangy)* occupied a subordinate place. In practice, sisters and their children retained life-long interests in their natal villages, where they often resettled between or after marriage, and remained to be buried. Thus, in practice, villages grew from ancestor-descendant ties identified with fathers and sons into larger clusters of masters of the land and strangers, organized around core groups of siblings, which eventually broke up again into smaller hamlets organized around married couples, brothers and their wives who were soon joined by brothers' sisters and sisters' husbands.

While villages grew by incorporating strangers through marriage and other ties, they also reincorporated the ancestors of the tompontany of the community as well as other spirits. The ancestors, whose dead bodies remained entombed 'in the forest' outside the settlements of living people and gradually rotted into the earth, were raised up from the ground in trees called 'quiet/peaceful' *(togny)*, interspersed among the houses of people who identified themselves thereby as their descendants. Majestic evergreen mangos *(manga)* and tamarinds *(madiro, kily)* were the commonest forms of togny, although other kinds of trees *(mandresy, aviavy, foraha, hasina)* also served as ancestors' places.[5] After the spirit had made its choice, a diviner would 'stand it up' *(mañangana azy)*, thus 'making it generative' *(mampamasina)* as the process was commonly described. The cool peace that grew from the togny kept the community healthy as well.[6] Persisting disputes or matters involving the community were usually settled at the togny by residents as a whole, guided by an older, usually male master of the land, who served as *sefo* or chef de village. The togny was also a 'means of pleading for goodness' *(fangatahaña tsara)*, where people could make vows to the ancestors in the land, petitioning them for rain, plentiful harvests, children, and good health.

Sometimes a royal ancestor or a forest spirit *(tsigny)* would possess a person and demand a place in his or her community. In contrast to the togny associated with the ancestors of the tompontany, these 'powerfully generative places' *(tany masina)*—the spirit's tree and the ground in which it was rooted—might be fenced to protect them from contact with dirt. Some places consecrated to royal spirits or other powerful historical figures had acquired regional fame. The togny for which Antognibe (At the Great Togny) was named—an enormous baobab located at the Grandfather's doany on the high ground over-looking the bay—served as a place for vows of all sorts. Another togny on the site of the Father's doany down below—an enormous mango inhabited by a python *(dô)*—was renowned as a 'means of pleading for rain' *(fangatahaña mahaleny)*. The 'generative iron' *(vy masina)* near Andronjona, the coastal village on the Ambolobozo Peninsula where the guardians of the Mahabo were relocated during the colonial period, was another well-known place of requests, though not a togny. Fiaroa, remembered as a Makoa, an African slave sold to people in Moromany (the Komajara Peninsula), became a famous diviner during the Grand-father's time. He dredged the vy masina from the bay and brought it to Andronjona. According to one man from the community:

"Fiaroa could walk on water. If he was out in an outrigger canoe with others, then wanted to get back to shore, he could walk back without drowning. He brought the vy masina to Andronjona out of the water. It used to stand upright, but gradually it has been leaning toward the ground. When it lies flat on the ground *(mandry)*, then the country will rest *(mandry)*. It will not be necessary to carry a knife anywhere in Madagascar. It was already close to the ground in 1959 when the French left."[7]

Each one of the rural communities in the Analalava region was known for special qualities associated with the people who lived and had lived there, its togny, the nature and availability of fields, water, animals, and plants, and the general atmosphere of the place, all grow-ing out of the ancestors in the land. I provide brief accounts of two communities, here called 'Tsinjorano' and 'Andonaka.'[8] Tsinjorano was like most of the communities in the area, ranging from 80 to 120 inhabitants, including several 'kinds' *(karazana)* of people. Andonaka was organized more around 'children of men,' an idea to which men especially aspired in going off on their own. Although neither community exemplified a regional norm, they shared some features. The particular experiences of people living in them also reflected more common concerns involved in searching and settling. The first point they emphasized was that even the smallest communities included both tompontany and vahiny, masters of the land akin to one another and strangers.

TOMPONTANY AND VAHINY: MASTERS OF THE LAND AND STRANGERS

Andonaka, an inland village south of the Loza River on the east side of the bay, was founded by a Sambarivo at Tondroko's doany in Antognibe, who purchased his own land early in the colonial period. The village was still occupied mainly by his descendants—his son and son's wife, Malaza and Rafotsy, a couple in their mid-seventies, and their children, of whom eight out of ten survived (Figs. 7 and 8).[9] Three grown sons and a daughter were living with their parents in the dry season of 1973, when we lived there, while the others con-

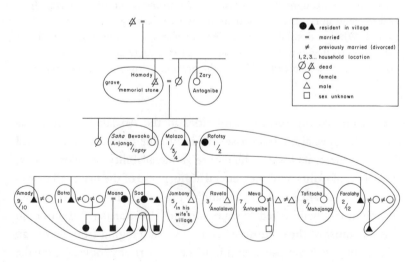

Figure 7. Partial genealogy of tompontany in Andonaka.

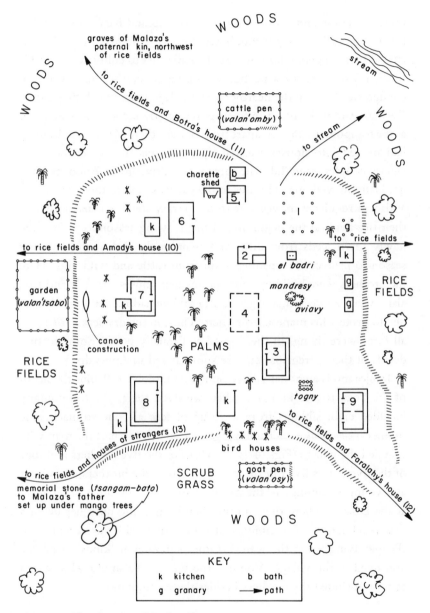

WOODS

graves of Malaza's
paternal kin, northwest
of rice fields

stream

WOODS

WOODS

to rice fields and Botra's house (11)

cattle pen
(*valan'omby*)

to stream

charette
shed

b

5

to rice fields and Amady's house (10)

k

6

l

g

to rice fields

garden
(*valan'tsabo*)

2

el badri

k

RICE
FIELDS

7

k

mandresy

aviavy

g

g

canoe
construction

PALMS

4

RICE
FIELDS

3

togny

8

k

9

to rice fields and houses of strangers (13)

k

bird houses

to rice fields and Faralahy's house (12)

to rice fields

memorial stone (*tsangam-bato*)
to Malaza's father
set up under mango trees

SCRUB
GRASS

goat pen
(*valan'osy*)

WOODS

KEY

k   kitchen   b bath
g   granary   ⟶ path

Figure 8. Sketch map of Andonaka.

tinued to come and go. During the growing and harvesting seasons (from around February through September), Andonaka was also occupied by strangers whom Malaza had allowed to cultivate one of his fields in exchange for a portion of the yield because there were not enough rice fields in the nearby coastal village from which they came. Even as Andonaka grew by incorporating strangers, it was dividing as the tompontany moved apart from one another. Malaza and Rafotsy had moved into houses vacated by their sons, living separately as elderly couples often did. The three sons cultivating in Andonaka had gradually moved out to houses in the gardens next to their rice fields. Villagers regularly moved out to temporary shelters *(banda)* next to their rice fields at the beginning of the growing season to protect the newly sown seeds from birds and again at the end of the growing season to protect the ripening grain from cattle and wild pigs. Here the brothers were building more permanent houses. Amady and Faralahy were between marriages. Botra said he had moved into his garden to protect his manioc from theft. Thus, in the dry season of 1973, all three were living 'in the forest,' as Faralahy put it. Some further details of their peregrinations are summarized in Appendix 1.

Tsinjorano is a coastal village on the Ambolobozo Peninsula, north of the Loza River. In 1973, when we lived there, the tompontany included eight siblings from a group of ten, all 'one stomach, one mother' *(kibo araiky, nini araiky)*, great-grandchildren of the man who founded the village (Figs. 9-12).[10] Three of the five brothers and four of the five sisters lived in the village. Two of the brothers, the oldest and youngest siblings in the group, had died. The other sister lived at the Doany, where their mother had been living until her death a few years earlier. The siblings identified themselves as Antandrano (People living along the water). Other karazana or 'kinds' of people also lived in the village. Vondro, the wife of Talañ'olo who served as sefo, included three others besides the Antandrano:

"Antandrano [first naming the tompontany, to whom her husband was related through his mother]. Sambarivo [her husband's kind, Sefo's mother having married a Sambarivo]. Antantety—Trefy, Vita's father, is that kind

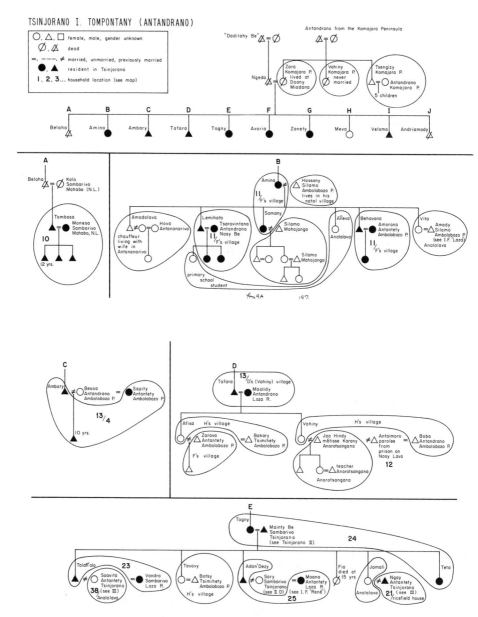

Figure 9. Partial genealogy of tompontany and vahiny in Tsinjorano.

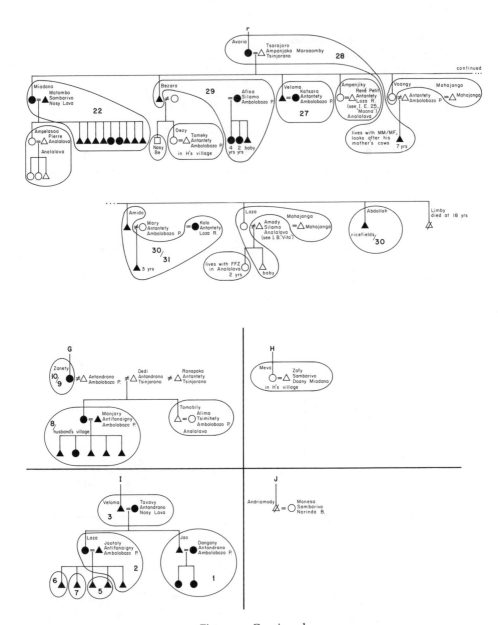

continued ...

Figure 9. Continued.

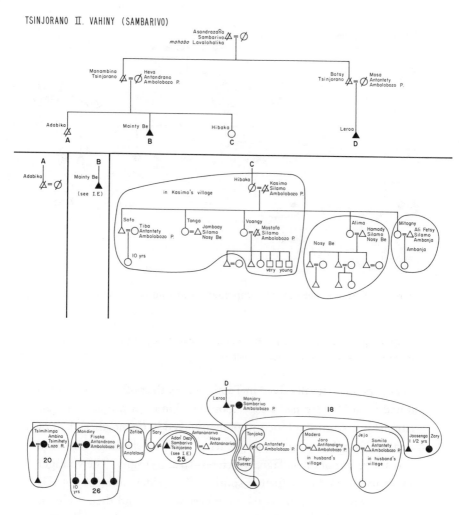

Figure 10. Partial genealogy of tompontany and vahiny in Tsinjorano.

[her husband's former wife was Trefy's sister]. They live in the southern
half of the village. And Ampanjaka Maroaomby [her husband's MZ
husband]. Tafara's grandfather [naming the eldest male sibling, not the
eldest living sibling who was female] was the first to settle here [and thus
tompontany], but he is not the head *(tale)* of the Antandrano. Making the
royal drums *(mañandria)* is his work. Ngoly [from another stranger group]
was made the big one among the Antandrano, stood up *(atsangana)*,

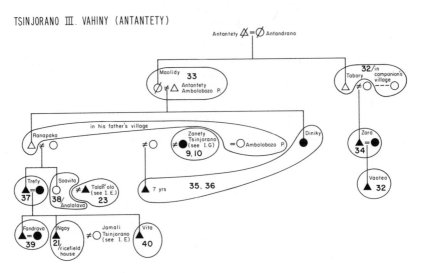

Figure 11. Partial genealogy of tompontany and vahiny in Tsinjorano.

because he gets Antandrano *(mahazo Antandrano)* from both parents, not just from his father's side *(ilan' ny baba)."*

Where people actually lived in Tsinjorano both confirmed and complicated what Vondro had to say about the 'kinds' of people and their relationships. Almost all the tompontany lived in the northern half of the village. Only one of the sisters lived south of the huge tamarind tree in the center of the village, which served as its togny. The younger siblings had settled ever further south of their elder siblings, but this trend was reversing itself as the youngest siblings and their children had begun to settle in northern places vacated by their deceased elders rather than among vahiny in the south to whom they were not related by ancestry. The southern half of the village was settled by Antantety, strangers descended from two siblings, a brother and a sister, whose father had married into the community (Fig. 11). They were thus 'children of women,' like the descendants of the sisters among the current generation of tompontany siblings—but two generations removed from them.

The other vahiny in Tsinjorano were clustered around the tom-

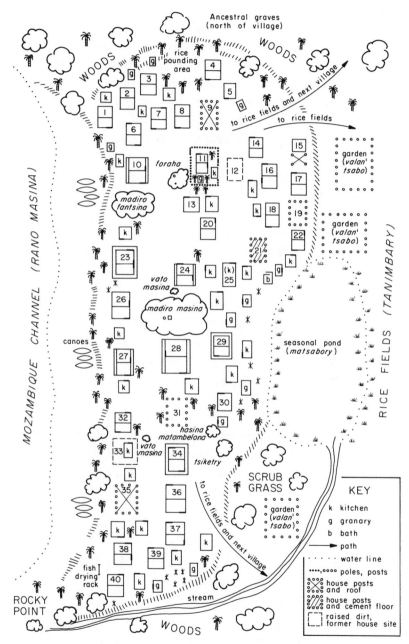

Figure 12. Sketch map of Tsinjorano.

pontany siblings to whom they were related by marriage. In other words, the north-south orientation of tompontany and vahiny, parents and children, elder siblings and younger siblings was offset by the tendency for siblings to form their own clusters of households organized around ties to their spouses, including spouses' kin as well as their own children. But finally, the youngest siblings had chosen to live with their ancestral kin rather than among vahiny connected mainly through earlier generations, the three current marriages among them having ended in divorce. Some of the particulars involved in these comings and goings are indicated in Appendix 2, focusing on the siblings, beginning with the oldest.

In Andonaka and Tsinjorano, as in other communities in the region, women were more likely to marry out than their brothers. But men also left to follow their wives, while their sisters returned home and often managed to stay there by marrying local strangers. People in the region often said that villages were organized around 'what people bring from their fathers' (fitondrasaña am baba) or what they 'get from their fathers' (mahazo am baba). Andonaka seemed to confirm that. Yet, as Vondro noted in discussing the kinds of people in Tsinjorano, Ngoly not Tafara was recognized as the local head of the Antandrano in the community because he got his Antandrano identity from both his parents, not just from his 'father's side.' So villages that were said to be organized around ties between fathers and sons came, in living, to be organized around brothers and sisters born of one mother, one father, more in keeping with another common assertion, that every person has valondrazaña—'eight ancestors'—which they got from both their parents, sometimes without being sure which came from whom.

VALONDRAZAÑA: EIGHT ANCESTORS

The eight ancestors represented by a person's great-grandparents mark the limits of cognatically related kin in many parts of the world. Matombo from Tsinjorano (Fig. 9, F22) explained the phrase:

"Eight ancestries—eight on a side, eight on a side. From my father eight ancestries, from my mother eight ancestries. Because the mother carries, the father carries from the grandfathers [grandparents]. They each bring everything." *(Valo firazanana—valo añila, valo añila. Am babako valo firazaña, am mamako valo firazaña. Satria manday mama, manday baba am dadilahiny. Ireo samby mitondra jiaby.)*

The generations of a person's eight ancestors on their mother's and father's sides were not seen as exclusive groups, because (as has often been observed of cognatically related people elsewhere), they overlapped. Furthermore, from the perspective of their descendants, people's eight ancestors could differ. Even siblings who were 'friends of one stomach or womb' *(namana kibo araiky)*, born of the same mother, could have different ancestries from different fathers. Characteristically, people in the Analalava region emphasized these unique differences, or, as MamanDjoma in Analalava put it: "Each to his own ancestors" *(Samby amin' ny razañan'any):*

I asked MamanDjoma and Tavavy, her daughter-in-law, "Who is the more powerful royal ancestor—Ndramisara [the founding ancestor of the Zafinimena dynasty enshrined at Mahajanga] or Ndramamahaña [the Father buried at the Mahabo]?" MamanDjoma answered: "[They are the] same. Each to his own ancestors" *(Miraña. Samby amin' ny razanan'azy).* I asked how, and she said, "Each person has different ancestors, whence the expression 'eight ancestors.' You have yourself, then you marry, you get the ancestors of your husband. You have children who marry, who have children who marry, and so on." She said she didn't know why people stop at eight. "You marry another person, your children marry other people, your grandchildren marry other people, the children of your grandchildren marry other people. It just goes on and on." *(Anao manambady am olo hafa, zanakanao manambady am olo hafa, zafinao manambady am olo hafa, zanaka ny zafinao manambady am olo hafa. Mahay rôso foño zigny).*

A person's eight ancestors were important in helping him or her to 'find kin' *(mangala havana)* in other places, especially at the post, as we shall see in Chapter 5. But the significance attributed to that term *havana*, the main way that 'kinship' was marked—by invoking the same ancestral names and prohibiting marriage among their descendants—derived from how people defined the relationship between the brothers and sisters, children of men and children of women, who came closest to being alike in sharing their eight ancestors. They could not marry, because sexual intercourse between them was incestuous. Furthermore, although everyone had eight ancestors and 'they each bring everything,' as Matombo put it, nevertheless, the children of men were considered superior to the children of women, in being closer to their common ancestors. The divisions between them were most evident in work, especially rice cultivation, where siblings depended on 'friends,' especially their spouses, for help. Yet tensions in relations with spouses brought siblings back to their kin. And because, as was commonly said, and almost invariably done, 'the father is master/owner of the children' *(baba tompon' ny zanaka),* sisters often ended up raising their brothers' children. Zanatany throughout the Analalava region—whether they identified themselves as Sakalava, Tsimihety, or Makoa—saw the prohibition of sexual intercourse between children of men and children of women as being the most distinctive feature of their relations with kin and strangers, so we will begin with that.

MANANTAMBO: CREATING CALAMITY

People in Tsinjorano and Andonaka—like zanatany throughout the Analalava region—defined their marriage practices by saying that people could marry whomever they liked, except kin. To marry kin would be 'to create great calamity' *(manantambo, mandoza).*[11] When I asked what *manantambo* or *mandoza* meant—it was not a common topic of discussion—people almost always responded first by interpreting it as "sleeping with" one's brother or sister, then going on to explain that it referred to "sleeping with" kin (havana) generally. Sexual intercourse between people related as *anadahy* and *anabavy* was considered to be the worst, so bad that people swore by it: *angosan-anadahy (-anabavy),* 'If what I say is not true, then I will sleep with my brother (sister),' referring especially to siblings of one stomach, but also children born of siblings. Sexual intercourse between people related as parents and children was also considered extremely dangerous. In describing these prohibited relationships, people almost always noted the contrast between 'Sakalava' practices and those of 'Silamo' and 'Hova' or 'Merina.' Speaking of a 'Silamo' family in Analalava, Tavavy said:

"According to Silamo custom, kin ought to marry each other, children of men should marry children of women, people related as brother and sister should marry one another (*Araka fomba Silamo, olo ampihavaña tokony mifanambady, zanakan'lahy tokony hanambady zanakan'vavy, olo mpianadahy mifanambady*)." I asked what 'Sakalava' did when they married 'Silamo,' since they considered such relationships incestuous, for example, MamanDjoma (her mother-in-law who had married a Comorian who had since returned to the Comores). "They don't like it, but, for example, her children in the Comores, things like that with the father there [are] things not seen, distant. But if they were here, she wouldn't agree to it."

MamanDjoma herself commented on another occasion that according to Silamo belief, the daughter of her oldest son could marry the son of her youngest son:

[Sakalava too?] "Oh, no. Nor the children of my brothers and sisters, or my mother's brother. All impossible. If they really wanted to marry, it would be necessary to invoke the ancestors to ask them not to make them sick. If close relatives like that married, they would have no children, or if they did, the children would come to nothing—one would come to nothing, the next would come to nothing . . ."

People invariably emphasized the horrendous consequences of incest. They differed only in whether there was any remedy for it. Having mentioned that people could go to royalty to be cleansed of wrongdoing, Sefo said, in response to my question, that for people who had committed incest, "there's no place they can go, nothing can take it away" [the dirt of wrong-doing] (*tsisy tany mboany, tsisy mahafaka azy*). Then he added:

"There is medicine, however, malagasy medicine. Committing incest creates festering sores called *drehy*. People have to ask for their food, fire, water, they can't walk. Other people have to bring them everything. They can only sit. Close kin may not [have sexual relations with each other]! Or [siblings] with the same father and different mother. But Silamo may— [siblings] of one father, one mother may sleep together." His younger brother and sister-in-law later echoed his words in saying, "There is no way of removing the prohibition *(fangalaña fady)* in incest. No way. Get drehy, covered with wounds, sit in the house, sick, all open sores *(boloñboloño),* eaten with wounds." *[Boloñboloño?]* "Toes and fingers as if they were cut off, like leprosy, but it's not leprosy. Sit inside the house until dead. Close relatives may not [sleep together]!" They both said that emphatically, while AdanDezy added: "Silamo may however." Then he said, "Distant relatives you don't know—then you invoke the ancestors, and tell them, 'These related children didn't know each other.' Only that is a little acceptable *(Zegny fo mety hely)."*

Others, perhaps responding to ourselves—the Vazaha—with views they associated with French colonists, also emphasized that the children born of such a union would be monsters *(sampona).*

One young man explained the bad consequences of marrying kin by citing a local proverb: *Lay olo hanelim-bato, tokanazy hañeny azy foño* (The person who would swallow stones, just one will suffice to fill him up), then drew a picture of a man about to swallow a big stone to illustrate its 'bad' meaning, saying: "It has to come out the other end. If you believe that something will have bad consequences, then don't do it. If you don't believe there will be bad consequences, then go ahead and swallow the stone."

MamanDjoma was more explicit about the motives of people who willfully committed incest, comparing them to sorcerers, because they knowingly did something that would kill others:

Alan mentioned that Tsimihety were said to have a medicine for incest. MamanDjoma responded, "You mean, a woman marrying her brother *(mañangy manambady anadahy)?* Everyone does—Tsimihety, Sakalava, Antaimoro—they all have. If anyone told you there wasn't one, they were lying, they just weren't saying." She said she didn't know exactly what it was, but she'd heard that you go to a person with special powers *(olo masina)*—it would have to be a great curer *(moasy be).* "He cooks up something in a pot, and while it's cooking, he pronounces words over it, and then he says to you, 'You swear!' *(Anao mamosà!),* meaning, 'Talk about what you did.' So the person says, 'It was my father who handled me, my father bedded me. I wasn't wanting this, but my father wanted this.' Then the *moasy* asks that nothing bad happen, that there will be no sickness, no infirmity *(kombo),* no drehy. If a person doesn't take away the wrong, then she or he will get drehy. Can't move around, just sit in a little house [she imitated a person all hunched over in a little house]. 'Give me fire!' Someone brings in fire, throws it down, and you cook your little bit of rice porridge. Or they might see some *kabaka* [or *rô,* meat or other accompaniment to starch] and throw it at you, 'Here's your kabaka! Here's your rô!' [in a cold voice]. Or they might just leave you to eat dry food. They might not bring you water when you wanted it. Because people don't like that. Because such people are like sorcerers *(ampamoriky),* doing things that are known to murder *(hamono).* Knowingly, knowing that they murder and yet doing."[12]

Perhaps because of the sharp contrasts in ethnic affiliation associated with different ideas and practices concerning incest, zanatany in the Analalava region were not openly divided about their commitment to their prohibitions against incest like people in highland or southern Madagascar.[13] I never heard of any publicly celebrated cases of incest during the almost two and a half years I was in the Analalava region in the 1970s, nor later in 1981 and 1989.[14] Perhaps because of the strong prohibitions against incest among local people with whom they had intermarried, even Arabo who argued that marrying kin was good, especially marriages between brothers' children, fulfilled this goal by defining 'kin' broadly as people from 'the same village' *(samby tanàna araiky).* Any ambivalence that siblings might have felt—ambivalence that might be inferred from the continued closeness of brothers and sisters especially in child-rearing—was expressed more in persistent structural parallels between siblings and spouses—for example, speaking of a royal spirit and its host as spouses if they differed in gender and as siblings if they were the same—than directly. Otherwise, brothers and sisters born of the same parents were taught as soon as they were old enough to 'know shame' *(mahay heñatra),* or 'know dirt' *(mahay loto),* as one man put it, to avoid using sexually suggestive words or actions with one another: not to sit on the same bed, not to be alone in the same room together, not to walk alone together, and so on. Even in joking *(samonga)* between children of men and children of women, participants avoided sexually suggestive remarks typical of other joking relationships (especially affinal relationships). They joked instead about who was the biggest nothing, hierarchy being the main feature of relations between children of men and children of women differentiated through prohibitions against sexual intercourse.

MAHAZAKA FOMBAN-DRAZAÑA: GOVERNING ANCESTRAL CUSTOM

As I have already indicated in Chapters 2 and 3, the tantara of the Southern Bemihisatra in the Analalava region, set down by guardians at the Mahabo and the Doany, portray the "ruin" of Sakalava monarchy as the disastrous outcome of an incestuous marriage between a brother and a sister. Yet the current division between the Northern Bemihisatra of Nosy Be and the Southern Bemihisatra of the Analalava region, seen as children of men and children of women respectively, is said to result from Andriantsoly's betrayal of his sister Oantity, and subsequent reversal of the hierarchy between them. Younger people, without the guardians' knowledge of royal history, explain the relationship between children of men and children of women in more contemporary imagery that illustrates their continued vitality in political life in the region and more broadly:

Mahasoa was living with his mother's brother (Mamoribe) in Analalava while he went to the high school [C.E.G.] there. (His mother was living in her husband's village south of Analalava near Andonaka.) He talked about children of men and children of women, using the language of Sakalava royalty interspersed with French political terms widely adopted during the colonial period: "Children of women do not govern ancestral custom *(tsy mahazaka fomban-drazaña).* For example, they can't invoke the ancestors *(mijoro)* in Andreba [his father's ancestral land in north-central Madagascar]. *Mahazaka* means *mitondra* [to bring, lead, rule over, the root of *fitondrasaña*]. Those children of men are the rulers (ampanjaka) there. They have honor. We [children of women] are not rulers. The children of men are independent, they are able to command *(mahavita mikommandy)*, they are completely free *(libre tsara be)*."

He continued with an example. "During the time of the troubles [May 1972, when then-President Tsiranana was thrown out of office], there was a big gathering in Majunga at which all the kinds (karazana) were represented. A Hova spoke, saying 'We are all Malagasy, all one ancestry *(firazaña),* we can all intermarry, we are all one,' and so on.[15] But later, a Muslim got up to speak, 'We [Muslims] are children of women.' They are still Malagasy, still masters of the land, born here, but lesser. For example, if a child of women builds a house in Andreba, cultivates, settles in there, and then for some reason, children of men want him to leave. They can say to him that they want him to leave, to return to his father. And if he refuses, answers back, doesn't agree, doesn't follow, then his mother's ancestors will be angry too."

Residents of Andonaka and Tsinjorano described these places as founded by men.[16] Malaza explained how his father founded Andonaka in these terms (Plate 7).

Malaza said his 'people'—referring to his father's forebears, himself, and his sons—were not 'people from here, but people from Menabe, Antaimoro who came north with Sakalava royalty.' His grandfather came to the Analalava region when the ampanjaka settled here. His father and himself were both born here. Both married 'Sakalava' women. He married Rafotsy, descended from a collateral royal line living in a neighboring village, fifty-six years ago [in 1917]. Malaza's father, Hamady, had served as fahatelo for Ndramahaña [Tondroko]. The French, seeing that he was trusted, made him sous-gouverneur [perhaps also because Tondroko himself was only about ten years old at the time]. Malaza showed us the certificate in which French authorities, after the fashion of the Merina before them, awarded 8 *Honneurs* to Hamady, Sous-Gouverneur Sakalava of Antognibe on 26 Janvier 1900. Hamady served as Sous-Gouverneur until Ndramamahaña replaced him [in 1905, his studies in the "section politique" of the École Normale d'Instituteurs Indigènes in Analalava having been completed]. His mother's younger sister, Zary, still living in Antognibe, had served as wet nurse for the current ampanjaka's oldest daughter [born in 1955]. Another kinsman was serving as the current living ruler's fahatelo. He said he no longer lived any length of time at ampanjaka's Doany because he disagreed with how they were doing things. But royal officials often wrote to request his presence there.

Plate 7. Malaza in front of his house (A. Harnik, 1973).

According to one man who served as the head of a neighboring royal district: 'His livelihood *(velon'teñan'azy)* lies in his rice fields, but his knowledge of royal custom is what makes him great *(mahabe azy)*.' Malaza said that Hamady had purchased the concession on which Andonaka was located. Hamady's house was located immediately east of the one Malaza then occupied. The house itself had long since been incorporated into more recent buildings.[17]

The historical priority of children of men as founders of new settlements was built into the structures of both villages where ancestors, masters of the land, parents, and brothers were usually north and east of living people, strangers, children, and sisters to the south and west.[18] Where unpredictable events may have led to dislocations of this overall pattern in the ongoing reconstruction of houses, gatherings to invoke ancestors *(mijoro)* consistently rectified them. Men in order of seniority always sat north of women in these gatherings, and men usually led them, although an older woman would take the lead if none of her brothers was present. "Men are the bigger ones" *(Lehilahy fa bebe)*, as one of the women in Tsinjorano explained. "The man is the strong one" *(Lahy mahery)*, as MamanDjoma put it, when she adopted Alan as her son and I became her daughter-in-law.[19] "Men command" *(Lehilahy mikommandy)*, said the ampanjaka's chief official, explaining why all the positions in the royal administration were occupied by men.[20]

Some of this emphasis on ties through men over ties through women clearly derives from the practices of government administrators. Asked about their 'kind,' most people in the Analalava region responded first with their father's ethnic affiliation. This was the expectation during the colonial period, in keeping with the conscription of men into labor brigades and into the army and the head tax on all men over twenty-one. Post-colonial census takers made the same assumption. As the mayor's assistant put it, "Men are the strong ones" *(Lehilahy mahery)*.

In rural villages like Andonaka and Tsinjorano, the preeminence of men as 'leaders of the masters of villages' *(mpitondra tompon-tanana)* in relations with the ancestors buried in the land they farmed, was also based on assumptions about the greater rootedness of men in the land as compared to women. Sons were said to 'stay on the piece of land [on which a house is built]' *(mipetraka am tokotany)*, while daughters moved, even though this was not born out in practice. AdanDezy expressed this idea in explaining the inheritance of work associated with specific ancestries from father to eldest son:

AdanDezy explained that all the children of the Ampanjaka Maroaomby belonged to that kind, everyone in the family [the children's children] except the mother [Avoria, one of the tompontany-siblings]. The Ampanjaka Maroaomby differed from other kinds in that they had the right to wrap the dish used to invoke ancestors in red cloth, and also the right to dispense *tany fotsy*, white clay with healing powers. They were also able to invoke the royal ancestors to plead with them to forgive people who had sworn false oaths in their name *(mipoko)*, and were therefore dying of their anger. Tsarajoro no longer did the work. He gave it to Bezara [his oldest son]. [Why Bezara and not Miadana, his oldest child?] "Because men stay on the piece of land [on which a house is built]; women go off to marry" *(Satria lehilahy mipetraka an-tokotany; mañangy mandeha manambady)*. He gave it to Bezara when Bezara cleared ground for his own rice field three years ago, thus settling in Tsinjorano.

Marriage negotiations indicate that a man tried to bring his 'friend' *(namana)*, that is, his spouse, to his own natal village rather than follow her to what was usually her 'father's village.' Successful men were those who could give the wealth in cattle and money necessary to 'divide [the] woman' *(manoko mañangy* from the root *toko)* or 'force oneself in/compel to agree' *(miletry)*, as the wealth was called.[21] Brides' parents, especially fathers, benefited from this.

Commenting that 'Getting a woman is expensive/difficult' *(Sarotro mangala mañangy)*, AdanDezy (Fig. 9, E25) said he was going to offer the father of Moana, his bride-to-be, already living in Tsinjorano, a *didinkarena* of four cattle and 15,000 FMG, with 1,000 FMG for the *joro* (Plate 8). Moana said later that she did receive wealth at marriage amounting to 12,500 FMG [about $50], but her father kept 10,000 FMG of it, and gave her only 2,500 FMG. They had a signed note, which said that 10,000 FMG was due to AdanDezy of Tsinjorano. They expected to get the rest of the money during the coming dry season. That was when they planned to build their own house with two rooms, a bed, and a table. AdanDezy's brother, Bezara, would make the furniture.

Although the marriage wealth was meant to go to the woman, fathers played a strong role in negotiations over first marriages of young women, which is perhaps why the women were more con-

Plate 8. AdanDezy in Analalava for marriage negotiations (A. Harnik, 1972).

strained than men to move from their natal villages, despite their own interests in 'searching,' to which we will return. Women marrying for the second or third time were better able to negotiate to their own advantage, independently of their kin. They were more likely to be able to keep the wealth—cattle, money, and other gifts—that they acquired through marriage. They could also reverse conventional practice by 'searching for a man with cattle' *(manjengy lehilahy amin' ny aomby)*. This way, as in *jôloka marriage,* a woman does not have to leave her household at her father's and gets to stay in her father's village *(tsy miala tokantrano am baba . . . makazo mipetraka am tanànan'ny babany),* as women put it. Women saw 'searching for a man with cattle' as the adoption of a man's strategy.[22] Faralahy, recently separated from his second wife, described women who negotiated their own marriages bitterly as 'whorish things' *(raha koetra)*. Older men, who had to pay more in bride wealth, also had trouble inducing wives to move to their villages, unless they had the support of their siblings or were independently wealthy.

Saha Ambary in Tsinjorano (Fig. 9, C13/4) was in the process of negotiating a new marriage, in which he was expected to give his bride, who had already been married once, a cow and calf and 6,500 FMG. When I commented to Sefo that it seemed to be a lot, he said, "Yes, costly! Because he's an old man. Hard to get a woman, have to pay more. 'Dividing [the] woman' *(manoko mañangy)* is what it's called—getting a woman by giving wealth, making an agreement about what a man will pay. The father asks one thing, a man may disagree and suggest another. Ambary is going to get her on Wednesday, return to Andronjona [where he lived with his first wife], after which he may come up here. He doesn't have a house here, he builds one east of [his yZ] Zanety's house when he comes."
[Why is Ambary living in Andronjona and not Tsinjorano?] "Ambary did *jôloka* in Andronjona.[23] He has his own manioc and corn fields there, but he had to borrow land for growing rice." [I thought she came from Port Bergé.] "Yes, they were living there for a while, then Andronjona for a while, then they came up here for a while. But she had a royal spirit [Ndramamahaña/Tondroko] who told her that she had to live in Andronjona, probably because it was close to the Mahabo on Nosy Lava, so she moved back there. He—compelled by love *(tery fitiavaña)*—he went

with her. Also, she didn't see eye-to-eye with Ambary's kin here in Tsinjorano. They all didn't get along."

Men followed women because they were compelled by love. Sometimes they followed women because of their friendship with their brothers-in-law. Nevertheless, it was mainly men with few alternatives who settled in their wives' villages for any length of time. And they went there, not at the behest of men who invited their brothers-in-law to live with them, but rather at the behest of women who chose to remain with their brothers and sisters.

Mainty Be (Fig. 9, E24), the husband of Togny, the fifth-born of the siblings in Tsinjorano, was descended from people who had been Sambarivo at the mahabo of Lavalohaliky, north of the Ambolobozo Peninsula. He said his father settled in Tsinjorano because he married a woman there. Sambarivo at the Mahabo suffered more severe restrictions than those at the Doany, like Malaza's father, especially restrictions on land.

Matombo (Fig. 9, F22), the husband of Avoria (the sixth-born eldest child), came from a village on Nosy Lava, where the penitentiary was located. When Miadana married him, she moved out to Nosy Lava, where they lived for at least a decade. They moved to Tsinjorano six years ago. According to Matombo, he moved to his in-laws' village because of the prisoners' roaming around. He was always worried about his children, that they would get killed by prisoners wandering in the woods. He got rice land from Tafara (Fig. 9, D). He does only *ketsa* (transplants rice), gets a yield of 50–100 *daba,* depending on the rains. He also has rice fields in his natal village [on Nosy Lava]. His older brother is able to take care of them for him, because there are no wild pigs on the island.

TOGNY: PEACEFUL TREES

Children of men—village founders, their sons, and their sons' children—were closer than children of women to togny, the 'peaceful' trees identified with the ancestral tompontany of the place. In Andonaka and Tsinjorano, as in most rural communities in the region, ancestral tombs were located north of the houses of the living. Malaza's kin were buried in graves at Andonaka; Rafotsy's kin were buried in graves near her father's village a half-hour's walk west of Andonaka. The ancestors buried at Tsinjorano included Sambarivo and Ampanjaka Maroaomby married into the village as well as the tompontany Antandrano, which their descendants had put "in whatever place they liked," as Bezara said. No one lingered around the 'dead' *(faty)* buried 'in the forest' *(anatiala)*, as their place was described. They saw their 'ancestors' in the trees and stones that they 'stood up' *(manangana)* among the houses of their living descendants. Being stood up, or standing up, put a person in a position of being *velono* (living) and being *masina,* full of growth or able to achieve growth. As we will see, living and growing were often spelled out by planting the shrubs called *matambelona* (dead-living) and *hasina* (generative) as a pair, together with a stone for offerings. These elements in different combinations, often set apart by a fence, established the 'remembering ground' *(tany fahatsiarovaña)* on which authority rested. The 'standing stone' *(tsangam-bato)* that Malaza put under a mango tree just outside the southern edge of Andonaka served to remember his father. The togny in both Andonaka and Tsinjorano were associated with the ancestral tompontany of each community as a whole.

Children of men stood up these trees, and they also led the services in which both 'masters of the land' and 'strangers' continued to pay their respects, that is, continued to recognize the differences between them, embodied in the togny itself.

When we first stayed in Andonaka, Malaza showed us three togny. Malaza did not 'shout commands in vazaha' *(mibeko vazaha),* the common expression for speaking French. Even so, like a Sakalava royal official speaking to Charles Poirier about the Vy Lava in 1926—he explained them to us as *églisenay,* 'our *églises'* (churches), using the French word (with a Malagasy ending) to make sure there was no confusion about their standing.[24] The oldest of the three, which he described as being 'in the middle of the village' [along its eastern side] consisted of a enormous *aviavy* [*Ficus* sp.] that had grown together with a *mandresy* tree [*Ficus* sp.]. Years ago, forest spirits *(tsigny)* had told him to plant the pair of trees, now entwined together, as an 'asking place' *(fangatahaña),* especially for people wanting children. The trees, which were unfenced, also served as a meeting place.[25]

More recently, Malaza had arranged for a powerful Muslim 'medicine' *(aody)* called *el badri* to be planted in the northeastern corner of the village, just east of his wife's house. The el badri consisted of a *mangarahara* tree and a pile of stones topped by an overturned iron cooking pot, to its west, surrounded by a low rectangular fence. A Muslim, a Comorian named Jamboay in Antognibe, had 'set it up,' had 'invoked el badri on the tree' *(nijoro el badri),* to protect the village from harm. Faralahy later explained that his father had gotten the Muslim to set up the el badri two years ago, after people from a nearby village, jealous of the large rice fields of Andonaka, had attempted 'to do evil things to him' *(nikafiry azy).*[26]

The most recent togny, at the southeast corner of Malaza's house, had been set up just a month earlier by a royal spirit possessing his sister who lived in a village in the Ambolobozo Peninsula. We will return to this later.

In Tsinjorano, the 'generative tamarind tree' *(madiro masina),* the main 'means/place of asking,' also marked the center of the community. It was an enormous old tree with huge roots above the ground.[27] As in Andonaka, the men among the tompontany had set it up, and they usually led the services honoring the tree, though here it was sisters who lived closest to it.

Togny and her sister Avoria, the tompontany-siblings who lived immediately north and south of the tamarind tree, pointed it out to us when we first came to Tsinjorano. They described it as a "generative tamarind for asking things" *(madiro masina fangatahaña).* "Elders in the past made it regenerative, the first people here to cultivate land. The tree is a place for asking good fortune." People could sit anywhere under the tree, except on the 'generative rock' *(vato masina)* on the west side, reserved for offerings. In fact, Togny, Avoria, and other women from their households often worked there during the daytime. But here, in contrast to Andonaka, the madiro masina was paired with a second tree north of Sefo's house, which served as the community's meeting place. This was called the *madiro fantsina* (tamarind calling place) in contrast with the madiro masina, even though it was actually a *foraha* tree.[28] Behind the rock, right against the trunk of the madiro masina, was a small wooden stand with two shelves, a 'table' *(latabatra)* on which people offered food to the ancestors when invoking them (Plates 9 and 10).

Togny's son Sefo said that the table was for cooked rice and for beef, if

Plate 9. The ancestral tree (togny) of the "masters of the land" in the center of Tsinjorano, looking south (G. Feeley-Harnik, 1973)

there was any. He explained that after the first rains fell, people in the community gathered around the tree to ask for more rain and no sickness. "Tafara (Fig. 9, D13) does it because his grandfather was the first to get a house here. Women on his side could also do it; all the children of that man are eligible. It's done in the morning. People gather around and sing—no special songs—anything they know. Money is also given. Actually only a couple of people really give money, but it stands for all. Men cook the rice south of the tree. No special men; we all did it last time." I asked, "Why men?" and his brother AdanDezy said impatiently, "[That's] its customs! Women may not!" *(Fombany! Tsy mety mañangy!)*[29]

VALY TARIMO: RESPONDING TO CARE

The close ties between siblings, especially as children of still-living parents, and the divisions among them as they sought to complete

Plate 10. The offering table in front of the togny at Tsinjorano, looking east (G. Feeley-Harnik, 1973).

themselves through strangers, were most evident in everyday reciprocity, especially in work. As ancestors, elders, and parents blessed and nurtured their descendants, so their children and grandchildren were expected to 'answer their care' *(mivaly tarimy)* by watching over them in turn: working for them, giving them gifts, and feeding them when they got too old to work for themselves. Marriage was a major turning point in these relations because once sons and daughters married and, together with their spouses, established houses, fields, and granaries of their own, they were increasingly able to support their fathers and mothers (parents and their siblings). The turning point was marked by gifts in which the bridegroom also responded to the care taken in raising the bride by giving money to invoke her fathers' and mothers' ancestors to inform them about the marriage, thank them, and ask for their continued blessing. Though both paternal and maternal ancestors were invoked on such occasions, maternal ancestors usually received half of what paternal ancestors received.

Parents, especially mothers, were often said to be closest to their youngest child, because the youngest child would care for them in old age. Nevertheless, in Andonaka, all the siblings living in the village supported Malaza and Rafotsy by giving them food, building materials, clothing, money, and by working for them. Malaza also got 10 *daba* of unhulled rice from everyone using his fields, including his children.[30] In Tsinjorano, Amina—the oldest sister—was the only one of the tompontany-siblings who did not work her own fields. She often noted with pride that she had six children living nearby, who gave her all her food, clothes, and whatever else she needed.

Marriage also marked a turning point in relations as siblings gradually replaced their parents as the persons to whom they turned for support in marriage exchanges and other major endeavors. The generalized reciprocity supposed to persist among siblings and their children was expressed in the notion that even if they lived with their spouses in separate houses, housedness being marriage, the house of one was the house of all.

A few days before we arrived in Tsinjorano, AdanDezy had quarreled with his FZ Zanety, so they were 'antagonists' *(ampirafy)*, as his wife put it. That was why Zanety refused to respond to their greetings. AdanDezy's wife explained that one evening he had been walking by the house [Zanety's BS's house] where Zanety was living (Fig. 12, house 10). He heard her talking about him, and went inside. People heard them quarreling and went to say 'Leave!' He left, but went back under the *madiro fantsina* (community meeting tree) south of the house, and continued to shout from there while Zanety answered from inside the house. He argued that he had every right to go into the house because it was the house of "the mother's brother of us all" *(zama atsika jiaby)*. Had it been the house of her daughter's father (Fig. 12, house 4), then he would never have entered. She answered, "You aren't my kin! *(Tsy havako anao!)* You have taken the name of my father in vain *(mañozoño ny babako),* and therefore owe me compensation." Sefo called the community together under the madiro fantsina the next day. They eventually decided that AdanDezy had not taken the name of Zanety's father in vain, so she was 'beaten in the dispute' *(resy)*. That was why she refused to respond to their greetings.

In fact, the community could have decided either way since houses were identified in different ways with both husband and wife. AdanDezy benefited by appealing to the ideal of reciprocity among siblings born of 'one stomach' where in practice there was considerable ambiguity and choice derived from the 'one house' each formed with his or her spouse.

This was evident in the case of Saha Ambary's new marriage, which took place after the parents of the tompontany-siblings in Tsinjorano had died. As indicated earlier (p. 182) and also in Appendix 2, Saha Ambary introduced the topic to his siblings in March by returning to Tsinjorano from Andronjona where he had been farming with his former wife. He reintroduced the subject the day after he arrived by arranging a gathering to announce the impending marriage to Ndramañavaka [Andriantsoly], the more powerful of the two royal spirits who possessed him. The spirit urged his kin to support him in this undertaking. Saha Ambary constantly reminded his kin and us in daily conversation that he needed money for his new bride. About two weeks later, after he had returned to his former wife's village, he sent a letter addressed to all of his six siblings and some of their children (Togny's two sons, Avoria's two eldest sons, Veloma's daughter and son, and Veloma's daughter's two eldest sons) explaining that his bride had arrived; the agreement was a cow and calf and 1,300 FMG (about $6.00); he needed 200 FMG "from you who are all my kin" *(aminareo jiaby havako)*; they should "send [it] quickly, Monday at the latest. We will be coming to visit you a week from Monday." They had not visited two weeks later, nor had Saha Ambary's kin given him any money. AdanDezy's father explained that since the rice was not yet ripe, there was no money to give him.

Profiting most clearly expressed the reorientations of new *toko,* households *(tokantrano)* grounded in their own houses *(trano)* and hearths *(toko),* among siblings born of 'one stomach, one mother.'

MANAO PROFITE: PROFITING

Although money was a valued, even required gift, especially in re-lations with ancestors, exchanging money for goods ran the risk of 'profiting' *(manao profite)* rather than reciprocating, or 'getting a benefit' *(mahazo benefice)* where none should be taken. People in Andonaka and Tsinjorano said in different contexts that buying and selling was inappropriate for relationships on ancestral land, and did not used to be practiced there. Yet, except for exchanges with fathers, mothers, and grandparents, relations between people outside households were often calculated in monetary terms.

The Malagasy wife of an elderly Chinese shopkeeper in Analalava said that during the colonial period, before they were married [in 1957], 'Patron' (her husband) used to have a shop in Tsinjorano—"a big house with a veranda and many rooms"—where he bought sea slugs and salted fish, which he sent in Analalava and Antananarivo, and sold goods like cloth, salt, kerosene, and matches.[31] The shop was long gone when we lived in Tsinjorano. Sefo had a memo from the administration in Analalava listing the percentages permitted to people who wanted to profit by wholesaling and retailing certain goods. When I commented that no one had started a shop here, he said, "Yes, people here are accustomed to each other *(fifankazatra);* they don't like to bring out prices *(miboaka vidiny)* of things. They are reluctant to profit from each other. There are people who do. It's seen, but nothing's said *(mañgina fôño)."*

Even though no one in Tsinjorano planned to open a shop, everyone was involved in monetary exchanges of goods with known values in shops that provided standards against which bartered exchanges were measured, because people could always sell goods there with impunity.

AdanDezy said that his parents had sold ten ducks to other people in Tsinjorano during their new year's celebration in January. Big live ones brought 150–200 FMG each. They had only two left and some babies. People also sold chickens at 100–200 FMG each, rice-breads at 5 FMG each, and home brews of various sorts. The price of these per liter varied depending on whether they were made from palm sap, mangos, or sugar cane. Highly alcoholic drinks were also more expensive because they required more equipment, especially large containers like oil drums. Many people in Tsinjorano sold chickens mainly to the police at the penitentiary on Nosy Lava, because they could get there and back in a day, rather than in Analalava where they would have to stay overnight. They also sold eggs, and therefore received money to compensate for their losses when someone's dog ate them.

These relationships could include siblings, siblings' spouses, and their children.

In Tsinjorano, when AdanDezy and Ngoly went out fishing together, AdanDezy gave fish to his parents, his younger sister who lived with them, his older sister who was visiting for the day from her husband's village, and to us, but not to his elder brother Sefo and his wife. Others did likewise, giving to some but not all close kin, and selling the remainder for 25–50 FMG a bunch, prompting Sefo to say that in the old days, before he was born, people who got fish used to give it to everyone for nothing. Now people "know money, love money."

In Andonaka, Botra was the only sibling to have made a *valakira* to catch fish.[32] Faralahy said that Botra was able to construct a valakira only because he had a wife; without a wife, it would have been impossible. The brothers were planning to construct a valakira for their father. They had already collected the poles, which would have cost Malaza 50 FMG/ bundle, or 1,000–1,500 FMG/fence, if he had been unable to collect them himself.

Botra and his family ate fish daily, and he also provided Malaza and Rafotsy with fish. He sold what remained to his brothers. The brothers' sister's husband got his own fish by line-fishing. Amady, the oldest brother, did his own cooking, but he had taken one of his sister's children to raise, so the boy could help him by finding *rô*—fish, meat, or vegetables to go with their rice—and by doing other work. Amady paid his sister-in-law, Botra's wife, to wash his laundry.

During the hunger months in March and April, before the earliest harvests, people also bought and sold paddy rice, the staple food, by the *daba,* a point to which we will return in the next chapter.

MITSABO: GROWING

Most kinds of work *(asa)*, though known to have monetary value, were not separated from personal relationships in the same way as the things sold in shops.

Sefo said he had been the sefo in Tsinjorano for fifteen years (one of three chefs de quartiers and twenty-one chefs de village, according to one of his official documents, but he said two were not on the list) in the canton of Ambolobozo. The sefo before him, not a local person, moved to Marovato. Back in 1962, the chef de canton and a gendarme had come to announce a new law; if people didn't like their sefo, they could chose a new one. Now a sefo with a bad disposition towards others *(ratsy fanahy)* wouldn't last a week. The sefo's work was to collect taxes, settle quarrels, take care of strangers like ourselves, and do jobs, like get the sacks of D.D.T. that the government left off in Ambolobozo to put on fields, though perhaps he would distribute some of it for killing the bed bugs. "There is no salary—it's work on ancestral land *(asa antanin-drazana).*" He had read in a newspaper that sefo were supposed to get salaries this year, but so far he hadn't seen one.

The people who tended cattle in both Tsinjorano and Andonaka were allowed their choice of one animal each year as a wage, but according to Faralahy in Andonaka, there was no 'wage' *(karama)* for cutting cattle. "You give a chicken; it's not allowed to give money; something just not done *(raha tsy fomba fona).*" Likewise, as AdanDezy once pointed out, the people who speak for the father during his son's circumcision (while the boy and his mother are still with the mother's brother), work "not for wages, but just for love *(tsisy karama—fitiavaña fo).*"

Asa included the work involved in growing crops and raising livestock. People in Tsinjorano and Andonaka made a clear distinction between 'growing/attending/nursing crops' *(mitsabo)* and 'working for people' *(miasa amin'olo),* which they identified mainly with working for wages (*mikarama, mangala karama,* from Swahili *gharama,* expense) by 'getting day labor' *(mangala journée)* at the post. These two involved different kinds of relations among people. Wage labor was associated with the work of purchased slaves. The work involved in growing crops was inseparable from the networks of exchanges among kin and affines through which people raised children and communities, by which they 'gave themselves/their spouses life' *(mamelontena mamelom-bady).*

People in Andonaka and Tsinjorano, as in other rural communities in the region, cultivated a wide range of plants and trees in their 'lands' *(tany)* and 'fenced cultivations' *(valan'tsabo,* or simply *vala),* including several kinds of rice, manioc, yams, maize, beans, greens, sugar cane, pineapples, coconut palms, bananas, mangos, orange trees, and breadfruit trees. They raised several kinds of animals—especially cattle, goats, and diverse birds. They hunted, fished, and gathered foods— especially fruits, nuts, and honey—as well as medicinal leaves and roots from the 'forest.' In Tsinjorano, where there were rocks along the shore, women also gathered shellfish.

Of all this work, rice growing was the most important. Rice, the basis of every meal, was considered the only substantial food—whence its common name 'filling' *(mahavoky)*. Growing rice also involved a wider range of social relations than other kinds of cultivation because trampling the ground for seeding, then harvesting, required more people than even the largest households could provide. People throughout the region solved this problem by organizing *fikambana* or unions. Yet, rice cultivation also required the most weeding and especially watching of any crop. Thus, where the need for unions might have encouraged people to value large collectivities,[33] in this area, it confirmed the value of the 'friendship' between spouses as the basis of rice growing and all other forms of cultivation as well.

Manioc and maize were usually planted with the first rains in November and harvested in January and February. Rice was planted in December, January, or even as late as February or March. Planting depended on when the rains came, the locations of fields in relation to water, the size and strength of their canals, the kinds of rice to be planted, the sequences of work parties, and the dispositions of planters. The most commonly planted kinds of rice matured in three months, but several other kinds of rice took four months to mature and a few took five months. People in Tsinjorano calculated that if rice has not 'birthed' *(teraka),* 'put out its flesh' *(miboaka nofony)* by late May, then it will die from lack of water. Most people had at least two parcels *(toko)* of rice land in different places, sometimes different villages, where they planted different kinds of rice, in order to avoid this.[34]

Although people were most heavily involved in rice cultivation during the rainy season and early dry season, the work as a whole was spread throughout the year, seen in the round. As people commonly responded when they had finished a particular piece of work, 'In the future too!' *(Amin' ny ho avy koa!).*

Saha Ambary went to his new wife's village in Andronjona to cultivate a second crop of rice during the dry season *(vary jeby* as opposed to *vary asara).*[35] Except for Ambarijeby (At the Jeby Rice), Antognibe, and a few other areas mainly south of Analalava, most of the Analalava region was not well enough watered to support dry season rice farming. People who did not grow vary jeby began to repair the canals *(kanaly)* in their fields after the harvest was done. Matombo (Fig. 9, F22) and Tabory (Fig. 11, 32) were among the few who started rice seedlings as the standing water *(matsabory)* east of the village (of which Tabory was tompony) began to fill during the first rains, and later transplanted them.

Once the rains were well established and there was running water in the canals *(rano velono,* living water), they prepared the ground for sowing *(mañosy, mandrevorevo).* Noël's description of how people in northwest Madagascar prepared ground for sowing rice still applied to the Analalava region in the 1970s. "To clear fields that they want to seed, the Sakalava simply put their cattle there for a while; the grasses trampled under the feet of these animals mix with their manure, forming with the earth a thick mud on which the rice is sown without any other preparation. . . . When the rice begins to grow, the Sakalava pull out the plants that are too close, build up the earth around those they leave, and pull out grasses that could be harmful to their development."[36]

In the 1970s, people still pastured their cattle in rice fields during the dry season so their manure would provide some fertilizer, but preparing the ground for seeding *(mandrevorevo)* required more intensive trampling. This was one reason why people relied on unions. Participants brought cattle as well as helped to drive them round and round counterclockwise, trampling the grass, manure, and earth into mud. Men broadcast the seed immediately afterwards. People in Andonaka and Tsinjorano used 10 to 20 *daba* (an oil tin holding about 7½ kilos of paddy rice) to reseed each of their fields.

Rice-watching *(miambigny vary)* began immediately after, first to make sure that birds—notably the *fody* *(Foudia madagascariensis)*, a species of weaver finch—did not eat the sown seed, then that cattle did not trample the young plants during the day. As the rice matured, people had to stay up all night watching for wild pigs, as well as birds during the day. Around Tsinjorano, where there were a lot of wild pigs, fires were lit every night to keep them away. While people had different concerns, depending on the area where they lived, they came to similar conclusions, as in these observations from Ndremahazo Jean-Pierre's wife Mariamo in Antognibe: "The problem with growing rice is *fody*, there are a lot of *fody* around Antognibe, because of the fody, one person can't do it!"

How soon householders moved out to their rice fields depended on the distance of their fields. Tompontany in Tsinjorano began by going out in the morning and returning in the evening, moving out only in the few weeks before the harvest. The Antantety in the south and the Antandrano related to Zanety's second husband moved out almost immediately because their fields were more distant. Malaza's sons lived in their fields, close by Andonaka, all year around. During March and April, most people weeded *(mikapa)* their fields at least twice, repaired water ditches, and worked in fenced gardens they had planted next to their fields. They also repaired or built the *bandra* or shelters, in which they finally lived as the rice got fully 'cooked' *(loky)* or 'grown' *(tombo)*.

Harvesting stretched over several months, beginning with the harvest of three-month rices in April and May and ending with four- and five-month rices in June, July, and early August. Men cut *(mandidy)*, while women tied bundles together *(mamehy)*. Together, they collected *(mamory)* the tied bundles and stacked them at right angles to one another in heaps *(tomy)* on top of mats in the fenced gardens.

People in Andonaka and Tsinjorano used different methods of harvesting. In Andonaka, they beat the grains off. Botra and his wife—threshing the last of their rice in early October—stood facing each other, knocking the heads of the bundles upwards and downwards with sticks, while the grains fell on the mat between them. Botra explained that the government had made it illegal to thresh grain by walking cattle over it, thus mixing in rocks, which made people sick. This was the common method of threshing for residents in Tsinjorano. After cutting the stalks, they put them down on a mat and walked cattle over them. Some put the stalks directly on the ground, explaining that it was the quickest way. Even so, people often complained about stones in the rice. Women throughout the region routinely sorted through *(mitsingôra)* paddy rice to pick out straw, stones, and dirt before pounding *(mandisa)* it, then separating *(mañôfa)* the seeds from the chaff *(mongo)* used to feed birds. Sefo's wife used a stone-remover *(fangalaña vato),* a rectangular piece of metal with the sides turned up and holes punched in the bottom with a nail, in which she sieved paddy rice for stones before pounding off the husks.

Once the rice was threshed, householders put it in their granaries or bagged it for sale in gunny sacks, which people in Andonaka purchased from a store-keeper in a neighboring village and people in Tsinjorano purchased in Analalava. The straw *(mololo)* was saved to stuff mattresses and chair cushions.

Like trampling and harvesting, cooking rice provided opportunities to turn communal "work" into playful performances of virtuosity. Thus, when women worked in community groups, pounding the husks off rice for meals at weddings, funerals, and the like, they made games of their strength, dexterity, and coordination, turning their work into kinds of dancing, which they described as *soma.* In *fanôpy* (throwing), four to six women would pound with three pestles, throwing them across the circle to every second person; in *tangariary* (silliness), four women would pound with two pestles, handing on the pestle from one to the next; in *kokofo* (joint work) or *telo telo* (three three), three women passed three pestles around the circle (Plate 11).

FIKAMBANA: UNIONS

The unions that people in Andonaka and Tsinjorano had formed to help in preparing rice fields for sowing and harvesting averaged twelve to fifteen people. The core of such unions consisted of parents, children, and children's spouses, not kin broadly conceived. People in Andonaka (including the tompontany and the two related toko of

Plate 11. Young women pounding rice and older women winnowing it for a funeral in a village north of Tsinjorano (A. Harnik, 1973).

strangers) were joined in a fikambana with people in Rafotsy's natal village. AdanDezy said that Tsinjorano used to have only one union, but the number had gradually increased to three as the amount of work had grown. His group had twelve people in it, including himself, his brother Sefo, his father and his father's kin (Leroa, Tsimihimpa, and Mandiny); friends, including Ngoly and Adapiso (the two younger brothers related through marriage to his mother's sister Zanety), and some in-laws from a neighboring village. His mother Togny's younger sister Avoria, her husband the Ampanjaka Maromaomby, their children and spouses formed the core of the second union. The Antantety at the southern end of the village formed the third. People living temporarily in a place could form unions on a one-time basis simply by calling together whoever they could find and providing them with food for the day. According to Faralahy in Andonaka, many men 'get a living' *(mangala viloma)* in that way, but the day's work did not entail any further obligations on either side.

Trampling rice fields and harvesting were meant to be *maresaka*, festive occasions full of talk, in contrast to the intervening rainy season when people became increasingly isolated from one another. At both times, the *tompon' ny asa* or masters of the work—the man, woman, or husband-wife pair whose field it was—contributed rice, fish or meat, and sometimes home brews. People came from as far away as Analalava to attend the trampling of the ampanjaka's rice field in a village near Tsinjorano. Young men drove cattle round and round to trample the field into mud, wrestling with them *(toloñaomby)* to show their boldness and strength, while young women followed in groups, singing. As one man commented, rice work *(asa vary)* was a rare occasion to eat meat and play *(misoma)*. Women also saw rice work as an opportunity to make money from liaisons (Plate 12).

Even so, participation in unions was notably irregular. Both men and women in Tsinjorano and Andonaka attributed this to the fact that everyone had different prohibitions concerning when they could and could not work.

According to the sisters, Togny and Avoria, "the real work in Tsinjorano is done on Friday, Saturday, and Monday. Sunday and Tuesday are

Plate 12. Field-trampling for a royal rice field *(mandrevorevo tsimirango)* east of Tsinjorano (A. Harnik, 1973).

prohibited for everyone [they are the days on which the Father and Grandfather died]. Some people are also prohibited from working on Wednesday and Thursday." People may be prohibited from working on the other days because they are possessed by a royal spirit for whom that is a prohibited day, the day the spirit died, or because it is a prohibited day for them personally.

Togny and AdanDezy's wife Moana identified the following days as prohibited for spirits that possessed people in Tsinjorano: Wednesday is prohibited for Zafinimena spirits Ndramaro and Ambilahikely; Thursday for all the Zafinifotsy spirits who drowned in the Loza River; Tuesday for the Zafinimena brothers Razamany and Raleva; and Saturday is prohibited for Ndramañavaka [Andriantsoly]. No one possessed by a spirit could work on its death day, although washing clothing was alright.

Tuesday and Sunday were prohibited days throughout the Analalava region. People in other rural communities confirmed what people in Tsinjorano and Andonaka had said about the role of prohibited days in the organization of labor. One of the Sambarivo at the Mahabo began by explaining that when a person gets their field trampled depends partly on the sizes of fields and thus the number of people working, and then went on to say:

"If it is an area that requires little work, four or five men can finish it quickly, then go on to the next, then the next. But if it requires a lot of men, then you end up doing one man's field one day, then another man will have to wait until the next good day, sometimes the next week, and so on and so on. It gets late. Because people at the Mahabo don't work every day, they only work Thursday, Friday, Saturday, and Monday. They can't work the other days." [What makes Wednesday prohibited?] "Day medicine" *(Aody andro)*. [Royal spirits' days?] "No, there aren't so many of those compared to these. These are days that become prohibited for a person because they have seen that everything they do on that day comes to nothing, ruin, they don't get even the smallest thing from their work. They go to a diviner. He does a divination. He says, 'Thus and such a day is plaguing you' *(andro karaha zegny migôdaña anao)*."[37]

Participation was hard to enforce even with close kin and affines. This may be why unions tended to multiply so that even small villages of 150 or so people like Tsinjorano, had as many as two or three of them.

Unions were not important in maintaining relations among households during the late rainy season when people lived out on their fields, watching first for birds and cattle during the day and later for wild pigs that could ruin a whole field in a single night. Nor did unions serve as networks for sharing rice, mitigating shortages at the end of the growing season.

VADY: SPOUSES

Cooperative work groups have long been seen as fundamental to the organization of agriculture in Madagascar.[38] Yet fikambana in the Analalava region may be a relatively recent form of labor organization that arose as people adapted to changes brought about by colonial administration—the gradual reduction of herd sizes that resulted from taxation, the emigration of young men and women to towns, and the loss of children to schools. For people in Andonaka and Tsinjorano, the most important relationship in rice cultivation was not the fikambana, which workers did not always take as seriously as their hosts. The heart of rice cultivation—begun at marriage, when a couple established their own fields, house, and granary—was 'living in the woods' day in and day out. Anyone in a union might be described as a *namana*—companion, supporter, friend—even, in the case of siblings, a *namana kibo araiky* (friend of one stomach). But of all the namana with whom people in Andonaka and Tsinjorano worked, the closest personal friend was said to be the *vady* or spouse.

Şaul's recent study of the coexistence of work-party labor, wage labor, and household labor documents similar preferences in Upper Volta and some other parts of Africa. Although work parties were widely used, they were considered to be the most costly of the three, in contrast to household labor, which was considered to be the least costly.[39] Even wage labor cost less than work parties "largely due to the inefficiency of party labor, where volunteers are careless, cannot be pushed, and try to combine work with diversion."[40] The main factor preventing all but the largest farmers from employing more wage laborers was that the poorest farmers had access to land, and therefore did not depend exclusively on wages to live. Wage laborers were and are scarce in the Analalava region for the same reason, so it is difficult to evaluate whether farmers there would be more willing to pay workers than participate in fikambana. Still, Şaul's general observation is relevant here too: "the existence of important flows of labor between households in Upper Volta does not contradict the existence of those households as independent production units in terms of farming decisions, allocation of resources, disposition of the produce, and accumulation. The full effect of these flows can be evaluated only when this fundamental independence is recognized."[41]

Şaul notes that he has deliberately focused on short-term, voluntary relationships with nonkin in work parties rather than long-term relationships involving a "morality of kinship."[42] Nevertheless, he concludes: "The relative equality with respect to the distribution of wealth in rural West Africa . . . stems not from some diffuse ideological principle or mysterious quality in the nature of the traditional community but rather from a structural principle in the organization of the economy: the lack of full private property in land."[43]

This separation between ideology and practice is not so easily made in the Analalava region. This is not simply because, as Bloch argues about the organization of work in Imerina, kinship relations (including affinal relationships, since marriage in Imerina is ideally endogamous) cannot be reduced to economic interest.[44] In the Analalava region, where people marry strangers, there is also a morality involved in relations between spouses *(vady)*, which contrasts with relations among siblings.

Spouses epitomized ideals about inseparability expressed not only in vady as commonly used to refer to the mates of all kinds of pairs, but also in explicit statements about the necessity for even numbers *(raha mahampy isaka)*—as opposed to 'insufficient' odd things *(raha tsy ampy isaka)*—to guarantee harmony and authenticity in a wide range of social contexts. The counterpoint between single and paired persons and things, which together compose whole bodies, is the most salient feature of royal service, as we shall see.

Faralahy explained the essential partnership of spouses in Andonaka in terms of work:

After explaining that his brother Botra had been able to make a *valakira* only because he had a wife—"it's not possible without a wife"—Faralahy went on to say that Botra's wife was his third. He had given no cattle for the first and three cattle for the second. He gave his current wife three cattle when they married, and he had just given her a fourth. Then Faralahy said, "You really suffer *(mijaly)* if you have no wife; it's really unthinkable *(tena tsisy hevitra)*. Tying rice is where it's most difficult. Men don't know how to do that. They don't know how to do some things. That's why Tsihy [an unmarried kinsman from a neighboring village] came over to find women in Andonaka to help with separating the grains from the chaff."[45]

The closeness of spouses in growing crops had to do with how they fulfilled each other in ways that kin did not. To begin with, spouses were not kin, except to subsequent generations born from their union.

AdanDezy kept referring to Tsimihimpa's wife Ambina (Fig. 10, D20) as his 'sister' *(anabavy)*, but when I asked him how she was related, he said, "I call her anabavy, but in fact she's not an anabavy even in the smallest way" *(tsy anabavy ata hely)*. [She was the wife of his FFyBSS, whom he called his 'brother-in-law' ever since he had been married, since divorced from Tsimihimpa's sister Sary, his FFyBSD.] AdanDezy said that sibling-in-law's spouses were called by the same terms as siblings, but the term was a way of honoring them *(fañajañ'azy); they were not 'real kin' *(tena havana)*.

Mahasoa, about AdanDezy's age, whose mother came from a village near Andonaka used the same words in emphasizing that the common joking phrase—*Vadiny zama vadin'tsika jiaby,* 'The mother's brother's spouse is the spouse of all of us'—was simply a way of 'talking not doing' *(fomba tsy fanao),* 'spouse only in talk' *(vady amin' ny koraña fona)*. "You can marry your *zena* (mother's brother's wife) only if your *zama,* who is dead or divorced, had no children. If he had children, then marrying your *zena* is prohibited, because her children are your brothers and sisters. Until they have children, the *zena* is not kin. Using kin terms with people who aren't kin is simply a 'way of showing respect' *(fañajan'azy)* or 'love for a friend' *(fitiava-namana)*."

Talk about friends was invariably associated with talk about the treachery of kin. Quarrels among kin, especially siblings, were as much a reason why people moved to other places as marriages among spouses.

Ambary had first moved out of Tsinjorano, because he quarreled with his kin over his first wife, with whom they did not get along. The next oldest brother among the tompontany-siblings in Tsinjorano, Tafara, had quarreled with Amina, the oldest of the siblings, which was why he had gone to cultivate with his married daughter and her husband in the husband's village down the coast.

Spouses represented equity that kin, even siblings born of the same stomach, same mother, did not share. But they were also the image and means of *not* sharing equitably with kin, *not* responding to care. When Tafara explained why most people in Tsinjorano planted rice by broadcasting seed rather than transplanting *(mañetsa),* even though transplanting resulted in a much higher yield, he mentioned problems getting workers first, then problems of sharing with kin. It was the end of July, and he had just gotten the last of his rice into his granary.

"It's all in the granary. Didn't get much, the weather was too dry, so trampling got later and later. Seventy baskets. They will last until the next harvest if I don't sell any, but I need twenty of them to reseed the field. People here don't transplant. They are afraid." [Why?] At first he said he couldn't explain why, then went on, "Work! Work!" He went through all the work involved. "Yes it's true that transplanting takes much less seeds, four baskets [not twenty]. It's not a question of not having enough water. If the trampling is done in January, then there is plenty of water for transplanted rice *(ketsa)*. But kin come and ask for food. Ashamed *(meñatra)*, you give them a *daba*. Another sees it—'Where did you get that?' 'There.' They come and ask too. Ashamed, you give to them too. Pretty soon, everyone has nothing together *(jiaby miaro-tsisy)*."

Throughout the Analalava region, people condemned fences as inappropriate to the reciprocity that should exist among kin and affines. In fact, fenced yards were rare in rural villages, except where Silamo traders had settled or people had adopted Silamo customs, like Amina in Tsinjorano. The palm-stalk walls for which houses were named *(trano ketikety)* stood as a contradiction to reciprocity and harmony, containing that which should ideally be shared.[46] Yet even more than these palm-stalk walls, the walls of the granaries represented the separateness that came between siblings as they married and established hearths of their own. People in both Andonaka and Tsinjorano said they had begun to lock their houses. In Andonaka, Malaza and Faralahy, who had no locks, moved their things to Rafotsy's house only when they planned to be away overnight. In Tsinjorano, people locked their houses even in the evening when they went out to walk around, sing under the trees, or visit in other people's houses. AdanDezy's wife said that otherwise adolescent boys would break in and steal their things.

Though people saw themselves as only beginning to lock their houses, they had long since kept their granaries locked day and night. Perhaps in keeping with this central image of keeping rather than giving, talk about conflict was most often phrased in terms of food and people who ate rather than fed others. As Malaza's son Amady commented about a long-standing enmity, "Ambantrofiky [a kind of manioc]—its bitterness never fades *(Ambantrofiky tsy lany faiky);* even the children and grandchildren continue to hate each other."[47]

Nurturing was the most important expression of kinship, but people also said, 'Each one eats in his own village, each in his own house, each in his own stomach' *(Samby mihina antanànany, samby an-tranony, samby an-kibony).* This was expressed most succinctly by a woman who was one of the royal guardians at the Mahabo.

We were at the Mahabo in early September for the second of the pair of services that inaugurate the new year in the royal calendar. Zarakono said that "it is only in *fanjava mitsaka* [the first month of the royal new year] that the Sambarivo wait until the moon is really full to start the services honoring the royal ancestors. In *asara be* [the third month, when the second of the pair of services was held] and in all the other months, they start right away as soon as the moon reappears and the first good day comes along. They had killed a cow last Monday, they will kill another tomorrow. They won't kill a cow at the Mahabo Avaratra [the second of the pair of royal cemeteries on Nosy Lava], only here because the work is here. Because they aren't working there, they won't be feeding people there either." She said, "Each one eats in his own village, each in his own house, each in his own belly," and laughed.

Each to his or her own village, where ancestors are buried and crops are cultivated; each to his or her own house, where children are conceived and food is cooked and eaten; each to his or her own belly where food is put and babies are grown. Since people used *kibo* to refer to inward dispositions as well as to stomachs and wombs, what she also implied was: each to his or her own preference.

Searching for companionship, an inseparable part of searching out one's own unique fate in life *(anjara)* began when 'children' *(tsaiky)* started 'growing' *(mitovo)*—being 'ardent,' 'daring,' or 'wanting to be ardent/daring' about men *(mazoto lehilahy, mahasaky lehilahy, mahasaky mazoto lehilahy, te-hazoto lehilahy),* as it was expressed more often about women than men. It was marked by girls and boys moving out of their parents' houses when they were ten to fourteen years old. A girl usually lived with a grandmother (FM or MM), in a separate room of her own, or sometimes her own house when she got older. A boy built a small house of his own or moved into a house with other boys his own age, like Veloma's daughter's boys (Tsinjorano, Fig. 9, I5).[48] Being a 'growing boy/girl' *(tovolahy/vavy)* was associated with increasing personal autonomy, including the freedom to give gifts without involving others and to keep gifts without redistributing them, which was especially important for women, as we will see in the next chapter. Growing men and women were eventually expected to settle down among their kin when they married, becoming *trano araiky* or 'one house' with a spouse. Nevertheless, some walls remained—houses of spouses that were not 'the house of all of us' *(trano atsika jiaby)*, as AdanDezy put it when he quarreled with his mother's sister.

"Are you still one house?" I was asked when I returned without my husband in 1981 and 1989. Marriage was, above all, a housed union between strangers, focusing on their mutual relationship as spouses *(mpivady)*, 'alone in the house' *(tokana antrano)*, whence *tokantrano*—household-living, housework, spouse—they made together, exclusive of the living that either achieved through their parents or their other kin. The closeness between spouses was articulated in their common dwelling, and its shifting relationship to outsiders, and embodied in their creation of children in the 'one bed' for which the 'one house' was a common circumlocution. Yet here were their deepest differences expressed. If a couple did not have children within the first year of marriage, they were brought back to the wife's ancestral village, where her kin could beg their ancestors for their blessings in the form of children.

During the time we lived in Tsinjorano, Bezara's oldest daughter Dezy and her husband returned to Tsinjorano to invoke the ancestors to bless their union with children. Bezara officiated. His father, older brother, and blood-friend Leroa, also attended the ceremony. Bezara's sister Ampenjiky, who was visiting, and Dezy herself were the only women there. Bezara's mother did not attend. She was at the rice trampling of one of the two fields she worked with her husband, the Ampanjaka Maroaomby. Besides, as Sefo's wife observed, she was not a descendant of the Ampanjaka's ancestors upon whom Bezara called first, followed by his father who made a second invocation, using his own dish.

Spouses were expected to follow each other's familial and personal prohibitions, especially during pregnancy.

Faralahy in Andonaka commented that his brother-in-law, married to Soa, was doing *joloka,* living in his wife's village, "because he loves the ocean. Every day he's down there. Not a day passes when he's not. When they lived in his [inland] village, he ate fresh-water shrimp and wild pig, but they are prohibited for Soa, for people in this village. So he was told that he would have to follow her prohibitions, because otherwise their children would be sick. So he came here to be able to get fish for *rô.*"

According to Noël, the French consular agent in the Nosy Be area during the 1840s, "The art of birthing babies *(faha-melou),* although usually practiced by women, is familiar to a great number of men; the most distinguished among them do not consider they have lowered themselves in gathering from the breast of its mother the infant to whom they have given the light of day. Andrian-Souli, ex-king of Bombetoka, acquired a kind of celebrity by the skill he often deployed in delivering his numerous wives."[49]

People in the Analalava region confirmed Noël's observations. Saha Barimaso, for example, 'made-living' both of his children, born during the growing season, when he and his wife were living alone near their fields. It was common practice to speak of men 'giving birth' *(miteraka)* to all the children of whom they were 'master,' a point to which we will return. Husbands also served as kinds of midwives for their wives' spirits, spirits to whom the medium was said to be married because their relationship was so close. Even if they had since separated, they continued to cooperate in important events in their children's lives, like circumcisions, holding them together as if they were still married.

Conversely, the most intensely antagonistic relationship *(ampirafy)* was not a pair of disputing kin, like Zanety and AdanDezy mentioned earlier, but a pair of co-wives. As MamanDjoma in Analalava put it, a co-wife *(rafy)* is "a person who is inherently bad" *(olo ratsy an-tena)*. The badness of co-wives and other women who came between husband-wife pairs was the topic of popular country songs like this one:

> *Tsakalabanga Zaina, fandroba-tany Zaina.*
> *Jibona ny tianao Zaina.*
> *Anao tsy mitovo, tsy manambady Zaina.*
> *Manana amato sary ny vadiaña.*
>
> Saw grass, Zaina, ruiner of land, Zaina.
> Jibona [Food-snatched-from-a-plate] is the name of who you love,
> Zaina.
> You are not growing, you are not married, Zaina.
> [Your] having a lover just looks like marriage.[50]

Some women also sang songs expressing Zaina's point of view, lamenting, for example, that they did not "call on the ocean, which knew how to murmur" to reveal their secrets rather than calling on "people's fathers who knew only how to tell." These songs, created and sung by women, also blamed women for their circumstances. While married women were supposed to be faithful, married men were expected to keep sleeping with many women, just as they had always done. MamanDjoma echoed widespread sentiment when she said:

"Men are the only ones who create rivals (*mampirafy*, have more than one spouse or lover). Women are prohibited from doing it. Rather they aren't prohibited, they don't like it. I'm angry [if that would happen to me] because my spouse is giving money to the other woman that would otherwise come to me, giving money, buying cloth, giving other things."

Another day, when I asked whether women's affairs were not just the same, she answered:

"Oh, no, that's really bad. If a woman goes with another man when she is married, she will have trouble finding another husband. People won't marry her. That is the way of men *(fomba lehilahy)*. But women are the ones who really hold on to customary practice *(mitana fomba)*. Their work is to stay in the house and take care of everything for their spouses. But he shouldn't go out on his wife in front of her, for example, in the evenings, when she is sitting at home alone [with the children]. That's what Djoma did, and he was wrong. He went out in the evening, didn't get back until 11:00. I told him that 'Your wife didn't marry a house, but you.' A man should go during the time he is out working."

Here the closeness of spouses ran into rough and twisted waters. Hidden infidelities were ignored, but if a wife caught her husband swearing *(mipoko)* falsely, then he had to beg pardon from the royal ancestors, or die.

Mipoko (to inflict oneself, to experience a blow while inflicting one) was usually used to refer to quarreling, especially starting quarrels. In quarrels between spouses, it referred to swearing by ancestors by saying: 'If I slept with someone else, may the ancestors [one's own, the royal ancestors] strike me dead.' As some women in Analalava described this experience, "The wife asks, and the husband says 'No.' Then the wife says, 'Swear on it!' *(Mipoko!)* If he doesn't mipoko, then she knows he did it. If he dares to swear, then she knows he didn't, because if he swore and did it, he'd die *(maty anteña)*. If he did something, he doesn't swear."

As AdanDezy and his wife Moana explained it, "If someone has been made afraid by his wife *(mampatahotra vady)*, and so lies to her about having slept with another woman, then he must cleanse the lie *(mampadio vandy)*. If he did it [swore a false oath] on himself [his own ancestors], if he did it [by swearing] on sacred ground [royal ancestors], dead! But if he hurries to beg pardon for the lie *(mangataka poko)*, then he won't die. That is what Bezara does [Avoria's eldest son, the Ampanjaka Maroaomby who inherited the office from his father]. People go to Bezara to *mangataka poko:* 'This is the poko that I did. . . . This is the poko that I did.'[51] Before that, he says that he desired a woman, but he feared his wife, so he lied to her, and they give money [for the ancestors]. They go to Bezara in secret, and he doesn't talk about things like that—just keeps quiet *(mangina fo)*."

If, as often happened as a result of quarrels about lovers or the money they involved, the couple finally separated and returned to their kin, then 'the man is owner/master of the children' *(baba tompon' ny zanaka)* and almost always did claim them. Women—if they were married more than a year—kept the marriage wealth and, as men saw it, got richer and richer at their expense.

TAVAVY'S STORY

The closeness of siblings born of the same parents, yet their opposition in relation to spouses, was expressed in contrasts between 'people of one belly' *(olo kibo araiky)*, who formed the basis of 'unions' *(fikambana)*, and 'people of one house' *(olo trano araiky)*, 'one bed' *(fandriana araiky)*, who formed pairs of spouses *(ampivady)*. These differences were built into the walls for which houses were named, and the locked granaries with which each house formed its own complete pair. Yet, despite some salient exceptions—couples like Malaza and Rafotsy in Andonaka and the two sisters, Togny and Avoria, and their spouses in Tsinjorano—friendships between spouses rarely endured either. So people moved back and forth between siblings and spouses. The complexity of these changing relationships, and their different consequences for men and women, emerge from accounts in which people evaluated for themselves the odysseys of kin and affines over the long run. I heard such accounts mainly from people I had known almost from the beginning of our stay in the Analalava region.

Djoma's wife, Tavavy, a woman in her mid-twenties, came from the village of Marosely, south of Analalava, about four hours walk from Andonaka. She was akin to Malaza on her mother's side, and more distantly connected to him through marriage on her father's side. She had lived in Analalava since she had started going to school there at age eight. Now she was married to my foster mother-in-law's eldest son by her last marriage, had one young girl of her own and was expecting another. For the past week or so, she was taking care of her younger sister, the child of her FyB who still farmed in Marosely. The child was currently staying with Añemboka, her FZD. She said that Añemboka had two boys, but they were already pretty big (fourteen and eleven years old). Añemboka wanted more children, but hadn't been able to have any, so she asked for this one to take care of. "[She] likes caring for children" *(Tia mitarimy zanaka)*.

I asked where her father was living. He is now in a village west of Mahadrodroka [near Mahajamba Bay, south of Antognibe], but he comes from Marosely. All the Silamo there and in the neighboring village of Ambohibao are his kin. Her mother and father separated when she was about six years old. There were four children. The oldest, a girl, and the youngest, a boy, died young; she and her older sister, married in Marosely, are left. I asked if they died when they were just born or later. She then explained how the boy died.

"When my mother died, my father married again, south of here. He lived in the district of Andribavontsona with a Sakalava woman from Antantiloky [east of Antognibe]. But the woman didn't like the children of the first spouse." Just the boy was with them. Tavavy was living with her FZ [Zalifa] in Analalava, Añemboka's mother. "The stepmother (*mamakely*) didn't treat the little boy well. That often happens with new spouses. They like their own children and their spouse, but not the [earlier] spouse's children (*zanakam-bady*). They are always treating them badly. One day she and the little boy were walking to a rice-trampling. The boy was little. He couldn't go fast, but she kept pushing him along, hurrying him along, pushing him along. She pushed him. He fell down, hit a root. He vomited blood from then on, and eventually he died. The root didn't pierce his body, but must have hurt something in there. When asked, she claimed she hadn't done anything. But there were people walking behind them, and they had seen what happened. Furthermore, people had also seen about a week earlier, she had been pounding rice and the boy was nearby. She hit him on the back [pointed to the center of her back] with the big pestle, hard! It swelled up big, turned green. The little boy couldn't sleep on his back without crying. Sick for a week. Then shortly after, this happened and he died."

[What did the father do?] "He didn't say anything. He still loved the woman, after all. But the grandfather [FF] said: '[I] don't need a woman who murders my grandchild,' and sent her back home to Antantiloky." Tavavy's father followed her. They lived there, then they separated after six months. [Why didn't his kin take the woman to the tribunal or something?] "People in the country don't like to fight with people (*tsy tia miady olo*). They are afraid of the government [so] they just keep quiet (*mangina fo*)."

"When he separated from this woman he took another woman from Antantiloky and moved to Ambodimañary [a town south of Antsohihy]. He lived with this woman about a year, then they separated. He moved to the place west of Mahadrodroka." [Why did he move?] "Ambodimañary was too small, and also there was not enough room for rice fields, not enough rice fields. There were lots of rice fields in this other place. He cleared a field, then took a wife, a local person, Sakalava like the others. Eventually they separated. He is still living there, but now he is married to another woman, from Antognibe. He was just up here with the new wife a little over a week ago." [Were all his wives Sakalava?] "Yes." [Why didn't he marry Silamo?] "Because they are all his kin—in Marosely, Ambohibao—all his relatives."[52]

A few days later, still trying to understand the story, I came back to these topics, and Tavavy went further into the relationships involved.

[Which children went with the father when he moved away with the second wife and why?] Tavavy said her younger brother died when they were still in Marosely. She was always sick when she was staying with the two of them, so her *dady* (FM) took her away from them and took care of her. Her older sister went with her father's sister Zalifa. "Zalifa—her children [were] all big, [she had] no one to order around to go get things, so she took my older sister [Zalifa's BD]. Zalifa lived some thirty years in Analalava. When she was fourteen or fifteen years old [in Marosely], a man came along and wanted her, [and] she got pregnant. But the man refused to marry her. Her parents were angry at her for getting pregnant. When the child was born, it slept with her in the same bed, and it was constantly sick. The mother and father said she was making it sick, and sent her to Analalava, while they kept the child to take care of. After a month, she yearned *(ngôma)* for her child and returned to get it and came back to Analalava. She slept in one bed and the baby in a little bed of its own. It didn't get sick, so the grandparents didn't send for it back again. Now the child [Añemboko] is all grown up."[53] Añemboka went back to Marosely [her mother's village], where she got married and had two children. Her first husband died, and she married a man from a village south of Marosely, where they lived for a year until they separated. Añemboka returned to Marosely, then went back to Analalava where she had been living about ten years, and where she was now taking care of her MyBD. Tavavy said, "This happens very often among kin. But if someone came along and asked for Meva [her daughter], I would refuse to give her up until I had another to take care of. The man really had a bad disposition *(ratsy fañahy)*. Zalifa was sick for a week giving birth to Añemboka because the man refused to invoke his ancestors [to beg them] to bring the child out *(miboaka tsaiky)*. He'd absolutely refused to marry her. Later he married another woman. He just didn't take Zalifa [to be his spouse]. Only later, when Añemboko was big, did he like her." When

Tavavy was eight years old, she came to Analalava to study because there was no school in Marosely and she stayed with her father's sister, Zalifa.

[Where again did your father move and why?] "When his father sent his second wife away from Marosely, he yearned *(ngôma)* for her, and went after her. But she refused to return to Marosely where the in-laws didn't like her. So he found land to cultivate [in a village near his wife's village], set up a house, and went to get her to live there. Eventually [having separated from her and married another woman from Antantiloky] he moved to Ambodimañary. Eventually [after separating from the third wife], he moved west of Mahadrodroka because Ambodimañary was too crowded, could only grow rice. He wanted more land to grow corn, other things. There is a kind of medicine *(aody)* that people use to send people away to other villages if they don't like them.[54] This is medicine-that-sends-away *(aody mampandefa)*. People with bad dispositions *(olo ratsy fanahy)* use this medicine to get people they don't like to move to another village. [I] don't know the power of the medicine *(Asa herin' ny fanafody)*. They go any place—whatever place they get to *(zay tany hazony)*—they see a place they like, settle down. People who make the medicine don't care where they go, only that they don't get the idea of returning. It could even be kin, even kin, even friends of one stomach [full siblings], if they don't like them. If the person doesn't leave, s/he will die."

"There is another bad medicine that makes people separate. If they don't separate, then one of the pair gets deathly sick *(matimaty)*. Its name is *famakitrano* [house-breaker]. A person who wants your spouse, and you aren't separating on your own, will give you this medicine. Or the parents of the boy or girl who don't like the parents of the other. Or a boy or girl who don't like their in-laws." [Where do people know to get these medicines?] "People with good dispositions *(olo tsara fanahy)* don't like handling bad medicines. People with bad dispositions who use these medicines mutually understand the people of bad dispositions who make them. They can tell another person with a bad disposition because they are that way themselves."

[Did someone use that kind of medicine on your father?] "Yes. Tinamby [his FZS] used medicine." [Why did he use the medicine on your father and not on your father's elder brother?] "Because my father was especially hard-working *(mazoto)*, clearing rice fields, fixing up his house. Tinamby didn't have a rice field. He was reluctant *(malaigny)* to clear a rice field. Also the inheritance was spread among a lot of children. So Tinamby gave him the medicine in a dish of water at the foot of an orange tree near his house. Every morning when it was still dark, Tinamby would go out and sprinkle water from the dish onto their house." [Why didn't he put the medicine in the house?] "Because it would have been too close to them there. They would have gotten sick or separated because of the medicine— bad medicine. If he [Tavavy's father] hadn't left he would have died. Other people saw it, but he *(izy tompony)* never saw it. The other people saw, but they feared in their hearts *(mavozo fo)*." [Afraid?] "Yes, they were probably afraid. That is why the [second] wife killed the boy, and they moved away. There has to be some talk that makes people leave *(tsy maintsy misy kabary hely hampandeha olo)*. Having gotten the medicine, her mind became turned around *(Hazon' ny fanafody, manjary mivadiky ny jery)*." [Does your father want to go back to Tsaratanana now?] "Not at all, although his kin want him to return."

[How did people know it was Tinamby?] "He said so. They fought about something. Tinamby left for Majunga shortly afterwards, where he bought the medicine. And after my father had left, he went around saying something like 'Isn't it good he's gone.' He was so glad that people knew he'd used medicine. No one likes him there, but they won't ask him to leave. He has to go to people, they don't come to him. But they don't say anything. It's just in their thoughts that they don't like him *(Anatin' ny jery fo tsy tia izy)*. He has a bad disposition, and he's proud *(miavona)*." [Miavona?] "*Miavona*. There's no one who knows Silamo custom if not he, and yet he's not really Silamo. There's nothing to do that he doesn't know *(Tsisy raha atao tsy hainy)*. If someone else kills an animal, he doesn't eat it—'There's no one who knows the prayers for killing an animal if not I.'"

[Did Tinamby get your father's rice field?] "He didn't. He didn't dare to ask for it, although that was the reason he wanted him to leave." [What field did he farm?] "His wife's rice field, inheritance from her father. Ever since we were little, he has farmed only on the rice fields of his wives."

Later, in talking about others of her father's kin, she commented, "The father of ZamanViloma [FBS] is known. Tinamby called him *Baba,* but he wasn't his real father *(tena baba)*. Only Tinamby's father is not known." So it turned out that Tinamby was a child of women only; there was no place that he was also a child of men. But Tavavy did not say this in telling the story, and perhaps would not have mentioned it later if we had not happened to go on to talk about her father's kin in neighboring villages.

Tavavy's story turned on contrasts between outsides and insides, superficial likenesses and deeper differences, revealed in seeing but not speaking. People claimed to be Silamo, even when they were not 'real

Silamo,' but 'Sakalava,' called men *Baba* who were not their 'real father,' but one of their mother's brothers. As she herself went further into the events surrounding her father's moves from place to place and from wife to wife, her own telling of the story began to change. She began with events involving mainly him—his household together with his new wife and the children from his former marriage. Then she gradually drew in his parents, his father, his sister and sister's child, and finally his brother who turned out to be related to him as a child of women to a child of men. She began with choices—to marry, to follow a spouse, even after parents had sent her away, to separate, to move again, searching in other places for new land and new companions. But she ended with more complicated contributions to choices—'bad medicines,' 'house-breakers' that 'turned people's minds around' so that they murdered covertly, driving others to force them openly to leave. She began with a problem that seemed to arise from relations between spouses, but turned out to have its roots in earlier relations with siblings. She brought up the structural constraints that they faced—like insufficient land (but not, at least directly, the subordinate position of children of women in relation to land)—but she kept coming back to the unpredictably different dispositions of people faced with such recurrent problems. Where some people were *mazoto,* interested and hard-working in clearing new land for themselves or in searching elsewhere, others were *malaigny,* reluctant and unwilling to work and search. So they continued to farm on their wives' land, while using medicines to harm the fortunes of their brothers, medicines that could transform even such dispositions.

People saw with their eyes and kept quiet, but finally "there has to be some speech to make people go," itself an indirect way of saying that there had to have been some dispute open enough to occasion formal speech in which people would be asked to leave directly. Other participants in the dispute may well have seen it differently, just as Tavavy herself gradually widened the range of issues she considered relevant. The unresolvable contradictions between siblings and spouses provoked such reflection. Before we go on to reexamine these relations in the larger regional context that Tavavy's story implies, we need to return from the wives her father sought to the children of women—the father's sister, and their sometimes fatherless children—which she kept bringing into her own account.

ANGOVAVIKO TIAKO ANGOVAVY: MY FATHER'S SISTER, I LOVE FATHER'S SISTER

Tavavy's father remarried after her mother died, but even if they had separated, he could still have kept the children. The primacy of ancestral ties through men, compared to ties through women, was most succinctly expressed in the repeated claim that the man was the *tompon' ny zanaka,* or 'master of the children,' 'things' *(raha)* in the belly, who first entered the house, or not, as 'strangers' *(vahiny)*. The strength of this claim was evident in the number of men in Andonaka and Tsinjorano who were able to keep their children by earlier unions. Children left with their mothers continued to be described as 'outside children' *(zaza antany)* in contrast to 'children in the house' *(zaza antrano),* even if they were royalty. Tavavy's father's sister's daughter, Añemboka, was such a child; so, too, was Tinamby. As Tavavy explained: "Tinamby's mother was my father's sister. I don't know his father. His mother went far away, got a belly and returned home with a belly" *(nandeha lavitra, nahazo kibo, nimpody misy kibo)*. One of the royal ancestors in the Analalava region—called Tompony Andronjona, 'Master of Andronjona' for the place where he was buried—was a well-known sister's child. Tompony Andronjona was often present at the gatherings of the royal spirits from the Mahabo. Soatoly—a sister's child of guardians at the Mahabo, who had returned there to keep the royal spirits from killing her and her sisters, still in Nosy Be, with their anger—explained:

"Tompony Andronjona and Ndramamahaña [the Father] were brothers *(mpirahalahy),* but Tompony Andronjona was an outside child, his father didn't take him *(zaza an-tany, tsy nalain' baba)*." [Who was his mother?] "I don't know, people in Andronjona would know. He didn't rule during his lifetime. He's dead, he's gone, he rules [now, by possessing people] *(Izy maty, izy lasa, izy manjaka)*. He gets people from far away. There are only two around here . . ." She went on to mention his two mediums, one from the Ambolobozo Peninsula in the north, the other from a village south of Analalava.[55]

In other words, such children remained children of women, no matter where they were, even if their mothers were not known. There were no places where, nor people with whom, they were also children of men.

The father's claim to children is most evident in the exception required of people who married Sambarivo. Sambarivo required an exception because, owing to their work as guardians of royal places, they were, in principle, people who "never left the mahabo" [or doany], as AdanDezy's father insisted concerning his own forebears, even though—as the moves of his own father, Malaza's father, and Soatoly's father's mother indicated—they did.[56]

Matombo (Fig. 9, F22), the husband of Avoria's oldest child in Tsinjorano, said that he 'follows' his mother's kind. His mother was a Sambarivo at the Mahabo. His older brother followed his father [Antandrano]. He said, "It is custom (fomba) that one of the children follows the mother's kind." But as he continued, it turned out that following the mother's kind was customary only when a person married a Sambarivo at the Mahabo or the Doany. Then one of the children must follow the mother's kind. "'I need one to carry out my part (anjara, that is, allotted work),' says the mother to the father. 'Take that one,' he says." Matombo said he followed all his mother's prohibitions; his siblings followed his father. He will not inherit from his father, only from his mother "because such a person's lot in life is there [at the Mahabo, where he or she has been chosen to replace the parent]. There is where he gets the anjara of his mother [her work at the Mahabo and whatever else she might pass on to the chosen child]."

Matombo emphasized that some people followed the customs of both parents, some followed the customs of neither. He was describing only the customs of Sambarivo at the Mahabo. "If a person marries a woman from the Mahabo, and they have only one child, then it goes with the father. But if they have more than one, then the mother gets one, but no more than one." He said that all his children followed his customs. He had not yet given a child to his wife. "[We're] not yet separated, after all! If people separate, the mother may take a child. When grown, some [choose to] remain, some return home [i.e., to the father's village]. But she cannot take more than one. The father is master of the children *(Baba tompon' ny zanaka)*."⁵⁷

Thus, as in Tavavy's story, the same differences between children of men and children of women that separated brothers from one another and women from their children, brought brothers together with their sisters. The father was master/owner of the children, but because a man's later wives were commonly reluctant to raise other 'spouses' children' *(zanakam-bady)*, the father usually gave them to his own kin to raise—his mother or sister. Or, as Tavavy's story also illustrates, and as happened in Tsinjorano and Andonaka, sisters who were unmarried or between husbands, asked their brothers for children.

The importance of sisters in raising their brothers' children was recognized in a small sum of money known as "a little pinch of greens" *(tsongotsongo feliky)*, which a groom gave to the woman who raised his bride. Diniky, Mahasoa's twin sister, whose mother came from a village near Andonaka, explained:

"It is usually given to the father's mother or father or to his sister in that order of preference, 50 FMG or so [about 40 cents]. The mother's sisters don't get it, and the mother's brother only rarely. This is because the child is most often cared for by the father's mother or sister, they often foster children. Father's sister because the man is master of the children *(Angovavy satria lehilahy tompon' ny zanaka)*."

The importance of sisters in raising their brothers' children was expressed in the trees and stones interspersed among the houses of living people in Andonaka and Tsinjorano. These included not only the togny associated with ancestral tompontany, but also trees and stones associated with royal spirits. Invariably these proved to be togny founded by sisters, sisters' spouses or even sisters' daughters' spouses (Plate 13).

The third togny that Malaza showed us in Andonaka stood at the southeast corner of his house. Bevaoko [a Zafinifotsy royal ancestor], who

Plate 13. Malaza standing south of Bevaoko's togny in Andonaka (A. Harnik, 1973).

possessed his sister from Anjango [a village on the Ambolobozo Peninsula, near the Loza River, where Bevaoko's doany is located] had directed him to set it up. The togny consisted of four shrubs—two kinds of *hasina* (*hasim-be* and *hasim-bola, Dracaena* sp.), a *matambelona*, and a *maimbogoaka*, east to west in that order—surrounded by a high rectangular fence made of thin poles. He had begun the customary procedures *(fomba)* to set up the togny in *fanjava mitsaka* [the first month of the royal year], but could not complete them then because he had been called to the Doany. In *asara be* [when the second royal service of the year was held], he would pour fermented honey (tô mainty) over the togny to clean it, using the same gourd they had used the first time they had called Bevaoko. He pointed out several places in the branches where people, sometimes from far away, had already taken 'medicines' *(aody)* from the togny.

There were several such shrines in Tsinjorano. When we returned to Tsinjorano, Avoria talked again about the *madiro masina* in the center of the village. Then she said that the *foraha* tree east of the meeting tree (the foraha called madiro fantsina) was also masina:

"Kotomena [one of the Zafinifotsy royal ancestors with shrines along the Loza River] said that it was masina, that it was his tree. 'This is mine, to cultivate. . . . This is my togny, my good choice of where to live' *(Ty ninakahy, mitsabo. . . . Ty togninakahy, mifanga)."* She said that people who want to make an oath can go either to Kotomena in his medium or to his tree. Someone else later mentioned that Avoria herself was a medium of Kotomena. AdanDezy said that Avoria (his MZ) had set up Kotomena's togny before he was born, when her first children were still babies (Plates 14 and 15).[58]

Another day, when we were sitting in the shade of her son Amido's unfinished house (Fig. 12, house 31), where Avoria often wove palm-leaf bags, she pointed out other togny that had been raised by royal spirits who had possessed people born in Tsinjorano but were now dead. Ndramanetsiarivo (the Grandfather), who possessed Maolidy (Fig. 11, 33), had directed the community residents to plant a pair of trees, hasina and *matambelona,* together southeast of her house. If there was any sickness in the community, people poured cold water at the base of the trees to take it away. Like Kotomena's tree, Ndramanetsiarivo's pair of trees had a stone west of them, where incense could be burned or offerings could be put. Burnt remains of copallier *(mandrôfo)* were still lying there. Avoria pointed to places where people had taken parts of the tree to make medicines, just

Plate 14. Avoria with her daughter Ampenjiky (kneeling) and some of her other children and sons' children, and her husband, the Ampanjaka Maroaomby, between their kitchen and their son's unfinished house to the south (G. Feeley-Harnik, 1973).

as Malaza did in talking about the growing reputation of Bevaoko's two pairs of trees in Andonaka.[59]

There was a large rock at the southwest corner of Togny and Mainty Be's house (Fig. 9, E24). People said in response to my question that Ndramamitranarivo (the Great-Grandfather) had set it up. The husband of Mainty Be's father's sister was one of his first mediums (Fig. 10). Mainty Be's father's sister had moved to his village just north of Tsinjorano when they married, but they had frequently returned to visit. The stone was used as a place to "cool" people who were fighting.

Men established themselves through togny associated with the an-cestral masters of the land who originally founded the village. Their sisters integrated themselves, their spouses, their children and chil-

Plate 15. Looking south from the togny of the royal ancestral spirit Kotomena toward the togny of the "masters of the land" in Tsinjorano (G. Feeley-Harnik, 1973).

dren's spouses more tightly into their natal villages by establishing their own togny as mediums of royal ancestors. Here, in contrast to the ancestral togny, associated with men, the idiom of 'growing, raising, tending' *(mitsabo)* was more explicitly used. As Avoria reported Kotomena saying about his togny: "This is mine, to cultivate, my togny, my special choice as a place to live." Like crops, these trees did not grow by themselves; people raised them up. Even trees 'in the forest' were assimilated to that image by saying 'God cultivates them' *(Zanahary mitsabo)*. While some togny having specifically local associations were cultivated by ancestors connected to their descendants especially through men, others that acquired regional renown were the cultivations of royal spirits most often embodied in women— sisters and sisters' children. Together they stood as kinds of growing commentaries on how people rooted themselves in the land and spread out in different ways through brothers and sisters, kin and strangers by growing, tending, nurturing one another.[60]

It is perhaps relevant to the roundabout way in which sisters re-established themselves in brothers' villages that the commonest of the royal spirits involved in establishing togny were junior figures in their respective royal lines: Ambilahikely was the current ruler's younger brother who never ruled. Bevaoko and Kotomena were Zafinifotsy, 'Grandchildren of the Silver,' descendants of the junior branch of royalty with which the Zafinimena, 'Grandchildren of the Gold' including the Bemihisatra, were paired. The Zafinimena and Zafinifotsy, senior and junior branches of Sakalava royalty in the Analalava region, were viewed much like children of men compared to children of women. The Zafinifotsy were represented as an ancestry headed by a brother and sister, the father and father's sister of the rest. In the words of one of the songs honoring them:

Bevaoko namaitry, Ampela Be nitarimy

Bevaoko [B, F] gave birth, Ampela Be [Z, FZ] gave care.[61]

When women in Tsinjorano gathered around Kotomena's tree in the evening, or in spirit possession meetings honoring Ambilahikely and other spirits embodied in their own kin, they evoked these images. Zanety (Fig. 9, G) was usually the lead singer in the following song, which praises the father's sister, Ampela Be:

Angovaviko,
Angovaviky,
Eeeeeeeeeeee Angovavy,
Angovavinakahy!
Vondraka malemilemy Angovavy.
Angovaviko Angovavy,
Angovaviko,
Eeeeeeeeeeee Angovavy!
Mitarimy tsara Angovavy,

Oy zaho mbola hely Angovavy.
Fa zaho koa be Angovavy,
Oy mamaly tarimy Angovavy.
Oy vadinao tsara Angovavy,
Oy nin'tsika aroy Angovavy.
Oy vadinao ratsy Angovavy,
Oy ny anao araiky Angovavy.
Angovaviko Angovavy,
Angovaviko eeeeeee Angovavy,
Eeeeeeeeeeee Angovavy,
Eeeeeeeeeeee Angovavy,
Angovavinakahy!
Angovaviko tiako Angovavy.
Tiako tsy malaigny zaho Angovavy.
Angovaviko tiako Angovavy,
Angovaviko tiako Angovavy!
Eeeeeeeeeeee Angovavy
Eeeeeeeeeeee Angovavy. . . .

My Father's Sister,
My Father's Sister,
Eeeeeeeeeee Father's Sister,
My Father's Sister![62]
Succulent, soft Father's Sister.[63]
My Father's Sister, Father's Sister
My Father's Sister,
Eeeeeeeeeee Father's Sister!
Father's Sister [you] cared for me well,[64]
Oy when I was still small, Father's Sister.
But now that I'm big too, Father's Sister.
Oy [I'm] responding to care, Father's Sister.
Oy your husband's wonderful, Father's Sister,
Oy he's both of ours, Father's Sister.[65]
Oy your husband's awful, Father's Sister,
Oy he's yours alone, Father's Sister.
My Father's Sister, Father's Sister,
My Father's Sister eeeeeee Father's Sister,
Eeeeeeeeeee Father's Sister,

Eeeeeeeeeee Father's Sister,
My Father's Sister!
My Father's Sister, I love you Father's Sister.
I love [that you] are not indifferent to me,
Father's Sister.[66]
My Father's Sister, I love (you) Father's Sister,
My Father's Sister, I love (you) Father's Sister!
Eeeeeeeeeee Father's Sister,
Eeeeeeeeeee Father's Sister. . . .

ANCESTORS, SIBLINGS, AND SPOUSES

The communities of people who happened to be living in Tsinjorano
and Andonaka when we were there extended far beyond the villages
where they farmed and stored grain to encompass many other kinds
of places in the region: the other villages where they cultivated, the
fields where they watched their crops, the villages where they were
born, the villages where they visited kin and friends, where they married, and where their children were living, the post where they
searched for wage labor, the Doany and the Mahabo where they served
living and ancestral rulers in exchange for their blessing. People
thought of the relationships constituting these communities from different perspectives—'what's brought from the father' and what is
brought from 'eight ancestors,' the need to marry out to avoid calam-
itous relations with kin, the differences between 'children of men' and
'children of women,' in which 'the man is the strong one,' while the
'father's sister is soft and succulent.' To make any one of these primary
would distort a range of alternatives that participants themselves resolved situationally, perhaps because of the strong sense of personal
destiny *(anjara),* and thus choice *(fidy),* with which I began.

Anthropologists working in Madagascar have noted broad areal
contrasts between people in the central and southern highlands, who
emphasize cognatic forms of relationships, and people in the northeastern and western parts of the island, who emphasize more lineal,
agnatic ways of relating to one another.[67] While Merina villagers emphasize cognation to the point of endogamy, the Betsileo villagers
with whom Kottak worked stressed both cognatic and agnatic ties in

different contexts. While Kottak sees the contrast between the two as being the major feature of Betsileo kin relationships, he rightly emphasizes that "the use of labels like 'patrilineal' or 'ambilineal' to characterize Betsileo descent would mask the dynamics of a cultural system where both operate simultaneously, but variably, at different levels and in different contexts."[68]

In Southall's view, kinship relations throughout Madagascar are best seen as "cumulative": "what seems to be distinctive about all Malagasy kinship systems is not their qualities of cognation or agnation, but their emphasis on kinship and descent status as something achieved gradually and progressively throughout life, and even after death, rather than ascribed and fixed definitively at birth."[69]

The optative, situationally variable use of many different ways of relating to kin is also a prominent feature of daily life in northwestern Madagascar. Here, however, I have tried to focus more on how participants themselves experience their choices in terms of tensions between siblings—'children of men' and 'children of women'—and their 'friends' or spouses. The emphasis on 'men as the strong ones' contributed to divisions between children of men and children of women, who were forbidden to marry one another. Yet the emphasis on the father as the 'master of children,' dividing spouses, re-created an interdependence between brothers and sisters, who thus often raised their ancestors' descendants together.

Where Kottak finds parallels between Betsileo descent groups and those of other Malayo-Polynesian speaking peoples, I see a strong common emphasis on siblingship and on the equivalence of siblings and spouses.[70] In Oceania and in Southeast Asia, relations between siblings and spouses are complicated by different attitudes toward endogamy and exogamy that have not been systematically studied in that context.[71] Kipp's analysis of Karo Batak (Sumatra) terms of endearment, which equate lovers and spouses with siblings, is one exception.[72] Kipp analyzes these metaphors as resolving structural oppositions that Karo Batak see between sexual love and love between kin, incest and alliance, siblings and cross-cousins.

Much of the literature on connections between siblings and spouses in Southeast Asia is written in the context of discussions concerning preferential, if not prescriptive, marriage systems. Weiner's reanalysis of Trobriand ethnography suggests the value of going beyond preferential marriage systems to the analysis of cultural conceptions of reproduction in looking at sibling-spouse relations in Madagascar, as I hope to do in later work.[73] But here, too, different attitudes toward endogamy and exogamy complicate the picture. AdanDezy's brief marriage to his FFBSD suggests an interest in endogamy, but it was unusual. The sole requirement concerning marriage, on which people in Andonaka and Tsinjorano insisted, was that people should marry out. Recognizing that 'Hova' in highland Madagascar and 'Silamo' in the northwest preferred to marry kin, they emphasized that they considered marriages with kin to be incest, from which 'there is no place to go' *(tsisy tany mboany)* to be cleansed from the wrong-doing. Preferences for marrying exogamously have been noted among other people living in northeastern and western Madagascar, in contrast to preferences for endogamy expressed by people living in the central highlands and the south.[74] Closer attention to the relationship between spouses who are strangers, yet siblinglike, and siblings who together raise brothers' children, might help to achieve a more integrated understanding of reproduction in these different contexts.

Data from northwestern Madagascar, where many different 'kinds' of people coexist, indicate that these questions about reproduction cannot be resolved without accounting more explicitly for the importance of 'strangers' and 'friends' in some Malagasy communities. Studies of rural villages in Madagascar have generally concluded that they are based on kinship.[75] While some early travelers and missionaries noted the creation of 'blood ties' *(fatidra)* to form friendships among strangers, the variable nature of such ties has not been widely studied. Bloch found that fatidra was of "little significance" in Imerina, owing to the sharp contrast between kin, whom one married if possible, and completely untrustworthy strangers.[76] In contrast, both *vaki-dra* and fosterage have long been important features of social relations among Betsileo villagers.[77] Kottak notes possibly historically based parallels to Southeast Asian cases, but argues essentially that fosterage and vaki-dra are forms of "kinship modeling." They are both ways that "traditional, kin-based cultures" deal with rapid social change by assimilating unfamiliar strangers to familiar social categories.[78]

Kin relations are an important feature of farming communities in northwestern Madagascar, as I have already indicated, but these are not "kin-based communities." Even the smallest rural villages include 'strangers' as well as 'kin,' reflecting strong emphasis on the uniqueness of every individual, and the search for fulfillment through strangers transformed into friends, of whom the most important are spouses.[79] Social relations based on 'friendship' are not only long-standing, but they seem to have more autonomy than they have in the highlands, in that they are not simply ways of assimilating strangers to familiar categories. Friends are important in their own right, precisely because of their differences from kin.

Here I would follow the lead of people in the Analalava region by suggesting an alternative to the kinship-contract model still implied in many contemporary studies of kinship, migration, and social change.[80] In northwestern Madagascar, 'searching' *(mitady)* is no less important than 'getting a place' *(mangala toerana)*. While kinship is commonly contrasted with residence—a black box containing all that kinship is not, but especially individualistic self-interest and other historical contingencies—searching involves 'friendships,' differently productive relationships connecting pairs and networks of companions to many different kinds of places. While 'friends' may join together by 'choice,' as people in northwestern Madagascar emphasize, the 'places' they create together may systematize these productive relationships in ways that facilitate the mobility of some, while constraining others. By following the lead of local people in focusing on natives and strangers and the different kinds of places they produce through their friendships, we may avoid the need to fall back on dichotomies between primordial and instrumental ties. Their interests also draw attention to the role of different places—houses as well as burial grounds—in the processes of nativization and alienation through which transformations between kinds of strangers and friends are achieved.

If all the places in northwestern Madagascar were farming villages of varying sizes, it might be possible to speak of extended family forms, characterized by the differential development of branches from a common tree. But in fact, the 'places' in and out of which people in this area now move originated, as we have already seen, from different kinds of 'friendships' among 'children of land' and 'strangers,' not limited to descent and marriage, but including 'mastery,' 'slavery,' and 'salaried' forms of reproducing relationships across generations. The question posed by the pairs and networks of people in these places, for local participants as well as observers, is not how people may extend one common set of sometimes contradictory kin terms to encompass a region, but rather how people—be they siblings, spouses, or the strangers they bear and raise, pioneers or latecomers—achieve any kind of common understanding about what, why, and for whom?

The historical sources discussed in Chapters 2 and 3 suggest that people who differentiated themselves as 'Sakalava,' 'Silamo,' 'Hova,' and 'French' came to share a common language about ancestors that was indispensable to representing and re-creating their different claims to land and laborers. The emphatic way in which people in the Analalava region define themselves in contrast to others through categorical statements about incest indicates the persistence of such controversies, but not the means by which they are created. In following local people as they move out of farming villages into the 'post' of Analalava, searching for wage labor, we will be able to examine in more detail just how they systematize their understanding about social differences and partnerships in their daily practices. We will explore how, as farmers, traders, wage laborers, and royal servants, people in the Analalava region build their diverse understanding of *kibo* and *trano*, stomachs, wombs, and houses, into other kinds of *tanàna*, settled places with controlling properties of their own.

Ampositra: At the Post

There aren't many children of the land *(zanatany)*
here. People come from other places to walk
around, to settle down, to look for work.

Ampenjiky, about Analalava and such places

AMBODIMANGA: AT THE FOOT OF THE MANGO TREES

The central square of Analalava is marked by a large red, white, and
green map of Madagascar, which in the early 1970s, commemorated
independence in these words:

Tahionao Ry Zanahary
Ity Nosin-drazanay ity
Tsy ho hadinoina
14 Oktobra 1958
26 Jiona 1960
Ph. Tsiranana

Bless, O Lord
This Island of our Ancestors
Not to be forgotten
14 October 1958
26 June 1960
Ph[ilibert] Tsiranana[1]

In 1971, the map stood in front of the Tribunal, which formed the
east side of the Place de l'Indépendance, formerly the Place Lyautey,

Plate 16. Ambodimanga (At the Foot of the Mangos), the central square in Analalava (A. Harnik, 1971).

locally known as Ambodimanga, At the Foot of the Mango Trees (Plate 16). The four-story building, made of cast iron prefabricated in France and put together in Madagascar, once dwarfed every other structure around it, including the long, low mud-brick offices of the local functionaries across the road on the western side of the square (Fig. 13).[2]

Lyautey, who served with General Galliéni in Tonkin, was his chief military officer during and right after the conquest of Madagascar, and later a prominent Governor-General of Madagascar in his own right. As French colonial capitals were reoriented to France, so through the *tache d'huile* policy that Galliéni and Lyautey originated in Tonkin and developed in Madagascar, were foreign countrysides reoriented to colonial capitals. By "oil spot," Galliéni referred to the spread of power from a single administrative center commanded by a single *soldat-colonisateur* whose military and administrative powers

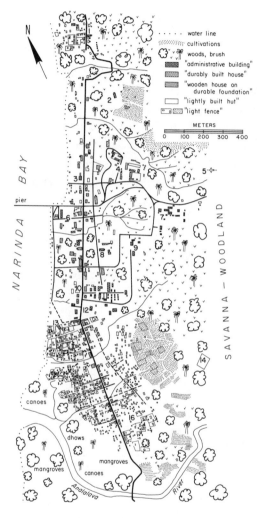

water line
cultivations
woods, brush
"administrative building"
"durably built house"
"wooden house on
    durable foundation"
"lightly built hut"
"light fence"

METERS
0   100   200   300   400

N

NARINDA BAY

pier

canoes

dhows

mangroves

mangroves

canoes

Analalava River

SAVANNA — WOODLAND

Figure 13. Sketch map of
Analalava. *Key:*
1. Ampasikely (Protestant
Church); 2. veterinary
service; 3. post office;
4. prison and gendarmerie;
5. air strip; 6. customs,
Forestry Service; 7. clinic
(formerly a regional hospital);
8. Catholic Church and
school; 9. Residence (of the
Chef de Province, then Préfet,
then Sous-Préfet, then head
of the *Fivondronam-pokontany,*
now empty); 10. *bazary*
(covered market); 11. schools;
12. Ambodimanga, Place de
l'Indépendance; 13. Friday
mosque; 14. Vazaha graveyard
(*Fasimbazaha*); 15. mosque;
16. Anjialava, Anjiamaeva.
(The original map did not note
the Protestant Church in
Ampasikely. It did include the
following not indicated here:
the former hotel and Air
Madagascar buildings, just
south of the customs building
on the main road; the
atelier in back of the market;
the soccer field west of the
atelier; and the buildings of
the then subprefecture and commune west of Ambodimanga. The cemetery
for local people, known as Ambodibonara [At the Foot of the Bonara Trees],
is on a hill south of the Analalava River.)

were co-extensive. The military post was to achieve both the pacification of the countryside and its reorganization along the lines exemplified by the post itself.[3]

Analalava began "a properly administrative life" when Captain Toquenne, head of the military expedition that pacified the region, settled
there on May 14, 1897. The post was formed by combining the European settlement in the middle with the Merina settlement of Ampasikely to the north, and the "Indians, Sakalava, Makoa or *zazamanga*
[a Merina term for slaves], and Silamo," in two villages, Tanambao
and Ampasoy, to the south.[4] The Merina settlement of Ampasikely—
by far the largest with 1,500 inhabitants in November 1897—was to
furnish the interpreters, petty officials, traders, and craftsmen.[5] The
two southern settlements were to furnish traders (Indians, Silamo) and
workers (local Malagasy).

The construction of the Tribunal and the Résidence, completed by
the time Galliéni visited a year later on July 23, 1898, established the
post as a new center of growth and development.[6] Judging by their
counterparts in French West Africa, the mango trees around the Tribunal may have been seen in the same light:

> From one town to the other, from one end to the other of the
> former French domain of black Africa, the commonest tree in the
> old administrative quarters is probably the mango (*Mangifera indica,*
> Anacardiacées). It is also the one whose bearing best expresses the
> idea of solidity, of hardiness, of equilibrium; it is the tree in ball-
> form, well built, of hard wood, the least accessible to all the assaults
> from tornadoes. The mango is also the most popular; its fruits excite
> bands of children; for that and for the density of its shade, for the
> moderate height of its foliage (the trunk branches at a man's height),
> it is equally appreciated in African yards. It is the chestnut of Africa,
> with less brilliant flowers, but with foliage constantly renewed by
> shoots of young pink-brown leaves . . . the other tree symbolic of
> the colonial town [besides] the irreplaceable flame tree (*Delonix regia,*
> Légumineuses) . . . the administrative tree *par excellence*.[7]

With independence in 1958–1960, all that began to change. A French
Catholic priest in Analalava expressed the consensus of local residents

concerning the direction of change a few months before the fall of Tsiranana's government in May 1972. His remarks were prompted by a rumor about who was working for whom. When a high government official called for workers to transplant his rice fields north of Analalava, eight people responded. When the ampanjaka called for workers a week later in the same area, four hundred people responded, bringing three hundred cattle, an accordionist and other musicians, and they sang and danced while they worked. He commented:

> French colonial officials tried to suppress the Bemihisatra rulers, yet their strength increased after independence [because] Analalava was cut off from everything. Antsohihy took over, because of the influence of President Tsiranana. Even though Analalava had buildings left over from the colonial period . . . Tsiranana chose to build up Antsohihy, located near his birthplace. . . . Now the only things left in Analalava now are the Tribunal and the hospital. And he wants to build both of those in Antsohihy, though he hasn't been able to raise the money yet. As soon as it is raised, they will be moved too. . . . Analalava is now the last in everything of all the sous-préfectures in the entire province of Majunga—the last in collecting taxes, in public works, economically, socially, in everything. That is why they don't get any aid, because they don't submit any taxes. The Sakalava don't care about working. They just catch a fish and eat a banana and go back to sleep. They don't pay their taxes, they don't work. Of the 40,000 in the préfecture, 10,000 are Sakalava. There are many other kinds in the préfecture of Antsohihy who have come here for land, to earn a little money taking jobs that Sakalava won't do. They take on Sakalava ways in order to be accepted.

During the night of December 6–7, 1971, a week before President Tsiranana was due to arrive in Analalava for a visit, someone poured kerosene over the archives on the top floor of the Tribunal and set them on fire. The square filled with people watching while the building burned to the ground in an hour, the generator-driven water pumps having been broken for a month. The administration of the Tribunal was moved to Antsohihy shortly after the fire. The hospital followed a decade later.

Implicit in the priest's appraisal was the knowledge that the current shift from Analalava to Antsohihy associated with independence had been preceded by a similar shift from Sakalava royal centers to Analalava, now perhaps reversing itself. While he saw the monarchy as his main obstacle in converting local people to Catholicism, his loyalties to other aspects of his French heritage were mixed with his respect for the efforts of the Malagasy to create an independent state. Ironically, given his own sense of isolation, he was not alone in his contradictions, although the loyalties of others were divided along different lines.

NY POSITRA: THE POST

In the early 1970s, Analalava was still called the *positra* and its residents often referred to themselves as *saovily,* civilians (Plate 17).[8] Yet the place had taken on local dimensions in the course of its transformation from a military post to a colonial administrative center, and finally the 'chief place of the subdistrict' *(voenam-pileovana).* These made it clear to all that whereas most highlanders had been assimilated to the position of the French living and working north and east of the tree-

Plate 17. Aerial view of Analalava, looking southeast (A. Harnik, 1973).

lined Place de l'Indépendance, most local people had been assimilated to the position of children of women in the south and west.

The government offices around the Place de l'Indépendance separated the chef-lieu du sous-préfecture, the northern half of the town, from the *quartiers* clustered in the south, while the shop-homes and eating places along the main road separated east from west. As in rural villages, 'big people' or 'higher-ups' *(olo be, olo ambony)*—here, government functionaries, clerical workers, and shop-keepers—lived north and east. 'Little' or 'simple people' *(olo madiniky, olo tsotra)*—mainly people who did unskilled labor, domestic work, and petty marketing—lived south and west.

The shop-homes *(dokany)* and eating places *(hotely)* along the main street reproduced the same hierarchy in a more linear form. The five shops in the north were run by second-generation immigrants from the European periphery, a French-Lebanese and a Greek, a Taiwanese immigrant from the Chinese periphery, a Merina and an Indian who still represented the Compagnie Marseillaise, which had moved to Antsohihy in 1970.[9] The Indian shopkeepers were descended from immigrants, mainly from Bombay, who had come to supercede the Silamo traders when they first settled here in the late nineteenth century. In the 1970s, most of them—five, including a shop run by a Merina merchant married to an Indian woman—were located in the south, interspersed with the small hotely or eating places run by Malagasy women.[10]

The smallest shop-homes were run by Silamo, eight families of second and third-generation descendants of the Swahili-speaking Muslim traders—*mpitondra botry*, 'dhow-captains' as they described themselves—mainly from the Comoro Islands, but including members of three large groups dispersed throughout the area, who identified themselves as Arabo from Muscat and Kuwait. They were dispersed in the quarters on both sides of the road, mainly in the west. The official *bazary*, mud-brick walls with a corrugated iron roof, where local farmers and butchers sold produce and sometimes meat in the morning, was located just north of the Place de l'Indépendance. In the evening, local women sold leftover produce and cooked food from little tables and pieces of cloth laid out along the edges of the southern half of the road. Some local women also sold small amounts of vegetables and cooked food from the porches of their homes in the quarters.[11]

A small chapel in the village of Ampasikely north of Analalava served 350 Protestants in 1971, according to the "Resumé de l'Historique de la Station d'Analalava" compiled that year by the Catholic priest. Catholics, numbering 528 parishioners (including 70 catechumens), attended a large church constructed in the northeast quarter of Analalava between the former Résidence and the main street when the mission was founded in 1901.[12] The four mosques were all located in the southwest quarter of the town. Two, including a 'Friday mosque' (moskeriny zoma) and a smaller mosque that some called the 'Thursday mosque' (moskeriny kamisy), belonged to the 693 Silamo or Sunni Muslims of the Shaf'i branch of Islam. The other two belonged to the 75 Indians, all of whom were Ismailian Shiites, most of them followers of the Aga Khan. The Bohra (Bohoro) mosque was no longer used because there were not enough worshippers to take care of it. The "pagans," identified as followers of the Sakalava monarchy, numbered 11,099 in 1971. Although there were no sectarian cemeteries, people whose bodies were not returned to their tanindrazaña were usually buried near the part of town where they had lived. Ampasikely had its own cemetery for local residents, mainly Merina.[13] Europeans during the colonial period were buried in a separate cemetery east of Analalava beyond the Résidence. People in the southern half of the town were buried in the cemetery of Ambodibonara south of Analalava.

The overall order of the town was reproduced on a smaller scale in each half. The homes in the northern half were located in the north and east, while most of the shops, where shopkeepers lived, were located in the south and west. The more densely populated quarters in the south were separated from one another by small streams running down from the hills east of the town. The northeastern quarter was settled mainly by highland and inland immigrants to the area, employed as teachers, clerks, and crafts people. Most of them lived in 'mud houses' (trano fôtaka) with galvanized iron roofs in the highland style, also characteristic of the houses in the north. The southeastern quarter, formerly a Muslim graveyard where the ampanjaka was settled as a child in 1926, was still occupied mainly by her followers who lived in small, unfenced 'palm stalk houses' *(trano ketikety)* with thatched roofs like those in rural villages.

The southwestern quarters of the post were settled during the colonial period not only by Silamo traders, but also by rural people identifying themselves as Sakalava and Makoa, who came to the post to work as laborers and domestic servants. When most of the European settlers left after independence, many of these settlers also returned to their ancestral villages. Indian merchants, who bought up the empty houses and houseyards, were the principal landlords to whom more recent immigrants from the countryside were paying rent in the 1970s. We rented one such house, which was standing empty because the previous renter had died there.

The southwesternmost quarter of the town was settled last, as people gradually moved further south to build their own houses in their own yards. The marginality of this area, implied in its name—Ambalahonko, At the Place Surrounded by Mangroves—was evident mainly during the spring tides *(samonta be)* at the new and full moons, when sea water flooded paths, yards, and low-lying houses. People who had the money built palm-stalk houses on cement foundations. Otherwise, they brought in sand and dirt to build up their houseplots. MamanDjoma, who had recently petitioned the town government for permission to move her house (formerly in the yard owned by her daughter who had returned from Diégo Suarez after her husband there left for the Comores) to an empty area further south, was still in the process of doing this in 1981. Every now and then, she paid a prisoner 10 FMG for each *daba* of sand he carried to the site.

LAKORO: FENCES

Residents of the post had adopted many features of French architecture, like windows *(lafenêtra)*, verandas *(lavaraña)*, kitchens *(lakozy)*, and bathhouses *(ladouche)*, as well as materials like cement *(siment)* for foundations and galvanized iron *(tôly)* for roofs. Highland style, wattle-and-daub 'mud houses' *(trano fôtaka)*, predominated in the northern and eastern quarters. Although mud houses were admired for being fire- and theft-proof, most residents of the southeastern and western quarters considered them to be hot, dirty, and expensive. They continued to build 'palm-stalk houses' *(trano ketikety)*, walled with more mobile and permeable panels of palm-stalks like those in farming villages, adding cement foundations and tin roofs, in that order, as they could afford them.

The most distinctive feature of the spatial organization of the post was undoubtedly the *lakoro* (from Fr. *la cour,* referring in Malagasy to the fence and yard alike). Lakoro were identified first with Silamo. As one man explained, 'That's Silamo custom. They do that to keep people in and keep people out.' As I have already indicated, fences were considered inappropriate to the reciprocity that should exist among kin and close affines. They were also prohibited to royal followers as being too like royal custom.

Except for the royal compound, there were few fences in the southeast quarter of the post, which most closely reproduced the form of a rural village. But elsewhere, especially in the densely populated quarters of the southwest, residents built pole-fences as high and closely set as they could afford, both to keep people out and keep people in, just as Silamo were said to do. I saw the use of fences to create distances between people most clearly when two women in Analalava, whom I came to know through their kin in Tsinjorano, first spoke to me through the intact part of the fence around our yard rather than through the broken place a couple of feet away. People were also explicit about the value of fences at the post, even describing lakoro as a "Sakalava trait."

A couple of months after arriving in Analalava, we were going with Somizy to visit a *kalanoro,* a kind of diviner. She left her sister's little girl, who was staying with her while she went to school, to watch her own place because—as she explained—she had fixed the kitchen, but there was still not a lock on the door, so it was not safe. The same was true of her own room; she had to sleep there with no lock on the door. She had been going to go to the *bal* the next night. But now, because the place was not

yet secure, she was afraid she would be robbed. She put on head and body
wraps over her blouse and skirt, and we started out toward the house of
the kalanoro's medium who lived on the southern edge of town. Passing a
big fenced yard with a small house in it, she said (in response to my
question) that people are afraid of having their land *(tany)* taken, so they
build a big fence around everything. She commented that it was "a
Sakalava trait" to build fences around their houses. All Sakalava do it that
way. Tsimihety don't do that. Later, when I asked her why Sakalava
should build fences, she said, "They take more than one wife *(mampirafy)*.
They don't like their wives getting people *(Tsy tia ny vadiny mahazo olo)*.
[The opposite is also implied.] When the wife goes out into the fenced
yard to cook in the kitchen, she can't see anyone who passes by" [and
can't be seen].

Somizy's emphasis on theft may have been prompted in part by the
fact that we were on our way to the kalanoro to inquire about who
had recently robbed us. But her remarks, made a couple of months
after we arrived, were reiterated on many later occasions in different
contexts. MamanDjoma, then living in her daughter's compound
while her daughter was in Diégo with her husband, explained how
her eldest son and his family came to be sharing it with her, living
now in his sister's house:

MamanDjoma explained that MamanTiba [Tavavy, her daughter-in-law]
was going to the government midwives, rather than the independent
midwife [like myself], because "There's no money." [What about all their
new chairs?] "Credit!" *(Bon ke!)* She said Djoma only made a small
salary—7,000 FMG/month [as a mechanic for the Veterinary Service]—
though it would increase a little with the birth of their second child. She
had often urged him to go to Diégo, a big city, where he would make a
big salary. When I said his expenses would be bigger too, she agreed,
noting that she had paid more money there for a smaller room with
carried water than here. But salaries were really big there, and "money
would also come when he went back and forth from work, encountering
people with broken cars, broken bicycles and the like. There is none of
that here." But he was "reluctant to go" *(malaigny mandeha)*.
[Why did they move into his sister's house?] "Because the old woman,
with whom they had been living, was robbed. Djoma [and his wife] was
the only other one living there. The police asked them if they had heard

anything during the night, which they hadn't. With no one else in the house, suspicion fell on him. And if they hadn't seen the tracks the thieves made in leaving the house [the commissaire had found those], they would have locked up Djoma. [How were the former prisoners caught?] The daughter-in-law [Djoma's wife, Tavavy] suggested it to the old woman, asking her if she trusted those men who came every day to sell charcoal. 'They are former prisoners who have done bad things in the past. Don't trust them!' So the old woman ran to the police and said she suspected them. And the police rounded them up and the story came out." [She repeated her account of how the former prisoners robbed the old woman; how the woman had been married to a Vazaha who stayed on after independence in the house he built in this quarter; how he died there; and how the woman now lived by selling second-hand clothing from abroad, including those of her husband.]

[Why did they ever move there in the first place?] "The old woman called them. 'Come, I need someone to live in this house with me. I am often gone, I need someone to watch that nothing is stolen while I am gone.'" MamanDjoma said she had warned them what would happen, but they wouldn't listen. The old woman had offered them the place rent-free, and they were tired of living in a house with no floor, in which every day the mat rots and you need a new one. "So they moved in there, and it happened exactly as I said it would."

As our child, Vanessa, grew older, and began to walk, warnings and cautionary tales took different forms:

MamanDjoma said, "You notice how we don't let our children out very long without asking where they are, or going to find them?" [In a lower voice] "[We] don't trust kin" *(tsy mahatoky havana)*. Likewise Mamoribe, "Never let Vanessa play with others when one of you is not around. You never know when someone evil might try to feed her something not right, a sorcerer" *(raha tsy mety, ampamoriky)*.

More than anything else, these high fences and the many narrow paths running between them, epitomized the contradictory nature of life at the post: creating many different opportunities for 'walking about' *(mitsangatsangana)*, while concealing the potential for treachery associated with 'searching for wealth' that inevitably led people to the post.

SAMBY MITADY VOLA: EACH SEEKS MONEY

Searching *(mitady)*, as Mahasoa explained from his perspective as a C.E.G. student, means two things: searching for what you don't see, like something you have lost, or searching for wealth *(hariaña):*

"If you say, '[I'm] going searching!' *(Handeha hitady é!)*, it always means wealth, going to do business, to search your fortune. That's how my grandfather got to Antsohihy [from Andreba in north-central Madagascar]—searching *(fitadiavaña)*—and he settled there. Only later, when he died, were his bones brought back to the same tomb where his father was buried. People go to the east coast because there are a lot of crops there, to Diégo, Sambavy, Mahavavy, to work coffee, vanilla, ylangylang, cacao. They leave at eighteen. Some don't come back until they are fifty, though some come back after only a little while. Their kin are astonished because they hardly recognize them; they don't recognize their face."

Wealth included money. As I was told repeatedly, 'It's human practice to seek money' *(Fomban'olo mitady vola).*

AdanDezy and Moana brought us up to Tsinjorano in an outrigger canoe he had borrowed from a brother. Shortly after arriving, AdanDezy came by his brother-in-law's house, where we were going to stay in the north room, and said the master of the house needed to rent the room for 450 FMG/month. He had already paid Tsimihimpa 250 FMG; he needed the rest from us. We said that we should pay it all. He insisted that we were vahiny—guests, not strangers, in this context—it wouldn't do; we should just pay the 200 FMG, which we did. Shortly afterwards, he returned with a group of men—his two mothers' brothers [the tompontany of Tsinjorano], his father, his older brother and another brother (MZS), introduced them all by kin terms as a formal welcome, then brought out a bottle of mango wine, which we all drank to celebrate our stay. In the evening, when I was cooking with Moana and AdanDezy's mother, Togny, I mentioned what had happened. Togny went out and returned to say that there was no rent, AdanDezy had lied to get money for alcohol. "Where would he ever have 250 FMG?!" she said to his wife, laughing. Hurt that he had called us kin in order to treat us like strangers, I commented that AdanDezy had asked even more than the going rate in Analalava. Moana answered: "Yes, they were trying to take advantage

(manao profite). Some Malagasy are like Vazaha, each seeks money"
(samby mitady vola).

The next Tuesday—a prohibited day when no one was working—
Tsimihimpa and Ambina returned to the village from their rice-field
house. He did some repairs on the house, while his wife went with the
other women in Tsinjorano to pound rice for a funeral in a neighboring
village. We went too. When we got back to the house, he gave us a
formal speech. He said that people were driving him crazy, asking if the
Vazaha were renting his house, but he would never rent a house to visiting
strangers. No one should ever think that we were renting his house, that's
not customary. But if we wanted to give him something—300 FMG, 250
FMG—he would take it. All people—himself black, us white—when their
skin is cut, they bleed alike.

Seeking money, a long-established practice on the coast, intensified
during the colonial period when French officials imposed a wide range
of taxes, while restricting previous means of getting money. They
monopolized trade and prohibited the unregulated cultivation of tobacco, which had served as a cash crop in the past.[14] The head tax
was levied in 1897, when Toquenne established the post at Analalava.
Other taxes, including a house tax, land tax, cattle tax, and goat tax,
came shortly afterwards.[15] These changed in detail, but the head tax
and cattle tax continued to be required in some form until 1972, when
General Gabriel Ramanantsoa, as Madagascar's new president, abolished them.[16] While government officials described their job as a constant search for people they could never find, local people described
the sound of the loud knocking in October (after the notices had been
sent out in June), when the chef du canton or the chef du village started
going door to door, and his words: "Hurry up—collecting money!"
(Malakilaky—mitaky vola!). Malaza's sons emphasized that they even
had to pay for the *carte d'identité*—*karatra vatan'lehilahy* (man's body
card)—used to keep track of their whereabouts.

Two men passed through Andonaka, walking north toward Analalava.
After they left, Amady took out his *carte d'identité* and his *carte mobilier*. He
said, "If you don't have the second stamped '*payé*,' then you are struck
with a fine *(voa lamande)*—3,000 FMG. If you don't have the *timbres fiscaux*

[100 FMG each], then you are also struck with a fine. If you don't have a *carte d'identité,* you are fined. If you don't have the photo in it—a fine." He added that this was also true under the French. Hova go around the countryside taking the photos, 200 FMG each.

The taxes were intended to incite local people to work on cash crops, identified by 1899 as rice, raffia, paka, beeswax, cattle, cattle skins, and coconuts.[17] French officials also promoted new businesses, beginning in 1904–1905 with a rum distillery, a coconut-oil crusher, a soap works using coconut oil, a cord maker using coconut fiber, raffia presses, and a salt works. Toquenne had hopes of turning Analalava into a resort, which never materialized. The salt works reached the height of production in 1908 with almost 1,000 tons of salt per year.[18] None of these industries remained in the 1970s, except for a small sawmill in the south. Generators provided electricity for the Catholic Mission and the C.E.G. district school in Analalava in 1971–1973. The generator, which the government installed to bring water to pumps throughout the town, had quickly broken and had yet to be repaired.

There were eleven raffia presses in Analalava in 1905, the high point of production.[19] But neither raffia nor paka was very profitable compared to coffee, spices, or tobacco, and the price of both fell after the introduction of artificial fibers in international markets in the 1950s.

According to Indian merchants in Analalava, raffia sold for 95 FMG/kilo in the colonial period. It had since fallen to 35 FMG/kilo, so local people did not bother to cultivate it any more. Paka, which used to pay 65 FMG/ kilo during the colonial period, now paid 20–25 FMG/kilo. Commenting that few people grew paka and raffia any more, though they used to be big money crops, one man described how he had gone down to Ambarijeby to collect local produce, and no one bothered to show up; they were all away at a royal service at Andampy. In the 1970s, the factory in Majunga, where paka fiber was made into bags used to export Malagasy produce, had to import almost half of its raw material from Thailand.[20]

Lumbering also became an important industry during the colonial period. Two of the four grass strips that once served as airfields in the Analalava region were located at lumber mills. The other two were built for Analalava and a military base at Andranosamonta in the northern Ambolobozo Peninsula; the Analalava airstrip was the only one still in operation in the 1970s. The area was then so bare of trees that the Malagasy government had instituted reforestation programs, using primarily *Eucalyptus* species. A few small mineral deposits were found in the early years of colonial administration (1899–1901), including bitumen in the region of Antognibe and gypsum at Andranosamonta. The extent of these deposits was never explored and eventually only the limestone on Nosy Lava was actually used to construct the penitentiary there and other government buildings in Analalava.

A French priest, formerly stationed in the area, recalled how a French settler, Flauraud, without help from the colonial government, built the roads connecting Antognibe to Analalava, when he constructed his sawmill at the base of the bay. In the beginning he said, "the Sakalava dug huge camouflaged pits in the road, so Flauraud's trucks would come along and fall right into them, because they didn't want the operation there." Flauraud's sawmill was still operating in the early 1970s. Faralahy was working there to earn a little money when he met his second wife, who lived in a nearby village. Local people never spoke to me about the businesses that failed, or about their forebears' efforts to make them fail. They recalled the past in images of cattle herds that had gradually dwindled in size as people sold animals to raise money for taxes, while other means of raising money were prohibited. We were watching Botra herd the cattle into the pen on the north side of Andonaka, and his brother Amady said:

"That is the wealth of the Malagasy. In the old days before taxes, people used to have two to three thousand cattle. They cost 150 FMG then. Then the French struck *(mamango ny Frantsay)*. Now you don't see one person with a hundred." Malaza described the French as having "enslaved" *[magnidevo]* the Malagasy. He quoted [then-] President Tsiranana ironically as saying, "There are no more ampanjaka in Madagascar, only *ampañarivo* [rich people]."[21]

People in Tsinjorano expressed the same opinion in almost the same terms.

Talking about what foods would be offered at the togny in the middle of the village, AdanDezy's mother said that beef, if available, would be included with the rice. This led her and her husband to comment on how few cattle there were these days. AdanDezy's father said that in the old days, most people had one to two hundred cattle; these days most people had one, two, or three, thirty or forty, one hundred at most. I asked why so few, and he, who was usually quiet, said heatedly, "The French wanted money, wanted money, wanted money. People sold their cattle to raise the money to pay the taxes of the French—the head tax and the cattle tax. The tax on one animal was *telopolo sy krobory [kirobo] efatra* [31 paraty]. How much would that be if there were a hundred?!" On other occasions, people in Tsinjorano commented that the ampanjaka was said to own three to four hundred cattle, while one prominent merchant in Analalava, who specialized in cattle-trading, was said to own six to seven hundred animals. He sold his cattle at the biweekly sale in the inland town of Mandritsara, where the average price was reputed to be 25,000 FMG/animal, compared to 15,000 FMG in Analalava.

At another time, Sefo and Vondro commented that people used to be able to fire the land. When the grass grew back heavy and thick, they got food for their cattle, and the fires also kept the wild pigs down. Now no one dared to use fire; they would be imprisoned. So the cattle have started to die out, while the wild pigs have multiplied. They also said that people in Tsinjorano used to grow tobacco in the precolonial period. The land was good for growing tobacco, even if it was not good for coffee. After the Vazaha came, they were not allowed to grow tobacco any more. If they did, they were imprisoned.

Beyond taxes, people sought money to pay for the services of spirit-mediums, diviners, and other specialists, and also for buying an increasingly wide range of goods: fruit, fish, building materials, and other local resources sold by people in the region; tobacco, coffee, and some manufactured goods sold by itinerant peddlers; and manufactured goods sold in stores, still known by the Swahili term *dokany*.[22] Store-bought goods included cloth and clothing, enamel-ware and other kinds of containers, kerosene, matches, soap, salt, sugar, tinned milk, tinned tomatoes, notebooks, passbooks, suitcases, fishhooks and nylon cord, gunny sacks, batteries, and medicines like Nivaquine and aspirin.

The goods they most commonly traded or sold in the early 1970s were surpluses of rice and manioc, oranges, mangoes, bananas, co-conuts, cattle and goats, chickens, ducks, and *sadôko* (a kind of duck-goose cross), gathered resources like guavas and other wild fruits, fish, raffia, palm leaves, grasses, and other building materials, and hand-made goods, especially woven palm-leaf bags, and sometimes cloth-ing.

Faralahy noted that not everyone around Andonaka cultivated. Some, like a 'Tsimihety,' working for his wife's family in a neigh-boring village, built a *valakira,* where he caught shrimp and traded them inland for rice, or sold them for 95 FMG/*daba.* "People who want rô [or *kabaka,* food accompanying rice in a meal, usually meat] come to them with a daba of rice [about 8 kilos of unhulled rice]. A daba of rice is exchanged for a pile of meat, the amount in the pile varying according to the current price of rice in the market. It has to be about right *(leralerany)* or people won't buy." Such specialties worked because, as a visitor to Andonaka commented on another occasion:

"Rice and rô are rivals. When there's rô, there's no rice; when there's rice, there's no rô. The two never come together."

Nevertheless, as Faralahy's example of his brother-in-law implies, it was mainly people like men in *joloka* marriages, without direct access to rice land except through affines, who specialized to the point of not raising their own rice. Most people, while they willingly sold food to others and occasionally bought food to complement what they had, worked to keep from buying staples. Faralahy brought this up, speak-ing about peanut oil, which then cost 200 FMG/liter (the price of a daba of unhusked rice during the harvest season):

"People don't use oil here—don't know how, stingy. Of those who do, people say, 'They're acting like Vazaha—they don't eat water!' Wealthy people use oil. Sakalava aren't people to eat boughten things. If they eat like that for two or three days, they wail and complain, sad. If you can eat at the end of the month too, then eating money every day doesn't matter. But if not . . . !"

An Indian shopkeeper in Analalava commented on the same behavior from his own perspective:

"You have to talk to people here to get them to buy things. Is it like that in civilized countries? People here are proud *(miavona)*. They walk in. If they don't see what they want first off, they don't discuss, they walk right out again. You have to talk to them. Talk all the time, that is the most important thing."[23]

Despite widespread ideals of self-sufficiency, people in Tsinjorano had to buy rice during the 'hunger months' *(volana mosary)*—March and April—before the new rice was harvested, when the price of a daba of unhusked rice rose from 200 FMG to 250–325 FMG/daba, whether it was bought from others in the area or from merchants in Analalava.

People in neighboring villages traded in small amounts. Most bulk trading was with merchants authorized as *"Receveurs des Produits Locaux."* During the colonial period, many of them had established branch stores *(succursales),* managed by kin, in rural villages; or local Silamo set up shops, which they stocked with goods from 'their Vazaha'—usually an Indian merchant—in Analalava. Some merchants still owned so much local land, employing residents as share-croppers, that they described themselves as 'owning' whole villages. Nevertheless, the number of rural shops had dwindled since independence. Furthermore, their prices—though set by law—tended to be lower for the goods they bought and a fourth to a third higher for those they sold.[24] People in Andonaka dealt mainly with a Merina shopkeeper from Antognibe, who ran a branch store in a nearby village, and a Silamo, to whom they were related through marriage, who worked as an itinerant collector for several Indian merchants in Analalava. People in Tsinjorano dealt mainly with an Indian merchant south of Analalava's central square because his was the closest shop to the place where they usually beached their canoes when they came to the post.

Rural people did some work for money. Women sewed—Malaza paid 500 FMG ($2) for a pair of trousers. Men could occasionally 'make a living' *(mañano viloma)*, or get food, in exchange for helping others with their work. Or they could *mangala journée Somapêche*, making 100 FMG/day on the French and Japanese boats that fished the bay. But apart from Flauraud's sawmill and a few concessions, Analalava was the main place in the region to get day-labor *(mangala journée)* or other work, and it was widely recognized that Analalava did not offer many choices. People living around us in Analalava claimed that prisoners had all the available jobs, but they usually hired prisoners to haul water and weed their gardens. Functionaries and storekeepers said they hired prisoners because they cost less, and they were more reliable. Local people did not want to work; even though they got higher wages, they would not show up regularly.[25]

As indicated in the preceding chapter, people in Tsinjorano and Andonaka contrasted 'growing/tending/nursing crops' *(mitsabo)* and 'working for people' *(miasa amin' olo)*. The work involved in raising crops was inseparable from networks of exchange among kin and affines through which people raised the communities of their descendants. Wage labor—'getting a wage' *(mikarama, mangala karama*, from Swahili *gharama*, expense) or 'getting a day's work' *(mangala journée*, from French *journée de travail*, day's work)—was associated with the work of purchased slaves who worked for others with little benefit to themselves.

Mahasoa expressed this idea when he commented one day that "Tsiranana does not like the ampanjaka because she employs people" *(manarama olo, mikarama)*. [What does that mean?] "To make slaves [of people] *(manao andevo)*. He doesn't like the ampanjaka because she enslaves people."

Followers of the monarchy in the Analalava region did not agree with this judgment. On the contrary, they defined the andevo of the ruler as 'people who agree to serve the ruler' *(olo mañeky manompo ny ampanjaka),* as we shall see in the next chapter. Conversely, they saw the evil spirits that possessed people—spirits like 'Mother Cold' *(Nja-rinintsy),* 'Big Blows' *(Be Hondry)*—as the salaried agents of evil sorcerers, in contrast to the beneficent royal spirits who freely possessed people to return them to proper practices.[26] To appreciate their perspective, we need to look more closely at 'working for people' *(miasa amin' olo).*

MIASA AMIN'OLO: WORKING FOR PEOPLE

Some women in Analalava grew plants in their yards, including greens, onions, sweet potatoes, squash, tomatoes, sugar cane, coconut palms, mint for tea, and flowers. Both men and women had larger gardens in the hills east and south of the post, where they grew manioc, corn, pineapples, special varieties of mangos, and other crops. Because of the land, water, and labor needed to grow rice, almost no one living mainly in Analalava grew their own rice, so they still had the daily expense of buying rice—an average of one kilo (three *kapoka,* a Nestlé can) per person per day, at an average of 20 FMG per kilo of unhusked rice or 35–40 FMG per kilo for husked rice. Having to buy rice, and having to work for people to get the money to pay for it, were the defining features of life at the post even for people who owned their houses.

Local residents explained their coming to live in Analalava in many different ways, all of them having to do with work, often mixing slavery with wage labor. It was in part the contrasting ways that different people came to the post that contributed to the local characterizations of the 'kinds' (karazana), or ethnies, that developed out of precolonial political distinctions during the colonial period—'Merina,' 'Tsimihety,' 'Sakalava,' 'Makoa,' and the like. Most of the highlanders at the northern end of the post, who had been in Ampasikely since the post was created at the turn of the century, had been forcibly relocated like this elderly Merina couple:

The husband, Robert, spoke first. He said his father had lived in Maromandia [northeast of Analalava], where he was a soldier in the

Merina army. He was born there in 1893. When they were conquered by the Vazaha, they escaped to Bealanana [in north-central Madagascar]. "The Vazaha made a whole lot of Hova in Bealanana move to settle in Ampasikely. The Vazaha said, 'Hova live north—Ampasikely—and Sakalava live south—Antanambao.' The Hova weren't allowed to leave Ampasikely, because they didn't want the Hova and Sakalava to mix." His father had been 'some person's slave' *(andevon'olo),* some rich man, a Malagasy, who had bought him to cultivate, to do all kinds of work: "He bought people, then enslaved them" *(mividy olo, magnindevo).* His wife, Marie, then said that her mother was a Betsileo from the Fianarantsoa region. She was out playing, "when people stole me" *(nangalaran'olo).* They took her all around (including Analalava) until she ended up in the Maromandia area where, as a 'person's slave' *(andevon'olo),* she cultivated tobacco.

Robert said that when they first arrived in Ampasikely, there was manioc, but no rice fields. His father had to buy food. People still have to buy food. "Hungry! No food. The French didn't provide any, because they thought people had brought food with them." Abdallah Haschim, a rich merchant who cultivated on Nosy Lava, had a huge warehouse of rice there. There was a fire, and it burned down. He sold the rice, which was only burnt around the edges, in Analalava to the Hova and the Sakalava.

His father became a *canotier* (oarsman) for the Customs Office. His brother became a washerman for Vazaha in Majunga. "He, a man, that was the work he did, for Vazaha. Because there was no other work; that was the only work." Family members were buried all over. He said, "it's customary to bring the bones back, but they don't have the money to do it."[27]

Robert had done clerical work in a government office. Marie did some sewing. People might occasionally fish to make money. There was no land to farm, but some people raised pigs. They had a large garden of fruit trees (bananas, mangos, one breadfruit, fifty coconut palms), and one pig. Other families came to Ampasikely later. Robert mentioned names of people who became teachers, interpreters, and tradespeople during the colonial period. Marie said, "they are all gone now, gone up to Tananarive or out to the countryside to cultivate—searching for money! *(mitady vola)."*

The other Merina families who settled later in Ampasikely or in the northernmost part of the post, had come of their own accord, looking for work in provincial towns during the colonial period. They came mainly from Antananarivo and surrounding areas, and still retained many ties to their kin there, which enabled them more easily to send their children back to school and eventually to the university.

People who identified themselves as Tsimihety and Sihanaka had moved into the area in the past two or three generations to take jobs as teachers, medical workers *(sage femme d'état, infirmier)*, and clerical workers, like Mahasoa's Tsimihety father who had worked as a teacher in Analalava during the late 1950s and early 1960s. One of his father's brothers had come in the late sixties to work as an infirmier in a large village south of Analalava. When Mahasoa visited there, he stayed with his father's brother, helping the infirmier's then pregnant wife with chores, rather than with his mother's kin who also lived there. The day following the night in which his wife gave birth to the baby, the infirmier described the migrations of Tsimihety in terms very like those of French scholars ten years earlier:

"See—the Sakalava are getting squeezed out as the Tsimihety are growing *(mitombo)*. Tsimihety used to be further east, then they moved closer to here *(bosesika aty)*. As the Tsimihety expand, they are pushing the Sakalava toward the sea. Here they have long been mixed. Along the sea, there are still few Tsimihety. Many women come from the east, because women leave their parents to follow men. This is the opposite of Comorians, where the man leaves his family and follows his wife."[28]

People who described themselves as original settlers, 'children of the land' (zanatany) usually identified themselves as 'Sakalava' or 'Makoa.' Zanatany had migrated to the post gradually, and retained their ties to rural villages. Even those who did not return to live in rural villages following independence usually returned there to cultivate during the rainy season.

AdanDezy, passing through Analalava in November after visiting his wife Moana's (Tsimihety) family in a village to the east, commented that his relatives in the yard behind us had already returned to Tsinjorano to cultivate: "Analalava has fewer people during the rainy season because people leave to farm." When I asked about another family, he said they have rice fields, but they are "reluctant to cultivate—they like working for people" *(malaigny mitsabo—tia miasa amin'olo)*. Others used almost the same words in speaking about how some people in the area kept two houses, one in the countryside and another in Analalava, while others lived there all year around. According to Tavavy, "They come to Analalava because they don't know how to work rice, or they don't like to. They marry, or they take in laundry, work in the shops, work for the Vazaha [Indians], whatever, whatever. . . ." I asked AdanDezy how much a person could make working for Indian storekeepers, the main employers, and he responded as others had: "A man makes 3,000 FMG/month (100–125 FMG/day); a woman makes 1,000 FMG/month, or at most 1,500 FMG, washing clothes, ironing, cooking—it's not enough to live *(tsy mahavelo)*." On another occasion, his mother Togny responded to my comment that I'd been working at the post with astonished disbelief: "Work at the post?!" Likewise Matombo, her sister's daughter's husband, whose oldest child was married to a man at the post: "It's a nice place, but there's no work, no [French] companies *(tsisy lacompagnie)*, just Indians there."

The one public protest about wages that occurred during the years we were in Analalava was a notice that appeared in mid-September 1972 at Ambodimanga, tacked to the trunk of one of the mango trees along the main road, opposite the functionaries' offices.

Addressing himself 'to the government,' the writer stated that he had worked for an Indian merchant for ten years, and he still earned 3,000 FMG/month, though he had children and also a wife. He worked from early in the morning until *midi,* then all afternoon until 6:30. He concluded: "It makes us sad" *(Mampalahelo zahay)*. Policemen were sent out to all the stores to question workers on how they felt about their jobs (as they periodically sent in children to check that storekeepers were giving full weights), but salaries remained unchanged.

Women from rural villages also came to the post to look for work, but they were more apt to settle there when they married; and more apt to try to find ways of supporting themselves at the post year-round, even after they had separated, rather than return to cultivate in rural villages. Matombo's daughter, in her early twenties, who already had three children of her own, had come to the post when

she married, had not been back to Tsinjorano for two years, and
thought she would never return. Avoria's daughter, Ampenziky, had
gone to live in Antsohihy when she married. She had since divorced
and returned to Analalava to live, but she too had no intention of
returning, although she had visited recently, wearing very emphatically, her fancy town clothes. Be Moana, the daughter of one of the
brothers from Nosy Lava who had moved to Tsinjorano to cultivate
(owing to their ties with Zanety's first husband, Fig. 9, G), had—like
Tavavy's father's sister—moved to Analalava as a girl some thirty
years ago. She married a Vazaha there, and later, after he returned to
France, continued to support herself by dress-making, sending her
two daughters to Antananarivo to be educated as midwives. Soavita
(Fig. 11, 38) had moved to Analalava a couple of years earlier, after
separating from Sefo. She still kept a house in Tsinjorano, like her
father's sister Diniky (Fig. 11, 36).

Such women who had chosen to settle at the post were more apt
to describe people leaving rural villages for the post, rather than the
other way around. So Tavavy described her father's village, Marosely,
south of Analalava:

"About 80 to 100 people live there. There used to be more, but now a lot
of the houses are empty. People live in places like Analalava. They may go
back to work in the rice fields during the growing season, but they don't
live there the whole year around."

Tavavy had been born and raised in Marosely before coming to
Analalava to stay with her father's sister at age eight. After going to
school there, she married Djoma and was then expecting her second
child. While she was married to Djoma, she did almost no outside
work. By 1981, they had divorced, and she was living alone. While
Djoma and his third wife had all his children, Tavavy was still caring
for one young child by another man, and expecting a second. She had
begun to work like her former mother-in-law, MamanDjoma, and
like most women in Analalava, at a variety of different kinds of jobs:
selling food at the morning and evening markets, washing, ironing

Plate 18. A tinted photograph of MamanDjoma with her first husband and their first child, in formal dress. MamanDjoma kept the picture above the east door of her bed-sitting room, the northern room of her two-room house. The embroidered door curtain says *A ANJARA AMINY ZANAHARY ALA MALAHELO ATSIK* ([Our] Lot with God/Royal Ancestors We Are Free from Sorrow), originally beginning with *ALA. . .* before it frayed and was resewn at the ends (G. Feeley-Harnik, 1972).

and sewing, pounding and winnowing rice. Recently, a Silamo had hired her to run his bar.

MamanDjoma had come to the post from a village on the Komajara Peninsula when she married a Comorian who was stationed in the area as a policeman (Plate 18). Eventually he returned to the Comores, while she remained in his yard in Analalava with their young children. When we knew her, she still had two young children from a subsequent marriage living at home—a boy about twelve, and a girl about seven. Djoma and Tavavy had just moved into the second house in the yard. Her son

Abodo, then about seventeen, had not slept at home for a couple of years, but he still stopped off there to cook for himself in the kitchen.

MamanDjoma did some washing, ironing, and sewing for neighbors (including for us). She charged less than the going rates to get more customers (150 FMG/dress rather than 300 FMG, 125 FMG for a blouse or 150 FMG, if the material was thin and slippery). She made most of her money by selling produce and cooked food. She had two gardens—in her yard and outside the post. But in contrast to some women who grew food to sell, she specialized mainly in greens bought from rural traders, cooked meat and fish, and occasionally cooked breads. For example, she bought large *bika* (*Mugil robustus,* mullet) for 25 FMG each, cut them in half and sold each half for 20 FMG/each, but had to reckon with the cost of oil and salt, and the possibility that some might not sell. If she sold in the bazaar, she had to pay 20 FMG/day, so she also sold from the porch in her yard "to friends who might not have gotten meat at the bazaar." Regardless of what she was selling, she calculated her profits by trying to ask at least double her monetary costs. Djoma also helped her with occasional gifts (Plates 19-21).

Plate 19. MamanDjoma making breads to sell at the market, while her daughter Soa looks on (G. Feeley-Harnik, 1972).

Plate 20. Djoma at the window of his workshop in Analalava (A. Harnik, 1972).

In 1981, buying raw fish and selling them dried or cooked was MamanDjoma's main way of making a living. Her daughter Sikina had returned from Diégo-Suarez, after her husband had gone home to the Comores. Sikina had moved back into her house in her father's yard, which she had lent temporarily to Djoma, her younger brother. Djoma and his third wife had moved to a house in the same quarter. His wife had inherited the house from her mother, a Sambarivo from the Mahabo, who lived in Analalava during the rainy season when her children were going to school, also trading to make ends meet. MamanDjoma had moved her house from her daughter's yard to a place in the southwesternmost quarter, close to where most of the fishermen landed. Now Sikina helped her more than her grown sons, perhaps because they, unlike their sister who was childless, had several young children. MamanDjoma said, "She buys rice, gives me half and keeps half for herself; buys soap, gives some to me, buys cloth on credit, gives me some. My daughter gave me that cloth I was wearing this afternoon. She loves me" *(Tia zaho)*.

Plate 21. Tavavy nursing her second child in her husband's sister's courtyard, which she shares with her mother-in-law in Analalava (G. Feeley-Harnik, 1973).

A few women who could afford the license (some seven to ten during the time we were there) ran small restaurants *(hotely)* along the main road.

When we first met Laza Be, her hotely was a rented room in the former store-home of Indian shopkeepers who had moved to Antsohihy, leaving their building in the hands of kin who remained in Analalava. She later closed and reopened her hotely in three different Indian-owned storefronts on the main street, living all the while in a small house in the southeastern quarter of the post, where she served the ampanjaka as a laundress. Like most people in the town, except some storekeepers who had stoves that ran on bottled gas, she cooked on charcoal burners *(fatampera)*. She sold rice, with and without rô, by the half and full plate, tea and coffee, at prices ranging in 1971–1973 and still in 1981 from 30 FMG for a half-plate of dry rice to 100 FMG for a full plate with fish, or 130 FMG with "meat" (chicken or beef), and tea and coffee, with or without sugar, at 15 FMG (25 FMG with condensed milk) and 25 FMG (30 FMG with milk) respectively. Her sister Somizy, and kinswoman MamanDjoma, occasionally worked at her hotely during the earlier part of our stay to earn money. Her mother and another sister, Asara, came up periodically from their *tanindrazaña* south of Analalava, where they still farmed, usually after they had attended royal services at the Doany, which was already half-way to Analalava. They brought coconuts to sell. All the women worked to remove the coconut meat from the shell. Somizy then took it to Antsohihy to sell. Asara stayed on a while to make a little money by selling food, then returned south with their mother. She later sent her daughter to stay with Laza Be, then Somizy, while she went to school in Analalava.

Somizy opened a hotely of her own a couple of months after we arrived, while MamanDjoma started selling food from her home and in the bazaar. Somizy moved the location of her hotely once again while we were there, because her new spouse had helped her to finance a better location closer to the center of town. When it was rumored that the South African government was going to build a supertanker port at the base of the bay (a plan that was cancelled after the government changed hands), she wanted to move down there where she could make money from the workers. As she pointed out several times: "There is nothing here—no food, no customers," but she was also afraid to go to the proposed site on the Komajara Peninsula, because she did not already know people there. After we left, she moved to Nosy Be to live with a husband whom she eventually left because he drank too much. In 1981, she had returned to Analalava and opened a new hotely on the southern edge of town. She said it was a poor location, since she was too far out for people to return after going into town to sell their goods, so she planned to move in toward the center as soon as a place opened up.

Searching was supposed to end when a person found wealth and a 'friend,' wealth *in* marriage, and returned to root that fertile seed in ancestral ground. In practice, it never ended. People moved from rural villages into the post, because they had to supplement subsistence farming with some form of wage labor. They returned to the countryside, because there was never enough work as day laborers, seamstresses, or small traders to support them at the post year-round. Furthermore, searching worked out differently for men and women. While men usually returned to their ancestral land (usually their father's land) to farm, women were more apt to try to stay in town, marrying or staying there after they separated. So villages, organized in principle around households headed by men, drew more men back to them, while the post—where local people occupied the position of children of women—tended in practice to be organized around households headed by women.

MANGALA HAVANA: GETTING KIN

When people came from the surrounding farming villages to the post to sell produce, get medicines, see the doctor or the midwives, put their children in school, or simply walk around *(mitsangatsangana)*, they sometimes bought food, but they did not pay rent. They stayed with their kin, who—because there was little work for men—were usually their sisters and daughters. Besides finding kin who were already known to be in particular places, people who were searching were always trying to 'get kin' *(mangala havana)*, ultimately a spouse. Women's houses at the post, and their hotely along the main street, were the central locations where these new ties to kin and new friendships, some of which became marriages, were formed.

Residents of Analalava maintained themselves as 'people with kin' *(olo misy havana)* by constantly renewing the sometimes far-flung connections they already had, especially to their parents' natal villages. The main way to keep from 'loosing' or becoming 'lost' (very) to kin after moving away from ancestral land was to continue participating in networks of exchange involving work, hospitality, letters, money and other gifts, and especially children. People in Analalava also 'got kin' by creating personal ties, through whatever common relationship of descent or affinity they could find, to people with whom they had already become friendly.

Commenting that there were as many kinds (karazana) of Comorians as there were Sakalava, MamanDjoma said that when people meet, they ask "What is your kind?" (Ino karazanao?) If it is the same, then you know you are kin. I said I would like to learn more about her family. She said "yes, when there's more time." But later when I brought it up again, she was embarrassed that she could not remember all her kin beyond her grandparents' generation. [She was embarrassed because short genealogies suggested that people had formerly been slaves, but in fact most people in the area did not recall ancestors beyond their great-grandparents' generation.] She said her mother was a "Tsimihety from inland." Her grandfather (MF) was "a really important man, Zaman Karoka. He was living southwest of Analalava, when he got very sick, went to the hospital at Majunga, and was told there was nothing to do about it, so he returned to his ancestral land in the Antsohihy area, where he died almost right away. He was a rich man. Forty cattle were killed at his funeral." Her mother's father kept a big book of his ancestors, but it was with his descendants there now. She had often wished they had the book. "For example, if a man in the family sees a girl, you can look in the book to find out if they are related or not.[29] But Djoma got married without that." When I suggested that they could get the book, she said they were too far away, they were not really in touch with them.

Her mother's father was one of three brothers, Tsimihety from the Mandritsara area [there were sisters, but she didn't know them]. "They were descendants of a Zafinifotsy ruler who was so cruel that he took the best children in the place and fed them to his crocodiles, which he kept in a huge pit. Finally he got too cruel, and his slaves—the Tsimihety—killed him." The brothers migrated from inland to different parts of the coast— the Nosy Be area, the Antsohihy area, and the Antognibe area—in the course of searching. Her mother's father settled in the Antsohihy area, where he married a local Tsimihety woman, then moved to the Komajara

Peninsula, where he farmed and raised cattle. [Why did he go there?] "Searching" *(Mitady)*.

MamanDjoma's mother finally settled in Analalava in the course of her marriages. She had taught her children their ancestral prohibitions *(fadindrazaña)*, for example, their prohibited day—Thursday—so that they would not be "lost to the ancestors *(very razaña)* and become like the people around us." MamanDjoma concluded: "Our kin are many, many! In Diégo, Nosy Be, Antsohihy, Ankerika. Those kin over east of here [in the Antsohihy area] kept saying, 'Come over, come over. Copy the book!' And I kept telling my sons to go do it, because they know how to write. But they wouldn't and wouldn't. And now the old man there [her MF] is dead. And here they are, as if they were lost to their ancestors, lost *(karaha very razana, very)!* They don't know how to say the names of their own ancestors, how to say 'brought . . . brought . . . brought . . .' *(ndesigny . . . ndesigny . . . ndesigny . . .).*[30]

MamanDjoma and Laza Be had discovered they were kin through their mothers. Laza Be called MamanDjoma's mother Mama Be. They met in Analalava when Laza Be married here, and MamanDjoma was just married and didn't know anything about her kin. They got to talking about their kin, and found that they were both descended from the same *dady* (lineal and collateral female kin in and above the second ascending generation) who had given birth to MamanDjoma's mother's mother and thus were children of sisters. Laza Be's kin had settled in the Antognibe area. MamanDjoma's mother and Laza Be's mother then talked and confirmed that they were related. Since then, "The two families can't intermarry—it would be incestuous *(manamtambo)*. When we invoke the ancestors, we say all the same names."

Later, when I returned in 1981 and asked MamanDjoma again about her ancestry, she asked me in turn if I knew about 'eight ancestors' *(valo razana)*. She then answered by listing them, beginning with the ones she had told me about earlier, but then going on to name several more. In other words, when one person asked another, "What is your kind?" *(Ino karazanao?)*, to find out whether they might be akin to one another, they had the option of choosing among what was, in all the cases I learned about, a wide range of alternatives.

While MamanDjoma's experience shows how people 'got kin' and marked them as such by invoking ancestral names and declaring marriages between them to be incestuous, Tavavy's experience shows how people separated themselves from those they knew to be kin.

MamanDjoma had married an immigrant from the Comores. Most marriages between Muslims and non-Muslims in the area were between men who were second or third generation descendants of Muslim immigrants to the area, who still called themselves Silamo after their forebears married local women, and the daughters of such unions or converts to Islam, who were called Kisilamo (Little Muslim), if they were called Muslim at all. Because it was much more common for local women to marry into Silamo families rather than local men, Silamo and Kisilamo were sometimes used to differentiate men from women as well as 'true Muslims' from 'Malagasy Muslims.'[31] Tavavy was the child of a third generation descendant of a Silamo immigrant who married a local Kisilamo woman. In fact, MamanDjoma said she had chosen Tavavy to be her son's wife precisely because she was Silamo. In contrast to MamanDjoma who talked mainly of her mother's kin,[32] Tavavy talked only of her father's kin. She claimed not to know any of her mother's kin because her mother had died when she was little. Unlike MamanDjoma's 'Tsimihety' mother, through whom she was linked to Zaman Karoaka and to Zafinifotsy royalty, Tavavy's mother's kin had been slaves—not royal slaves (Sambarivo), like Malaza (her FMB), but Makoa, ordinary slaves, to whom she, like other branches of her family, sought to deny any connection. This came out accidentally when I asked if all her father's wives had been Sakalava. "Yes." [Why didn't he marry Silamo?] "Because they were all his kin, all those in the village where he lived and in the neighboring villages." [Then you are related to the head of a family that distinguished itself among the Silamo as being Arabo?] "Yes, he is my mother's brother. He is Silamo, but he gets Sakalava on his mother's side too." [What about the Y, another Arabo family?] "Yes, they are also kin." With an embarrassed laugh, she said "We're dirty *(maloto)*. They don't like to recognize the relationship with Makoa, people below them. They have straight hair. It's like people who have things are liked by everyone. People who don't have things aren't liked by anyone."

MAHAZO DRAKO ANAO! YOU'VE GOT A FRIEND!

When we first came to Analalava, we got to know Laza Be, whose hotely was in the next room of the storefront where the *maire* had found us a room to rent. Knowing we planned to move from there to a house in one of the southwestern quarters, Laza Be introduced us to her sister, MamanDjoma. In the beginning, when MamanDjoma and I were walking some place together, I would hear other women calling out to her, *'Mahazo drako anao!*, You've got a friend!'[33] In fact, people also searched by trying to 'get kin' who were decidedly not kin, namely, 'friends' *(jirany, drako, namana, [ampi]kamarady, sakaiza)*, that is, people who were like kin in giving without immediately expecting something in return, but explicitly not kin. As Tavavy put it, contrasting proper friendship with the apparent friendship of the woman who later robbed me: "One day you need a paraty [5 FMG piece] to buy some matches, your friend lends it to you. You don't ask too often like Be Moana—that's just work *(asa foana)*."

Usually friends addressed one another in just these terms: to women—*Drako ô! Lakely ô! Jirany é! Somo ô!*; to men—*Oa Zalahy é!* Kin terms like *Njariko* (My mother), or affinal terms like *Rañao* (Sibling-in-law), were used 'simply to show respect' *(ndesigny foño fañajaña)*, as various people emphasized, but not because friends were 'real kin' *(tena havana)*.

Apart from exchanging food and cooking together *(mandoky drako)*, one of the most important expressions of friendship was spirit possession meetings. Women held spirit possession meetings together with friends and the spirits themselves expressed many important characteristics of friends and many important values associated with relations between friends. As MamanDjoma herself said:

"If you have kin possessed by a royal spirit, and you want to go to someone to bring the spirit out *(mampiboaka tromba)*, you go to a friend— *jirany*. People fear going to people they don't know. If they are not familiar with them *(zatra an-teña)*, they are afraid, whether they are strangers or whether they are masters of the place. People who clap [to bring out] royal spirits are mutual friends, not kin to one another" *(ampijirany, tsy ampihavaña)*.

The royal spirits themselves were constantly compared to living people in their likes and dislikes. The immediate purpose of a meeting was usually curing, bringing life, fruitful unions between the spirit and its host and among other spirits and their hosts, out of the deadly illness caused by not knowing the identity of the 'stranger' (vahiny) who possessed the person. In fact, successful cures established a 'marriage' between the spirit and its host, formerly lethal strangers. Most cures involved 'bringing the spirit out' into the company of others, who assembled to praise the spirit and present him (almost always him) with gifts, which he would then return to them. For this, the spirit's own 'friends' had to be present, or he would become sad and angry, refusing to appear and declare his identity. The importance for spirits of having their friends around them was apparent even to young men who were usually much less informed about such things than their sisters. So Mahasoa explained—when his mother's younger sister's husband became possessed—why there were two other royal spirits present in him at the same time, besides the angry one who had first made him sick.

"The royal spirit probably called them. With bad spirits, there is only one, but with angry spirits [that is, good royal spirits who are angry at not being recognized], often there have to be friends, probably because they see that their friend is sad, so they come. They are kind of like lightening, because they don't come singly. Accompanying the big one there are always lots of little ones. They pair up *(mikambana)*."

Meetings might be held for other purposes—to cleanse a spirit, to announce some change in the life of its medium. Very often they were held simply because the spirit wanted to get together with its friends or make some announcement to its followers. In this, they were like their 'grandchild,' the living ruler, whom Laza Be described as living in her quarter "surrounded by her friends" *(drako)*. In fact, the emphasis on friendship in *tromba* gatherings for royal spirits may be another way of expressing not only the importance of friends as sources of support, but also the suspicion of kin who—in the case of royalty—are explicitly excluded from the compound of the living ruler.

Spirits were also like friends—friends who might turn out to be distant kin—in coming from all over. The majority of spirits who possessed people—mainly women—at the post were not the living ruler's immediate ancestors, buried on Nosy Lava just off the coast. They were spirits who came from many different distant places, mainly in the Mahajanga area and further south. And ultimately, they were descended from strangers who had come to Madagascar from abroad.

TSY AZO MIÔVA VAZAHA! TURNING EUROPEAN IS NOT ALLOWED!

The celebration of people from far away places coming together in friendship in spirit possession meetings was in keeping with the outward, as well as inward, orientation of the post. Global hierarchies had assumed local forms in the course of their reproduction there. Like MamanDjoma, these immigrants from the peripheries of South Asia, China, Europe, and the West Indian Ocean also anguished about becoming 'lost' to their kin. One Indian storekeeper described how a formerly wealthy merchant, having married locally, had become a poor trader in fresh-water shrimp. No longer financially able to return to his homeland, he would become "lost in Madagascar." "Manioc is already entering his stomach!" he repeated as he told the story.

All of the shopkeepers retained ties to kin elsewhere in Madagascar and abroad. One Indian family had relatives in Bombay, but also in Lourenço Marques (as they still called Maputo, Mozambique), in Leopoldville, Kinshasa (Zaire), Mombasa in Kenya, Egypt, and Canada, where one of their sons later emigrated. Another family had close ties with kin in Bombay, France, and Belgium. The Chinese shopkeeper and his wife corresponded with kin in Taiwan, Honolulu, Toronto, and Columbus, Ohio, while Silamo retained ties to kin in the Comores, Zanzibar, and the Gulf states. Meanwhile they continued to cook and speak in their own languages—Swahili, Gujarati, Hindi, Chinese, and Greek. The government functionaries, though no longer French, were mostly from other parts of Madagascar, to which they too retained their ties, as expressed in the dialects they spoke and the special regional 'customs' *(fomba)* they publicly observed (Plate 22).

In coming to the post, people with their roots in the countryside were searching outwards along the broader networks of connections that presented themselves there. Young women, starting in school, kept 'friendship books' *(livres d'amitié)*, notebooks in which they had pasted postcards, letters and photographs from their friends (mostly

Plate 22. The girl's dance group of the *Société Paraty Dimy* (Five *Paraty* Society, after the money paid to join), led by the *imam* of the Friday Mosque, a flute *(anjomary)* player, and the group's leader (a well-known spirit-medium), making their entrance at an entertainment for visiting government officials in Analalava in 1973 (A. Harnik).

other girls, but sometimes boys), songs in French and English, drawings, and magazine pictures.[34] People used the postcards, photographs, and letters they received from elsewhere to decorate the walls of their houses. One woman, converted to Catholicism, framed the photographs of distant kin, together with their letters and birth and death dates. Decorations in sitting rooms, where spirit possession meetings were held, consisted of calendar, newspaper, and magazine pictures of exotic people and places, and sometimes the boxes that cigarettes and medicines came in. One especially wide-ranging group in 1972 included magazine photographs of Roman ruins, a classical Greek vase, the American pop singer Junior Wells, a gilded head from Tutankhamen's tomb, and a French calendar pin-up.

Internationalism flourished in the popular sayings printed on body wraps—for example, *Ah chérie aza kivy zaho mbola ho avy,* "Ah, darling, don't be heartsick, I'm coming"—and in the love letters of young men, written in Merina, using French and English words and phrases.[35] Women gave their hotely inviting names, like *Karibo Jirany* (Come In Friend) and *Fanantenana* (Hope/Expectation [of good fortune, of meeting]), and these too could have an international character. Shortly after becoming 'one house' with a sailor from Nosy Be, Somizy changed the name of her hotely from *Marodady* (Many Grandmothers)—which her friend had earlier explained to us as *Hotely Luxe*—to *Marodady It is Very Nice.* Somizy said that her friend, who sailed between Mahajanga and Nosy Be, had thought of the idea. "He is always studying, always has a little book in his hand, teaching himself English," though she was not sure if he had yet been to England or America.

This exuberant openness had controversial limits, which we heard about most bluntly through the indirect statements of older men, many of whom had fought in Europe, the Middle East, and Africa during the First and Second World Wars. AdanDezy's father, Mainty Be (Fig. 9, E; Fig. 10) had spent some three years in Paris, Marseilles, Aleppo, and elsewhere in the Middle East, and also in Djibouti. Taodraza, a Sambarivo from the Mahabo, had been in Paris, then Bordeaux, Les Eyzies, and Marseilles.[36] AdanDezy's mother's brother, Saha Ambary (Fig. 9, C), who was taking us up to Tsinjorano in his canoe, had picked up two other men traveling north. Probably because he was going to Tsinjorano to persuade his kin to give him money to get his new wife, they got into a conversation about getting spouses. One of the men was brother of the elderly woman, formerly married to a Vazaha, who had recently been robbed. He talked about how his daughter had moved away when she married, and recently had taken to wearing *pantalon* even though he had told her, as he said in a slightly louder voice, "Turning Vazaha is not allowed!" *(Tsy azo miôva Vazaha!)*

Other limits, imposed from without, led to bitterness and disillusionment. Seeking *(mitady, mitady hariaña)* was not just a matter of making one's fortune through a broad range of amicable relationships with various people, and finally finding wealth and companionship united in marriage. People sought to find their 'lot in life' (*mitady anjara*), which could only be discovered in forming close paired relationships with others. As Be Moana said to me toward the beginning of our own friendship:

"It is not good to make too many friends. Too many friends is bad. It's good to have one close friend, while knowing some other people. I have just a few close friends, the people in my yard and a few others."

Since Be Moana had initiated our friendship so she could later steal from me, her remarks were probably already intended toward that end. Nevertheless, most people we came to know during our stay in the region maintained their closest relationships with only a couple of people. Had I not been so absorbed in challenges to 'friendship' from my own perspective, I might have thought to ask more about how people in the Analalava region found their personal destinies through intensely close relationships with 'strangers' as well as with kin. Without my asking, the paradoxical combination of opposites in friendship came out most prescriptively in the ways that people evaluated individuals and pairs of persons or things over a wide range of contexts. Intense closeness with difference confirmed the truth of both partners, fulfilling each through the other, against the constant threat of reversal.

For example, on the morning of a circumcision, the boy's mother's brother is expected to arrive and wait outside the boy's village, where the circumcision is done. He then orders two older boys to tell the boy's father that he has arrived. They carry a flag, a body-wrap attached to a stick. As AdanDezy explained, "Two boys are sent because you can't trust just one. With two there are no lies, one is the *témoin* ['witness,' another French loanword] of the other. Then the mother's brother comes parading along by himself afterwards, strutting proudly, taking his ease, wiping his face with a cloth [like a colonial official], followed by the crowds of people."

Several kinds of medicine came in pairs. Concerning kinds used to catch fish, Bezara in Tsinjorano (Fig. 9, F29) said: "There are two of them. It's necessary to get both. One cannot be separated from the other; they are like a married couple *(fivadiaña)*. If you take one and not the other, the medicine doesn't work *(tsy masina ley aody)*." Many medicines were made of pairs of ingredients—two, four, or six (but not eight, associated with royalty) leaves or pieces of wood. Growth medicines in particular required pairs of people for their creation. For example, the *sodifafaña* leaves used to make *aody be* (growth medicine) for premature and sickly babies had to be pounded in the rice mortar by two people simultaneously, not alternately as when pounding rice.[37] Twins were thought to have healing properties, conveyed through their hands. In general, any observances concerning growth or the regeneration of new life required the leadership of a person, or pair of people both of whose parents were still living.

When royal spirits possessed someone, their kin and friends tried to begin the process of bringing them out in the first month of the royal lunar new year, *fanjava mitsaka*. Like Malaza, who still had work to do on his sister Bevaoko's togny, they planned to continue and ideally complete the work in the third month, *asara be*, with which fanjava mitsaka is paired. Conversely, odd numbers of anything were avoided on the grounds that they were 'incomplete' *(tsy ampy isaka)*, but this was especially true in royal service.

The two closest kinds of companionship—blood friendship and marriage—illustrate the complexities involved in people's attempts to realize these contradictory unions in their daily lives.

FATIDRA: BLOOD FRIENDS

As Bezara's relationship with Leroa (his MZHB) in Tsinjorano shows, affines could make their relationship closer by binding it in blood *(fatidra)*.[38] Early accounts indicate that blood friendships have long been an important feature of social relations in western Madagascar, although they also suggest differences of opinion concerning how and why they were made. For Noël, the French consular agent in Nosy Be during the early 1840s, fatidra was "the most remarkable custom among the Sakalava . . . without contradiction," even compared to their unusual practice of judging their kings after death through praise names. Noël went on to explain how fatidra was done with a mixture of fresh and salt water. In concluding, he noted that people who betray fatidra will not prosper. The partners are considered to be so close that when one dies, the other will die soon after.[39] According to Richardson, who prepared his islandwide dictionary for the London Missionary Society in the 1880s, fatidra, "a mutual and solemn pledge of friendship or brotherhood," was "performed by each party partaking of a small piece of liver, etc., mixed with the blood of the other party." He therefore explained the term as a combination of *fatitra* (incision of the skin so as to draw blood) + *ra* (blood). Nevertheless, "there are natives who contend that the above words as given in the original dictionary are really derived from *fatotra* [bound, confined, fettered, enchained], which constant use has changed to *fatitra*.[40]

Rare historical descriptions of actual fatidra relationships in western Madagascar suggest something of the circumstances in which differences about the practice and significance of fatidra developed. George Herbert Smith, a missionary from the Society for the Promotion of Christian Knowledge, heard about fatidra at the beginning of his travels among Sakalava royal followers in the southern domain of Menabe during the 1890s: "This covenant gives an absolute guarantee for safety and assistance from the king or chief with whom it is made." Thinking that fatidra might be advisable for himself, he spoke to one of the local Christian converts (nearly all of whom were Makoa, former slaves) to see what he thought about the idea. The Christian condemned the practice as idolatry, saying that the covenant rested on the sanctity of the *hazomanga* [an ancestral shrine] where idolatrous ceremonies were held. "Besides this," said he, "it is not a ceremony for a Christian, for to seek for a bond of union by drinking another man's blood is to make light of the Blood of Christ, which is our bond of union." Smith thereupon abandoned the idea, but was assured by the same man that "an exchange of gifts, in the presence of the people, would be accepted as an equivalent to the *'fato-dra'*."[41]

Gardenier, an ethnographer working among followers of southern Sakalava royalty in the Besalampy area in the 1970s, confirms the importance of fatidra there. He found that almost every adult had one or more such ties, cross-cutting gender, locality, and ethnicity. He attributed the high frequency of fatidra relationships to "the geographic mobility of the Sakalava and their mistrust of non-relatives. . . . For instance, while traveling around one may want to spend the night in a village where one had no close relatives. In that case it would be advantageous to have a blood sibling on whom one could count for a hospitable reception, a meal and a place to sleep. It is especially with this in mind that these relationships are entered into."[42]

According to Gardenier, fatidra, which he translates as "blood siblings," were as close as siblings. Siblings might come to mistrust one another in the course of disputes over inheritance and the like. But with fatidra, "no conflict is likely to arise and their relationship tends to remain pure and trusting." Violations of that trust were considered to be so serious that participants "can, and do, put full trust in each other." The relationship extended, in principle, to encompass all the participants' kin; but in practice, "ties of blood siblingship are primarily meaningful to the immediate partners involved."[43] Like siblings, fatidra could not marry, nor should any of their kin.

In the Analalava region in the 1970s, fatidra relations were similarly widespread and binding, but more hierarchical. Even people who saw one another as siblings, used 'Older' *(Zoky)* and 'Younger' *(Zandry)* in addressing their partners, just as they did with the siblings who were their kin. Friends more different in age formed fatidra as if they were parents and children, or grandparents and grandchildren, using these terms of address.

Like other strangers, I learned about fatidra in part through personal experience. In Andonaka, Malaza advised us to introduce ourselves to his friends as his fatidra (although we were not), in order that they would trust us. In Tsinjorano, one of the first questions people asked me was, 'Is your spouse AdanDezy's fatidra? If he is, can I become fatidra with you?' One of AdanDezy's kinsmen asked us for money AdanDezy owed him, saying that AdanDezy had told him that all he had to do was ask his fatidra. We said then and on other occasions that we were not fatidra, just *kamarady*. Seeing that the Vazaha clearly considered kin to be more basic than friends, AdanDezy's father responded to our words with a formal speech, explaining to us that kamarady, for Malagasy, were *havana*, or kin. So we all tried to control the nature of our exchanges by imposing our own terms for our 'friends' and our own definitions of what they meant.

Muslim immigrants to the Analalava region may have experienced similar differences of opinion concerning the significance of *jirany*. People I knew in the Analalava region, described jirany not as fatidra, but as friends *(namana, sakaiza)*, especially a woman's female friends, though jirany could become fatidra if they wanted. Yet, judging by Gueunier's ethnographic research in Mahajanga during the late 1970s, the word meant much more to Comorians. According to what Gueunier told me in 1981,

Comorians in Mahajanga "have a custom called *jirany*, meaning *voisin* [neighbor]." When they travel in the Comores, they ally themselves with other Comorians in a relationship of jirany. A person can ask his or her jirany for anything, from an amount of sugar to any other kind of assistance, without having to pay. When they came to Madagascar, they developed these ties with Malagasy families. Every Comorian family had a Malagasy family as a jirany. The "massacre in Mahajanga" [in 1977, riots against Comorians, in which over 1,000 people died] was so terrible, not simply because so many people were killed, but because the custom of jirany was shown to be totally valueless. There were some very moving stories of times when the jirany saved their people. But for the most part they did not. Gueunier noted that some observers attributed the riots to outside agitators, but others saw them as originating in local political-economic relations, in which Vazaha and Indians were the capitalists, highlanders were the *cadre* or managers, and Comorians and coastal people—*Betsirebaka* [a name given to a heterogeneous group of people from diverse places along the west coast and inland]—were the workers, *proletariat* and *sous-proletariat* respectively. An official review of factories in the area had led to some improvements in Comorians' working conditions. This intensified the already bitter competition between Comorians and coastal people for the lowest paying jobs, and perhaps led highlanders to encourage violence against Comorians to keep them from entering the cadre, as they appeared to be doing. The violence may also have been exacerbated by divisions within the Comorian community, which were deeply rooted in the complex political history of the Comores.[44]

Thus, blood ties, while appearing to be islands of stable predictability in relations with strangers, were sociolinguistically and historically diverse phenomena, with uncertain consequences in practice. As people in the Analalava region saw it, there was always the possibility that they might 'turn' *(mivadiky)*, as illustrated in the relationship between MamanDjoma and the fatidra of her oldest daughter, Sikina.

MamanDjoma's *Zoky* (Elder Sibling), as she addressed him, arrived from Antsohihy in mid-January 1973. I asked why he had come to Analalava. "To search. He is searching for money, selling grasses, medicines" *(Mitady. Mitady vola izy, mandafo ravin'ahitry, fanafody).* [Is he havana?] MamanDjoma said yes, he was a fatidra of her daughter, Sikina, living in Diégo, a Tsimihety. He had been a prisoner on Nosy Lava, when her husband was stationed there as a policeman. He did work for them, various little things, came over to the house a lot. "We gave him a little food, tea. One day, he came and said he wanted to be fatidra [with Sikina], so she would be his sister. So they did fatidra. They can't marry one another, down to the children of their grandchildren and beyond, until people no longer know the tantara [history], no longer realize that they are fatidra. As long as they know, they cannot marry."

MamanDjoma said, "If a fatidra comes like that and asks for lodging or food, you have to give it to him. To go back on fatidra *(mamadiky fatidra)* is very bad. For example, if the one comes asking for something and the other yells back [demonstrating], 'I don't have anything!' Going back [on such an oath] is like committing sorcery, murder *(mamadiky—mamoriky, mamono).* God sees it and brings badness *(haratiaña)* on such a person. Difficult! *(Sarotro!)* Fatidra is difficult! That's why fatidra is so important with Malagasy, because it is so difficult." [Don't kin and affines go back?] "Yes, for example, if your husband says something bad to you, you can answer back *(mamaly),* because he turned *(mamadiky).* But not with fatidra. When Sikina did fatidra with this man, everything was written down: She has this mother and this father, and they have these children, and this person and that person lives here, lives there, and so on. And her name. So it is all written down in his notebook. Fatidra are like kin (havana)." She said that several times. Alan asked if it was good to do fatidra, given how difficult it was, and her daughter-in-law Tavavy quickly responded, "[You] get kin!" *(Mangala havana!)* In response to further questions, they both asserted that kinds of people (karazana) did not matter in fatidra— "Anyone can do it" *(Zay olo mañano).*[45]

Two days later, MamanDjoma spoke to her fatidra about how his "son," who was also staying with them, had stolen something, taking the same opportunity to tell him that he was not doing his share of work like a proper guest. Seeing him through the fence as he was coming along the path, she whispered to Tavavy, 'Mangorohoro!' as they referred to him in his absence.[46] When he came in, she immediately asked him to sit down and began her formal speech—"I say . . ." *(Hoy zaho . . .)*—calling him 'My Father' *(Babako)*, while he referred to her as *Mamako*.[47] She said, "We give birth to the body *(vatana)*, but not the mind *(jery)*. . . . Your son has quick fingers *(malakilaky tañana)*." He had taken a package of cigarettes from the daughter of Saha Tsialana to the west, just after she had bought them. The girl followed him back here, but he had already gone, so she spoke to Abodo [her second son]. "She didn't say much *(tsy mijijy)*, just asked, 'Was he here?' 'No.' 'When he comes back, tell him to return what he took.' Then she went home."

MamanDjoma told her fatidra that she was afraid. She had nothing of value in her house, but there were people's things in her son's workshop. If anything there was stolen, he would be locked up for all those losses. People take things and sell them in the countryside. "I am afraid!" *(Atahorako!)*, she repeated several times. "People would ask, 'Who is this person?' And everyone would know he is staying with MamanDjoma. 'What is she doing putting up people like that, in the same yard?' Furthermore, there are the police, many of them now, spies. They are going to come around and ask, 'Why are you sheltering a former prisoner?'"[48]

Having begun to speak very formally, she ended bluntly by saying: "Also, when people stay with someone, they should help out—see rice to be pounded, pound it, see firewood, cut it up. Yet you are up and out in the morning—up, out, up, out, up, out *(foha, roso, foha, roso, foha, roso)*." Her fatidra listened without saying anything. When she finished, he began telling a story about how he had some twenty palm stalks for house-building at 125 FMG each. Shortly afterwards, he and his younger brother moved to another place in Analalava.

Friendship in the Analalava region was rooted in relationships with different kinds of strangers over time—Malagasy (fatidra), Silamo, and perhaps especially Comorians (jirany), and Europeans, especially French (kamarady). Its multiple and not wholly shared meanings were clearly negotiated differently in different situations. People expressed their awareness of the propensity of relationships to turn, or reverse themselves, in talk about 'appearances' *(fizahaña)* as opposed to 'really it' *(teña izy):* pairs of things that looked the same, but in fact were different, looked as if they had identical interests, but were actually opposed. Appearances were a major issue in spirit possession, where the enduring question, throughout the time the spirit was being brought out and even afterwards, was whether the spirit truly possessed the medium or whether 'just the clothes came to rule on her.' Was their relationship a true marriage, as it should be? Was it a 'lie'? Or did they need to 'care for' *(mitaha)* the afflicted person longer to allow the spirit to emerge more clearly?[49]

For people who defined themselves in part by marrying strangers, marriage was like other forms of friendship in being subject to different, often conflicting interpretations. People could marry according to *fombandrazaña* or *fomba vazaha*. In other words, marriages could be contracted through exchanges of money, cattle, and household goods, in forms that were themselves the product of the colonial period, enforceable by laws originating in the colonial period, or they could be 'written' *(soratana)*. Most people married according to ancestral custom in not having their marriages recorded by the government. But the ways in which participants handled the exchanges that constituted marriage still evoked disputes about whether the relationship was 'marriage' or 'deception.'

VAÑAVAÑA TSY MAHAZO RAHA: IF YOU'RE SLOW, YOU WON'T GET THINGS

People in the Analalava region usually distinguished *mitady,* searching for wealth, from *manjengy,* searching especially for a spouse. Yet, perhaps because of the imponderability of who got together with whom and how, or perhaps because of the way in which the closest pairs were thought to complete one another, there was a sense in which searching for a spouse epitomized searching for destiny *(mitady anjara)* in its broadest sense. Richardson's dictionary of 1885 includes the phrase *lany zara,* "used of a number divided by another without any remainder or of a man or woman whom no one wishes to marry." I never heard those words, which would have been a terrible pronouncement. On the contrary, popular wisdom urged even those in the worst circumstances not to lose heart, as in this saying, which MamanDjoma embroidered into her bedspread to celebrate *Bonne*

Plate 23. MamanDjoma's bedspread celebrating the French *Bonne Année:*
"Do Not Renounce Me Sir/Madam [for presuming to advise you] Even If
[You] Act But Do Not Flourish Do Not Be Easily Disheartened Because
[Your] Lot Is Still To Come" (G. Feeley-Harnik 1972).

Année in 1972: "Do Not Renounce [Me] Sir/Madam [for my pre-
sumption in advising you] Even If [You] Act But Do Not Flourish
Do Not Be Easily Disheartened Because [Your] Destiny Is Still To
Come" *(Aza Fadi Tompoko Na Dia Manao Ka Tsy Mambinina Aza
Mora Kivy Fa Mbola Ho Avy Ny Anjara)* (Plate 23).[50]
    The importance of anjara in the creation of marriages was itself a
widely shared idea.

As the wife of one of the Indian shopkeepers said, explaining how her
daughter had rejected a perfect marriage prospect: "It wasn't her anjara."
When finally, and unexpectedly even to herself, the daughter ended up
marrying a dumpy man, with a big stomach, a year younger than herself,
whom she hadn't even wanted to marry at first: "It was clearly her
anjara." [How?] "Some things seem so easy to do, yet they don't get
done. Others, despite difficulties, happen anyway. Anjara."

According to one marriage song sung in the rural villages around
Analalava, 'We're waiting for our destiny still to come eeeeeee!'
(Miambigny anjaranay mbola ho avy eeeeeee!), the most popular song
went like this:

Vañavaña homan-draha, tsy mahazo raha . . . Vañavaña homan-draha, tsy mahazo raha . . .

Slow to eat things, won't get things . . . Slow to eat things, won't get things . . .

These lines were repeated several times, interspersed with individual responses like *Vañavaña eeeeeeee!* (Slow eeeeee!), or *Vañavaña atsika eeeeee!* (We're [all-inclusive] slow eeeee!), or *Vañavaña anao ôôôô!* (You're slow ooooo!), culminating in a chorus of:

Tsy mahazo mañangy!!!!!

Won't get a woman!!!!!

This was followed on one occasion by a man's spoken response to the female singers:

Ndra anao koa vañavaña tsy mahazo lehilahy!

Even you too if you're slow won't get a man!

to which some of the women responded on the next chorus: '[You] won't get liquor eee!' *(tsy homan'toaka eee!),* ending up finally with 'Won't get things!' *(tsy mahazo raha!)*[51]

After first hearing the song, I asked a friend about the word *vaña-vaña,* without mentioning the song. She said:

"*Vañavaña*—a person who doesn't get things *(tsy mahazo raha).*" [Why?] "Doesn't get things *(tsy mahazo).* For example, I say, 'Take this!' You don't take it fast enough, I get it, you sort of let it lie." She started singing the song, '*Vañavaña tsy mahazo raha. Dabidaby*—don't get things.' She put a fan between us and said, "Reach for it!" She was faster, I was *dabidaby, tsy nahazo.* "*Mavitriky* is to be really quick at getting something."

Beyond searching for wealth and getting kin, people searched especially to find a spouse. Many of these searches—perhaps an increasing number as rural villages dwindled in size during the colonial period—led people to the post. AdanDezy met his second wife, Moana, at the house of his sister and brother-in-law who lived next to Moana's brother and sister-in-law in Analalava. Even Kasimo, from a village just north of Tsinjorano, who wanted to marry a kinswoman, a *métisse Arabo* like himself, decided that his village was too small for him to find the right person locally. When he did not find a spouse in Analalava either, he finally 'ordered' *(mañafitra)*—as one of his kins-women put it—the third child of Raschid's second wife (Malaza's daughter), who was then staying in Mahajanga with her older sister. "And when they took too long in coming up here, he went down and got her," she said laughing (Plates 24 and 25).

Men, who planned to resettle in rural villages, searched for a spouse who could become their 'friend in the forest.' But, as the song also indicates, searching for a spouse brought out women as well, whose goals were not invariably the same as those of men. Some, like AdanDezy's wife Moana, married and moved to Tsinjorano to cultivate. Others, like MamanDjoma, Laza Be, and Somizy married people at the post, then continued to live there after they divorced. Still others, like Diniky from Tsinjorano (Fig. 12, 38), kept a house in their ancestral village, but lived most of the time in Analalava, where they were more apt to be able to support themselves until they met their true friend.

MAÑANGY TOVO: GIRLS GROWING INTO WOMEN

Both women and men saw men as living more from work, while women lived more from gifts, especially the gifts they received from men. "Balls make money!" *(Kabojy maniry vola!)*, as Abodo said jokingly, when MamanDjoma said he shouldn't go around in such a tiny pair of shiny stretch shorts.

Another time, she added: "Your character is not good *(tsy tsara ny toetranao)*, going back and forth alongside your mother, alongside your own sisters in shorts like that, with your balls all sticking out." He went off down the path, saying, "But we're Vazaha!" while she turned to me

Plate 24. Friendship in Analalava, sometimes exuberantly multilingual, as in these closing lines of a love letter:

Veloma hoy ilay tsy manadino anao/A bientôt mon Amour/24,000 baisers sur tes joues merveilleuses/Bye-bye my love (May you live says the one who does not forget you/Till soon my Love/24,000 kisses on your wonderful cheeks/Bye-bye my love.) (G. Feeley-Harnik 1981).

Plate 25. Saha Barimaso and second wife Amina in their yard opposite his son's yard (G. Feeley-Harnik, 1981).

and asked if this was really Vazaha custom—"Many people are saying that!"

Women's gifts began with the gifts they received from their lovers, as they grew into womanhood, and continued with the gifts they received from their spouses. The wealth that women from Tsinjorano and other rural villages acquired in moving to the post to 'walk about' *(mitsangatsangana)* was expected to come mainly from such gifts, often called *gadô* (Fr. *cadeau[x]*), not from the small wages *(karama)* they might earn by working, which averaged about two-thirds less than men's wages. In fact, there was some sense that women should not work like men (Plates 26-28).

MamanDjoma was repairing her fence with strips of *sely* bark, helped by 'Big Daughter-in-law,' Tavavy's older sister. She said that when we didn't

Plate 26. Net fisherman returning to Analalava, where people are waiting on the shore to buy his catch (A. Harnik, 1972).

Plate 27. Tavavy's father's sister's daughter Añemboko, Tavavy's first child Meva, and Vanessa in MamanDjoma's yard. The work group included MamanDjoma, Tavavy, and myself, MamanDjoma's adopted son's wife (G. Feeley-Harnik, 1973).

Plate 28. MamanMamoribe with her daughters-in-law and grandchild in Mamoribe's yard (G. Feeley-Harnik, 1972).

come by, she started doing other things. "There is never any loss for work, [I'm] getting like a man" *(manjary lehilehy)*. I asked where the *lehilehy* were, her two sons. She gave me a look and said that Abodo had been there, but left a while ago.[52]

One Malagasy-Indian shopkeeper, whose mother was a descendant of Bemihisatra royalty south of Antognibe, used this association between men and work to explain why women had ruled in the Antognibe area since the introduction of wage labor in the colonial period:

"Doria [older brother] and Anatrona [younger sister] were children of Djerman, the ruler at Morafeno. They had the same mother. Anatrona became ampanjaka after Djerman because she was a woman, had no money. She got the *direction* [French loan word] to make it easier for her

to get money. She got the people *(pon)* for that reason. Avoria of
Antsakoabe was another. She became ampanjaka because she was the
youngest child and a girl. Her three older brothers all had salaries.
Anatrona married a Silamo who stayed in Antsakoabe where he came
from, while she lived and died in Morafeno. She had no children. Doria
had two girls: Fañahy and Anarena. Doria took the oldest girl, Fañahy.
She stayed in Ambarialoha. Anarena was an outside child whom her father
adopted. Her father's sister [Anatrona] took her. When she was just one
and a half years old, Anatrona gave word that Anarena was to get the
direction. Anarena has no children either. Her successor will be her
brother's child [the child of another father's sister's son]. She will take the
child to stay with her."

When a man said, like AdanDezy did: "Getting a woman is difficult/
expensive" *(sarotra mangala mañangy),* he invariably referred to the
cattle, money, and other gifts required to contract a marriage. In exchange for these gifts, including the man's promise to build her a
house, the woman was expected to provide household goods, especially bedding and cooking pots. If the marriage failed in the first year,
the man remained the 'master/owner of the children,' while the
woman was required to return the wealth with which he and his kin
contracted the marriage. If the couple separated after more than a year,
a man could still claim the children and almost always did, but he had
to return the woman's wealth. This obligation evoked the bitterest
differences of opinion. Malaza and Rafotsy's youngest son, Faralahy,
said that he had recently divorced his second wife.[53]

He had paid 1,000 FMG to invoke the ancestors on her father's side; 500
FMG to invoke the ancestors on her mother's side; and a *miletry* of three
cattle (two *tomboay* and one *vantony*) plus 4,000 FMG.[54] He said, "If the
girl is old enough, she makes the terms, like a whorish thing *(raha koetra).*
Then you go to her father. She [his second wife] was bad *(maditra),* so I
sent her home. But it was over a year, so she got to take everything." He
wasn't going to agree, because she hadn't brought any household goods
(entana) the way she was supposed to—a bed, mattress, kitchen
equipment—"not even one thing." He said that everything he has—
buckets, plates—comes from his mother. But his father and older brother
made him return the *miletry,* because his father was "afraid, afraid of the

Vazaha." [Vazaha?] "Government." Later, he added: "There's no point in getting married, because there's no respect *(haja)*. Women don't respect their husbands."

His older brother, Amady, who had divorced several years ago and had yet to remarry, was even more bitter.

"Marriage here is just deception *(mikatramo foño)*, nothing but deception. Because of the *miletry*. Give cattle—three, four, five, six . . . money, the tax on the cattle, 12,500 FMG. Then if a year goes by, it's all theirs, the women. They go home, go get someone else. But if it happens too often, then all the cattle die. They die because men who were struck too hard *(voa loatra)* appeal to their ancestors that this woman should be struck for having hurt them too much. All women can get *miletry,* even if they are old."

Aly, an older man living at the post, an Arabo who came from a village north of Malaza to whom he was related through marriage, made the same argument in talking about work at the post and other ways of getting money:

"Prisoners do all the work. Local people don't work; they get money to buy things by selling the cattle they keep in the countryside. Almost all the people who own cattle are women. Very few are men. Women get them through marriage. Their parents, who receive the cattle, are only caretakers for their daughter. The cattle belong to the daughter. *Volambita* is the name of the engagement, which is a year long.[55] *Taimboraka ny lany*—'What's left is excrement,' since the woman and her family get to keep it. That is what [that phrase] means.[56] It is a signed agreement [enforced by law]."

Mahasoa, in his last year at the C.E.G. school in Analalava, contrasted 'Sakalava' with 'Tsimihety' marriages in the same terms. His 'Sakalava' mother came from a village just east of Andonaka, where she had returned and remarried after separating from his father, a 'Tsimihety' from an inland town, who had been stationed as a teacher in the northern part of the post.

"Expensive cloths *(patribe, setroka lagera, tomboay)* make people separate. The wife says she wants one of those cloths. That's very expensive, might cost a cow. The husband is reluctant. The wife gets mad: 'After all I do? I'm going home!' Sakalava women are really like that, always in competition with other women, about cloths, about things in the house. One has such and such a cloth, the other has to have it too, only better. One has a cast iron bedstead, the other has to have one better. That more than anything is what turns Sakalava women into whores *(mahery mahakoetra mañangy Sakalava)!* Part of it, they like to anger their friends *(hahatezitra namana)*—they want this, that, against this person, that person. That's all that's in their heads. It's not too bad here. It's really bad in the province of Diégo. *Moa!* Ruined land! Land with nothing desirable about it! *(Tany robaka. Tany tsisy raha ilañ'azy!).*"

"Tsimihety aren't like that. When important people lead a household, it's not like that at all. Tsimihety just need things to be strong. The person who marries a Sakalava—all his wealth is ruined, he's destitute. Also his mind is not at rest. His wife will say one thing to his face, then behind his back, she will sleep with other men. It breaks up marriages. What also often breaks up Sakalava marriages is that they are just made, not written in the Tribunal. Sakalava marriages are not strongly rooted *(tsy mafy origny).*"[57]

Women's perspectives on these relationships were altogether different. They had their own visions of deceptive appearances that 'ruined land,' like the song about Zaina, which was popular in rural villages: '[Your] having a lover just looks like marriage.' They condemned the use of 'house-breakers' *(famakitrano)*, medicines effective in breaking close relationships, especially marriages, as being the work of evil people, sorcerers. They noted in several different contexts that some people had 'prohibitions against girls who do not give birth in their house-yards [that is, in marriage]' *(fady tsaiky tsy miteraka am tokotany)*. One of the greatest dangers for a woman in labor was a man who refused to acknowledge a child and thus did not invoke his ancestors to bless the woman and child with a good delivery, in which both came out alive.

MamanDjoma also brought up the phrase, *Taimboraka ny lany,* in talking about "when people marry off a child." But in contrast to Aly, she illustrated it with an example of how men could harm women:

"They [the bride's kin] take the child to the man and give him a formal speech, saying that he must treat the child well. If he beats her, then *taimboraka ny lany*—they will take her back home."[58]

By her own account, mothers were as concerned as fathers to assure that their sons married *mañangy misy jery*—women with discernment, intelligence. At the same time, she made it clear that—as she put it in another context, and as other women reiterated—"A discerning woman, eager for men, should seek money" *(Mañangy misy jery, mazoto lehilahy, tokony hitady vola)*.

I asked MamanDjoma about beauty. She began by speaking about what people looked for in women. "A beautiful face is not what's sought in a woman, but rather her character *(toetran'any)*. When I was looking for a wife for Djoma, I got the Daughter-in-law, because she had a beautiful face, light-skinned. But it's always necessary to look to the mind *(jery)*, even if a woman's hair is wiry, not beautiful. Get a woman with a good mind, and the man likes her kin, then there will be only great joy in their household. If he doesn't like his in-laws, then he will be angry when he sees his wife's younger siblings come into the house to eat. I don't like stinginess with food *(Tsy tia matity sakafo)*."

She said there was no one standard of beauty; different men liked different things in women, all kinds of women. Then she concluded: "It doesn't matter if a girl is beautiful, her husband will always get a woman outside, that is the custom of Malagasy men. It doesn't matter how beautiful she is. Parents look around for the girl. They ask questions about her mind. They talk to people who know her. They confirm that her mind is well seated *(Mahita jerin'any mipetraka tsara)*. They don't want some kind of bandit *(bandibandy)* who is going to run around after she gets married, or who is going to run off with the marriage wealth after a year is up. If it happens before a year is up, then everything can be collected. But if it happens afterwards, [the man's] kin don't dare to get it back. There were people from Ambolobozo here recently getting a woman— Tsengizy's child in Anjiameva. The wealth was 20 or 25,000 FMG and a cow and calf. If more than a year goes by, then the wealth can't be taken back. A girl known to have a bad disposition, no intelligence *(ratsy fanahy, tsisy jery)* would never be married; no one would take her."

In response to my question, she said that what is considered good-looking in men depends on the woman. Then she added: "Now when a girl is growing into a woman *(mañangy mitovo)*, a man will come to her and say, 'I want you' *(Zaho mila anao)*. She might look him over, and whether she liked him or not, she might say: 'It's alright with me' *(Ah, zaho mety)*, because she needs to get money—500 FMG, 400 FMG, 250 FMG. She asks how much he will give her before, and if it's not enough, she refuses. That's not the way it used to be done. In the past, a woman, if she liked the man, accepted. She invited him in, gave him a clean bodywrap from the suitcase to wear. They stayed together talking, sleeping, talking together. In the morning when he woke up, he slipped a little money under the pillow of her bed. Under the pillow. But kids just coming up these days don't do that."

"If, by the second or third day, she is already tired of the man, she will tell him, 'Add more money *(ampianao markay)*, or I won't sleep with you any more.' If he doesn't, she kicks him out. She brings in some other man, so that the first one sees he's there and just leaves. But that is not what happens in the countryside. All the young men in the village get together clapping him, 'Eh, Oh, Fallen é! Who's this?' *(Eh, oh, latsaka é! Azôvy?!)* over and over again. They follow the man around the village all night. Meanwhile, they board up the door to the girl's house with a stick, so she and the new friend can't get out in the morning."

Her kids were falling asleep. Perhaps because she was hurrying them out rather than focusing on her choice of words, she concluded with what might have been the most important issue: "Some girls, even if they are ugly—thick *makoa* lips, bad hair, black—get men, Indians, Europeans. Then there are other girls—beautiful Arabo girls—who just sit there. No one comes to marry them. Some have bad minds, but some have no good fortune *(Misy ratsy jery, fa misy tsisy riziky)*."

Aware that they earned about a third of what men earned for low-paying domestic work, women sought to expand their incomes through the gifts they received from men. Mothers explicitly counseled their daughters to benefit from their relations with men, and recognized other women as doing the same. When the girl with whom Abodo had been sleeping for some time became pregnant, and MamanDjoma was dealing with her father who was extremely angry about the 'bandit' (her son) who had 'ruined his child' *(mandrobaka zanakan'azy)*, the girl who was still in school, she said:

"It's her fault." [Even though she's still so young?] "Yes, it's always the woman's fault. Men don't know shame—They see a woman, want her,

see a woman, want her. Men don't know shame, so it's women who have
to be careful. But the girl needed this." She rubbed the money I had just
paid her for the washing and the fried fish and bananas she was selling. I
asked if Abodo would be working to earn the money to support the baby.
She said, "There's no work here. He wants to go to Diégo. He would go
by boat to Nosy Be, cross over to the mainland, and go by car from
Ambanja to Diégo. But there's a bridge broken on the paved road there,
and everyone has to go by plane, so he can't go."

She made the same argument later, in 1981, when I first asked after
Tavavy, whom Djoma had divorced to marry a third wife by whom
he now had an eight-month-old baby.

[Is MamanTiba married again?] "No, she *mitovo,* she hasn't married. A
man came along and said, 'I want you.' She got pregnant. A lot of women
live like this because there is not enough work. Men can't support a
family. Like Abodo. When women *mitovo,* men are still masters of the
children."

Places where men gathered provided opportunities for women who
sought to benefit from their gifts. These included work parties, like
trampling royal rice fields, and other royal services at the Doany and
the Mahabo. The post provided other opportunities. 'Walking about
elsewhere' *(mitsangatsana am tany hafa)* was the main way of talking
about liaisons. As Sefo from Tsinjorano said one time when he stopped
by in Analalava, laughing at each change in the meaning of *vady:* "Got
to be going, look for a new wife, wife at the post. Wife left behind
in Tsinjorano, need a new wife." *(Handeha, mizaha vady vaovao, vady
ampositra. Vady tavela Tsinjorano, mila vady vaovao).*

In the past, the post included more lucrative opportunities in the
form of the Europeans living there. In the 1970s, women in Analalava
imagined the northern port town of Diégo Suarez, the site of a French
naval base, as one of the main places where such opportunities still
abounded.[59] As Ampenziky, now living in Analalava, described it:

"A lot of people go to Diégo. It's like Analalava. There aren't many local
people *(zanatany)* there. People come from other places to walk around,

stay, look for work. People who compare Diégo with Mahajanga say that Mahajanga is nicer, more beautiful. But a lot of people like to go to Diégo! Lots of young women *(tovovavy)*. It's lively, and there are lots of Vazaha." [But when the Vazaha go, they usually leave the women and children behind.] "Yes, for example, the children of the woman who lives south of here, the boy and girl. Other kids do tease them. They say, 'Fatherless Vazaha, rotten Vazaha, worthless Vazaha.' But a lot of women just throw the children away. Give birth, come out, and throw the baby away. If it's still living, another woman coming along might pick it up. Many are strong willed *(mahery toetra)*, little white Vazaha there in the woods. But women like it there [in Diégo] because they get all sorts of things from the Vazaha, and when he leaves, he leaves it all with them."

She said she knew about this first hand because the son of her father's older brother, who lived in a village east of Tsinjorano married the daughter of another kinsman's sister who lived in Analalava. "They separated after a while, and she went up to live with her mother in Diégo. There were four houses in the courtyard, all rented by different people. A woman in one of the houses had a Vazaha for a *vady,* and one day he brought back a friend. The friend looked at her and looked at her. She knew that he wanted her, but she was very embarrassed. She said to the woman, 'What do you do? You don't know how to speak their language. They don't know how to speak Malagasy. How do you talk to them? Besides, I don't have any clothes.' The girl said, 'Don't worry about a thing. If you have any questions about anything, come and ask me.' Her vady spoke a little bit of Malagasy, not much. 'He will give you anything you ask for. Just say to him how you feel, having no clothes, and such.' So when he came, she said how embarrassed she was, how she was dirty, he was a Vazaha, she had no clothes, no household goods *(entana),* nothing, she was a visitor in town, just staying there with her mother, and had nothing. He said, 'It doesn't matter.' [Ampenziky repeated this a couple of times.] He said, 'It doesn't matter. Let's go to the Compagnie [store].' He was their commander. Lots of money! They still hadn't gotten together *(miharo),* still weren't one bed. So they went and he bought everything: bed, chairs complete with couch, frigidaire, everything for the kitchen, lamps, then moved everything into a different house—a *trano étage* (house with many floors)—at 2,000 FMG/room. Visitors came there and she told them it was like dreaming, she couldn't believe it was all hers.

The only work they have is to go get their vady at noon, bring him back, cook lunch while he drinks his beer, siesta, then take the vady back to work, then get him again at the end of the afternoon. If they don't do that, there will be another woman who will get him. Also they will suspect the vady of taking another woman. A lot of those légionnaires like to keep more than one woman. But if they [the légionnaires] catch their vady with another, they will knife *(mipoignard)* him. Sometimes they destroy all the household goods. Then if they make up, the woman will say, 'But now my household goods are all ruined,' and he will buy everything all new for her. Pretty soon, it is all new again. Knives are used *(atomboko meso)*. No man may be admitted into the house. If a kinsman comes, she has to introduce him to the vady and say exactly who he is, for example, 'This is the child of my mother's brother, my brother, or whatever.' Diégo progresses! *(Diégo mandroso!)*"

TRANOM-BAZAHA TSY LAPA: EUROPEANS DON'T KEEP OPEN HOUSE

Men spoke bitterly of money as being the real 'passport' *(pasipaoro)* enabling people to go wherever they wanted. One man echoed Malaza in citing Tsiranana's post-independence rallying cry—"There are no rulers (ampanjaka), only rich people *(ampañarivo),*" then said "I am just as much a king *(roi)* as these former ampanjaka are princesses because I have money. [Speaking of a local merchant and his young wife] It doesn't matter what you look like. It is money that makes him so attractive—the universal passport." This, too, was a widely held idea.

A son of one of the Indian store-keeping families in Analalava was planning to emigrate to Canada, where he already had relatives. While his mother and I were talking about plane travel, his father kept rubbing his thumb and forefinger together and repeating, "But you need this, but you need this . . .!" Then he said that there was a song to that effect: 'Money is your mother, money is your father, money is your sister, money is your brother . . . Money is your kin (havana).' Seconded by a man from another of the Karany families, he explained: "That means, if you've got money, you've got kin. If you don't, you don't. The words are Malagasy, but it is an Indian, not a Malagasy, song."

In fact, most local men, even though they received higher wages than women, did not have full access to the universal passport. The proverbial phrase, 'Vazaha's houses aren't royal halls' *(Tranombazaha tsy lapa)*—meaning, as one man explained, "it's not allowed for many people to come in, it's not allowed to stay long" *(tsy azo adira olo maro, tsy azo mipetraka)*—was understood in the broadest terms. The homely imagery referred to all the places that Vazaha were seen as having created, like the post, or like Diégo, where they and those representing their interests still had a hand.

Malaza said, "When the French were here, they didn't mix *(tsy miharo)*. They thought of Malagasy as animals, something not human *(biby, raha tsy olo)*. Indians even up to today think the same way. If one of them bore children from a Malagasy, they killed the child." He then went on to talk about a female ruler who had married an Indian, whose children did not look to their mother and to the customs of the ampanjaka. Another time, he commented: "The French take our women, but they don't give us theirs, probably because they are afraid of letting them in for a hard life."

His sons echoed his words almost exactly. His oldest son Amady said: "There are two kinds of people who never mix *(miharo)* with Malagasy— Indians and Vazaha. When the French went on *tournée*, they were really mean. They would arrive in the village, eat everything—chicken, rice— without paying for it. Then at the end of their stay, they would collect the head tax. The men who didn't pay were chained and taken to jail in a huge line. They never slept with women in the village. Only those Frenchmen who didn't work for the government. If the Indians saw a child born to a Malagasy, they killed it. When Tsiranana came into power, he told them that if they didn't want to marry Malagasy, they should go home. A lot of them don't have any relatives there in Bombay. Some don't know how to speak Indian. Lost to their ancestors, lost!"[60]

Women were more able to make 'friends' of such higher-ups than were men. In keeping with the growing autonomy of both men and women as they 'grew into adulthood' *(mitovo)*, the money and other gifts they received from such relationships were less accessible to their kin than the wealth exchanged in marriages with local people. Because, as women themselves recognized in handling their pregnancies, 'Vazaha don't mix' *(Vazaha tsy miharo)*, they were even more able to keep what they received from these relationships. But for the same reasons, these beneficial relationships were most often temporary, leaving them vulnerable to accusations of *mandranto*—'trading in sexuality for profit'—both from those who asked them into the 'Vazaha's house,' and from those who were allowed in only as the lowest kinds of workers or closed out altogether.

Mañangy, the commonest local word for a woman or women, is an active verb derived from the money *(tangy)* men are expected to give women in expressing their desire and persuading them to agree. *Mandranto* (trading for profit), never used in this way, was associated with other words for women, some Malagasy *(koetra, [fi]janga),* but most of French origin. *Amato* (whence *mañamato),* already current in the early nineteenth century, though perhaps of Portuguese origin, was in keeping with the appraisals of Noël and Guillain of the 'Sakalava' as loose-living people, which were central to their interpretations of royal succession, as I have already indicated in Chapter 2.[61] Other terms—*bandỳ, dépôt, makorelly, mañano passage, mañano pratik, mirôndy*—probably came into use during the colonial period.[62]

In local usage, these terms, together with their negative meanings associated with practices of mixing while not mixing, transformed the way that people talked about *mañangy tovo,* girls growing into women in the course of relationships with men, and about older women between husbands. As AdanDezy said, when asked whether one of his kinswomen was married:

> *"Mitovo,"* adding to make sure we understood, *"Koetra." Koetra* clearly meant, as Somizy in Analalava explained it in a series of Malagasy-French words: "a female bandit *(mañangy bandỳ),* a woman who acts like a bandit *(mañangy manao bandỳ),* big business *(pratik be),* a woman who makes the rounds *(mañangy mirondy)* in the evening and collects men. There are lots of them in Majunga. They go out in the evening and work all night until morning, going around the boats."

Yet when I asked Tavavy about the name of a woman—*Njarikoetra,* 'Koetra's Mother'—in her grandparents' generation, "Isn't that a kind of oath?" (since proper names are usually blessings), she corrected me brusquely: *"Koetra* means woman!"

The tensions expressed in these different perspectives on relations between men and women encompassed the region. In fact, they ex-

tended beyond the region to all the major towns east, north, and south
of Analalava. Nevertheless, local people associated them with the post
as a place. Thus, AdanDezy, speaking together with his new wife
Moana, made a clear distinction between *mañangy tovo,* young single
women in rural villages, and *koetra,* young single women at the post.
Yet they both concluded by saying, "Each gets money!" *(Samby mahazo vola!),* merging their differences again.

Speaking about the sister of one of the Antantety men in the southern part
of Tsinjorano, Moana said: "She lives in Antsohihy; she *mitovo* there.
Women who live alone at the post are called *koetra* or *makorelly.*" [What is
the difference between *koetra* and *mañangy tovo?*] "If a girl lives at the
positra, she is a koetra. If she lives in the countryside by herself, it is called
mitovo, mañangy tovo. If a girl goes to the post, people say: 'There are a
lot of koetra in Analalava é!' *(Misy koetra maro Analalava é!).* Each one gets
money *(Samby mahazo vola).*" AdanDezy then said: "In Majunga, there is
a special quarter called Manga, where women hang out, lots of them,
beckon to men with their hands, though they don't say anything. Then
when the guy gets in the house, they ask for the money—100 FMG, 150
FMG." Moana then said: "It's like that in Antsohihy too. I was there with
a friend, and we saw all these women sitting out in front of a building
between two trees. Lot of them Indians—pretty too. They call out, make
little cries. They get 10 FMG, 20 FMG. Some people who feel sorry for
them give them 100 FMG." They both added, "Sakalava don't do that;
they don't solicit like that." Then Moana said, "Yet they do say things in
order to make men want to sleep with them: 'When did you get here?
Long time since you were last seen. Ah, Rañao. How are you, Rañao?' If
the man isn't interested, then he doesn't respond. Or he might even
answer back: 'I'm not your rañao. Since when am I your rañao?' It's
embarrassing! Girls say this to some man they don't even know. I
wouldn't dare." [Why rañao?] "Rañao is the husband of the *rahavavy* [a
woman's Z, MZD, MBD, FZD, FBD, etc.]. People related as rañao
(ampirañao) are not forbidden to sleep with one another. Especially if they
see a man who has come in to sell things, anything. He has money. They
would like to get that money from him."

Thus, social life 'at the cultivations' (antsabo) organized around
ancestors and descendants, and epitomized in men who were the 'mas-
ters/owners of the children,' contrasted with social life 'at the post'

(ampositra), the place of wage labor, associated with new forms of slavery, settled primarily by single women. The feeling of malaise— 'This place is dead,' 'ruined land'—permeated the region as a whole. But its clearest focus was on the women—children of women *(zanakan' nyvavy)*—whom people could choose to interpret as mañangy tovo or as koetra, depending on their own changing fortunes.

MITADY TOKO, NAHITA VATO: LOOKING FOR A HEARTH, I FOUND STONES

One day, visiting with Laza Be, I met a functionary who had come into her hotely, Come In Friend *(Karibo Jirany),* to drink the beer he had bought at the Indian-owned bar across the street.

He said he was a development worker at Animation Rurale south of Analalava. He came from Mandritsara [a large inland town]. There was a competitive exam to enter the C.E.G. school when he first came to Analalava in 1949. Analalava was big then and famous too. He lived out at Animation Rurale. He liked it there, "because it is close to the peasants. There is such a big gap between the functionaries and the peasants. In spite of efforts to close it, the gap increases. A lot of people come to a town like this to look for work. They get a little work from commerçants, Indians. They spend money on things, they buy *tergal* [a highly prized French polyester]. They find the money is not enough to live on, so they finally turn to theft." He agreed that many local people suspected the prisoners from the regional and national penitentiaries, released to work in the area, took time out to steal from them. Laza Be didn't say anything during this time, simply played with Vanessa.

He evoked a very common image of the post, especially the people living in the southwestern quarters, which one teacher's son compared to Isotry, the poorest quarter of the national capital of Antananarivo, settled by recent migrants from the surrounding countryside. In fact, local people did not live only at the post, stealing when there was not enough work. Their lives at the post were inseparably intertwined with the rural villages in which they continued to live part of the year, through kin ties, friendship, and marriage, their movements back and forth, the ceaseless round necessary to make a living by combining occasional wage labor with other kinds of work, mainly cultivation. Farming was still the mainstay of their many efforts to make a living, yet other kinds of work had become so essential that farming villages were no longer the centers from which people moved elsewhere. Even while searching that never ended was being redefined as *vagabondage*, ancestral villages were becoming more like the *banda* or temporary shelters that rural villagers built to live in while they were watching their fields. Thus, progress or 'moving ahead' *(fandrosoana)*, may have led to growth and prosperity in other parts of Madagascar. But people in the Analalava region—tompontany and vahiny alike—saw it as having led not only to impoverishment and theft, but also lost ancestors, lost generations. Searching was supposed to end in finding a spouse in marriage and the establishment of new centers of growth and prosperity. Instead, as the popular saying has it, *Mitady toko, nahita vato*, 'Looking for a hearth, I found stones.'[63]

People from farming villages came to the post in the course of searching their fortunes, especially searching for money. In the processes of searching, they got kin through friendships, blood bonds, and marriages formed with nonkin, including strangers like Indians and Europeans. Yet all these relationships were thought to have the potential 'to turn,' to return to the condition of 'not mixing' *(tsy miharo)*, characteristic of relations among strangers. While historical sources substantiate the long-standing practice of incorporating strangers into local communities through a wide variety of means, contemporary practice in the post was surrounded more by the imagery of buying and selling, profiting and prostituting, still associated with slavery, than by the imagery of cultivating ancestries in rural villages. In seizing and taking advantage of the best opportunities for lucrative employment that were most available to them, growing women—*mañangy tovo*—were acting in what scholars, writing about women in comparable situations in, for example colonial East Africa or the contemporary urban United States, have characterized as economically rational ways.[64] These women sought to advance themselves by forming liaisons with people of higher political-economic and social standing, even as they continued to marry up into Silamo and Arabo families. Because of the autonomy associated with mitovo for both men and women, but also because these higher-ups 'didn't mix,' they were more able to keep these benefits for themselves. In providing places for their kin to stay while selling produce at the post, while going to school, while looking for work, or simply while visiting, they did assist their families in these enterprises and were encouraged to do so. At the same time, they were condemned for their self-interest.[65]

While women in the Analalava region benefited from such strategies, they bore the burden of representing the subordinate position of local people as 'children of women' in a new sense, exemplifying a process of subordination by feminization documented in other postcolonial contexts as well.[66] Followers of Sakalava rulers may have contributed to such processes, playing into assumptions about politically inconsequential women in order to keep the monarchy from being destroyed. But the colonial and postcolonial officials who took their rulers' places also put them in the subordinate position of women, children, and slaves when they reoriented the region around the post as a center of growth and development that would rival rural and royal villages alike. The arrangements now necessary to making a living, which in practice divided women at the post from men who continued to work at cultivations, cut into their own efforts to recognize ancestors and thus to produce strong concentrated bodies of descendants. The coexistence of these different forms of companionship through work has been renewed every time people identified with the post have tried to maintain their position as children of men on a larger scale, and people identified as children of women have continued to question their alleged mastery.

Words—the socioculturally and historically complex words with which 'children of the land' and 'strangers' in the Analalava region evaluated 'woman,' 'children of women' and 'children of men,' 'creating calamity,' kin of 'one stomach,' 'paired' friends, ties 'in blood,' 'spouses' and their 'one house,' giving 'money-gifts' and 'trading for profit'—have been an integral part of this struggle. Diverse speakers used these same images to represent their conflicting views on changing processes of social reproduction on a regional and national scale. Their strategies are powerful examples of Bakhtin's arguments concerning language from a dialogic perspective:

> Any concrete discourse (utterance) finds the object at which it was directed already as it were overlain with qualifications, open to dispute, charged with value, already enveloped in an obscuring mist—or, on the contrary, by the 'light' of alien words that have already been spoken about it. It is entangled, shot through with shared thoughts, points of view, alien value judgments and accents. The word, directed toward its objects, enters a dialogically agitated and tension-filled environment of alien words, value judgments and accents, weaves in and out of complex interrelationships, merges with some, recoils from others, intersects with yet a third group: and all this may crucially shape discourse, may leave a trace in all its semantic layers, may complicate its expression and influence its entire stylistic profile.
>
> The living utterance, having taken meaning and shape at a particular historical moment in a socially specific environment, cannot fail to brush up against thousands of living dialogic threads, woven by socio-ideological consciousness around the given object of an utterance; it cannot fail to become an active participant in social dialogue. After all, the utterance arises out of this dialogue as a continuation of it and as a rejoinder to it—it does not approach the object from the sidelines.[67]

The very choices of such complex words—*mandoza, havana, zanakan' ny vavy, zanakan' ny lahy, namana, vady, mitovo, amato, koetra, jirany, kamarady, fatidra*—just saying them in particular contexts, were already powerful acts of definition in their own right. One could say that their coercive power lay above all in their particular resolution of ambiguous social relations.[68] By this argument, words were the overriding factor in determining the 'real thing' among socially and historically variable alternatives—whether, for example, children were the growing tips of vital ancestries, or fatherless dead ends. Yet the actual practice of these relations in the Analalava region shows that these controlling representations were spatial as much as social. They point to social-spatial processes by which people went or were put in places where they had more or less control over their choice of companions, more or less support, compared to other places in the region.

I have described how people in the Analalava region have to move from place to place and have asserted that they need to do so in order to make a living by undertaking different kinds of work. I would derive the power of the words they use to describe and explain their migratory circumstances from the very places inside and outside of the 'Vazaha's house,' where they work. Yet, I have not yet shown in detail just how *in working,* people are drawn or put into the different positions they represent in these words. This is the topic of the next chapter, focusing on the 'royal halls,' with which 'Vazaha's houses' are contrasted—the Doany and the Mahabo—and the work that people do there in 'serving' royal ancestors, much of which is by its very nature, unspoken in words, even—for many different reasons—unspeakable.

C　H　A　P　T　E　R　6

Vala: Pens

Samby am-pilasiny, samby an-kolafikolafiny.
Each to his own place, each to his own kind.

Mbaraka, guardian at the Mahabo, on royal service

AKOHON-ZANAHARY: GOD'S CHICKENS

When Alan got hepatitis, MamanDjoma said sympathetically, "Living people are God's chickens" *(Akohon-Zanahary ny olombelo),* which I took to refer to the enormity of God and thus misfortune that strikes human beings regardless of their different ancestries and actions. A few months later, she was talking about how there were no longer any really great curers *(moasy)* in the area, people who would know how to heal people with incompatible fates *(tsy tokam-bintana):*

"Curers *(moasy)* who know how to take care of fates *(mitaha vintana)* don't exist any more. There is only one big curer now—east of here in the Antsohihy region—Rabemanana is his name. There are no moasy here. When people get sick, they go to a royal spirit *(tromba)* or to a diviner *(ampisikidy),* who tells them whether someone has used sorcery on them, whether a royal spirit has possessed them, or whether God has made them sick." [Why would God want to cause sickness?] "You remember I said that living people are God's chickens—*Akohon-Zanahary ny olombelo?* You know how we keep chickens, ducks, geese in pens. One day you want to eat one. It's the same thing."

Zanahary—a single one, like the Zanahary of the Muslims or the Andriamanitra of the Christians, or the several who were one's own ancestors or those of royalty—were all renowned for their limitless capacities to inflict misfortune. The greater or higher they were, the more deadly was the anger expressed in their curses and realized in personal misfortune or the misfortune of one's closest companions. In contrast to wholly evil spirits, the kind whom sorcerers paid to kill, wrathful ancestors were not thought to act at random. MamanDjoma had tactfully ignored our own responsibility for Alan's sickness. Although some misfortunes were the result of others' evil doings, most misfortunes happened because of one's own wrong-doing, although what and according to whom, how to treat them and who should do the work were matters on which people disagreed and acted differently, as these abbreviated examples illustrate:

Diniky had come from Mahajanga, where she was staying with her father's sister, to visit with her mother's brother's family in Analalava, where her brother Mahasoa was also staying while he finished his last year at the C.E.G. She brought her infant boy, Kidroa. The boy's father was still in Mahajanga. She stayed in Analalava for about three months, then returned to Mahajanga, where Kidroa died shortly afterwards of diphtheria. Diniky went to a diviner in Analalava who told her that a rejected lover had used sorcery on the baby. Later, a diviner in Mahajanga, having elicited the story of her recent journey from her maternal kin in Analalava to her paternal kin in Befandriana, then back to her maternal kin in Analalava, and finally back to her father's sister in Mahajanga, attributed the baby's death first to the "death" money that Diniky's mother's brother's senior wife had given her in exchange for helping to bring baggage back to Analalava from Antsohihy on the recent trip, then to her relationship with Kidroa's father. Diniky's mother, who came up to Analalava from where she farmed south of Analalava, attributed the death to Diniky's 'bad milk.' Royal spirits in Analalava finally told her that she would have to return to Mahajanga to inquire with royal spirits there, which she did. They told her that the baby died because it 'needed its father' (mila baba), that is, needed to be claimed by the father's ancestors. Against the wishes of the father's father's sister, Diniky and the baby's father subsequently married. With the further assistance of Sakalava royal spirits, embodied in mediums in the Mahajanga and Analalava areas, they went on to have five more children, despite efforts from his sisters to kill Diniky using sorcery.

Jaohindy was an Indian merchant whose family came from Mahajanga where they first settled when they emigrated from Bombay in the late nineteenth century. He, another brother, and a half-brother, born of a Malagasy mother, had lived in Analalava for some thirty years. During this time they had bought so many rice fields in one area of the Ambolobozo Peninsula that his daughter described them as "owning the village" occupied by the farmers who worked the fields. His wife had four daughters and still no sons. He made an oath to an important local shrine tended by the members of the farming community—another of Fiaroa's shrines, indirectly connected to the monarchy (see Chapter 4). The next child was a boy. The boy was nine years old when the family began ailing. The oldest daughter in her mid-twenties was still unmarried. The second oldest, though married and living in Mandritsara with her husband, was not getting pregnant. Jaohindy's wife felt sick all the time, and there were problems with his business. He went to a local diviner, who told him that he never did fulfill his oath. He fulfilled it by returning to the shrine and sacrificing a cow, with the assistance of the farmers in the community who knew how it should be done. Shortly afterwards, the second daughter became pregnant.

Avoria, one of the tompontany-siblings in Tsinjorano (Fig. 9, F) became angry with Bezara, her oldest son, because he did not participate when their union got together to trample the rice fields she worked with her husband, the Ampanjaka Marojao. After the quarrel dragged on for a couple of weeks without being resolved, Bezara's sisters entered into it. Avoria's two oldest daughters—Miadana who, with her husband Matombo, was part of the union and Ampenjiky who was visiting from Antsohihy—called down to their mother the more powerful of the royal spirits whom she served as a medium—the Son (the ampanjaka's brother), Ambilahikely. They told him that they supported their mother in her quarrel with their brother. As they explained later, they were afraid that if they didn't make their own positions clear, then Ambilahikely, offended by the affront to his medium, would avenge himself on those whose primary concern should be their mother's well-being. Bezara, working with his union to prepare someone else's rice fields for sowing, did not attend the meeting. Ambilahikely let the sisters' gift of 100 FMG lie where they had put it, while saying that Bezara himself had to come to pay his respects and ask forgiveness for having quarreled with his medium. His refusal would be reported to the supplicator (ampangataka) at the Mahabo and the ampanjaka's chief official (manantany) in Analalava who would forbid him to pay his respects to the ampanjaka or her ancestors at the Doany and at the Mahabo [which, given any illness, was equivalent to threatening him with death]. While Bezara's sisters sang praise songs in

Ambilahikely's honor, Ambilahikely spoke to Bezara's father and brother [the husband and son of Bezara's MZ Togny], ordering them as Sambarivo to notify these officials. Bezara's sisters, having made offerings to Ambilahikely to induce him to come and hear their petition, also pressured Bezara to respond to the spirit's demands. During the following week, Bezara came to beg pardon from the spirit and to pledge a cow to cover the grief he had caused his mother who served as the spirit's medium.

A couple of months after arriving in Analalava, I was robbed by one of the first persons who had befriended me. Not knowing who it was at the time and hoping to get some good out of bad, I took the advice of my foster kin to go to a *kalanoro,* a kind of forest-being reputed for its success at finding lost things. Speaking through its medium, the kalanoro said that the thief, perhaps thieves, lived southeast of me [they did]. But they were merely the immediate source of my misfortune. The real source was the anger of my unborn babies whom I had never allowed to live until now when I was finally pregnant. Yet my being pregnant was a sign of my good fortune in coming to this place. The ampanjaka had blessed me. Alan and I should beg Andriamanitra (the Merina/Christian term for God) and Zanahary (the local term for God and for the royal ancestors) for their blessings, using water to which the crushed leaves of sun's chronicle *(tantara masoandro)* had been added.[1] We should cleanse ourselves inside and out by drinking the water, rubbing it on our bodies, and then asperging the interior of the house. We should go to the ampanjaka and pay our respects, and then go to the Mahabo and pay our respects to the royal ancestors there, saying that we have come to the masters of the land (tompontany) to beg them for their blessings.

> This is Sakalava custom. When you went to the Mahabo on Nosy Lava, did you pay your respects to the Sakalava royalty there? You should go there, say you have come to offer your respects to the Masters of the Land. [Sudden whisper] The father of the ampanjaka is buried there. Those are tombs! Go and give *ariary valo* [eight five-franc pieces, about seventeen cents], and say you have come to pay your respects to the masters of the land and ask for their blessing, a good pregnancy and good health.[2]

Somizy, who had taken us to the kalanoro, showed us how to supplicate the ancestors for their blessing. As she left, she said, "You should speak to the landlord and get the fence fixed so people can't get in."

Soatoly returned to Analalava from Nosy Be, where her father's mother had gone searching, then settled down to stay. She made her living by taking odd jobs. When Somizy was caring for her sister's baby, she asked Soatoly to wash clothes for her, including the baby's clothes. When other women began telling Somizy that she was employing (mampiasa, making to work) a spirit's medium to wash her clothes, she told Soatoly that she had to seek work elsewhere. As she explained it:

> When I asked Soatoly, she said, 'Yes, that's right, but I got permission from the spirit *(tromba)* to wash clothes, everything except clothes with excrement on them is permissible.' I am still afraid—there could be a little bit of urine on something, something overlooked. But people who aren't afraid still have her work, for example, T. who lives near the tamarind tree. Soatoly told me that she had gotten an important man, the supplicator from the Mahabo, to call the spirit. When the spirit came, she told him: 'I am without a spouse. I am tired of pounding [to remove the hulls] a *daba* full of paddy rice for 50 FMG. I have no money, no spouse. I have to earn money some way. Can I wash clothes?' The tromba said, 'Yes, provided you carry the dirty clothes in your hand, or tied over your arm, not on your head.' Because people sitting on the ground might accidentally pick up some excrement on their clothes. Once the clothes are clean, she can carry them on her head. So, although she cannot wash clothes with excrement, she can wash other clothes, even baby's clothes. This happened quite a while ago. She got her request *(nahazo hataka)*, but those who are afraid [of somehow incurring the spirit's anger] still don't dare.

The people who paid homage to the royal ancestors at the Doany and the Mahabo came from all over the region, and sometimes far beyond it. One man had married a woman from the Mahabo. They had ten children—two were sailors in France, some were living in Antananarivo, some in Mahajanga. "All over. But we still have to follow ancestral custom. My children told me to come. I am not staying long, because there are many prohibitions here—no mattresses, have to sleep on a mat on the floor." He had brought 1,000 FMG to pay his respects to the royal ancestors at the door to the tomb; *indroy valo* (two-times-eight five-franc pieces) for an offering at one tamarind tree, and *paraty valo* (eight five-franc pieces) for another, to fulfill special requests from his family, including one daughter "who has given birth, but wants to have another good birth."

On another occasion, we asked AdanNoro, a long-time resident of the

Mahabo where he came from, and he responded: "Where do you come from?" Alan explained our 'path/purpose' (dia, a person's purpose expressed in how she or he has come to be in a place). AdanNoro then said that he came from the Farafangana region (along the southeast coast of Madagascar). He lived in Mandritsara [a large town in north-central Madagascar] for a while selling cattle. His son, who came here with him, was born in Mandritsara. But then he got sick. He was sick all the time, never well, until he came here to Nosy Lava—"All better!" (Mahivaña!) That was why he was still living at the Mahabo. "I came here to pay respect to the ancestors (mikoezy). I went back to Mandritsara for a while. There I saw a royal spirit, Ndriamaro. Ndriamaro said, 'You are a person who has run away, fled. You should go back there, that place where you got better. There you had lots of children, you gave birth to many.'" So he went back to the Mahabo to stay. "Now if people ask where I come from, I say, 'Nosy Lava.' I don't tell people I come from Farafangana. This is my village (tanàna)!" Pointing to his manioc garden north of the village, he said: "The supplicator told me when we came back here that we must build our house up near his house because it's nice and open there. So we have our own house." [Do your kin visit you here?] "Yes, my son married the daughter of B. [the male head of the second most influential 'pen' of guardians at the Mahabo]; they have two girls. That is how I have become many."

As these examples indicate, the royal ancestors at the Doany and the Mahabo were meant to be at the top of a hierarchy of finders and healers, including other royal ancestors and people's other ancestors. Although all of the communities in the region were organized around tany masina, ancestrally regenerative ground, the doubly fenced compounds at the Doany and the Mahabo were the largest of these. Although almost all finding, blessing, and curing was achieved by purifying oneself inside and out, these processes were far more extensive at the Doany and the Mahabo. Like the farming villages and the post with which they coexisted, more or less compelling to different people for different reasons, the Doany and Mahabo could be compared to the jar in Wallace Stevens's poem:

> I placed a jar in Tennessee,
> And round it was, upon a hill.
> It made the slovenly wilderness

Surround that hill.
The wilderness rose up to it,
And sprawled around, no longer wild.
The jar was round upon the ground
And tall and of a port in air.
It took dominion everywhere.
The jar was gray and bare.
It did not give of bird or bush,
Like nothing else in Tennessee.[3]

These high light places—especially the Mahabo, built on the blinding white chalk of Nosy Lava—did visibly draw up the surrounding "wilderness" with all its dark, wandering by-ways. Royal places "took dominion everywhere" by reorienting the seekers along these paths to the royal ancestors, transforming those who recognized the ancestors' preeminence by washing them in light. The Doany and the Mahabo were like the jar in being clearly different from the "forest," to use the local idiom. But unlike the jar, made of hard, impermeable dead glass, they were made different out of the same bird and bush around them, so they would bring new life out of death, a regrowth that took unexpected turns. I would sometimes imagine the Doany and Mahabo placed like jars to resolve momentarily for myself what was always being contended—thereby killing, as Stevens seems to suggest, what really lived in them. Who did take dominion in these places: the ampanjaka, the royal ancestors, the commoners who were their mediums, or the guardians, former slaves who tended the shrines and gave the mediums their legitimacy? And what was, in fact, the nature of their dominion over such different kinds of people? Some people, like Bezara, belonged to communities that had long been associated with the Doany or the Mahabo, through the nobility and former royal guardians who lived there, through the royal spirits that possessed their kin, friends, and affines, and through their participation in royal services. They did gradually make their way through lower finders and healers to the Doany and the Mahabo. For Jaohindy, such a pilgrimage would have entailed an open, demeaning loss of his own ancestors. Diniky's mother's brother (like her father, but not her

mother) was seeking to 'progress' away from the backward enslave-
ment that he was not alone in associating with the precolonial monarchy. Diniky and Jaohindy used the lesser finders and healers to avoid
being drawn into the more demanding kinds of service associated with
the Doany and the Mahabo, yet they shared similar assumptions about
the regenerative powers of the royal ancestors buried there.[4] The royal
ancestors were formally recognized as the *tompontanana,* masters of
these places, and thus *tompontany,* 'masters of the land,' so we will
begin with them, then go on to the land of diverse people from which
and by whom they were made.

OLO ARAIKY: ONE PERSON

Sakalava followers spoke of royal lines, like the Zafinimena and Zafinifotsy, as being 'one person' *(olo araiky)* or 'one path/one purpose' *(dia
araiky).* An injury to anyone in the line was an injury to all, even as
the blessing of one was conceived as a blessing from all of them collectively. Within the one person, there was nevertheless a certain division of labor, as we have seen: Zafinimena were identified with the
land, Zafinifotsy with the water. All of them were seen and addressed
as individuals. Vows were made and repaid to particular spirits in
specific mediums. They were also seen as if they were different members of a common household. As indicated in Chapter 4, the Zafinifotsy were represented in the Analalava region by a brother and sister
and the brother's children. Just as "Bevaoko [the brother] gives birth,
Ampela Be [his sister] gives care," so too, they had different work to
do in ruling.

> Women: *O o o o e e e e e e e e e a*
> Men: *O o o o o o o o o* (repeated)
> Women: *Azôvy mandidy e e a?*
> Women & Men: *Ampelabe mandidy e e a!*
> Women: *Azôvy manjaka i i a?*
> Women & Men: *Soazara manjaka a a a!*
> Women: *Azôvy mangôty e e a?*
> Women & Men: *I Fotsy mangôty e e e!*

Women: *Azôvy ampimalo o o a?*
Women & Men: *Kotomena ampimalo o o o!*
Women: *O o o o o o e e e e a a a a*
Men: *O o o e e e e e e*
Man speaks: *Maro so(a) e e e*
Women: *Azôvy sataigny e e a?*
Women & Men: *Ndrandahy sataign(y) e e e!*
Women: *O o o o o o o e e e e a a a a*
Men: *O o o o o e e e e*

Women: *O o o o e e e e e e e e e a*
Men: *O o o o o o o o o* (repeated)
Women: Who commands *e e a?*
Women & Men: Ampelabe commands *e e a!*
Women: Who rules *i i a?*
Women & Men: Soazara rules *a a a!*[5]
Women: Who is spoiled *e e a?*
Women & Men: Fotsy is spoiled *e e e!*
Women: Who talks things over *o o a?*
Women & Men: Kotomena talks things over *o o o!*
Women: *O o o o o o e e e e a a a a*
Men: *O o o e e e e e e*
Man speaks: Many good/beautiful ones *e e e*
Women: Who is cruelly violent *e e a?*
Women & Men: Ndrandahy is cruelly violent *e e e!*
Women: *O o o o o o o e e e e a a a a*
Men: *O o o o o e e e e e*[6]

The characters of the Zafinifotsy rulers commemorated in shrines (doany) around the mouth of the Loza River were common knowledge because they possessed more people in this area than any other royal spirits. Thus spirit possession meetings often involved their interactions with one another. Diniky and her mother explained their dispositions in these terms:

"Fotsy is spoiled because he is the youngest. When he possesses people, they cry! Cry! Then Kotomena, his older brother, comes and takes him on his knee. Ndrandahy is cruel and violent because he has no use for a lot of people, just himself alone. His doany is Sohy out there, the island, the rock known as Ambatosohy. He is angry, mean. All the others have doany in the mouth of the Loza; he is the only one by himself. Kotomena is a person who discusses things, not like a judge, but like a person who loves to talk and laugh. Not mean, he is a simple, direct person. Ampela Be [Diniky's mother lowered her voice] commands because she is an elder, she is their father's sister."

As this version of the song indicates, people sometimes sang 'Soazara [instead of Bevaoko] rules.' Once, not long after the uprising, then elections, in the spring of 1972 when General Gabriel Ramanantsoa replaced Philibert Tsiranana as President of Madagascar, the lead singer's brother attempted to drown out his sister in every chorus by singing *Gabriely manjaka . . ., Gabriely mangôty. . . .*

Sister: *Azôvy mandidy e e e?*   (Who commands e e e?)
W & M: *Ampela Be mandid(y)* (Ampelabe commands e e e!!)
e e e!
Sister: *Azôvy mandidy e e e?*   (Who commands e e e?)
W & M: *Ampela Be mandid(y)* (Ampelabe commands e e e!)
e e e!

Brother: *Gabriely mandid(y) e e e!*
Sister: *Azôvy manjaka i i a?*   (Who rules i i a?)
W & M: *Soazara manjaka a a*   (Soazara rules a a a!)
a!

Brother: *Gabriely manjaka a a a!*
Sister: *Azôvy mangôty e e a?*   (Who is spoiled e e a?)
W & M: *I Fotsy mangôty e e a!* (Fotsy is spoiled e e a!)

Brother: *Gabriely mangôty e e a!*
Sister: *Azôvy ampimalo o i a?* (Who talks things over o i a?)
W & M: *Kotomena ampimalo o* (Kotomena talks things over o o o!)
o o!

Brother: *Gabriely ampimalo o o o!*

Sister: *Azôvy sataigny e e a?*   (Who is violently cruel e e a?)

W & M: *Ndrandahy sataigny e*   (Ndrandahy is violently cruel e e a!)
e a!

Brother: *Gabriely sataigny e e a!*

W & M: O o o o o o o o o o
o o o o o o o o o

Brother speaking: *Gabriely ampimalo! Gabriely ampimalo!*

As the singers suggested, the ancestral and living royalty of the Southern Bemihisatra branch of the Zafinimena were seen, like the Zafinifotsy, as interacting kin, in contrast to the Presidency of the Republic, in which one man governed in all ways, and ancestors had no role. Soazara was like the sister of the group (father's sister to the children)—the single female member of the group in both cases and like the brother (and father, too)—she ruled by command. Her own older brother, nicknamed Ambilahikely, but also referred to as the 'Brother,' was like the spoiled Fotsy. Never having ruled, he was always a child, if not always crying. 'Soazara's Father' was like Kotomena, remembered as warm and talkative, and reappearing that way in his mediums. 'Grandfather' and 'Great-Grandfather' were often assimilated to one another. The Great-Grandfather was the real *tompontanana,* or master of the community, since he was the first one buried at the Mahabo. Together, they stood for the royal ancestors as a whole in contrast to their living descendant. They were the "cruel ones" like Ndrandahy, isolated on his rocky island.[7]

What the living descendent of these kin commanded in the postcolonial period of the 1970s were the gifts and services by which the ancestral ones were honored throughout the year. She 'governed ancestral custom' *(mahazaka fombandrazana),* as Mahasoa had said of children of men in general compared to children of women. Whence the other titles by which she was known: 'master of the ancestors' (tompondrazana) or 'master of the cupped hands' (tompon' ny lambantàñana) with which royal followers give to royalty and receive from them.[8] Individuals and households gave gifts in making or fulfilling vows. Villages also gave tribute (paria) every year, sometimes twice a year, in rice, money, and cattle. Such gifts usually coincided with the main harvest time in the early dry season, which came at about the same time as the new year's celebrations at the Doany and the Mahabo. Villages with enough water to cultivate a second crop of rice during the dry season had to contribute some of that as well. Tribute averaged 50 FMG and 2 kapoka (8 oz Nestlé canned milk tin) of white rice, about two-thirds of a kilo, somewhat under the average amount that one person eats in a day, a "tiny pinch" as one royal official put it. Each village was expected to give a cow and also to contribute portions of other major harvests, such as manioc or corn, as well as the special wild foods of their area in season. They supplied food, shelter, and entertainment to royalty—the ampanjaka or mediums of royal spirits—whenever they passed through. Services ranged from herding royal cattle and cultivating royal rice fields scattered throughout the region to honoring the royal ancestors at the Doany and the Mahabo, to making and repairing the buildings there.[9] All of these were more time-consuming than their common counterparts because of the numerous prohibitions involved.

The ampanjaka was assisted in commanding these gifts and services by the manantany, one who has land. The position, associated with the Zafindramahavita ancestry, was supposed to be passed on from father to son. But if there was no appropriate successor, then 'you take who you see,' as one of the Sambarivo at the Doany put it. Malaza pointed out that the son and grandson of ZamanKaroka, who had been the Father's manantany, did not succeed him because 'they didn't look here' (tsy mijery aty), did not recognize the royal ancestors, having converted to Christianity instead. The manantany served as the main liaison between the ruler and her followers, 'announcing the ampanjaka's work,' sending out letters to district heads concerning the days on which services were to begin, and so on. Some royal followers emphasized that he had regular 'hours' *(lera,* from *l'heure)* like a government functionary, leaving home to work with the ampanjaka in her office around *setèra sy sasany* (7:30), returning about *onzèra sy sasany* (11:30), going out again and returning about *sizèra* (6:00), using the combinations of French and Malagasy words for clock-time now common in this area.[10]

While the manantany was associated with the region as a whole, the commoner who served as 'third in the service of the royal ancestors' *(fahatelo am' razan' ny ampanjaka)* or 'third' *(fahatelo)* for short, was associated with the Doany. He administered the activities of the Sambarivo surrounding the royal compound and the conduct of royal services like the menaty service. Both the manantany and the fahatelo lived at the Doany when it was still in Analalava, in the northeast and southwest corners respectively. The manantany still lived northeast of the royal compound in Analalava, while the fahatelo had moved with the Doany when it was relocated to the countryside south of Analalava.

Commoners who served to 'bind up the country' *(fehitany)* lived among their kin in surrounding villages.[11] They administered some ten 'tied or governed places' *(fehezana)* of three to six villages each. Besides providing a rice field each year, each district usually pastured part of the royal herd *(tanimbary tsimirango, aomby tsimirango).* Royal followers described the fehitany as a 'substitute for the living ruler in villages' *(solontena ny ampanjaka antanàna),* a *sefo* for the ruler, 'like the chef de village, but concerned with the ampanjaka's work.' In villages where there was no fehitany, the chef de village was asked to do his work.[12] The work of the fehitany was to collect *(mandano)* the tribute and other gifts, to recruit workers for royal services and to organize the royal services in their own districts. *Paria* refers to something scattered about like seed, as well as to something that has run away in every direction, like chickens or perhaps reluctant subjects. Malaza commented that the ampanjaka collected things from all over—turkeys and other kinds of birds, baskets of eggs, loads of mangos and other special fruits like *mokonazy:* "But when people hear that she is coming to collect, they are afraid, they run away. Because they are afraid that something might be done wrong and thus look as if they had tried to commit sorcery against her."

The regional services to work on the royal rice fields—preparing them for sowing and later harvesting and threshing the rice—were usually very festive events: 'Full of talk *(maresaka)*! Young men just have to come and wrestle cattle there,' as one man said. There was no communal meal, but meat was distributed, and many people attended mainly to have a good time especially during the all-night singing to honor the royal ancestors *(tsimandrimandry)* that preceded the work. Royal spirits possessed their mediums and sat together under trees talking, while the work was going on. Preparing the ground was done in the same way as commoners' own work, except that the cattle could only be driven to the right. As Diniky explained: "They have to go right because all royal things go right first, *ankahery,* toward strength. Just one direction. They can't go in two directions. Ordinary people do both. This is what separates *(mampihavaka)* the ampanjaka and simple people." It was also forbidden to thresh royal grain by laying the cut stalks on the ground and walking cattle over them; threshing had to be done by hand.

The fehitany also served to convey people's requests to the ampanjaka through the manantany—for example, their needs for blessing—as well as the ampanjaka's responses. Like all royal officials, he was expected to keep a portion of what passed through his hands for himself, although he was not supposed "to eat" more of it than he fed villagers in the form of royal benefits. Fehitany corresponded with other officials in writing. Some of them also kept their own notes concerning royal services or the activities of especially renowned curers or mediums in their district.

The population as a whole, termed *Tsiarô, Bemihisatra,* or *Sakalava,* was represented by male heads of kin networks who served as royal counselors *(ranitry,* sharp), two or more in large villages. They lived at the Doany when the ampanjaka called them there to deliberate *(mimalo, manao kofransy)* royal affairs or adjudicate disputes involving royal services. Royal officials described *malo* as an activity from which the ampanjaka was excluded. Young men *(fihitra, fihitry,* catch/caught)

and young women (*marovavy,* many women) were called to the Doany
and to the ampanjaka's compound in Analalava to sing and dance and
to serve as additional workers during special services.

Laza Be was a marovavy, a position she got from her father. She said her
father's family had served the ampanjaka since they came up from the
south. "He is the fourth of the men in his generation who are fihitra. The
women are marovavy. My mother, Tsimihety from the highlands, is just
people *(olo fona).*" [The children followed the father?] "Yes, the children
got the father's lot *(nangala anjaran' ny baba).* My mother didn't become a
marovavy by marrying him. She is with the Tsiarô." People living along
the shore (Antandrano) were recruited to work whenever royal services
required transportation by boat.

Ancestries of commoners known collectively as Ancestor People
(Razan'olo) prepared the royal corpse for burial, washed the regalia
at the Doany, and played the major role in rebuilding the menaty
fence around the royal tomb. Guardians at the Doany and the Mahabo
included ancestries known as the Sakalava Mañoroaomby, Ndrarameva, Jingo, and Antankoala in this group. According to Saha Barimaso, Ancestor People included Sakalava Tsiaraña, Sakalava Mañoroaomby, and Sakalava Ndrarameva, related to each other as a pair
of big and little elements.

"The Sakalava Mañoroaomby are only with the ampanjaka [the living
ruler]. They don't go to the Mahabo, they are prohibited from going
there. The other two can go there. The Sakalava Mañoroaomby are the
big ones of the three, who are like the Bahary Be and Bahary Bitiky [a
paired group of Sambarivo]. They get to stay wherever they want [in the
countryside and at royal centers, unlike Sambarivo, who must stay in
specific places]. Ancestor People get to do that. Very small is the difference
between the Sakalava Mañoroaomby and the ampanjaka. Their work is to
serve as the supplicator at the Doany [they are in charge of sacrificing
cattle *(mañoro aomby)* to the royal ancestors at the Doany]. The Sakalava
Tsiaraña and Sakalava Ndrarameva are the little ones. They may serve,
may go to the Mahabo. Jingo and Antankoala are different, they are kinds
of people who work, kinds of people *[iregny karazan'olo miasa, karazan'olo,*
as if they were not ancestries, *razan'olo].* The Sakalava Ndrarameva don't

work. They are people who go there [to the Mahabo], but don't work.
Jingo go in front, Antankoala follow." [Why are they called Ancestor
People, what makes them Ancestor People?] "Because they may do things
that shouldn't be done with the ampanjaka. Things that people don't dare
to join together, they dare" *(Satria izy mahazo mañano raha tsy tokony atao
amin' ny ampanjaka. Raha tsy sakin' olo mañambitra, izy mahasaky).*

Sambarivo from the Tsimazava and Mosohery pens closest to the
Ancestors' House at the Doany—usually a man, but sometimes a
woman—served as the ampangataka (supplicator), who received offerings and spoke for the people who came to the Doany to petition
the royal ancestors during the new year's ceremonies and throughout
the remainder of the year.

The positions of manantany and ampangataka were duplicated at
the Mahabo, but their importance was reversed, reflecting the fact that
the work of the guardians at the Mahabo was around the tomb, not
throughout the region. Furthermore, all the positions were held by
the guardians themselves, not by commoners. The ampangataka was
the major official there, selected from the Antibe group of Sambarivo
in the southeast part of the settlement considered closest to the tomb.[13]
One man and then three of his sons had held the position since early
in the colonial period. The ampangataka was sometimes called a fahatelo because he was also in charge of organizing royal services at the
Mahabo. He too sent out notices to surrounding villages telling them
to 'Come to the Mahabo, we're going to serve!' *(Avia Mahabo, atsika
hanompo!)*

A manantany, selected from the Antiravaka group of Sambarivo in
the northern half of the settlement, assisted the ampangataka. As one
of the brothers explained it:

"His work is to honor the monarchy according to ancestral custom, but
there is no work. He doesn't talk. Only the ampangataka speaks to the
ancestors in the tomb *(razana)* or to the Zanahary [ancestors embodied in
mediums]. The manantany is second to the ampangataka, like the adjoint
to his district."

Nevertheless, the logic of the sequence was different. Whereas the
emphasis in the royal administration associated with the Doany was

on the sequence descending from the one person at the top, here it was on the pair, each of which served to correct the other.

Jaotogny, who belonged to the group from which the ampangataka was chosen, talked about the shame of discovering that some royal official had eaten too much from the offerings. "Shame. Shaming, shaming. Visitors come from far away, from the Doany, from the royal quarter in Analalava. They find there is no money in the coffer or only a little left. They know it must be the supplicator. The offering dishes come from the *zomba vinta* ('house of destiny' inside the burial compound). Two men and two women go into the enclosure to bring them out. The ampangataka and the manantany are the men. The women could be anyone, but one from the south, the place of the ampangataka, the other from the north, the place of the manantany. The ampangataka goes in first. That key he took was the key to the zomba vinta. He and the manantany always stand to the south and north respectively. He pays his respects *(mikoezy)* at the menaty [the innermost fence around the tomb], if this is the first time he has gone in. The manantany doesn't mikoezy, but he has to be there. Then they go into the zomba vinta and open up the coffer in there and put the petitioners' money into it. Then they get the white clay *(tany fotsy/ malandy,* conveying ancestral blessing) and bring it out." [Why do the women put it on?] "Custom! *(Fomba!)*" [Which one?] "The one from the south [then he hesitated], because southern people get [the position of] ampangataka." [What is the work of the northern one?] "There is no work. If the ampangataka couldn't get a woman from the south, then he would take one from the north, and she could put on the tany fotsy."

Later he contrasted the work of the ampangataka and the manantany in similar terms:

"The work of the manantany is to ask for the formal speech of the people who have come to pay their respects to the royal ancestors *(manontany kabarin'olo avy mikoezy).* The work of the ampangataka is to ask for the formal speech of the royal ancestors *(manontany kabarin' ny Zanahary).* If they possess people in the council house, then he is there to ask for their speech *(manontany kabary).* He is the one who supplicates at the door *(mangataka ambaravarana).*"

Besides these two officials, there was also a 'door-keeper' *(ampi-tanambaravarana),* selected from the Tsimandrara *(be* or *bitiky)* groups in the north. The Antiravaka had the key, which was kept in the house of the manantany, even though the door-keeper who did the work belonged to another group. "But then he got old and died, and his children didn't know anything about the procedures, so we Anti-be [the ampangataka's group] took the key."

DOANY

The *tompon'tanana*, 'masters of the village,' at the Doany and the Mahabo, were royalty with officials to assist them in 'governing ancestral custom.' To explore the nature and extent of their mastery, it is necessary to go further into the places themselves, in and through which their mastery over land and people was articulated. It will soon be apparent that the first purpose of these places was to distinguish royalty from others by separating them from surroundings with which they 'don't mix' *(tsy miharo)*, or at least should not mix. The long-term purpose of these separations was to transform their followers, but in a different direction. In practice, the reorganization of the relationship between 'leaders' and 'followers,' 'heads' and 'feet,' was achieved through the spatial reorganization of the entire countryside in the unique structures of the Doany and the Mahabo, combined with the prohibitions governing people's movements in these places. As we have already seen, these reformations of surrounding life underwent significant changes during the precolonial and colonial periods as 'leaders' and 'followers' were put and placed themselves in different positions in relation to one another and to other sources of power and authority like the French and Merina. The menaty service of the mid-1970s still stands as the most intensive royal reform in this area since independence.

The clearest point of entry into these recurrent reformations through rebuilding is to examine the structures themselves. One contradiction in these relationships between leaders and followers, heads and feet, should be kept in mind from the outset. The ampanjaka commands with the assistance of the manantany who 'has land,' suggesting perhaps that the ampanjaka commands like a stranger at the behest of indigenous land-owners. Royal followers do emphasize the foreign origins of the Maroseraña royalty, and they do see themselves as masters of the land in the sense of being the original inhabitants of the area. Yet the very presence of the Doany and Mahabo contradicts that view, while the ways in which they are organized serve to transform masters of the land into servants of royal ancestors. Royalty are acknowledged tompon'tanàna, masters of the respective places they occupy, but their status as tompon'tany, masters of the entire region, asserted by the central position of their tombs in the land, is still more open to dispute. The structures of these places, especially their fences, contain divergent opinions.

The Doany, known as Miadàna (Move Slowly, Peacefully, Prosperously), was moved from the southeastern quarter of Analalava to its present location, about a day's walk south of the post in the early 1950s.[14] Royal followers explained that they had to move the Doany in order to separate the ampanjaka from the Vy Lava, which was preventing her from conceiving children, and to protect it from the dirt and disregard of prohibitions associated with life at the post. In fact, the practice of having two locations for the living ruler—one in the post and one 'away from all that,' in Velondraza's words—goes back to the establishment of the Southern Bemihisatra in this area, as we have already seen in Chapter 3.

The ampanjaka's house at the post was built in the mid-thirties when Launois was chef de district.[15] It was four to five times the size of the houses around it, made of wooden planks with a veranda on the west and south sides, on cement pillars raising it about six to eight feet above the sand on which the surrounding houses were located. It was roofed in galvanized iron. As Malaza commented, a house of stone would also have been acceptable, but 'mud houses' *(trano fotaka)* were prohibited because of the dirt. The house stood in the northeast corner of the compound. The ampanjaka's daughters' house was located in the southern half of the compound, which also included a *magasin* (as followers described it) for coconuts and manioc and another building with a *magasin* for rice in one half and a kitchen in the other. Besides the manantany's house outside to the northeast, the compound was surrounded by the houses of Sambarivo and followers on all sides.

There was a togny outside at the southwest corner—a *mandrofo* tree. Laza Be explained that "this is so they don't have to struggle to find incense (copal) when they supplicate the ancestors." The tree, which had been there a long time, was located on the former house-site of a Sambarivo, whose house was taken down after he died.[16]

The Doany Miadana, consisting of the royal compound surrounded by guardians' houses, was moved to a site along the coast, on high ground overlooking Narinda Bay.[17] The royal compound included the ancestors' house where the royal regalia were kept, the house of the living ruler, a kitchen, bathhouse/urinal, and a council house (Fig. 14). The orientation of these places was opposite to that of ordinary settlements. While north was primary in relations among the living and northeast was the place of contact between living people and their ancestors, north was still primary in relations among royalty living or embodied in living people, but the meeting place between living people and royal ancestors in their nonliving forms was in the southeast.[18] Thus the royal ancestors were honored in the northeast corner of the living ruler's own house, but they also had their own house, surrounded by its own fence, in the southeast corner of the compound. The Doany differed from surrounding settlements in another way as well. The living ruler's children had no place there. The compound articulated in space the principle of unrivaled rule embodied in the 'Long Iron Without Equal That Rules Alone.' The daughters, then about seventeen and fifteen, could come to the Doany, but they could not enter the compound. They slept in the southern half of the settlement among Sambarivo who had cared for them since childhood.[19]

The ancestors' house (Fig. 14.1, 2) was known variously as royal ancestors' house, royal men's house, royal house of blessing, and great royal house *(zomban-drazaña, zombalahy, zomba mitahy, zomba be)*.[20] The size of the house, which was said to vary according to the importance of the doany, was about eight by sixteen feet. It was constructed like a 'Malagasy house' *(trano gasy)*, in a north-south direction, with walls made from panels of palm stalks. The difference was that the corner posts had to be made of the *teza* or hearts of a hardwood known as *mañary*. French features like windows and verandas were

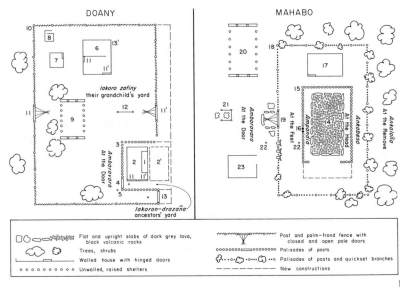

Figure 14. Outlines of the Southern Bemihisatra doany and mahabo. 1 (see 14), *raha sarotra*—difficult, precious things; 2, 2' (see 17), *zomban-drazaña, zomba be, zombalahy*—ancestors' house (big house, men's house) in August 1972, with new house (2') under construction; 3 (see 15), *valamena*—red fence; 4 (see 19), *varavara, varavara mitahy* (L)—door (of blessing); 5 (see 22), *toha (tombony) mañandria*—support for mañandria drums; 6, *zomba ny ampanjaka*—ruler's house; 7, *fanisara*—royal kitchen; 8, *moraba faly*—taboo walls (bath house, urinal); 9 (see 20), *fantsina*—place of summons, council; 10, *tsirangôty*—not (to be) scratched/harmed; 11, *varavara ny Sambarivo, varavara Tsimaniha* (L) (east)—door of the Sambarivo (Tsimaniha); 11', *varavara omby, varavara be* (L)—cattle (great) door; 12, *toha, tombony*— supports (for drying meat, fish); 13, 13' (see 16), *varavara menalio, varavara faly* (L)—red-blood door, taboo door, with counterpart (11') in ruler's house (L); 14 (see 1), *raha sarotra*—difficult, precious things; 15 (see 3), *menaty*—red inside; 16 (see 13), *varavara menalio*—red-blood door; 17 (see 2), *zomba vinta*—house of fate; 18, *fiaro-aomby*—protection against/for cattle; 19 (see 4), *varavara*—door; 20 (see 9), *fantsina*—place of summons, council; 21, *toha (tombony) bekiviro*—supports for bekiviro drum; 22 (see 5), *toha (tombony) mañandria*—support for mañandria drums; 23, *zomba bekirivo*—bekiviro house.

prohibited.[21] The two sliding doors were both at the southern end (Fig. 14.11, 11'). The eastern door—the 'great door' or 'door of the cattle' *(varavarambe, varavara aomby)*—was used only by the living ruler and her officials. The western door—'the door of the Sambarivo' *(varavara Sambarivo)*—was used only by Sambarivo from the groups nearest the ancestors' house, who were charged with caring for the ancestors at the Doany, as opposed to the living ruler.[22] Anyone else who entered there, even accidentally, would become a Sambarivo, followed by his or her descendants as well.

The ancestors' house was surrounded by a high palisade (Fig. 14.3) of closely set, pointed stakes called the "red fence" *(valamena)*.[23] A door (Fig. 14.4) was located in the southern end of the west side of the fence, which people in the past called 'the door of blessing' *(varavara mitahy)*.[24] A post for the pair of royal *mañandria* drums, kept in the ancestors' house, was located just outside the enclosure, south of the door (Fig. 14.5). The door was opened only during the services honoring the royal ancestors when the drums were played. When the services were done and the drums were put back in the ancestors' house, the door was shut. Once it was shut, even the living ruler was prohibited from entering the enclosure.

The *valamena*, referring to the fence and enclosure alike, was sometimes called the 'ancestors' fence/court' *(lakoron'drazana, lakoron' ny zomba be)* in contrast to the fence around the royal compound as a whole, called 'the grandchild's courtyard' or 'the courtyard of the ruler's house' *(lakoron-zafiny, lakoron' ny zomba ny ampanjaka)*. The ampanjaka ruled by virtue of the ancestors, as seen in their adjacent houses. Royalty in nonruling lines were prohibited from constructing 'red fences' (valamena) around their ancestral shrines or in keeping the mañandria drums associated with the ancestors. Nevertheless, the two places were clearly separate. Sambarivo at the Doany emphasized that the ancestors had their own house surrounded by their own fence, whereas the living ruler lived in a separate house surrounded by a separate fence.[25]

The ampanjaka's house *(zomba ny ampanjaka)* was located in the center of the northern half of the compound (Fig. 14.6). Like the

ancestors' house, it was built according to "Malagasy custom." French
features, like the metal roof, windows, and wide veranda of the royal
house in Analalava were prohibited at the Doany. It had a floor of
palm stalks, but the floor was near the ground to assure that even the
living ruler was lower than the ancestors, resting on a 'bed' *(kibany)*
in the ancestors' house (Fig. 14.1). Even so, it was somewhat larger
than the ancestors' house, about ten feet wide by twenty-four feet
long, including two rooms in contrast to ordinary houses, which elsewhere might have two or occasionally three rooms, but here had only
one. An interior wall, with a door at the east end, divided the bedroom
on the north from the reception room on the south. There were three
outer doors: the 'Bemihisatra door' *(varavara Bemihisatra)* in the east
end of the south wall, for the ruler, her officials and followers; the
'Sambarivo door' *(varavara Sambarivo)* in the west wall, just south of
the inner partition, for Sambarivo going to and from the kitchen and
reception room; and the 'prohibited door' *(varavara faly)* in the north
end of the east wall in the bedroom, reserved for ruler's communi-
cations with the ancestors.[26] The two ribs of raffia palm extending
beyond the ridge of the house at each end were a sign of royalty
common elsewhere in Madagascar.

Fire was prohibited in the ruler's house, so the ampanjaka had a
separate 'royal cooking place'—*fañisara,* as opposed to *lakozy* (Fig.
14.7)—even before laws requiring separate kitchens were enacted in
the colonial period.[27] The kitchen was located west of the house,
roughly opposite the Sambarivo door. The bathhouse/urinal—*moraba
faly,* prohibited walls, as opposed to *ladouche* (Fig. 14.8)—was north
of the kitchen in the northwest corner of the compound. The bathhouse was made of five panels of palm ribs, arranged in the form of
a square with overlapping ends to baffle the eye. The bathhouse was
prohibited to all but the ruler and the Sambarivo known as 'Strong
Pots' *(Vilany Mahery),* whose particular work was to wash 'dirty'
(maloto), even 'filthy things' *(raha makota).*[28]

The 'summons place' *(fantsina)* was the last building to be constructed when a doany was built on a new site. It was located in the
western half of the compound, toward the south (Fig. 14.9). It was

made out of the same materials as the other buildings, except that it had no walls and was elevated to catch the breeze. As Malaza explained, it had no walls "because it is not a place where people sleep [which is also why it could be raised]. It's built to provide shade as a judge's office, where adjudication is done" *(birao ny juge, ao fitsaraña)*. Shade trees were planted nearby to make it cooler. The fantsina was organized like a house around an outer pole *(anjovery)*, known in a royal context as *mongory*.

The fence around the entire compound, seen as the 'ruler's fence' as opposed to the 'ancestors' fence, was called the *tsirangôty* (does not scratch) (Fig. 14.10). It was about six feet high, made of six overlapping tiers of thornless ravinala palm fronds supported on posts made from the hard cores of rosewood *(mañary)* set at seven to ten foot intervals. Other materials were prohibited. Its name and materials distinguished it from the thorny enclosures *(fatsimbala)* that people throughout Madagascar use to fence animals and gardens. The privilege of building tsirangôty around their houses was allowed to non-ruling royalty, but they were prohibited from using the same materials. The leaves of another local palm *(korompanjara)* had to be used instead. Like the dimensions of the ancestors' house and its fence, the dimensions of the tsirangôty were said to vary according to the importance of the ruler within, the only restriction being that the posts had to add up to an even number. The fence at Miadàna was about sixty feet wide by one hundred and ten feet long. In the mid-thirties, people were prohibited from touching or looking over the tsirangôty.[29] This was still the case in the 1970s, and we were also prohibited from taking photographs over or inside it. The palm fronds between the posts had fallen down owing to age and storms. The guardians were in the process of building a new ancestors' house east of the old one. Once that was finished, they planned to rebuild the tsirangôty on the eastern side.

The ruler's fence had two doors: the 'big door' or 'door of the cattle' in the middle of the east side and the 'Sambarivo door' in the middle of the west side, named like the east and west doors in the ancestors' fence and the comparably placed doors in her own house (Fig. 14.11,

11′). The doors in the fence were neither sliding rails, like those in cattle parks or gardens, nor 'carpentered' *(saripatiay)* doors, made of wooden planks, like those in most houses and house-fences in the region. They were made of palm stalks strung from one end on a cross-bar. Sambarivo opened the door by placing the loose ends in a large forked branch, just inside the fence. A raised sill, made from a stationary row of palm stalks about a foot high, kept the door shut and prevented it from being opened outward.[30] West of the main door on the east side were two comparable forked branches, supporting a pole used as a drying rack for meat and fish (Fig. 14.12). They were probably earlier door forks, turned to new uses, suggesting that the ancestors' house had been rebuilt at least twice since the Doany was relocated.

A third door, at the southern end of the eastern side of the outer fence, immediately south of the ancestors' fence, was a carpentered door known as the 'forbidden door' *(varavara fady)*, which had a counterpart in the northeast corner of the ruler's house (Fig. 14.13, 13′). It was prohibited to everyone except the Sambarivo and Ancestor People who served as intermediaries with the royal ancestors: the supplicator (ampangataka), and her assistants from the Mosohery and Tsimazava pens. The ampanjaka sacrificed cattle to the ancestors in the narrow place between the two fences of living and ancestral royalty, facing east toward the forbidden door.

FADY: PROHIBITIONS

The reorientations articulated in the walls and fences surrounding royalty were incorporated into the bodies of the people who lived in and around these structures through restraints on their behavior. Visitors to the Doany learned these fady before anything else.[31] They were designed to reproduce precolonial circumstances. Prior to the French conquest of the area and the creation of the fenced houseyards known as *lakoro,* the continuous space occupied by royal followers was broken only by the royal enclosures at the Doany and the Mahabo and the fences of Silamo and Indian traders. As ancestry among commoners was not to interfere with their common subordination to the royal ancestors, so houses were not to contain followers in any way that constrained royalty.[32] While commoners had begun—with some ambivalence in farming communities—to build fences around their houses, the Doany was explicitly created to be a "chronotope," to use Bakhtin's term, of precolonial arrangements of persons by excluding as Malaza said succinctly, "all things there weren't before" *(raha jiaby tsisy taloha)*.[33] Thus, royal guardians lived as royal followers were thought to have lived before the conquest: in small one-room houses, without the windows, verandas, and other French features that had since become common.[34] Four-cornered mosquito nets were prohibited as resembling too closely the gauzy cloth covering the regalia in the ancestors' house. Beds and chairs were still prohibited during the early colonial period as elevating people to the height of royalty. Guardians slept on mats on the floor until they petitioned the royal ancestors for permission to make carpentered beds with stuffed mattresses and to buy "Salama"-brand folding chairs and kerosene lamps made of Nestlé tins.[35] Malaza said that kerosene lamps were still prohibited in the ancestors' house; only beef tallow was used there.

Prohibitions against other European manufactured goods like portable radios and flashlights were still observed in the 1970s. There were further prohibitions against European and other tailored or closed forms of clothing within the tsirangôty. Belts, hats, trousers, dresses, bras, underpants, and closed shoes *(combotte)* could be worn outside the compound, but not within it.[36] People dressed for the royal compound as if they were preparing to be possessed by a royal spirit: in an unsewn body wrap *(sambelatra)*, with their braids down and their heads and shoulders bare.[37] For that reason, they also had to be 'clean' *(madio)*, free of bodily 'filth' of any sort.[38] They had to give to royalty and receive from them with both hands, that is, with their whole bodies, just as they had to carry royal objects on their heads while holding them with both hands; to give, receive, or support royalty with one hand was prohibited.[39] They had to enter and leave royal enclosures and buildings with their right foot first because it was the 'oldest,' the left foot coming 'last' because it was 'younger.'[40] Prohibitions on movement included prohibitions on the places where guardians and visitors could live, to which we will return later.

Restraints on time suggest that the recreation of the Doany in the precolonial form was inseparable from the recreation of a place in time that was not simply before or 'ahead' *(taloha)* in years or generations, but a specific time *(fotana)* related to royal death and burial. Sunday, Tuesday, Wednesday, and Thursday (reckoned from sunset to sunset) were all 'bad' because these are the days on which Southern Bemihisatra rulers had died. Days of the lunar month, when the moon was 'rotten,' 'sick,' or 'dying,' that is, waning, were also prohibited.[41] The second and last months of the lunar year also fell into that category. Royal services could only be done on 'good days' (Fridays, Saturdays, and Mondays) in good months, during a 'living' or 'growing' moon and a rising sun.

The point of these prohibitions was to distinguish Malagasy from Europeans and rulers from followers—to make then 'not the same' *(tsy ampitovizana)*—while exposing followers to royal direction. The fences surrounding royalty enforced the prohibitions against assimilating oneself to royalty or seeing the royal ancestors, contributing to their inaccessible hiddenness, while the prohibitions concerning commoners contributed to their openness and visibility in relation to royalty. Some prohibitions against European manufactured goods achieved both these ends. Chairs *(seza,* from *chaise)* and iron bedsteads put ordinary people on the level of royalty instead of in lower places. Closed shoes *(combotte,* from *bottes de combat[?])*, said to be prohibited 'because when the French arrived in combat boots, people were afraid and ran away,' also hid the body, closing it off from royalty. These prohibitions enforcing the separateness of royalty and exposure of their followers, achieved through doors and fences, were the main source of the 'difficulty' of royal work. While they were a well-known feature of life at the Doany, they were most strictly enforced in the community of guardians, mediums, and pilgrims who lived around the royal tomb.

MAHABO

The Mahabo was located in the southeast part of the island of Nosy Lava, on high chalky ground overlooking the bay. The 'difficult things' (Fig. 14.14) were at the eastern edge of the village formed by the houses of their guardians and mediums. Like the ancestors' house at the Doany, the tomb was also surrounded by two fences: an inner fence known as the menaty immediately around the tomb, and an outer fence, the fiaraomby, that enclosed a 'royal destiny house' *(zomba vinta)* as well (Fig. 14.15, 17, 18). The house was used for storing the material belonging to the spirits—the dancing costumes, cloths, pots and baskets used in royal services, the white clay with which pilgrims were blessed, the money and other offerings they brought, and the clothing, jewelry, and other gifts that mediums who were now deceased had bought to clothe the spirits when they possessed them. Decary, who saw the tomb in the late 1920s, after the Father's death when it was still guarded by one man, described it as "a single mass of rocks, seven to eight meters on a side by about two meters high." Conch shells *(antsiva)*, blown during royal funerals, were placed around a small bush. North of the tomb was a hut for storing ritual material. Decary notes, "When I visited this mahabo, it was guarded by an old native with completely white hair, who told me coldly that he was one hundred and twenty years old."[42]

In the Analalava region, the menaty (Fig. 14.15) was a rectangular palisade of thick posts made from the cores of hardwood trees *(teza)* cut six to eight feet high and closely set, like the *valamena* at the Doany. The fiaroaomby (Fig. 14.18) was made from quick-set branches of *matambelo* and other kinds of shrubs *(sandrahaka)* that got bushier as they grew higher. Those that did not take root were periodically replaced. Such 'living fences' *(valavelona)* were used to make gardens and cattle parks throughout the area, but the fiaroaomby was the only such fence around royalty.

The term *menaty*, 'red inside,' may derive from the phrase 'red pith' *(mena + aty)*, that is, from the cores of the ideally red hardwood trees from which it is made, perhaps alluding indirectly to the corpses within or to their royal status as Zafinimena, 'Descendants of the Gold/

Red.' *Fiaro,* from the root *aro,* refers to any kind of protective barrier. The fiaroaomby served like a garden fence as a 'protection against cattle,' comparable to the fans (*fiarolalitra,* protection against flies) that Bemihisatra used to protect the materials used in royal services from dirt, or like the royal coffin known as *fiarovonotro,* 'protection against moisture.' The name of the fence can also be understood as 'protector of cattle,' like the *fiaro* that Richardson describes as "a charm rubbed on a fighting bull to preserve him from being wounded by his antagonist,"[43] or to the *fiarotanàna,* 'protector of the village,' as ancestors' trees (togny) are known among royal followers in Menabe. The royal ancestors were often compared in their strength and grandeur to prize bulls. These two fences were the prerogative of rulers. Lesser nobility were allowed to fence their ancestral tombs, but the enclosure had to be made of smaller pieces of wood than the menaty and called by a different name (*kizohizohy,* cavelike place).

The fiaroaomby had an inward-opening door (*varavara*), made of palm stalks like the doors in the ruler's fence at the Doany. Here the door was located only in the middle of the west side, because it was prohibited for people to walk on the east side of the tomb, known as Ankalaña, At the Remove, unless they were doing royal work requiring them to throw things from the interior of the enclosure out there. The royal guardians explained the menaty as the counterpart of the *valamena* or red fence around the ancestors' house at the Doany. It was sometimes called 'red fence,' for example, mediums expelled from the Mahabo were described as having been 'thrown out of the red fence' *(roasigny valamena).* Like the valamena, the menaty had a single door (Fig. 14.16), with a post for the ancestors' *mañandria* drums to the south of it (Fig. 14.22). But here, the door was located in the middle of the west side, and its name—'red-blood door' *(varavara menalio)*—linked it to the door in the southeast corner of the ruler's fence, where sacrifices were held at the Doany. Furthermore, the menaty door, composed of the two tallest posts in the fence, one next to the other, could not be opened or closed by any ordinary means. The menaty was 'opened' only when the entire fence was removed during the menaty service. It was 'closed' only when the fence was rebuilt and the door sealed with the blood from a sacrificed cow.

The red-blood door is named in the guide to the menaty service. Sambarivo belonging to the Antibe group at the Mahabo also mentioned the door in discussing the service, always to emphasize that it did not open. One of the brothers who served as supplicator put it this way:

"There is a door in the menaty, in the center of the west side. There is no other door in the menaty, no east door. The door is in the center, opposite the fiaroaomby door *(varavara fiaroaomby)*. It is made of two posts, side-by-side. Just the two. Both of them are sharp at the ends. That is how you know it is the door; the other posts are blunt. Sakalava Manoroaomby construct the red-blood door. The posts are sharp, so you know it's a door, yet it may not be opened." He kept repeating that—"yet it may not be opened" *(tsy mety biafigny eky—tsy biafigny eky)*. He concluded: "Two cattle are sacrificed in front of the door—one is the mat, one is the cow. It may not be opened. Once the menaty is built, there is no more entering in."

Even so, when I asked one of the long-time mediums of the Father at the Mahabo whether the menaty had a door, he said it did not and could not. The 'red-blood door' was the door in the fiaroaomby. Furthermore, the 'real door' was the two posts on either side, not the poles by which it was closed.[44] Royal guardians said in 1973, before the menaty was completed, that they would sacrifice the cow, whose blood was used to anoint the tops of the door posts, in the area in front of the door (to its west, facing east) between the two fences. But in 1981, they said that the sacrifice was done at the southeast corner between the southern ends of the menaty and the fiaroaomby, which is in fact the closest spatial counterpart of the place where cattle are sacrificed to the ancestors at the Doany, except that there is no comparable 'forbidden door' in that place at the Mahabo.[45]

Pilgrims to the ancestors gathered to honor them in the raised area west of the tomb known as Ambaravara, 'At the Door' (of the fiaroaomby). The ground here, like the ground inside the burial compound, was called 'oil' *(famonty)*. As one guardian explained, "Dirt *(fôtaka)* cannot be used at the door." The rocks used to keep the earth around the door from washing away in the rains were usually referred to as 'supports' *(tohana)*, but royally speaking, they were 'waves' *(riaka)*.

The stand for the mañandria drums was located to the south or right of the door, facing in (Fig. 14.22). Pilgrims made their offerings in lines facing east toward the tomb in front of the stand for the large *bekiviro* drum (Fig. 14.21). The council house *(fantsina)* where royal spirits in mediums met with their guardians and petitioners was located in the northern half of this area (Fig. 14.20). The 'royal drum house' *(zomba bekiviro)* was located south of the door (Fig. 14.23). Only Sambarivo could walk between these buildings and the fiaroaomby. Their houses and those of spirit-mediums stretched out 'behind' and 'below' the burial compound to the north, west, and south.

The prohibitions against European features in the construction of houses and European manufactured goods were more exacting at the Mahabo than at the Doany. The restrictions on clothing were the same, but they applied not simply to the royal compound (which petitioners were not allowed to enter anyway), but to the entire village. A special *ampisikina,* 'dressing place,' where visitors could change their clothes, was located just outside the main path into the settlement. Decary, writing in the late colonial period, noted that Merina villagers a generation earlier (ca. 1920) used to put on their shoes and socks at the entrance gates to Tananarive, whereas in 1950 almost everyone there wore European dress. He goes on to argue that clothing evolves together with housing as a measure of progress toward civilization. Such practices were still common in the Analalava region in the 1970s. Diniky, for example, prepared to return to Mahajanga after Kidroa's death by unbraiding her hair and redoing it in a bouffant style, changing her body wrap for a white dress with black and white loafers, and covering her right wrist with a clean cloth where her mother had tied a 'medicine,' so people would think she had just sprained it. At the Doany and the Mahabo, the chronotopes that people made of themselves through clothing were designed to achieve the opposite.

The prohibitions against European-style folding chairs and bedsteads, which were lifted at the Doany, were applied at the Mahabo. The Sambarivo were allowed to put their mats on beds made of unbarked poles, cushioned with loose straw, but they were still forbidden to use stuffed mattresses and pillows. Other prohibitions on housing rendered them more open to royalty. Outer doors had to open inward and could not be covered, although curtains were permitted inside.

The bodily prescriptions on cleanliness and on handling, carrying, and moving right foot foremost were likewise similar.[46] But the hiddenness of royalty, in contrast to the openness of royal followers was even more pronounced at the Mahabo than it was at the Doany. Anyone, except the living ruler's descendants, could enter the outer fence at the Doany as long as they observed the prohibitions there, but only the living ruler, the manantany, the Ancestor People, and certain Sambarivo at the Doany were permitted to enter the ancestors' enclosure and the ancestors' house itself. A still smaller number—a royal substitute, the Ancestor People, and the guardians at the Mahabo, were allowed to enter the fiaroaomby at the Mahabo. Only the substitute and the Ancestor People could enter the menaty, and then only during the menaty service itself. The greater separation of the royal ancestors at the Mahabo was accentuated in royal service. Whereas the valamena at the Doany was opened every year so the ancestors could be washed, the menaty was opened only once in every generation. Although the tomb was washed then, the ultimate purpose of the service was to close the menaty, which had been broken open in the course of the preceding burial and covered only with a cloth.

Just as there were two royal residences, the royal compound at the post and the true doany in the countryside, so there were two mahabo on Nosy Lava. The Bemihisatra mahabo, known in this context as the 'southern' or 'upper Mahabo' (mahabo ambalaka/ambony) was paired with the 'northern' or 'lower Mahabo' (mahabo avaratra/ambany), about an hour's walk to the north. The pair of tombs reproduced other oppositions as well, between southern 'Sakalava' or 'Malagasy' royalty and northern Muslim royalty, and between Bemihisatra and Bemazava royalty. The northern Mahabo was the tomb of a Bemazava ruler, Ndramatikoarivo, 'Noble Who Separated Thousands.' As

Sambarivo from the southern Mahabo explained it, he came over to Nosy Lava from Tsinjorano in the Mahajamba Bay region south of Antognibe because of fighting between the Bemazava and the Bemihisatra long ago (probably during the early 1800s).[47] After he arrived, he got sick and died. His followers buried him here because 'it is prohibited to move [the body]' *(tsy mety hifindra)*.[48]

The burial compound was similar to the one at the southern Mahabo, and so was the arrangement of the council house north of the door and the houses of the guardians to the north, west, and south. But there was no drum house; the number of guardians was much smaller; they were not organized in pens like those at the Doany and Mahabo of the Bemihisatra; and they were subject to far fewer restraints. Guardians at the southern Mahabo explained the lack of 'Sakalava' features, by saying that the Bemazava—whom they considered to be a junior branch of Sakalava royalty compared to the Bemihisatra—'left [their ancestors to become] Muslim' *(rôso Silamo)*. They said that they requested the Bemazava to send people over from Tsinjorano to attend the tomb, but of these immigrants, only a brother, sister, and the sister's child remained. The Silamo immigrants observed some services of their own, especially invoking the ancestors on Maolidy *(mijoro Maolidy)*. But the major services honoring the royal ancestors, organized around the new year, were carried out by the guardians from the southern Mahabo who came there on the day after they had finished their own (Plates 29-31).

One of the spirit-mediums at the southern Mahabo explained the relationship between the two groups of royalty by comparing them with the brother and sister pair at the head of the Zafinifotsy. I was asking why royal officials were going to Bevaoko's doany when they were preparing for the menaty service. Saha Tahiry answered:

"They are going because they need direction *(mila lalàna)*, because Bevaoko'used to be a diviner-healer before. They go to ask how the work should be done—'How should I act to complete this work?' *(Akory ataoko mahavita asa 'ty?)*. Then if they go to Bevaoko, they have to go to Ampela Be also. It's the same as going to both the southern Mahabo and the northern Mahabo. They have served together a long time. The master of

Plate 29. The supplicator (ampangataka) at the northern Mahabo on Nosy Lava giving 'white earth' (tany malandy) to petitioners (including A. Harnik), while royal spirits possess their mediums in the meeting house (fantsina) to the north (G. Feeley-Harnik, 1973).

the northern Mahabo, he isn't a ruler who should have people. The one with people, the one with lots of slaves, in the south, asked for a place from the one with no people because he was there before him. Then he made a vow—a path of action *(làla)* since Ndramamitranarivo [the Great-Grandfather]—that whenever they served south, they would serve north too."

Like the royal compound at the post, the northern Mahabo also served as the second member of a pair against which to evaluate the unique rigor and authenticity of the royal services at the first. As one of the guardians from the southern Mahabo said: "The northern Mahabo has no prohibitions. People can wear pants, shoes. . . ." [Why are there so many prohibitions at the southern Mahabo?] "Sakalava!"

RAHA JIABY BOKA AM'MPANJAKA MIÔVA: EVERYTHING ABOUT ROYALTY CHANGES

The fady governing relationships with royalty included prohibitions on speech. Tsivery, an ampanjaka from a nonruling group who lived

Plate 30. Sambarivo women serving in the 'cleaning service' (fanompoaña kongo) at the northern Mahabo by taking cloth-loads of sticks and leaves out from the burial compound, while spirit-mediums gather in the meeting house (fantsina) behind them. Men are clearing fallen leaves and branches from the perimeter of the compound (A. Harnik, 1973).

south of Analalava, was talking about the words that had to be used in talking about royalty. Looking at some photographs taken of royal followers during the mid-1930s, he commented:

"That woman sitting in front of the ampanjaka was her *nanza.* She is a Sambarivo. All those women around her are Sambarivo. Nanza is just the word used for people who care for the ampanjaka *(olo mpitarimy ampanjaka),* not her actual name. Other people have to nurse the ampanjaka and take care of her. It is forbidden to say 'to breast-feed' *(mampinono).* The word for the person who nurses the ampanjaka is *ampitritry.* Ampanjakas' children never stay with their own mother. Once they are living, they are sent to another place *(Izy koa velono, ndesigny an tany hafa).* When I bore children, my children were raised by someone

Plate 31. Sambarivo women carrying fresh water to make mead (tô mainty) into the burial compound at the northern Mahabo, while Sambarivo men play the mañandria drums south of the door to the compound, other Sambarivo men cook the mead inside, and other women, Sambarivo and petitioners, sing praise songs (kolondoy) to the royal ancestors (A. Harnik, 1973).

other than their own mother. The fan that the girl is holding is called *fihimpa*." [Is it prohibited to say *kepakepa?*] "Yes, say *mikopokopoko*. Everything concerning the ruler has different words. Everything about ampanjaka changes, everything changes."

In defining the Doany and the Mahabo as being what ordinary places, especially the post, were not, the royalty identified as the 'masters' of these places defined themselves as being what ordinary people were not. Royalty were above all *olo araiky,* one person, who ruled alone, in contrast to the large numbers of followers who surrounded them. They were defined not only in contrast to rural villages and to the post, but also to other royal centers, sharpening differences still further, so followers should clearly discern what was the 'real thing' *(tena izy)* in these places as opposed to what was 'wrong' *(diso)* in others.

Royalty, ancestral and living, were 'one person' like siblings were one in having been born from 'one father, one mother.' The descendants stood in wholly for their ancestors, just as ancestors who were their head or source, encompassed wholly their descendants. The difference with royalty was that their 'one person' was achieved by cutting away siblings and offspring, as Tsivery indicated. Prior to the French conquest, they were sent away to more distant places, but even in the 1970s, the ruler's children were still removed from the royal compound as soon as they were born and given to others to raise. So royalty were also 'one person' in the sense that they had no living descendants who could replace them.

In contrast to the unity of siblings born of one father and one mother, the 'singleness' of royalty was born of dying. Saha Barimaso was talking about the few people who had ever been mediums of the Great-Grandfather, the master of the Mahabo, who numbered about one in each generation since he had died around 1865. Saha T., the current spirit-medium of the Great-Grandfather had appeared shortly before Saha Aly (Mainty Be's sister's spouse) died. A new medium— a woman from another village in the Ambolobozo Peninsula—was recently legitimated, but she had yet to live at the Mahabo. "She probably does not live at the Mahabo, because if she did—the two of them there—one of them could die. You see—Saha T. came to the Mahabo, and Aly died, the one died."

Royal followers moved the Doany away from the living ruler in Analalava for comparable reasons. The sharp edge of the 'Long Iron Without Equal,' the reason why the Bemihisatra had so few descendants compared to their junior rivals, the Bemazava, was preventing her from having children. After it was moved, she finally became pregnant and bore one girl on January 18, 1955, then another girl two years later, both of whom were raised outside the royal compound, like Tsivery's children.[49]

We have already seen some of the ways in which 'simple people' *(olo tsotra)* reshaped kinship relations among royalty by seeing Zafinifotsy and Zafinimena as children of women and children of men respectively, and how they reinterpreted each of them as sibling groups in their own terms. The Doany and the Mahabo also reshaped kinship relations among royalty, but according to a completely different model. Stripped of their kin, so that they lived alone inside the fences by which they were defined, they were surrounded with new 'friends' of a completely different sort, slaves who were also strangers without kin, but estranged from their kin by different means. Judging from the 'battles among kin,' by which the Bemihisatra characterized the precolonial period, rulers actively transformed themselves. But I infer from the events of the late nineteenth century and the colonial period that some royal officials and guardians became increasingly interested in directing these transformations to achieve their own 'mastery' over the places where they lived. 'Everything about royalty changes' in the temporal as well as spatial dimensions of people who are 'one path.' But to evaluate the nature of these different kinds of changes, it is necessary to examine more closely the reformation of working relations among kin and strangers that the Doany and Mahabo were oriented to achieve, the nature of the 'mastery of ancestral custom' embodied in the very people guarding these places.

SAMBARIVO: EVERY ONE A THOUSAND

Sambarivo is a generic term meaning 'every one a thousand,' that is, an infinitely great number, in contrast to the single 'noble who conquered, joined, or fed infinite thousands' whom they serve. In the precolonial period, their number included strangers as well as local people: Africans purchased from Arab traders, Malagasy from other parts of the island purchased through the internal slave trade or captured in warfare, slaves seeking refuge from other rulers, as well as a variety of kinds of commoners. Commoners might be enslaved for trying to emulate royalty in wealth and power, typically by expanding their own networks of kin, clients, and slaves. Commoners could also be enslaved for other infractions of ancestral custom or, as I mentioned above, because they stumbled inadvertently into places, especially through doors, restricted to Sambarivo.

When talking about how people became Sambarivo, the guardians
at both the Doany and the Mahabo acknowledged, after I asked, that
Sambarivo in the past could be bought with money. What they emphasized was 'wrong-doing,' 'wrong people' *(olo diso)*. As Velondraza
put it:

"If the wrong is really serious, then they go to the Mahabo to discuss
what should be done: whether money will suffice; whether an ox will
suffice; or whether only the body will do" *(vataña foana manêfany)*.

His brother, Mazaka, went on to mention that some people could
come in by their own choice *(sitrapon'dreo)*, but as he described it, this
choice too resulted from prior wrong-doing.

"For example, [they say] 'We're consumed, sick to the point of dying!'
(Lany zahay, matimaty!) Everything is going wrong. These are people
afflicted by the curse of royalty *(olo misy tsigny)*. It kills if nothing is done
about it. They come to the big people at the Doany or the Mahabo. 'What
thing will cure me?' *(Ino raha mampijanga zaho?)* 'Give your child, put your
grandchild into the service of the ampanjaka.'"

The root of wrong-dong lay in not recognizing the royal ancestors
as the true 'masters of the land,' the true source of well-being derived
from working in the land. The underlying connection between land
and people, lostness from ancestral places, and isolation from kin providing alternative sources of support, was most evident in talk about
ordinary slaves *(andevo)*. They came from so far away that negotiations
about 'wrong-doing' were irrelevant; they could be bought and sold
with impunity. Their complete vulnerability to manipulation was a
direct consequence of their lostness. As Saha Tahiry explained, when
I asked about the origins of such slaves:

"From Morima, Afriky. They don't know where they come from. People
sold andevo for guns and shot, like selling oranges." [Why didn't they run
away?] "There was no way *(làla)*, they didn't know the community
(tanana)." [Did they have a special house?] "You, your own master, alone
know the place you put your slaves, their food, their clothes—they're

your slaves, after all. 'Go [do this, do that]. . . .' You just nod your head." [Could they invoke their own ancestors?] "They could invoke them, but they didn't know their kin because they were left behind. Their owner was their only kind, their owner. He was their kin *(Igny fo karazandreo, ley patron igny fona. Igny havandreo)."* Later, talking about the children of andevo, he said: "Slaves' children were like your cattles' children—still yours. You could make a slave like a child *(miraña zanaka).* Do fatidra—'I make you my child' *(Ataoko zanako)."* [This was how slaves were freed.] "You could marry them into your family, or marry them to another slave. They were slaves after all—do/make anything with them *(Andevo ke, zay atao izy fona)."*

Whether they came from Morima, from elsewhere in Madagascar, or from the immediate region, people enslaved as Sambarivo were also separated from their kin. They were required instead to honor the royal ancestors, a relationship derived not from specific relations of descent but from the work associated with the specific places they occupied around royalty. They were put together not to regenerate themselves, but to work to regenerate royalty. Even so, although they worked like purchased slaves for royalty, they were also more like ordinary royal subjects than purchased slaves. As one of the guardians at the Doany said:

"Sambarivo are not forbidden to invoke ancestors. They can have their own ancestors." [Do they give *miletry*—marriage wealth?] "There could be marriage wealth. Sambarivo and people are similar. There are some who can marry Sambarivo unless it is prohibited for them. Ancestor People are all forbidden to marry Sambarivo. These days, they just do it. Sometimes they're sick, sometimes they go crazy. It's forbidden, but they just do it. The person who wants to marry the Sambarivo goes to the father first. When that's done, he goes to the ampanjaka, need a path/permission *(mila làla).* He gives money, there are certain customs. Eight five-franc pieces, ten. Not much is taken, but the practices have to be observed. The name of the money is *vidihefigny,* to leave the ampanjaka. *Vidy* [bought] because the work is bought, because the Sambarivo is finished with the work. *Hefigny* [anything that protects, defends, covers something else] is the work. The Sambarivo does not live there [at the Doany or Mahabo again] unless separated, having gotten a path/permission."

In the precolonial period, Sambarivo were prohibited from living anywhere except the Doany and the Mahabo, where they had the use of royal rice land to support themselves. In the 1970s, royal officials emphasized that Sambarivo were completely free to come and go from these places, as they chose. Like Laza Be, who described the ampanjaka as surrounded by her 'friends' *(drako)* who are her 'kin' *(havana)* in her royal compound in Analalava, so the manantany explained about the Sambarivo at the Doany:

"Royal slaves (andevo) are people who agree to serve the ruler *(olo mañeky hanompo ny ampanjaka)*. The people at the Doany are simply guardians, not people who have been captured and then enslaved *(olo ampiambigny fõño, tsy sambory)*. When the elders decide on a time, they come and stay. Otherwise they can go home like the female attendants *(marovavy)* who live around the ampanjaka here in Analalava. They come, and if they need to go back to the countryside, they just go back. They don't have to stay."

Some Sambarivo who had 'run away' *(milefa)*, as Malaza described it, were indeed living elsewhere in the surrounding countryside, especially in the Antognibe area where Sambarivo stayed when Tondroko was brought up to Analalava in 1908, but also in the Ambolobozo Peninsula. Some had been compelled to return. When I asked Soatoly whether she served as a medium for one of the royal ancestors at the Mahabo, she said:

"What people are saying about that is a lie. People around here who don't know things think that everyone who goes out to the Mahabo is a *saha* [medium of one of the founding ancestors or one of the ancestors at the Mahabo]. But it's not true. I am not yet [a medium]. The reason I go out there is this. My grandmother who bore my father came from Nosy Lava, [she was] Antimahabo [from the Antibe pen of the ampangataka, who had called the royal ancestors so Soatoly could request the dispensations Somizy had described, which applied to Sambarivo as well as spirits' mediums]. You know how women walk around from one place to another. Then they get married somewhere and stay there. That's what happened to her. She went walking north, then married up there and didn't return. My father was her only child. Since then, me and my older

sisters have all been sick." On arriving, Soatoly had said that six of her kin
in Nosy Be had since died—the oldest sister, a child of the oldest, and a
child of another older sister, besides the deaths we had already read about
in the earlier letters she had showed us. She mentioned it again now. "I
myself was sick for two years. We went to a diviner who said that the
grandmother [father's mother] was making us sick. She wanted us to
return to Nosy Lava and serve, to carry out the customary practices there.
When I got well enough, I was the one who went. I was here about a year
when you arrived. I am not allowed to go home yet." She planned to visit
her siblings and their kin in Nosy Be right after she came back from the
new year's service at the Mahabo. She wouldn't stay more than a month
before coming back here. "All my older siblings want to come down here
too, but they won't."

In other cases, Sambarivo had stayed near the royal center where their
forebears had served, while looking elsewhere in other ways.

Malaza several times spoke of a Sambarivo associated with the Father's
former doany at Antognibe who wanted to sell some of the doany's rice
land. He went up to Analalava to speak to the ampanjaka about it, but she
didn't agree, saying it was her father's field, and he had no right to sell it.
Returning from Analalava to Antognibe by outrigger canoe, he got caught
in a storm that ripped his sail apart. Malaza told both his sons and his
grandchild, who visited while we were there, that they should never travel
with this man in his canoe because they could die if they did.

VALA: PENS

While some Sambarivo had run away and others had returned in different forms, descendants of the original Sambarivo who served
Southern Bemihisatra royalty in the past were still the sole permanent
occupants of the Doany and the Mahabo. They were not organized
around royalty in terms of ancestries, because in principle—having
been taken forcibly from their kin or having been forced themselves
to sever relations with their kin—they were lost to their kin. They
were organized instead by 'pens' (vala). These pens were called by
the name of the fences (vala) that commoners build around their gardens and livestock, except that here they enclosed people. Furthermore, they were not actually fences made of wood; they were places.

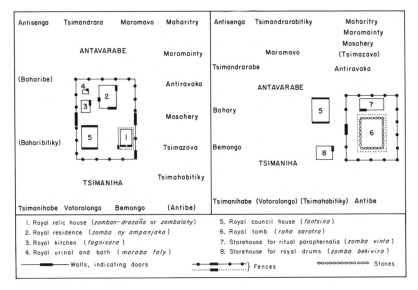

Antisenga	Tsimandrara	Maromavo	Maharitry
	ANTAVARABE		Maromainty
(Baharibe)			Antiravaka
			Mosohery
(Baharibitiky)			Tsimazava
	TSIMANIHA		Tsimahabitiky
Tsimanihabe	Votorolongo	Bemongo	(Antibe)

Antisenga	Tsimandrarabitiky	Maharitry
		Maromainty
		Mosohery
	Maromavo	(Tsimazava)
Tsimandrarabe		Antiravaka
	ANTAVARABE	
Bahary		
Bemongo		
	TSIMANIHA	
Tsimanihabe (Votorolongo) (Tsimahabitiky) Antibe		

1. Royal relic house (*zomban–drazaña* or *zombalahy*)
2. Royal residence (*zomba ny ampanjaka*)
3. Royal kitchen (*fagnisara*)
4. Royal urinal and bath (*moraba faly*)
5. Royal council house (*fantsina*)
6. Royal tomb (*raha sarotra*)
7. Storehouse for ritual paraphernalia (*zomba vinta*)
8. Storehouse for royal drums (*zomba bekiviro*)

—■■— Walls, indicating doors   •—•■•—•} Fences   ∘∘∘∘∘∘∘∘∘∘∘∘ Stones

Figure 15. Pens (vala) at the doany and mahabo, including those in parentheses that no longer have people.

Each pen had a different name. Sambarivo said that the names referred to the 'places they occupy,' 'the kinds of pens they occupy' in relation to the royal compound (Fig. 15).

The fahatelo from the Doany summarized Sambarivo as "people who govern the rulers' places there *(olo mahazaka pilasin' ny 'mpanjaka ao)*— [they] manage entering *(mahaleo miditra),* do the washing, her sweeping up, her clothes, her food. The Sambarivo attached to the one still living are Antidoany. When they die—Antimahabo." He emphasized that Antidoany were prohibited from staying at the Mahabo and vice versa. Each can only visit in passing the place of the other.

As the fahatelo indicated, the places that Sambarivo themselves occupied in relation to royalty defined the kind of work they did. At both the Doany and the Mahabo, the pens of Sambarivo in the southeast, closest to the royal ancestors, were dedicated to the service of the royal ancestors. At the Mahabo, where everyone served the royal ancestors, the Antibe in the southeast served as the leaders of the group as a whole. At the Doany, the pens in the north and west were dedicated to the service of the living ruler. Those to the north and east assisted the manantany, who lived in one of the houses in the northeast corner. Those in the southwest assisted the fahatelo who lived at the southwest corner. Those in the lowest position in the northwest were dedicated to services concerning the person of the living ruler, especially her cooking and cleaning.

When I asked how it was decided where new people should go, it became clear that the distinctions between north and south at royal centers encompassed the region as a whole. Furthermore, the groups of Sambarivo in their different places, although they were all 'pens,' reproduced social distinctions inherent in their origins. Ngeda at the Mahabo said:

"If they are Antavarabe [from the north of the Mahabo, i.e., the Ambolobozo Peninsula], then the manantany chooses which pen they enter. If they are Tsimaniha, then the fahatelo chooses." [How is it known which they are?] "It depends whether they live north or south. If the mother and father come from different places, then they take the place of the father. Unless the father gives the child to the mother. Husbands and wives always keep their own work."

The western pens of 'Strong Pots' who did the lowest kinds of work, in close and dangerous contact with the living ruler, had been filled in the precolonial period by purchased slaves or Malagasy from elsewhere captured in warfare.[50] The pens that served the royal ancestors were filled by local people who had been made into Sambarivo for some wrong-doing. The Antibe group who served the royal ancestors at the Mahabo was the most salient example of this process. It was widely known that they had once been a large and wealthy local ancestry.

As Saha Barimaso said, "They were not captured (tsy samborigny) . . . [it was a matter] not of boughten things, but love (tsy vangain-draha, fa fitiavaña). They were friends (kamarady) of the Great-Grandfather. But they needed to become great/many *(be)*, they wanted to get great, above the ampanjaka [whence their name as Sambarivo, 'At Greatness']. Ndramamitrañarivo was friends with their big people. He asked their big people to come to his community *(tanàna)* and follow him. They refused. The Antibe came to the place where the ampanjaka was and made a cattle pen [a huge cattle pen for their enormous herds], using skins from cattle they had sacrificed for that purpose. They did this in their community, while he was still living, to show that they were just as big as him. Then when he died and their big people died, descendants started to get sick. The royal curse *(tigny)* made them sick. The cattle gone, the later ones [descendants] assented *(mañeky* [becoming Sambarivo at the Mahabo]), because they were getting sick."

Rather than agree, the Antibe chose to flaunt their ancestral roots; finally they were forced to agree or die out.

But as Béatrice, one of their affines, remarked: "The Antibe are people who make themselves independent *(olo mahaleoteña)*. They can really make their own living. They do well, have lots of things, don't depend on anyone else. They can be Sambarivo if no one else is there, but they aren't really Sambarivo. The Antiravaka are like them, the only others like them. They, like the Antibe, are only at the Mahabo, not at the Doany. The Antibe can be made Sambarivo, but they aren't really; their job is to hold the keys."

    The pens of Sambarivo were combined into two larger groups of eight, also named according to their place relative to royalty: one south (Tsimaniha) and one north (Antavarabe) of the royal compound or royal tomb. Tsimaniha and Antavarabe worked on the southern and northern halves of royal services respectively. Like the number two, eight *(valo)* was used in many different contexts to represent the most complete possible number of things, notably the 'eight ancestors— eight on a side, eight on a side' *(valondrazana—valo añila, valo añila)—* with which people throughout the region summarized their entire ancestries. "Two times eight!" *(Indroy valo!)* Saha Barimaso's wife exclaimed, after hearing a companion at the market conclude an account of her kin ties to diverse 'kinds' by using that phrase. At the

Doany and the Mahabo, there were eight pens in each of the southern and northern halves. Their combined force was represented as 'two times eight' *(indroy valo)*, rather than by the ordinary term for sixteen—'six more than ten' *(tsiot'ambinifolo)*—thus doubling the completeness they already represented. 'Twice eight' evoked one of the most inclusive images of kinship in order to create a condition of kinlessness. Reckoning people by eights was common practice in royal services, as we shall see. Explaining why eight people were required to do a particular kind of work, one of the guardians at the Doany said: "so that there are spouses upon spouses *(fivadiaña fivadiaña)*—two and two for four, four and four for eight."[51] Perhaps not accidentally, this emphasis on even numbers, notably eights, in Sakalava royal practice, is exactly contrary to historical organization of royal practice in Imerina, where odd numbers had priority in most contexts, especially seven.[52]

The paired eights of "Those [at the place of] the Doany" *(Antidoany)* were paired and contrasted in turn with "Those at the Mahabo" *(Antimahabo)*. The arrangements of the pens at the Doany and the Mahabo were exact replicas of one another except that living rulers, in becoming ancestors, moved from the center, where they were surrounded on all sides by their guardians, to the east, the 'head' of the community of the dead, while their guardians moved around to their 'feet' (Fig. 14).[53]

FANOMPOAÑA: ROYAL SERVICE

The relationship between royalty, the 'one person' inside two fences, and Sambarivo, 'every one a thousand,' grouped in 'pens' around royalty like a third fence made of living people, was the model for the division of labor by which royal services—*fanompoaña*—were organized. The term itself is a substantive of an active transitive verb *manompo ny ampanjaka,* that is, 'to make a *tompo*—master, owner— of one who rules.' People made ampanjaka masters over themselves by their very service.

Tompo (master/owner, 'Lord' in Christian usage) is widely used in Madagascar to indicate authority, seniority, responsibility, possession, as in such phrases as *tompontany* (master/owner of land), *tompon' ny asa* (person in charge of work), or *tompoko* (my master/owner/superior/boss, female or male). Shortly after independence, President Tsiranana ordered the islandwide use of "Salama Tompoko" in salutations to eradicate divisive greetings based on rank. Royal followers in the Analalava region use tompoko to address government officials and Europeans, their own ancestors and royalty. For example, when MamanDjoma said that Tompony had prescribed certain medicines for her daughter-in-law, she explained that as meaning 'the one who sits on my head' *(tompony mipetraka am lohanakahy)*. The reciprocal of *tompo/ko* is *ampanompo,* but royal followers use the reciprocal and related terms like *fanompoana,* 'royal service,' only in that context. *Ampanompo* were all those who served royalty in whatever capacity, thus recognizing their superior position.

Catholic and Protestant missionaries since the nineteenth century borrowed the term fanompoaña to refer to 'service,' acts of 'faith' as opposed to the 'works' of the New Testament, which they translated as *asa* (work/s). French colonial administrators, who condemned fanompoaña as corvée labor, borrowed the term to refer to statute labor, which people throughout the Analalava region still call *asa.*[54] Royal followers emphasized that fanompoaña was not like ordinary work. They were shocked when I asked whether *fehitany* (administrators at the village level) received a salary: 'No that's royal service, there is no wage' *(zegny fanompoaña am' mpanjaka fôño, tsisy karama).*

There were two kinds of royal services: the royal funeral, known as the 'hot service' *(fanompoaña mafana),* and every other kind of work for royalty, from preparing rice fields for sowing to washing the royal ancestors. Services were distinguished as 'big' or 'little,' depending on how many people and resources they required. But regardless of size, their common model was the royal body, ultimately ancestral, with a single, sharply defined head, commanding the work of a large body of people who followed behind. The relationship between the two was conveyed repeatedly through images of pairs. Inequality between pairs in one context was transformed into equality in another, but the inevitable outcome of these exchanges was the recreation of hierarchical distinctions among participants according to the ancestral prototype.

The single head of Sakalava monarchy, the 'one person' of ancestral and living royalty, was represented in sharp, powerful, potentially deadly objects like the sharp posts and spear heads that decorated royal architecture, or the Long Knife itself. Royal cattle (*aomby ranitry*, sharp cattle) were marked by cutting their right ears into sharp points. The male heads of kin networks appointed as royal counselors concerning the people as a whole were likewise described as 'the ruler's sharp or empowered ones' *(ragnitr'ampanjaka)*, or 'sharp/empowered' *(ragnitry)* for short. "Round things are prohibited because there is no head" *(raha bory fady—tsisy lohany)*, said one royal guardian; canoes have to have a prow, just as much as workers have to have a leader. The common use of *ragnitry* to describe circumcision *(mandragnitry,* to sharpen), and conversely, the use of *bory* to describe a childless woman *(tany bory,* barren land) or a hornless cow *(omby bory)* conveys the broad ranging power of 'sharpening' persons and things in contrast to the futility and weakness, sometimes speechlessness, of bodies without heads.

Royal service had this same sharp form. In small services carried out by ancestries like the four kinds of Ancestor People, the 'master of the work' *(tompon' ny asa)* was the head of the ancestry—its *tale,* or *baba* (father) since it was usually a man. In services at either the Doany or the Mahabo, the work was directed by the fahatelo or ampangataka, depending on whether it concerned the living ruler or the ancestors. In work like the reconstruction of the innermost menaty-fence around the tomb, which involved royal officials and guardians from the Doany and Mahabo as well as different kinds of people from the region, workers were appointed to recreate a model of the royal administration, including a *jadô* or substitute ruler, a substitute manantany and fahatelo, as well as Ancestor People and commoners who stood in for their ancestries and for the people in the region as a whole. In such work, the ancestors at the Mahabo were represented by a pair of spirit-mediums, accompanied by an even number of Sambarivo from the Mahabo who served as their 'dressers' *(ampisarandra).*

Royal service retained this sharp form—at least in principle—not only because labor was divided along clearly hierarchical lines, but also because no one worker was allowed to do or even know in detail the work of any one else. To complete even the most menial task required royal guardians to cooperate in keeping their divided places.

SAMBY AMIN' NY PILASINY: EACH TO HIS OWN PLACE

Like the 'one person' within whom specific royal ancestors and the living ruler exercised different kinds of authority, so royal followers were distinguished from one another according to their work. These different kinds of work were described as 'portions' *(anjara)*, as if the widespread idea of individual destiny, like the idea of the wholeness embodied in 'eight ancestors,' had been taken up and turned to new uses. The importance of distinguishing workers according to their different anjara in royal service came up almost immediately whenever anyone talked about royal service. Thus the first time I heard about fanompoaña, Dimby, the wife of Mamoribe, who came from a village south of Analalava, differentiated the work of the fehitany there from the work of the Antidoany who looked after the ampanjaka's cattle in the area: "It is prohibited to mix the work of different kinds of people" *(Tsy mety miharoharo asa amin' ny karazana)*. Royal officials and Sambarivo made the same point repeatedly and in many different ways when they were exhorting fellow workers to do things right: 'each to his own lot,' 'each to his own work' *(samby amin' ny asany)*, 'each to his own task' *(samby am' devoiran'any)*, 'each to his own royal service' *(samby am fanompoan'any)*, 'each to his own way of doing things' *(samby am' fomban'any)*, 'each to his own place, his own seat, his own side' *(samby am' pilaspilasiny, pitrapitrahany, fipetrapetrahany; samby am' kolafikolafiny)*. The manantany at the Doany said he could speak about the work of lower officials like the fahatelo, fehitany, or ranitry to whom he delegated specific tasks. He claimed to know nothing of the work of specialists like the Ancestor People, nor would others associated with the Doany. "Only they know their own work."

The Sambarivo at the Mahabo, who arranged to have the guide to the menaty service typewritten in 1962, made exactly the same point: "Those Ancestor People know all about those various customs of theirs" *(dia ireo Razan'olona ireo no mahalala izay rehetra fombafombandr'izareo)*, so he does not include their work in his general account.

The Ancestor People were a prime example because their work was to create distinct ancestors from living, then dead rulers, but the principle applied to all royal service. The anjara epitomized in royal service accounted for why Sambarivo women, unlike most other women in the region, were entitled to get at least one of their children. The child was their replacement in the pen to which they belonged and from which they and their descendants should not move. The efforts of royal followers to hold on to their children, even in the face of such demands, was reflected in their emphasis that only one child was required to replace his or her mother and not necessarily the first. Meanwhile, the mother continued to carry out her own work, not her husband's work, if she married into another pen.

The fatal, inescapable curse *(t[s]igny)* of angered royal ancestors was the ultimate sanction on staying in place. To take on the anjara of another *(mandray anjara)*, which royal followers also expressed spatially as 'entering into another person's lot' *(miditra amin' ny anjaran' olo)*, suggested that a person 'wants to commit sorcery against the royal ancestors' *(mila mamoriky ny razan' ny ampanjaka)*. Thus a person who did the work of another would be struck *(voa)* by their anger, as evident in his or her fatal misfortune. Depending on the gravity of their imposition, for example, attempting to do the work of Ancestor People, they could be 'struck down on the spot' *(toraña sur place)*, even become 'suddenly dead' *(maty tampoko)*. Even if the living ruler were to order people to do work that was not theirs, they should refuse, or they could 'fall in a faint' *(toraña)*.

Such failures to observe the royal division of labor were said to have been among the 'wrongs' that transformed people into Sambarivo. Royal followers still asserted in the 1970s that anyone who did the work of Sambarivo or infringed even accidentally on places like their doors at the Doany or the strip of ground between the council house and the burial compound at the Mahabo was thereby transformed into a Sambarivo. This point was so well known that Mamoribe, who was not a royal follower, refused to allow his sister's son to go with us to the Doany or the Mahabo for fear that he might be cursed or changed into a Sambarivo through some unknowing misstep. By the same token, people who ran away from their appointed service, no matter how far, were said to suffer and their descendants after them. Nothing they attempted would succeed, and finally they would sicken and die unless they returned to beg pardon from the royal ancestors for attempting to abandon them. Saha Tavela, a senior medium living at the Mahabo, exemplified this inexorable fate. As one of his guardians explained: "Saha Tavela comes from Ankabinda. His father was a Sambarivo from the Mahabo who left to wander around and forgot the customs. So the monarchy *(fanjakana)* came to rule on the son [possessed him] and brought him back to the Mahabo for that reason. He is Maromavo, and his children are the heads of the royal service that Maromavo do *(tompon' ny fanompoana Maromavo).*"

OLO NY MANORO, OLO NY MIHILAÑA: PEOPLE OF THE LIVING, PEOPLE OF THE DEAD

The pens were intended to prevent people from 'mixing' *(miharo)* with one another, meeting and forming ties other than those binding them to royalty. But the pens also showed clearly how the paired separations supporting the singularity of royalty were subverted over time, especially through the formation of kin ties. Kinship drew royalty out from the royal centers and into the surrounding countryside, grounding them in ways that ran outside and sometimes contrary to the hierarchy of royal service. Anjara applied with the greatest force to the separation between the 'people of the living' *(olo ny manoro)* and 'people of the dead' *(olo ny mihilaña),* as Antidoany and Antimahabo were called. Yet it was precisely here that the greatest mixing occurred, or at least the mixing with the greatest consequences for the question of who were the tompon'tany of these larger places.

In contrast to the ampanjaka of the Northern Bemihisatra and the Bemazava, the living ruler of the Southern Bemihisatra was prohibited from setting foot in the Mahabo or even on the island where it was located.[55] She honored the royal ancestors annually, and sometimes more frequently, by sending people from the Doany to the Mahabo with offerings *(takitaky)*. For royal services requiring the cooperation of both groups, like the menaty service, she sent a substitute *(jadô)*, the descendant of a local branch of nonruling royalty.

People disagreed about whether spirit-mediums from the Mahabo could stay at the Doany. Some said they could not because they were ancestors and their place was therefore at the Mahabo, away from their 'child' or 'grandchild' at the Doany. Others said that mediums who had not been legitimated could not stay at the Doany, because they could be sorcerers. Legitimate mediums could stay there, because 'After all, a medium has a good mouth!' *(Saha vava tsara ke!)*, and would not attempt to harm the living ruler. Mediums themselves said that they went to the Doany only when summoned, and otherwise stayed away. The ampanjaka called the four main spirit-mediums from the Mahabo to the royal compound in Analalava in December 1972 to discuss plans for the menaty service, and they were called about other questions concerning royal services. They also visited the Doany at royal rites of passage to honor their grandchild with gifts that they paid for by selling cattle *(joro velo,* living prayers), which petitioners had given to them. They all emphasized that as soon as their *dia,* path/ purpose, was finished, they left.

Similar prohibitions governed the conduct of royal guardians. Just as the pens of Tsimazava and Mosohery, who worked for the ancestors at the Doany, were prohibited to work for the living ruler, so Antidoany could not do the work of Antimahabo and vice versa. Neither could attend the services of the other unless specifically required, as in the menaty service, after which they left. Malaza said that even photographs of living and ancestral rulers should not be placed next to one another or stored in the same box. Then he added that his own picture as an Antidoany should not be mixed with pictures of Antimahabo on the same page of the book I wrote: "They [Antidoany and Antimahabo] don't want one place, one thing all different. Each to his own service."[56] (Plate 32).

Plate 32. Sambarivo and visitors at the Doany (A. Harnik, 1972).

The difficulty in separating the 'people of the living' and the 'people of the dead' lay in the links of kinship and marriage between them. Despite the principle of anjara and the practices by which the dead were continually set apart from the living, the one case when members of one group became members of another was when a ruler died. All of his Sambarivo should 'follow' him to his tomb. As one of them spoke for the ruler: "If my child is here, I leave some of them with him." The officials at the Doany then appointed Sambarivo from each of the pens there to be sent with the body from the Mahabo, where they would continue to serve his ancestral spirit. These Sambarivo were described as 'cattle separated from the herd' *(avak'aomby)*.[57] The ancestor's avak'aomby eventually became the chief judges of the legitimacy of his mediums.

Saha Barimaso confirmed Sambarivo from the Doany and the

Mahabo in saying that the "big people" in those places decided who was to be "separated from the herd," not the Sambarivo themselves. If Sambarivo had money, they could buy slaves to do some of their own work. (The Antibe's 'book of ancestors' [bokindrazaña] included slaves by name.) But according to Saha Barimaso, no Sambarivo could use such slaves as substitutes for themselves in relation to royalty. As he put it, "I don't know your slave, I just know you" (Zaho tsy mahay ny andevonao, fa anao fona haiko). I asked what happened if a Sambarivo did not want to go to the Mahabo, and he said:

"Yes—'I'm old, here's my substitute' (solo)—either a child or a grandchild. Other people cannot substitute for him, just his children. He is not allowed by buy slaves to replace him, just his children, because slaves can't substitute for him! (Fa andevo tsy misolo azy eky!) The ones who should go are the ones who grew up with the ampanjaka. Children can't go, they don't know anything. There were many [avak'aomby] at the time of Ndramamahaña [the Father, around 1925]. Just two are left [in 1981], a man living in A. [on the Ambolobozo Peninsula] and a woman living in A. [near Antognibe]. Bahary Be I think. There were also some at the time of Ambilahikely [the Son, around 1924], but they are all dead." He went on to talk about where Sambarivo were buried when they died at the Mahabo. Later, when we were discussing joking relations between parents, their siblings, and their children, he returned to the subject: "The mother's brother is a real animal! (Zama koa biby!) He can sell his sister's son. The father cannot sell his own son, but he can sell his sister's son. Just the mother's brother, just the mother's brother has a bad disposition (ratsy fanahy)."

Thus, the majority of Antimahabo were the descendants of Antidoany. Except where they had run away or died out at either place, or were placed only at the Mahabo (like the Antibe), almost every pen of Antimahabo had its corresponding pen of kin at the Doany, possibly related as children of women to children of men.

Antimahabo were meant not to move from the royal tomb or at least from the island. They had land around the Mahabo, and they were also considered to be the 'masters' of Nosy Saba, six kilometers off the coast of the Ambolobozo Peninsula, the only other island besides Nosy Lava to have fresh water. Both of these places had the great advantage of being free of wild pigs, which were major pests on the mainland. The problem—among others—was, as the head of the Tsimanihabe group said, "The prisoners are our wild pigs." French officials built the penitentiary on the island in 1910–1911. Finding that the residents of the Mahabo were helping the prisoners to escape, they forced them to move to a coastal village on the Ambolobozo Peninsula 1916. Although the guardians eventually succeeded in returning to Nosy Lava some eleven years later, most of the members of the Antibe pen, from which the supplicator was chosen, continued to farm in the mainland village during the rainy season, and they also married local people there (Plates 33 and 34).

The Tsimanihabe, west of the Antibe and comparable to them in size, continued to live during the rainy season in a mainland village south of Analalava, where they had access to land through Antidoany forebears. The village was not far from the place where the Doany was relocated in the early fifties. They, too, married locally.

Antimahabo continued farming on the mainland not only because of the prisoners, but because land around the Mahabo has become scarce owing to the increasing numbers of mediums there. Spirit-mediums had priority over Antimahabo in the apportionment of rice land because, as royalty, they were considered to be the 'masters of the village,' while the Sambarivo were merely the caretakers.[58] The male mediums all had land on the mainland in the village where they were born or into which they had married. Female mediums and guardians without spouses were most likely to stay on the island where they could hire prisoners to help them farm and also benefit from their gifts.[59] The supplicator and *chef de quartier* of the Mahabo called a meeting to urge the guardians not to sleep with the prisoners on the grounds that this was not their ancestral land, but that of royalty. They were simply guardians, and the prisoners would steal not only from the storage house in the royal cemetery, but also from the guardians themselves. Nevertheless, the practice continued, in part because of the reluctance of Antimahabo and other Sakalava men to marry women associated with the Mahabo.[60] Thus, the prisoners had driven

Plate 33. A Sambarivo from the Mahabo and his wife in
their mainland village (A. Harnik, 1973).

out those with opportunities to farm on the mainland, mostly male
guardians and mediums. But their presence had led greater numbers
of women, mediums and guardians, to stay at the Mahabo, who would
formerly have returned to their natal villages to farm or moved to
Analalava.

The two most important groups to live on the mainland during the

359

Plate 34. A Sambarivo from the Mahabo and his wife and child in their mainland village. The child's forelock *(tsokotsoko)* shows that the Zafinimena royal ancestor, Ndramaro, is also raising him (G. Feeley-Harnik, 1981).

growing season were from the largest, wealthiest, and most important pens at the Mahabo, having the most to loose from insufficient land and theft. They were both from the southern or dominant half of the community. The Antibe served as ampangataka; the Tsimanihabe were their chief assistants and substitutes. The other pens at the Mahabo did lesser work and were fewer in number.[61]

These two pens were meant to be united by the intermarriage between them and by their common lot as Tsimaniha, people of the southern half, and as Antimahabo, but they had long been opposed. The Antibe, close to the spirit-mediums because of their work as ampangataka, had become associated with the northern portion of the royal domain where they farmed perhaps because Antibe had never served at the Doany. The Tsimanihabe were more closely associated with the Doany just south of the mainland village where they farmed. There was also a large pen of active Tsimanihabe at the Doany, who continued to be powerful in Doany affairs since the fahatelo who administered the Doany was selected from among them.

During the 1960s, some Antimahabo went so far as to elect the head of the Tsimanihabe pen to fill the position of ampangataka associated with the Antibe pen. His stay in office was very short because of the fears of other Antimahabo combined with the warnings of spirit-mediums concerning the dire consequences of an action so clearly contrary to ancestral custom. When asked who had voted the Tsimanihabe into office, Saha Fiara, one of the Father's mediums, said:

"Some of the community (fokon'olona) who want to see things ruined did it. No spirit-medium (saha) chose Angatahy. How could they—being royal spirits—when it is a wrong thing? It is not his lot (anjara). But the spirit-mediums could not do anything about it either. It was a question of people from far away [meaning both the mediums, ideally strangers to the area, and the royalty they represented] against the masters of the community (tompon'tanàna). As soon as the spirit-mediums are gone, the people there just do what they want. As soon as the spirit-mediums return, they say: 'We've done it!'"

SAMBY AMIN' NY ANJARANY: EACH TO HIS OWN FATE

Sambarivo were meant to be completely separate from the royalty they served like slaves, but over time they became oddly similar. They were meant to protect royalty, especially from theft. This was less of an issue in the postcolonial period, but many older Sambarivo and others in the region, who were not involved in the monarchy, remembered how the Malagasy nationalist Ralaimongo had attempted to 'steal' the ampanjaka Soazara in the mid-thirties, when she was still a child.[62] Sambarivo were also meant to contain royalty. This came out most clearly in discussions concerning the dangers of direct contact with royal bodies, even the body of the living ruler. After Malaza explained why people ran away when they heard that the ampanjaka was planning to collect in their district, he went on to say:

"Also if she goes around visiting, they are afraid to receive her because it is so difficult. Where would she exert herself [*mangery,* move her bowels]?[63] Where would she pee? If a person stepped on it by accident, it would kill them, they would die. [You] try to have her pee against the side of a tree. At the Doany, she exerted herself down by the shore, where very few people walked. When she goes down there, she always says hello. My house is at the southwest corner. Then she returns to the *moraba faly* [bathhouse/urinal]. Only that pee can stay inside the doany [royal compound]. A special kind of Sambarivo takes care of this at the Doany— the ones who were actually bought with money, known respectfully (*fañajaña*) as Strong Pots (*Vilany Mahery*). They are in charge of the *moraba faly* and fetching the water used there. They wash everything filthy (*makota*). She can't touch her own menstrual cloths. Others must handle them and wash them. Strong Pots."[64]

Similar contradictions were characteristic of the cattle imagery most often used to picture the relationship between rulers and their guardians. Sambarivo were compared to cattle, corralled in pens and separated like herds. Rulers occupied the position of wealthy cattle barons in these images, but they were also celebrated as 'great bulls' *(aombilahibe, jaolahy),* monsters whom Sambarivo alone could capture and control, as in these praise songs *(kolondoy):*

Mitregny anao mitregny.
Tsy mitregny fa misy zaka tregnany.
Aombilahy sarotro é!

You bellow like a bull, bellow.
[It is not I who] bellow but some thing that bellows.
Precious/difficult bull é!

Bibianala, kaka manda.
Savao lala, fa hiditra é!
Boana e e e e e!

Animal in the forest, monster under guard.
Clear the way, for [we are] entering in é![65]
Boana e e e e e!

Similarly, Sambarivo as slaves were children. Indeed, they stood in for the royal descendants who had been excluded from the Doany. Yet their main task was to care for living and ancestral royalty as if they were their own children. In practice, close relationships, 'friendships,' did develop between the 'caretakers of royalty,' the nanza that Tsivery and others mentioned, who were sitting close to the young Soazara in the photographs he was looking at. They became her drako, as Laza Be pointed out about the people living around the ampanjaka in Analalava during the 1970s. "Those are her kin (havana), her friends in everything. They cook for her, help her to fall asleep, talk to her, her kin."[66] She relied heavily on them for their knowledge about royal practice. The relationship between the Sambarivo at the Mahabo and the spirit-mediums who lived there was even closer, not only because the Antimahabo were more broadly knowledgeable, but also because they judged the legitimacy of royal ancestors embodied in mediums. Diniky made the same point about Sambarivo who themselves became mediums: "Once they come out *(miboaka)* from being slaves, they are like ampanjaka because they are so close to them."

Sambarivo were also supposed to be completely different from commoners. In fact, when I asked Velondraza again in 1981 about Tsiarô, one of the general terms for royal followers besides Bemihisatra or Sakalava, this is how he explained it:

"Tsiarô are people who are not Sambarivo *(olo tsy Sambarivo).* They can serve royalty, but they aren't Sambarivo. They can get work in the forest [referring to the menaty service when Tsiarô cut trees], but they can't enter into the places where Sambarivo go."

Tsiarô means 'unfenced,' even 'unprotected,' perhaps an allusion to their differentness from both royalty and Sambarivo. But in practice, there was a thin line here too. Commoners might cross that line in 'doing wrong,' as Velondraza emphasized most strongly during that visit. They also crossed it in doing 'right' by serving royalty. Although both Sambarivo and Bemihisatra emphasized the difference between them, the practice of royal service—temporally and spatially—was clearly oriented to turning one into the other, turning a highly heterogeneous collection of pilgrims with different ancestries and different anjara into one person with Sambarivo, and through Sambarivo, into one person with royalty.

I have already tried to sketch out in broad terms some features of political-economic relations between local people in the Analalava region and their would-be masters in the 1970s following independence. I began by examining the changing places of 'masters of the land' and 'strangers,' children of men and children of women, at cultivations in which they were differently rooted through ancestors embodied in the trees and rocks interspersed among their houses and granaries, some more centrally than others. I then examined 'the post' through which French colonists sought to transform themselves from strangers into masters of the land by localizing themselves through their own ancestral togny centered on the Tribunal. While claiming that these reorientations of living people around new lines of descent, new ancestries, were essential processes by which relations of domination and subordination were systematized, I focused mainly on the language with which people represented these new households of masters and servants to one another.

Beginning with this chapter, I hope to show how people in the Analalava area work, and are worked, to build the systemic relations of mastery and servility into the very ground over which they are contending. A key element in this process, implicit in contested representations of 'children of men' as 'children of women' with diminished relations to ancestors, and 'children of women' as suspected traffickers in their generative powers, is the underlying connection between the land, which is being reworked, and the workers themselves, their living bodies. While speech is one critical element in the representation and reincorporation of these new relations, people also reincorporate these relations in working, making and remaking them into new forms out of materials that include themselves.[67]

This chapter has focused on representations of living and ancestral royalty, defined in terms of separations and prohibitions experienced in speaking and doing, whether leading or following. These separations are marked at the Doany and the Mahabo by repeated fences made of dead and living materials, but they are achieved regionwide by their outer, most encompassing fences, which are made of people. The very qualities of these people—formerly slaves 'without ancestors,' 'lost' to the places from which they came, even 'separated' from one another like cattle—exemplify local processes of depersonalization and estrangement basic to efforts to create new forms of mastery and subordination. Through the 'division' of workers, these processes are extended beyond situational negotiations to encompass places and people in the aggregate. We have also seen that Sambarivo have their own interests in maintaining their guard over royalty, especially over royal ancestors. Although they are supposed to remain in their 'pens' for generations, they find ways to move out into the region, contributing to the expansion of their followers through the creation of spirit-mediums in surrounding communities. We have also seen how people who may or may not be spirit-mediums are drawn up to the feet of royalty through their own concerns about ancestry, fertility, sickness, and death. In the last three chapters, we examine how, by participating in royal work, they are drawn through 'Every One a Thousand' into the very body of royalty, how in working, they recreate images of ancestry encompassing even their own.

A Green Estate

Filthy Land

Navy vazaha—robaka fanjakaña malagasy. Fiaroa—
tsisy varany—vazaha navy, namono teña. . . . Zahay
mangataka, tsy mboany, tsy ekeny, tsy mboany.
'Tabataba,' hoy ireo. 'Olo mivory tsy mitsabo,' hoy
ireo. . . . Fanompoaña, maro fomba, tsy vita.
When Europeans came, Malagasy government
[Sakalava monarchy] was ruined. Fiaroa [the great
diviner-curer]—there was no point any more—
when the Europeans came, he committed
suicide. . . . We asked [for permission to do
things], they didn't agree, they didn't consent,
they didn't agree. 'Trouble,' they said. 'People
who assemble don't grow crops,' they said. . . .
Royal services, many customary acts, weren't
completed.

Malaza at Andonaka

FOLAKA NY TANY: THE LAND IS FILTHY

The ampanjaka Tondroko died at eight o'clock on the morning of Sunday, September 20, 1925.[1] Thereafter it was forbidden to call him by his living name.[2] He was renamed Ndramamahaña, 'Noble Who Nurtured Thousands,' praised like his father and grandfather before him, for unifying the region into one domain until the French cut their efforts short. As Ngeda from the Mahabo explained:

"The Great-Grandfather of the ampanjaka did not have many followers because he was the first to establish *(mamoraña)* a government in the Analalava‹region. He was still setting things right *(mañajary)*, still uniting people *(mamitrañ'olo)*, gathering people together *(mamory olo)*. That is why his praise name is 'Noble Who Joined Thousands Together in One Group' (Ndramamitrañarivo). The Grandfather, who inherited the monarchy, had many followers. In his time, many people moved all over doing lots of things *(mietsiketsiky maro)*. So they gave him the praise name 'Noble Who Activated Thousands' (Ndramanetsiarivo). The Father, who ruled during the time of the French, was called 'Noble Who Nourished Thousands' (Ndramamahañarivo) because he was so generous, but already his support was waning. There aren't many people now. Soazara has few people now."

As Ngeda indicated, Sakalava royal ancestors took lifetimes to bring 'thousands' of followers together in one place. Although he avoided any mention of their deaths, the work of 'making them great' *(mahabe azy)* actually began when their descendants enlisted royal followers to bury the royal corpse, thus cleansing the land of its filth. The burial began with the year-long 'hot service' *(fanompoana mafana)* in which workers dried out the corpse and broke through the fence around the royal tomb to bury the bones. It ended with the 'menaty service' *(fanompoana menaty)*, when royal workers were called up again to remove the broken fence from around the tomb, enlarge the tomb to make room for the next burial, and recover it with a new fence.

When Tondroko died, French authorities curtailed his funeral from a year to less than two months. Southern Bemihisatra officials hired a lawyer who got the burial service extended by a month, but it was still cut short a month early "under administrative pressure."[3] They requested permission to complete the reconstruction of the tomb, but their requests were denied. So the body, which had been scraped of its flesh to achieve its premature burial, remained in a half-open grave for almost five decades. Here we ask how successive generations of royal followers worked to close Tondroko's grave, so they could raise from it the ancestor Ndramamahaña.

TONDROKO'S BURIAL

L'Inspecteur des Provinces Charles Poirier, who investigated the circumstances surrounding the choice of the infant Soazara as Ndramamahaña's successor, ended his report of December 27, 1926 with an account of Tondroko's burial.[4] Poirier was not sent to Analalava until the spring of 1926, so presumably he got his information by questioning participants, including those he would have come to know when he was chef de province of Analalava in 1914–1916. In 1971–

1973 and 1981, there was no way of 'taking away the prohibition' *(mangala fady)* against talking about the funerals of specific royalty, and thus no way of learning the details of how Tondroko's corpse was buried. I did learn about some general features of Sakalava royal burials from my own fieldwork and from other sources that I have included here because they are relevant to the later reconstruction of the menaty, the one context in which such matters can be discussed. These are bracketed in my summary of Poirier's report, so as not to mix different accounts.

Poirier states that four of Tondroko's followers were present at his death: "Mbaraka, Djouma, Tiandraza, Mazavabe." [As indicated in Chapter 1, death is identified with the moment that 'the breath of life is gone' *(rivotra ny aina lasa)*, expressed as 'the clouds are gone' *(lasa zavona)* in the case of royalty, as indicated by holding a mirror up to the mouth of the dying person. The corpse, ordinarily called *faty,* 'dead one,' is here called *fanompoaña (mafana),* '(hot) service,' because, as one man put it, "He's the work." It may also be called *zanahary,* 'royal ancestor.']

Telegrams were sent to the Sakalava in Nosy Be, Majunga, and Ambilobe, informing them of Tondroko's death. Two groups of Ancestor People—Jingo and Antankoala—washed the corpse and wrapped it in a piece of plain white cotton *(bafota).* It was forbidden to move a royal body on Sunday, Tuesday, or Thursday. On Wednesday, September 23, the corpse was wrapped in a piece of silk embroidered with silver thread (sobayia), laid in a canoe lined with red cotton, taken over to Nosy Lava, and put in a house oriented east-west, opposite to the orientation of houses of living people.[5] [Poirier describes the house as being an "antechamber of the tomb," but according to contemporary royal followers, the royal corpse is dried out in a house called a *zomba mañitry,* 'sweet-smelling mansion/royal house,' on a small point of land below the Mahabo known as Antsandrarafa.] The body was laid out on a "bed," called *kibany,* with its head to the east. [*Kibany* is the usual word for 'bed.' The full name for this bed is 'gold bed' *(kibany fanjavamena)* or 'gold trestle' *(savaly fanjava).*[6] The house was similar to MamanDjoma's image of Pepony in Silamo doctrine (see Chapter 1): cool and sweet-smelling, like a place under a tree next to running water or the sea.]

Pieces of white cotton cloth were laid under the bed to catch the liquids from the decomposing body. Every Monday, during the night from Sunday to Monday with which the new day begins, Jingo, Antankoala, or Sambarivo, emptied the viscera of decomposing material, washed the corpse in a mixture of fermented honey mixed with water called *taodrazana,* and scraped off the flesh from the bones with a wooden scraper [Poirier uses the term *raclette*], made especially for that purpose.

[According to royal officials in the 1970s, no one is allowed to enter the house except the Razan'olo and the Jado, or royal substitute, who is there as a 'witness' to make sure that nothing is done wrong. The Sambarivo from the Mahabo, led by the supplicator there, take the remains from the body at the door and throw them away on a small island nearby. One person said that eight people fan the body without stopping, to make sure that no flies or dirt get on it. "Without sleeping. Four fan, while four sleep; four men and four women, working in groups of two each, so that there are spouses upon spouses *(biaka fivadiaña fivadiaña),* two and two to make four, four and four to make eight." The fanning is done until the body is put into the grave. The same man said that the body is washed with two honey mixtures, first *ontso velo* (an uncooked mixture of honey and water widely used for cleansing dirt associated with sickness and death), then *tô mainty,* a fermented mixture of honey and water used only to cleanse the royal ancestors. Two holes are dug underneath the bed for the liquids to fall into: one at the east end for the tô mainty, and one west of it for the ontso velo. One official said: "Plain water is never used, only reddish water *(rano menamena)* for royalty." No one mentioned to me such details as scrapers, but royal officials at both the Doany and the Mahabo did say that the flesh should fall from the bones, just as sacrificial animals should submit to their death without making a sound, these being premier examples of the willing submission of royal followers, which is one of the most prominent parts of royal service, as we have already seen. One man said: "It's not necessary/desirable to take it off forcibly" (*Tsy mila mangala forisay* [forcé]). This was one of the main reasons given for the length of royal funerals: the body should dry out of its own accord. The raclette seems to have been necessitated by the fact that Tondroko's body had to be buried in less than two months, so his followers had to commit acts that must have looked and felt like the worst form of sorcery to achieve this end, compounding acts already dangerously similar to sorcery.]

Incense—an Arabian perfume known as *tibou*—was burned around the body to cover the odor of decomposition. [Cow bones may be burned as well as incense. It was prohibited to say that the corpse smelled bad *(maimbo)*; it was sweet-smelling *(mañitry)*.]

While six to eight men from the Jingo or Antankoala groups guarded the body inside the house, six to eight Jingo or Antankoala women sang "forbidden songs"—*antsa faly*—very low whenever the drums sounded in the mornings, at sunup, at ten o'clock, and in the evening, at sunset.[7] The crowd of five to six hundred, who stayed on Nosy Lava during the burial services, was organized spatially around the southern, western, and northern sides of the house. Poirier notes that seated people had to cross their legs and fold them under their thighs. [It is prohibited to sit with the feet sticking out toward the east, that is, toward the ancestors, even in one's own house.]

"In the South, the Tsimania took their place: *clans* Tsimandrara, Mananadabo, Antifarimay, Antambovozavaka, Zafindramahavita, Antevinanibe, Antevinanikely, Tsimazava, Antiromba, Andranomeva, Vezo, Antsamby, Bahomy, Maromary—in the North, the Antavarabe: *clans* Marorandro, Joaty, Bemongo, Manantsaka, Antiravaka, Manoromby, Antankandrafana, Mosohiry, Tsimaniribe, Antankoala, Antifanivana, Jingo, Tsarana, Antibala—in the West, all the strangers who were not subject to the kingdom."[8] [These names include names of ancestries, some of whom serve as manantany and as Ancestor People, and some names of pens of Sambarivo.]

Mourners cried from dawn until dusk, but it was forbidden to cry at night. Men worked on the tomb—bringing up rocks and slabs of stone to reconstruct the tomb following the burial. Others slaughtered the animals with which the workers were fed. Women sang praise songs (kolondoy) honoring the royal ancestors.

Izaho Boana malilo andriaraiko.
Izaho Boana malilo lolohaiko.
Izaho Boana malilo mananahy.

I Boana beg pardon of my noble father.
I Boana beg pardon of the one I bear on my head.
I Boana beg pardon of the one who possesses me.[9]

Izao Tompontsik'izao fa zafiny Andriamisara.
Tsy manjaka tsy entiny zafiny Andriamandisoarivo.
[Refrain.] *Fa ny zafiny Andriamandisoarivo o o o o o!*

Our Lord now is Andriamisara's grandchild.
Andriamandisoarivo does not rule if he does not bring along his
  grandchildren.
[Refrain.] Andriamandisoarivo's grandchildren o o o o o![10]

According to Poirier, no nails, teeth, or hair were taken from the body, "because the Bemihisatra do not make 'dady' to conserve relics." Instead: "When the corpse was reduced to a skeleton, two gold pieces were placed between the jaws; it was enveloped in a piece of stuff called *dalahany* [a precious Arabian silk, restricted to royalty], a red cloth, bordered with two yellow stripes, then it was put into a coffin made from a tree trunk, hollowed out like a canoe." [In his report, Poirier states that 4,000 francs in five-franc pieces were buried with the body, two in the mouth and the rest on the chest. In his published account, he states first that 8,000 francs were laid on the chest and two gold coins were put in the mouth, and later that 150 francs of gold were put in the coffin and 776 piastres taken to the tomb.[11] The coffin was called *fiarovontro*, 'protector against moisture.' Royal officials in the 1970s said that the coffin was not made until after the body had been washed and dressed. One said, 'As soon as the body is in the coffin, they are together called *fanompoana* to show that everyone else is a server *(ampanompo)*, a slave of the ampanjaka

(andevon' ny ampanjaka). Anyone can carry the coffin, even Vazaha.'
The coffin is constructed at the place known as Antsandrarafa. Likewise if the bearers stop at the foot of a tree on their way up to the
Mahabo, that place is also called Antsandrarafa. The movement of
going there is described as *milay*, 'to sail like a canoe on the sea,' which
one man explained by saying: 'The Service moves, the slaves (andevo)
follow, not fast, not slow, but steadily.']

"At the very moment of burial, the Jingo, Antankoala and Sambarivo dig the grave, resting very often because it is forbidden to sweat
during this task." [Digging the royal grave is described as 'breaking
open the sky' *(mamaky lanitra)*, as opposed to 'breaking open the
ground' *(mamaky tany)*, the phrase used in digging up the earth to
plant crops or to bury commoners. According to Mellis, who lived
in the northwest for some two decades during the early colonial period, the grave itself is called 'a hole in the sky.'[12]]

"The coffin was put at the bottom of the grave, on a bed of 1,600
silver five-franc pieces. The burial took place in the middle of the
night; these burials are forbidden in the day." [Mellis says Sakalava
royal burials are always held on a Friday, beginning at sunset and
ending at midnight, which would make them early Saturday, the second of the three 'good days' in the week by Sakalava reckoning.[13]
Southern Bemihisatra said the burial could be done on any of the good
days, but the actual burial—the digging of the grave and placing of
the body—'can only be done at night, when it's dark, so people can't
see.'] "The hole where the coffin was put was recovered with stone
slabs. It is forbidden to fill these graves with dirt; the stones then pile
up in cubical form and enclosures of poles raise up all around this
mausoleum." [Mellis states that a trench is dug in the bottom of the
hole and filled with four black stones taken from the sea *(riana mainty,*
black waves), on which the canoe-shaped coffin *(laka,* canoe) containing the corpse is placed. The tomb is surrounded by black stones
known as 'black waves' *(riaka mainty)* and sand from the sea known
as 'white waves' *(riaka malandy).*[14] The phrase *añivon' ny riaka* or *añ-
ivondriaka,* 'in the midst of the waters/waves,' is used in contrast to
antety, 'on land.' It is also an expression for the whole island of Mada-

gascar, dating back at least to the early nineteenth century. Radama I, ampanjaka of Imerina in 1810–1828, had these words engraved on his silver coffin: *Tompo' ny anivon' ny riaka,* "Lord of what is in the midst of the waves," that is, Lord of Madagascar.[15] Mellis emphasizes that while the mourning ceremonies are public, the actual burial is attended by only those immediately involved in the work.[16]]

The burial services ended on November 15, 1925.[17] During that period, from September 20 to November 15, royal followers were forbidden to wash their clothes or their bodies. [Current officials and guardians say that they were allowed to wash their faces when they got up, preferably by wiping their eyes with a moistened index finger.] Even those in charge of cleaning the body were not allowed to wash their hands; they could only wipe them on their hair. Neither men nor women were allowed to dress their hair. Women were required to let their hair down and loosen their braids. It was forbidden to say that the corpse smelled bad or to spit, to say the word "Tondroko" or any other word resembling it. [Southern Bemihisatra still refer to 'fingers'—*tondro* elsewhere in Madagascar—as 'branches of the hand' *(rantsan-tàñana)*.] Poirier adds that men were forbidden to wear more than a single thickness of cloth. [Since men do not customarily wear double thicknesses of cloth around their bodies, this may mean that they were forbidden to cover their heads with a second piece of cloth. In 1971–1973 and 1981, both men and women had to remove their head cloths when addressing royal spirits embodied in mediums or at the doors of the Doany and Mahabo.] Among these prohibitions, Poirier notes that "Every man took the woman that it pleased him to choose and no woman had the right to refuse."[18]

Chef de province Philibert reported that the Sakalava "gave themselves up to veritable acts of savagery on the remains of Tondroko," by which he probably meant to include the sexual license to which Dandouau and then Poirier alluded.[19] These included songs that Sakalava themselves described to Poirier as *antsa vorery, ompa, sy asaha,* which Poirier translates as "voluptuous, insulting and injurious songs."[20] *Asaha* does refer to acts, including speech, insulting and injurious to the ancestors, like swearing by them falsely, for which they kill in response, unless the actor begs their forgiveness *(mangataka poko)*. *Ompa* is even stronger, suggesting abuse or vilification with intent to commit sorcery. *Vorery* is typically used to refer to bodily fluids, not voluptuously, but as filthy and defiling substances. The singers, men and women, told Poirier that they could not understand the archaic language of the songs, prompting Poirier to suggest that the songs "present as much interest for linguists as for ethnologists, because they bring us back to the sources of primitive thought *(la pensée primitive)*."[21] Poirier claims that the songs expressed "the natural attractions which are practiced freely at night in the course of these ceremonies . . . of native groups overexcited by the mysteries of the cult, the libations, and the instinct of complementarities." But he hastens to add that "no immodest gesture mimics these intimacies of the consciousness *(conscience)*."[22]

FANOMPOAÑA MENATY: THE MENATY SERVICE

The first obligation of an ampanjaka to the royal ancestors was to carry out the funeral of his or her predecessor.[23] The second major obligation was to replace the menaty or innermost fence around the royal tomb. The menaty was ruined when the royal spirit suddenly compelled the coffin bearers circulating around the outside of the fence to break through it to bury the corpse in the tomb within. According to Mellis, writing in 1938:

> The will of the deceased is respected; some do not enter by the door; the porters of the body are generally drunk, they go around the enclosure with advancing and retreating movements—rituals—which indicate on the one hand that the deceased wants to stay among his own, and on the other hand, that his faithful want him to return to God. After two or four tours, it happens that one of the ends of the poles [with which the porters carry the coffin] touches the enclosure; it is there that the deceased wants to enter. A few posts are then demolished to permit him to penetrate into the enclosure.[24]

Southern Bemihisatra confirmed this, but as Saha Barimaso said, having noted that there was no door in the menaty, just in the outer fence:

"To get in, the menaty has to be ruined *(Miditry tsy maintsy robaka ny menaty)*—when an ampanjaka dies. It's difficult to talk about this."

The menaty service *(fanompoaña menaty)* takes its name from the reconstruction of the fence, but the work actually involved the cleaning and rebuilding of the whole tomb as well. Until the fence was replaced, the tomb remained dangerously open: the corpses exposed to the depredations of would-be sorcerers and the living vulnerable to the malevolence of the recently deceased. The critical event in the timing of the menaty service seems to have been the reemergence of the deceased as a 'royal ancestor' *(razan' ny ampanjaka)* through the body of a legitimate medium. In this case, the process was complicated by people interested in keeping Ndramamahaña buried.

TALKING ABOUT BEGINNING

Dandouau, in a paper published in 1911, not long after the first reconstruction of the menaty in the area, and Poirier, in his account of Tondroko's funeral written in 1926, report that both of the fences surrounding the royal tomb are repaired or rebuilt in the course of the royal funeral. Mellis states that the opening in the fence closest to the tomb is first covered with a piece of white cloth; "the hole is stopped up only two or three years later, apparently when a *sahoa* [*saha*, medium of a local royal spirit or founder of the monarchy, usually a commoner but sometimes a guardian] declares itself and is recognized."[25] Explaining why they were reconstructing the menaty in the mid-1970s, Southern Bemihisatra said that it could be rebuilt any time after the burial. They did not mention the mediums, probably because Ndramamahaña already had at least ten recognized mediums by the time the menaty service was begun in 1972. Indeed, there was some controversy about who was to be considered the senior medium.

The emphasis of these royal followers of the 1930s on the reemergence of the dead ruler's voice in political affairs is illuminating. Only after the ancestor had emerged from the tomb, by possessing a commoner through which he could speak and act, would his supporters be able to bury the corpse completely by closing up the tomb altogether. According to Sambarivo at the Mahabo, there were no mediums resident at the Mahabo during the years following the Great-Grandfather's death (ca. 1865). It is also unclear to me what happened with the menaty following the Grandfather's death around 1892. Hova incursions into the area during the 1890s, then the French occupation of Analalava and Antognibe in 1897, must have made it difficult to organize such a large service. The immediate precedent for the menaty service in the mid-1970s was a service that Tondroko held for the master of the northern Mahabo, conducted by the supplicator who was the father of the brothers who occupied that position at different times during the 1960s, 1970s, and 1980s. The service was done at Tsinjorano on the coast of the Ambolobozo Peninsula. It was begun in 1914. According to one of the brothers, they crossed back over to Nosy Lava on April 15, 1916. As soon as it was completed, they had to move people and cattle to the mainland, perhaps in 1917. [As indicated in Chapter 3, Poirier's letter to the Governor General of Madagascar states that he removed all the villages on Nosy Lava on April 19, 1916.]

The royal ancestors were represented by the Grandfather, Ndramanetsiarivo, from the southern Mahabo and his 'friend' *(namana)*, the Bemazava ruler, Ndramatikoarivo, from the northern Mahabo in the persons of the first of their mediums. The Grandfather's first medium was a Sakalava man, probably from an inland village a couple of hours walk north from Antognibe where the Grandfather's doany had been located.[26] The Bemazava ruler's medium was a woman from a coastal village on the Ambolobozo Peninsula. They were joined by the Great-Grandfather, also in the person of his first medium. He was not officially part of the service, because the Great-Grandfather as the tompony of the Mahabo, is not supposed to move from there. But his medium—Saha Aly, married to Mainty Be's sister (Fig. 9, E; Fig. 10) came from the village immediately north of Tsinjorano, where the work camp was located and where his wife had been born, so he came as a visitor. All these mediums were deceased at the time of the menaty service in the 1970s.

Some Sambarivo remembered one other menaty service in the area. This one was also for Ndramatikoarivo, the Bemazava ruler buried in the northern Mahabo, maintained by the guardians of the southern Mahabo. The service was held at a village on the Komajara Peninsula some time during the colonial period after the southern Mahabo was reoccupied (in the late 1920s). No one that I spoke to remembered just when it was. The royal ancestors were represented by the same spirits as before, in the persons of the mediums who were respectively the third and second they had possessed. The Grandfather's medium was a Sakalava woman from an inland village ön the Ambolobozo Peninsula. The Bemazava ruler's medium was a Sambarivo woman from the southern Mahabo, the second child of the supplicator there and older sister of the brothers who have served as supplicators at the southern Mahabo since their father's death. These mediums were also deceased at the time of the menaty service in the 1970s.

After Tondroko was buried at the end of 1925—but I do not know exactly how soon after—Ndramamahaña began to speak through 'simple people' living in the region. Sambarivo at the Mahabo named a 'Sakalava' woman, a mother's sister of the supplicators in the Antibe pen, who had married into their mainland village from Antognibe, as the Father's first medium, now deceased. According to another long-time medium of the Father, she was actually the second to become possessed. The first was a 'Sakalava' woman from a village about an hour's walk south of Analalava, who had married into a coastal village on the north side of the Loza River. She still came to the Mahabo to pay her respects, but she had "never really stayed there." At the time of the menaty service in the mid-1970s, Ndramamahaña had ten recognized mediums. Their very number indicates that other factors besides the emergence of the royal ancestor in his first medium, other voices besides his, were important in initiating the menaty service.

The service was actually the work of the ancestor's successor. It could only be carried out if the living ruler could muster the necessary labor over the long time. Although the royal funeral requires a large number of mourners, the workers are drawn only from the Ancestor People and the Sambarivo around the Doany and the Mahabo. Indeed, others are prohibited from doing their work. Furthermore, in the case of Ndramamahaña's funeral, workers were involved in the service for less than two months rather than for a whole year. During the royal funeral, the doany had to be moved to a new location. Ndramamahaña's former doany was renamed Tsimahasenga (Not a Royal Body/ Does Not Cure), his death having rendered it uninhabitable.[27] The work required to move the doany was carried out by the guardians there, who might be expected to have strong personal interests in supporting the efforts of a new ruler to found a new doany. According to the Antidoany in the 1970s, the service was completed within one dry season. The actual move was restricted to a single day. The work required only the people of the living ruler and some people from the domain. Antimahabo were excluded. It was concluded long before the royal funeral. Even though Ndramamahaña's funeral lasted less than two months, the new Doany was already established in Analalava by the time it was done.

The Mahabo was never moved as we have already seen. It was always rebuilt on the same spot. Nevertheless, the rebuilding of the menaty required much more time and many more workers and other resources than either the royal funeral or the relocation of the Doany. Thus it must have served much more than those services as both test and proof of the regrowth of the monarchy under a new ruler. This may help to explain the paradox that Mellis notes with some amusement: "Such a modest monument [as a royal tomb] would not seem to require substantial maintenance, but to think so is to be ill-acquainted with the Malagasy. When it is necessary to change a fence-post, there are innumerable complications and that can last one and even several years; also an administrative authorization is necessary in view of the ceremonies that follow one after another during this time."[28]

The observations of Bemihisatra followers concerning the menaty service of the mid-1970s confirm Mellis's general points in detail. Besides the 'people of the living' and the 'people of the dead,' the menaty service required workers to be drawn from the region as a whole. In the precolonial period, they served at least twice as long as the year required of mourners, and perhaps longer than that. Some guardians at the Doany and the Mahabo remembered the menaty service at Tsinjorano as having lasted six or eight years, and said that was obligatory in earlier services. The scope and length of the service required more planning on the part of the royal administration as well as more support from royal followers, both in tribute and in the extra work needed to make up for the loss of absent kin. Thus, it seems reasonable to suppose that the reconstruction of the menaty recognized not only the reemergent voice of a royal ancestor, but also the superior abilities of his or her living descendant in mobilizing large numbers of people and extensive resources. As long as the dead ruler was not completely buried, his successor was not completely confirmed as the living ampanjaka either. The deliverance of the ancestor from the grave accomplished both.

The menaty service in the precolonial period was likely to have been part of a process by which living rulers and their officials tried to retain their forebears' followers around them through their undeniable respect for the royal ancestors. Incorporating the 'people of the dead' as well as the spirit-mediums around the Mahabo into a service, controlled and organized by the ampanjaka at the head of the 'people of the living,' must also have helped to prevent the Mahabo from developing into a separate, independent center of ancestral power and authority.

The praise names of the Southern Bemihisatra rulers in the Analalava region speak to the gradual growth of royal power in the course of each reign as well as over generations of reigns, moving from the Great-Grandfather, the 'Noble Who United Thousands' (Ndramamitrañarivo), to the Grandfather, 'Noble Who Made Thousands Move About' (Ndramanetsiarivo), to the Father, the 'Noble Who Nourished Thousands' with his generosity (Ndramamahañarivo), a progression from which the Brother who never ruled—the 'Noble Who Compelled Thousands Unwillingly' (Ndranteronarivo)—stands distinctly apart. Although exalted in praise names, the activities of joining, building, feeding, and growing were part of everyday experience. *Mamitraña* was used to refer to seaming or joining together any kind of separate pieces—mats, cloth, boards, people—into one thing with greater size and strength. *Mietsiketsiky* implied the liveliness and growth that was seen as both cause and consequence of moving around a lot. The same term was used in speaking about the development work financed by international aid programs. Mamahaña encompassed a range of acts in which one person or thing gave strength, energy, support to another, as in feeding and fattening people and animals, weaving a weft or filling into the warp, or charging a gun. It was also used of a person's own efforts to stand fast in supporting or resisting persons or things.[29]

Similar processes of growth are critical to the authentication of mediums, both the lesser mediums known as *tromba* and the mediums of the four founders of the monarchy or of the royal ancestors at the Mahabo, known as *saha*. The emergence of a spirit in the body of its mediums, its recognition as a particular historical being, could take months, even years.[30] Even after a spirit's identity had been publicly recognized and his relationship to his medium routinized through many reappearances, he, in the person of his medium, still had to establish himself as a powerful diviner and healer among people outside the immediate circle of kin and friends of his medium in which he first came to being. Mediums were usually well known by the time they sought legitimation at the Mahabo. Once there, they had to establish themselves in relation to their 'elder siblings,' that is, the mediums of their spirit(s) who had been recognized before them.

Colonial rule inevitably affected the continual growth of ancestors from deceased rulers, including Ndramamahaña's forebears as well as Ndramamahaña himself. In principle, permission was required for every kind of royal service, as it was for the burials that commoners conducted for their own kin. Malaza's sons said that they and others throughout the region continued to honor the royal ancestors secretly, for example, holding spirit possession meetings in the forest. Mellis's comments suggest that as the colonial period wore on, French administrators collaborated in these subterfuges as long as they did not directly threaten the exercise of French authority: "The populations [of northwestern Madagascar] have a veritable cult for the princes, in whom they see representatives of a GOD inaccessible other than by their intermediary. To destroy that force would be more than a mistake, wrong, especially since most of these princes are disposed to help as far as possible, on the condition, 'understood,' that no one concerns himself or intervenes in the practice of the 'cult of the ancestors.' They are more intelligent about knowing to use means of attenuating these practices than we might admit."[31] This was one of Malaza's arguments for why the Doany was moved from Analalava to the countryside:

"The French—they enslaved. Peed, shat from the palanquin while Malagasy were carrying it. Savage. They didn't follow the customs at the Doany. That was why it was moved—struck too much with their shit *(voa loatra taitaindreo)*. Weren't permitted to do *tsimandrimandry* [all night celebrations of the ancestors]. Evenings it wasn't permitted to carry on until dawn—said it created trouble."

In fact, royal followers were not permitted to move the Doany until the early 1950s. The menaty service was also too large to be carried out without the explicit approval of local colonial, then postcolonial, functionaries. This is evident from Bemihisatra correspondence dating from the time of Ndramamahaña's funeral, which also confirms that the menaty was reconstructed after, rather than during, that service. On November 14, 1925, the junior kinsman representing the Northern Bemihisatra ampanjaka Amada at Ndramamahaña's funeral wrote to Amada on behalf of all the people involved in the service, asking for his help with the French government in getting them more time than the two months they had been allowed: "We need a prolongation because . . . it has already been more than ten years since the guardians of the mahabo here on Nosy Lava left, so all the things *(zavatra)* here have fallen to ruin *(nirotso)*.[32] So we would like to serve [to rebuild] the *fiaro omby* because the *mena aty* is no longer able to cover the difficult/precious things *(tsimaharakotra ny rahasarotra)*. We cannot keep silent; we are informing you, master of the ancestors *(tompondrazana)*."[33]

Southern Bemihisatra in the 1970s said that it was especially difficult to get permission to do services requiring many people, such as the menaty service. For example, Sefo in Tsinjorano commented:

"In the time of the Vazaha, some were nice *(tsara fanahy)*, some were reluctant about the ampanjaka. Some said people couldn't serve. Others said, 'Do it!' But both in the time of the French and in the time of the Malagasy, it is necessary to notify that a service is to be done, no matter what it is, how long it will take, and so on. Then when people gather, it is already known why. People don't come around asking questions. For example, if you ask for six months to do the *fanompoaña fiañitry* [service to get incense], you get four. The 500 FMG for spirit possession meetings used to go to the commune, which no longer exists [under General Ramanantsoa's government]. No money needs to be paid for doing services. The [chef de] canton is informed first, then the [chef de] district."

A Sambarivo at the Mahabo added to Sefo's remarks about service during the colonial period:

"Permission was usually given, but not for long. It was because she is a female ampanjaka, not a male ampanjaka. Because she doesn't have much of a head, like a man's head *(Fotony izy tsisy loha loatra karaha lohan'lehilahy)*. Women need to follow what people tell them. Look at Amady [ampanjaka of the Northern Bemihisatra at Nosy Be]. What he asked for, he got. He just asked, they let him do what he wanted. Asking [was possible], but [services] didn't last long, they had to be done quickly. It wasn't necessary to give money, just make a request. Elders went to the ampanjaka, then the ampanjaka sent the letter to the government. It is still done like that now."

Other Sambarivo at the Mahabo and at the Doany made similar connections between the conduct of French officials and relations among Bemihisatra. Responding to our comment that we could not see the menaty at either the Mahabo Ambalaka or the Mahabo Avaratra, one Antimahabo leader said:

"Yes, for a long time it's been like that. Couldn't get permission to serve the menaty in the time of the Vazaha. Kills too many trees. Too many people gather together. And it takes a long time, don't do any other work, play every day. They couldn't collect the head tax that way. They gave permission to get guava and [some other fruit], but not *teza* [cores of hardwood trees], which is what's needed. She [ampanjaka] is stingy! stingy! Has lots of money. She could give money to get the *patente,* but

she doesn't. She is stingy! See her house!. . . . Built long ago, broken
down. The house of Amady, her grandfather in Nosy Be—beautiful, a
house of stone, with floors! She should build something like that, but
stingy. The mahabo up there is finished in *tôly*. All the mahabo are like
that, all finished in *tôly*. . . . Only Nosy Lava is left. Stingy! She has lots
of money, gets money from all over here [gesturing outward with his
hands]. A rich person *(ampañarivo)*! And those around her don't work, just
eat. She is a woman. She is not married, she should be taken care of
(mitarimy). The big people, the men, should tell her what to do. 'Let's do
such and such.' Then she would agree and do it. But the big people don't
work . . . they just eat."

Another man, who had formerly been associated with the Doany,
but who had moved away, made similar comments in the context of
a general discussion of changes in the region. Even though, on other
occasions, he had described the living ruler as the premier ampanjaka
in Madagascar, this time he began differently:

"The big people at the Doany, they probably collect thirty cattle, but only
use up three or four. Then they sell off the rest and keep the money or
give very little of it to the ampanjaka. . . . The reason is that she doesn't
look after things. In the past, they wouldn't have dared, they would have
been hit with the royal curse. But now they do because they don't fear the
way they used to. The reason they got rid of M. [a supplicator] at the
Mahabo was because he didn't eat enough. Stingy! 'What do you need all
that for?' he would ask. A. [his immediate successor] is always calling for
alcohol for all the royal spirits, for all the young men. . . . Now the
ampanjaka doesn't follow the customs . . . eats anything on the road. In
the past, the ampanjaka ate inside. People had to taste the food before,
drink the drink before, to make sure it was alright. He was surrounded by
people everywhere he went, stepped out [to relieve himself] with people.
Couldn't walk over it. His spit was collected in a special dish by a child
who followed him. If it hit the ground it would kill, because he was a
masina person. Wouldn't touch a snotty baby, always surrounded by
people, everywhere watching everything. He coupled, people watched.
She does everything alone, none of that. It's not right. She hates to go to
the Doany. As soon as she gets there, she wants to leave. They were late
this year—you see? Arrives, then 'Have to go, have to go.' People sing
songs for her. They dance for her. She doesn't see! Doesn't see! Doesn't

see even the least bit. Did you see the car they [her followers] bought her
because they were so joyful about the birth of the [first] child. It's just
rotting there in her courtyard. . . . I don't like to go to the Doany any
more unless I am called. I stay here, work here. I was the one who got all
the guns for the birth. Had to tell her, 'You have to follow the customs! If
you don't follow the customs, everything will be bad, it will come to
nothing.' Doesn't see. . . . The plane trip when she came back from
France. Some people like myself were waiting in Analalava the whole time
she was away, waiting for her. Others came up when the date was
everywhere made known that she would return. Analalava was not big
enough to hold all the people who came to receive her on the air strip and
in the town (Plate 35). The French were really surprised to see how the

Plate 35. The ampanjaka Soazara, surrounded by followers who welcomed
her back to Analalava from France around the time of independence
(Service Photo—Cinéma du Ministère de l'Information; TY 13, no. 317)
The Service dates the photo to 1958. But according to the written records
of her Bemihisatra followers: "The date *(daty)* the ampanjaka came back
from abroad and arrived here in Analalava was September 10, 1962 and the
total number of people who met her at the airstrip was four thousand and
the cattle killed forty [and] white rice one hundred daba and three people
gave birth on the airstrip and there were ten female people pregnant and
the number of cars was twenty-seven."

Sakalava loved their ampanjaka. In Mena Be, no one follows the old customs any more. The ampanjaka are just names. In Nosy Be, they don't even have a *tsirangoty* [royal fence], just a house. All the difficult things are in the house. They don't even have a special place for them."

The colonial administration stood in the way of the reconstruction of the menaty not only because it prohibited people from participating in lengthy royal services, but also because it drew them away from the Doany and the Mahabo. As independence moved closer in the 1950s, royal followers became more divided in their loyalties, so that no clear consensus could be achieved about whether to support the ancestors or to turn away from them. Thus, in the course of waiting to get permission to do the menaty service, at least two different ideas seem to have developed about how the menaty should be reconstructed: with posts made from hardwood trees as before or with cement *(siment)* and galvanized iron *(tôly)*. According to Southern Bemihisatra in the 1970s, the wooden menaty had been replaced by a cement wall at every other Bemihisatra and Bemazava mahabo on the northwest coast except the mahabo at Lavalohaliky, Berafia, and Nosy Lava.[34] For tombs, as for houses, cement and iron were considered more desirable than wood—more resistant to fire and more impervious to rot, requiring less work to maintain. In contrast to the perishable materials demanding continued renewal, the more inert materials would have buried the royal corpses in a more lasting way.

Some guardians at both the Doany and the Mahabo had favored this plan, as we have seen. Malaza said:

"Soazara's father ruled for ten years before the French came. Then when they came, it was incredible, couldn't do anything, they never agreed to anything." [For example, the menaty service?] "Yes, the Mahabo was abandoned for twelve years. They are just repairing the things now that fell into ruin then. No menaty, only the fiaroaomby. I told the ampanjaka to put a wall of cement around it, the way they have elsewhere, for example, at Nosy Be. But she said the royal spirits don't want that. I thought they should have made a wall of cement and reconstructed all the roofs with tôly."[35]

Independence in 1960 (June 26) brought renewed hope. Royal followers in the Analalava region, like many Malagasy elsewhere, thought that independence would free them to combine *fandrosoana* and *fombandrazana,* 'progress' with 'ancestral ways,' on their own terms. The typewritten copy of the *Customs of Royal Service Concerning the Menaty* was completed on August 20, 1962, three weeks before the ampanjaka returned to Analalava from France. The *Customs . . .* required wood, though some guardians had purchased sheet metal and were negotiating for cement. Antidoany asked permission to do the service, but they were refused. Spirit-mediums, who had initially agreed to the use of the materials, said finally that it was not right.[36] The sheet metal was sold to a series of buyers, finally a Malagasy woman and her Vazaha husband, who subsequently died. Saha Barimaso, who served as one of the Father's mediums, explained in 1981:

"The Father and the Grandfather said no. The tôly had been bought, thirty pieces from Nosy Be. They had almost gotten the cement, but they were still negotiating at this time. Before, the royal ancestors had agreed, but finally they said they couldn't agree *(irô tsy mety)*. M., an Ancestor Person—Antankoala—bought the tôly, all thirty pieces. Then, 'can't be done' *(tsy mety)*. His children were afraid. 'We don't need this,' his children said. 'Send it some place else.' So M. sold it to V., a policeman. He got it, his wife and children also said 'can't be done' *(tsy mety)*. V. sold the thirty pieces to A. [she was Tsiarô, a royal follower]. She was married to a Vazaha, a Frenchman who worked on Nosy Lava, don't know what he did—Directeur [of the prison]? The Vazaha bought them and gave them to his wife. The house completed, the Vazaha died there inside it. A. didn't stay around. She went to Antsohihy, to this place, to that place. Then she crashed in a car *(tampônay [tamponnée])*, broke her collar bone. Went to Majunga, got a little better. She was still in Majunga when Ambilahikely [the Brother] came and possessed her *(mipetraka amin'azy,* sat on her). [He was] following the tôly. [She] got royally cursed *(nahazo tigny)*—Ambilahikely came and sat on her—because she had sold that difficult/precious tôly. Royal ancestors don't usually possess people who are cursed *(olo misy tigny)*, but he was just following the wrong. Unless a person goes to pay their respects *(mikoezy)*, to cover themselves with the living ruler *(mifono amin' ny ampanjaka)*, they stay sick. It's really incredible! *(tsisy hevitra boka io!)* Too much wrong can't be taken away.

Little wrongs might be taken away, but too much wrong just can't be taken away! When Saha K. [the Grandfather at the menaty service] did wrong, he covered himself with the ampanjaka, bringing money, and his sickness went away. 'I'm not angry at you any more, I'm making you good/beautiful/well' *(Zaho tsisy heloko aminao eky fa mahatsara anao)* [is what the ampanjaka said to him]. He was sick until then, until he covered himself. He got permission to return to [the Mahabo at] Nosy Lava, but he is still not really well. A. was sick until she died. She married a policeman down there, never returned here. Ambilahikely came out [*niboaka*—identified himself as the spirit possessing her, which is expected to cure the afflicted person], but she didn't get better. No one dares to buy the house. Her kin who live south of Analalava can't sell it. People come up from there who have kids here in school." [Why do they stay there?] "Some people don't know. There's no rent, they just stay. If they learn about it, they leave. That's the house, just west of here."

People in the Analalava region, as elsewhere in the country, were disillusioned by the results of independence. While highlanders saw President Tsiranana as favoring coastal people and the French who supported him in office, many people in the Analalava region—tompontany and vahiny alike—saw him as favoring his own ancestral land at the expense of nearby people he saw as competitors. Tsiranana had publicly declared his aversion to the "slavery" associated with precolonial monarchies throughout the island. Observers in the Analalava region dated his hostility to Sakalava monarchy to the years he had gone to school with the ampanjaka, when Analalava was still a provincial capital. In building up his own ancestral land by moving all the public services, except the penitentiaries, from Analalava to Antsohihy, he had ruined Analalava. A highland functionary, who had been stationed in Analalava for about a year, spoke from his own perspective, but his views were shared by a broad range of local people as well, including those who supported the monarchy:

"Analalava is a *ville de condemnation* for prisoners from all over Madagascar. Formerly they were also sent to Sainte Marie [an island off the east coast], but now they are all sent here, the worst of the worst from all over the country. . . . The government does nothing for Analalava because of the 'mpanjaka. . . . Analalava doesn't progress because of this. Before [in the

colonial period], Analalava was capital of the province, comparable to
Majunga now. Then it became capital of the prefecture. Tsiranana moved
the capital of the prefecture from Analalava to Antsohihy, and all the
services that had been here were moved to Antsohihy. . . . there is no
mutual love, and that is the reason why Analalava is ignored by the
government, why it has become dead, dead. In Nosy Be, the Sakalava
'mpanjaka follows the government, there is mutual love, and for that
reason Nosy Be progresses and there is a lot of life there. While here there
is nothing, no progress. The place is dead and filled with thieves."

Southern Bemihisatra continued to ask permission to do the menaty
service during the 1960s and early 1970s, and to prepare themselves
by various 'studies.' One of these from the Mahabo, headed "Studies
concerning the menaty service—supplication at the red-blood door"
(Fianarana fanompoana mainaty—fangatahana aminy varavara menalio)
and dated July 16, 1970, shows a pencilled diagram of the positions
of kinds of persons and the quantities and dimensions of things around
the menaty before and during the sacrifice, which completes the service. The nationwide news of Tsiranana's hospitalization in Paris in
February–August 1970, was interpreted by some people in light of
these concerns.[37] As one man said:

"Tsiranana said that there are rich people *(ampañarivo)*, but no rulers
(ampanjaka). Royal ancestors, slaves, prohibited days—there are none of
these. But she is *masina*. In saying this, he was struck *(voa)*. She answered
and he got sick. Now there *are* lots of spirit-mediums. Some have it, some
don't *(Sasany misy, sasany tsisy)*. They used to club them to death in the
past, if they lied. If they went to the Mahabo and didn't pass the trial.
Everyone cried when T. [the current medium of the Great-Grandfather]
had his trial. Everyone was sad, crying, because he was the real thing. He
came from Mandritsara, yet he knew all the Great-Grandfather's people.
He [Tsiranana] became afraid because of what he did *(Nitsôha am raha
nataony)*. Struck in France. Weak. The medicines in the hospital there
didn't do him any good. The Grandfather possessed him. . . . He
[Tsiranana] said, 'There are no Zanahary [Royal Ancestors, God], I am
Zanahary. The rich people are the rulers here.'"

The deciding factor in the menaty service was the *rotaka* in May
1972—the 'commotion' in which President Tsiranana was replaced

Plate 36. The ampanjaka Soazara, together with the wives of local
functionaries and other leading women in Analalava, at a political rally for
President Tsiranana in 1972 where many wore his face on their clothing
(A. Harnik).

by General Ramanantsoa—though no one drew attention to the association between national politics and the permission when it finally
came.[38] While Tsiranana and his supporters used their long-time
knowledge of the area to appeal to the royal ancestors for their support,
Ramanantsoa appealed to local people not to listen to spirit-mediums
(Plate 36). He also followed through on reforms that his supporters
hoped would achieve a second independence through Malgachization,
including a People's Assembly, the selection of a balanced, multiethnic
cabinet, the nationalization of numerous businesses in French hands,
the abolition of the head tax and cattle tax, and the elevation of workers' wages. Ramanantsoa won the referendum held on October 8,
1972, and was confirmed in office in November, by which time plans
for the menaty service were already underway.

The ampanjaka sent an offering *(takitaky)* to the royal ancestors at
the Mahabo in August 1973, following *fanjava mitsaka,* the first month

of the new year, indicating that she planned to do the service in their honor. The offering was brought by the people who would be in charge of the service, the Jado, or substitute, representing the ruler, and the Manantany and Fahatelo, representing the manantany and fahatelo at the Doany. She herself was accompanied to the new year's ceremonies at the Doany by the newly appointed sous-préfet of the Analalava subpréfecture, stationed in Analalava. This marked the first time that a member of the national administration had ever accompanied the ampanjaka to the Doany. His presence provided the most public evidence of the new government's support and esteem for the monarchy.

Once the time of the service was set, Southern Bemihisatra officials had to choose where the timber would be cut and who to enlist as workers from the Doany and the Mahabo and from the royal districts. In contrast to the timing of the service, which depended on Sakalava relations with outsiders, these choices were made on the basis of relations among people in the region.

CHOOSING WHERE TO CUT THE TREES

The menaty service began and ended at the Doany, but the trees were cut at a 'camp' *(toby)* in the forest, while the work of taking down the old fence and putting up the new one took place at the Mahabo. The longest time was spent at the toby, unavoidably distant from most settlements. Royal officials had to choose a place remote enough to have large stands of old hardwood trees, which neither the Bemihisatra, in previous services, nor the several French lumber companies seeking hardwoods during the colonial decades, would have depleted. The camp also had to be near enough to existing villages that it would attract the largest number of workers who could not be forced to participate.

The ampanjaka favored a place east of the Doany, near the crossing of the Analalava and Antsohihy roads. She was supported by most Antidoany because the location was not too far from kin and friends. The spirit-mediums at the Mahabo wanted the service done at Tsinjorano, because it had been done there successfully before. The ampanjaka was against this location, because she considered the Ambolobozo Peninsula to be a Mahabo stronghold in which so few people attended the Doany that she might not be able to muster enough participants to conduct the service, which was supposed to be the work of the living sovereign. According to one Sambarivo from the Mahabo who farmed in a coastal village on the Ambolobozo Peninsula:

"A lot of people would like to have it here in the north. But she won't agree, doesn't favor the idea of doing it in the north. 'The people there,' she says, 'don't like me much.' Because there in those northern villages, people do not readily come forth to go to her. In the south, the area around Antognibe, if she calls, many people come. Here if she calls, not so many people come. . . . Also the place is far away—a half-day's walk [from Tsinjorano] to get to where the trees are. Thus, only get a few each day, takes a long time. Now life is changing. People want to get things done quickly. Last time there [in Tsinjorano], it took six years. This way, we will go to Komajara, need 1,200 *teza* in all, get fifteen or so a day, done fast. Probably we will be finished this year."

Tsivery, a noble from south of the Doany pointed out other problems:

"It's not going to be done in the north because there are no trees in the north. There are trees of course, but the cores are too small. Yet, the people at the Mahabo want it done in the north, but the people in Analalava and the Doany want it done in the south, because it's closer to their food. Tsinjorano is far from their food, [they] won't be able to feed themselves *(mamahaña tsy efa).*"

As I have already indicated, divisions between the Mahabo and the Doany, associated with the northern and southern halves of the region respectively, widened when colonial officials moved the Mahabo to a mainland site on the Ambolobozo Peninsula. Ndramamahaña (Tondroko) had toured the southern part of the peninsula, attending local work parties and visiting villages, to join the gap between the two. Perhaps this is one reason why his brother by another mother, who became known as "Tompony Andronjona" after he died there, came to live in Andronjona, where Tondroko himself had been circumcised. The current ampanjaka rarely made such tours, except to the south and then mainly to Antognibe. In fact, Bemihisatra did not so much turn away from the monarchy as they chose between its diverging centers.

As followers associated with ancestral and living royalty, north and south, debated their differences, officials at the Doany moved to consult the royal ancestors of the Zafinifotsy. While the Zafinimena were acknowledged masters of the land, Zafinifotsy were seen as governing the water, in which they had drowned themselves rather than submit to Hova rule, and where their bones still lay buried. Besides evoking these oppositions, they were identified with Tsimihety who had migrated out to the coast from inland, in contrast to local Sakalava followers of royalty. Like the Zafinimena, the Zafinifotsy led by Bevaoko and Ampela Be also raised questions about rightful relations between brothers and sisters and their children. Representatives from the Doany went to Bevaoko first. As one Sambarivo from the Mahabo explained, "He's people's brother after all! *(Azy anadahin' olo ke!)*." He made it known through his supplicator that he favored a location on the lower Narinda Bay rather than the Ambolobozo Peninsula, precisely because the service had already been done in the Ambolobozo Peninsula once before. His choice was supported by Antidoany because of its proximity to their sources of support. Ampela Be, who was consulted second, agreed.[39]

Saha Barimaso once explained why the many recently legitimated mediums at the Mahabo did not participate in discussions about the menaty service: "Talk going every which way *(karbary mivadibadiky)* is not suitable, [we] follow just one path, the path of the earlier mediums." Concerning the question of where to cut the wood, no agreement was reached after almost a year of debate. Neither side could force a decision on the other, because although the ancestral spirits were above the ampanjaka, it was her work in their honor that was to be done, the work of Antidoany not Antimahabo. The differences of opinion were finally resolved when a woman who had married into Antognibe, but otherwise had no kin there, had a dream in which a 'thing' possessed her, insisting that the service be done on the Komajara Peninsula. Saha Fiara, a long-time medium of the Grandfather, explained the outcome this way:

"The Great-Grandfather and the Grandfather liked Tsinjorano because the natal village of his medium [the medium of the grandfather who was chosen to accompany the menaty service] is A. . . . nearby. The ampanjaka likes the Antsohihy road crossing. What brought it about to Komajara [Peninsula] was that a woman down in Antognibe had a dream *(nofy)* in which she was told that the menaty service should be held at Komajara. It happened three times in a row. It was like a thing *(raha)* that possessed her. The first time it happened, she kept silent. The second time—they were always on the same day of the week—she still kept silent. The third time it told her, 'If you don't speak formally to the people of the village council *(olo fokon'olona)* about this, I will kill you.' So she got scared and spoke to the village council of Antognibe. They asked her if she dared to go to the ampanjaka with this dream and she said, 'I dare.' So eight people accompanied her, people from there, women. And the ampanjaka listened and she had confidence in the dream. They all followed—the ampanjaka, the royal ancestors at the Mahabo, and everyone else." [Was she a Sambarivo or an Ancestor Person?] "No, she was just some person who had married in, people marrying people *(olo manambadimanambady, olo ampanambady olo)*." [He did not know the person who was her husband or whether he was a Sambarivo or Ancestor Person.] "The spirits of the Father and the Brother also liked Tsinjorano. All four of them did. But they were *all* overpowered—the ampanjaka and the royal ancestors. They followed the woman's dream. She said she would dare anything—drinking gold *(migiaka volamena)*, the *tanguin* trial, whatever test they proposed she was ready to do it to prove that she was not lying."

I heard about how the location was finally chosen just before I left, so I was unable to find out what connection, if any, the woman's husband or other friends or kin might have had with either the Doany or the Mahabo. It is notable that her solution—the Komajara Peninsula—was a good compromise between the two main alternatives advocated by people at the Doany and at the Mahabo. The Komajara Peninsula west of the mainland lay outside the north-south orientation that divided the rest of the region, but the proposed location at its northern end was equally accessible to both. It had been more heavily populated during the precolonial period, when there was more local sea traffic, and it had also served as a common place of refuge when the Hova started moving into the area. It had never been heavily populated over a long period of time by partisans of any description, and since the early colonial period, the population had slowly dwindled, except for sharecroppers working the rice fields and coconut plantation of a long-time Réunionaise settler. Furthermore, the location had been proposed by a woman widely seen as a complete stranger, possessed by a deadly 'thing,' which would have killed her had she not conveyed its words exactly.

Spirits, as strangers who possessed strangers (though many mediums were locally born, as were their rulers), were meant to be above the deceptions *(politique)* associated with local politics. In practice, petitioners assessed them in terms of their ties to kin and friends, just as they assessed diviners or curers. In this case, there was wide disbelief that the most vociferous spirit-mediums at the Mahabo, known to be tied by marriage and other bonds to Antimahabo, were completely neutral. Yet even the revered medium of the Great-Grandfather, was not followed. The woman's dream was seen as a kind of possession, but what spoke through her was not a royal ancestor with particular ties, but a 'thing' *(raha)*. Its 'apartness' was intensified by the marginality of the woman's position in Antognibe as a person who had simply married in there from outside and thus presumably had no local ties. Perhaps—although I never heard the phrase used in this instance—the truth of the thing was also assured by the fact that its medium was a woman, who, not having a 'man's head,' could only have followed what the thing said.

SAMBY AM FIPETRAHAÑA: EACH TO HIS OWN POSITION

Royal followers referred to the work camp as 'At the Temporary Shelter(s)' (Antoby), toby including the shelters built next to rice fields during the rainy season as well as the lean-tos put up as extra housing during the annual services at the Doany and the Mahabo. The camp was located on the site of an existing village to which additional structures were added, reorienting it so that it reproduced a royal center.

To prevent the cut timbers from being "struck by dirt or filth" in the middle of the village and to keep them dry, members of the work party constructed a raised platform south of the village known as the 'royal sitting place' *(fitambesarana)* or 'golden trestles' *(savaly fanjava [mena]* or *fanjavamena)*. Northeast of the royal seat, they constructed a small house for the tools. This was called a *zomba* or royal house like those at the Doany and the Mahabo. As one man explained, "If it's a place for putting royal service, then zomba is its name" *(Izy koa fa pitrahan' fanompoaña, zomba anaragny)*. European features like windows and verandas were prohibited just as they were at the Doany or the Mahabo. Had they used a local house, it would have to have been built in 'Malagasy style only' *(trano gasy fo)*.

Finally they constructed a fence around the platform and the house, 'so that no thing or no person could get in to defile the service or steal from it.' The fence was called a *tsirangôty*, like the outer fence around the royal compound at the Doany. It had a single door in the west side, so that residents could sit in front of the door on good days, facing east, to pay their respects to the royal ancestors. Everyone worked to construct the compound without the distinctions made in constructing the buildings and fences at the Doany and the Mahabo. Sambarivo from the Doany were appointed to guard the royal enclosure once it was finished. A large tamarind tree in the village was designated as the council house *(fantsina)*. The reorganization of the village in setting up the work camp was similar to the reorganization that Antimahabo did when they moved the Mahabo to the mainland. Then, according to one of the men from the Antibe pen, they "put *(nitambesatra)* the difficult/precious things at the base of a tamarind tree (not already consecrated to a spirit) south of the village." They built a 'destiny house' *(zomba vinta)* for them like the one at the Mahabo, and then enclosed everything with a fiaroaomby, like the outermost fence at the Mahabo.

The pens of the Sambarivo provided the model by which the workers from the mainland were organized. The person appointed to serve as Manantany was associated with the Maharitry pen in the northeast corner of the settlement, like the real manantany, while the Fahatelo was associated with the Tsimanihabe pen in the southwest corner, like the fahatelo. Sambarivo took up places corresponding to the places of their pens at the Doany and Mahabo. Malaza explained this when Ravo from the Tsimanihabe pen, appointed the head *(tale)* of the southern group of Sambarivo at the Mahabo for the service, came with a friend to ask Malaza's advice about the 'places' *(pilasiny)* where the people from the Doany should be put when they came to the Mahabo and then the work camp. Ravo also said there were three kinds missing [three pens vacant at the Mahabo]—Tsimazava, Maromainty, and Jirany. Malaza answered:

"Jirany? [Friends?] I never heard of that one. They all have kin there [at the Mahabo]. Each of the kinds of Sambarivo at the Doany have kin and therefore a place to stay out at the Mahabo. Only the Marovavy and Fihitry [the women and men recruited from the region] and the Ampanjaka [the jado or royal substitute]—may what my mouth says be prevented from happening—have no places there." He strongly emphasized how each group had to be in its own place, how the 'different kinds' *(karazana sambisany)* had to be separated. "There are heads of the Marovavy and the Fihitry and the Sambarivo, south and north. Each to his/her own place. They may not mix."[40]

The Jado stayed with the Maromainty, whose work was to serve as royal bodyguards and enforcers.[41] The women and men recruited as Marovavy and Fihitry from the Tsiarô, the general population of royal followers, were not lodged in specific pens. They were incorporated into the southern and northern groups of Sambarivo at the Doany and Mahabo, Tsimaniha and Antavarabe, depending on whether their fathers's ancestral villages were south or north of the Doany and Mahabo, which made an east-west dividing line. The placement of the spirit-mediums also reproduced practices characteristic of the royal centers. As Ravo had once explained at the Mahabo, in response to my question about which of the Sambarivo there served which of the spirit-mediums:

"The spirit-mediums from the north are dressed by the women from the north. Those from the south are dressed by those from the south. The spirit-mediums from the north become possessed in the north. This is because everyone who sits in the council house [fantsina, where spirit-mediums, Sambarivo, and petitioners 'meet/mix' *(miharo)* to talk], sits north or south of the central pole *(anjovery)* according to whether she or he lives north or south in the Mahabo.[42] Those from the north sit north, those from the south sit south. Each to his/her position *(Samby am fipetrahaña)*. When the spirit possesses the medium, she or he might move over toward the east. Or, if it is really crowded, the ampangataka might come over to where the spirit is sitting to hear his/her formal statement *(saontsy)*."

The Ancestor People and the Antandrano lived outside these arrangements. They were not associated with the land of the ampanjaka in the same way as the Sambarivo from the Doany or the women and men recruited from the region. The Ancestor People were identified with royalty so closely that their head—the Sakalava Mañoro-aomby—took the role of the ampanjaka's partner when she danced in honor of the royal ancestors.[43] Their work was organized into northern and southern halves, as we will see in the next chapter. But when representatives of these groups came to the Doany or the Mahabo, they were not settled in any of the pens. As Saha Barimaso said, "Ancestor People can stay wherever they want. Their thing is unique *(Zakandreo tokana)*. They have no prohibitions, just their own preferences. They can't settle at the Mahabo, but they can settle wherever else they want. Whatever place they stay is alright." The Sakalava and Ndrarameva kinds of Ancestor People stayed near the Bemongo, who worked for them, while the Jingo and Antankoala stayed just west of the Antibe to which the supplicator belonged.[44]

The Antantety, or uplanders among the workers recruited from royal followers in the region, worked at chopping and trimming the trees and also lived on the land, in the camp. The Antandrano, people from the general population who lived by farming and fishing along the coast, served only in work relating to the water, for example transporting the rocks and sand from the shoreline required to finish the tomb.[45] They were expected to continue living next to the water for the duration of the service too, coming up to the camp, or to the Mahabo or the Doany, only when their work required them to bring something there, or when they came to pay their respects. At the regular new year's services, the Antandrano usually made a special request to the ancestors to 'take away the prohibition' *(mangala ny fady)*, so they could live in the community. Then they lived like others, north if they came from the north, and south if they came from the south.

A GREEN ESTATE

The monarchy of living and ancestral royalty in the Analalava region was, in Shakespeare's terms, "a green estate." Their power to rule did not emerge full-grown. It grew over time from the efforts of people who "planted their joys in the thrones of the living," "spending the harvest of one king" to "reap the harvest" of his child.[46] In north-western Madagascar, the green estate of monarchy was cultivated by people who willingly and forcibly planted their joys in the burial places of dead rulers in order to raise up ancestors who would guarantee the rule of their living successors. Since the early nineteenth century, when Hova and French rivals sought to intervene in the transformation of these deaths into rebirths, Sakalava monarchy was also "green and yet ungoverned. Where every horse bears his commanding rein and may direct his course as please himself." In the colonial and postcolonial periods especially, it was "green [and] should be put to no apparent likelihood of breach."[47]

In Madagascar as in Europe, these images of growth were cross-cut with images of coercion and violence. But here, more clearly than in the European example, it is possible to see the work—'service'—by which guardians and farmers, who formerly served merely as slaves and followers, sought to cleanse the land made filthy by Tondroko's death under colonial rule. In different ways, for varied reasons, they tended the growth of the "Noble Who Nurtured Thousands" and his forebears into independence. The timing of this menaty service was clearly influenced by the intervention of political leaders who sought to incorporate the growth of regional communities into their own visions of national regeneration. The placing of the service involved similar considerations on the part of local people who had not become rich after independence. They negotiated over a long period to achieve some consensus on the location of a work camp to which people of diverse orientations would come willingly from all over the region. We turn now to these workers and their work.

Serving in the Forest

The essentials in this are: *First of all*: The following
from the living ruler: it is necessary to appoint a
Manantany and a Fahatelo [and] a Ruler master of
the cupped hands (a substitute), those are first,
[then] Rangitra ampanjaka, Marovavy, Fihitra, and
Razan'olona, these Razan'olona: JINGO,
ANTANKOALA AND SAKALAVA.
The following things must accompany them:
Axes, Shovels, Large Knives, and Mead, if only
one Demijohn. All of the above must be presented
to the royal ancestors at the Doany first. Once
they have been properly presented, then go to
Ankaliava (Mahabo).

Opening lines of the *Customs of Royal Service Concerning the Menaty*[1]

VOALOHANY: FIRST OF ALL

The workers in the menaty service reproduced the hierarchical organization of the Southern Bemihisatra region, just as the work camp
reproduced the structure of the Doany and the Mahabo. The workers
were directed *(manendry)* to serve. The direction in their appointment
was evident in every feature of the work itself, which was organized
around 'heads' and paired groups of 'friends' together reproducing the
royal body. I will follow their lead in discussing first how representatives of royalty and royal officials were appointed to serve; how
royal officials assembled the tools for the service; how they recruited
volunteers from the ampanjaka's people; how royal followers should
serve; and how they did serve.

REPRODUCING THE LIVING

The workers from the Doany included people who reproduced the
domain of the living ruler, but not in such forms that they could usurp
it:

—a substitute manantany
—a substitute fahatelo
—a substitute for the living ruler (jadô)
—counselors (rangitrampanjaka)
—female (marovavy) and male (fihitry) followers
—Ancestor People (Razan'olona) of different kinds.

The workers associated with the living ruler were primary because the menaty service, although it concerned a structure at the Mahabo, was considered to be the living ruler's service honoring her ancestors and thus the work of Antidoany. Spirit-mediums came from the Mahabo to represent the ancestors there, with whom the living ruler was paired. But, as they emphasized, the guardians from the Mahabo came simply to care for the ancestors' needs, not to cut wood. Therefore they were few in number by comparison to the people from the Doany and the region.

The Manantany and the Fahatelo were named first because they would actually conduct the service *(mitondra ny fanompoaña)*, just as their prototypes, in their view, administered the domain. They were selected in deliberations between the manantany, fahatelo, and counselors (rangitry ampanjaka) at the Doany. The Manantany they chose was a descendant of the Zafindramahavita ancestry with which the position is identified. He came from a village along the southern bend of the Loza River that was closely associated with an important former manantany of the current ruler (Fig. 16).

The Fahatelo was appointed to serve in two positions at once: as Fahatelo and as a representative of the senior subgroup of the Ancestor People, the Sakalava Mañoroaomby (almost always shortened to 'Sakalava'). These were actually three, since the Sakalava Mañoroaomby, which usually served with the Ndrarameva subgroup of the Ancestor People, opposite the junior pair composed of the Antankoala and Jingo members of the group, was to take the place of the Ndrarameva as well.[2] The man chosen as Fahatelo-Sakalava (Ndrarameva) was a 'Sakalava' from a village a few kilometers south of the Doany, who was also related to the Tsimanihabe pen at the Doany, the location

403

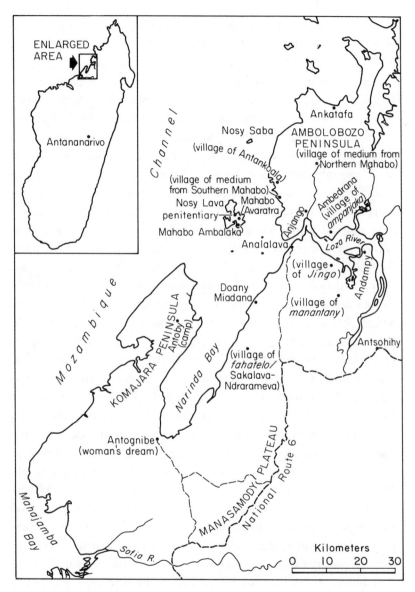

Figure 16. Places in the menaty service.

identified with the fahatelo there. As a Tsimanihabe, he was also related to the Tsimanihabe at the Mahabo, being a mother's father's
brother of the head of the Tsimanihabe at the Mahabo.

Both of them were older men, selected at least in part for their
knowledge and for their ability to gather people around them to work.
The Fahatelo-Sakalava was particularly respected for his knowledge.
As Fahatelo, together with the Manantany, he was in charge of administrative details, seeing that there were enough workers, enough
food, enough housing, and so on. As Sakalava (Ndrarameva), together with the other Ancestor People, he was in charge of all the
work directly associated with the royal ancestors and their tomb.

In contrast to the Manantany and Fahatelo, the ruler's substitute
was a child. The practice of using a *jadô*, or 'substitute for the royal body'
(solomahasenga), to represent the living ruler at services held at other
doany and mahabo along the coast was common. In this case, the
living ruler was also prohibited from going to the Mahabo.[3] The Jado
had to be male, even if the ruler was female. He also had to be the
descendant of Zafinimena royalty, but of one of the 'little' groups of
descendants who did not reign, of which there were three in the Analalava region. If the service was to go north, for example, to Nosy
Be, then the substitute was selected from the Zafinimena line headed
by Riziky at Ankatafa north of Analalava and the Doany. If the service
was to go to south, for example, to the doany at Mahajanga, the Jado
was selected from the Zafinimena line headed by Harosy at Anjiajia
to the south of Analalava and the Doany.[4] The substitute to the
Mahabo was always chosen from among the Zafinimena at Amben-
draña, at the mouth of the Loza River east of the island of Nosy Lava
on which the Mahabo is located. Royal officials at the Doany emphasized their subordinate position by explaining that they were the
'sisters' children's grandchildren' *(zafiny zanakan' ny vavy)* to the
Zafinimena at Anjiajia, not descendants in the male line. The boy in
his late teens, said to have been chosen to go by an elder kinsman,
was described as a 'child' *(zaza)*, rather than a 'youth' *(tovolahy, tsaiky
lehilahy)* like others of his age.

Except for the Fahatelo who also represented the Sakalava Ndrarameva, the representatives of the other groups of Ancestor People were 'boys' *(tsaiky lehilahy)* like the Jado. They were enlisted by sending letters or messengers to the heads of their local ancestries, commanding them to select people to represent the group at the service: a 'head' *(loha)*, together with some 'friends' *(namana)*. Under the leadership of the Sakalava Ndrarameva, foremost among the Ancestor People, they were to handle the work directly involving the royal ancestors: cutting and debarking the timber, removing the old fence, and constructing the new one.

Like the leaders of the work, the materials for the service reproduced the organization of the monarchy in their numbers, the hierarchical order in which they were carried, the ways in which they were handled, and the term 'service' (fanompoaña) by which they were collectively known. The tools included eight each of the axes, shovels, and large knives, two demijohns of mead, one curved knife, and one black cow with a white face, a coloring known as *mazava loha* (clear, bright head), which made the cow look as if it had just received the ancestors' blessings conveyed in an upward mark of white clay *(tany fotsy/malandy)* on the forehead.

The number eight expressed the total number of tools the service would require; more axes, shovels, and knives were taken over later without ceremony.[5] Two demijohns of mead were considered more appropriate than one, in keeping with the emphasis on pairs of people and things throughout the service. The guardians at the Doany made the mead during the same lunar month (around May 1973) when they made mead for the annual new year's services there.

The *jambia* (from Arabic, *shibriya*) was a small, curved 'fighting knife,' for the Jado to wear at his waist, like Sakalava rulers did in the nineteenth century, perhaps a kind of mobile, lesser counterpart of the Vy Lava, like the Jado himself.[6] A new jambia was bought especially for this service to replace one that had been burnt in a fire at the Mahabo in 1953. Doany officials said they once purchased such weapons in the Comores, but this one was bought 'quite a while ago' from a Silamo man in Analalava for 30,000 FMG (about $120). The handle was made of silver, the broad, curved blade, ridged in the center, was made of iron.

The cow from the royal herd was the customary gift with which the ampanjaka announced to the royal ancestors a service in their honor. The cow was kept in the royal cattle pen at the Doany *(val-an'aomby tsimirango)*. The rest of the equipment for the service—known as 'the service' *(fanompoaña)*—was kept on a mat in the Fa-hatelo's house, not outside because 'It's service, after all!' *(Fanompoaña ke!)*.

REPRODUCING THE ANCESTORS

The royal ancestors were represented by:

—one ancestor, through his medium from the southern Mahabo, where the work was to be done; and

—a 'friend' *(namana)*, the Bemazava 'Lord of the northern Mahabo' (Ndramatikoarivo), through his medium.

They were to be accompanied by sixteen 'dressers' *(ampisarandra)*—guardians from each mahabo, who would call them into the bodies of their mediums, dress them, hear their requests and speak for their petitioners, as well as cook and clean for them.

The guardians were to care for the equipment from the Mahabo, which would be used for making offerings to the royal ancestors and for entertaining them. This included:

—a white offering dish;

—together with a whole number, two-times-eight, or otherwise even number of pieces of white earth;

—a small basket with a four-cornered lid holding eight pieces of incense;

—a pair of royal mañandria drums, the 'mother' and its slightly smaller 'child,' played when the door to the royal enclosure was open and shut on good days, and during the dancing battles com-

memorating the historic conquests of Zafinimena royalty over their
adversaries; and

—the costumes for the two lead dancers who play the royal roles.
Two of the male guardians were appointed to play the drums, which
women were forbidden to touch.[7]

The royal ancestors were represented by two spirits, one from the
southern Mahabo, where the work was to be done, and the other from
the northern Mahabo. The first was the important one; the second
was there simply as a 'friend,' to make the pair. Many participants
emphasized that the fewest possible number was best. As Malaza said,
"Only one spirit is needed. It's not necessary to have many. They just
raise trouble *(mitabataba)* and give people a hard time *(mampijaly olo)*
with their disagreements. And besides, there is no work for them to
do." Mediums agreed with this. In Saha Barimaso's words, what was
needed was "one path" *(lala araiky)*, not many divergent opinions.

The Great-Grandfather could not move from the southern Mahabo
because he was its 'Lord' (Tompony), being the first one buried there.
The Bemazava spirit was also a 'Lord,' being the first and only burial
in the northern Mahabo, but he had to participate for each of the spirits
to have a companion. As one of the Sambarivo from the Mahabo said:
"One spirit-medium is appointed, a friend is added; there must be a
friend, a grandchild," the elder representing ancestors, the younger
representing descendants, as the two together stood in for the ancestors
in relation to the Jado who stood in for the living ruler.

The supplicator from each Mahabo had the most influence in deciding which spirit-medium was to go. As in the two earlier menaty
services, the Grandfather was chosen to represent the southern
Mahabo. At first he was the only other ancestor there besides the
Tompony. He continued to be chosen because of his seniority. The
Father was considered too junior in relation to the two senior ancestors, and the Brother was ineligible, never having ruled. His partner
would have been the Lord of the northern Mahabo, except that the
Bemazava ruler's only medium was blind and no longer left her farming village on the mainland. Reluctantly, his 'grandchild' Ndraman-

isoko, buried elsewhere but represented by a local medium, was chosen instead.

There was little leeway concerning which royal ancestors were to attend the service. Most of the controversy surrounded which of their mediums were to be chosen. As indicated earlier, the relationship between spirit and medium was seen as a kind of marriage. In principle, a spirit was supposed to be embodied on all important occasions by his 'eldest' medium, the first or earliest of his living mediums to have been legitimated. In practice, they were often not. Four 'big mediums' *(saha be)* had embodied the ancestors from the southern Mahabo at important events over the past several years, including the time when the ancestors were called to the Doany to discuss the menaty service in December 1972 and the gathering at the Mahabo on the night before the workers left for the camp. The mediums of the Great-Grandfather and the Brother were the 'eldest' of their co-spouselike groups. The other two were thought to have established their superior position over older mediums by marrying members of the Antibe pen from which the supplicator at the Mahabo is chosen, and by reciprocity (some said bribery).[8]

Officials at each mahabo responded by selecting the 'eldest' medium in each case, but both posed problems. The medium from the northern Mahabo had long been suspected of being a sorcerer and 'lying medium' of whom it was said that 'the royal ancestor is not acting, the body is acting' *(Zanahary tsy mañano, vata fo mañano)*. The medium from the southern Mahabo was widely considered to be shiftless, as evident especially—from the perspective of Antimahabo—in the fact that he had come to the Mahabo in the dry season for forty years without building his own house. Despite having been allotted a place among the Tsimanihabe group in the southwestern part of the settlement, he had lived first with one guardian, then with another, and finally ended up in the kitchen of the current supplicator with whom he was close friends. Antimahabo said privately that he got the appointment because he had always wanted it so much and kept demanding it as his rightful due. He was very bitter that a younger medium was regarded as the 'big medium' of the Grandfather, when she was only the sixth to have been possessed, while he was the fifth.

Suspicions concerning the medium from the northern Mahabo were soon confirmed when she was found dancing on the cut timbers inside the enclosure at the work camp in the middle of the night, an act comparable to dancing on the corpses in the tomb itself. The clothing, silver jewelry, and prayer dish belonging to the royal spirit were taken away from her, and she was forbidden ever to return to Nosy Lava. Since she was the only medium of Ndramanisoko in the area, she could not be replaced. The Grandfather's medium remained the only representative of the royal ancestors in the menaty service, until a few months later when he too was banished for sorcery. The woman who was his immediate junior and rival, the Grandfather's 'big medium,' was appointed in his place.

The spirit-mediums were to have been accompanied by sixteen guardians from the royal cemeteries, eight from the south and eight from the north, four of them senior and four of them junior. The fours, eights, and twice-eights or sixteen, young and old from south and north, were complete numbers (as discussed in Chapter 6), to encompass the full range of kinds of people at the royal cemeteries. Seven young men and women were appointed at first: four from the southern Mahabo and three from the small community of the northern Mahabo. The ones from the southern Mahabo were divided equally according to their sex, residence in the southern or northern half of the settlement, and affiliation to the ampangataka and manantany respectively:

—J., male, South (Tsimaniha), Antibe, a kinsman of the supplicator;
—A., female, South (Tsimaniha), Antibe, kinswoman of the supplicator;
—M., male, North (Antavarabe), Antisenga pen; and
—F., female, North (Antavarabe), Antiravaka pen, kinswoman of the manantany.

Other young relatives and friends accompanied the four from the southern Mahabo, but the four were the only 'really appointed ones' *(teña vaotendry)* who had to stay at the camp until the work was finished. The northern Mahabo was represented by only three guardians—two young women and one young man—because the village as a whole had so few people. There are no divisions between north and south or among pens, so these distinctions played no role in their selection.

The 'big men' at each mahabo chose who was to go. They emphasized that only a few of their people were involved because the menaty service was basically the work of people associated with the Doany. Nevertheless, the scant number and young age of the participants, like the lack of involvement of 'big mediums,' suggests that few people wanted to go. In the past, according to a former supplicator, more than the required number would have volunteered to go.

The first big crisis of the menaty service occurred when the Fahatelo leading the group from the Doany was greatly angered to discover that no 'big people' *(olo maventy)* had been appointed to accompany the royal ancestors, only "little children who know nothing" *(tsaiky madiniky tsy mahay raha)*. He discovered this only after the workers from the Doany had arrived at the Mahabo, stayed there a few days, and were about to depart for the work camp. The procession of persons and things associated with the service was forming in front of the burial compound to move down to the canoes and dhows on the beach. Evidently, none of the guardians from the Mahabo had told him before. The supplicator of the southern Mahabo did not address the head of the Doany group himself, nor did any of his elder brothers, all of whom were present. Since all of them had served as supplicator at different times in different ways, there was some ill-feeling among them. For that reason, and to avoid an open confrontation among senior people, they sent their youngest brother, who had never occupied any position of power at the Mahabo. He addressed the Antidoany leader placatingly as 'mother's brother' *(zama)*, thus putting himself in the subordinate position of a sister's child, reassuring him that the Antimahabo would discuss the issue *(mimalo)*. When the supplicator realized that the Antimahabo had no 'big people' to represent them at the work camp he would surely appoint some.

One of the brothers later said that no important people went because the supplicator did not appoint any: "After all, if he doesn't say anything, you just sit there." There should have been four ranitry ampanjaka [at the Mahabo, the term means heads of pens], two from the southern half, two from the northern half; the children would follow after them. He described the situation as 'not good to eat' (tsy tsara homaña). But later he added that no one wanted to go:

"Many are needed, but there just aren't many. [Hushed whisper] Many are needed, but people will not go. 'Ah, [I'm] sorry, [I'm] sick. I this, I that . . . ah, ah, ah.' It's long work! People can't surmount it. Long work!"(Mila maro fa maro tsisy ke. Mila maro fa olo tsy mety handeha.'Ah, malahelo, marary. Zaho zegny hoe . . . ah, ah, ah.' Asa ela! Tsy dingan'olo. Asa ela!)

He noted as an afterthought that there was one 'big person' there in the sense that she was an 'adult' (olo be), but being a woman she did not know anything and therefore did not count as an important person. He added that if the ampanjaka ever heard of what had happened, she would be very angry. On getting to the camp and running into some difficulty that the 'children' could not handle, the Antidoany leader might well send her a letter informing her of the absence of important Antimahabo in the service."After all, who knows what might happen there. If she should know, then the supplicator is really going to get it!" He was exactly right. Nothing happened during the first two months of work at the camp (when we were still in the Analalava region). But in the course of the next year, one of the brothers, highly respected for his knowledge of ancestral custom, was appointed as supplicator to replace the man who had made all the initial Antimahabo appointments, at the insistence primarily of Antidoany. As they explained it later, in 1981, he was replaced because he did not know how to lead a service (tsy mahay mitondra fanompoaña) and he 'ate too much money,' which had long been the major complaint about his service as ampangataka. "It's like replacing a president!"

ENLISTING WORKERS

In addition to the officials and the Jado who represented the Doany, the Ancestor People, and the spirit-mediums and their dressers from the southern and northern Mahabo, workers were appointed from people in the royal districts throughout the region to serve as:

—counselors (rangitry ampanjaka)
—female and male followers (marovavy, fihitry)
—followers in general (Tsiarô or Bemihisatra).

People living in royal districts were ordinarily represented at the Doany by esteemed elder people in their ancestries, who also served as royal counsellors. As workers in royal service, they were recruited not according to their own ancestries, but as 'people' (olo). Royal followers repeatedly emphasized that any act in the service of royalty should be done freely, from a glad heart, in harmony with others. When I asked how much money they considered appropriate to give when paying their respects to royalty, the answer was invariably prefaced with the statement: 'Whatever money you yourself see' (Zay fanjava hitanao an-teña), after which people would provide examples of what they had given, which did vary widely. Asking what determines whether someone will donate one of his cattle to feed the workers at the service, I got similar responses: '[You give] according to your preference, you being in charge' (Araka sitraponao tompony).

The emphasis on willingness and choice in royal service was completely consistent with the emphasis on choice in every other area of life. Even so, if it dates back to the precolonial period, it is likely to have been intensified in the course of colonial rule, as Bemihisatra sought to refute the allegations of forced service that the French used in trying to get rid of the monarchy. Commandant Toquenne stated at the very outset of his administration in 1897:

> Finally, let us note a special belief in the region, according to which each 'mpanjaka' becomes God, after his death. Thanks to this superstition, the natives believe that every complaint made against a

'mpanjaka,' every disagreeable testimony against him, will be punished, in the future, by a misfortune striking the plaintiff and his family. This sort of cult, which we must apply ourselves to making disappear, makes our inquiries into the acts of native princes very difficult.[9]

Southern Bemihisatra explicitly refuted these allegations as indicated in correspondence from the period. Some of the ampanjaka Riziky's officials wrote to the administration in Analalava in July 1926, emphasizing that the people there were giving tribute 'of our own free will' *(sitrakanay),* in expectation of royal blessings; people would protest its prohibition.[10] A letter from Tondroko at Manongarivo, dated June 5, 1925, requests the services of Totobe at Anjiajia in the same language: "May you live! *(Veloma!)* I appoint you to go to serve at Majunga if you are eager *(mazoto),* but [you are] not forced *[forise,* from *forcé].* In this service, the eager will go to serve. No one may say anything of any sort to prevent them *(tsy azo ilazana tambana na inona na inona).* People who are reluctant may explain what prevents them from going. But this service is urgent. Answer my words within two days. May you live!"[11]

In fact, this was the language—*tambana,* unanticipated problems preventing a person from doing what she or he was supposed or had planned to do—that people were still using in the 1970s at the Doany. As Laza Be said, explaining why most people stopped going to the Doany and the Mahabo after the second of the new year's services in the month of *asara be* (around September), as people prepared for the new growing season: "They are unexpectedly prevented—much work" *(Tambana—maro ny asa).*

Even though such explanations were allowable, they still left royal followers open to accusations of sorcery. Thus, when the workers were preparing to leave the Mahabo for the camp, the supplicator called on his more knowledgeable brothers to help him, because it was so critical that the 'service'—the offering dish, and other materials—be carried out in the correct order. As one of them explained later, he called them together the night before and said, "'I don't know the customary practices. You have to tell me what to do. Think on it! *(Hañano hevitry é!)*. If you don't tell me, then you are committing sorcery! *(mamoriky anareo!)*' That is why we were in the *zomba vinta*, even though we weren't part of the service."

With somewhat more leeway than 'cattle separated from the herd' *(havak'aomby)*, the Sambarivo whom royal officials chose to move from the Doany to the Mahabo when a ruler died, a worker appointed to the royal service could send one of his own siblings or one of his descendants as a substitute. No other people could serve in his place.

The stories that circulated during the months in which people were being recruited for the menaty service reflected people's efforts to wend their ways through conflicting obligations, often by attempting to do while not doing. One of the royal officials at the Mahabo sympathetically explained the poor participation of other Antimahabo by emphasizing the difficulty of having to stay away from one's house, fields, and livestock for such a long period of time—not merely a few weeks, but a few years. Kin could not always be counted on to care for things without taking them, and fields, livestock, houses, and other valuables could disappear or fall into ruin. People were also afraid to go because the service—like all royal work, but especially work involving the ancestors—was known to be very 'difficult.' Two people died suddenly at the work camp within the first nineteen months because, it was said, they transgressed ancestral custom. And later, in 1981, Laza Be counted six people who had died shortly after the service was completed.

One of the Sambarivo at the Mahabo told me how he had gone to a mainland village on an errand and found everyone gone because they were afraid he was coming to collect money or volunteers. People seem to have been more willing to give money than labor to the menaty service. Malaza raised 5,500 FMG, but only one volunteer from households of his kin living in four villages.

Those persons who were directly appointed to participate by a member of the administration, either the supplicator of the Mahabo or a fehitany in one of the regional districts of the domain, were required to serve or face the possibility of being cursed. Asked if a person could refuse to serve if appointed, an Antimahabo said yes, but that such a refusal was "bad, bad, not good at all. You have to agree. In the end, if you don't agree, one day you are going to be sick and need a royal blessing through the supplicator, and he won't do it. He won't do it."

Appointed persons could not refuse, nor could they replace themselves with a sibling or a descendant except in cases of grave illness or death. Even then, the substitution had to be announced to the royal ancestors at the Doany and Mahabo, to whom every single participant was known through just such prior announcements. One of the cautionary stories that Malaza told the Sambarivo from the Mahabo in this context concerned the Jingo group of the Ancestor People who replaced a dead relative in an earlier menaty service without announcing it to the royal ancestors. He was struck down shortly after he entered the menaty to begin work on the royal tomb and taken for dead, leaving that portion of the service uncompleted.[12]

Mahasoa's Mother (also mother of Diniky) farmed in a village south of Analalava, not far from Malaza. In late October, six weeks after the work party had left for Komajara, she was staying a while with her brother Mamoribe in Analalava. We started talking about the menaty service because she said that two of the little children in her brother's yard were really sick. She had gone to the manantany so he could divine by *sikidy* what was wrong with them. He said that evil people living near them had put sorcery in the children's food, and gave her medicine *(aody fankaboka)* to take away the sorcery.

"While I was there, a man came to him to ask what to do. He was appointed to go serve the menaty, but he couldn't go, he was sick. He had gone to his fehitany [local royal official], but the fehitany had insisted he should still go. But he couldn't, he was sick. So the manantany said he should stay for the time being until he was well, then join one of the later groups appointed to go. . . . There was also a woman who had gone to the ampanjaka be and said she couldn't go, because she was troubled *(sahirana)*, people were sick. . . . The ampanjaka said that she had to go. 'Can't' [she told the manantany]. The manantany told her to go and plead with the royal ancestors out there, the masters of the work. When she receives white earth, she will be cured. Drink the water of the supplication. People who are sick go out there, and plead to him—cured."

I asked if people from A., the village where she farmed with her husband, had gone to serve the menaty, and she said: "Three from A. were in the orders, in the writing, but they are getting more people all the time. Now they are asking for ten people from each village, each month. This month, ten people from one village go as soon as the moon is living and return when the moon is small. Ten from another village replace them the following month. The first ones who were appointed are not allowed to go home, except to pass by for a little food, then return [to the camp]. Ravao's Father [her former spouse, named after the child] was appointed, but he didn't go. He has a sister down there who is married, who gave birth to a little girl not long ago. Her in-laws have been saying to her constantly, 'What is your brother doing? He is appointed to go serve the menaty, and he is not going. We're [inclusive] going to die! You have to speak to him. You have given us a grandchild. You have to go and speak to him.' They are also afraid that the grandchild is going to get sick. He had said, 'The canoe wasn't big enough, the canoe wasn't big enough.' He took the name of the ancestors in vain (nipoko). If you swear falsely, then the ancestors of the ampanjaka kill, murder. Ah! People fear the ampanjaka! So when I came up here, I went with Ravao [her child with the man] to B., the supplicator at A. [who takes care of lying and false oaths]. I said, 'The father of my child made false claims concerning the royal ancestors. He is appointed to serve the menaty, but he is not going. We are afraid of getting sick. . . .' He said, 'Leave the house! You go back home [to your father's village]!' He thought we were still married. I said we were not. He said, 'Oh, he's staying in a different house?' 'Yes, a different house.' 'Oh, it doesn't matter.' He pleaded [to the royal ancestors] to take the child [Ravao] and sister's child from him so they wouldn't be affected, no one but him. I also said I wanted to separate from my [current] husband, because he constantly makes my two little children sick. He hit them with a stick too often, too hard. He hit one of them hard with a stick. Then he was really sick to his stomach. I took him up here to the doctor, who was really worried about him. Now he is alright, but I want to separate from him and move up here to my brother [Mamoribe]. But B. said it was prohibited during the time of the menaty service for people to separate from their spouses. They have to wait until the service is completed. If they separate before then, they will be sick. . . . Now the children are well, but I cannot separate yet. Overstepping the ampanjaka's words is not allowed, overstepping is not allowed. . . . If people get sick because of the menaty service now, they can be cured. But if they do wrong things, they may not get sick until

after the service is over, and then they will die! That is what makes it bad
(maharatsy azy)."

Other royal followers confirmed what MamanMahasoa said about
overstepping royal prohibitions concerning royal service, especially
prohibitions against any kind of open conflict. When I asked Saha
Barimaso about forbidden behavior during the menaty service, he
began by saying:

"People may not truly separate *(misaraka marina)*. People who are serving
need speech that follows *(kabary fanaraka)*. Separating breaks things into
little pieces *(mampotipotiky raha)*. . . . It is forbidden to wear gold [as if one
were in a royal enclosure]. It is also forbidden for women to fight with
other women. If a woman sees that her husband is making rivals of
women *(mamparahy mañangy)*, she has to remain silent. When the service is
completed, then she can fight or do whatever. Any kind of fighting is
forbidden because it ruins the service."

One hundred and sixteen people were finally entered on the official
list—called 'appointments/orders' *(tendry)*, 'writing' *(soratry)*, and
'passport' *(pasipaoro)*, that accompanied the service from the Doany
to the Mahabo.[13] Others were appointed to shorter periods of service
later, as MamanMahasoa indicated. Some short-term workers were
urged to serve by their elders to bolster the reputation of their ancestry,
or they joined for a while, because the camp was reputed to be lively.
No one was prohibited from working.

The officials and the workers on the original list were obligated to
serve until the very end when they returned from the Mahabo to the
Doany to report to the ampanjaka and her ancestors there that the
service was completed. They could not return to their homes, except
very briefly to get food, by permission from the leaders of the service,
although their kin were permitted to visit or stay at the camp.

The workers cultivated corn and manioc at the camp. They brought
rice and received rice from relatives and from the common store that
was purchased with the initial money contributed for provisions (9,000
FMG from the living ruler and 5,000 FMG from the royal ancestors

at the Mahabo—a kilo of unhulled rice was then about 15–20 FMG), and by subsequent donations, raised from tribute levied monthly in the villages of the domain. There were also donations from others: a spirit-medium gave a cow to the Antidoany party while they were still at the Mahabo, which they then gave to the Antimahabo. Another spirit-medium gave them a demijohn of palm wine, which they kept. An Indian merchant (who was possessed by two lesser Sakalava royalty and who came to the southern Mahabo ceremonies during the first and third months of every new year to sell his goods to participants) gave one gunny sack (about 20 kilos) of unhulled rice and one gunny sack of hulled rice to both parties jointly. A long-time French settler, who had a coconut plantation on the Komajara Peninsula and depended on local people for labor, gave the use of one of his two trucks to haul the timbers from the forest back to the camp. Royal followers from Sakalava mahabo and doany on the northwest coast also supported the service, as was customary with large services. Royalty in the Maromandia, Nosy Be, Mahajamba, and Majunga areas were said to have sent money. The royal ancestors at the mahabo at Lavalohaliky and Berafia, closer by, were said to have sent people as well.

MOVING IN ORDER

The menaty service began with the assembly of workers and tools at the Doany and their reassembly at the Mahabo, before moving on to the camp in the forest. The first two moves took the first pair of good months in the lunar year. Workers were expected to remain at the camp cutting trees for at least two years, possibly longer, even though they had only been granted one year for the entire service. As it turned out, they spent two years at the camp and six before the service was done.

The logs could be stripped at the camp or at the place below the Mahabo known as Antsandrarafa, where the royal corpse was dried to bone. Once all the trees had been stripped, they were taken up to the Mahabo together. The tomb was cleaned, the old fence was cleared away, the new fence was raised, and the 'door'—actually door posts—

in the fence was sealed with the blood of a cow. The workers informed the ancestors at the Mahabo that the service had been completed, and then informed the ampanjaka at the Doany. They were then free to go home.

The workers from the mainland, together with the tools, were presented to the ancestors at the Doany at the first month of the new year (June–July 1973), during the services honoring the royal ancestors, which were also attended by the newly appointed sous-prefet. The ampanjaka arrived too late in the lunar month for the Antidoany group to get to the Mahabo while the moon was still growing. Having announced their departure to the ancestors, they left the Doany as required. They went on foot, with eight Sambarivo, four men and four women, divided equally between the southern and northern halves of the Doany, carrying the 'service' on their heads and shoulders. They spent the last quarter of the moon and the next lunar month—the 'bad month' of *asara maimbo*—in the village north of the Doany, where Tsimanihabe from the Mahabo farmed during the rainy season. They could have crossed over to Nosy Lava, but they would have had to camp on the cove below the Mahabo. Since it was a bad month, they could not have announced their arrival to the ancestors, and thus stayed at the Mahabo itself. In fact, most of the people from the Tsimanihabe pen at the Mahabo were in the mainland village during this time, trying to finish threshing rice they had harvested just before the new year's service in June and July.

The Antidoany crossed over as a group on a Monday, a good day, but the last day of the lunar month when the moon was going down (August 27, 1973). Traveling on that day broke the prohibition against serving royalty on bad days, but the next good day—Friday—was reckoned to be too late to accomplish everything at the Mahabo and then at the work camp before the moon of *asara be* was down again, so they took off anyway. The move took fifteen outrigger canoes and three dhows, although some of the worker's own baggage had to be left behind and brought over later. The service was carried in a *fiara* type of outrigger canoe, one of which was built especially for that purpose. The *lakafiara* is distinguished from all the other kinds of

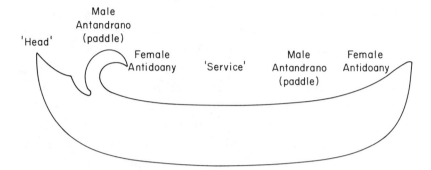

Figure 17. Order of the 'service' in a fiara-style outrigger canoe.

outrigger canoes in the area by its distinctively carved prow or 'head.' The service was carried in the center, with the two Antandrano 'masters of the canoe' and two of the Antidoany women who served as its porters seated in the order shown in Figure 17.[14] The other outrigger canoes were also handled by Antandrano as their part in the service, the dhows by the Silamo, from whom they were hired.

When the Doany group landed on Nosy Lava, they went straight up to the Mahabo and gathered in front of the door to the tomb. The supplicator at the Mahabo announced their arrival and the purpose of their visit to the royal ancestors. The Antidoany presented him with the service, which he directed junior Antimahabo to put on a mat in the storage house inside the burial compound. The visitors were then taken to the places where they were to eat and sleep during their stay at the Mahabo. Everyone brought their own food, although the two groups—Antidoany and Antimahabo—also exchanged some food as gifts.

The service left the Mahabo on a Monday (September 10, 1973), two weeks after the Antidoany had arrived and two days before the full moon. The door to the burial compound was opened on the two preceding good days (Friday and Saturday). Everyone sang and danced in honor of the royal ancestors from sundown on Thursday until dawn on Friday.[15] During the morning, the Antidoany, Antandrano, and Antimahabo paid their respects to the royal ancestors in separate groups. In the afternoon, they 'played' *(nisoma)* by dancing out battles of Zafinimena conquest. Singing and dancing continued Friday night, and some participants—mainly Sambarivo and a few spirit-mediums from the southern Mahabo—went up to the northern Mahabo on Saturday morning to pay their respects to the ancestors and honor them with dancing there.

From sundown on Saturday to sundown on Sunday, the door to the burial compound was shut, Sunday being a bad day. That afternoon, Antimahabo held a meeting among themselves, then with Antidoany, to discuss whether the service, which now included material from the Mahabo, should be carried in canoes or in a dhow. During the singing and dancing for the royal ancestors, which began again on Sunday night, the ancestors possessed their principle mediums for the first time since the Antidoany and Antandrano had arrived. They were joined by Ndramañavaka [Andriantsoly] in the person of Saha Ambary from Tsinjorano, and by Tompony Andronjona ('Master of Andronjona') in the person of his medium from Andronjona, both of whom usually joined the ancestors from the Mahabo when they gathered in the *fantsina* during the services in their honor. They expressed their approval of the workers' service so far, blessed them, and wished them a safe journey to the timber camp. Their collective appearance also made it clear who the big mediums were and who were not—notably the two mediums about to leave for camp, neither of whom became possessed at any time during the service at the Mahabo. Meanwhile, people said goodbye to one another throughout the day, using a phrase reserved for departures of people involved in royal services: 'Blessed cattle may you return home safely and flourish' *(Aomby mazava loha soa mody soa mandroso)*.

The service left the Mahabo for the camp early the next morning. The supplicator at the Mahabo, who was in charge of removing the service from the burial compound, insisted that his more knowledgeable brothers be present to supervise the order in which the material was taken out. To ensure that they did everything right, they referred to the relevant passage in the *Customs*. . . . The writer, their father, warned participants to "be very careful because those things mentioned above are the ancestors' share of the equipment." Then he itemized "the order of the service when opening things out in preparation for leaving the Mahabo" *(raha hivavatra hiala eo Ankaliava),* stipulating "what may be put in front and what may be put in back":

What is to be carried *(hibohoena)* first of all, what is to go in front, is:
1. offering dish with white earth
2. four-corner-covered basket then incense
3. mead
4. dancing hats
5. [the pair of] mañandria drums, it comes at the very end of these.

As one of the brothers explained it, they had to be sure that the most important elements of the service—the offering dish and white earth—were brought out first, at the head of the procession, not somewhere behind,

"because that's the head of what's going, of the procession. If what goes first is put last, it doesn't go. It must go first, there must be a head to it, its head. If the dish was put at the end, if it was reversed to the end here *(mivadiky afara aty),* it wouldn't go. Some of these don't go ahead, because that's what's the biggest, the offering dish and white earth there."[16]

Although no one made such a comparison, carrying a body head first signifies that it is alive, even if it may be ill or injured. Carrying a person head last, as in a funeral procession, states openly that he or she is dead.

Antimahabo, guided by the Antibe, carried the service out of the burial compound on their heads, and lined up north to south in front of the door to the compound with the offering dish and white earth at the head of the procession. All of the participants in the service, led by the supplicator, paid their respects to the royal ancestors, then group by group. The supplicator asked for a special blessing on the Jado, and concluded by formally announcing the departure of the service for the camp.

The officials and the Sambarivo realigned themselves to go down to the cove below, with the women carrying the offering materials on their heads in the lead.[17] They were followed by the Sambarivo men from the Doany who carried the tools. The Ancestor People came next, wearing white shoulder belts *(savôko)* akin to ammunition belts.[18] They were followed by the two Sambarivo men from the Mahabo who had been chosen to play the mañandria drums. The two spirit-mediums came last, together with their attendants.[19] The crowd joined in at the end, as they left the Mahabo and headed down to the cove.

Antimahabo had announced the night before that people with canoes might be required to transport workers to the camp, because no one on the original list could be left behind. As it turned out, the service filled forty-two boats of different kinds: twenty-two outrigger canoes with triangular sails and a dhow rigging *(lakarakisy)*, ten outrigger canoes of the *drao* and *jilo* kinds, three *lakafiara,* and seven dhows. As before, Antandrano sailed the canoes as their part in the service, while the Silamo handled their own dhows.

Several of the leading men from the Mahabo who were not officially part of the service went along too. These included the supplicator's two brothers as well as the head of the Tsimanihabe pen and his brother-in-law, kin to the Fahatelo. Two cattle were killed at the camp on Monday to celebrate the workers' arrival. The men from the Mahabo returned home the next day, from which the supplicator went to Analalava and the brothers returned to their mainland village where they were soon to start farming.

SERVING IN THE FOREST

Once they arrived at the camp, the workers stored the service in the royal compound south of the village and waited for the first good day to start working (the following Friday at the earliest). My brief account of the remainder of the menaty service is based on how participants said the service should be done and on what they said actually happened, since I was not present at the camp or when the menaty was rebuilt at the Mahabo, five years later.

The timber can only be cut on good days—Friday, Saturday, and
Monday—reckoned from sundown to sundown. The day begins with
singing and dancing honoring the royal ancestors during the night.
The next morning, the workers go into the forest, taking the offering
dish, basket of incense, mead, drums, and axes. They carry the mead
in a gourd known as *tsôntso* in the royal vocabulary (*voatavo* in ordinary
usage). The equipment is carried in the royal order, but in this case,
the Sakalava Ndvarameva or senior representative of the Ancestor
People takes the lead.

The Ancestor People are in charge of cutting the first tree, which
will be the first post that is put into the ground, forming the southeast
corner of the menaty, the head of the fence. The next three trees are
set aside to be the other three corners. Like the dominant element in
many pairs, they are referred to as the 'mothers' of the fence, in contrast to the rest of the posts, which are its 'children.' The leading men
in the group choose the trees from which the Sakalava selects the first.
One of the Sambarivo from the Mahabo lights the incense; the Antankoala pours the mead into the offering dish and at the foot of the
first tree, the Sakalava leads the prayers of the assembled workers,
and the Jingo cuts the tree. The two Sambarivo men from the Mahabo
play the drums throughout the procedures and the women sing royal
praise songs. The Sakalava asks the royal ancestors for their blessings,
especially that no one will be cut by the axes and knives and that no
one will be sick.

Both Antidoany and Antimahabo said that it was not prohibited
for Antimahabo to go into the forest, but that there was nothing for
them to do as far as cutting the trees was concerned. Later, they usually
stayed in the village, where they served as supplicators for people
wishing to speak to the royal spirits through their mediums. As one
person explained it, "Those royal spirits are their work *(asan'azy)*,
they just stay with the royal spirits."[20] The ancestors cared for workers' illnesses, pardoned their willful and inadvertent wrongs, heard
and received oaths, and called for celebrations, in which they could
be joined by any other royal spirit that possessed a person in the community.

The Ancestor People asked the royal ancestors for their blessings when the first tree was cut. Workers cut the rest without ceremony. Six trees were cut on the first day, ten on the second. The number always had to be even: 'insufficient numbers' *(tsy ampy isaka)* were forbidden. Some participants said that the numbers of trees on subsequent days should be ever greater, making the entire service at the camp hierarchical, but this was not actually done.

Workers transported the trees back to the camp in the French settler's truck and stored them on the Royal Seat to keep them dry and protect them from dirt. The tree-felling was completed in March 1975, nineteen months after the service arrived at the camp. Two-thousand tree trunks, each four meters long, were said to have been cut. The process of stripping the trunks was begun in the first month of the next lunar new year (June–July 1976).

STRIPPING THE TRUNKS TO THE CORE

The tree trunks could not be made into posts as they were. They had to be stripped down to the hard durable core known as the *teza* by removing the leaves, branches, and bark with the large knives. The stripping process was described by a word in the royal vocabulary *(manasona),* based on a common word used to refer to cleaning or making something spotlessly white and to praising someone, possibly ironically or mockingly. Participants that I knew in the menaty service never mentioned implications of praise or mockery, nor were these suggested in the written *Customs. . . .* The author of the *Customs . . .* clarified the meaning of the word from the "Sakalava royal vocabulary" in a mainly Merina text by explaining it in French: "Here it must be kept well in mind that all those pieces of wood must first be cleaned (that is to say, all the wood must be debarked or planed by Antidoany)."[21]

Workers can strip the trees either at the camp or at the place below the Mahabo called Antsantsarafa or Antsandrarafa. The work can only be done on good days. Depending on the number of people involved and the speed with which they worked, participants estimated that the whole job would take two to six months. In fact, it took two years.

The workers from the Doany do the work under the guidance of the Ancestor People. Participants emphasized that only the Ancestor People knew exactly how it was to be done. Everyone has a general idea of what needs to be done, because they have made fences for themselves, but only the Ancestor People know the details of this particular work, and therefore only they can direct the work. The stress on the category of people in charge of the work is in keeping with the hierarchy and clarity of the division of labor at both the Doany and Mahabo. Commenting on the fact that only the Antidoany can help to strip the trunks, a Sambarivo from the Mahabo said: "Everyone has their own unique kind of work once they are there [at the Mahabo]" (Jiaby tôkaña asa izy koa fa agny). The tree trunks cannot be taken up to the Mahabo until all of them have been stripped to the core, the teza. They are taken up only when they are ready to be placed directly in the ground. As several participants emphasized, they should be 'beautiful, similar' (tsara, miramira). Until then, none of the workers can go up to the Mahabo either.

Once all the trunks have been stripped—and now they are described as menaty wood (kakazo Menaty), not simply as wood—they are taken up to the Mahabo and put directly into the burial compound between the outer and inner fences. The rest of the service is put in the storage house right next to them, as it was when the menaty service began. As before, the order of things in the service is critical. Now the menaty wood comes first. Every last post must be taken up to the Mahabo and put in the burial compound before 'the dish and its friends' can be moved. They are to be carried up last, in the same order as they have been carried before. The workers from the Doany take the service up to the burial compound. The workers from the Mahabo put it inside.

CLEARING THE INSIDE

The workers begin serving inside by first 'serving Kongo' (manompo Kongo), that is, clearing the interior of the burial compound of the

dead leaves and branches that have fallen on the ground since the last
Kongo service, which would have been done at the end of the preceding year in preparation for the new year's service.[22] In other words,
the 'difficult things' are "cleaned of everything or cleared of leaves,"
as one Antimahabo leader said, just like the tree trunks themselves.

The Kongo service that is done now is basically the same as the
Kongo service that is carried out every month during the dry season
when the new year's services are held. The difference is that in the
annual services, only the areas between the inner and outer fences and
immediately outside and around the burial compound are cleared of
dead leaves and branches. In the menaty service, the interior of the
menaty and the tomb itself are also cleaned. Sambarivo at the Mahabo
were perfectly familiar with the Kongo service, which they did several
times a year. But the workers from the Doany would not be so familiar
with how the tomb was cleaned.

The workers begin by opening the 'red-blood door' in the middle
of the western side of the old menaty fence. This is done in the morning
with the rising sun. Guardians from the Mahabo provide the materials;
the Ancestor People are 'masters of the lot of opening it' *(tompony
anjara mampisokatra azy)*. The door, consisting of the two adjacent
door posts, is 'opened' by offering eight five-franc pieces to the ancestors within (40 FMG, about 16 cents). In fact, participants didn't say
that the Ancestor People 'open' *(manokatra)* the door; they 'cause it to
open' *(mampisokatra)*. Walking in front of them and behind them,
perfuming them with incense, and shielding them from dirt by constantly fanning them, Antimahabo bring six gourds of mead from the
'destiny house' over to the 'red-blood door.' The Ancestor People
then pour the mead into the ground around the posts, half on one
side, half on the other.[23]

The Jado can enter inside the menaty because he is a descendant of
Zafinimena royalty. Otherwise, only the Ancestor People are 'masters
of the lot of entering inside the difficult [things]' *(tompon' ny anjara
hiditra ao anatin' ny sarotra)*. Even the guardians of the Mahabo are
prohibited from going into the very innermost part of the burial compound or touching the tomb. Everyone who enters the burial com-

pound must have washed themselves, but the Ancestor People and Jado must be especially thorough about it. While they are still gathered in the open-air meeting house before the service, the Ancestor People, Jado, and supplicator must clothe themselves in their shoulder belts. The Jado must also arm himself with the fighting knife. While the Ancestor People do the Kongo service inside the menaty and the Jado watches over their work, the supplicator stands at the opening of the red-blood door and watches from there.

The tomb is a rectangular pile of dry stones, oriented lengthwise in a north-south direction. The Jado climbs up the west side and sits 'on top, in the center' *(ampovoany)*. The Jingo climb up on the southern side and the Antankoala on the northern side.[24] 'On top, in the center' *(ampovoany,* locative *am + vovo[na])* is another term clarified in the *Customs . . .* by translating it into French *(au centre)*. Sambarivo at the Mahabo uttered it only in hushed tones. *Vovo(na)* refers to the ruler's head among royal followers in Menabe.[25] The Bemihisatra in the Analalava region used *kabeso* to refer to the ruler's head, including the head(s) at the eastern end of the tomb, and *vovona* to refer to rooftops of dwellings, royal or common. Both might have been relevant here, since the royal corpses were buried with their heads 'up' to the east, and—at least in the case of Ndramamahañarivo [Tondroko]—in a coffin carved to look like a house, the lid being the roof.

The Jado should then center himself on the highest part of the tomb, the head of the tomb identified with the royal corpses. He sits there to 'watch them,' as one Antimahabo explained, while the Ancestor People clean the dead leaves and branches from their respective halves of the tomb. He is armed to ensure that neither they nor anyone else attempts to steal some part of the difficult thing to use in making deadly medicines and "in order to honor the Monarchy by embellishing or ornamenting it" *(mba ho rangin' ny Fanjakana)*. The most likely people to attempt sorcery were those who were already close to royalty. This was why the powerful spirit-mediums known as saha were often suspected of sorcery. One of the Sambarivo at the Mahabo said that in the past, the Jado would have killed such persons by cutting their heads off. Another man said that the jambia marked its bearer as being a 'true ampanjaka': "That beautiful thing is there in order that it can be seen that he leads the government. You know that there is an ampanjaka! Carrying a thing like that, he's a true ampanjaka *(ampanjaka marigny)*." The Sakalava Ndrarameva directs the work from inside the menaty, and the supplicator, standing at the doorway, directs the work on the outside. The Jado was not expected to give any orders. One of the Sambarivo at the Mahabo explained: "He's a child, there's nothing he knows" *(Zaza io, tsisy raha hainy)*.

The workers must stay in their places until the service is completed. If anything should bring the workers down before the service on the top is finished, they are prohibited from climbing back up on the tomb. The top has to be left as is, whether or not the service there has been completed. Together with the fear of sorcery, this contributed to the tension of the work inside the menaty, because Antimahabo like Malaza and other Antidoany, also remembered what had happened during the last menaty service at the northern Mahabo. In retelling the incident, the Antibe reemphasized their points about workers' substitutes: if an appointed person has to be replaced, his or her replacement must be announced formally to the royal ancestors at the Doany or the Mahabo (as the original person was), or else the replacement will die. No person who is unknown to the royal ancestors as part of the service may climb up on the tomb.

As Antimahabo recalled the event, the service was still at the camp in the forest, when the head Jingo, a man from the same village as the head Jingo in the current service for Ndramamahaña, died. His kin chose his younger brother to replace him without notifying the royal ancestors. When the time came to clean the top of the tomb, the Jingo's younger brother climbed up together with the Jado and the Antakoala. The Antimahabo had just brought in the second of eight loads of gravel, which the Ancestor People were to spread on the top, when he dropped in his tracks. His fellow workers took him down and the supplicator and others crowded around him. The Jado and the Antankoala, assuming that the royal ancestors had killed him, and not seeing the supplicator, rushed down from the tomb, fearing death or accusations of sorcery. Without a witness to their proper conduct, they could later have been accused of stealing from the difficult things to make deadly medicines. As one of the Sambarivo from the Mahabo commented: "It is best that people down here below keep watch [on those up on the tomb]. The supplicator watches people work. In case, sometime, someone might put something in their clothes, take some difficult, precious thing, take it away. [He watches] for fear that [someone might] take things, make medicines, do wrong things. To climb up there to take something is wrong, it may not be done."

That part of the menaty service at the northern Mahabo was never completed, although some participants in the current service argued that it could have been salvaged. According to one of the brothers who had formerly been supplicator at the southern Mahabo, the royal officials should quickly have asked the ancestors' pardon and their blessings, and then announced the substitution of another Jingo, whom they would have cleansed and clothed with the shoulder belt to be "strong! strong!" *(fatatra! fatatra!)*. He said they did not do that because they were afraid that local French officials would think they had sacrificed the man to the royal ancestors, as the Sakalava were reported to have done in the past. Later they found that the man had not died, but "fainted on the spot" *(toraña sur place)*, still a serious condition attributed to ancestral intervention. By then, it was also late in the day and the rest of the Kongo service had to be finished before sundown.

Once they have finished cleaning the top of the tomb, the Antankoala and Jingo notify the supplicator of the Mahabo who orders Sambarivo from the Mahabo to get fresh gravel called 'tiny waves' *(riaka madinika)* to spread over the top. All the stones used to construct the tomb, from sand to the slabs of rock around the sides, were called 'waves' *(riaka)*. They differed in being 'tiny' (the gravel on top of the tomb), 'black' (the slabs of rock around the tomb), or 'white' (the sand around the base of the tomb inside the menaty). The gravel was always taken from the same place northeast of the royal cattle pen at the Mahabo, where people rarely walked. The Antimahabo get eight loads of gravel; the Ancestor People spread it on top of the tomb.

Only after they have finished recovering the top of the tomb, do they come down to complete the Kongo service around the base of the tomb. When that is done, they come out of the menaty, and the Antimahabo 'take the part' *(mandray anjara)* of doing the Kongo service.

The Antimahabo clear the area between the menaty and the fiaroaomby and around the outside of the burial compound just as they do ordinarily. They cut back the grass and pile it together with fallen leaves and branches onto cloths and carry the wrapped bundles out to the Ankalana, 'At the Remove,' east of the tomb. Workers also referred to this place as *tany rotsohana*, 'land into which things are put or thrown out or down, laid to rest, sleep, die.' They emphasized that only Sambarivo from the Mahabo could walk around there, and only on such occasions. The complete Kongo service takes most of the day. Workers return to their households to eat only when the work is done.

PUTTING THE OLD MENATY OUT AND DOWN
Once the tomb and the surrounding area is completely cleared of dead leaves and branches, and the top of the tomb has been refinished with 'tiny waves,' then the old menaty is 'put out and down.'[26] The men leading the service decide when this is to be done because some people may be out of food or other supplies and need to return to the mainland to restock. Workers begin taking the menaty out of the ground by pouring mead at the base of the corner posts, beginning at the head or southeast corner.

The supplicator appoints Sambarivo from the Mahabo to get eight gourds of mead from the storage house in the burial compound and give them to the eight women from the Doany, whom the Fahatelo has appointed to wait at the door of the house.[27] The women must move counter-clockwise around the tomb, from the storage house, south along the foot *(ampandia)* or western side of the tomb, then east to the southeast corner post where they pour the first two gourds of mead around the base or root of the post *(ampototra)*. This is the head of the four posts. Then they move on to do the same at the northeast, northwest, and southwest corners. It is forbidden to go in the opposite direction.

Once the mead has been poured at the base of the corner posts, cleansing the place, the Ancestor People unearth the posts. With the Antankoala working on the northern half and the Jingo working on the southern half, they begin at the middle of the east side, 'At the Heads' *(Ankabeso)*. They end in the middle of the west side, 'At the Feet' *(Ampandia)*, where the red-blood fence is already open. The old posts are put with the grass, leaves, and branches from the Kongo service in the Ankalana east of the tomb. Residents of the Mahabo are forbidden to use the old posts for firewood or any other purpose. They should decay into the ground of their own accord.[28]

PUTTING UP THE NEW MENATY

'Setting the menaty up high' *(mampizoana, manangana menaty)* must be done in a single day, like the royal burial and moving the Doany.[29] Some time before that day, the Antimahabo are to ask the Ancestor People to determine the dimensions of the new fence. These are fixed by moving the place of the southwest corner post two to three meters south of its present position to make room for the next burial. This purpose was never once mentioned. Participants simply emphasized that only the Ancestor People would know just where the post should go.[30] Sambarivo from both the Doany and the Mahabo emphasized the speed with which the new menaty must be built. Ignorance or clumsiness would prevent them from completing it in time. Antimahabo said that this was another reason why it was necessary to write the procedures down, so they could give a lot of orders without hesitation.

The Ancestor People begin erecting the new menaty by putting in the corner posts, first the southeast post, then the other three in the same order as before. Then they 'wash' each post, beginning with the southeast post, using meter-square serviettes *(sarivety)* made from new white cotton cloth bought especially for that purpose.[31] The Jingo and Antankoala do the washing at the southern and northern halves respectively. The process of setting the four corners is concluded by pouring two gourds of mead at the base of each one in the same sequence. The eight gourds are brought around by eight Sambarivo

women from the Doany, who have gotten the mead from Antimahabo
at the door of the storage house as before.

  The Ancestor People—Sakalava Ndrarameva directing, Antankoala
on the north, and Jingo on the south—put up the rest of the posts,
beginning 'At the Head' in the middle of the east side and moving
towards the west side. When they have reached the middles of the
north and south ends, they stop and call the 'Bemihisatra'—all the
rest of the people in the service, including the Sambarivo from the
Mahabo—to come into the burial compound and complete the service.
The Bemihisatra take up where the Ancestor People left off, continuing around until they reach the middle of the west side, 'At the Feet.'
Like the Ancestor People, they are divided spatially. Members of
southern pens work on the south side, members of western pens on
the west side, and members of northern pens on the northern side.
The eastern pens at the Doany arrange themselves according to
whether they are from the northern or southern half; there are no
eastern pens at the Mahabo. The posts must be set together so closely
that it is impossible to see through them. Antimahabo said that whenever people served to reconstruct parts of the burial compound—for
example the menaty, the storage house or the council house—they
were offered alcohol *(toaka)* to drink. The toaka was kept in the storage
house, in a demijohn that once held rum, but rum was forbidden as
the cause of Ndramamahaña's death, so other kinds were served instead. Sambarivo from the Tsimandrarabitiky and Tsimandrarabe
pens at the Mahabo were in charge of distributing the toaka.

  Only men work to set up the menaty. When I asked one of the
Sambarivo from the Mahabo why women did not work at this too,
he said, "Many do. There's no work, but singing." [Why?] "Eh eh,
it's not customary. Singing, singing is their work. They come, but
come to sing, to give courage *(manome courage)*."[32]

  Once the menaty has been erected, the Ancestor People must go
back inside to 'wash the royal ancestors' and lay down fresh beach
sand around the tomb before closing the door. As before, eight Antidoany women bring gourds of mead, which they have gotten from
the Antimahabo in the storage house, to the Ancestor People who are

waiting inside the menaty. They begin with 'the one royal spirit' *(ny zanahary iray)*—the spirits are not mentioned by name—who is the eldest, the Great-Grandfather of the current ruler buried at the northern end of the tomb. They clean the spirit by pouring eight gourds of mead over the large slabs of stone at the north end of the east side of the tomb. Then they rub them with two meters of new white cotton cloth. They clean the Grandfather next, using eight more gourds of mead and one and a half meters of cloth. The Brother is cleaned next, using eight gourds of mead and one meter of cloth. The Father, buried at the southern most end of the tomb, is cleaned last, also with eight gourds of mead and one meter of cloth. Antankoala clean the two royal spirits in the northern half of the tomb. Jingo clean the two in the southern half.

Participants in the service described the actual work as 'pouring' *(mañidina)* and 'cleaning' *(mañadiovana)*—though not 'washing' *(mañasa)*. The general process is described as *mañasona* (or its reduplicative, *mañasohaso*), the same term used to refer to the process of stripping the tree trunks of leaves, branches, and bark, which is also thought of as cleaning and possibly as praising. Royal spirits, angered by departures from custom, could curse the offender. Coaxing, cajoling, and flattering the royal ancestors with praise songs, dances, gifts, and services were among the main ways in which supplicants sought to 'take away anger' *(mangala heloko)*, whatever its source. Cleansing the royal spirits with mead and other mixtures of honey and water was another important way of assuaging their anger.

Once the royal spirits are clean, the Ancestor People prepare to "pour white waves *(riaka malandy)* lightly over the tops of all the royal ancestors," as one Antimahabo described it; that is, to lay beach sand down around the perimeter of the tomb, from the edge of the tomb to the edge of the menaty. Antandrano were appointed to get the sand. They carried it in ordinary, uncovered baskets, but they had to get it from a beach, which he said was "from way out there in the forest where people rarely go" *(Bok'agny anatiala agny. Ampassy fa mandeha anatiala andranomasigny agny, lavidavitra. Tany tsy diavigny olo loatra, mahalaña)*. In the past, it was always taken from a small cove (Amboanio Kely) west of the northern Mahabo. Sambarivo from the Mahabo emphasized in this context that, in reconstructing the menaty, "nothing is required from the mainland, except, of course, the posts" *(Tsisy raha alaigny an-tanibe izy koa tsy kakazo eky).*

Antandrano bring the baskets of sand around to the southern end of the island by canoe, and carry it up from the cove to the door of the burial compound. Sambarivo from the Mahabo take it from there and bring it to the opening in the menaty. The Ancestor People take it from there and lay it around the tomb in the same order they used in putting up the posts. They begin at the head of the tomb in the middle of the east side and work around to the foot in the middle of the west side, Antankoala on the north and Jingo on the south.

The white sand is the froth on top of the sea. Participants in the service used the same word, *mañidina,* to describe their spreading the sand over the ground as they used to describe their pouring the mead over the royal spirits.[33] The Ancestor People are expected to cast the sand 'carefully, nicely' *(moramora, tsaratsara)* on the ground, moving backwards at the same time, to avoid stepping on it. Having begun 'At the Head,' they leave through the gap in the fence 'At the Foot.'[34] Once the white sand has been laid down, no one may enter again except to bury the next royal corpse.

CLOSING THE DOOR

Once the menaty is up, the royal ancestors have been washed, and the white waves have been poured over them, then the red-blood door should be 'walled shut' *(mandriba).*[35] The "real custom" *(tena fomba),* as Saha Barimaso expressed it, is to complete the reconstruction in one day. The door should be shut before sundown. This time, even though participants' houses extended up as far as the Dressing Place (Ampisikina) outside the Mahabo, they were not able to finish before dark. But they did begin on a Friday and end on Saturday.

The door consists of two pointed posts. The door is shut by brushing the sharp heads of the posts with the blood of a sacrificed cow from the royal herd, then putting them side-by-side into the open space in the fence.[36] A pair of cattle are killed because a second cow is required to serve as a 'mat' for the sacrifice. As a gift to the royal ancestors, the sacrifice could not be allowed to touch the ground. But having two animals, when there were two partners to a sacrifice, was common in the region. When participants called upon their ancestors in a circumcision ceremony, both the father's kin and the mother's kin provided cows, known as the 'father's cow' *(omby ny baba)* and the 'mother's brother's cow' *(omby ny zama)*. The father's cow was 'for invoking the ancestors' *(ho joroana)*, and the mother's brother's cow 'for eating' *(ho hanina)*. They were both washed, as they are here. Participants also urge them to 'Lay down quietly, don't move, because we are invoking the ancestors!' *(Mandria tsara, kaza mihetsiky, fa zahay mijoro é!)*. After washing the animals and before sacrificing them, the person invoking the ancestors says: 'Dead today, thankful tomorrow' *(Maty niany, misaotra amaray)*. As AdanDezy from Tsinjorano explained: "Even if this cow is killed, its generations will not come to an end" *(tsy ho lany ny taranak'aomby)*.

The animal to be sacrificed—called the 'service' (fanompoaña)—is the ampanjaka's gift to the ancestors, from her herd. It must be a young female of calving age that has not yet born calves *(sakaña)*, with the dark body and white face *(mazava loha)* showing that it has been blessed by the royal ancestors. The 'mat' is a 'people's cow,' which can be a male or female of any age. Its color also 'doesn't count' *(tsy mikonty)*, as long as it is not one of the kinds that are prohibited under any circumstances. Both of the animals are kept with the royal herd that is penned at night in the *tsimirango* cattle pen just outside of the Mahabo to the northeast. Sambarivo from the Maromainty pen at the Mahabo serve to bring them in and tie them down.

Colonial scholars, including Dandouau in 1911 and Decary in 1962, have written that humans were sacrificed at Sakalava royal funerals to provide the 'mat' on which the royal corpse was laid.[37] Antimahabo participating in the reconstruction of the menaty said that the human sacrifice did not take place until later when the menaty was rebuilt, when human blood was used to close the door. They explained the European point of view by saying that if a leading participant in a service, for example, the supplicator at the Mahabo, happened to die in the course of the year-long royal funeral, then he was buried at the door to the Mahabo when the royal corpse was buried in the tomb. Cattle were substituted for humans in the colonial period. The cattle stood in for humans who have voluntarily subordinated themselves to the monarchy.

The two animals are put down on their right sides, their heads to the east and their feet to the north, the mat west—behind, thus down from and under—the service, as the sacrifice is called. In 1973, Antibe from the Mahabo said that the cattle were laid in front of—west of— the red-blood door, following what was stated in the guide. In 1981, they said that they laid the animals down at the new southeast corner of the menaty, between the southern ends of the two fences, the counterpart of the place where royal sacrifices are made at the Doany. Six Sambarivo women from the Doany bring six gourds of mead to clean the cattle that serve to close the door, just as six women brought the six gourds of mead with which the old door was opened. They pour *(manidina)* the mead over the two cows while they are still alive, beginning at the head and ending at the tail, four on the sacrifice in front and two on the mat behind. The mead is to remove any trace of dirt.

The head of the sacrifice first 'puts [the service] to sleep' *(mampirotso)*, then the mat, that is, he lays each animal down on its side, just as people 'lay down/put to rest or sleep' *(mampandriana)* the animals they sacrifice to their own ancestors. Participants used the same root from the royal vocabulary that is used in referring to the ampanjaka's 'sleeping' or the old menaty's 'decaying' *(mirotso)*, explaining that in this context it means 'to kill' *(mamono)*. Both Antidoany and Antimahabo said that the sacrifice used to be carried out by the leader of the Ancestor People, the Sakalava Mañoroñaomby, or by one of the people from the Mosohery or Antiravaka pens who serve the royal ancestors at the Doany, using the ceremonial dagger (jambia). Today, many Sakalava are descended from or married to Silamo or follow Silamo customs, including the prohibition against meat from animals that have been killed by a non-Muslim without the appropriate prayers *(kopinda)*. Therefore Silamo are chosen to kill all the animals sacrificed and eaten during royal services, using an ordinary knife, though one man pointed out that the head of the Antankoala subgroup of the Ancestor People participating in the menaty service was Silamo and could therefore do the work.

The 'killer' of the cows *(ampamonoana)* catches blood from the sacrifice in two dishes; no blood is taken from the mat. The blood is referred to by the royal word *vonotro*, meaning dew or moisture in ordinary speech. Regardless of who kills the animals, the Sakalava who is head of the Ancestor People, must anoint or cleanse the posts with the blood. The term *manosotra* (smearing, washing, cleaning, anointing), used here, is related to *manasona*, used of the mead in earlier contexts. With the tail cut from the sacrificial cow, he brushes the blood from one dish on one post and the blood from the second dish on the second post. The blood is brushed upwards, on the sharpened heads of the posts, just as white clay is applied in an upwards streak on the foreheads of petitioners receiving ancestral blessing. It is prohibited to brush it downwards toward the feet of the posts. One Sambarivo from the Mahabo compared the two actions in using the verb *tsontsôrany* to describe the motion, perhaps suggesting that it is the same blessing in blood. Once the heads of the posts have been brushed with blood, they cannot be left lying down on the ground; they must be stood upright in their places *(atsangana am pilasiny),* thus closing the door.

The meat from the service is given to the Jado and the Ancestor People, who can take from it what they like. The meat from the mat is divided among the Sambarivo from the Mahabo. Other cattle are killed outside in the usual way for the Sambarivo from the Doany and the Tsiarô—the workers from the royal districts. As they did at the beginning, the Sambarivo from the Mahabo bring out an offering dish and some white earth so the Jado and the Ancestor People can formally declare to the royal ancestors *(afantoko)* that the service they have done in their honor has 'grown to full size' *(tombo).* They must stay for a week or two afterwards to praise the ancestors with songs and dances. If the ancestors do not possess their mediums of their own accord, they must be coaxed into possessing them to say goodbye and to give gifts like money and jewelry. The members of the service will take their gifts back to the ampanjaka at the Doany in thanks for the respect that she had shown the ancestors in reconstructing the menaty. All the gifts must be formally announced to the royal ancestors at the door before leaving.

Once that is done, the Jado, the Manantany, the Fahatelo, the Ancestor People, and the Tsiariô in the original list return to the Doany to tell the ampanjaka in person that 'the service is grown' *(tombo ny fanompoaña)*, to present the gifts, and stay a while to celebrate. Then they are free to return home to their own villages. In 1981, leaders of the service said they had gotten permission for four years, and the service had lasted four years: two at the camp and two at the Mahabo. Some spirit-mediums said that it had lasted six. Saha Barimaso and Laza Be, who was one of the workers, said that it had actually lasted five: two at the camp, and three at the Mahabo. This meant, in Laza Be's words, that they needed a 'friend' (namana) to make an even number of years. Having completed the work at the Mahabo and paid their respects to the royal ancestors in *asara be* of 1977 (the second of the good months in the new year, when they left the Mahabo to go to the work camp in 1972), the original group from the Doany had to leave the Mahabo and return to the mainland. They went back to the village north of the Doany, the farming village of the Tsimanihabe from the Mahabo where they had stayed before. As Saha Barimaso explained,

"They waited until there were a full six years, need paired/married years *(mila taona manambady)*." [Why there?] "Because it is close to the Doany. They cannot go up there [to the Doany] if it's less than six years. When they increased to six years, they went home to the ampanjaka, and they paid their respects to the ampanjaka too. They left [the mainland] during asara be, so they had to wait until then to return. They went to pay their respects in asara be [August–September 1978]. Later, representatives from all the other doany came to pay their respects. The ampanjaka's younger siblings [her children], they were all there. Once all those people were gone, then the spirit-mediums came with the Antimahabo to pay their respects to the ampanjaka." [Why did it take so long?] "Difficult! That is a really difficult thing. Difficult to stay with it!" *(Sarotra ke! Raha sarotro boka io. Sarotro pitrahaña!)*

THE DIFFICULTIES OF ROYAL SERVICE

Like the 'government' (fanjakaña) of Southern Bemihisatra royalty, the work involved in the menaty service was organized in pairs consisting of a 'head' and the head's 'friends' or 'partners,' reckoned by seniority, age, gender, and location. Choosing people to make such unions, being chosen, or volunteering to participate, inevitably involved controversies concerning the abilities of some to lead and the willingness of others to follow, given conflicting demands on the labor and loyalties of all.

Leaders of the menaty service, and its other advocates, were careful to instruct workers recruited to the service, as well as outsiders, in the significance of many specific restrictions. Such efforts are also reflected in the multilingualism of the *Customs . . .,* written in Sakalava, Merina, and French. Participants constantly emphasized the need to follow the correct order, and they outlined the necessary steps, beginning with the head, necessary to accomplish otherwise familiar work in this difficult way. They never elaborated on why that form was right, perhaps because the greatest difficulty in royal service lay in resolving tensions between diverse heads and feet in the direction of royalty. The purpose of the concluding chapter is to explore that unspoken possibility.

Rooting Ancestors

Tsy tany miherinkerigny, fa olombeloño.

It is not land that comes and goes, but living people.

Malagasy saying, Analalava region

OLO TSOTRA: SIMPLE PEOPLE

Laza Be once said, "Sakalava are simple people *(olo tsotra)*. They don't know how to make fancy speeches. They just know the customs." Such disclaimers were essential to good etiquette, which discouraged open boasting about personal skills. Yet Laza Be's words were also based on an awareness of the power of knowledge concerning proper conduct—that embodied knowledge, unwritten and often unspoken—that could only come from living in a place. As Malaza put it, "Masters of the land are people who know the customs; that knowledge of local ways is what makes them masters of the land *(mahatompon'tany azy)*."

In the case of the menaty service, royal officials in the colonial period finally outlined these ways in writing to ensure that when it could eventually be done, then it would not be 'done wrong.' The authors of *Customs of Royal Service Concerning the Menaty (Fomba Fanompoaña Momba ny Menaty)* followed their names, printed and written as in a legal document, with this statement: "Those Grandfathers presented [this book] to their Descendants, Great-Grandchildren and subsequent generations, in order that the Service to be done will not be done wrong."[1] Nevertheless, the *Customs . . .* were only a rough guide to

441

the detailed knowledge of its diverse creators, articulated in the fence itself. The menaty service had to be done because the old fence was *mirôtso*—broken in death, decayed in time, and thus liable to loss.

As long as the fence remained unrepaired, the distinctions between the dead and the living from which ancestors emerged, were obscured. The *tany masina* or powerfully generative place of the ancestors, marked by the menaty, was vulnerable to theft, but also open to oblivion. The prisoners who worked around the island during the daytime were most likely to try to steal money and other valuables from the royal storehouse north of the tomb. Far more dangerous was the unspoken possibility that evil people might try to steal the 'difficult/precious things' themselves. What sorcerers could do by design, royal followers could do by looking and going elsewhere. To remake the fence was to realize the knowledge incorporated into its structure. To 'do it right' was to rewrap the entombed ancestors in recognition of the distinctive features of royal order embodied in the fence, and in recreating them in the fence, to reproduce them in one's self.

The key to this process was expressed in a remark that an ampanjaka, descended from one of the nonruling royal ancestries in the region, made about the royal burial:

"As soon as the body is in the coffin, the coffin and corpse together are called fanompoaña, to show that everyone is a servant *(ampanompo)*, a slave *(andevo)* of the ampanjaka. For the Sakalava, a slave is a servant of the ampanjaka. The Hova understand something different by slave: there are nobles *(andriana)*, commoners *(hova)*, and slaves *(andevo)* like common slaves *(andevo)*. For Sakalava, there is the ampanjaka and the andevo, all the same kind. Besides the ampanjaka, there are only andevo. In the hot service [*fanompoaña mafana,* royal funeral], everyone is a royal slave, including other ampanjaka."

The key was service, encompassing worker and work alike. In the royal funeral, the service was the royal corpse, into which royal followers were assimilated through prohibitions on mourning that put them in a 'filthy' condition analogous to death. In the menaty service, the service was first the tools with which the new fence was to be reconstructed, but finally it was the menaty itself: the fence made of teza, the enduring hearts of trees planted around the cleaned tomb. The menaty service clarified the form of the tomb (enlarged inside to receive the next royal corpse), but also obscured it from view. To see something of the relations among leaders, followers, and pilgrims to the site they restored, we must look more closely at the service itself, that is, the teza in which they are joined.

TEZA: HEARTS OF TREES

The teza of a tree is its heartwood, the hard, durable wood at its core, in contrast to 'the whiteness' (*tapotsiny, kotofotsy*), the soft outer sap-wood between the core and the 'skin of the tree' (*hodi-kazo*). The dense heartwood keeps the tree upright, while the porous sapwood conducts the 'water of the tree' (*ranonkazo*), from which it grows ever bigger, taller, and deeper. The heartwood is darker than the sapwood, increasingly impervious to air and water, thus more nonliving, toward the center. As the tree grows older and larger, its heartwood also expands in size. Teza are so widely prized as building materials for houses and memorials throughout Madagascar that teza is synonymous with 'fixity,' 'permanence,' and 'uprightness.'[2] For Bemihisatra in the Analalava region, the right to use teza in building was a royal prerogative. Thus, like all the objects of royal service, organized into heads and pairs, after the model of the royal body, teza were identified with royalty, first the living ruler, but finally the royal corpse.

Ngeda at the Mahabo emphasized that "nothing is required from the mainland [to rebuild the menaty], except, of course, the posts" (*tsisy raha alaigny an-tanibe izy koa tsy kakazo eky*). The same was true of the royal funeral. One of the main purposes of the 'hot service' was to move the royal corpse from the mainland to the island where it could be buried in ground that was central yet separate and distant. The parallel between the menaty service and the royal funeral was affirmed in the central role of workers from the Doany, especially Ancestor People, in every part of the menaty service. In keeping with the strict division of labor, Antidoany served in cleaning and repairing all the parts of the Doany, while Antimahabo cleaned and repaired most parts of the Mahabo. The menaty service was the one exception besides the funeral. All the participants in the service emphasized that it was the work of people from the Doany, in which Antimahabo simply cooperated, just as they did in the funeral itself.

Several prohibitions governed the selection of the teza from which the menaty was built. The hardwood trees from which they were made had to be 'red' like ebony *(piro)*, 'white,' or 'yellow' like *katrafay* and *famoalambo* (*Dichrostacys tenuifolia* Bth.). The yellow was considered least desirable because it lasted only about four years, while the red—the color with which the Zafinimena were identified—was considered to be the most durable, as evident in the fact that the 'red' posts were the only ones still standing in the menaty of the northern Mahabo. *Ficus* species, like *aviavy* and *mandresy*, which were praised for their conquering habits in surrounding villages, were prohibited in royal constructions like the menaty on the grounds that they twisted around other trees, their 'friends' (namana), and killed them.[3]

Besides being hardwoods of particular colors and kinds, the trees had to be 'dry,' not 'wet.' Dry trees were 'dead, but standing' *(maty izy, fa mitsangana)* in the words of one Antimahabo, for example, trees having withstood lightening fires without falling to the ground and rotting. Such trees were sometimes called 'dead wood' *(ala maty)*. In contrast, he said "wet trees, living ones, are prohibited because they quickly become ruined, rotten" *(Hazo lena, velona, tsy mety satria malaky mirôtso, motraka)*. The trees had to be stored on the 'Royal Seat' *(Fitambesaraña)* above the ground to keep them dry. It was prohibited to lay them on the ground where they might get wet and begin to decay.[4] The Royal Seat was also known as the Golden Trestle *(Savaly Fanjava[mena])*, like the structure on which the corpse was laid while the Ancestor People washed and dried it for burial. Their seat, together with their storage house, was further enclosed inside a *tsirangoty* fence (implying a living ruler), at the door of which people addressed their petitions to the royal ancestors. Once all the trees had been cut, they were taken to Antsandrarafa below the Mahabo, where the royal corpse was first taken after leaving the mainland. Antimahabo described this place in hushed and abbreviated terms as 'the place where the hot service *(fanompoaña mafana*, the royal corpse) is put in order *(mañajary).*' The royal corpse, laid on a slatted bed, was washed with mead, while the flesh turned to water and fell from the bones (as the decay of corpses was described in other contexts), thus 'drying' the body.[5] The bones were put into a coffin, made from the hollowed 'male' and 'female' halves of a tree, thus standing in for the heartwood or teza of a new kind of tree to be planted in the tomb.

The trees cut to make the menaty were likewise 'washed' *(mañasona)*—stripped of leaves, branches, and bark—to expose their hard centers. The Ancestor People were in charge of both kinds of work. They also led the Kongo service in which the tomb itself was cleared of the leaves and branches that had accumulated on its surface and re-covered with the various sizes of stones called 'waves,' ending finally with the froth on top of the sea.

Once the 'wood' *(kakazo)* had been 'washed' by stripping it down to the teza, then the 'menaty wood' (kakazo menaty) took precedence even over the offering dish when the service was carried from place to place. In both the royal funeral and in the menaty service, the service—the corpse and the teza—could not be taken up to the Mahabo until the work at the Antsansarafa was completely finished. Then the wood, like the corpse, had to go directly into its proper place. As Velondraza said concerning the teza: "Once carried up, it's there! It's put in its place. It's not necessary to wander all over; what's wanted is a finished thing!" *(Izy koa manonga . . . avy! Mbo mipetraka ampilasy. Tsy mila mitetitety, mila raha vita!)*

In short, workers in the menaty service handled the trees like royal bodies, and they handled the teza like royal corpses. The transfor-mation of trees that had died on the mainland into posts reburied in the ground around the royal tomb thus paralleled the transformation of the fleshy corpse into a skeleton, enclosed in a tree trunk and buried in the tomb itself. The workers accomplished this transformation by 'opening' an unopenable door, unwrapping the royal ancestors by removing their decaying fence, cleansing the stony surface of the waves around the land where the ancestors' bones lay housed in trees like heartwood, and rewrapping them in a new fence made of the hard, dead, 'bone-ish' cores of trees, surrounded by an outer fence of quickset branches. In reburying the 'difficult things' at the now more powerfully dead center of an outwardly living forest on the island of Nosy Lava, they raised them again over the Analalava region as a whole.

REBUILDING AND REBURYING

The menaty service could be described as a kind of secondary burial (*famadihana,* turning) of the sort that have been well documented in the ethnography of highland Madagascar.[6] Its manifest purpose is simply to repair the fence around the tomb, not to rebury the royal corpse. Furthermore, reburial as such is not practiced in the Analalava area, by royalty or their followers. Nevertheless, the menaty service is virtually identical in its structure to the pattern described elsewhere in which the bones are exhumed, unwrapped, cleaned, and reordered, rewrapped in new coverings and reburied.

The reconstruction of the tomb and sometimes even of the participants' houses appears to be an integral part of the famadihana ceremony, at least among the Merina and Betsileo where the most extensive research has been done, although scholars have not elaborated on this point. Furthermore, if Sakalava royal service is taken as a whole, the bones—at least the relics—of royal ancestors are actually removed in the annual new year's ceremony at the Doany. The Vy Lava of the Southern Bemihisatra is not removed from the ancestors' house at the Doany, like the relics at doany further south. Yet it is taken from its cloth-covered 'bed,' cleaned and replaced there. Such royal baths—called *fitampoha* among Southern Sakalava and *fandroana* in Imerina—have been found in varying forms in at least five other precolonial monarchies, although they too have not been linked to the famadihana, which is generally associated with commoners.[7]

Despite these similarities, it is clear that what was being reburied in the menaty service was not the same as what was buried in the royal funeral that preceded it. In rebuilding the menaty in 1972–1978, the Southern Bemihisatra served Ndramamahaña, who died in 1925, by unwrapping the 'difficult things' from their old fence, broken in his burial, cleaning them of the filth associated with death and disregard, and then recovering them with a new fence, enlarged to make room for a new burial in the future. In taking the form of the posts, the royal corpse multiplied, and in multiplying, it became identified with commoners stripped of their associations with kin in the process of reorganizing as individual 'followers' around royalty.

The royal corpse was not the only body moved from the mainland to the island, where it was buried. Serving in the menaty service also removed royal followers from their living places through the same series of steps. People from all over the region were required to move from the rural villages where they were tompontany or vahiny—masters of the land or strangers, children of men or children of women—for weeks, months, even years in the case of the original group inscribed on the official list of workers. Although they were represented in the royal administration through rañitry, who served as the heads of local kin groups, they were recruited into the menaty service (as in other royal services) as individuals. Indeed, the service entailed the separation of people as kin and their reassociation solely as royal followers, that is, solely in terms of their common subordination to royalty.

In moving out to the work camp through the Doany and Mahabo, and in returning through the Mahabo and the Doany to their homes, they had to resettle themselves around royalty; either north or south, depending whether their own paternal ancestors came from the northern or southern part of the domain centered on these royal places. Doing the service right required them to conform to rules considered inviolate to the point of forcing even enemies into friendly cooperation. Following these rules about 'heads' and 'pairs,' 'whole' and 'insufficient' numbers, 'good' and 'bad' days reformed relations among them according to the model of government embodied in the relationship between ampanjaka and Sambarivo, at least so long as they worked.

I would go on from there to make more generalizations about royal work than participants themselves stated. Their convergence in the menaty service, in the fence itself, speaks to the separation yet interdependence of royalty and followers implied in the various forms of fences surrounding royalty, including the pens of guardian-slaves. The menaty service has 'grown' *(tombo)* to its full size when it has produced just such a complex pen. This pen is still larger than the pens containing royal slaves, for it includes people from the entire region.

The menaty-pen embodies the *Trongay magnidevo* of royal praise songs, Sakalava rulers who enslaved by assimilating people of diverse origins, ancestries, and personal destinies to the positions of infinite numbers of Sambarivo, 'Every One a Thousand.' Sakalava rulers 'tie' their followers together like bundles of sticks, 'pen' them together like cattle, grouping them according to their common service. The cut trees convey the death of a living ruler and his removal to the royal cemetery, accompanied by 'cattle severed from the herd' to watch over his remains. They also convey the cutting or uprooting of royal followers from where their ancestors are buried, places that are also 'in the forest' by comparison to the Doany and the Mahabo. The stripping that changes a living ruler into a royal ancestor is repeated over and over in the experiences of royal followers. In addition to being stripped of their kin, they are stripped of their customary practices in the course of conforming to royal ways of carrying out the simplest forms of work. In serving to rebuild the menaty, workers are transformed from trees scattered in a 'forest' of local communities into a trimmed, orderly, cultivated fence centered on the royal ancestors. In taking up places around the 'difficult things,' workers themselves complete the structures with which royal ancestors are raised above their own.

The isolation and reorganization of workers around the royal ancestors reproduces the isolation and reassociation of living rulers with their followers and ex-slaves. Like the workers, living rulers have been cut from the forest of their kin. Alone in the royal compound, Bemihisatra rulers serve as heads of households including the descendants of all the ancestries in all the places that are tied to their place. Yet deprived of their own descendants and brought up by guardians who become their closest friends and companions, living rulers are like children of the people, whom their followers 'raise' *(mitarimy)* in pens of their own making. Royal followers work to raise living rulers up to maturity. Perhaps they can be said to raise royalty to the maturity of ancestorhood as well. But age and death also begin to reverse the relationship between royalty and commoners. In growing bigger, the wild, unruly child also grows more 'forceful' *(mahery)*, 'cruel' *(masiaka)*, 'difficult, albeit precious,' even 'very difficult and precious' *(raha sarotra indrindra)*, as the royal ancestors are sometimes known. In contrast to 'simple people,' the extremely difficult value of these 'things' derives precisely from their combination of extreme violence with their unlimited capacities to heal *(mitaha)* and bless *(mitahy)*. Like the Long Knife with which they are identified, they are protective because of their deadly powers. The formal praise names of the royal ancestors extol their beneficence in saving, unifying, and feeding infinite thousands as living rulers. Yet the epithets applied to them collectively express the 'great violence' *(bisata)* of these 'difficult/ precious bulls' *(aombilahy sarotra)* or 'monstrous things' *(kaka, zaka)*. So commoners uniting around the royal ancestors may be said to have 'captured' them in pens made by and of themselves together with the guardians who are ex-slaves.

Yet the older the royal ancestors are, the weaker they become, as exemplified in the solitary wickedness, yet frailty of the Great-Grandfather and the Grandfather of the living ruler, compared to the conviviality of her Father and Brother. The older ones possess fewer people, finally only one. They are much less sociable. They speak far more quietly, to fewer people in fewer words. As they become less visible, more hidden, they lean more on the strength of their grandchildren to conduct the government, the same grandchildren who enlarge their burial places in anticipation of future dying.

In the words of one of Ndramamahaña's funeral songs: *Tsy manjaka tsy entiny zafiny Ndramandisoarivo*, 'Ndramadisoarivo [one of the four founding ancestors of the monarchy] does not rule if he does not bring along his grandchildren.' One of the guardians at the Doany explained this by saying: "Ndramandisoarivo does not rule without descendants. When a ruler gets old, the children and grandchildren bring the monarchy up, they raise it, grow it, make it great *(mahabe ny fanjakana)*. There is no government if his children and grandchildren do not replace him *(misolo azy)*."

Through the living ruler, royal followers serve to 'make the royal ancestors great' by enlarging and 'elevating' (*mahabo*) their place in the land. Royal followers protect the ancestors in surrounding them just as the Maromainty, the royal bodyguards with whom the Jado stayed, are said to have 'screened' *(manakona)* the living ruler from his or her enemies in the precolonial period. The menaty is thus a monument to their collective strength. Royal followers also make the ancestors great by replanting themselves in their powerfully regenerative ground—this ground incorporating the land as a whole—and growing from their union a new person.

OLO ARAIKY: ONE PERSON

Participants in the menaty service compared the *kongo* service, in which they cleared the burial ground in preparation for setting up the menaty fence, to their work in clearing land for planting, or weeding a garden so it would grow properly. Ravo at the Mahabo explained: "Serving kongo means cutting, chopping down trees, clearing. Everything that's not right, that doesn't belong, is thrown out for the time being. [It means] cleaning up." *(Manompo kongo—mikapa, manapa kakazo, manjava. Raha jiaby tsy manjarinjary, adoso tsendriky. Mañadio.)*

Weeding is typically the activity of the early rainy season when people begin to turn from the royal centers to their villages and eventually their isolated shelters 'in the forest' where their own fields are. Here their clearing, bringing light into the darkness of the royal tomb, achieves a very different kind of growth. They cleanse the royal ancestors by washing away the dirt associated with rotting, sickening, obscuring, and dying. In removing the old leaves and branches from the tomb, washing the headstones with mead, taking away the old fence, putting up the new one, and laying down a fresh layer of white sand, 'white waves,' around the perimeter, before finally closing the door— they clarify the form of the tomb within the thicket of trees that continues to grow ever higher around it.

Workers regenerate the royal ancestors by forming new ties among themselves as individuals joined together on the basis of their common subordination to royalty. The reunion with royalty, which they accomplish through all this cutting, trimming, tying, and penning, produces a body with the form of an enormous tree-person made of stones, trunks and living branches, bones and flesh, dead and living persons, including rulers, followers, and their former slaves. The east side 'at the royal head(s)' is the body's head, identified with royalty; the west side 'at the feet' is its feet, identified with guardians and followers. The menaty or innermost fence made from the dead cores of hardwood trees, is the body's trunk; the fiaroaomby, or outermost fence made from the quickset branches of 'dead-living' *matambelona* branches, forms its leafy arms *(sandry)*.[8] The royal ancestors, buried at the center, are the fertile roots or genitals *(faka, vôto*—doany in the royal vocabulary) from which it grows.[9]

'Dead things with no life in them' *(raha naty tsisy veloño)* must indeed be buried to keep living people from dying. But living 'people' *(olo)*— men and women working together—must eventually combine with them again to create the ancestries from which future generations will emerge. In moving about the camp, carrying out their allotted work according to the pervasive requirements of heads and pairs, participants in the service are drawn into the very body of ancestral royalty, even as the royal ancestors are regenerated through their incorporation into the bodies of their living followers. Together they form one person. To my mind, Saha Barimaso's explanation of the Ancestor People's name suggests that radical union: "Because they may do things that should not be done with the ampanjaka. Things that people do not dare to join together, they dare" *(Satria izy mahazo mañano raha tsy tokony atao amin' ny ampanjaka. Raha tsy sakin' olo mañambitra, izy mahasaky)*. Under the guidance of these 'masters of the work,' Southern Bemihisatra serve to make the royal ancestors great by joining to stand them up as a person with the outward appearance of a huge branching tree. This new body does not 'represent' the one person of royal ancestry, it *is* the royal ancestors. They are not 'just names,' but people in this place. Like all ancestors in this region, royal ancestry grows from the repeated union of the living and the dead, but the feet of this body come out of different ancestries, different places in the land around the royal tomb.

In cleansing the body of the debris and dirt associated with death and forgetting, royal followers saturated it with a liquid akin to blood and finally with blood itself. Honey, conceived as the sap or blood of trees (*lio*—the term is the same), was renowned for its purifying powers. It was added to dirty water to make it potable. Mahasoa once claimed that people could eat excrement if they put honey on it. Spirit-mediums cleansed themselves with raw and cooked mixtures of honey and water to remove urine, excrement, semen and other bodily fluids, but also the dirt of wrong-doing and the filth of death. Removing the dirt removed the spirit's anger, inducing it finally to remove its fatal curse as well.

The life-giving properties of honey derived from its capacity to cleanse away the dirt of anger and death. Honey was the chief ingredient in the majority of Sakalava medicines. It was used to make children grow, and was also the favored food of old people, who could no longer eat rice or relishes. Perhaps for that reason, it was seen as the favored food of spirits as well, so their petitioners left bottles of honey at the foot of spirits' trees as gifts. As mead, honey was compared to blood, not just the sap of trees, but human blood. The sticky black liquid resulting from the mixture of cooked honey and water, called by the royal word 'black spirits' *(tao mahintigny)*, was known to royal followers as *tamberoño*. Tamberoño was prescribed to drink in all cases in which there was considerable blood loss, "so as to replenish the blood" *(biaka mimpodipody ley rahaben'azy, lion'azy)*, as Ngeda from the Mahabo once explained it, adding "Like wine too, for that matter" *(Karaha divay koa boka)*.[10]

The door was finally sealed with blood, uniquely binding, if the practice of blood friendship (fatidra) is any indication. The blood came from a pair of cows, including the sacrifice given by the living ruler and its mat given by a royal follower. Like all those who served the ancestors, they too were expected to submit soundlessly, 'willingly.' The blood from the sacrifice was used to anoint the sharp heads of the door posts, closing the fence between the royal ancestors and living people, even the living ruler, while remaining their crucial connection.

THE BREATH OF SPEECH

The ancestor person made from the bones of trees, the flesh of leafy branches, and the blood of sap is animated by the powerful breath of speech embodied in the mediums who come to live around the place where it grows. Royal workers could close the door in the menaty with blood, thus burying Tondroko's corpse, because Ndramamahaña had already emerged in the body of a medium recognized as being the 'real thing.'

Silence is a major feature of death: being silenced, but also keeping silent. The speech of the living ruler, buried by death, emerges again through living 'channels' *(saha),* as mediums are called. A medium supports the spirit with her whole body, but the spirit is thought to sit on her head. Judging by the medium's practice of cleansing her mouth before the spirit speaks, the spirit is thought to communicate with its petitioners especially through its speech. While the supplicator 'asks for speech' *(manontany kabary)* from ancestral spirits, their formal statement of why they have come, the manantany 'asks for speech' from their petitioners. Most of what happened with the royal ancestors at the Doany and the Mahabo was in fact talk, as I have already indicated. But just as a new body emerges from reburying royalty in the menaty service, so too does a new voice, and eventually many voices. Royal ancestors speak through commoners legitimated by their former slaves. In the fifty years that passed since Ndramamahaña's death and burial, he was recognized not just in one medium, but in ten whom Antimahabo had confirmed as the 'real thing,' and he was emergent in others still out in the countryside.

This new ancestral person lived in the speech of its mediums. It also lived in the speech of participants in the service itself. Southern Bemihisatra could not talk about the royal corpse, which revealed all too graphically the corrosive effects of death. In fact, prohibitions on speech were one of the major ways in which dead rulers were buried not only in the ground at the center of their domain, but also in the very bodies of their followers. The menaty service regenerated the royal ancestors by repeating the royal funeral in a more accessible, thinkable, talkable form. The service transposed the unspeakably 'difficult things' onto 'simple people' and things, lending themselves to more open discussion and reflection. The royal funeral was carried out secretly in the dead of night. The crucial technical details were known only to a few specialists who were bound not to communicate them. The menaty service was also in the hands of the Ancestor People, but the general requirements of the service were broadcast far and wide. Participants could talk at length about how they select timber and fell it to make a fence or how they weed gardens. Such matters were common knowledge. Indeed, the service required by its very nature the comprehension of a great many people, not merely as observers, but as active participants.

Judging by what I heard at the beginning of the service, much of their speech did have to do with the service itself, providing means by which participants and observers could reflect for themselves on the changing significance of royal deaths and burials, the major unspoken subject of royal work. Yet, what workers themselves emphasized was talk having nothing to do with their service. Their own talk accounted for the great length of the service. Yes, so many trees were required; the right kinds of trees were difficult to find; there were many days, weeks, and months in which royal work was prohibited; the work had to be organized according to pairs, including pairs of years. But finally, as Velondraza explained, speaking of the menaty service for the northern Mahabo held in Tsinjorano, which he said lasted eight years:

"You know why it takes so long to cut down those trees? Because nobody does any work! They sit around and drink. We used to bring up those barrels of alcohol from Ambanôra. Friday would come [the first auspicious day for royal work]. We still wouldn't have left [for the forest]. Eating, singing, drinking! Friday, we just drank, we didn't go and serve. There were months we went only once into the forest! People just wanted to have a good time."

Judging by the annual services, many new friendships would have been formed among participants during the reconstruction of the menaty, ranging from lovers' liaisons, to economic exchanges, to marriages and blood ties, persisting after the service had grown to its full size and the workers had gone back to where they came from.

DARKNESS AND LIGHT

The menaty service expresses the power of Sakalava royal ancestors to enslave people, but also the power of their followers to capture royalty and define it on their own terms. The work clarifies the relationship between ruling and following before obscuring it again. The construction of the fence suggests parallels to house-building, born out by the fact that the top and bottom of coffins are sometimes described as the roof and walls of a house. There are also clear parallels to cattle-raising, as I have indicated. But taking into account the burying as well as the burgeoning, the closest parallels in the menaty service are to agricultural work. To govern *(manjaka)* is to impose burdens, but most local expressions of how some people control or contain others are derived from activities like 'cutting' *(manapaka, mandidy),* 'slitting, separating' *(manetra),* 'clearing' *(mikapa, misava* or *manava),* 'sharpening' *(mandragnitry),* and 'binding' *(mifehy).*

The structures of Sakalava monarchy hide royalty, while exposing their followers to scrutiny. The menaty service contributes to their hiddenness by hiding the royal ancestors behind a new screen of trees, retrenching people as their followers. But these related purposes are accomplished by cutting, clearing, and washing, which open royalty to the examination and manipulation of those who serve them. Every act of covering and obscuring is matched with movements of elevation and clarification, reproducing the paradox on which the royal funeral is based: that burial in the ground *(mamaky tany)* is burial in the sky *(mamaky lanitra),* where darkness *is* light. In the words of one of the songs (kolondoy) honoring the royal ancestors:

> *Bibianala, kaka manda.*
> *Savao lala fa hiditra é!*

Animal in the forest, monster under guard
Clear the way for [we are] coming in!

In reconstructing the menaty, Bemihisatra followers assert that the royal ancestors are the roots and trunk of existence on which living followers grow like leaves and branches. But they also reestablish themselves as the living ground in which ancestors grow. In the menaty service, as in rural villages and in the post, creating ancestors is inseparable from claims to living people, and, through people, claims to land. The 'one person' regenerated from the royal tomb does not speak an obscure language. Claims to people and land, long disputed between Sakalava royalty and local ancestries, multiplied with the addition of new contenders like the Hova and the French. The ancestral tree made out of the royal tomb in reconstructing the menaty stands as a clear alternative to the togny of farming villages and to the "administrative trees *par excellence*" of the post. All of them extol competing images of fruitful reunions among people paired as 'friends,' each comparison confirming just one as the 'real thing.' Royal followers work to establish the Doany and the Mahabo as a single transcendent alternative. But even the guardians and spirit-mediums who work the hardest cannot live by that irreducibly contradictory partnership alone. Nor would they. Because of enduring oppositions between royal ancestries and those of 'simple people,' because of their persisting interests in entering freely into the 'Vazaha's house', which still dominates the national economy, even they do not stop moving.

I have suggested that royal service in the Analalava region—in all its various forms, including spirit possession—is comparable to processes of unearthing and reburying the dead found throughout Madagascar, the best known being the reburials celebrated by the Merina and Betsileo of the highlands. As Malagasy ethnology indicates, there are many ways of understanding the significance of these 'turnings' (*famadihana*), depending in part on the scope of the analysis. The parallels among them suggest that they would benefit from comparative analysis in a regional or national context. To do so would expand Kottak's argument[11] about the involvement of Betsileo funerals in political-economic relations among the Betsileo and between the Betsileo and the Merina. Such analysis might also modify Bloch's argument about the role of Merina reburials as a refuge from change,[12] and his later interpretations of "ritual" as "an attack on the value of human creativity," which works because of the collusion of inferiors, embodied in women, who have "made their humiliation their pride."[13]

The menaty service derives from competing ideas and practices concerning work for kin, compelling devotion to royalty, wage labor, *corvée* and *engagé* labor, and slavery, which do not divide into "ritual" and "work," even as ideal types. I see the menaty service, together with other kinds of Malagasy reburials in a regional and historical perspective, as ways of making ancestors that embody diverse visions of social reproduction. Ancestors are unwrappd and rewrapped to make some speak or others speechless, to separate people who have found ancestries from those who have lost them, those who have seized ancestries or separated others from them. Openness and hiddenness coexist not because of any mystery or confusion about the contradictions in political-economic relations, but because no one fully controls them. Circumstances are always turning, yet for people in the Analalava region, those who fail to recognize their own kind are as 'lost to their ancestors' (*very razana*) as slaves and with the same results. They are exposed to the cutting and grafting of others.

Merina and Betsileo persist in burying their ancestors, while honoring royalty. In the very process of concealing them in layers of precious silks, they single them out. Men appear to bury them oratorically, while women bring them back to life in their shrouds.

Among Sakalava royal followers in the Analalava region, the ambiguity of competing allegiances is also embodied in the shroud. Rewrapping the royal tomb in the hard cores of trees multiplies royalty, but it also celebrates the collective power of commoners. The menaty service calls into question the single voice of royalty by making it the creation of commoners. In spirit possession, royalty are brought to life in the very bodies of commoners, typically women, aided by men. Enshrouding these mediums makes them speak, but they may speak as much for themselves and their companions as for others.

The ambiguity, the potential for turning, seen as inherent in all social relations, is embodied in the hard and soft materials with which ancestors are remade: earth, stones, teza, and leafy branches, analogues of shrouds and corpses, tombs and bodies, the bones, flesh, blood, and skin of humans, female and male. The interconnections of these different materials, and their transformations back and forth in time between fragile and more enduring states, is the root of Malagasy burial rites. In their transformations, they are commentaries on the complex composition of human beings and of human relations, especially relations of domination and subordination that call for silence as well as speech, concealment as well as open confrontation. Strategies like these have drawn on both the strengths and the weaknesses attributed to men and women in ever-changing combinations throughout the precolonial, colonial, and postcolonial periods in Madagascar.[14]

In the menaty service, the creation of a new ancestor person, in which rulers and followers were conjoined, could be seen as redefining and confirming a set of abstract values—the 'real thing' (tena izy) concerning work for royalty. These values were abstract in the sense that they were produced by the abstraction of workers from their specific places and their relocation into one common place designed to obliterate their differences. They were abstract in turning individual distinctions—'personal lot' (anjara), 'eight ancestors' (valo razaña), 'spouses/friends/pairs' (namana/vady)—into the common properties of people. They were also abstracted in numbers—the twos, fours, and eights—by which the value of different kinds of companionship could be ostensibly compared and measured. These numbers, abstractions about fruitful relationships, could then serve as standards by which to organize work groups, rank and pair people, and measure the buildings through which their redefinitions might be incorporated into workers' bodies, and workers themselves might be transformed and reoriented. The abstractions were achieved when royal followers relinquished their claims to the construction, for example, when Velondraza explained why the guardians had to receive petitioners from the penitentiary, even though he feared their motives for coming to the Mahabo: "It's not your door, it's the government's door" *(Tsy varavaranao, fa varavara ny fanjakana).*

With the menaty service, Bemihisatra followers marked their own end to the colonial and neocolonial periods, in which such loyalties were forbidden. They also affirmed, in reconstructing the royal tomb in trees that would eventually rot, requiring rebuilding in the future, the continued importance of the royal ancestors in the contemporary life of the region. Yet "every machine contains a cow path," as Burke says about "bureaucratization" in another context.[15]

I think that participants in the menaty service walked this path too. They recreated a structure that could stand as an abstraction about moral relations between royal ancestors and living people. But in reconstructing the menaty, they dismantled the royal funeral, which was its prototype, exposing the roots of these abstractions in earth, bones, trees, and diverse kinds of people with their own varying ideas about who should work for whom to make whose ancestries grow or die.

In making the menaty, participants exposed their own connections, embedded in the land on which they worked, over which they moved. They could look to what was hidden in the ground as a way of examining what lay buried within themselves through prohibitions on their movements, including their speech. Then they could talk about the bodies made from these questionable combinations of persons and things, the abstractions derived by abstracting people from their places and stripping them of their particular defining features in order to turn them into a common body of workers.

INTELLECTUAL ARCHAEOLOGY

I have tried to use this same ground to examine the roots of my own intellectual assumptions. But whereas it is easy to impute such noble motives to others, it is hard to carry them out in practice. Reexamining the menaty service in the light of social and historical phenomena that I have seen as antecedents, one could retrace a history of notably French scholarship on space. It could begin with Durkheim, whom recent

Marxist theorists of the politics of geography still credit with being one of the main originators of the concept of social space.[16] It could continue through other scholars of classification and seasonal migration in the Annales school, notably Mauss. It could also include Van Gennep on rites of passage, Lévi-Strauss on binary and tertiary structures, Bourdieu on *habitus,* and Foucault on other asymmetrical forms of spatial discipline.[17] They all share a premise that Lévi-Strauss once attributed to the Salesian Fathers seeking to convert the Bororo in Brazil:

> So vital to the social and religious life of the tribe is this circular layout that the Salesian missionaries soon realized that the surest way of converting the Bororo was to make them abandon their village and move to one in which the huts were laid out in parallel rows. They would then be, in every sense, dis-oriented. All feeling for their traditions would desert them, as if their social and religious systems (these were inseparable, as we shall see) were so complex that they could not exist without the schema made visible in their ground-plans and reaffirmed to them in the daily rhythm of their lives.[18]

What Lévi-Strauss observed about the Salesian Fathers, and pursued in his own studies of asymmetry, Bourdieu made the basis of his theory of lived experience as social capital, invested here in ancestors. Foucault explored the close connections between "surveillance and punishment," rooted unmistakably, it seems to me, in the scrutinizing *regard* of Louis XIV and his royal and republican successors, although, curiously, Foucault reaches for Bentham's Panopticon as his main example, and does not mention such latter-day *oubliettes* as Devil's Island and the other penal colonies in French Guiana (1851–1951), to which Malagasy prisoners, who did not go to Nosy Lava, were also sent. In fact, French Guiana was initially a colony with insufficient local labor. Prisoners were first sent there to provide the colony with badly needed workers.[19]

To pursue these parallels properly would require a far closer analysis of French scholarship on space in its own social-cultural and historical contexts at home and abroad, including its Anglo-American colonies of the mind.[20] Without making a clear escape from this hermeneutic circle in which I am also caught, I will return to the image of the *ville de condemnation,* the image of social life from the perspective of the post as an enormous prison, which many people there shared with Foucault and about which they have their own perspectives to contribute. Perhaps the hidden abode of production in the Analalava region is to be found in this overarching image and its competitors: the hidden 'pens' that hold Sambarivo around royal centers; the invisible 'Vazaha's house' encompassing working relations at the post; the buried ancestries determining who are masters of fertile rice land and who are strangers.

Foucault uses prisons to talk about social transformations in France occurring during the late eighteenth into the mid-nineteenth century but persisting into the present. Curiously, his argument is very like Rose's concerning transformations in American slavery prior to abolition, which I see as persisting into the present day here as well. Beneath what appears to be the increasing leniency of punishment, moving from tortures of the body to trials of the soul, there is actually a displacement of punishment to a body more extensively conceived. This new punishment, involving a new political economy of the body, is all the more draconian for being the less visible and apparently more humane.[21]

The key structural features of "disciplines" creating "docile bodies" could apply not only to the creation of 'pens,' but also to the creation of the 'quarters' at the post distinguishing children of women from children of men: "the distribution of individuals in space" through enclosures, partitions, and the redefinition of sites in functional terms; "the control of activity," exemplified in timetables; "the organization of geneses," creating new beginnings and ends; and "the composition of forces."[22]

Yet it is already evident that 'the state' in any of its historical or contemporary guises—as precolonial, colonial, or postcolonial monarchy, as colonial power, as independent nation-state, at the administrative post or at the togny of rural farming communities—nowhere holds total sway in this area. Furthermore, some people 'choose' to become caught in pens, while others manage to avoid them. This is the import of recent work inspired by Foucault, for example, O'Brien's study of French prisons in the nineteenth century and Nye's study of French medical models of national decline from the mid-nineteenth century into the belle époque, prior to World War I, focusing on forms of deviance called 'criminal'.[23]

The pains of imprisonment in nineteenth-century France revolved especially around the efforts of officials to isolate and dehumanize prisoners through the bureaucratic methods of dispersal, regimentation, and normalization that Foucault describes. Yet O'Brien argues that prison officials were not completely successful in this. She focuses especially on how prisoners created their own underground networks through the use of secret languages, whispered through walls, tapped on heat ducts, projected ventriloquently through the air, scratched on slop tins, and tattooed on their bodies. Much of the talk with which prisoners thwarted the watchful eyes of their wardens was about friendship, desire, and love in many guises, ranging from idealistic and egalitarian to brutally dominating.

If one takes Sykes's earlier study of the maximum security prison at Rahway, New Jersey, into account, these social relations would have involved guards as well.[24] Sykes also uses prison life as a model of broader social processes. While his study, too, would confirm Foucault's insights into contemporary "disciplines" of the body, he focuses especially on "the defects of total power." "Total power" can be exerted by individuals upon one another in the form of torture. I see the bureaucratic strategies that Foucault describes as attempts to achieve the same effect on a larger scale, where thousands might control thousands as effectively as one might dominate one. According to Sykes's analysis, such totalitarian institutions do not work as they are supposed to because even the most extreme efforts to coerce others involve people in forms of exchange that inevitably compromise the totality of the control they wield over others.[25]

Sykes analyzes how guards, charged with the actual implementation of totalitarian power, are drawn into the social relations of prisoners. Nye examines how popular sentiment contributes to the spread of the coercive forms of professional expertise that Foucault describes. Thus, the medical model of cultural crisis, in which 'deviants' became labeled 'criminals,' was not just a matter of doctors who sought to expand and find new constituencies in formally nonmedical domains. It also involved various interested citizens who actively sought their new-found expertise.

The opposing poles of antagonistic relations are all too clearly seen. What is far more difficult to grasp, what remains shrouded in often deliberate ambiguity, is the exchange, unequal as it may be. While people in the Analalava region distinguish such poles by locating them at different places in their land, by creating different places out of them, they are deeply entangled there too. They use these places to make critical distinctions between 'masters of the land,' rooted there through ancestors, and 'strangers' who are 'people without kin,' though as differently as Sambarivo and ampanjaka. These strangers without kin are indeed aliens serving as instruments of power, as Coser describes some of their European counterparts.[26] But even these social processes of estrangement and localization remain too much at the poles. The focus for people in the Analalava region is 'friendship' in all its ambiguity, celebrated in polyglot languages of love and trade as well as in narrowly standardizing number-talk.

The Euro-American theories of prison life as a paradigm for domination and resistance are relevant because French colonial authorities did indeed use police and prisons to supplant military control in the early colonial period, and these are still one of several key sources of political-economic power in Madagascar. Already by 1910, the Analalava region was considered sufficiently isolated to warrant the construction of a national penitentiary there. This in itself should serve as a reminder that French prisons derived not only from ideas about *surveillance,* but also ideas about the powerfully oppressive force of isolation and exile, which Malagasy would share. The paradigm is useful not because, following Foucault, it helps to explain the achievement of total control, but because, following O'Brien, Sykes, and Nye, it helps to convey the ongoing, often underground, struggles for control in the pluralistic circumstances of many countries that experienced colonial and neocolonial rule.[27] The "dark house" *(trano maizina)*, as the *maison de force* is locally known, conveys something of that shadowy world where, by keeping what is given, taken, or stolen, showing what is hidden, elevating what is buried, some are trying to keep alive what others are trying to kill. But from a local perspective, it is just one of several "houses" in the Analalava region competing for the labor and loyalty of a moving population.

In the Analalava region, enclosure acts, and similar means of swiftly relocating workers in Europe, have not occluded the view from the post of other houses in other landscapes. The perspective from this periphery thus helps to expose a different footpath in the machine, namely, the more recognizably human dimensions of the verbal, visual, and spatial strategies underlying estrangement and replacement in prisons of social control. The more powerful local paradigm for imposing and contesting domination, from abroad or from within, is the manipulation of ancestries for the creation of an open-ended, changing range of 'ones'—individuals with unique destinies, unrivaled rulers, would-be corporate 'persons,' identifiable ethnicities. In this area, the royal ancestors are still the only ones whom some would not allow to become 'mud' *(fòtaka)*, but all these possibilities of 'oneness' stand against the single alternative embodied in those who are one because they are 'without kin,' as 'lost to their ancestors' as slaves. The local paradigm shows how relationships of inequality may continue to be reconstructed and contested even after some words have been suppressed and others instated in their place.

TREES

This book is about growing, grafting and chopping ancestries to seize the land in which they are rooted and capture the laborers who are their descendants. In organizing my account of these movements around trees—the branching structure of expansion celebrated in "Trongay enslaves," the togny and other spirits' trees of farming villages, the "tree in ball-form, well built, of hardwood, the least accessible to all the assaults from tornadoes" of the post,[28] and the tree-person of the royal tomb—I have followed the local idiom. These trees do not "represent" the diverse common grounds where masters of the land and strangers articulate their differences about growing and dying; they *are* the common grounds.

The tree-person of the Southern Bemihisatra tomb does not speak a parochial language in this region, nor in Madagascar as a whole. Writing in the aftermath of the savagely repressed revolt of 1947, in which 80,000 to 100,000 people died,[29] Decary concluded his assessment of *Moeurs et coutumes des Malgaches* (1951) with this image of "autonomy in the best sense of the term":

> Evolution, but not revolution. The [Le] Malgache ought to progress in his personal path, in his traditions, while remaining 'himself.' The young Malagasy plant grows, protected by the shade of the French tree. Once adult, it will be a matter for her *[la jeune plante madécasse]*, not of autonomy, which is a brutal and definitive separation, but of autonomy in the best sense of the term. The political association which will then be envisioned can be no better compared than to the vegetable associations of botanists, in which varied plants prosper in a harmonious whole, but where the disappearance of one of them risks breaking the equilibrium and bringing in turn the extinction or at least the decline of the others.[30]

The prototypes of Decary's imagery could have been Malagasy or French—e.g., *togny* or the *arbres de la liberté* of the French Revolution, adopted from widespread popular practice.[31] Ethnographic and historical data on the Ndembu, Bemba, and Fang of central Africa, the Rotinese in island Southeast Asia, as well as Europeans and Americans provide other well-documented examples of the central place of botanical, especially arboreal, imagery in political-economic relations.[32] A recent account of "where the planet is loosing its life forms," owing to "the ungentle agency of human activity," focuses on seven "species-rich nations," including Madagascar. The account concludes: "By identifying what Russell A. Mittermeier, the head of Conservation International, calls 'megadiversity' countries, which have an unusually large number of species, biologists say they hope to awaken the world to what they regard as the loss of the intricate, interconnected body of the living planet."[33]

These transcendent concerns need to be placed back in the social-cultural and historical contexts from which they originate. Further ethnographic and historical research would be required to do this properly. As an anthropologist, I see these tree-persons as part of a more extensive metaphorical field, which Salmond, from English usage, has called "knowledge as landscape." Despite the elaboration of the metaphor, she finds that "there is no literal sense (at least as far as I'm aware) in which knowledge does resemble the physical environment, spatially or in any other way, and so these landscape metaphors present major difficulties of explanation for 'similarity' or 'analogy' theories of metaphor." Salmond asks, "Why landscape, then?" As an answer, she suggests that Max Black's observation—"a metaphor might be self-certifying by generating the very reality to which it seems to draw attention"—might apply to this case. She goes on to test the comparative validity of English epistemological metaphors against some Maori metaphors of knowledge, finding these both like and unlike in emphasizing "landmarks and certain buildings," but also "knowledge as wealth."[34]

The answer to "Why landscape, then?" may lie in what seems, from widespread experience and some recent research, to be a close association between space and memory.[35] I wonder if the English and Maori metaphors might have shown more similarities with more extensive analysis of both, including ideas and practices outside academic and other specialists' circles—for example, such competing claims to land and laborers as we have considered here.

There is ample evidence for the specific social-cultural and historical roots of English, Maori, French, or Malagasy knowledge—indeed, knowledges—about how people work to make some grow and others die out. But in practice, people forge common languages for generalizations transcending their particularities in the process of relating to one another. The heteroglossic arguments about death and development, still circulating among Malagasy and between Malagasy and Europeans, are expressed more in terms of trees, fences, houses, paths, and bodies, than in the abstractions of social theory. Perhaps such images recurrently facilitate the apprehension and articulation of differences across linguistic boundaries, because they derive, like the spatial dimensions of memory, from more general human capacities of laterality, movement, or uprightness.[36] Perhaps these capacities for creating root metaphors are comparable to the generalized linguistic capacities for sound that enable human beings to create open sets of what linguists still agree to call "phonemes," while still disagreeing about their "reality." Yet these generalized capacities are socially and historically constituted, and thus ever-changing. From a political-economic perspective, I wonder if the successive debates among Western scholars concerning "Europe and the people without history," as Wolf succinctly puts it,[37] have not obscured more local concerns about who is with and without the land in their landscapes, and thus more or less exposed to laboring on the landscapes of others, ancestral, historical, or still living.

"Only connect . . ." says E. M. Forster, in following different paths of death and rebirth through the house, tree, and abyss of England's "Age of Property."[38] I have kept hearing these words throughout my own journey.

Comings and Goings of People Living in Andonaka in 1973

Appendixes 1 and 2 provide some more information about the comings and goings of people whose interrelationships (including spatial relations) are partially indicated in Figures 7 and 8 (Andonaka) and Figures 9–12 (Tsinjorano), respectively. Appendix 1, concerning people and places in Andonaka, centers on the spouses Malaza and Rafotsy, at the core of the community, and the places of their children's houses around them. Appendix 2, concerning people and places in Tsinjorano, focuses first on the siblings, who are the masters of the land in Tsinjorano, and secondly on the clusters of their descendants living around each sibling and his or her spouse. The numbers before the names (in Appendix 1) and after them (in Appendix 2) indicate the house or clusters of houses with which people are associated. Because they are not always adjacent, they could not be so indicated on either the maps or the partial genealogies. These differences express a few of the several overlapping perspectives from which people in the Analalava region viewed community life as well as different times in the developmental cycles of households and communities.

(1) Malaza and Rafotsy had lived in a house in the northeast corner of the village until the house burned down to the posts a couple of years earlier.

(2, 5) At that point, they chose to live separately. Rafotsy moved into the house (5) of the couple's third son, Jombony. Last rainy season, when the roof began to leak, their fifth son and youngest child, Faralahy, gave Rafotsy his house (2) and moved out to his garden. Rafotsy used the kitchen east of (2) until it was damaged in a cyclone. Now she cooks in the south room of Jombony's house (5), since Jombony is still living with his wife in her village.

(3, 4) Malaza moved into the house (3) of the couple's fourth son, Ravelo, who had moved to Analalava and was still living there. We stayed with Malaza in Andonaka, sleeping in the northern room on our first trip and in the southern room on our second trip, since he had moved his bedroom from south to north in the meantime. His sons planned to build him a new house (4) in the center of the village, immediately west of the pair of trees—*mandresy* and *aviavy*—that served as Andonaka's togny.

(6) When Soa, their eldest daughter, first married, she lived with her husband in his inland village. When Soa became pregnant, her father and brothers persuaded her husband to move closer to Andonaka, where both would be better able to follow her ancestral prohibitions against eating certain inland foods. They lived in a coastal village about a fifteen-minute walk away, and she also kept her house in Andonaka (6). They were away visiting kin in other villages and in Analalava during most of the dry season of 1973.

(7) Meva, the second daughter, married a 'Vezo' from southwest Madagascar, who worked on a twenty-three-ton ship that stopped periodically in the bay. They lived in Andonaka when they were together. When they separated, she moved to Antognibe, where she had a child by an earlier marriage. She was still living in Antognibe with her child, leaving her house unoccupied for the time being.

(8) Tafitsaka, the third daughter, was living in the port city of Mahajanga, so her house was also unoccupied. When she was the second wife of Raschid's (see p. 156) kinsman, a man belonging to one of the three main Arabo groups in the Analalava region, she lived in his village north of Andonaka. They had four children. The oldest girl

lived in Diégo Suarez with her Indian husband, the second girl with her mother in Mahajanga, and the third girl with her father's current wife in his village and sometimes with his younger brother in Analalava. The boy had built his own house in his father's village, where he farmed.

(9, 10) Amady, the couple's eldest child, lived in (9) south of his parents when he was married. His house no longer had a kitchen because, as Faralahy explained it, "his wife left long ago." After she left, he moved out to the temporary house in his garden on the eastern edge of his rice field, a five-minute walk west of Andonaka. He fixed up the house and took in one of his sister's (Soa) sons to help with the cooking and other housework.

(11) Botra, the couple's second son, lived in a garden-house next to his rice field five minutes north of the village, together with his third wife, their baby, and his children from his first wife. The family moved to Analalava, near his brother, in October 1973. They were living there again in April 1981, but were back in Andonaka in 1989.

(12) Faralahy lived in (2) when he was married. He and his first wife divorced after the birth of their first child, and she returned to her father's village. Faralahy continued to live in the same house with his second wife until their divorce a year or so later in 1972. When the rains came and Jombony's house (5) started leaking, Faralahy gave his house to his mother and moved out to the fenced garden next to his rice field just outside the village to the southeast (12). In the dry season of 1973, he was building a sturdier house so he could live there year-round. As the youngest child, he was expected to care for his aging parents. While all the sons provided their parents with food, Rafotsy continued to cook for Faralahy. She also looked after his two-year-old child, old enough to have been returned to him in a quick visit that his first wife made with her father one day in August.

(13) 'Two related households' *(toko aroy, fehiny),* two married couples from a nearby coastal village where Malaza had a rice field, lived in a grove of mango trees south of Amady's garden-house during the growing and harvesting seasons when they were cultivating the field

north of Amady, which Malaza had allowed them to use. They had
no house in Andonaka, but they kept an ox-cart in the shed next to
Jombony's house, where Malaza, his sons, and his daughter's husband
could also use it. They planned to return to their own village when
they finished harvesting their rice.

A P P E N D I X   I I

Comings and Goings of People Living in Tsinjorano in 1973

Please refer to Figures 9–12.

Beloha (9?) (1, 2, 3, 6). Beloha, the eldest sibling, lived in the northern part of the village during his lifetime, in the open area where his yZ Zanety was building a house (9) or perhaps in the area where the youngest of the siblings and his descendants now have houses (1, 2, 3, 6, 7). Beloha married a Sambarivo from the Mahabo on Nosy Lava. He was also the first person in the Analalava region to become possessed by the spirit of the Brother, Ambilahikely, although Beloha died before he was able to build a house at the Mahabo.[1]

The tompontany of Tsinjorano serve royalty by making the royal drums (mañandria) used at the Doany. Beloha made the drums. When he died, his younger brother Tafara inherited the work. Beloha's son Tombosa, who also married a Sambarivo from the Mahabo, was skilled at playing the drums. Tombosa played them for his FyZ Zanety, so she could learn how to dance the war dance *(rebiky)* done at the Doany and the Mahabo. He and his family had moved out to their rice field house early in the rainy season of 1973, so Zanety, who had been living at the Doany during the preceding dry season, could live in their house (10) until her own house was finished.

Amina (11). Amina, the oldest living sibling, then in her late sixties,

lived in "Zara's *tokotany*" (11), as one of her sibling's children described it, the place where her parents had lived, although her M Zara
spent part of the year down at the Doany Miadana where her D Meva
moved after her marriage to a Sambarivo there. Amina had married
a Silamo and moved to his village immediately north of Tsinjorano,
where they had six children. When they divorced, and her parents
died, Amina moved back to Tsinjorano and settled in her mother's
tokotany, surrounding it with a fence in the Silamo style she had
adopted during her marriage.

Two of Amina's daughters also married Silamo men (the third was
still unmarried). Amady, the husband of the youngest daughter Vita,
was formerly married to Avoria's youngest daughter Laza (WMyZD,
see Tsinjorano Fig. 9, F) (Amady was related to the siblings Ravo,
Tsarajoro, and Somary [Fig. 11] through his FZ). Amina lived part
of the year with her siblings in Tsinjorano and part of the year in her
former husband's village with her children, three of whom—two married sons (the younger one married a woman from his father's village)
and a recently divorced daughter—alternated between their father's
and mother's villages, staying in Amina's courtyard when living in
Tsinjorano.

Ambary (13, 4). Ambary, a man in his sixties, had been married to
Besoa, an Antandrano from the northern Ambolobozo Peninsula.
They lived in Tsinjorano, but had to move because Ambary's siblings
did not like his wife. According to one of his brothers, they chose to
move to Andronjona because Besoa was possessed by one of the royal
spirits from the Mahabo who had told her to live there. Ambary was
possessed by two royal spirits—Ndremanjiarivo from Lavalohaliky
north of the Ambolobozo Peninsula and Ndramañavaka [Andriant-
soly], renowned for his Silamo ways, which perhaps accounts for the
Silamo name of Ambary's only child, a ten-year-old boy, born when
he was in his fifties.

Ambary and Besoa divorced. During the rainy season of 1973, Ambary was in the process of negotiating for a new wife. Most of his
dealings with his siblings and their children were conducted through
Ndramañavaka, the more powerful of his two spirits. Ambary was

staying with his brother Tafara (13) in March 1973, but by September, he had brought his new bride from her natal village to Andronjona and finally to Tsinjorano, where they settled into the northernmost house in the village (4), formerly occupied by his yZ Zanety and her deceased second husband. His new wife brought her children because they were still small; her former husband had returned to Port Bergé.

Tafara (13). Tafara, in his sixties, was married to a woman from one of the Zafinifotsy doany along the Loza River. The older of their two daughters was visiting them during the rainy season of 1973. Her son cultivated in his father's village immediately south of Tsinjorano, but maintained close ties with his mother's kin in Tsinjorano, where he too visited frequently.

The younger daughter had lived with her first husband, a *métisse karany* (Indian father, Malagasy mother) in Anorotsangana, north of the Ambolobozo Peninsula (see Chapter 2). When they divorced, she had to leave their children with the father in Anorotsangana, where they still lived. She returned to Tsinjorano, where she married a parolee from the penitentiary on Nosy Lava, an 'Antaimoro' from southwest Madagascar who asked to stay five years in Tsinjorano, then liked it so much that he stayed on for two more years.[2] They built a house in the open area northeast of Tafara (12). The parolee introduced a style of building with woven strips of flattened bamboo that other residents 'studied' (as Sefo put it) by building similar houses in their rice fields. When he left in 1971–1972, he gave the materials to his neighbor Ravo (16), who used the walls to make a new kitchen and the posts to fence his grove of orange trees. In 1973, Vahiny had moved to her third husband's natal village, Andronjona, where her parents had started cultivating after Tafara quarreled with Amina.

Togny (20, 21, 23, 24, 25). Togny, a woman in her late fifties, married a Sambarivo from Tsinjorano. They lived in a small house (24) immediately north of the togny in the center of the village. They had two sons and four daughters, one of whom died. The two sons (23, 25) and one of the daughters (21) had their own houses in Tsinjorano; the youngest child still lived with her parents. Togny's oldest child Talañ'olo ("Sefo") (23), who lived next to the large tamarind that served as the village meeting place, was then chef de village. Sefo was formerly married to Soavita, an Antantety from the southern half of the village (38, see Fig. 11). His younger sister Jamali married one of Soavita's kinsmen. He had moved up to the northern half of the village, next to her parents, where he built the only house in Tsinjorano with a cement floor and metal roof (21). In 1973, they had separated. She had moved to Analalava, and he was in the process of moving the house out to his rice field; only the posts stuck in the cement were left.

The younger son's first wife was also a local person, one of his father's kin living in Tsinjorano. Almost all the tompontany siblings were surrounded by the households of their children, both sons and daughters. Togny was the only sibling whose spouse had kin living near them as well. Mainty Be was descended from Sambarivo (Antibe), some of whom still lived at the mahabo Lavalohaliky north of the Ambolobozo Peninsula (see Fig. 10). Mainty Be's F settled in Tsinjorano after marrying a woman who lived there. He was followed by a younger brother who married a woman from a neighboring coastal village. Mainty Be was the middle of three children. His eB brother lived in Tsinjorano, but died childless. His yZ Hibaka moved to her husband's village just north of Tsinjorano. A son and two daughters still lived in their F natal village; the other two daughters lived with their families in Nosy Be and Ambanja.

Mainty Be's FyB had one son Leroa. Leroa still lived in Tsinjorano (18), as did his two eldest children, his sons Tsimihimpa (20) and Mandiny (26). The marriage between Mainty Be's son AdanDezy and Leroa's daughter Sary (a FFyBSD) was the only instance of endogamy that I heard about in Tsinjorano. They separated shortly after they married, but AdanDezy still called his former wife's older brothers 'brother-in-law' *(valilahy)* rather than 'brother' *(rahalahy)*. Sary married a Hova policeman who worked at the penitentiary on Nosy Lava, and moved with him to Antananarivo, when he was transferred. AdanDezy then married Moana, his MZD's husband's sister, whom he would also have called *anabavy,* the term including female siblings. They met at the house of his MZD (his anabavy) and her B (anadahy) in Analalava. After their marriage, they moved to Tsinjorano, where they lived in his yZ's unused kitchen (25) and cultivated part of his parents' rice field, while they planned to build a house and granary of their own.

We met AdanDezy in Analalava, shortly after his marriage to Moana. He invited us to stay in Tsinjorano, where we lived in the house (20) of his 'brother-in-law' (FFyBSS) and his wife, Tsimihimpa and Ambina, who had already moved out to their garden-house.

Avoria (19, 22, 27, 28, 29, 30, 31). Like Togny, Avoria, a woman in her late fifties, had married locally and remained in Tsinjorano. Tsarajoro was an Ampanjaka Maroaomby. Like Togny's husband, he was a second generation resident, his father having moved to Tsinjorano from a village on the Loza River; unlike Mainty Bc, he had no other kin living in Tsinjorano.

Avoria and Tsarajoro lived in a large house (28) just south of the togny in the middle of the village, surrounded by the houses of all four of their surviving sons (27, 29, 30, 31).[3] Three of their daughters had married out, but they returned frequently to visit. (Togny and Mainty Be also raised one daughter's child, until it was old enough to be turned over to its FZ in Analalava). The daughter who was their oldest child had lived some ten years in her husband's village on Nosy Lava. Around 1967, they had returned to Tsinjorano and built a house (22) near her parents and close to a large garden they planted on the east side of the village. Their oldest child was living with her husband in Analalava, but their next oldest, a boy about to marry, was in the process of building a house (19) next to his parents.

The clusters of households around the two sisters, Togny and Avoria, were also linked in other ways. Togny's son, AdanDezy ('Dezy's Father'), who (like his elder brother Sefo) had yet to have children, was known respectfully after the name of Avoria's son's daughter Dezy (Bezara's daughter). AdanDezy's second wife was the husband's sister of Bezara's yZ Ampenjiky. Conversely, Bezara had formed a 'blood tie' (fatidra) friendship with AdanDezy's paternal kinsman, Leroa, formerly AdanDezy's *baba* (FFyBS) and now his 'father-in-law.' AdanDezy's marriage to Sary had separated his maternal and paternal kin as kin, but reconnected them as in-laws. The bond between Leroa and Bezara affirmed the status of Leroa and his kin as strangers by blood-tying the two men individually as brothers (Leroa was otherwise Bezara's 'male in-law,' *rafozana lahy*, MZHB). While AdanDezy (Dezy's Father) was called after the name of Bezara's daughter, Bezara was known respectfully as AdanMandiny (Mandiny's father), after Leroa's second son. The formation of 'blood ties,' linking people as brothers, sisters, (grand)parent-child, is discussed further in Chapter 5.

Zanety (4, 8, 9, 10, 14, 15, 16, 17). While the two middle sisters married men from Tsinjorano and settled there like their elder brothers, Zanety, like the oldest sister, moved out of Tsinjorano when she married a man from Andronjona, returning to Tsinjorano after they divorced. Her second husband lived in Tsinjorano (4). He came from a village on Nosy Lava, but like Avoria's daughter's husband (22), who came from the same place, Dedi had asked permission to live in Tsinjorano because he feared the prisoners who roamed the island. Dedi was eventually joined by paternal kinsmen from the same village—a pair of brothers who settled nearby (14, 15) and later a second pair of brothers (16, 17) in his children's generation. They were well situated in the northern half of the village, but their fields were farther from Tsinjorano than the next village, an hour's walk away.

Zanety and Dedi had two children before he died. The older daughter married a man from a village immediately south of Tsinjorano, but they kept a house (8) near Zanety in the northern half of Tsinjorano, where they also lived and cultivated. The younger son lived in Analalava during the dry season, when he was looking for wage labor. During the rainy season, he cultivated on the island of Morintsa, where his father's elder kinsmen also had fields. Tomobily was married to one of two sisters, whose mother worked for an Indian merchant in Analalava. The sisters were widely known as thieves who stole clothing drying on the banks of the stream south of Analalava where women did their washing, and took them out to the countryside to sell.

After Dedi died, Zanety often stayed at the Doany Miadana where her mother lived before she died and where her younger sister Meva had married. She and her sister were the only women to play the roles of royalty in some three dozen rebiky dances that I saw in 1972 and 1973. Their older brother's son Tombosa played one of the mañandria drums on that occasion.

Zanety's third husband, Ranapaka, was an Antantety from the southern part of Tsinjorano, related to the Antantety that Togny's children had married (see Fig. 12). Like Sefo's wife and Jamali's husband, Zanety's husband moved up to the northern half of Tsinjorano. They were in the process of building a house (9) east of Zanety's daughter's house (8) when they divorced, and Ranapaka moved away to his father's natal village to cultivate there. When Zanety returned from the Doany to cultivate in Tsinjorano during the rainy season of 1973, her brother's son and his family moved out to their rice field so she could live in their house (10) until she finished her own house.

Meva. Like Zanety, Meva also left Tsinjorano when she married a Sambarivo from the Doany Miadana. She still lived in her husband's natal village, where her mother used to live part of the year, and her siblings and siblings' children continued to visit, especially her older sister, Zanety.

Veloma (1, 2, 3, 5, 6, 7). Veloma and his wife (1) lived close to the households of their daughter and son (3, 2). Veloma's daughter (3) married a man from the village immediately south of Tsinjorano, related to the husband of Zanety's daughter (8). Veloma's son married a woman from the village immediately north of Tsinjorano, where his elder sister Amina's children were married (11). The son's two girls still lived with their parents, but the daughter's two oldest boys had already established their own houses (6, 7) south of their parent's house, while the youngest boys had begun to live independently in the "boys' house" *(trano gaoño)* nearby (5). The youngest boy was named Beloha (the name of his MFeB, the eldest of the tompontany siblings). The names of deceased relatives are usually prohibited. This is the only instance of a child given an ancestors' personal name that I learned about in Tsinjorano.

Antandrano–Antantety (32–41). The *toko* south of the cluster of households including Avoria, her husband the Ampanjaka Maroaomby, and their children, were the descendants of two siblings—a brother and a sister, whose father had married into the community (see Fig. 12). They were thus 'children of women,' like the descendants of the sisters among the current generation of tompontany siblings.

Maolidy, the second person recognized by Sambarivo at the Mahabo as a legitimate medium of the Grandfather, had lived in what people remembered as a 'very large house' in the southwestern part of the village (33). Her brother, who lived north of his sister (32), had since built his kitchen on the site. Tabory, then unmarried, had "followed a woman north," as his son put it. He was expected to return to Tsinjorano in the dry season; meanwhile his grandson was living in his house.

Tabory's son, Zara (34) and Maolidy's daughter Diniky (36), both of them in their forties, had houses and cultivations in Tsinjorano. Diniky was building a new house (35) east of the one in which she was currently living. She also had a house and rice field in the village on Nosy Lava to which Avoria and Zanety were connected through spouses and children's spouses. She cultivated there, and also—being between husbands—she *mitovo,* sought lovers from the many men there whose gifts provided her with scarce cash and goods like cooking oil and soap. Having no children of her own, Diniky had 'taken' *(nalain')* one of her brother Ranapaka's sons to care for.

Maolidy's son, Ranapaka, was first married to a woman from Ambolobozo, the village from which his father had come. Children and grandchildren from the marriage were still living in Tsinjorano (37–41), though one of them—a woman between husbands, like her FZ Diniky—also rented a house in Analalava. When Ranapaka later married Zanety, he began building a new house in the northern half of the village (9), but after they divorced, he returned to his father's village to cultivate.

Population Statistics for Analalava and Ampasikely, 1972–1973

Category of Population	14 years or less		15–20 years		20+ years		Total
	M	F	M	F	M	F	
Analalava							
Sakalava	214	821	31	120	918	1184	3288
Tsimihety	298	320	18	6	161	229	1032
Comorians	52	86	12	28	54	68	300
Indians	10	6	3	3	16	18	56
Vezo	7	3	—	—	3	9	22
Chinoise	1	2	—	—	1	(1)	4
Bara	1	—	—	—	4	—	5
Merina	56	52	11	8	58	52	237
Antandroy	2	—	—	—	5	—	7
Betsileo	12	14	—	2	12	8	48
Antimoro	6	22	—	—	18	3	49
Betsimisaraka	4	60	—	—	10	7	81
Makoa	189	101	21	28	169	106	614
Français	—	—	—	—	1	3	4
TOTALS	852	1487	96	195	1430	1687	5747

Category of Population	14 years or less		15–20 years		20 + years		Total
	M	F	M	F	M	F	
Ampasikely							
Merina	28	36	1	13	30	28	136
Betsileo	11	16	—	10	15	17	69
Tsimihety	13	23	6	—	8	12	62
Tanala	—	—	—	—	8	—	8
TOTALS	52	75	7	23	61	57	275

(compiled by the office of the Canton d'Analalava, Sous-Prefecture d'Analalava, Province de Majunga) (M = male; F = female).

Notes

Notes to Preface and Acknowledgments, pp. xix–xxiii.

1. Richards 1941.
2. Malinowski 1961:3.

Notes to Introduction, pp. 1–17.

1. Hocart 1970:135.
2. See, for example, Althabe 1969; Baré 1977; Bloch 1971, 1982; Decary 1962; Gueunier 1977; Huntington 1988; Kottak 1980; Rabedimy 1979; Rajaonarimanana 1979.
3. Deschamps 1959:247, 41.
4. Hocart 1927:231.
5. See Evans-Pritchard 1940:16–50.
6. Kantorowicz 1957; Giesey 1960, 1985.
7. See Fischer 1976.
8. Thompson 1967.
9. See, for example, Atkins 1988; Cooper 1977, 1980; Marks and Rathbone 1982; Mintz 1977, 1978; van Onselen 1976, 1982.
10. Mintz (1977:265) on labor relations in the Caribbean; see Cooper (1980:4, passim, 1977) for discussions of similar issues in European colonies in Africa.
11. See especially Cooper 1980:18–19.
12. Cooper 1980:3.
13. Johnstone 1976:193; Thompson 1967; van Onselen 1976.
14. Delelée-Desloges 1931:58.
15. Thompson 1967; see Harvey 1985:xii–xv on the "strong and almost overwhelming predisposition to give time and history priority over space and geography" on the part of "social theorists of all stripes and persuasions."
16. Decary and Castel 1941; Deschamps 1959.

17. Chevalier 1952:63.
18. Rose 1982.
19. Ibid.:28, 29.
20. Ibid.:30.
21. See, for example, Stack 1974.
22. Coser 1974.
23. Hayden 1976:33.
24. Giesey 1960, preface.
Giesey's account of the *hanouars* is one of the most graphic examples of this phenomenon.
25. Hocart 1937:345.
26. Bakhtin 1981:293.

Notes to Chapter 1, Ancestry, Land, and Labor, pp. 21–64.

1. Dez 1956:122; Bloch 1971:124–127; Baré 1977:94, 95; Kottak 1980:211.
2. Andriamanitra is the term for 'God' most often used by highland Christians in contrast to *Zanahary,* used locally for 'God' and for royal ancestors. *Doniàny,* or *donia* derives from Swahili *dùnia* (earth, the world, universe), which derives in turn from the Arabic term *al-dunya,* the "here and now," in contrast to *al-akhira,* "the other, viz. the other world, the end" (Krapf 1964:54, 302). See Lambek (1981:26) on the expression of these ideas among Malagasy speakers in Mayotte.
3. Basso 1983; Cohen et al. 1989; Fox 1979; Kuechler 1987; Kuipers 1984. See Simmel 1965.
4. Yates 1966.
5. See Bakhtin's 1937–1938 essay on "Forms of time and of the chronotope in the novel: notes toward a historical poetics"

(1981:84–258). In concluding remarks written in 1973, Bakhtin notes that the study of the temporal and spatial relationships in literature has just begun. Yet the focus has been mainly on temporal relationships apart from "the spatial relationships indissolubly tied up with them" (ibid.:258). See also Frank 1945; Knapp 1985; Lestringant 1982; MacDonald 1987. Casey's (1987) phenomenological study of remembering attempts to redress this same imbalance in philosophy.
6. Letter to Gillian Feeley-Harnik from Walter Woodman Wright (my MMZS), Paris, Maine, July 22, 1989.
7. The penitentiary on Nosy Lava, which had been one of three main penitentiaries in Madagascar, was made into the national penitentiary around 1970.
8. Occasionally, comparisons are made to people like *Sinoa* (Chinese), for example, how Sinoa eat pythons, but Malagasy don't— 'Ah! It can't be done. There might be spirits in them.' The most important points of comparison are to Silamo and highlanders, like the Merina.
9. Renel 1920–1921:162–163; Molet 1959; Deschamps 1959.
10. Deschamps 1959:63–64.
11. Ibid.:159, 180–189, 194–195, 269.
12. Association des Géographes de Madagascar 1969–1970, planche

21. The most recent census, held in 1975, was not published in its entirety. Assuming a population growth rate of 3.1 percent per annum, Covell (1987:xiii, 10) estimates the total population of Madagascar in 1984 at 9.9 million people.

13. The *firaisampokontany* is the second of four levels of government, including the *fokontany* (village or urban neighborhood), the *firaisampokontany* (district), the *fivondronampokontany* (region), and the *faritany* (province). See Covell (1987:111–113) for a discussion of the 1976 Charter of Decentralized Collectivities.

14. See Donque 1972.

15. Population density ranged from five to ten persons/sq km in the canton of Analalava, to two to five people/sq km in the Ambolobozo Peninsula and the northern Komajara Peninsula, to less than two persons/sq km in the Antognibe area. The town of Analalava had 1,433 residents in 1906 (Guide Annuaire 1906:383) and 1,787 residents, including 42 Europeans, around independence in 1960. Antognibe had a population of 981 in 1906. (I am grateful to Professor Pierre Vérin for showing me his copy of the *Monographie d'Analalava* for 1960. The more recent census followed the change of government in 1972–1973.)

16. Thompson and Adloff (1965:17) note that Anglo-French rivalries, dating back to the early nineteenth century, persisted into the colonial period with the identification of Merina aristocrats with English Protestantism and *côtiers* with "French Catholicism or secular republicanism, or both." These entanglements are still evident in relations between Protestants and Catholics in the Analalava region.

17. Fortes 1976:7.

18. Some people referred to the house where the body was prepared for burial as the *trano mañitry,* 'sweet-smelling house,' perhaps one source of the imagery in MamanDjoma's vision of Pepòny.

19. These differences in orientation, discussed further in Chapters 4, 5, and 6, were supported by other taboos distinguishing the places of the ancestors achieved through burial from the places of living, for example the taboo against sitting with the feet outstretched, or 'rising up towards the east' *(manonga antiñanana),* as if the living person were stepping down on the ancestors.

20. Richardson (1885:98) identifies the *bonara* tree as the leguminous *Albizzia Lebbek* Bth., noting that the common term comes from the French, *bois noir.*

21. Immediately after the burial, the siblings were embroiled in a bitter dispute over the inheritance of their parents' money and land.

The dispute began when the sister in Analalava was robbed of a valuable radio during the wake held in her home, and various brothers' sons were suspected of having taken it. The inheritance dispute derived from tensions between 'children of men' and 'children of women,' considered in subsequent chapters.

22. According to Dandouau (1911:157–158), who noted this prohibition, the eldest relatives of the dead person purified the interior of the house and the exteriors of neighboring houses by asperging them with chalk mixed in water. [This would have been *tany malandy*—the substance used for purifying, blessing, and assuaging pain in the context of royal service.] The accompanying statements, which he cites, suggest that people's fears about the retribution of the dead were accentuated when they were prevented from carrying out ancestral custom by burning the house: "May all the inhabitants of the village be well! May few persons die! May no one be rendered responsible for the violation of the prescriptions of the ancestors."

23. In Analalava, we rented a house owned by an Indian merchant. We wondered at our luck in having found a house on the water, where many people preferred to live because it was cool. Neighbors explained that it had been empty for some years because its former occupant—a policeman—had died there. In 1989, it had been turned into a bar.

24. The Malagasy phrase is *mitaña hidy,* "to grasp the lock". Hidy refers to anything used to shut or lock something; to the state of being locked or closed "comme les dents d'un mort"; and to anything prohibited. The reduplicative *hidihidy* refers to clenched teeth, obstinate silence, or angry words. The verb *mihidy vava* (literally, to close/lock the mouth) means to clench the mouth shut without being able to open it, or, figuratively, to keep an obstinate silence (Abinal and Malzac 1970:244–245).

25. Although I never heard anyone say it, "Sakalava" would also contrast with at least some other Malagasy ethnicities in this respect. For example, according to Kottak (1980:11), when a Betsileo man died, his eldest son took his place to the point of assuming his teknonyms.

26. Cited in Mellis 1938:65.

27. Dandouau 1911:165–172.

28. Dandouau 1922:7.

29. Dandouau 1911.

30. This may be one source of the important practice of 'mirror divination' *(sikidy fitaratra).* It may also account for why royal ancestors, who must keep separate from death, are forbidden to see

themselves in mirrors. The mirrors in their mediums' houses are covered with cloudy whorls of the 'white clay' they use in blessing people.

31. According to Mellis (1938:69), a long-time resident of the northwest coast during the first decades of colonial rule, royal deaths were also announced by saying, 'We [inclusive] are all eating excrement' *(Atsika jiaby mihina tay)*. Current guardians claimed never to have heard such a phrase, which would ordinarily be a form of 'cursing with filth' *(manasaha fôtaka)*, in which people are told to 'eat shit.'

32. Ibid.:167.

33. Ibid.:170.

34. Malaza of Andonaka commented in this context that the current ruler's father had a mistress in a neighboring village, who refused to destroy photographs of the two of them together. 'They [the royal ancestors] Strike!' *(Mamango!)* [What happened?] 'Dead!' *(Maty!)*.

35. See Noël 1843:56–57, 59.

36. His mother's brother, possessed by Ndramañavaka [Andriantsoly], a Zafinimena ancestor, had dictated the list to Bezara's younger sister who could write it down because she had been to school.

37. This emphasis on vision, seeing things in their places, was also expressed in the distinction that people made between 'what I saw with my own eyes [and therefore know] and what I heard' *(honoko)*.

38. See Noël 1844:389, who describes *midzourau âmi ni raza-ni* as invoking fathers' spirits and praying to them to intercede for their descendants with "*Zanahari,* singular divinity, of which, in spite of our efforts, it would be impossible to give a definition even the slightest bit exact."

39. One of the special prerogatives of the ampanjaka Maroaomby in Tsinjorano was the right to wrap his offering dish in the red cloth of royalty.

40. Malaza explained that *mijoro* is expressed as *mitakitaky* in the royal vocabulary. According to Launois's (1938) account of the architecture of the Southern Bemihisatra in Analalava during the mid-colonial period, the *taky* was the "ancestors' shelf in the northeast corner [of the north room of the house], where were placed the sacred dishes with earth coming from the tombs of different rulers, some incense, the ebony scepter, and the crown (in the form of a mitre)." He also showed a "trône" in the northeast corner of the south room of the house.

41. 'Beautiful/good' *(tsara)* and 'bad' *(ratsy)* are also synonyms for 'living' and 'dead' in speaking about royalty, for example: 'The ampanjaka when she was still living' *(izy mbola tsara)*. The current

ruler's Father died on Sunday, the Grandfather on Tuesday, the Great-Grandfather on Thursday, and the Brother on Wednesday.

42. See Feeley-Harnik 1988.

43. In the *kongo* service, the workers clear out dead leaves and branches and cut back the grass that grew during the preceding rainy season. Kongo is actually a generic term for biting insects, evoking an image of an animal, perhaps the bull to which royal ancestors are often compared, being cleaned of the venomous insects afflicting it. Thus, when I asked Laza Be, who worked for the living ruler, about the meaning of kongo, she began by describing kongo first as 'dirty things' *(raha maloto)*, then as 'living things that sit on cattle—big, biting,' going on from there to mention a smaller kind of insect that sits on the grass, bed bugs *(kongo mantsy*, foul smelling insect), and the like.

44. Tô mainty is the royal counterpart of ontso velo, mentioned earlier. Ontso velo (living water), made from raw honey to which cold water has been added, is the substance that 'simple people' use for cleansing various kinds of filth, including the filth of death. Tô mainty (also *tao mainty* and *tô/tao mahintigny)* is restricted to royalty. In contrast to ontso velo, tô mainty is made by cooking honey until it is black (whence the name, according to some royal

followers), then adding water to which bark chips from the *katrafay* tree *(Cedrelopsis grevei)* have been added to speed the fermentation process. Some royal followers derive tô from *toaka* (liquor), as we have seen. Tao is also the root of the verb *manao,* to do, make, accomplish. Comparable constructions include: *tao-vary,* rice-reaping, collecting and threshing; *tao-vato,* masonry; *tao-volo,* hairdressing; and *tao-zavatra,* manufacturing. These constructions refer not to the ingredients (i.e., a black thing, in Malagasy *raha mainty)*, but to the result of the process of making, i.e., "blackness."

It should be noted that some Sakalava during the colonial period referred to it, at least in writing, as *tao mañitra,* that is, "fragrantness, perfume." A letter written by royal officials to the ampanjaka Riziky in the northern part of the Ambolobozo Peninsula in April 1925, around the time when the tô mainty is made, notifies Riziky that "the tao mañitra [service] of your ancestors is coming up and we will bathe them [the royal ancestors] in July," admonishing her—"the royal ancestors' grandchild"—"not to change the customs of her ancestors" by neglecting to carry out the royal service in which it is made (cited in Poirier's report of 1926:18–19—his translation of the term as *époque parfumée,* which would be *taona manitra,* is inaccurate).

Perhaps participants' understanding of the significance of this liquid has changed over the past fifty years. More likely it is understood in many different ways. The relevance of alcohol has already been mentioned. Sakalava in the Analalava region commonly perfume dead bodies—those of commoners and royalty alike—with incense and cologne in preparing them for burial. The perfume and incense are explicitly intended to cover the smell of death. Perfume and incense are also important in spirit possession meetings involving "redeaths" as well as rebirths for spirits and mediums alike. Tô mainty is also used to "wash" the royal ancestors during the new year's service. "Blackness" is no less relevant because, as we will see later, every act of cleansing and clarifying the royal ancestors is matched by acts of covering and reburying them.

45. Offerings are given and blessings received in both hands, cupped together *(mandamban-tañana, mikopokopoina).* It is taboo to give or receive with one hand in relations with ancestors of any sort and disrespectful in relations among the living.

46. *Tsontsoraka* is a line of chalk applied from the tip of the nose upwards onto the forehead. Royal ancestors embodied in spirit-

mediums may also draw a circle of chalk in the petitioner's right palm, signifying money. I never heard the term used in any other context, but according to historical sources— Richardson (1885:717) and Abinal and Malzac (1970:793)—*tsontsona, tsontsoraka,* and *tsoraka* are all species of plants—a fibrous shrub from which cord is made (*Pavonia bojeri* sp. Baker), a kind of rattan, and a kind of bamboo respectively. Tsontsoraka and *tsora-kazo* (*kazo,* wood) may refer generally to a cane, slender stick, or rod, and *tsoraka* has the additional meaning of "well formed, straight, upright". According to Richardson (ibid.), Merina used tsontsoraka in sacrifices to their ancestors, placing it together with other "things" in the northeast corner of the house during their prayers (see Bloch 1986:52–55 for an account of the wild plants, considered to be "of a living mother," quick growing, and prolific, which are currently used in Merina circumcision rituals). Richardson adds that in the provinces, tsontsoraka means "superabundance", while the verb form *manontsoraka (havana)* means "to surpass others".

The *New Malagasy-English Dictionary,* prepared by the London Missionary Society missionary J. Richardson together with J. Andrianaivoravelona and J. Rajaofera, fellow pastor and student respectively, was first published in

1885. It incorporated two earlier missionaries' dictionaries published in 1835 and 1853. The "provincial," that is non-Merina, definitions come mainly from the dictionary of 1853. The Jesuit Fathers Abinal and Malzac incorporated all three of these dictionaries in preparing a Malagasy-French dictionary for the Mission Catholique de Tananarive in Madagascar in 1909. I use these dictionaries here and elsewhere in this book to get a broader historical and regional perspective on the variant and changing meanings of terms that are currently used in the Analalava area.

47. 'Your words are clean' *(Madio ny teninao)* is one of the highest form of praise that can be given to speech, because it implies clear truth, as is sometimes stated in such phrases as the following: 'Your words are clean. The things you say are true! There is nothing wrong about them, [you] don't lie.' *(Madio ny teninao. Raha lazainao marigny é! Tsisy raha diso amin'azy, tsy vandy.)*

48. A baby may also be given a French name, marking the day it was born according to French calendars of saints' days. *Nomenjanahary* has its equivalent in *Dieudonné.*

49. *Mirôtso,* meaning 'fallen down, decayed; fallen asleep' in common speech, is a euphemism in the royal vocabulary for 'to die'. 'Struck down' *(mamango)* and 'hit'

(voa) are the commonest ways of describing all forms of misfortune. Downness implies death in contrast to 'standing up' *(mitsangana),* an act and image of life and living, which recurs in a wide range of contexts, from people, whom a curer instructs to 'stand up, because you live; the thing aggravating you is gone now' *(mitsangàna, fa veloño anao, fa afaka ny raha migodaña anao),* to trees which are 'stood up' *(mampitsangana, mañangana)* to commemorate ancestors in villages (see Chapter 4).

50. Kin or friends of the possessed person put their hands on the back of the head and on the chin and carefully turn the head to one side and the other. Sometimes the shoulders are also twisted. Then they press the limbs, especially the neck and shoulders, to get the hurt out. Participants in spirit possession gatherings also explained these practices in terms of the strength of the spirit, who was seen as 'coming [down] to rule' *(mianjaka)* on the head of the medium, and later 'rising up' *(misondotro)* to leave. One woman said it this way: "This [twisting the body and pressing the limbs] is done because the spirit is strong! *(Zanahary fatatra!).* He really exhausts the body. After he leaves, the whole body aches. This is to stop it, just to take away the ache, so [the medium] feels less exhausted."

51. See Feeley-Harnik 1989.

52. *Boana,* a Swahili term of address derived from Arabic *abuana* (our father), is one of the respectful terms of address used with Sakalava royalty. *Moana,* its female counterpart is used only as a woman's personal name. *Boanalahy,* 'male Bwana' or 'Bwana-man,' is an intensification of the male aspect of the term. The living ruler, a woman, is addressed as Boana in Malagasy. Some people also used the term *Princesse* that French colonial officials used. A very few, aware of the discrepancy, used the term *Prince* as a term of reference, though never as a term of address.

Sarovola is another praise name for Ndramisara, the first among the first four progenitors of the Maroseraña dynasty who, collectively known as Ndramisara, constitute the root of the monarchy, implying the monarchy as a whole. The word is a compound of *sarotra + vola,* difficult, demanding, valuable costly + wealth, money. Sakalava often refer to the royal ancestors collectively as *raha sarotra,* difficult, precious things. The addition of vola intensifies the idea of immense wealth implicit in the name of the senior branch of the dynasty, the Zafinimena (Descendants of the Red/Gold), short for Zafimbolamena (Descendants of the Gold) in the contrast to the Zafinifotsy/Zafimbolafotsy (Descendants of the White/Silver).

Whole and cut coins were central to the foreign trade on which the monarchy was based since its beginnings. Whole coins were used in paying respect to the ancestors, and coinage was also melted down to make jewelry. Silver coins are still essential to royal services, and the color red still serves to summarize the greatness of the Zafinimena to which the Southern Bemihisatra belong.

53. To describe something as fat, heavy, thick or dense, is also a way of saying that it is big, important, and well known. *Tavy,* fat(ness) also refers to the cultivations, usually rice fields, created by slash-and-burn agriculture. The singer interpreted *Sarovola . . . tsy lany tavy* to mean that "his wealth, opulence, and beauty is inexhaustible; I will just always love him; his goodness can never be bad." She repeated these sentiments in explaining "Honey mixed with salt" as being "something good and beautiful, sweet and salty, powerfully efficacious," the word *(masina)* for salty and powerfully efficacious.

54. Like the language of the royal blessing in which petitioners "receive the ruler," the words of the song seem to incorporate the language of New Testament Christianity in which English and French work ethics were often presented in Madagascar. If this is the source of the imagery, the

singer is using it to explain why such ethics are rejected. London Missionary Society missionaries founded a mission among Sakalava in Majunga in 1872 (Gow 1979:203). The following words from *Asa* [Works, i.e., Acts] 20:28 were printed across the top of the formal agreement to convert: "The Church of God which he hath purchased with his own blood" *(Ny Fiangonan' Andriamanitra izay novidiny tamin' ny rany)* (London Missionary Society Archives, Odds Box 4. "Betsileo/Merina words compared—and Sihanaka" by Dr. Mackay, written on the backside of an L.M.S. agreement form, *Fanekena Hataon' Ny Olona Vao Manatona Fiangonana,* dated 189–).

55. François, the Inspecteur Général de l'Agriculture aux Colonies, described the mango tree *(Mangifera indica)* in rich soil as "the most opulent species in the country [of the west coast] . . . a superb tree" (1937:45). Mango trees can grow to immense size in western Madagascar. The trunk *(tronga)* of medium-sized trees is more than human in height and girth. The mature leaves, six to sixteen inches long, with wavy edges and tapered ends, look like spearheads, the insignia of Sakalava royalty. The dark leathery green body of the tree is crowned with the dark to bright red leaves of the young shoots with which the tree continually renews itself. Its dense foliage provides shade throughout the year. Most kinds of mango trees produce two crops in succession at the beginning of the rainy season. One—*manga antongombato* or *manga Diégo*—fruits continuously throughout the year.

56. To describe someone as *malaigny,* 'reluctant,' is a common indirect way of saying they refuse to agree *(tsy mañeky)* to do what others claim they are obligated to do or wish them to do. Malaigny also means unloving.

57. The singer explained *Trongay* as "the place where the royal ancestors lived first when they arrived in Madagascar from abroad." The place name may derive from the root tronga, meaning tree trunk.

58. Zafinimena, which looks like 'Grandchildren of Red' is a shortened form of Zafimbolamena, 'Grandchildren of Gold'.

59. People in the Analalava region who identify themselves as "Tsimihety" explained the Zafinifotsy as Tsimihety from Androna, that is, from the uplands as opposed to the coast, like themselves. The Zafinifotsy committed suicide by drowning themselves in the Loza because, as one person put it, they were 'reluctant about the Hova *(malaigny Hova).* Better to go in the water than to assent to Hova rule *(mañeky fanjakaña hova).*' Their spirits are described as 'the royal spirits from the water' *(ley tromba boka an-drano),*

and the term *doany*, applied to their memorial places in the mouth of the Loza, was said to mean a 'grave in the water' *(fasigny an-drano)* as opposed to a *mahabo* or 'grave on land' *(fasigny an-tety)*. Throughout the area, Zafinifotsy royal spirits were consulted concerning issues having to do with the water, whereas the Zafinimena had priority in issues having to do with the land. Besides dramatizing far-reaching oppositions between highland and coastal people, land and water, they also play a role in representing differences among siblings and their descendants, between 'children of men' identified with the Zafinimena and 'children of women' identified with the Zafinifotsy, a topic discussed in Chapters 4 and 5.

60. Many of the slaves that Arab and later European traders imported into Madagascar from Africa came from northern Mozambique and southern Tanzania, where an ethnic group known as Makua is still recognized, whence the generic Malagasy terms (Makoa, Masombiky) for any slave of African origin. Richardson (1885:806) defines *amporia* (literally, at the asshole) as a provincial word for slave. I never heard that phrase, but the similarity in construction to *andevo* (locative + substantive) suggests that andevo may derive from the root *levona*, which Richardson defines as the condition

of being "consumed, dissolved, utterly destroyed; spread over the whole surface of the body, as scabies or leprosy . . . completely spoiled; fig., to be in great want or distress," whence perhaps *an-devona* or andevo (-na is often dropped), a person in a condition of extreme misery.

61. They were sometimes called 'ampanjaka who get respect' *(ampanjaka mahazo koezy)*, *koezy* being the respectful greeting given to royalty. They had the right to the greeting, but not the right to make the fence, known as *valamena*, distinguishing their ancestors from those of others.

62. See also Dandouau (1911:163), who quotes from a funeral oration given in the Analalava region: "You are not a person without relatives; you have on the contrary esteemed relatives, relatives who have ancestral spirits."

The monarchies of the Southern Sakalava of Menabe seem to have been organized along similar lines. Slaves were known as "no ancestors." Those permitted to have ancestors were ranked in authority by their ancestors, from the royal ancestors *(dady)*, to the ancestors of nobles and "masters of the land" *(raza be,* great ancestors), to the ancestors of commoners *(raza,* ancestors) (Lombard 1973:92). According to Rey's (1913:70–71) earlier account, only rulers and descendants of collateral royal lines had the right to ancestors. When rulers ennobled subjects, giving them privileges and duties transmittible to their descendants, they also gave them the right to recognize ancestors. The powerful ancestries that resulted became known as "people with ancestors" *(olo misy raza)* or "people that grow like the creeping, climbing, branching vine known as *vahy*" *(vahin'olo)*. Freemen and slaves "apparently had no ancestors," while "tributary or protected groups . . . conserved their ancestral traditions" (ibid.).

One slave who had recently escaped from an Arab ship told the S.P.G. missionary E.O. McMahon, traveling near the mouth of the Tsiribihina River in 1888, that captured women crying for water (and dying of thirst at the rate of three to five a day) were told: "You have no father and mother here" (McMahon 1892:392).

63. A ruler might grant some of these rights under certain conditions. In the 1920s, the current ruler's father granted a famous spirit-medium named Tsimijotso rights to use royal *mañandria drums* and to build a *valamena* (red fence) for the ancestral spirit's shrine because the ancestor was so far from Mahajanga, where its actual doany was located. Later, when French authorities arrested the medium on suspicion of subversion, the drums were confiscated and sent to the Prefet's Résidence.

64. Noël 1843:303.

65. Royal followers once used *Adabara,* an Arabic term for the star that forms the eye of the constellation of the Bull, to refer to the fourth day of the month and in divination (Ferrand 1902, vol. 3, p. 42). The qualifier *tokana*—one, alone, set apart—intensifies the uniqueness of the eye and the sea eagle, a solitary bird. Richardson (1885:54) identifies the sea eagle as *Haliatus vociferoides* Des Murs. In other words, Sakalava royalty is uniquely great everywhere. This open insistence on the personal singularity is specific to royalty. Despite the common emphasis on the unique fates of all people, discussed in Chapters 4 and 5, people in the Analalava region rarely singled themselves out as "I." When they did, it was usually used to draw attention to their personal inadequacy, for example, their meager speech, their meager gift.

66. The Bemazava branch of Sakalava royalty developed in opposition to the Bemihisatra branch during the early nineteenth century, and members of the two ancestries, as well as their followers, still define themselves and each other, in terms of their mutual oppositions. Bemazava, now concentrated in the Ambanja and Maromandia areas of northwestern Madagascar, do not

follow Bemihisatra prohibitions on kin. They see themselves as having numerous descendants because they chose to give up the Vy Lava to the Bemihisatra. They also contrast with the Bemihisatra in having converted to Christianity. Ndremahazo Jean-Pierre, from Maromandia, taught in the Catholic Mission in Analalava.

The Northern Bemihisatra officials to whom Baré spoke in the early 1970s expressed the same sentiments in almost exactly the same terms, describing the mitaha as something that makes an ampanjaka of someone *(maha ampanjaka)*, which is 'the companion of the Vy Lava,' and which royalty involved in wars between kin *(ady milongo)* use to kill each other, 'to mutually kill friends' *(mifamono naman')*. Like the Bemazava, the Northern Bemihisatra also claim to have had the Vy Lava, and then "abandoned it" because of its deadly power. See Baré 1980:241–242.

67. See Beidelman 1980.
68. Fortes 1976:7.
69. See Fortes 1961, 1965, 1981; Kopytoff 1971, 1981; Brain 1973; Calhoun 1980, 1981.
70. Fortes 1965:140.
71. See Glazier 1984; Feeley-Harnik 1989.

Notes to Chapter 2, Deadly Blessings, pp. 65–113.

1. Mitahy (to bless, help, save, carry carefully) is one of a group of related verbs with overlapping semantic fields, including *mitaha* (to care for, cure) and *mitahiry* (to care for, preserve, guard). Royal guardians and followers of the southern branch of the Bemihisatra in the Analalava region assert that the royal ancestors are called Mitahy, not Mitaha, and they use the term Mitahy in their personal correspondence. Their written histories refer to the royal ancestors embodied in relics and regalia as (Ny) Mitaha, and this is also the term in current use among the Northern Bemihisatra in the Nosy Be/Ambanja area (Baré 1980:240–241). Applied to the living ruler, the phrase *mitaha ampanjaka* means not only "to care for the sovereign, to keep him living," but also "connotes secrecy, [in the words of one of Baré's informants] 'in that sense the ruler does not go out, cannot be seen by many people'"(ibid.).

2. See Berg 1986.
3. See Bloch 1986.
4. See also Bloch 1971 and 1982 for earlier statements of this argument, based on analyses of Merina reburials.
5. Bloch 1971:156; 1982:227; see Feeley-Harnik 1989 for further discussion of women's roles in the use of cloth in Sakalava spirit possession ceremonies, which are comparable in form to Merina reburials.
6. Several tantara about the Maroseraña or Zafimbolamena rulers were put in writing during

the first three decades of French colonial rule. Some of these (Anonymous circa 1908a, 1908b, 1908c), probably composed in the Mahajanga region, may have been inspired by the publication of Merina oral traditions—the *Tantaran' ny Andriana* or *Histoires des rois,* collected by French Jesuit missionaries during the latter half of the nineteenth century and published in 1908. According to the heads of the guardians of the Mahabo in the Analalava region, their grandfather (FF) was the first to put the Southern Bemihisatra histories into writing in the late nineteenth century.

Although earlier Sakalava manuscripts have yet to be found, Kent (1970:191–192) believes that Sakalava in the Mahajanga area had an important history written in Arabic script, which was destroyed in a fire. Guillain (1845), who derived his *Documents sur l'histoires,* discussed in this chapter, from oral traditions current in 1842–1843, testifies that royal followers had a lively interest in the history of the monarchy:

> In all the places that we have visited in the Sakalava lands, we have found the events and the names that they recall still living in the memory of the populations, and exciting in them an enthusiasm and a veneration that can only be the result of faith; we have heard the Sakalava

invoke these names in all the important acts of their social life, recall with pride these events to those who seem unaware of their past grandeur and, in the presence of this testimony from an entire people, it was difficult for us to remain completely incredulous (ibid.:9–10).

People in the Analalava region, regardless of ethnic affiliation, describe tantara as 'true' *(marigny)* accounts of events, in contrast to *angano,* stories that are always asserted at the end to be 'not I [the teller] lying but elders before' *(tsy zaho mavandy fa olo be taloha).* Some guardians at the Doany and the Mahabo made notes on specific royal services, especially details concerning times, places, numbers of persons present, and the kinds and quantities of gifts. Their notes on the ampanjaka's return to Analalava from abroad (France) in 1962 are an example of this (see Plate 35). See Feeley-Harnik (1978) for further discussion of tantara in the Analalava region.

7. Since the Southern Bemihisatra histories were put into writing around the time of the succession battle in the mid-twenties, it is possible that specific dates and perhaps particular incidents may have been borrowed from French histories as a way of using French techniques of legitimation to defeat French efforts to delegitimize the Southern

Bemihisatra monarchy.
Nevertheless, the use of specific
dates seems to have been a long-
standing practice in the region. In
presenting oral traditions collected
in 1842–1843, Guillain notes that
traditions concerning the earliest
ancestors were not dated. He
extrapolates dates from a variety of
published accounts of Europeans
(e.g., 1845:8–9, 32, 369–370) and
reckons from lengths of reigns, a
common feature also in the
Southern Bemihisatra histories
(e.g., ibid.:22, 35). Beginning with
the reign of Andriantsoly, a ruler
who converted to Islam shortly
after becoming ampanjaka in 1824,
he provides dates in the Islamic
lunar calendar, still used in
northwestern Madagascar, with the
corresponding Gregorian dates in
parentheses (e.g., ibid.:67ff, 121,
128, 130, 131; see also Ferrand
1908:13–17). The correspondence of
the Southern Bemihisatra ruler
Añono in the Analalava region in
1865–1891 was all in Arabic, using
Arabic dates (Centre des Archives
d'Outre-mer [CAOM] 4 Z 8).

8. A second history—*Naviany
Razaniampanjaka*—incorporates
some details of the royal ancestors'
lives into the chronicle of their
births and deaths, concluding with
Soazara's birth. A third history,
consisting only of a list, identifies
"25 mpanjaka nanjaka," divided
into five numbered *fehiny* or
networks of kin related to specific

ancestors. These include
(1) Andriandahifotsy,
(2) Andriamandisoarivo,
(3) Andriamboeniarivo,
(4) Andriamarofaly, and
(5) Tsimisarakarivo, with whom
Andriamamahanarivo is shown to
be affiliated. A fourth, *Fomban' Ny
Ampanjaka Sakalava,* chronicling
the birth of the Soazara's first child,
a daughter born in 1955, begins the
same as the first history. Here, the
list is more explicit in identifying
the ampanjaka as "coming from
Basiroly in Araby, two male
ampanjaka descended from
Ibrahim" [the first two names],
who "crossed over to Madagascar,
landing at Toliameva on the
southwest coast [where] they
created Malagasy Sakalava
government" *(namorona fanjakana
gasy Sakalava)*. It also phrases the
list in terms of who gave birth to
whom, for example:

2. Marosiranana gave birth to
   Andriamiandrivola and
   Andrianalimbe did not give
   birth.
3. Andriamiandrivola gave birth
   to Andriamandimby and
   Andriantahoranarivo.
4. Andriamandimby gave birth
   to Andriamisara and
   Andriantahoranarivo did not
   give birth.
5. Andriamisara gave birth to
   Andriandahifotsy

The form X gave birth to

(niteraka) Y is also common in Merina histories. See Berg (1980) for a discussion of ideas about generation conveyed in Merina tantara.

Royal followers currently describe the Southern Bemihisatra as a branch of the Zafimbolamena or, more rarely, Maroseraña dynasty, terms that date back at least to the 1840s (see Guillain 1845:11). Nevertheless, these terms are not used in the histories. The royalty are simply "Rulers" (Ampanjaka), "Ancestors of the ampanjaka" (Razaniampanjaka), or "Sakalava Rulers" (Ampanjaka Sakalava); Marosiranana is an early ruler's name.

9. See Anonymous circa 1908b. The Southern Bemihisatra histories credit Andriamisara—as founder-ruler, or, according to other histories, as a diviner-healer *(moasy)* attached to the ruler Ndramboay—with conceiving the idea of the "Grandparents" *(Dady)*.

10. Grandidier and Grandidier 1903–1920, vol. 2, pp. 245–246; see also the observations of his contemporary, Père Louis Mariano, ibid., vol. 1., pp. 228–233.

11. Grandidier and Grandidier 1903–1920, vol. 6, pp. 127–128. According to Southern Bemihisatra histories, Andriamandisoarivo died around 1720, after ruling some thirty years; his son Andriamboniarivo died about ten years later. The relics of Andriamisara, Andriandahifotsy, Andriamandisoarivo, and Andriamboniarivo, known collectively as "Andriamisara four men" *(Andriamisara efadahy)*, have long been associated with the doany Andriamisara at Mahabibo (now Miarinarivo) near Mahajanga. These may have been the relics that the sailors from the *De Brack* saw in 1741.

12. Boudou 1941, vol. 1, p. 252.

13. Guillain 1845:31–32, n. 2.

14. Rey 1913:70. Rey also noted that the relics were entrusted to porter-guardians *(mpiboho)*, chosen from among "the greatest noble families," who were supposed to bear them away to a secure place at the first sign of attack, and who were always killed if they failed. Relics seized or recovered from enemies were purified by plunging them into clear streams every day for a month. These ceremonies included the sacrifice of large numbers of cattle as well as "immense orgies," after which the relics, confided to the care of new porters, were replaced in the *jomba* or "royal house" (Rey 1913:70).

15. Guillain (1845:19–20) names Andriamandisoarivo's doany as Tongaï, which he derives from *tonga (arriver, parvenir),* which would be analogous to *toly,* as in Toliamaeva, though he does not draw the parallel. The root, tronga, meaning tree trunk, may be an allusion to the image of the

Maroseraña dynasty as an enormous ever-growing tree.

16. Armstrong 1982, 1983–1984; Campbell 1983–1984; Filliot 1974; Rasoamiaramanana 1983–1984; Vérin 1986; and the special issue of *Slavery and Abolition* 9 (1988) on the Indian Ocean trade.

17. Armstrong (1983–1984:212–215), who notes that although data on Arab, Portuguese, and English trading is fragmentary, the activities of the Dutch East India Company in this area during the seventeenth and eighteenth centuries are well documented.

18. Armstrong (1982:13).

19. Ibid.:14.

20. Armstrong (1983–1984:213). One of the Englishmen, who had traded with Lahefoutsy (now called Andriandahifotsy) noted that he died in late 1683, "succeeded by his eldest son" (ibid.:220). Arabs are rarely mentioned as trading in southwestern ports, perhaps owing to problems of navigating dhows south of Cape St. Andre, about two hundred kilometers south of Boina Bay (ibid.:221). This may account for why local rulers, at war with one another, were able to establish control over the trade in the southwest, which may have assisted them later in taking control over the northwest as well.

21. Ibid.:214. An English account from 1640 notes that "country people, the Hovas" came in March and April to trade two to three thousand slaves with residents of the town, who resold them to Muslim and Portuguese traders (ibid.). A Dutch ship, trading in the northeast Antongil Bay, found that the local ruler had been "obliged" to sell all his slaves on the other side of the island (ibid.:214, 223).

22. Armstrong (ibid.:215) suggests that the Dutch report of August 15, 1686 may be the earliest use of the name "Sakalava" in European documents.

23. Ibid.:227; Filliot 1974.

24. Guillain 1845:33; see Gevrey 1972:112–113; Vérin 1986:120–130.

25. Armstrong (ibid.:220–221). Armstrong (ibid.:221) notes that the demand for guns gave Europeans an advantage over Arabs "who had few or no such weapons to trade." See also Rasoamiaramanana (1983–1984) for details concerning the slave trade from Mahajanga in the second half of the nineteenth century, involving the Merina who then occupied the area, and Campbell (1988) for the related use of forced labor in Imerina.

26. Rey 1913:70–71.

27. Ibid. Rey (ibid.:71–74) lists ennobled kin groups, some of which are characterized in terms of their work for Sakalava royalty, e.g., *Tiarea,* "guardians of the royal cattle"; *Ranontoaka* who "made alcohol for the king"; *vangohazo,* "carpenters or sculptors charged with the construction and ornamentation of royal buildings

and tombs"; *valahy*, "personal body guards." Neither Rey nor Lombard and Rabedimy, who later did ethnographic research in the region, discuss how these workers were organized.

28. Southern Bemihisatra often distinguish followers of the royal ancestors in Menabe, south of the Doany Miarinarivo in Mahajanga, as Sakalava Ambalaka (Southern Sakalava) in contrast to Sakalava Avaratra (Northern Sakalava), followers of the royal ancestors of Boina. This distinction dates back at least to the 1840s (see Guillain 1845:7).

29. Southern Bemihisatra tantara identify Andriamanentiarivo as ancestral to [Pierre] Kamamy, ampanjaka of the Southern Sakalava of Menabe, whose doany was located in Belo-sur-Tsiribihina. According to Raharijaona and Valette (1959:annexe), Kamamy, who was ampanjaka during the fitampoha or washing of the royal relics that they witnessed in 1958, had taken office in 1897. He died sometime between 1957 and the next fitampoha in 1968, when he was one of the ancestors (dady) who were washed (Lombard 1973:23).

30. According to both Noël (1843–1844) and Guillain (1845), followers of the Volamena or Maroseraña dynasty in the south (Menabe) and north (Boina) called themselves "Sakalava." I will use

this term in speaking of the accounts they document in order to distinguish them from the Southern Bemihisatra tantara from the Analalava region from around 1925. In most cases, I have changed their phonetic spelling of Malagasy words to my own.

Noël was an agent consulaire, stationed in Zanzibar (Decary 1960:25). He says about the king list, with which he concludes one installment of his account, that he got his information from *"un Sakkalava parfaitement instruit de l'histoire de son pays, Nahikou, principal conseiller du roi de Mayotte,"* in contrast to Guillain, whose information comes he says, from "diverse persons, as much Arabs as AntiBoina" (1843, vol. 19:294–295, 288). Later, Noël (1843, vol. 20:53) describes Nahikou as Tsiomeko's prime minister. Noël got other information, especially on Mayotte from an Arab whom Tsiomeko's followers killed after he left (1843, vol. 20:40–41).

Guillain was a capitaine de corvette in the French Navy. He cites the historical sources he uses, and he notes (1845:10, n. 1) that he follows Noël in linguistic matters, since he seems to be the most linguistically competent of the "very small number" who have studied the Sakalava language; but does not identify the people from whom he received oral accounts. Promoted to capitaine de vaisseau,

Guillain went on in 1846–1848 to do a comparable study of the East African coast.

31. Noël's (1843, vol. 20:63–64) point of departure is the deposition of Andriantsoly in favor of his sister Oantity in 1832. He then traces the decision back to the transition from men to women, endogamy to exogamy, beginning with the daughters of Andriamahatindriarivo, as does Guillain (1845:29–30).

32. See, for example, Noël 1843, vol. 19:289, 1844:416; Guillain 1845:143.

33. Guillain 1845:110–112.

34. Noël 1843, vol. 20:63.

35. Guillain 1845:72.

36. Ibid.:23.

37. Ibid.:26. Guillain also notes that the first of the six daughters born of their union was named "Tsafantouki (the independent, the all-powerful), alluding to her birth from the son and daughter of royalty which put her above every other member of the royal family." After her death, she was given the praise name Andriamamolakarivo, Noble Who Broke/Subdued Thousands, another allusion to great strength, which could also mean Noble Who Made Thousands Filthy. Since *Folaka ny tany* (The land is polluted) was used to announce royal deaths, the praise name might also have been an illusion to the disasters that royal followers now trace to this brother-sister marriage. Ndramamolaka—now remembered as a male ruler from Madirovalo near Mahajanga—was one of the ancestral spirits who most often possessed women in the Analalava region in the 1970s. Although he was the most aggressive of the early royal spirits, he still ranked below the founder-ancestors like Ndramandisoarivo, as expressed, e.g., in his sharing eating utensils with 'simple people'.

38. Noël 1843, vol. 19:292; Guillain 1845:30.

39. Noël 1843, vol. 20:63–64; see also Guillain 1845:23, n. 1, 30, 47. Earlier, Noël (1843, vol. 20:55) notes three kinds of Sakalava royalty: "*Ampanjaka mahery n'fanjaka* or princes skilled at ruling"; "Ampanjaka, distant or dubious kin of royalty"; and "*anaka n'driana,* the descendants of the principal families who have followed the Voulamena in their conquests."

40. Guillain 1845:31.

41. Noël 1843, vol. 19:287–289.

42. Ibid.:287, 288, 289.

43. Guillain 1845:31.

44. Even as Guillain, like Noël, supported Andriantsoly over his sister's daughter's daughter, Tsiomeko, so he also supported Maka's son Tsimandroho over Tsiomeko on the grounds that Tsimandroho's father was related to the Volamena dynasty solely through women in contrast to Tsiomeko's mother's mother's

father, Oza, who was related through both men and women. For his discussion of Maka and his efforts to seize power from Vahiny, see Guillain (1845:14, 21–31, 46–47). The relationship between the Bemihisatra and the Bemazava branch of the Volamena dynasty, which Southern Bemihisatra still see as their junior, exemplifying all that they are not, will be discussed in more detail elsewhere.

45. Guillain 1845:146.

46. Malagasy in the Analalava region describe highlanders, like the Merina, and Muslims living around them, as practicing endogamy, which they themselves see as a form of incest. Brothers and sisters, though very close, are expected to marry "strangers," people who are not kin (see Chapter 4; Gardenier 1976:104, 109; Baré 1974; Lambek 1981:21–22). See Bloch 1971; Huntington 1978; and Middleton 1990 on endogamous unions among the Merina, Bara, and Karembola in central and southern Madagascar.

47. *Andriamahatindriarivo nandova fanjakanan' i rainy Andriamboniarivo nanjaka roa ambiny folo taona 1786–1797.* *Andriamarofaly zanany nandova fanjakanan' i rainy nanjaka valo toana izy 1797–1804 robaka fanjakana tamin' io satria olona bekibo voatrahany olona ampianadahy ampivadiny niteraka iray izy*

1. *Andriamamelonarivo   vavy*
   Io koa nandova fanjakanan' i

rainy nanjaka dimi ambiny roa polo toana 1804–1828. Izy no niteraka Andriamandrangitriarivo lahy ary Andriamandrangitriarivo koa niteraka efatra:

1. *Andriamanesiarivo   lahy*
2. *Andriamanorinarivo   vavy*
3. *Andrianatolotrarivo   vavy*
4. *Andriamanavakarivo   lahy*

48. In this translation, *voatrahany,* possibly *voatrany,* is derived from the passive verb *voatrahana* (to be made erect, raised, lifted up, stood up with the head erect) (see Richardson 1885:673). One Malagasy informant derived it from voatrany, eviscerated, like a fish, explaining what she saw as a crude term for birth by saying that such a marriage was utterly prohibited and thus could only have such a terrible outcome. "A pregnant person eviscerated [like a fish] by people, brother and sister, husband and wife . . ." could conceivably refer to Andriamahatindriarivo, who married his sister, who is remembered as having pursued his rivals so brutally that he tore them as babies from their mothers' wombs; such an incident is included in the Sakalava tantara that Noël recounts, identifying Andriamahatindriarivo as the father of Vahiny. Noël provides no details concerning their marriages, incestuous, endogamous, hypergamous, or otherwise (Noël 1843, vol. 19:292). *Niteraka iray izy* could still refer to Andriamarofaly

who bore Andriamameloñarivo. In either case, the brother-sister marriage remains the source of ruin.

49. A little earlier, when I was peeling potatoes, she said, *"Pièces de terra? [pommes de terre]*—Ah! Makoa don't know!" using the term still applied to people who identified themselves or were described by others as the descendants of former slaves from Africa.

50. Doctrines based on European notions of race and racial purity, claiming that the Merina were descended from original Asian immigrants to Madagascar, while coastal people, mixed with imported slaves, were predominantly African, developed gradually during the eighteenth and nineteenth centuries and became widespread during the colonial period.

51. Mola is the root of Ndramamolaka, the praise name of Tsafantoky, the firstborn of the incestuous union (see note 37).

52. In 1989, in the wake of efforts by Andriantsoly's descendants to get back the Vy Lava a couple of years earlier, royal followers in the Analalava region insisted that Soazara was the rightful holder of the Vy Lava because she was a 'child of men,' as evident in the line of male ancestors buried on Nosy Lava. Earlier statements that she was a 'child of women' were 'all wrong.'

According to people in the Analalava region, Andriantsoly's descendants said they had given up the ancestors embodied in the Vy Lava so they could have numerous children. Now they had many children, but no money, so they wanted the wealth that followers (through the ancestral Vy Lava) would give them. These recent reinterpretations of royal history, related to changes in relations between children and wealth, will be discussed elsewhere.

53. Guillain's (1845) detailed description of Hova expansion correlates closely with archival sources from Imerina, as well as London Missionary Society accounts, Robin's journal from 1820, and Hastie's journal from 1824 (Gerald Berg, personal communication, July 1988). People in the Analalava region still use "Hova" to refer to Merina.

54. Guillain notes that "The sovereigns of diverse parts of Madagascar have always been in the habit of giving gifts to one another when they live on good terms" (1845:370, n. P). Sakalava told Guillain that Vahiny became so close with Andrianampoinimerina's sister that the sister made Vahiny her heir (ibid.:32). Vahiny's Hova affiliations are evident in the Merina form of her name, Ravahiny (Stranger), by which she is best known outside the Sakalava domains.

Another contemporary, James Hastie—"The British Agent" whom Farquhar, Governor of Mauritius, appointed as his representative to the Merina court—noted in his journal from 1824–1825 that during the exchange of oaths between Radama and Andriantsoly's emissaries in Antananarivo on November 14, following the invasion, Radama declared that the inhabitants of Boina were not his subjects but part of his own family. He also instructed the Sakalava to increase agricultural production for the market (Hastie 1968:113–115). I am grateful to Gerald Berg for drawing my attention to this reference.

55. Guillain 1845:54–67.

56. Raharijaona and Valette 1959.

57. Compare, for example, W. Ellis 1838, vol. 2, p. 477, see pp. 472–473; Poirier 1939a, planches II, III; Lombard 1976:175; Raison-Jourde 1984, planches 11, 19, 21, 28; Mack 1988, plates 48–49, 64. Guillain (1845:60) notes that Hova desecrated Sakalava tombs in 1821. The respect of the Merina for their *sampy,* embodiments of powerful spirits closely associated with royalty, is evident in Merina royal traditions known as the *Tantaran' ny Andriana,* collected during the second half of the nineteenth century (Callet 1974: passim). Though Ranavalona II burned many of the sampy on September 8 and 9, 1869, after converting to

Protestantism, they did not lose the respect of rural people (Berg 1986:191–192). A Malagasy correspondent for a Protestant magazine *Teny Soa* (Good Words) wrote about the "Sakalava royal ancestors" in Majunga in 1872. Describing the four relics encased in images of crocodiles' teeth, he commented several times on their close resemblance to Merina sampy (R-N-J-S 1872:45, 47). *Teny Soa* was the monthly magazine of the L.M.S. Theological College (founded 1870) in Antananarivo. Although edited by English missionaries, it became an important place for the expression of Malagasy views, selling some 3,000 copies a year in the 1880s (Gow 1979:138–139). S. Ellis's (1985) work on the *menalamba* rebels in Imerina in 1895–1899 shows the continued power of the sampy in highland politics even after their suppression.

58. Guillain 1845:67–68. Guillain attributes Tsolovola's conversion to Islam, after which he was renamed Andriantsoly, to pressure from Swahili traders wishing to increase their influence. Tsolovola may have been following the earlier conversion to Islam of the brothers' father Oza.

The information in Figure 5 is based on the "Sakalava" tantara from the 1840s (the dates in the upper half of the diagram are from Guillain 1845), on Southern

Bemihisatra tantara from the Analalava region, and on French archival records noted in discussing these relationships in the remainder of this chapter.

59. Guillain ibid.:77.

60. Ibid. The Malagasy correspondent for the Protestant monthly magazine, *Teny Soa,* described in 1872 the zomba in which Merina officials and soldiers watched over the "Sakalava royal ancestors" day and night; the ceremonies in which people paid their respects every Friday, before going to church on Sunday; and the annual "washing (or showing)" *(fampandroana na fampisehoana),* in which they were displayed on the backs of four men (R-N-J-S 1872:45–47).

An interpreter for the French colonial administration in Majunga, writing shortly after the conquest, said that when the Hova fled Mahajanga in 1895, they took the relics to force "the queen of Boeni, Ramboatofa" and her followers to follow them to Antananarivo, where they were all captured by the French, who eventually returned the relics to Mahajanga where they also used them to control the local population (Bénévent 1897:53).

61. Guillain 1845:69. Elsewhere (ibid.:47, n. 1), Guillain states that they had different mothers.

62. Ibid.:113.

63. Ibid.:104–105, 108.

64. Ibid.:107–108.

65. Gevrey 1972:122.

Andriantsoly was buried at Mahabo on the promontory of Mayotte known as Choa, where most of his followers had lived, opposite the island of Dzaoudzi where he had fortified himself.

Concerning his *acte de cession,* signed on April 26, 1841, there was some debate at the time. On April 31, Andriantsoly told Passot, representing the French in Mayotte, that he did not really say he wanted to cede the island, just establish friendly relations. It was wrong that the French took his letters that way: "this was just a way of speaking among Arabs . . . and the words should never be taken literally." Passot then provides a history of how Andriantsoly came to be Sultan of Mayotte, to establish his right to cede his claims (Passot to de Hell, 1 Juillet 1841, CAOM MAD c. 295 d. 737).

Like Passot, Noël (1843, vol. 19:286–287, vol. 20:40–55) also provides a history of Mayotte and a brief description of Choa, populated entirely by Andriantsoly's followers from Boina, and Dzaoudzi, where "the king of Mayotte, the sultan Andriantsoly," lived surrounded by some thousand followers from Boina (see also Gevrey 1972:123).

Writing about twenty-five years after Andriantsoly's death, Gevrey described his tomb as "a square mound of earth, without mausoleum or piled stones, surrounded by a double row of posts; between the first and second row is a little shed *(baraque)*, hermetically sealed and mounted on four posts. Each year, the Malagasy have ceremonies there, on the anniversary of his death. The tomb is shaded by two magnificent tamarinds" (ibid.:122). See Lambek (1981) for a study of spirit possession among contemporary Malagasy speakers in Mayotte, of whom "the descendants of Andriantsuly's followers presumably form the backbone" (ibid.:15; see also pp. 153, 156, 158).

Ironically, General Ramanetaka, a kinsman of Radama, whom Radama appointed as governor of Mahajanga in Andriantsoly's place, had to flee to the Comores when Ranavalona succeeded to Radama's place in 1828 and killed many of his kin and supporters. Ramanetaka became sultan of Mohéli (Anjouan).

66. Guillain 1845:129–130. In Imerina, there was also a seeming shift from male to female rulers in the early nineteenth century, when Ranavalona succeeded Radama as ampanjaka in 1828. According to Merina sources, Radama I (son of Andrianampoinimerina) and Ranavalona I were both adopted by Andrianampoinimerina's sister Ralesoka so that one of the children of their endogamous brother-sister marriage would succeed Radama I.

The earliest European (French) commentators on succession in Imerina, writing in 1777 and in 1816 or 1817, reported different preferences for male successors (Delivré 1974:235). Delivré's extended discussion (1974:235–283) of succession and legitimacy in the Merina monarchy indicates that a privileged group of successors known as the "Brothers and Sisters," Andrianampoinimerina's (and others) expressed preference for sisters' children called *zanak'anabaviny,* parents' identity with their children, and disputes concerning endogamy and exogamy, related to Radama's radical choice of the daughter of one of his Sakalava wives, were major issues for local participants and observers. The extent to which the Sakalava and Merina succession controversies of the early nineteenth century were related has yet to be explored.

Except for Radama II's brief reign in 1861–1863, cut short by assassination, four female ampanjaka ruled Imerina from 1828 until 1897, when the French abolished the monarchy and exiled Ranavalona III. Berg (personal communication, July 1988) infers from Ranavalona's own remarks in correspondence of 1831 that she had to justify the apparent change in gender: "I am not female but male, I am the changling of the twelve who rule" *(Tsy vavy aho fa lahy, fa izaho ny fanovan' ny roambinifolo manjaka).* She uses the term *fanovana* (changling), rather than *solo* (substitute), as the embodiments of ancestors made from the dirt of royal tombs were called. Despite her claim to be male rather than female, paralleled in the Sakalava case, it was during Ranavalona I's reign that the office of "caretaker of royalty" *(mpitaiza andriana)* originated, which is also paralleled in how Sakalava followers view the royal guardians around female rulers. In Imerina, the chief *mpitaiza* was the "Prime Minister," a position occupied mainly by three brothers who also served as Commander-in-Chief of the Army and as royal consort.

Among Sakalava in northwestern Madagascar, senior male officials are also described as mpitaiza. This is not a formal title, but work they share with the living ruler's guardians and with all her followers, dedicated to nurturing and protecting living and ancestral royalty. The shift in emphasis from male rulers caring for followers, as if they were children, to followers who care for feminized and infantilized royalty seems to have begun in western Madagascar during these decades when the Sakalava were being pursued by the Hova.

67. Northern Bemihisatra supporters of her successor Tsiomeko told Baré (1973:61–62)

that Andriantsoly gave the royal relics to his sister, then negotiated with the Merina governor at Mahajanga to capture and take her to Antananarivo, in exchange for his freedom to flee to Mayotte in 1932. They remember the sister as Agnitsaka. Tsiomeko's grievance against Andriantsoly for this reason is seen as one of her most distinctive characteristics as embodied in mediums.

68. According to Noël (1843, vol. 20:304) and Guillain (1845:128), Tahosy was praised as Tsimisarakarivo, which Noel translated as "the inseparable . . . because she remained constantly on the side of her mother [Oantity] against her uncle Andriantsoly." They also note that Tahosy was commemorated by a second praise name—"Andrian-Tangiani-Arivou"—which they translate as "The Regretted One . . . because she died in the full force of youth, and before her daughter Tsiomeko was in a state to govern the AntiBoina [the name of royal followers in the north]" (Noël 1843, vol. 20:304). "Noble Regretted by Thousands," from the root *hanina,* would ordinarily be rendered as Andriahaninarivo. The root *tangy,* reduplicated as *tangiangy,* means 'to be hired as a whore', by thousands in this context.

Oantity was also commemorated in at least two praise names:

Andriamangosiarivo, which Noël renders as "the steadfast queen [because of] the firmness she deployed against the Hovas" and Andriamanorigniarivo, "the queen who seized hold, because in fact, it was she who seized the power when her brother Andriantsoly was dethroned" (ibid.). Guillian mentions only the second of these two names, noting: "Manhorigni signifies what is planted in the ground, put, fixed, and alludes to the election of Oantity who was put by the people in the place of her brother Andriantsoly" (Guillain 1845:130, n. 1). Praise names may designate the "Noble" or the "Thousands" as the agent of the action, depending on the nature of verbal prefixes. Andriamanorigniarivo would ordinarily signify "Noble who set up, or established, thousands on a firm foundation."

Noël (1843, vol. 20:304) notes that just as rulers' own followers may remember them differently, so their enemies may invent their own mocking names of dispraise. Thus, the followers of Andriantsoly and Tsiomeko gave Maka, founder of the rival Bemazava branch of the monarchy, "a nearly injurious surname," and therefore the followers of Maka's son Tsimandroho were no less disrespectful toward Andriamandisoarivo. Perhaps these scornful praise names for Tahosy and Oantity have similar origins.

69. Guillain 1845:130–131, n. 2.

70. Ibid.:131, see pp. 130–133; Noël 1843, vol. 20:54.

71. Noël 1843, vol. 20:53–54; see Guillain 1845:133–139.

72. CAOM MAD 1 Z, 2 Z, 4 Z. To give his reader some idea of "the foolish ignorance . . . and the ridiculous pride developed in that child by the adulations of her entourage," Guillain describes how, during the redaction of the *acte de cession* of Nosy Be to the French, she was "very shocked" that the French placed S.M. Louis-Phillipe above her, "claiming to be considered as his equal, and to treat power to power" (ibid.:143). Leguevel de Lacombe, a French officer who witnessed this incident, conveys more of the great anger that Bemihisatra most remember about Tsiomeko: "Tsiomeko . . . showed a resistance that had not been expected. In her *sauvage naïveté* she found it very odd that his Majesty Louis-Phillipe had been placed above her; but, entirely dominated by her chiefs she was forced to hide her repugnance and give her consent not only to the acte of cession dated 14 July 1840 but to the dispatch of various chiefs to Boubon" [Réunion] (cited in Baré 1980:47).

Admiral De Hell, who represented the French government in these negotiations, also succeeded in getting several other small islands around Nosy Be and some land on the northwestern mainland from the Antankarana monarch descended from Sakalava royalty, Tsimiharo, with whom Tsiomeko had allied herself against the Merina. He got Mayotte from Andriantsoly a month later on April 25, 1841.

73. Northern Bemihisatra and French archival reports concur in identifying Rano's father as Derimany, younger brother of the Antankarana ruler Tsimiharo, allied to Tsiomeko; he was adopted by her Zafindramahavita husband and manantany, Tsifohy.

Rang, Commandant Supérieur de Nosy Be et Dépendances, informed his superior, the Ministre le Directeur des Colonies, of Tsiomeko's death in a letter on January 10, 1844: "Among the news that I have from Fédamari [a brother of Tsimiharo, whom Arab traders had captured with other 'Sakalava' and taken to Mauritius as engagé laborers] only one merits being reported to Your Excellency, it is the loss of the queen Tsiomëkou, who died in childbirth. A child that she already had has been recognized in her place" (CAOM MAD c. 296, d. 738). Baré (1973:63) notes that Tsiomeko died without ever having been able to fulfill her religious obligations to her mother Tahosy and grandmother Oantity, buried at Lavalohaliky.

74. Letter from Rang to M. Le Ministre, no. 6, February 28, 1844 (CAOM MAD c. 296 d. 738). Rang himself died in June.

75. Baré 1980:54–99.

76. Ibid.:15.

77. Baré 1973:64.

78. Ndramamalikiarivo's most prominent characteristic, according to Northern Bemihisatra, is her personal grievance against Andriantsoly for this reason (Baré 1973:61). Even Baré's most zealous informants were afraid to break the rule against revealing royal secrets in speaking of Tsiomeko, despite the fact that the current ruler Ahamady Andriantsoly, Andriantsoly's great-grandchild, had permitted them to do so (Baré 1973:64).

79. See, for example, Guinet's meeting with Añono and his notables at Antognibe in 1882 (J. Guinet, letter to the Commandant of Nosy Be, October 1882) (CAOM MAD 4 Z 71).

80. This was one of several revolts against the French administration, notably in 1843.

81. *Concerning Rano, Tehimbola, Añono:* Tsiomeko's son was called "Ranou" [Rano] in the reports of French officials in Nosy Be around the time of his birth and abduction from Nosy Be to Nosy Lava in 1844–1850 (CAOM MAD 1 Z, 2 Z, 4 Z).

Nevertheless, it was "Temboula ben Soultan" (with variant spellings) at Nosy Lava about whom Edmond Samat wrote on August 8, 1854 concerning the looting of a French boat by the followers of "King Rano," 10,000 of them, "all very poor," who do a lot of pillaging on the mainland to feed themselves (CAOM MAD 4 Z 61). Temboula himself, in 1854 and 1856, sent several letters in French to Commandant Dupuis at Nosy Be, noting he was "only a child" (CAOM MAD 4 Z 5).

André Dandouau, French head of the school in Analalava where Tondroko was educated in 1901, wrote down a genealogy which identifies Andriamamalikiarivo's successor "Andriamamitranarivu" as "(Tehimbula) father of Andriamanetiarivu (Iagnumanu)." Dandouau notes that "This list of Sakalava kings is one of the most complete that we have been able to draw up. It is the genealogical list of 'Tundruka,' king of Antunibe whom we have had as a student in Analalava in the political section, a kind of school for hostages added after the Sambirano insurrection to the École Normale d'Instituteurs. We have drawn it up according to information that he gave us himself and after those furnished us by 'Dzurundrazamandzari' today chef de canton at Ambudimadiru-Befutaka, descendent of the former manantani of Tundruka's family" (Dandouau circa 1911:24, n. 1).

The name Añono, which Northern Bemihisatra now use to refer to Tsiomeko's son Rano (Baré 1980:54–57), simply means "What's His Name." It may be a deliberate circumlocution following the long-standing prohibition against uttering the living name of a dead ruler or any similar word (see Noël 1843:304–305), or an elision of Rano's living name and his son's.

Concerning Rano's descendants:
According to Southern Bemihisatra tantara, Ndramamitrañarivo [Rano] died in 1868 or 1875 and Ndramanet(s/r)iarivo in 1890. The report of J. Guinet, a French naval officer who surveyed Narinda Bay in 1878 and again in 1882, states that "Anghono" [Añono], a young man between twenty and twenty-two years old [i.e., born about 1860 when his father Rano would have been about seventeen years old], was ampanjaka at Antognibe and also controlled the port of Analalava (CAOM MAD 4 Z 71). The name Añono may have been used as a circumlocution here too, since Dandouau, as indicated above, was told at the turn of the century that Andriamanet(s/r)iarivo's name was Iañomano, perhaps meaning "Praised, Blessed" (Ianoano). Correspondence between Añono (Tehimbola) and the Commandant of Nosy Be indicates that he became ampanjaka as a child in 1865 and probably died around 1891 or 1892 (CAOM MAD 4 Z 8). According to Southern Bemihisatra tantara, his son

Tondroko was born in 1890. Tondroko wrote to the "Administrateur Nossi-Be" (in response to his letter of two years earlier) to announce himself as his father's heir and place himself under French protection on April 1, 1894 (CAOM MAD 4 Z 32).

The most circumstantial of the Southern Bemihisatra tantara identifies Ndramamahañarivo's mother as real ampanjaka Bemazava descendant *(tena ampanjaka tara[na]ka Bemazava)* and the mothers of Ratsima and Soazara by name.

82. Cited in Guillain 1845:202–203.

83. See Mettam 1989; Mayer 1985.

84. The female ampanjaka "Souz" whom Andrianiheveniarivo (Fig. 4) made head of the Antankarana in the north, when he returned to oust his rival Maka, is another example (Noël 1843, vol. 19:292). Some Southern Bemihisatra tantara mention an "Ampela Be" (Big Woman) among the earliest rulers.

85. Noël 1844:413; Guillain 1845:21. According to Guillain's account, this was actually the idea of a "low-born Muslim" whom Andriamandisoarivo had initially appointed to the position in the hope of dividing the Muslims of Mahajanga against one another. The Muslim, afraid he would be killed, thought this arrangement would protect him.

86. Guillain 1845:86.

87. Ibid.:130. According to Southern Bemihisatra tantara, Andriamboniarivo named the first capital of the northern domain of Boina "T(r)ongay," after the first capital of the Zafinimena in the south.

88. Noël 1844:53–54; see Guillain 1845:133–139.

89. Guillain 1845:128.

90. Richardson (1885:787) identifies *voromahery* as the South African peregrine falcon (*Falco minor* Bp), describing it as "a hawk small in size, but noticeable for its strength and courage, whence its Malagasy name of 'powerful bird'." He notes that Voromahery is also a name applied to the Hova, who adopted the image as an emblem of the monarchy. Berg (personal communication, December 1989) says that the Voromahery in Imerina were ". . . the group of administrative cadres organized in Antananarivo after Andrianampoinimerina's conquest of Tana. Unlike the king's 'body-guards,' Tsiarondahy, who also acted on behalf of the king, the Voromahery were 'free,' i.e., they were granted tomb sites in and around Tana, and so became a kin group. By the time of Radama's first major attempt to conquer Menabe in 1820, they formed a special military unit."

91. Berg 1985.

92. Sakalava war dances *(rebiky),*

still performed in the Analalava region, suggest the existence of such exchanges between Sakalava and Hova during this period (see Feeley-Harnik 1988). According to Mantaux (1969:3), who does note cite his source, Andriantsoly "forged himself an embryo of an army, copied after that of Radama I."

93. Callet 1974, vol. 2, pp. 442–445.

94. The teller of the Merina tantara comments that "it began to be thus under Andrianampoinimerina and is still thus today." See Belrose-Huyghues 1983, plate 14, for a photograph of Ranavalona II's military encampment on the plain below the royal capital in Antananarivo, taken July 31, 1873, during the period in which the tantara were put together. According to Berg (personal communication, December 1989), "In 1820 in Menabe, the four geographical regions formed separate regiments in the Merina army, which I've called *tanin'drazana* regiments to distinguish them from professional, standing regiments. All these regiments (total number of troops: 96,000!) marched to Menabe in 1820 and manoeuvred in battle exactly in the spatial configuration of your diagram!!!"

95. Andriantsoly, surrounded by "a thousand Sakalava" followers, took refuge in the Muslim port of

Anorotsangana on July 25, 1825. When the Hova tried to capture him there, he fled to Muscat (Guillain 1845:181–185). He returned there after Radama's death on July 27, 1828, and started making his own incursions on the Hova at Mahajanga. Ranavalona sent a new group of Hova troops after him in 1831, which destroyed Anorotsangana on September 13. Andriantsoly rebuilt the settlement, naming it Tanan-Safikarany (Safikarany's settlement) after his daughter. After being deposed, he left for Mayotte on July 15, 1832. Tsiomeko stayed in the region until 1836, when the Hova attacked again and stayed on to build the fort from which they sent out the troops that pursued her up to Nosy Be. Whether the Hova fort might have adopted some Sakalava building techniques, or whether Sakalava might have learned here from Hova techniques is not clear.

96. Guillain 1845:185; Mantaux 1969:151–152. Guillain notes that the men were "more properly clothed than the other functionaries, but in the indigenous costume, the *salaka* [loin cloth] and the long and white *lamba* [shoulder wrap]." Mantaux (1969:152) notes that the construction of this fort, particular to the northern coasts of Madagascar, was "strongly inspired by European systems (English)."

97. Noël 1844:394–395.

98. See Campbell 1983–1984;

Filliot 1974; Rasoamiaramanana
1983–1984; Vérin 1986; and the
special issue of *Slavery and Abolition*
9 (1988) on the Indian Ocean trade.
99. Guillain 1845:117, n. 1.
100. Noël 1843, vol. 20:60; see
also McMahon (1892:390) who
comments on the mobility of royal
supporters, and the importance of
capturing the greatest numbers.
This was still how people expressed
tacit discontent in the Analalava
region in the 1970s. Noël
(1844:395) noted that Sakalava
either built their houses on the
highest possible sites in the interior,
surrounding them with deep
trenches and high palisades, or on
the coasts, on sandy beaches, where
they could get away quickly by
outrigger canoe. The "few
miserable huts" in the intervening
plains were occupied only by slaves
guarding cattle.
101. Raison-Jourde (1984)
provides a detailed discussion of the
innovations in the organization of
royal work, which the Merina
Tantaran' ny Andriana (Callet 1974),
collected during the middle to late
nineteenth century, attributed to
Andrianampoinimerina.
102. Guillain 1845:91. Berg
(personal communication,
December 1989) notes that Hova
troops under Brady in Menabe
fought the Sakalava ruler
Ramitraho at "Mahabo" in 1820,
and by 1822 and 1823, they had
established garrisons of their own at

Bondrony (Ambondro) and
Mahabo respectively.
103. Guillain 1845:121. Berg
(personal communication,
December 1989) notes: "*Fatidra* was
one of Radama's favorite forms of
'contract' with *foreign* rulers (he
concluded a fatidra contract with
Jean René on the east coast in
1817), but he *never* used such
contracts with the Sakalava.
Merina-Sakalava relations
in Menabe were instead
defined by giving *wives*.
Andrianampoinimerina gave to
Menabé in 1802, and Ramahitra
gave to Radama in 1823."
104. Baré 1980:52.
105. Chazan-Gillig 1983; Nérine-
Botokeky 1983; Raharijaona and
Valette 1959. Fitampoha have been
held in Belo-sur-Tsiribihana in
1939, 1946, 1958, 1968, and 1978
(Chazan-Gillig 1983:455;
Raharijaona and Valette 1959:10).
Spectators in 1958 were estimated
at 15,000 people (Raharijaona and
Valette 1959:23). Belo-sur-
Tsiribihina is the site of the
Kamamy branch of the Maroseraña
dynasty in Menabe, currently
divided into rival factions. The
relics are kept in a "destiny house"
(*trano vinta*—the same term used for
royal tombs in Menabe), near the
residence of the living ampanjaka in
the town of Belo (Raharijaona and
Valette 1959:12).
106. Rabedimy 1979:177.
107. Rakoto 1947–1948:111.

108. Ibid.:112.

109. Ibid.:112–114.

110. See Feeley-Harnik 1988 for more discussion of the rebiky in the Analalava region. Rakoto (1947–1948:114) mentions "warrior dances" of men, representing former kings, followed by women, held after the regular service in 1938.

111. Poirier 1939c:104, written in 1926.

112. Baré 1980:241. Baré (1980:240) says that Northern Bemihisatra have only some "very ancient" relics made from those of the four founder-kings at Mahajanga, which Galliéni, the first Governor-General of the colony of Madagascar, ordered restored to Andriantsoly's descendant Safy Mizongo.

113. Lombard (1973:135–139) mentions positions among the Southern Sakalava of Menabe comparable to the official positions associated with the doany in the Southern Bemihisatra region, including *manantany, fahatelo, ampitantara, ombiasy, masonandro [ragnitry]* and *fihitse [fihitry]*. The mpiboho, or porter-guardians of royal relics were and are heads of clans related as "brothers-in-law" to the living ruler. There were and are no other categories of people dedicated to serving the royal ancestors (Chazan-Gillig 1983; Nérine-Botokeky 1983; Raharijaona and Valette 1959).

For Boina, Guillain (1845) and the early military writers mention only the manantany and the fahatelo. According to an unpublished manuscript in the Académie Malgache, probably written or dictated by Sakalava in the Majunga region around 1908, spirit-mediums called *mpibaby (mpiboho)* served as guardian-porters (Anonymous circa 1908b). The manuscript does not specify whether they were commoners or slaves.

There are no Razan'olo among the Bemazava (Ndremahefa and Feeley-Harnik 1975).

114. Rey 1913:69.

115. According to Lombard (1976:176–177), these "sites funéraires" or "cimetières royaux"—neither he nor Rabedimy provides the Malagasy terms—mark the five historical periods in which Menabe expanded to its full size. The tombs (trano vinta, houses of destiny) seem to be built like the houses of living rulers (see Lombard 1976, photograph 2 for an example of one of the royal tombs at Mañeva).

116. Rabedimy, personal communication, December 1987. Rabedimy also said that the rites for cleaning commoners' tombs a year later were known as *fafalolo* (sweeping spirits), which could imply either cleaning the spirits or sweeping them away, or both. There were no further rites at commoners' tombs either.

Abadie (1947–1948) describes the tomb of a Sakalava ruler south of the Mangoky River: a rectangular construction of dry stone at the wooded summit of the highest hill in the area, two and one half hours walk from the nearest village. Local people were prohibited from cutting the trees surrounding the tomb. The tomb was aligned lengthwise north-south. Twelve coffins, constructed from the two halves of hollowed trees, were aligned east-west in a row down the length of the tomb. The top halves were sculpted like canoes, and the sides were ornamented with images of cattle, houses, and canoes. The coffins were surrounded by an "enclosure." Remains of old coffins and some household objects were piled east of the coffins within the enclosure. The tomb itself was surrounded by groups of tall hardwood posts, placed at the corners and mid-points of each side.

The tomb of Andriamandazoala, one of the earliest Sakalava kings, is identified with a grotto near the Mangoky River, but only his everyday possessions are said to be found there, not his body (Lombard 1973b:95). Andriandahifotsy is said to be buried at Mañeva near the town called Mahabo (Lombard 1973b:95), but there are no published accounts of his tomb. Andriamisara's descendants have the exclusive

privilege of building tombs like those of royalty, which are known as trano vinta (Lombard 1973b:95). There are no published accounts of these either, and in any case, they are associated with nonruling lines. Elsewhere among Southern Sakalava, the term trano vinta refers to the relic house (Poirier 1939a:13; Raharijaona and Valette 1959:281), which may also be called a zomba, using the word in the royal vocabulary for 'house' (Poirier 1939b:31). The zomba vinta next to Bemihisatra tombs is used to store ritual equipment, money, jewelry, and other valuables, but not relics or corpses.

117. Thomassin 1900:410, 411. Ramitraho and his two successors (Rainasy, Ratovonkery) are buried a few kilometers from their capital at Mahabo, in the village of Maneva on the banks of the Andranomena River. According to Lieutenant Thomassin's report on "the kingdom of Mahabo," then in the hands of Ramitraho's granddaughter Rasinaotra:

> This place was chosen by king Ramitraho. He had his country house there; he enjoyed himself greatly there when he was living; he wanted to stay there after his death. He chose, for reposing in his last sleep, a tiny knoll covered with a miniature forest including scarcely more than twenty trees, but [trees] of great beauty: gnarled baobabs, spear-like

palms, figs with deeply fissured trunks. Under their shade, there rest today, in a little house, three wooden shelters, which enclose his remains and those of his successors, father and brother of Rasinaotra. . . . About once a year, the same ceremonies [as those at the royal funeral] are carried out once again around the tomb, not at fixed dates but when, through the intermediary of a guardian of his tomb, the dead person makes it known that he would not be angered to hear, yet one more time, around him, his good people rejoicing.

Thomassin's report suggests that some of the other tombs in the south may also have been built relatively recently, rather than representing practices dating from the earliest Sakalava domains in the south.

118. Bénévent 1897:55; see Rakoto 1947–1948:112–114; Vérin 1986:286–287.

119. Bénévent 1897:55. R-N-J-S (1872:45) notes that the zomba at Mahajanga was considered the *fotony,* or 'root' of the others in Boina. The order of services at different doany may have replicated this image of the ancestral tree.

120. For Lavalohaliky (founded 1835–1836 at the deaths of Tsimisarakarivo/Tahosy and Ndramañorigniarivo/Oantity), see Renel 1920–1921:160; for Ambalarafia (founded in 1843 at the death of Ndramamalikiarivo/Tsiomeko) in about 1929, 1933, and in 1972, see Poirier 1939d, planche XVII and Baré 1980:296–304; for Choa (founded in 1846 at the death of Ndramañavakarivo/Andriantsoly), see note 65; for Tsinjoarivo (the first tomb of Ndramanjakamboniarivo/Binao, who died in 1923), see Poirier 1939d; for Manongarivo (the second tomb of Ndramanjakamboniarivo/Binao, built in 1938–1941 by her brother and successor Amada) and for the controversy surrounding its creation, see Baré 1973:139–146; 1980:37, 296–304.

Poirier's (1939d:113) diagram of an unidentified doany, made around 1929, is probably the doany of Binao's successor Amada.

121. Letter from Temboula ben Soultan to Dupuis, Commandant de Nosy Be, no date, with other letters dated 1854 and 1856 (CAOM MAD 4 Z 5).

122. See Baré 1980:293.

123. CAOM MAD 4 Z 8.

124. Renel 1920–1921:160.

125. See Baré (1980:240) for a description of the Northern Bemihisatra doany where the ancestors' house was located in 1972.

126. Giesey 1960; see, for example, Brown 1978, 1980, 1985; Giesey 1985; Hanley 1983, 1989.

127. Kantorowicz 1957; Hallam 1982.

128. Mayer 1985.

129. See Feeley-Harnik 1985:294–300. Whereas the absolutism of "divine monarchy" in Europe seems to have come into question only recently (judging from Mettam 1989, Chapter One), it was first to be questioned by scholars working in nonwestern contexts, who argued that African kings were more at the mercy of the people than vice versa (Feeley-Harnik 1985:273–287). Perhaps because of different assumptions about nonwestern polities, or perhaps because of the different nature of the historical and ethnographic data, scholars working in Africa have become especially aware of rulers' *many* bodies, created in the course of conflicts over the power, legitimacy, and continuity they represent.

130. Guillain 1845:371, n. R; Noël 1843, vol. 19:293.

131. Guillain 1845:120–121.

Notes to Chapter 3, La France Orientale et le Far-West Malgache, pp. 115–151.

1. Guillain 1845:144.

2. Ibid.:145.

3. Ibid.:145–146.

4. Ibid.:147. The French settlement of Fort Dauphin, named by an agent of the French Compagnie des Indes Orientales to honor the future Louis XIV, was established in 1643 and abandoned in 1674. Nevertheless, the concessions in Madagascar—first called "Ile Dauphine"—granted to the Compagnie des Indes Orientales by the French crown were the basis of the legalistic arguments for French sovereignty over Madagascar in the theoretical annexation of July 8, 1665 and the invasion and conquest that followed some three centuries later (Heseltine 1971:70–71). Louis XIV renamed the island *France Orientale* when he incorporated the Company's possessions into Crown lands by decree on June 4, 1686.

5. Guillain 1845:148.

6. Guillain (1845) mentions the exchange of gifts in his own account. See also the official requests to the Ministry of the Marine for the money for these presents—mainly guns, cloth, rum, uniforms, and money (CAOM MAD c. 293, d. 726). Such gifts are occasionally listed in other correspondence, for example, some gifts of food from Andriantsoly to French officials in Nosy Be (CAOM MAD c. 295, d. 737). Richardson (1885:308) includes *kado* (Fr. cadeau[x], 'a present') in his dictionary.

The SPG missionary, McMahon, compared the responses of Sakalava, Hova, and North American Indians on such occasions, based on his experience around the Tsiribihina River in 1888 (1892:388). He emphasizes especially the "pride" of the

Sakalava, who "think themselves quite the equals of Europeans and treat all foreigners accordingly," and how they mask their emotions. He recounts a story that people in that area used to explain Sakalava-European relations, in which the Sakalava was the rich elder brother who, because of his wealth, grew lazy; the white man was the smart younger brother who, because of his poverty, grew smarter until eventually he grew even wealthier.

7. Noël (1844:385–387) asserts that after the judgment of kings at their death [the practice of giving them praise names summarizing their accomplishments or contesting these], the most remarkable custom of the Sakalava is without contradiction that of fatidra or *identification du sang*. The SPG missionary, G. H. Smith, who traveled in Menabe, also commented on the practice of fatidra (1896:22–23).

8. CAOM MAD 4 Z 47.

9. S. Ellis 1985:223.

10. Cahuzac 1900:1–41.

11. Decary 1954a:48.

12. Decary 1960:25–26. Decary closes by citing other correspondence from 1883 showing that the treaty was not to be found at the Ministry of Foreign Affairs either. In his appendixes, he provides copies of the legal documents he could find (ibid.:187–221). J. Yates's (1989) analysis of changing labor relations in American businesses emphasizes the increased control over workers that managers achieved in moving from oral to written forms of communication during this same period (1850 to 1920).

13. See Ferrand 1902, vol. 3, p. 66.

14. Bénévent 1897:53. He goes on to describe the relics— combinations of beard-hairs, nails, and teeth in sculptured wooden boxes, ornamented with silver and gold, the relic of Ndramisara being the most elaborate—and the regalia with which they were associated.

15. *Journal officiel de Madagascar* 1902 (March 12):7183.

16. S. Ellis 1985:128.

17. Heseltine 1971:143.

18. S. Ellis 1985:129, based on the "Rapport concernant la translation des restes des anciens rois. . . ." Mars 1897 (ANRDM SS 30).

19. Heseltine 1971. Bastille Day (July 14, 1789) had become a French national holiday hardly more than fifteen years earlier in 1880.

20. Demortière 1905–1906:138. He goes on to describe four relics, each of which consisted of a tooth, a few beard-hairs, and a piece of skin taken from the shoulder near the neck.

21. For example, Ferrand (1902, vol. 3, p. 66) makes the connection between Merina and French tactics in his account of Islamic groups in

Madagascar at the turn of the century.

22. Cooper 1980:3.

23. Jacquier 1904:6, citing the words of Bernard's address to the Congrès International of 1900 on "Labor in the Colonies."

24. Jacquier 1904:5–6.

25. Cohen, Compans, and Gutkind, calling for more research on precolonial and colonial African economic and political history and neocolonial states, suggest testing the notion that "the 'true' history of colonial Africa is the history of labor" (1978:16).

26. Jacquier 1904:6. He qualified his assessment of Madagascar as a "notable" example of an exploitation colony by adding that it was really mixed: it was a settlement colony in the highlands [formerly governed by Merina royalty] and an exploitation colony on the coasts and in intermediate areas (see also Chevalier 1952:100–101; Isnard 1964:125–126).

The Analalava region presented additional problems because it was too dry for the cultivation of really profitable cash crops like coffee, spices, tobacco, and cotton, raised to the north and south. The commercially important products of the region, established within the first six months of French occupation in 1899, included rice, raffia, beeswax, cattle, cattle skins, and coconuts. Europeans needed local labor to produce these

commodities, as well as for public works in the region and nationally. Engagé labor for La Réunion was also recruited from the area, from the mid-nineteenth century, when the French abolished slavery in their territories to the north, to the early years of colonial administration, when they were able to turn their attention to the drought-ridden south of Madagascar (CAOM MAD 1 Z, 2 Z, 4 Z). Forced labor, a common solution to the problems of recruitment, was not legally abolished until 1946, although it persisted even later in some areas (Isnard 1964:104; see Kloosterboer 1960:107–118).

27. Jacquier 1904:53–54.

28. See, for example, Jacquier 1904:67–84; Sabatier 1903; André 1899.

29. Jacquier 1904:89. The emancipation proclamation was read on September 27, 1896. The deputies of the French Chamber actually voted to abolish slavery on August 6, 1896, the same day the law was passed, at their urging, which declared Madagascar to be a French possession rather than a protectorate, its status since the conquest on October 1, 1895 (Thompson and Adloff 1965:15). Thompson and Adloff comment that it was fortunate for the deputies' honor that the two events coincided. Perhaps the deputies did feel that the emancipation of Malagasy slaves somehow

compensated for the subjection of the Malagasy people.

30. In this, too, the French were not unique. Cohen et al.(1978:7) introduce their collection of articles on *African Labor History* with the Belgian King Leopold's directive to his district commissioners in the Upper Congo on June 16, 1897: "These people must submit to new laws of which the most imperious, as well as the most salutary, is assuredly the law of labor."

31. André 1899; Sabatier 1903; Jacquier 1904; Cherrier 1932.

32. Isnard 1950.

33. Kloosterboer 1960:107–118.

34. Thompson and Adloff 1965:xiii.

35. Ibid.:449.

36. Sabatier 1903:103–104.

37. Jacquier 1904:285.

38. Galliéni 1908:273; Cherrier 1932:88.

39. Cherrier ibid.:61, 92–93.

40. Ibid.:86, 94.

41. Isnard 1950:314–318. For studies of similar conditions elsewhere in Madagascar, see Augagneur 1927; Boiteau 1948; F.V. Esoavelomandroso 1975; Faroux 1980; Fremigacci 1975.

42. Thompson and Adloff 1965:449.

43. It could also be argued that French colonial labor law in Madagascar involved the enactment of essentially immoral kinds of legislation. This is Kloosterboer's (1960) argument about forced labor in general, but it is clear even from Thompson and Adloff's (1965:442–464) brief account of Malagasy labor history that many French citizens felt the same way.

44. The French kept soldiers stationed in some areas for several years after the conquest. In the words of one administrator, speaking of a part of the Analalava region where a detachment of Senegalese gunners was still maintained: "There, as everywhere for that matter, sanctions are necessary in order that fear will create habit" (Rapport politique et administratif, Année 1913, Analalava, CAOM MAD 2D 25). Plans were already underway for the prisons that were to take over the role of direct enforcement (You and Gayet 1931:146, n.1).

45. Barthes's "Grammaire africaine" defines "politique" by saying: "There is *la France* on the one hand and *la politique* on the other" (1957:157–158).

46. Galliéni 1908:37; see Jully 1907.

47. Decary 1957:2.

48. See Ozouf 1988:126–157.

49. See Feeley-Harnik 1980:560.

50. Decary 1957:1.

51. Rapport politique et administratif, Region d'Analalava, 1913 (CAOM MAD 2 D 25).

52. Jacquier 1904:89.

53. Sabatier 1903:87.

54. Rapport politique et Administratif du Cercle d'Analalava

pour la periode 1896 fin 1904, p. 31 (CAOM MAD 2 D 24). See Bouillon (1981) for a discussion of what he sees as two different, even opposed, conceptions of "the Malagasy soul," originating in the reports of precolonial French travelers and later used to justify colonial policy.

55. Rapport politique et administratif, Année 1906, Analalava, le 15 janvier, 1907 (CAOM MAD 2 D 25).

56. The French scholar and former colonial administrator Decary, writing in the early 1960s (shortly after independence), observed that the Malagasy knew French better than the French knew Malagasy. A *peuple colonisateur* should have learned the local language to get closer to the natives, thereby facilitating their civilizing mission. Yet this rarely happened. Courses in Malagasy were available in Paris and Tananarive, but "in the absence of any obligation, these measures were not very effective, and with a few exceptions, quite rare were those who, without claiming to be linguists, could speak the language of the country fluently" (Decary 1964:11). The Académie Malgache petitioned the Governor-General in 1935 to make knowledge of Malagasy obligatory for all administrators, but he never responded, presumably because he could not find the words to express

his approval and simultaneously his lack of power to carry out such a plan (ibid.). Although Decary spoke Malagasy, the collection of stories and legends for which these remarks are the preface is entirely in French, the language in which Malagasy school children were directed to write them down (Decary 1964:13). Dandouau (1922), director of schools in the Analalava region and former secretary general of the Académie Malgache assembled his collection of Sakalava and Tsimihety folklore in the same way.

F. V. Esoavelomandroso (1976) provides a detailed discussion of Malagasy and French language instruction during the colonial period.

57. *Guide Annuaire,* Rapport politique et administratif du Cercle d'Analalava pour la periode 1896 fin 1904 (CAOM MAD 2 D 24). Their political interpretation was taken as further evidence of the state of superstitious savagery in which they languished. Twenty years later, when the French were involved in legal battles with the Sakalava over the continuation of the monarchy, a "sorcerer" was found to be fabricating antilocust medicines. This time, the French linked the two cases as political. In fact, although the French seem to have regarded the man involved as nothing more than a fraud, suspiciously supported by a "secret

organization" of Sakalava royalists, Sakalava followers clearly regarded his divinatory power and medicines as inseparable from his status as a royal spirit-medium. Persons who failed to follow the prohibitions associated with the medicines were subject to royal wrath *(tigny)* (Poirier 1939c:84, 97).

58. Summary of the Rapport politique et Administratif, Année 1906, in Compagnon's letter #79, January 14, 1907 (CAOM MAD 2 D 25). One of Captain Toquenne's first acts after occupying the Analalava region in 1897 was to send out commissions composed of an officer, an interpreter, and a census-taker to all the villages in the region to make a complete census of the population and to gather information on topography, geology, agriculture, and industry (Toquenne 1897b:1121–1122). Chef de Bataillon Lecreux's report on the demography of the region in 1900 concluded that the Sakalava were "generally healthy and well built" and that the causes of their infertility were therefore to be found not "in defects of the constitution inherent in individuals, but in certain habits, certain customs, a general manner of living, which does not permit them to procreate and to have numerous children." Even so, he drew special attention to "the horror of work and an inveterate laziness" characteristic of the Sakalava,

suggesting that the first cure was to make them work, while developing their idea of private property (Rapport d'ensemble [for 1900], Analalava, le 15 janvier 1901 [CAOM MAD 2 D 24]). Most observers attributed their infertility to their laziness, apathy, filthy living conditions, and sexual vices (e.g., *Guide Annuaire* 1900:359; Camy 1905:72–73; Compagnon in his Rapport politique et Administratif, Année 1906, 14 janvier 1907, CAOM MAD 2 D 25).

59. The Southern Bemihisatra consistently claimed that they had many more cattle in the precolonial period, before taxation. A communication in the *Journal officiel* (September 28, 1897, p. 980), which confirms that the number of cattle in the region dropped sharply in the years following colonial rule, attributes the problem to pillaging following insurrections against French rule, and lack of maintenance of herds. The article cites Toquenne as estimating that it will take several years for the cattle herds to regain their earlier numbers.

60. See Baré 1980:79, 242, n.2.

61. Camy 1905:73.

62. Their use of the Malagasy word kabary, used throughout Madagascar to refer to formal oratory in contrast to various kinds of more casual talk, is meant to emphasize the seriousness of their

talks with local people as well as their knowledge of local custom.

63. Letter from Chef de province Compagnon to the Governor-General, Analalava, 17 juillet 1908 (ANRDM F 148).

64. Rapport politique et Administratif, Province d'Analalava, Année 1912, n.d. (CAOM MAD 2 D 25).

65. The *arrêté* was issued in 1848 to take effect in 1849. See Decary (1960:201) for a copy.

66. CAOM MAD c. 1, d. 5; c. 296, d. 739, 740.

67. From the island, Rano's notables (he was around eight years old) tried to maintain relations with the Merina, over land in both Anorotsangana and Antsohihy, and the French by sea, both of whom claimed the area as their own. Charles Fournier, Commandant of a war ship that visited the area in 1852, identified "Ranou" as "chief of all the Sakalava of Narinda Bay." He said that "at the beginning of his stay on land under Hova jurisdiction," Rano wrote to Ranavalona, ampanjaka of Imerina, asking permission for "Ranou's men" to settle on the mainland and live there peacefully "under the authority of Ranou, their king. Ranavalo responded that she granted them their request, but that if she agreed that Ranou was their king, she remained for her part the Queen and the Sovereign of Ranou." Emissaries were then sent to Tananarive, but finding no way, they turned back ("Rapport de la mission du brick *Le Victor* à la côte N.O. et Ouest de Madagascar," 12 Novembre 1852, CAOM MAD c. 146, d. 203). One of the Southern Bemihisatra histories says of Ndramamitrañarivo [Rano] that "He united with the Hova. Raimboana gave him 12 Honors."

Meanwhile, Rano, or those who wrote for Temboula ben Soultan during the mid-fifties, addressed the Commandant of Nosy Be as "our father" in letters written during the mid-1850s asking that he not forget to protect "us who are France's people" (e.g., Fatouma Ben ti Sultan, Nossilava le 28 aout 1854 to the Commandant Nossibe, CAOM MAD 4 Z 5).

The SPG missionary McMahon, who traveled around the Tsiribihina River area of Menabe in 1888, noted the number of "petty kings," including two or three powerful ones. He says: "Most of these, if pressed, acknowledge the Queen of Madagascar (Ranavalona III) to be their 'mother,' but some consider her as their 'sister,' that is, their equal. In their own country, however, they are supreme" (1892:390).

68. Toquenne (1897a:980) described Analalava as "a great center of population before the campaign of 1895," composed primarily of Muslim traders. The rice fields just south of

Analalava at Andampy, where Ndramanetsiarivo's doany was later located, and at Ovary (now Ovaribe and Ovarikely), were widely reputed for their rice fields (Guédès 1898:2384).

69. Toquenne 1897b:1121.

70. Rano's son and successor Añono, caught between the French and the Merina, also tried to deal with both while keeping both at bay. Judging by a letter of October 10, 1865 from the Commandant supérieur de Nosy Be et Dépendances to the Commandant at Nosy Be, the French saw themselves as having appointed Añono as Rano's successor. The Commandant supérieur informs the Commandant that he has decided this day that "the child Agnognou son of the deceased chief Temboula should be put back into the hands of the Sakalava population at Laphi-Minty[?], but that he should not execute this order until receiving particular instructions. Añono's own letters, written in Arabic, are stamped: "Protectorat Français// A'gnonou//Roi de Nareenda//et Nossi-Lava//Madagascar." Most of the correspondence now in French archives concerns the Commandant's reassertions to Añono that *"mon cher prince"* rules under French protection, and Añono's reassertions of loyalty and requests for guns and ammunition to fight the Hovas (CAOM MAD 4 Z 8).

When yet another French sea captain, J. Guinet, surveyed "geographical, commercial, and political" conditions in Narinda Bay in 1878 and 1882, Añono had his doany at Antognibe. He described Añono in 1882 as a young man of 20–22 years, light colored, with braided hair like people on the East coast, dressed in "semi-Arab" clothing, who did not speak one word while he was there. On this second trip, he posed several questions concerning the loyalty of the Sakalava to France, of which the first was whether, "despite the time elapsed since the death of Andriantsoly their ancestor, they still considered themselves allied to France in the terms to which their grandfather *(aïeul)* had agreed." Añono's ministers eventually responded to Guinet that "They accepted and had never ceased to consider the Commandant de Nosy Be as their Chef, that they had never ceased to accept all that Andriantsoly had done . . ." with other assertions of loyalty following from that (J. Guinet, "Voyage dans la Baie de Narenda October 1878 [vapeur Hardi]," Letter to Monsieur Le Commandant, October 1882, CAOM MAD 4 Z 71).

In 1890, Añono wrote to the Commandant from Nosy Lava, begging him for help, saying the Hova have taken his country and the port [of Analalava], and are in the process of building a fort [at Andronjona]. In one of the last of his letters in the file, dated November 1891, he pledged his loyalty again, declaring himself "son" and "grandson" of France, asked not to be forgotten, and signed himself, as in preceding letters: "Sultan Angnounou son of Andiamamihitanga arriva."

Last's report (1895:236) describes "Andrônjina" on the coast of the Ambolobozo Peninsula, opposite Nosy Lava, as a Hova settlement with an "officer in charge" and a "Ruva," a fortress. Last was glad to see them, because he found the area to be off the high road and seldom visited by strangers. He said the rest of the coastal area to the south was deserted, people having gone to the Komadjara Peninsula to escape marauding bands on the mainland.

The Hova had moved into the Ambodivohitra area near Antognibe by 1892 (Rapport, Province d'Analalava, 1 aout 1898 [CAOM MAD 2 D 24]). They pulled back to Antsohihy when the French entered the area in 1897.

71. Andampy is not to be found on contemporary or later maps, perhaps because all that remained in 1898 of Tondroko's doany were blackened posts indicating remains of 300–400 houses (Guédès 1898:2384, 2385), suggesting that the Sakalava may have burned the doany before leaving, or possibly

that they moved because it caught fire. Guédès, a member of the French army that occupied the area in 1897, attributes the move, which he says took place after they had been there about two years, to the nomadic habits of the Sakalava population.

72. Toquenne 1897b:1121. Malaza said that the 'telephone' was located on the former site of the zomba mitahy or ancestors' house at the Grandfather's doany. At the site of the Father's former doany down below, there was during the colonial period a big cleared area *(banja)* for public celebrations, because people had been afraid to build houses there. He concluded 'Now, in the Republic, it is covered with houses.'

73. Letter from Le Résident de Nossi-Bé et Dépendances [Toquenne] to the Résidence Général de France à Madagascar, 1 mars 1897 (ANRDM D454). Troupel continued to describe the geographic advantages of the site in still more detail.

74. Toquenne 1897a:972.

75. Ibid.

76. Guédès 1898:2385; ANRDM, D 10. The *Guide Annuaire* for 1906–1907, p. 383, estimates the population of the area at 6,580, of which Antognibe was 981.

77. Toquenne 1897a:973.

78. Arrêté du 4 avril 1897, no. 562, 563 (ANRDM D 454). The first of the four was the

Circumscription of the
Antankarana, headed by the
Antankarana ampanjaka Tsialana;
the second, the Circumscription of
the Bezamava, headed by their
ampanjaka Tsiarasso; and the third,
the Circumscription of the.
Northern Bemihisatra, headed by
their ampanjaka Binao. Toquenne
(1897a) hoped to use the district
heads in the royal administration
(fehitany) for similar purposes.
Southern Bemihisatra do likewise;
the chef du village administers royal
work in villages where there is no
fehitany.

79. Toquenne 1897a.

80. Letter from Le Résident de
Nossi-Bé et Dépendances [Troupel]
to the Résidence Général de France
à Madagascar, 1 mars 1897
(ANRDM D454).

81. Toquenne 1897a:973; Guédès
1898:2384; Camy 1905:32. André
Dandouau, the creator and
administrator of the Normal School
for Training Indigenous Teachers,
founded in Analalava in October
1900 (Galliéni 1901:6150), was
Tondroko's teacher in 1901. He
describes "la section politique" as a
"sorte d'école d'otages," which was
attached to the École Normale after
the Sakalava around the Sambirano
River near Nosy Be revolted in
1899–1901 (Dandouau ca. 1911:24,
1922:7). The revolt extended south
to the Analalava region (Lamolle
1899). Dandouau (1922:7) noted
that bands of rebels still held the

Moromany [Komajara] Peninsula
opposite Analalava (part of the
Antognibe sector) in 1901.
Toquenne never suggested that
Tondroko was in any way
involved. According to Guédès
(1898:2384), Tondroko had already
been moved from Antognibe back
to his old doany at Andampy, near
Analalava, "to withdraw him from
the intrigues of his entourage and
place him more directly under our
authority." Camy (1905:32) later
claimed that he was brought to
Analalava "in disgrace" to be
educated at the École Normale not
only to get him away from the
Silamo, but also because he was the
object of "too enthusiastic
demonstrations on the part of his
subjects" on several different
occasions. Lamolle (1899:3286)
described the Antognibe area as
"turbulent," but noted that
Tondroko was "intimately
associated" with the clean-up effort.

Toquenne (1898b:1121) wrote
that Antognibe was "occupied
peacefully" on September 30, 1897.
However, he established forty
Senegalese soldiers under a
lieutenant there. They were
removed in December 1900 to be
used elsewhere. But according to
Camy (1905:33), the fear that their
removal might lead to trouble from
the "still belligerent" population led
to reinstatement of thirty
Senegalese almost immediately.

82. Camy 1905:32.

83. The indigenous gouverneur was expected to transmit government orders and collect taxes (Toquenne 1897a:972). Many of them were men whom the conquering Hova had already employed for the same tasks. Governor-General Galliéni's (1899) voyage from Majunga to Diégo-Suarez in 1899 was primarily for the purpose of collecting workers to build a road between Tananarive and west coast port of Majunga (Mahajanga). He spoke to the ampanjaka on the northwest coast, who had to muster the labor among their followers. As sous-gouverneur, the ampanjaka Soazara still accompanied local officials on their tours of the region to collect taxes and muster labor.

84. Toquenne 1897b:1121.

85. Rapport politique et Administratif, Prov.d'Analalava, Année 1906, le 15 janvier 1907 (CAOM MAD 2 D 25).

86. According to guardians at the Doany in 1971–1973, Tondroko was supposed to go with three other Sakalava rulers by boat to Majunga, then to Tananarive to visit Governor-General Galliéni and personally pledge their fidelity to France (see Anonymous 1900a and ANRDM D 55 for a description and correspondence relating to precisely such a trip in 1900 by the other three heads of Circumscriptions mentioned earlier, whom Tondroko was to have accompanied). The Southern Bemihisatra guardians said that Tondroko's counselors persuaded him not to go, and that the French wrongly construed his action as revolt, stripped him of his governorship and moved him to Manongarivo where they could watch him.

87. Rapport politique et Administratif, Prov. d'Analalava, le 31 déc. 1907, M. Pont, Année 1907 (CAOM MAD 2 D 25).

88. Rapport politique et Administratif, Prov.d'Analalava, le 31 déc.1907, M.Pont(CAOM MAD 2 D 25).

89. Poirier 1939c:67, n. 34.

90. Rapport politique et Administratif, Année 1915, Prov. d'Analalava, le 17 fév.1916, M.Poirier, pp.4–5 (CAOM MAD 2 D 25).

91. Rapport 26-CF, 6 mai 1926, cited in the report of Inspecteur des Provinces, Charles Poirier, 1926, p. 37 (CAOM MAD 6[2] D 121). In subsequent notes, this report is noted as Poirier 1926.

92. *Guide Annuaire* 1901:369.

93. CAOM MAD 2 D 25; ANRDM D 438.

94. Rapport 26-CF, 6 mai 1926, cited in Poirier 1926:37.

95. Ibid.

96. Poirier 1926:61, 62.

97. In his brief account of Tondroko's funeral, Poirier says it ended on December 15 (1939c:104). In his account of the succession

battle, he says it ended on November 15 (1926:59). Correspondence with Northern Bemihisatra (cited in Poirier 1926:65–70), in which Southern Bemihisatra say that they have not been able to get permission for more than the two months originally granted, confirms that the funeral ended on November 15.

98. This is the date that royal officials give in a letter to the Northern Bemihisatra ampanjaka Amada, asking for his help (cited in Poirier 1926:66). Poirier also cites October 25 and 28 as the baby's birth date (ibid.:60, 64). The mother actually gave birth in a village three and a half hours walk south of Manongarivo.

Two of the written Southern Bemihisatra tantara state that Soazara ruled as of October 2, 1925. One, concerned to disprove "those recent lies that Andriamamahanarivo did not bear a child before dying" *(ilay vandy betiky tsy niteraka rantsy ny tany Andriamamahanarivo)*, states that Soazara was born on August 31, 1925, and started ruling on October 2.

99. Poirier 1926:39. The man was a Tsimihety, Antandrona, from the same canton as the child's mother, but not from the same village. He was identified variously as the mother's brother-in-law *in partibus* and the mother's mother's husband (see Poirier 1939c:77, 78,

82, 90). He is called "prime minister" (manantany) in Poirier's account of the dispute and trial (1939c, Part VI), but according to Soazara's current manantany in Analalava, he was "only a ragnitry," that is, a representative of an ancestry in the royal administration.

100. Rapport politique et Administratif, Année 1925, n.d.(CAOM MAD 2 D 26).

101. Poirier 1926:40. Later the Southern Bemihisatra told Poirier that they intended to found a new doany at one of several unnamed locations, all of them in the Antognibe region, having large rice fields around them (Poirier 1939c:99).

102. Poirier 1926:41, 48. According to Poirier (1926:26), the ancestors' house at Manongarivo contained the Vy Lava and a "hindu trunk in wood . . . which the administration broke to open." In a covered cavity on a shelf in the upper part of the trunk were "the relics," which included a five-franc gold coin, a two-franc gold coin, a gold drum about a third the size of a thimble, a piece of black and yellow striped silk known as *dalahany,* a piece of cotton—"white but blackened with dirt and stained with sweat," a white porcelain bowl broken in two places, two oval, white porcelain plates. Had there been relics made from the parts of the royal body, Poirier

would surely have mentioned them, the dady being his primary interest in his discussions of the Southern Sakalava (Poirier 1939a). In his description of Tondroko's funeral, Poirier (1939c:104) states that the Bemihisatra do not make such relics.

103. Poirier 1926:42.

104. Tondroko's followers had already hired one of these lawyers in 1923 and 1924 to plead Tondroko's right to return to his doany in Antognibe (Poirier 1926:43–49). Following World War I, French communists trained as lawyers and living in Madagascar, and those lawyers sent by the French Communist Party in France began to defend Malagasy forced to stand trial for antigovernment activities in Madagascar (see Thompson and Adloff 1965:27–28). The lawyers in the succession dispute, who were from Majunga, the largest town on the west coast, may have become involved in this way, and perhaps also the lawyer from Analalava whom the Sakalava hired to help them in prolonging Tondroko's funeral. I will present a more detailed analysis of these legal affairs elsewhere. Contemporary guardians at the Mahabo now remember the lawyer as being a Malagasy who really knew how to talk and who argued the case right up to Tananarive.

105. Ibid.:52–58, passim.

106. Ibid.:52, 1939:97.

107. Poirier 1926:1. In the edited version of the report, published in the *Mémoires de l'Académie malgache* (1939), Poirier omitted this passage and included another, in which he characterized the Sakalava themselves as "revelers" and "great sensualists," living for the moment and lying as much as they told the truth (Poirier 1939c:41–42).

108. Poirier 1926:57.

109. Poirier 1939c:101.

110. Poirier 1926:35.

111. Soazara was still living in Analalava in July 1928 (ANRDM D 454, no. 1447).

112. Poirier 1926:59–60.

113. Richardson 1885:96.

114. "Affaire Poirier . . . 1929–1931" (CAOM MAD 3 D 87, 3 D 121). Curiously, there is no documentation on the events surrounding Tondroko's death and Soazara's succession except what is found in Poirier's own report, written in 1926, filed in the colonial archives (CAOM MAD 6[2] D 121) and published in 1939 in the *Mémoires de l'Académie Malgache.* In 1936, the office of the Governor-General of Madagascar made a confidential request to the chief archivist in the colonial administration for the dossiers relating to "native affairs following the death of the Sakalava chief Tondroko" in the Analalava-Antognibe region during the years 1923–1926. He was particularly interested in information

concerning the death and succession
that put Soazara "at the head of the
tribes of the region," because leftist
nationalists were threatening to
kidnap her as a way of attracting
the Sakalava to their cause. The
files were missing then and have
not since reappeared (Governor-
General to Archivist, September 24,
1936, September 28, 1926 (CAOM
MAD 6[2] D 121).

115. Rapport politique et
Administratif, Années 1903, 1905,
1906, 1907 (CAOM MAD 2 D 24,
2 D 25; ANRDM D 438).

116. CAOM MAD 2 D 25.

117. Rapport politique et
Administratif, Année 1912,
Demarsy (CAOM MAD 2 D 25).

118. There were other islands off
the northeastern and western coasts
that would have been large enough
to locate a penitentiary. Remoteness
was probably one consideration in
the choice of Nosy Lava. By 1909
the French were beginning to
consider portions of the Analalava
region remote enough to punish
their own delinquent employees
(Analyse de la lettre no. 57-C.F. du
27 juillet 1909 du Chef de la
province, ANRDM D 438). Yet
after the prison was opened, the
Chef de province complained that
Malagasy so loved their country
that even Nosy Lava was no real
punishment; it was too bad that
exile to Guyana had been
suppressed (Rapport politique et
administratif, Année 1912, CAOM

MAD 2 D 25). It was later
reinstituted (You and Gayot
1931:146, n.2).

119. Thompson and Adloff
1965:11. Sakelika means to send out
new shoots or branch like a tree.
The name of the organization
conveys the combined strengths of
iron, stone, and growing things in
the image of a ramifying tree.

120. Rapport politique et
Administratif, Année 1915,
Analalava, le 17 fév. 1916, Poirier,
pp.7–8 (CAOM MAD 2 D 25);
letter no.2333 from Chef de
province Poirier to the Governor-
General de Madagascar et
Dépendances, 19 avril 1916
(CAOM MAD 6[2] D 87); canet de
tournée, 16–17 mai 1916 (CAOM
MAD 2 D 25). Archival data on the
move does not indicate who chose
the site or whether it was well-
known earlier as the location of
Fiaroa's shrine, the place of
Tondroko's circumcision, and the
village where Tondroko's half-
brother had lived and died. Saha
Barimaso said the guardians of the
Mahabo chose the site because it
was the closest to the island
cemetery.

Poirier's report of February 17,
1916 also discusses the possibility of
constructing a "huge leprosarium"
on Nosy Lava, a project first
suggested by his predecessor
Demarsy in 1912 as a replacement
for the one in the Antognibe
region, recently destroyed by a

cyclone (Rapport politique et Administratif, Année 1912, CAOM MAD 2 D 25). If the leprosarium was rebuilt on Nosy Lava, one doctor could then serve both lepers and prisoners. It should be located in the southwestern part of the island where there was plenty of water and arable land. In fact, this is where the first doany in the area had been located, the "real doany" of the Great-Grandfather. In 1922, a leprosarium with room for 500 persons was established in the "former" penitentiary, apparently abandoned because of cyclone damage, but it had yet to receive them in 1924 (Rapport politique et Administratif, Année 1924, Analalava, le 29 juillet 1925, CAOM MAD 2 D 26). The Alsatian Fathers established the leprosarium on the site of Tondroko's former doany around 1940. I do not know when the penitentiary was reestablished in its former location on Nosy Lava.

121. *Monographie du district d'Analalava* 1950 (CAOM MAD 6[9] D 35).

122. See the annual Rapport politique et Administratif, 1920–1925 (CAOM MAD 2 D 25 and 26).

123. See the annual Rapport politique et Administratif for the years 1921 through 1929 (CAOM MAD 2 D 26); miscellaneous economic and labor reports from the 1920s through 1940s (CAOM MAD 2 D 27, ANRDM D 438 and 439); the *Monographie du district d'Analalava* for 1950 (CAOM MAD 6[9] D 35); and the *Monographie* for 1960 (courtesy of Professor Pierre Vérin). In the administrative reports from 1905–1920, the reported law cases are almost all about work, whereas later administrators in the 1920s emphasize that there are no cases because there are no workers (CAOM MAD 2 D 25 and 26). French settlers, who used to use gifts to obligate workers, now used penal labor on their plantations. In the 1970s, people who identified themselves as "Sakalava" rarely migrated out of the region to seek wages as itinerant laborers on the large plantations north and south of the Analalava region, though it was recognized as "Tsimihety custom." In 1960, the only year for which I have figures, 400 Tsimihety men from the Analalava region sought seasonal wage labor in the tobacco plantations around Port Bergé and the coffee and vanilla plantations around Antalaha and Sambava on the east coast, in contrast to no Sakalava (*Monographie du district d'Analalava* 1960, p. 2). Ottino (1964:244–245, n.2) cites the observations of one resident of Analalava in 1961, who blamed women for the problem on the grounds that they did not demand enough cloth and other goods from men to make them work.

124. Poirier 1939c:101.

125. Decraene 1964.

126. Tsiranana suffered a serious stroke in 2/70, while attending a OCAM heads of state meeting at Yaoundé in Cameroon. He was flown to a hospital in Paris, where he was treated for seven months before being able to return to Madagascar. The stroke paralyzed him and made him unable to speak, and his doctors initially did not expect him to improve. It was two months before he regained his ability to speak (Covell 1987:43–44). According to Covell, "the supposedly hopeless illness, and subsequent miraculous recovery had the effect of opening the competition to succeed Tsiranana while forcing the participants to pretend it was not happening." Perhaps partly because the stroke affected Tsiranana's speech, some followers of the royal ancestors in the Analalava region interpreted his illness as the result of possession by a royal ancestor in retribution for his slighting their domain in national affairs.

127. Horton (1971) argued that decentralized polities in West Africa were not simply lesser versions of chiefdoms and monarchies on an evolutionary scale, but rather the common products of regional tensions rooted in a wide range of ideological, social, and ecological factors.

128. The available rice land in the Analalava area, which might

have enabled larger numbers of Bemihisatra supporters to settle around the living rulers at Manongarivo and Analalava, had they been permitted, was already in the hands of others, mainly outsiders, including the large groups of Hova and other highlanders whom the French had brought from Tsiafabazaha to act as functionaries, small-scale merchants, and craftsmen (see Toquenne 1897a:972).

Notes to Chapter 4, *Antsabo:* At the Crops, pp. 155–229.

1. *Ka nianavaratra ny fanjakana tao Fiherena; satria folaka ny tany tamin' ny Andriandahifotsy dia nifindra fonenana ry zandry raha efa tombo ny fanompoana mafana ary nibohoina ny razany fanjakana nianavaratra nankany Tsiribihina izareo* (from *Fanazavana Niantombohany . . .*). *Fonenana* (from the root *onina*) refers to a dwelling place, not house, spelled as it appears here, as in the highlands. According to Richardson (1885:201) the same term can also be used to refer to 'loss of memory,' 'obliviousness.'

2. Covell 1987:93.

3. The term taranaka derives from the root *anaka,* 'children'. Substantives formed with the prefix *ta-* refer to "those things having essentially the property of the root, as: *tafotsiny* (root *fotsy,* white), the white of an egg" (Richardson 1885:594).

Fehiny, from the root *fehy* (a tie

or knot, control, govern), refers especially to things tied together. The passive verb *fehezina,* derived from the same root, referring to the condition of being tied, controlled or governed, is the term for the districts, composed of three or four villages, governed by the royal administration (see Chapter 6).

4. Conversely, people 'ascend to villages' *(manonga antanana),* just as they are invited to 'ascend to the north' *(manonga avaratra)* in taking a guest's place of honor in the ancestors' corner (northeast) of a house. The contrast between high and low, cleared and uncleared ground is basic not only to founding villages and preparing gardens, but also to reconstructing tombs (see Chapter 1 and Chapters 7–9). In all of these instances, the clearing is preparatory to planting something that will grow: people, crops, ancestors. Richardson (1885:614) derives *tanàna* from *tanam* (Malay, Javanese), "to plant, to cultivate(?)."

5. One man, trying to respond to my probably wrong-headed question about connections between trees and royal ancestral spirits, said 'The trees are their houses. They are twisted around or entangled in them[?], tied' *(Tranondreo ny kakazo. Mifadiditra, mifehy).* Royal spirits who possess people by 'coming to rule' *(mianjaka)* on them are visualized as 'sitting' *(mipetraka)* on their heads, or people are said to

'carry them on their heads' *(miloloha)* as they would carry other royal burdens.

Togny are most often set up in mango trees or tamarinds. Mango trees grow new shoots throughout the year. The foliage of *Tamarindus indicus* is, as one French botanist observed, "if not persistent, at least partially permanent . . . representing in these places [the plains of the west coast] the most active life in drier soils" (François 1937:44).

6. Togny are known as *fiara-tanà,* protectors of the village, in southwestern Madagascar. People there also distinguish two kinds of togny: *togny-tanà,* or "togny of the village," associated with the founding ancestors of the village in which the tree is located, and *togny-tany* or *tognin'ampanjaka,* "togny of the land" or "togny of the ampanjaka," associated with Sakalava royal ancestors identified with the land as a whole (Rabedimy 1983:178).

7. Fiaroa's 'sacred iron' is a wheel-shaped piece of cast iron that was probably part of a ship that capsized in the bay. Last, who visited Andronjona around 1895, when the Merina had established a garrison with a fort in the village, said that a French ship had gone ashore and was afterwards broken up by the Sakalava. A few pieces of the ship's timbers still remained on the beach (Last 1895:237). Another

resident of Andronjona said that the Grandfather wanted the vy brought down to his doany at Antognibe, but it was too heavy to be transported by outrigger canoe, so Fiaroa set it up in Andronjona instead. The speaker's grandfather, who had been the Grandfather's fehitany or district head, based in Andronjona, had written down the details of the story, but the papers had since been lost.

8. We lived in Tsinjorano in mid-February and most of March, during the rainy season of 1973, and in Andonaka for two weeks in July and August and again in October, during the dry season of 1973, which followed.

9. The partial genealogy, which I made on the basis of information from Malaza and his sons, focuses mainly on their kin who were—in the dry season of 1973—most closely associated with Andonaka. It does not include the vast network of people throughout the region, mainly south of the Loza, whom Malaza, Rafotsy, or their children counted (in different ways) as kin.

10. The partial genealogies of the tompontany and vahiny: Sambarivo in Tsinjorano are based mainly on information that AdanDezy told Alan about his family. They focus primarily on the kin with whom AdanDezy lived in Tsinjorano. Though he knew about some of his parents' kin—for example his mother's siblings in the Komajara

Peninsula, they were only 'distantly acquainted' *(fifankahay lavitry)*. The partial genealogy of vahiny: Antantety, which I made on the basis of information from different sources, reflects their numbers in Tsinjorano, which were much smaller, and also the fact that we knew Tsinjorano more through its tompontany than through its vahiny.

Here, as in the genealogy from Andonaka, I have not included the children's children's names for lack of space and also because the discussions center mainly on the siblings, their parents, and children. Except where spouses came from the Doany Miadana, the Mahabo on Nosy Lava, or from Tsinjorano itself, I have simply noted the general area in which their natal villages are located: on the Ambolobozo Peninsula north of the Loza River (Ambolobozo P.), along the river (Loza R.), or around the bay south of the river (Narinda B.). Everyone in "Analalava" was living in one of the two quartiers inhabited by local people in the southwestern part of the post (see the map of Analalava in Chapter 5).

Connections through marriage among the siblings' children in Tsinjorano (Figs. 9–11) are indicated below:

a. Amina's youngest daughter Vita (Fig. 9, B) is married to Amady, the former husband of Avoria's youngest daughter Laza

(Fig. 9, F). Amady is related to the brothers Ngoly and Adapiso and their sister Somany (Fig. 11) through his father's sister in Analalava, with whom his child by Laza is now living.

b. Togny's oldest child Talan'olo (Sefo) (Fig. 9, E23), was formerly married to Soavita, one of the Antantety at the southern end of Tsinjorano (Fig. 11, 38).

c. Togny's second son, AdanDezy (Fig. 9, E25), first married his FyBSD Sary (Fig. 10, D).

d. AdanDezy (Dezy's Father), named after the second child of his brother's first marriage [Avoria's son Bezara (MZS), Fig. 9, F29], then married his sister's husband's sister [Avoria's daughter Ampenjiky's (MZD) husband's sister], whom he would have called *anabavy*, like a female sibling. They met at the house of Ampenjiky and René Petit in Analalava. Moana had moved to Analalava when her brother settled there, and AdanDezy was still living there after his divorce from his FyBSD.

11. People who identified themselves as 'Sakalava' or 'Tsimihety' (usually both in different contexts), identified manantambo as a Sakalava term and mandoza as Tsimihety. Loza, often translated as 'danger,' actually has much broader significance, including 'calamity, evil, distress, misery,' which is also the

significance of antambo. Overwhelming calamity has long been conveyed by combining the two, *loza amana antambo* (see Richardson 1885:56, 402).

12. Other people also use *kombo* (weak, paralyzed) as a synonym for drehy. The defining feature of the affliction was not being able to move: 'When it's impossible to move. Whatever sickness makes it impossible to move' *(Izy koa fa tsy afaka mandeha. Zay karazana aretigny mampa-fa-tsy afaka mandeha)*. Thus some saw leprosy as a kind of drehy, but this was always contested. So, for example, when one woman responded by way of explanation that her mother's brother's wife's older brother had drehy, the wife said vehemently, 'Lie! Lie!' One of the commonest local antidotes against the sickness brought on by incest was a glass bead called *tsy leon-doza* (not overcome by calamity), which could be carried or worn.

13. See Bloch 1978; Huntington 1978; Middleton 1990.

14. There was one incident in 1973, widely regarded as shameful and pathetic, in which a man molested a child to whom he was related as *dadilahy* (grandfather and men of the same generation in collateral lines).

15. Endogamy among the Merina and some other Malagasy ethnic groups are discussed in more detail below.

16. Except for the domains founded by the female rulers of the Zafinimena dynasty—notably Tsiomeko's last doany, discussed in Chapter 2, where she emphasized that her followers were free to choose whether they wished to settle there with her or not, and the doany was named for that freedom of choice—I learned of no other communities founded by women.

17. Though Malaza never said so directly, more distant kin described him as 'working for the ampanjaka, her person, her slave' *(olon'azy, andevon'azy)*. I do not know whether—like AdanDezy's father, descended from Sambarivo at the mahabo Lavalohalika—his father Hamady chose to purchase his concession near the village from which his wife came, in or near which he might have lived, since he had no father's or mother's ancestral land in the Analalava region. Malaza's wife, Rafotsy, did come from a village about twenty minutes walk from Andonaka. But his marriage took place after Andonaka had been established as an independent village with its own ancestral tombs.

18. See Feeley-Harnik 1980 for more discussion of domestic architecture and spatial arrangements.

19. Likewise, AdanDezy took Alan as his brother *(rahalahy)* and I became his sister-in-law *(rañao)*. Women also used the strong-weak contrast in distinguishing babies in the womb as male or female according to whether the mother's belly was 'hard' *(mahery)* or 'soft' *(malemy)*.

20. The living ruler, though described as an ampanjaka, an ungendered term for someone who governs the actions of another, and sometimes referred to as Princesse, following colonial usage, is properly addressed as Boana (see Chapter 1, n. 52).

21. *Manoko mañangy* or miletry were the local terms for these transactions, but some people also explained it by using the Merina term *didinkarena* (portion of wealth), which described the division of goods rather than the separation of a woman between her own kin and her husband's kin or the compulsion involved. Malaza said that there was no miletry proper, that is gift of cattle, in his father's generation. A man simply gave a small sum of money for the bride's kin to use to invoke their ancestors to bless the marriage. [These were actually two gifts of money—one to invoke the father's ancestors, the other, usually about half as much, to invoke the mother's ancestors.] Malaza had given for Rafotsy 150 FMG for invoking her ancestors and three cattle, a *mianaka* (cow and calf) and a *tomboay* (young gelding). His youngest son, Faralahy, had given four cattle and 6,000 FMG for his

first wife, not counting the
invocation money. The large
amounts of money, distinguished
from the miletry proper as 'leaves
of money' (*ravin'kariana,* bills not
coins), were related to the miletry,
or cattle, since they were meant to
be used to cover the first year's
taxes on them. But they were
mainly intended for the bride's
household goods (*entana*). Marriage
wealth in the 1970s for first
marriages varied from two cattle
and 5,000 FMG to four cattle and
10,000 FMG, 500–1,000 FMG for
the joro and a comparable amount
for the woman who had done the
most to raise the bride. People
living in Analalava sometimes
agreed to give or accept more
money, instead of cattle. Djoma
gave 30,000 for Tavavy in 1970,
but 20,000 for his second wife in
the late seventies, because she had
been married before. His younger
brother, Abodo, gave 15,000 for his
first wife in 1974, because she was
already pregnant. If he had not
agreed, her father threatened to
have him jailed, but his brother
helped him with some money, and
he found work and paid the rest.
Like the kinds of marriage wealth,
the other sums of money are
named. The invocation money is
called *fangala gadra* (lock remover),
for 'the child's grandparent to open
the mouth of the formal speech [to
the ancestors]' *(mampibiaña
dadan'tseke ny vavan' ny kabary),* as

one man described it. The gift to
the foster mother was called
tsongotsongo feliky, 'little pinch of
greens.'

22. After explaining that a
woman 'searching for a man with
cattle' gave a miletry consisting of
two or three cattle, one woman
went on to say: 'Women marry
women, more than one wife
*(mañangy manambady mañangy,
mampirafy*). My father's sister
Maromine was a woman who acted
like a man *(mañangy mañano
lehilahy).* She got two wives by
giving miletry. She made a
homestead with one on one side,
the other on the other. She lived in
the middle.' She then went on to
explain other ways in which
Maromine 'acted like a man.'

23. Joloka (entrance, admittance)
is the term used to refer to a
marriage in which the husband goes
to live in the wife's village, usually
because he cannot pay what the
bride's family or the bride
demands. It had a pejorative
connotation among men,
suggesting a man who had become
like a woman, who more often
follows her spouse. (Joloka is the
term for a woman's body wrap
elsewhere in Madagascar, see
Richardson 1885:305.)

24. A Sakalava royal official,
whom Poirier questioned during
the succession battle following
Tondroko's death, described the
ancestral Vy Lava, as "our église"

(Poirier 1926:28). Although Malaza did not 'speak French,' he often used French words that were common regionally for some features of rank and order in government, including the monarchy (for example, *galôño, cadre, konfransy, birao ny juge, mikommandy*), consumer goods (for example, *petrôly*), and parts of the house (for example, *lafenêtra*). In this same conversation, he also used a Merina term, *fivavahaña*—'place/ means of prayer' usually referring to Christian churches—as a way of interpreting for us the local term *fangatahaña*, 'place/means of supplication.' Like many others in the region, he often equated the Merina with Vazaha since the Merina had served as the main intermediaries of the French during the colonial period.

25. *Aviavy* is a species of *Ficus*, perhaps *Ficus megapoda* Bak. The white sap was used for bird lime. According to Debray et al. (1971:83), people in the highlands use the smell from the crushed leaves to stop coughs.

Mandresy (to conquer) has an edible fruit. According to Richardson (1885:425), "It is supposed by the Sakalava to have the power to destroy the effects of any evil charm whatever used against any one." Richardson thought it was the same as the tree called aviavy, but Malaza and others in the Analalava region

distinguished them. Zanatany in the Analalava region said that *Ficus* trees owed their conquering power to the fact that 'they're not good with their friends, they murder their friends' *(tsy tsara am namana, mamono namana)*. They kill anything to which they attach themselves by choking their growth. This accounted for their conquering power, but for this same reason, they were prohibited at royal centers, in keeping with other prohibitions at those places against disagreement, violence, and death.

26. Richardson (1885:427, 231) describes *mangarahara*, also known as *harahara*, as having a very hard wood, sometimes mistaken for *Lignum vitae*, used in making spade handles, and also as a remedy for indigestion. The scraped bark was an antidote to a poisonous insect sometimes drunk in water. Debray et al. (1971:91) identify harahara in the highlands as *Phylloxylon ensifolium* Baill., used there to bring down fevers and to combat dandruff.

27. Sakalava in the nineteenth century used infusions made from the leaves of *Tamarindus indica* L. *(madiro, madilo, kily)* as a vermifuge and as a cure for other stomach disorders. (Perhaps this was also the source of the black dye they used in making silk cloth.) The edible fruit was also used in making rum, and the seeds were used as the pawns in *sikidy* (from *kily*) divination

(Richardson 1885:336). According to Debray et al. (1971:17), the pulp of the ripe fruit was used in southwestern Madagascar as a laxative and infusions of the internal layer of the bark were used in calming coughs.

28. Richardson (1885:203) identifies *foraha* as *Calophyllum inophyllum* L. In some villages during the early colonial period, *fantsina* (calling place[s]) were constructed like houses raised up from the ground a foot or two, but without walls, as places to meet but also as cool places to work and rest (see Dandouau 1922:11, 37). During the 1970s, there was a fantsina in the royal compound at the Doany and next to the tomb at the Mahabo, for gatherings with royalty, but they were not common elsewhere in the region. Women in Tsinjorano often worked in the shade of the houses under construction, which served, like Togny's and Avoria's work groups under the *madiro masina,* to mark out smaller social groups within the community.

29. Other impressive trees had, for the time being, simpler uses. Avoria explained that the *tsiketry* tree south of her house in Tsinjorano had enormous fruits with deliciously fatty seeds. Its thick bark was good for making spoons. Bezara had brought back a large white rock from Nosy Lava and leaned it against the western side of his house because he liked it.

30. A daba, a oil tin holding about 7½ kilos of unhulled rice, was the commonest way of measuring rice in bulk. Ten daba was the minimum amount that people counted on saving from each crop to reseed a field the next year. Ten daba is a substantial amount to exchange for the use of a field. Lower amounts could also be negotiated. Strangers who wished to cultivate in Tsinjorano went not to Tafara, the eldest male tompontany (since Ambary was living in his wife's village), but to his sister's son who served as chef de village. Sefo called the members of the community together. If they agreed to accept the stranger, then the stranger made his or her own arrangements. Sometimes he paid rent *(karama)* for the field, sometimes not. The amount—for example five daba—was decided in advance, so that even if the stranger got a huge harvest, he only had to pay five daba.

31. Before that, he had worked in a village on the Komajara Peninsula and in Antognibe. He went from Tsinjorano to another rural village further north before returning for his bride to the Tamatave region on the east coast, and then settling in Analalava in 1957. Sea slugs, eventually exported to China, were still a major part of his business in the 1970s.

32. A valakira was a fence (vala) made from the ribs *(kira)* of raffia palm leaves after the outer coat had been removed to make twine or rope, interspersed with heavier posts for strength. The valakira was built along the shore to catch the fish trapped inside the fence after the tide went out. The productivity of valakira varied according to seasons of the year and places on the coast.

33. See Bloch 1971, 1973.

34. Fields purchased during colonial and postcolonial periods had names like villages, recalling features of the landscape. There were at least nine such fields around Tsinjorano. Descendants of 'masters of the land' and 'strangers,' who had bought land, had access to these fields through their parents and grandparents. Strangers who had no land had to 'rent land' *(mikarama tany),* which was usually calculated at the number of daba tins they used to sow the land, regardless of the yield.

35. 'Wet-season rice' (vary asara) is named after the time it is grown. Jeby means disordered, confused, irregular, perhaps referring to the fact that it is grown out of season. According to Richardson (1885:300), vary jeby was 'rice planted in a rough and ready manner,' but this is not currently the case in the Analalava region. Vary jeby, depending on year-round sources of water, is more

likely to be hand-planted or transplanted, as opposed to broadcast, than wet-season rice.

36. Noël 1844:405. In the 1980s, more people in the Analalava region cleared land by burning *(mandroro tany)* and planted by spading in the seed *(miantomboko vary).* These were the commonest methods of cultivation in 1989, not only among functionaries who had turned to farming to augment their incomes during the 1980s, but also among long-established farmers. These changes will be discussed elsewhere.

37. Parents also passed on prohibited days, identified with their own 'ancestral customs,' to their children: days on which they should not herd cattle, cultivate rice, trample fields for planting, or handle money. Children born to them on that day had to be given to one's spouse, and cattle born to them should be killed, since as one person pointed out, it would get no milk if it was given to someone else, so it would die anyway. Saha Barimaso's story, in Chapter 1, turns on such issues.

In addition to the prohibitions derived from royal ancestors' death-days and from one's own ancestors, the land itself, if it was inhabited by a 'spirit' *(tsigny),* might have a prohibited day. Cattle dedicated to spirits also had prohibited days.

38. Charsley makes this point about the silika of the Margoli in

Uganda, arguing that "apparently traditional work organization may in fact be a response to new circumstances" (1976:44). French colonial administrators in Madagascar ascribed indigenous origins for the cooperative work groups they sought to establish. From their point of view, these groups *(fokon'olona)* were a means of introducing beliefs and practices that would lend themselves to "modernization," for example, the organization of cooperatives for the purpose of buying agricultural machinery that individual households were too poor to purchase on their own (Decary 1951a, 1956). The contemporary agricultural cooperatives, renamed *fokon'tany* in 1972, have been justified in the same way (Serre-Ratsimandisa 1978).

39. Şaul 1983:87–88.

40. Ibid.:85.

41. Ibid.:92.

42. Ibid.:93, n. 3; see Bloch 1973.

43. Şaul 1983:93.

44. Bloch 1973.

45. People often said that boys did some kinds of work, girls did other kinds, for example, boys watched cattle, while girls gathered wild fruits and shellfish and wove palm-leaf bags. Carrying burdens was one of the few other areas where it was often insisted that men 'did not know how to carry on their heads' *(tsy mahay miloloha);* they carried burdens on poles balanced on their shoulders *(titiaña, lazaina).* Yet royalty—the spirits that possess people and the objects in royal services, which are identified as royalty—is carried only on the head, held with both hands.

46. See Feeley-Harnik 1980.

47. Perhaps not surprisingly, poisoning was said to be a favored weapon in undeclared enmities. Many sicknesses centered around food and the openness and hiddenness of things, including words, relations, and exchange. Sickness from eating prohibited foods was usually the first sign of spirit possession. Aching teeth were the forerunner of a systematic malaise centered on the *vava fo* or heart's mouth, which people located in the epigastrum. The spirit was finally 'made to come out' *(mampiboaka tromba)* by inducing it to speak, openly declaring its identity, its reasons for making a particular person sick, and the prohibitions having especially to do with food that would make the situation right again. Cases I know better from people in Analalava than from people in Andonaka and Tsinjorano suggest that spirit possession often had to do with righting relations among close kin.

48. Tavavy especially emphasized that a boy who gets to be that old "may not share a house with the

father! It is absolutely necessary to live in a separate house from the father's house" (*Tsy mety miharo trano am baba. Tsy maintsy misaraka trano am babany*).

49. Noël 1843, vol. 20:291.

50. The women in Tsinjorano who sang this song explained it as follows: "Tsakalabanga is a kind of grass that grows near water. Once it takes hold, it ruins the land. Zaina [the name of any woman] goes around grabbing people's husbands—that's her work, ruining people's relations with their spouses (*mandrobak'olo am vadiny*). She's no good, she grabs husbands. Jibona is the name of the man she likes because she takes people's husbands like grabbing food from a plate (*mijobo*). Mijoboño means to chose especially the husbands of people, the married ones. She is not a growing girl [who is expected to sleep with several young, unmarried men before she marries]. An *amato* is simply a man who wants to sleep with her, not a husband. Having a man, she looks married. Then she's after someone different (*Bok eo, mazoto olo hafa*)."

51. Others described this form of speaking specifically as *mamôsa*, "revealing hidden things that people shouldn't be told" (*manambara raha miafina tsy tokony hanambara olo*). MamanDjoma's use of Mamosàh! which she translated as Kabaria! (Talk!), in her discussion of incest earlier in this chapter, is another example of what was commonly involved in invocations to ancestral spirits. MamanDjoma regarded mipoko as another difference between kinds of people: "Silamo don't mipoko, just Tsimihety and Sakalava."

52. She then went on to talk about branches of the family in Analalava, and in that context commented on how "According to Silamo custom, relatives ought to marry each other, children of men should marry children of women, people related as brother and sister should marry. . . ."

Tavavy said that her FFF came from the Comores, she was not sure where. He married a local 'Sakalava' woman, as did all his male descendants: "his children just followed Sakalava custom, ate prohibited things. . . ." Her FM was the child of a Silamo father and Sakalava mother. She followed 'Silamo custom.'

53. Zalifa had since died and was buried in the cemetery of Ambodibonara, south of Analalava. She was not buried at her father's village of Marosely because it was too far away, and following Silamo custom, the body had to be buried within a day, two at the most.

54. Later she said it was called *tsiminindrano*—she said she didn't know what that meant—or *atolaka* from *atolakandreo*, "something with which they send them to a different place from where they are living"

(alefandreo am tany hafa izy mipetraka). According to Richardson (1885:654), tolaka and its derivatives have stronger meanings related to sending away than lefa, including: "to hinder, prevent someone from proving his innocence by the *tangena* poison through means of witchcraft, to throw the blame on another; in the provinces it means to throw a bone to a dog, to throw anything down, to drive out, to chase, etc."

55. The medium of Tompony Andronjona from the Ambolobozo Peninsula explained in 1981 that "Ndramamahaña had a younger brother, Moena Kely, same mother, different father. He lived at Nosy Be. Ndramamahaña called him to be near him while he was at Manongarivo. Then he [Moena Kely] got sick and died here. He was buried at Andronjona, because the mahabo was still there where the French government had thrown it out *(voaroasigny ny fanjakana frantsay).* He was buried east of the village." She identified herself as his only medium, saying "When there is a royal service, he comes to rule (mianjaka) out there. If the mahabo had been there, he would have been buried there." She was also possessed by Ambilahikely, their child.

Keeping in mind Malaza's perspective on these events, that Tondroko's (Ndramamahaña) followers did not accompany him when the French relocated him to Manongarivo, "because the French had gotten the government" [not because the French had prohibited him from bringing numerous followers], I wonder if Tondroko himself had sought to appeal to his marginalized status in the eyes of his own followers by bringing his brother through his mother from Nosy Be to live with him.

56. The only other exception I found in Tsinjorano and Andonaka was Laza's seven-year-old son (Fig. 9, F). His father came from an inland village a half-day's walk from Tsinjorano, nevertheless he was living with his mother's parents (Mbotisoa and her husband), looking after his mother's cattle, while his mother lived with her second husband in Majunga. In every other instance I encountered, the child living with the mother of a divorced couple, or with her kin, was due to be returned to the father's kin sometime in its second year, when it was considered old enough to be separated from its mother. To cite one example from Tsinjorano not included in Figures 9–11, Laika, a woman in her twenties, married to one of the younger pair of brothers linked to Tsinjorano through Zanety, had four daughters from three prior marriages. Two were living with their father in a village on Nosy Lava, the third was living with her mother in the same village

until, as Laika put it, she was old enough to 'stay with her own relatives' [i.e. her father's kin]. Laika, who had no children from her current marriage in Tsinjorano, was still caring for the youngest girl. Laika was born in her mother's father's village, Ambolobozo, where her mother continued to live after having married a man who had moved there from Ambanja in search of work. When Laika's father returned to Ambanja, Laika's mother moved to her second husband's natal village on Nosy Lava, to which Laika returned after her first marriage and met her second and fourth husbands.

57. I asked Matombo about divisions among his own children because I got confused. In fact, he can fulfill his obligations at the Mahabo with all of his children, of which he is the 'master.' Since Avoria's daughter Miadana is not a Sambarivo, she does not have to replace herself in the next generation at the place from which, in principle, no one moves.

In 1981, my "brother-in-law" Djoma had divorced Tavavy, his wife during our first visit in the 1970s, and married a Sambarivo from the Mahabo. According to MamanDjoma, he had to go out to the Mahabo to beg the royal ancestors for permission to keep the children, but she did not know whether he had actually done so.

So far, they had only one eight-month-old baby, and, as Matombo indicated, the problem would arise only if and when they separated.

58. Richardson (1885:203) and Debray et al. (1971:38) identify the foraha as *Calophyllum inophyllum* L.. He derives the Malagasy term, meaning "full of joy, happy, angelic" from "Swahili, *furaha*, gladness, joy." The tree produces a gummy substance that Betsimisaraka use as bird-lime. The fruit produces an oil that women use in their toilet (ibid.). According to Debray et al. (ibid.) Betsimisaraka use a decoction of the pits of the fruits, which has healing qualities, to stop post-partum bleeding. They mix the pounded seeds with rice to use as a rat poison.

59. Hasina (*Dracaena* sp., the name is a substantive of masina), is also a common feature of ancestral shrines and offerings in highland Madagascar (see Richardson 1885:236, who identifies it as *Dracaena angustifolia* Roxb.; Bloch 1986). *Matambelona* (dead and living) is a shrub whose quickset branches can be used to make bushy fences. The outermost fence at the Mahabo (the fiaroaomby) is made mainly from matambelona.

60. I could be more specific about the role of the royal spirits' trees in the community life of rural villages had I not imagined that trees just grew by themselves. I did

not think to ask about the circumstances in which royal spirits came into the community to grow their trees and how their work involved others over time, even over generations.

61. When I once asked why there were no 'mothers' and 'mothers' brothers' among the Zafinifotsy, I was told: 'Because they are from Marangibato, in the Mandritsara area [inland, in an area identified with 'Tsimihety,' which they are said to be]. They were running from the Hova, running right out to the edge of the water. They weren't from here, so people don't know who the rest of them are. Bevaoko and Ampela Be are brother and sister. He is the father, she is the father's sister of Kotomena, Ndrandahy, and the others.' While the Zafinimena are 'masters of the land,' the Zafinifotsy are 'masters of the water,' the Loza River where they committed suicide by drowning, rather than submitting to Hova rule, and where they are still honored at several shrines.

62. The lines indicate the brief pauses between melodic lines. The singer began by using the standard, Merina possessive ending -ko in the first line, followed by a made-up possessive suffix (-ky) in the second line to rhyme with the locally used possessive suffix (- [n]akahy) in the fourth line, while using the root "Angovavy" in the third line.

According to Richardson (1885:48), *angi* is a provincial word for a man in the father's generation; *angivavy*, referring to women in that generation, thus meant female F/ FB, etc. This connection is not linguistically emphasized in the Analalava region, where people use *baba*, not angi or ango, to refer to F, FB, FFBS, etc.

63. Vondraka could be used to describe a person who had a nicely plump body, but *botra* or simply *be vata* (big bodied) was more often used for that purpose, while vondraka applied especially to the fatty flesh of animals, grains, and beans, which made the most succulent meals.

Another common way of admiring a nicely plump person was to say: 'That one's really sweet' *(Mamy io é!)*, whereas 'ugly hair' or 'ugly faces' were described as 'not sweet' or as 'bitter' *(Maroy'nany tsy mamy é! Ratsy tarehy? Ah, tsy tsara, mafaiky é, mafaiky igny!)*. In daily life, people most often described women in these terms, but they also recur in royal praise songs. People responded to good songs by exclaiming Matavy! (Fat, succulent). Lively events were both *maresaka* (full of talk) and *masaka* (cooked, ready to eat).

64. The song is addressed to Ampela Be and thus can be understood as addressed to 'you,' Ampela Be. It can also be understood as describing the

singer's relationship to Father's Sister in general.

65. Or, *atsika aroy tompony* (we're both his owner/masters). These lines are taken from a popular joke between affines: *Vadiny angovavy [zama] vadin'tsika jiaby,* 'The father's sister's husband is the husband of all of us,' which is also said about the mother's brother's *(zama)* wife *(zena).* According to one joking song, which was said to have been very popular in the countryside not long before we arrived: 'Oa Zena, what should I do about you [my love for you]? If I sleep with you, Zena, your stomach will hold my younger sibling!' *(Oa Zena, akory atako anao. Zaho handry aminao, zena, kibonao misy zandriko!).*

66. Or, 'I love that you love me, Angovavy.' The singer increased the force of her statement by phrasing it indirectly, and also avoided the repetition that would have resulted from using the direct form, which would have been: *Tiako tianao zaho Angovavy. Tsy malaigny* (not reluctant/indifferent/ unwilling/lazy) is also an indirect way of saying *mazoto* (eager/ zealous/willing/hardworking), but in the context of love, *mazoto* refers to women's ardent desire to sleep with men.

67. See Southall 1971; Kottak 1980:309, n. 1; and Southall 1986 for summary comments.

68. Kottak 1980:180, see pp.

174–176. See also Huntington 1988, concerning Bara in the south-central highlands, who argues that although agnatic ties are critical to the definition of local descent groups, they are encompassed within larger collectivities based on ties through women.

69. Southall 1986:417. Southall reflects Huntington (1988) in arguing that where "the mystical bond of child to mother is extraordinarily profound" throughout the island, father-child bonds have to be built up over time, assertions that are not clearly born out in the Analalava region. Southall goes on to suggest that cognatically oriented people simply keep their options open longer than more agnatically oriented people for whom cattle-keeping is a major concern (ibid.:418). In keeping with his emphasis on the cumulative character of kinship in Madagascar, Southall would view Malagasy uses of agnation as being more like patrifiliation in practice (ibid.:421). Patrifiliation—or rather, fathers' repeated claims to children—better describes the position of 'children of men' in farming villages in the Analalava region. But neither of these processes account for the systematic use of lengthy patri-matrilineal genealogies supporting Sakalava royal ancestries described in Chapter 2, with which the ancestries of 'simple people' are explicitly contrasted.

70. See Kottak 1980:177–179 for his assessment from a comparative perspective. See Marshall 1981 on siblingship in Oceania, who notes the importance of siblings as the key reproductive pair in the creation of descent groups. See Kipp (1986:638) for a brief summary of research on the equivalence of siblings and spouses in Southeast Asia.

71. Schneider (1981) notes that research on siblingship in Oceania has not taken marriage practices sufficiently into account.

72. Kipp 1986.

73. Weiner 1980.

74. Baré (1986), Hurvitz (1980:250, 253), Gardenier (1976:104, 109), and Lambek (1981:21–22, on Malagasy speakers in Mayotte note preferences for exogamy among people in northeastern and western Madagascar. See Bloch (1978), Huntington (1978), and Middleton (1990) on relationships between incest and endogamy among the Merina, Bara, and Karembola respectively. Among Merina in highland Madagascar (Bloch 1978) and Karembola in southern Madagascar (Middleton 1990), there are also hierarchical differences between brothers and sisters, expressed in such terms as *anak'ampela,* 'children of women' in the south. Because in both cases marriage is ideally endogamous, the difference seems to be seen mainly

in terms of an inequality between wife-takers and wife-givers, though this too varies. Among the Merina, marriages should be between equals because they are between kin (Bloch 1978:23). Yet the wife-takers, or groom's family, are regarded as superior to the wife-givers because the wife-givers are having to give up the greatest good, namely child-bearing women. Bloch argues that Merina marriage ceremonies resolve the contradiction between equity in the long run and inequity in the short run by ritually reversing it. Among the Karembola, wife-givers are the ones who "shame" and "enslave" their wife-takers in "giving life" to them, an opposition that Middleton (n.d.) argues is redressed through Karembola funeral rituals. Among the Betsileo with whom Rajaonarimanana (1986:252–253) did research in the 1970s, 'children of brothers' and of brothers and sisters were preferred partners *(anjara vady),* in contrast to children of sisters, who were forbidden to marry *(vady fady).*

75. See Southall 1981; Baré 1986; Bloch 1971; Condominas 1961; Huntington 1988; Kottak 1980; Pavageau 1981; Schomerus-Gernböck 1981; Wilson 1967.

76. Bloch 1971:206.

77. Kottak 1986.

78. Kottak 1986. Bloch (1973) makes a similar argument.

79. Another feature of social

relations in northwestern Madagascar, which links it to the wider Malayo-Polynesian area is the importance of friends, expressed in earlier work on kindreds in Southeast Asia and reaffirmed recently in Gibson's (1986) work on the Buid of the Philippines.

80. Guyer (1984) argues that "naturalistic" models of production still dominate the analysis of African household organization, especially economic development. According to Packard (1991), the kinship-to-contract model has reemerged among scholars studying AIDS in Africa.

Notes to Chapter 5, *Ampositra: At the Post*, pp. 231–301.

1. Philibert Tsiranana proclaimed the independence of the République Malgache within the Communauté, a federation including France and its Territoires Outre-Mer, on October 14, 1958. He declared the independence of the République Malgache from the Communauté on June 26, 1960. Sometime after he was forced out of office in 1972 (and after we left at the end of 1973), his name and the earlier date were whitewashed from the monument.

2. This map is a slightly simplified copy (omitting street names and some paths) of the official map of Analalava in use in the early 1970s. The map, completed by the Section Topographique du Service de l'Architecture de l'Urbanisme et de l'Habitat (Ministère des Travaux Publics des Transports De La Construction et des Postes et Telecommunications, Repoblika Malagasy) on August 13, 1963, was based on an earlier map completed in 1953, combined with aerial photographs taken in 1963. The "conventional signs" *(signes conventionnels)* distinguishing durably built administrative structures in the north and east from the lightly built huts and fences in the south and west— *bâtiment administratif, maison en dur, maison en bois soubassement dur,* and *case légère, clôture légère*—were probably taken over from the earlier map, made toward the end of the colonial period. The key includes most of the structures indicated on the map (except the *terrain de sport* west of the Place de l'Indépendance). They were all in the north, except for the cemetery. I have added numbers 13–16 designating places in the southern half of the town.

3. Although the structure of the administration was centered on the Gouvernement Général, represented by Galliéni in Tananarive, it was expected to be locally various, relying heavily on indirect rule through indigenous authorities, which might vary from place to place, and especially on the judgment of the local *soldat-colonisateur* in charge, whom

Galliéni emphasized should be (in English): "The right man in the right place" (Gouvernement Général de Madagascar 1899:17–18, 121–125, see p. 122).

4. Cercle d'Analalava, Rapport économique, 1896–1904, completed in Analalava on February 9, 1905 by the commandant du cercle, Captaine H. Charbonnel (CAOM MAD 2 D 24).

5. *Journal officiel,* 25 novembre 1897; Toquenne 1897a:972. Many of the Merina in Ampasikely had been resettled there from the Merina fort at Anorotsangana discussed in Chapter 2.

6. *Journal officiel,* 23 juillet 1898, p. 2181; Charbonnel's report for 1896–1904 (op. cit.) notes that the Tribunal was constructed in 1898 according to the "système Espitellier et Wehrlin."

The French schoolteacher, André Dandouau, who lived in Analalava on and off between 1901 and 1921, claimed on the basis of censuses in 1912 and 1920 that "It would be difficult to find, in all Madagascar, a province where the population is more mixed than it is in the province of Analalava" (1922:19). The province of Analalava then encompassed most of the Boina basin north of the Sofia River (ibid.:15). Administrative boundaries have changed several times since then.

The administrative hierarchy of the country, transformed in the course of reforms in the mid-1970s (see Covell 1987:97–115), still followed the French colonial model in the early 1970s. The sous-préfet of Analalava described it as including the *fanjakana—pouvoir central* (the national government, headed by a president), province (chef du province), préfecture (préfet), sous-préfecture (sous-préfet), arondissement, canton (chef de canton, maire), quartier (chef du quartier), village (chef du village). At that time, Analalava was the capital of the subprefecture of Analalava (with seven cantons, including the town of Analalava), included in the prefecture of Antsohihy, in the province of Majunga. The town was governed by the maire, an elected official. Including five quartiers, its population numbered about 5,700.

Statistics compiled by the Canton d'Analalava for Analalava and Ampasikely in 1972–1973 indicate a similarly diverse population (see Appendix 3).

7. Haeringer 1980:290. *L'Arbre en Afrique tropicale: La Fonction et le signe,* in which the essay by the geographer Haeringer appears, includes papers by other geographers and economists at ORSTOM. It is evident from their presentations that African and French participants alike have long seen trees as powerfully direct expressions of the relationship between people and land, their

attitudes toward "civilization," its
growth, decline, and regeneration.
Ozouf (1988:145–146, 232–261)
uses the "Liberty Tree" to illustrate
how politicians drew upon popular
culture for the central images of
festivals celebrating the French
Revolution. Most of *les arbres de la
liberté* were oaks, chosen for their
hardness, suggesting strength and
longevity, "for (as a participant put
it) it would be desirable that these
trees, a symbol of liberty, should
be eternal" (Ozouf 1988:341, n.
108).

Saha Barimaso said in 1989 that
there used to be many more trees
throughout the post of Analalava.
Many were cut down, some fell
down, and when the Tribunal
burned, many were lost then too.
Analalava never had a togny. But
when I suggested that the big
mangos around the Tribunal might
have been like the togny of the
French, he said: "When JIRAMA
[the national electricity company]
tried to cut down the huge mango
at the northwest corner of the
square, the oldest and largest still
standing, blood came out of it
(niboaka lio). It had huge fruits, as
big as water jugs. So the workmen
refused to cut it down, just cut its
hands *(tañantañana)*, and left it
standing like a living person
(napetraka karaha olom-belona)."

8. Some people used the term to
distinguish local residents from
government functionaries; others

used it to distinguish themselves
from prisoners in the national
penitentiary and paroled to live in
the area.

9. The Taiwanese shopkeeper
had lived in several coastal villages
(including Tsinjorano). In 1957,
having married a Chinese-
Betsimisaraka woman from the east
coast, he established a store in the
lower half of a building owned by a
French merchant who continued
living on the second floor until he
left after independence.

10. The bars in Analalava
reflected the same north-south
divisions. During the colonial
period, only three places in the
northern half of the post were
authorized to sell alcohol—a hotel
run by a French *colon,* then his
Malagasy wife; a bar run by a
French-Lebanese immigrant; and
the Chinese shopkeeper. At
independence, in 1960, a local man
(the son of a local woman, whose
father was a government
functionary originally from
Morondava in the southwest) got
permission to sell bottled beer in
the southern half of the post. Two
other 'palm-wine bars' *(bar trembo)*
had since opened in the
southwestern quarters of the town,
run by Muslims with coconut-palm
concessions in the Ambolobozo
Peninsula. The trembo bars were
known jokingly as SOTEMA and
COTONA, after the trademark
(Vita Malagasy, Malagasy Made) of

Madagascar's two cloth factories, nationalized after 1972.

11. According to an early *Guide Annuaire* (1901:369) on the region of Analalava, "the Europeans prefer to engage in the business of alcohol," both importing and exporting large quantities, while the Indians restricted themselves to what were still their specialties in the 1970s: the purchase of local produce and the sale of household goods, tools, cosmetics, clothes, and especially cloth. Silamo merchants sold kerosene, cloth, matches, soap, canned tomatoes, Malagasy tea, spices, and incense in small amounts. Other local residents occasionally sold palm wine, cooked meats and fish, biscuits, candy, and white clay *(tany fotsy/malandy)* for people possessed by spirits. See Condominas (1968), Tsien Tche-Hao (1961), and Fanony and Gueunier (1980) for further discussion of Greek, Chinese, and Silamo immigrants in Madagascar.

In 1981, all of the shopkeepers relied much more heavily on locally made goods, including new items like cane syrup and yogurt. The bar in the northern half of the town sold only locally made rum *(betsa)*. Three Indian shopkeeping families, the one in the north and two in the south, who were not licensed as *receveurs des produits locaux* and who were thus supposed to buy bulk produce from the Compagnie

Marseillance in Antsohihy, had moved out.

12. Fathers of the Congrégation des Pères de Saint Esprit, from Nosy Be, founded the mission at the request of the then Commandant Lecaux of the Cercle Militaire d'Analalava. They were followed in 1947 by the Pères Capucins. The first sisters from the Congregation de la Divine Providence de St. Jean de Bassel arrived in 1953. One Père, one nursing sister for the leprosarium at Tsimahasenga, and three to four teaching sisters (mostly French) represented the Catholic Church in the early 1970s. In 1989, two Pères and about the same number of Soeurs (mostly Malagasy) represented the church in Analalava in 1989. The Italian Catholics had moved to a place outside of Antisohily.

13. No law prohibited others from being buried there, but people who identified themselves as "Sakalava" or "Silamo" said that they could not be buried in Ampasikely because the highlanders there kept pigs, which were unclean.

14. Sakalava rulers collected tribute *(mangala paria),* including money *(mitaky vola)*. The ruler's presentations to the royal ancestors were and are still known as *takitaky.* Merina rulers taxed people in their provincial colonies, but Ranavalona III was still in the

process of trying to occupy the
Analalava area at the time of the
French conquest in 1895–1896.

15. Toquenne 1897a:973; Guédès
1898:2384; Arrêté du 31 décembre
1900, Arrêté du 4 juin 1901, *Guide
Annuaire* 1901:462–463.

16. In the early 1970s, when
there were 250 Malagasy francs to
the dollar, dropping to 210 FMG to
the dollar in 1973, annual taxes
included a head tax *(latety,* from Fr.
la tête) on adult males, beginning at
age 21, when a man got a *carte
d'identité,* which had to be renewed
every ten years (officially 2,875
FMG, but usually described as
3,000 FMG); a cattle tax (130 FMG
each); a dog tax (300 FMG); a gun
tax (1,000 FMG); a charette tax
(500 FMG); a tax on houses with or
without metal roofs, but varying
according to location and walling
material (in Analalava or in the
countryside: palm-stalk walls (287
FMG, 86 FMG), mud or brick
walls (575 FMG, 86 FMG). In
1973, under the new administration
of General Ramanantsoa, the head
and cattle taxes were abolished.

Freehold land was not taxed;
people owning concessions were
expected to pay revenue taxes on
what they sold. People who ran
businesses *(dokany, hotely, bar,
boulangerie*—Muslim bread-sellers)
paid for licenses renewed annually
(averaging 14,000–25,000 FMG/
year) plus revenue taxes.

Explaining why the census

figures for most years were
"probabilities—because people keep
moving around"—a government
official from the highlands, who
had married a local woman, went
on to say: "It is really hard to
collect taxes around here; it creates
such difficulties *(mampanahirana
marè).* You go out and you don't
find them there. They've gone off
some place and are not expected for
several months. They give their
stuff to their elders to look after
while they are gone. The problem
of collecting taxes is never finished;
it goes on and on. We are still
collecting last year's taxes (in April
1973). Some people constantly keep
moving because of the taxes—in
one place one year, in another year,
and so on."

A young man from the
countryside came in. The official
told him to remove his hat. He
took it off and sank to his knees,
the way people do *(mirefaka)* when
speaking formally to their elder kin
and which some still do in speaking
to the ampanjaka in her office,
though not publicly. He was still
on his knees, talking to the official,
a few minutes later when we left.

17. These were already the main
resources that were traded in the
Analalava region. One reason they
were established so quickly was
that besides the local people,
including Silamo and Indian traders
who produced and traded in these
resources, there were also French

creoles from Réunion who had begun to settle in the area after Nosy Be and the adjacent mainland became a protectorate, especially since the 1880s. All of the four concessions in the canton of Analalava in 1971–1973 were planted with coconut trees. By far the largest (322 hectares) was that of a creole who had bequeathed it to a former slave who served as his foreman. The other three, much smaller (16, 6, and 3 hectares), were owned by Malagasy.

18. *Guide Annuaire* 1909–1910:143.

19. Ibid. 1905:478.

20. *Association des Géographes de Madagascar* 1969–1970, planche 35.

21. The early colonial guide books for prospective settlers also speak of the impressive numbers of hardy, healthy cattle in the region. The numbers of cattle in the canton of Analalava (including Analalava, twenty-one villages south of Analalava, one village on the Komajara Peninsula, and Nosy Lava) were 11,197 in 1960; 14,807 in 1961; 11,720 in 1962; 12,034 in 1970; 10,424 in 1971; and 9,630 in 1972. The total population of the canton of Analalava in 1961 was 9,430 and in 1972–1973 was 12,388 (statistics compiled by the Canton d'Analalava).

22. Dokany derives from *dukani,* a locative form of the Swahili term *duka.* Most of the shops in the region were located in Analalava,

Antognibe, and Ambarijeby. Smaller shops, operated by Silamo merchants, were located in a few rural villages north and south of the Loza River. Judging by the experiences of local people, the prices at which goods were sold in rural shops were one-fourth to one-third higher than the prices in Analalava, while the prices at which goods were sold were correspondingly lower.

Apart from those who deal in identity photos, highland peddlers specialize in small manufactured goods like needles, thread, cloth, fishhooks, and the like, though occasionally highlanders peddled carved wooden furniture in Analalava. Most of the other itinerant peddlers in the Analalava region were migrant laborers from the plantations in the Sambirano and Sofia river valleys to the north and south, who sold the tobacco and coffee that was raised there. In Tsinjorano and Andonaka, whoever had money bought as much as they could, then sold it to others in the village. Like alcohol, tobacco was bought and sold freely, even among kin.

23. The Malagasy phrase for such talk is *tenim-bola* (money-talk), which is already in Richardson's (1885:639) dictionary as "words used in order to get money." Most words for manufactured goods in the Analalava region—for example, *savôño (savon), dipoivre (du poivre),*

petroly (pétrole), sezy (chaise), tirkôt (tircot), jipo (jupe), tergal (tergal), charbony (charbon). Likewise, most talk *about* money in buying and selling—*marikè (marque), manao profite (profiter), mahazo benefice (bénéficier), be depense (grosse dépenses), bon-por (bon pour,* debt coupon), *kontiny (compter), patenty (patente), mipezy (peser)*—were derived from French usage.

24. They were allowed to charge extra for the cost of transportation in some instances.

25. According to the reforms initiated after the change of government in the spring of 1972, government functionaries (except for the schools, on the grounds that they desperately needed regular workers) and private persons were not allowed to employ prisoners as day-workers, but it is unclear how closely this reform was followed. People in Analalava with concessions in the countryside were using prisoners as workers again in 1981.

26. This idea was already well entrenched in the first decade of the colonial period, if not earlier. Dandouau cites a funeral oration in which the dead person's spirit is admonished: "Never return to make women and children afraid; do not make your kin sick. Do not give money, do not give a salary to bad spirits *(tsigny)* for them to make your descendants sick" (Dandouau 1911:161, 163).

27. I asked if there was a togny in Ampasikely. Robert said that there was already a togny here when they arrived, what they called 'the madiro [tamarind] of the Hova.' A second tree—'the togny of the Sakalava'—was set up later near the ferry-landing, north of Ampasikely, when the landing was built. They identified togny as the trees of royal spirits (tromba). Robert had heard that when Sakalava rulers died, they could not be buried in the ground, but were put *(ahantona)* on top of a madiro tree while their bones dried out. Their followers removed the nails and teeth, then the bones were taken over to Nosy Lava and buried there. He said that people don't go to the old [Hova] togny any more; they do tromba at the Sakalava tree. And yes [in response to my question], also in their houses. "Lots of people. Didn't you hear the tromba meeting in Afongony yesterday. All the women from here went down there to it." Maria started naming names, and Robert said quickly that we were not interested in that business.

28. See Deschamps 1959; Molet 1959. A schoolteacher at the C.E.G. made the same argument in 1989. He identified himself as "Betsimisaraka" from the east coast. There, "you can't tell Tsimihety and Betsimisaraka apart. You ask one day, and a person calls himself Tsimihety; you ask the

next, he says Betsimisaraka." In
contrast, the Sakalava in the
Analalava region are retreating in
the face of "more industrious
people, like Tsimihety, from
inland." But then he went on to
complain about "how proud
(miavona) the Sakalava are,
especially the women. They never
speak to you directly; they always
speak away, as if they were talking
to someone else."

29. She had explained earlier that
people from the same karazana,
who were therefore akin to one
another, could marry if their elders
invoked their ancestors on the head
of a cow to beg them not to make
the couple sick. This required at
least three grandparents, three
generations. Otherwise the
incestuous union would have only
disastrous consequences.

30. 'X brought Y' *(X ndesiny Y)*
is the other main way of speaking
of the connections between
ancestors and descendants besides
'X bore Y' *(X niteraka Y),* whence
fitondrasaña (am baba, am mama),
'what's brought (from the father,
from the mother).'

31. *Ki-* is a prefix used in
making diminutive substantives out
of adjectives, which are often
reduplicated to intensify their
diminutive quality. The use of ki-
prefixes is common in Swahili
(Richardson 1885:230), from which
the form may have been borrowed.

32. She may have done this
because she was talking to me (who
is not Muslim); or possibly because
her father's Silamo kin had not
chosen to recognize his connection
with a local woman; or possibly
because she did not know the kin
on her father's side who were
mainly in the Comores.

33. When I returned in 1981,
having written in advance,
MamanDjoma told me how happy
she had been to hear that 'my
Vazaha' was coming back, for
whom she used to do all the
washing and ironing, which we
ourselves had seen as a way of
entering networks of exchange that
she already had with other people.

34. A school teacher from
Analalava told me in 1981 that he
had asked for penpals in America
and England when he was a
secondary student at the end of the
colonial period (1959). He got two
in America—one in Arlington,
Massachusetts and another in
Connecticut. He sent them orchids,
which he collected in the woods
around Analalava, and they sent
him articles about Bob Dylan and
records of his music. Now, some
twenty years later, he had given his
young children names that
commemorated those connections:
Dôlo [Doll], Dilan, and Dorrice.
His mother later mentioned that his
father had been a Vazaha who had
chosen not to keep his child, even
though she had taught the boy to
speak only French in the hope that

his father would take him to France when he left.

35. Merina and French were the standard languages taught in school, but English was not. The prisoners who made souvenir baskets to sell to travelers en route to Nosy Be, occasionally incorporated English catch phrases that French tourists were known to like. Local people also bought the baskets. One of them, decorating MamanDjoma's living room in 1981, read "Make Love Not War."

36. Taodraza commented that he liked Paris and Marseilles the best, because there were the most Malagasy and Vazaha who spoke Malagasy in those places. Mainty Be said he had been in the army around 1920, Taodraza said around 1929. Judging by their ages—late fifties—I think they both fought in World War II. Estimates of numbers of Malagasy who "volunteered" for service in France in World War I range from 34,386 to 45,963, and in World War II (recruited in 1939–1943) some 43,000. Sources differ on whether the majority came from the central plateau or from the coasts and on the numbers of thousands that died in France (Thompson and Adloff 1965:21, 34, 37; Covell 1987:24–25). Veterans of World War I and World War II were prominent contributors to Malagasy nationalist movements in the postwar periods, including a massive revolt in 1947 (see Tronchon 1974).

37. Richardson (1885:579), who identifies *sodifafaña* as *Bryophyllum proliferum* Salis., comments that besides its use in poultices for gout or rheumatism, it was put with other plants in the ancestors corner [northeast] of a newly built house "to insure good luck. This was done because the plant is very retentive of life."

38. See Figures 9, F29 and 10, D18, Chapter 4, p. 206, and Appendix 2, "Avoria."

39. Noël 1844:385–387.

40. Richardson 1885:173–174. I think fatidra is a substantive form of the locative phrase 'in blood' *(f- + aty + [d]ra)*.

41. Smith 1896:22–23. According to the *Journal officiel de Madagascar* (20 mai 1897, p. 489) and Sibree (1897), fatidra was a common way of guaranteeing food, lodging, and protection in trading, traveling, or warfare. See also Dandouau's (1908b) account of a "Tsimihety" ceremony in the Analalava region in 1905.

42. Gardenier 1976:111.

43. Ibid.:111–112.

44. Noël Gueunier, personal communication (Fieldnotes 4/1981). See Fanony and Gueunier (1980) for a discussion on conversion and Islamic brotherhoods in northern Madagascar, based on fieldwork in Muslim communities during this same period, and Robert (1979) and Covell (1987:85) for further discussion of Comorian-Malagasy relations in the late 1970s.

45. They then went on to explain two of the "many ways!" of doing fatidra: "drinking gold"; or, for people tabooed from drinking gold, "eating blood," guided in both cases by an "oath-maker" *(ampañozoño)*, an important person who knows formal speech, but *not* a relative. Drinking gold in water or eating blood on rice were the ways of making fatidra that others mentioned before and after.

46. MamanDjoma's daughter-in-law called him Mangorohoro (to make something/one shake, like an earthquake or a fearsome person). When I then used the name (not yet recognizing that proper names praised and blessed people, while nicknames usually teased), they laughed and said it was not really his name. The kids had started calling him that because he rumbled in his throat when he talked, mangorohoro. Later MamanDjoma made a point of explaining, "You know his name isn't really Mangorohoro [she repeated its origin]. His real name is T. . . ."

47. 'His son' was actually a younger brother whom MamanDjoma called 'his son' as a way of emphasizing her fatidra's responsibility for his younger brother's behavior.

48. She explained the next day that the person who had taken the cigarettes was actually her fatidra's younger brother. He had also been imprisoned. She did not know

why, "probably cattle theft. Those Tsimihety—the Antsohihy area where he comes from is full of Tsimihety—are always stealing cattle."

49. See Feeley-Harnik 1989.

50. Richardson 1885:796. A sixteen-year-old girl in a farming village south of Analalava embroidered a similar saying into a bedspread for her trousseau when she became a paramedic's sixth wife in 1989: "Don't be disheartened because [you are] young [your] destiny is not lost" *(Aza kivy fa tanora tsy very anjara)*.

51. A saying printed on a body-wrap, produced by the SOTEMA cloth factory in Mahajanga, and widely worn in western Madagascar, expressed a similar sentiment: *Miambiny edy tsy ho azon-draha,* 'S/he who waits will not get things.' Guillain reports the Merina ruler, Radama (following his return to Antananarivo after conquering Mahajanga in 1824), justifying the royal division of labor in similar terms: "The entire island is mine. . . .I am the father of the orphan, the protector of the widow and of the oppressed, the redresser of wrongs, and the remunerator of what is good and just . . . the duty of others is to work. To you then the care of cultivating the earth. . . . If you do not work the ground, you will be, like the cattle-herder before your eyes, without father, or mother, or anyone who

might have care or pity for you. Reeds grow from the ground; gold and silver do not fall from the sky!'' (1845:89–90).

52. MamanDjoma and other women said that women were really the ones who 'kept up the customary ways of doing things' *(mitaña ny fomba)*. They should 'stay in the house and take care of everything for the husband.' Since they also commented from time to time about how the French women they had seen had never done any work, having servants even for their children, perhaps they were expressing ideas about the division of labor between men and women that had some French origins.

53. He identified her as coming from her father's village, south of Antognibe. Her father was dead, but his older and younger brothers still lived there. He had met her in a village nearby Andonaka where her mother lived, but it was one of her father's brothers who came with her when she brought back the son born of their marriage.

54. As indicated in the preceding chapter, men and women in the Analalava region used several terms to refer to marriage wealth: *didinkarena* (portion of wealth), most common among highlanders, and miletry (something permitting one 'to force oneself in' or 'force to assent'), or *manoko mañangy* (to divide the woman), most common among people born in the area.

55. *Volambita* was said to be the Tsimihety word for what Sakalava call fanjava mitsaka, the first month of the lunar year.

56. Richardson (1885:601) defines the phrase as meaning, ''dung from the inside of a bullock; fig. things obtained by violence.''

57. The root *origny (orina)*, fixed, firmly established, well founded, is used in compounds typically referring to the foundations of houses *(fanorenana)*, the deep-rootedness of trees *(orim-paka)*, and the groundedness of standing stones *(orim-bato)*, set up as witnesses or memorials (see Richardson 1885:467).

58. She then gave two other instances in which the phrase is used: ''When two people make a bet, the winner may say to the looser, '*Taimboraka ny lany, tsy nahazo raha,* you didn't get anything'; or when a person plants a crop of rice and it doesn't fruit, nothing comes of it *(tsisy raha nahazo amin'azy)*, then s/he may also say this, but it's most often used when people marry.''

59. Some sixty Vazaha were residents of Analalava at the close of the colonial period. Most of them were gone by the early seventies. Diégo Suarez was the site of a French naval base until 1972, when the base was turned over to Malagasy authorities following the fall of Tsiranana's government. Antseranana, as it is now called, is

still "one of the best natural harbors in the western Indian Ocean." It operates as a port with naval repair facilities capable of serving supertankers as well as smaller ships and, more recently, as the location of a Soviet-run air base. It is one of the three main areas of the country where nonagricultural work is concentrated, the others being the Antananarivo-Antsirabe areas and the Mahajanga area (see Covell 1987:10–11, 71, 148).

60. These were common sentiments among men who had grown up during the 1930s, 1940s, and 1950s. One of the most eloquent was Abdallah Be, a Silamo farmer-trader from a village about two hours walk north of Tsinjorano. He was related to the man who married Mainty Be's father's sister from Tsinjorano. His kinsman, as one of the Great-Grandfather's earliest mediums, had set up a generative stone in Tsinjorano (see Chapter 4, pp. 220–221). Abdallah Be knew the stone. He said: "It's not for making vows *(fanaovana tsakafara)* [like some standing stones]. There is medicine buried underneath it. In the time of the French, when they came to a village, they were always very ferocious *(masiaka),* knocking people around with sticks if they couldn't instantly produce their karatra [carte d'identité], accusing a person of lying if they caught someone en route who claimed his

karatra was back in his house, collecting the head tax, whatever. The French government was hot in those days! So Ndramamitranarivo [the Great-Grandfather] possessed Aly ben Tsimatavy, and he said, 'Bury this medicine. Put the big stone over it. Then when the Vazaha are coming, pour cold water over the stone in order that the government will come coolly, without hitting.' They always came with a lot of soldiers who did the translating. They used soldiers from faraway places in this area. Sakalava from this area they used as soldiers elsewhere, Malagasy soldiers."

He itemized the taxes that were charged during the colonial period, compared to the current taxes. Then he continued: "If they wanted nice land, and you happened to be working on it, they could kick you off. For example, Le Sueur on Ambariovaliha, or Matthieu on Berafia, where all my kin were cultivating. Some left. Those who wanted to stay had to give part of their crops to the Vazaha. Or if you built a house on a really nice piece of land, and they wanted to build their house there, they could just take the land, tear your house down, and build their own stone house with many floors. The schools were separate. The Malagasy got schools with palm-leaf roofs, the Vazaha got metal roofs. Only a Malagasy who was a French citizen could go to the

Vazaha school. Otherwise they all went to the Malagasy school, including the Hova. Indians went to the French school. If a man couldn't pay the head tax, he could run and hide on a Vazaha concession and the soldiers would be afraid of going in to get him. The Vazaha would chase them off. It didn't matter if he didn't pay. But if the owner of the land was Malagasy, then they would drag him [the tax-evader] right in. If men didn't pay the head tax, then ten, twenty, thirty would be tied together and sent out to walk into Analalava, where they would be put in prison. A long walk, all tied together in a long line, to make them suffer. In the revolt of 1947, everyone listed in the opposition against the French were sent up to Nosy Be. They dug big basins, filled with water, and put hot peppers in them. Men who tried to lift their heads out were struck with clubs. Or men were shot and killed. The French were *very* ferocious here."

61. See Chapter 2 and Noël 1843, vol. 20:299–300. Richardson (1885:500, 617) defines mandranto as "to trade, to traffice, to engage in commerce" from the root *ranto*, "trade, commerce, traffice, used of a journey to a distant part for commercial business" and *manangy* as "to hire a harlot." Noël (1843, vol. 20:299–300) comments concerning "adultery" *(mangamato):*

If a husband catches his wife's lover, he can make him pay a fine called *rehetsi* (cicatrization); there is no shame attached to the status of a deceived husband; a woman is excused because of the love she must have for her lover and "by the weakness and facility of her nature"; the lover is excused by the passion he must feel and fined less for his offense to the husband than for his inability to keep the affair quiet; children born to a married woman belong to her husband, who may recognize them or not, as he chooses. Noël's rendition of *mañamato* (to take a lover) as *mangamato* suggests a European origin for the word *manga,* still the name of one of the poorest quarters in Mahajanga and another term that people in the Analalava region used to refer to the women who worked as prostitutes in the larger towns in the northwest.

62. In French usage, *le bandit* usually refers to a 'thief' [its meaning when applied to men in the Analalava region], *le dépôt* to a 'deposit, store, dump, or point of sale'; *la maquerelle* to a 'madam'; *le passage* to 'a short stay' or, in a commercial context, to 'passing or casual trade'; *la pratique* to 'practice, experience' or, in a commercial context, 'custom, clientéle'; *la ronde* to 'the round(s)' of a soldier, policeman or night-watchman. One of Dandouau's first papers on life in the Analalava region concerned

"The laxity of Malagasy morals"
(1908a), as exemplified in Malagasy
ideas of "feminine virtue".

63. Toko refers here to the
family living on their tokotany,
'piece of land' or houseplot, as well
as to the hearth, the trio of stones
on which the cooking pot is placed.

64. See, for example, White
1987; McCrate 1989.

65. White (1987) discusses the
coexistence of different kinds of
prostitution in Nairobi in ca. 1899–
1939. She emphasizes the important
role of *watembezi* prostitutes, young
women from formerly wealthy
pastoralist families in Kenya, in
helping their fathers to build up
their herds after they had been
decimated by drought, disease and
world economic conditions. In
contrast to the watembezi, who
worked the streets and were known
for their aggressive techniques of
solicitation, *malaya* women, who
worked more discretely from their
houses, came from much poorer
circumstances. They went into
business primarily to benefit
themselves. White suggests that
colonial officials tolerated the
malaya women because their
activities contributed to colonial
goals by providing housing and
other domestic services for badly
needed male workers. When the
malaya women became so wealthy
as to rival the economic interests of
government officials, they were
condemned and driven out.

Mañangy mitovo did provide such
services for workers in Analalava,
but the area was poorer, and so
activities were also less
economically interesting to colonial
and later government officials.

Ottino (1964) and Waast (1974)
describe the Sakalava in wealthier
circumstances in the Nosy Be area
in the late fifties and early sixties
and in the Soalala area near
Mahajanga in the early seventies
that are more closely comparable to
the situation that White describes
for Nairobi. Noting that "the taste
for moving around is one of the
characteristic traits of the sakalava
style of life," Ottino (1964:227 and
passim) analyzes how women's
demands were related to the
increasing incidence of divorce and
remarriage in the Nosy Be-
Ambanja area. In the Analalava
region during the same period, by
contrast, Ottino found "the
country, the activities, and people
seemed . . . strangely struck with
immobility." An old man in the
then mainly Comorian
southwestern quarter of Analalava
complained to him that young
Sakalava did not want to do
anything. He blamed young
women for this, for having so few
needs that they did not incite the
men to work (Ottino 1964:244–
245, n. 2). Waast (1974) examines
how Sakalava women in the Soalala
area, long crowded with lucrative
plantations, take concubines rather
than marrying.

66. Compare, for example, Comaroff 1985; Stoler 1989; Vinogradov 1974.

67. Bakhtin 1981:276–277.

68. See Bakhtin 1981:293–294 and his essay, "Discourse in the novel," passim. Harding's (1987) analysis of the dialogue involved in fundamental Baptist witnessing in the U.S. is a valuable example of the coercive power of verbal images to reshape experience as listeners become speakers. Fernandez's (1982) detailed analysis of the reformative power of words in Fang Bwiti in Gabon focuses on the way in which words are embodied in other sensory forms, to which we are now turning.

Chapter 6, *Vala:* Pens, notes to pp. 303–364.

1. Sun's chronicle *(tantara masoandro)* got its name from the fact that it faced the sun, following it across the sky all day, and closing at night. Leaves of tantara masoandro and the leaves of the shrub known as matambelona (dead-living) were very commonly used in supplicating the ancestors and in cleansing afterwards. Many people grew them in their yards for that purpose. MamanDjoma said that she had tried to grow tantara masoandro (pointing to a broken pot full of water, where it had been), but the chickens kept eating it.

2. Later, neighbors said that they could see it coming. They said that Be Moana, whom they had nicknamed the "White Cat" *(Piso Malandy)*, had acted friendly in order to get inside the house. She had given in order that she could eventually take. Her vady had helped her by watching while she slipped inside. They had bought a large tin trunk worth 4,000 FMG, two gunny sacks of white rice, and enough cloth for two wrapped outfits and one fitted dress.

Be Moana was called "White Cat" because of the way she snuck around, taking whatever she could. No one said anything to her directly. They just made sure someone was always with her when she came to call. They said they would have warned me had they known me better. But they didn't, and perhaps I too had an 'evil disposition.' My being pregnant was generally regarded as a sign of royal blessing, and when Vanessa was born, MamanDjoma suggested that one of her names should be Mosarafa, Royal Gift.

Piso, seen as European's pets, played thieves in riddles in the Analalava area. Rakoto (1947–1948:110) notes that cats called *kalodoany* roamed the doany of Andriamisara at Miarinarivo near Mahajanga when he was there in 1938. *Kalo* are plaintive songs of praise to royalty. One royal spirit from the Mahajanga area (Andriamandzoala) prohibited his mediums from keeping cats because they were "ruinous animals of luxury. Their incessant meowling: *'Omeo!, Omeo!'* [Give! Give!] makes of them dangerous parasites" (Estrade 1977:220).

3. "Anecdote of the Jar" (Stevens 1982:76).

4. There was one Indian merchant, married to a spirit-medium, who came to the Mahabo every dry season and stayed there during the several weeks in which the new year's festivals of the first and third months were held. He gave major gifts to the royal spirits and guardians at the Mahabo, and also participated as the junior, Zafinifotsy, ruler, in the danced battles (rebiky) that were staged in the afternoon (see Feeley-Harnik 1988). Several ampanjaka in the area south of Antognibe had married into the families of Indian merchants during the colonial period (see Chapter 5).

I think that the *tsintsoraka*, the royal blessing conveyed through the line of white clay drawn upwards from the tip of the nose to the hairline (or sometimes put on the forehead between the eyes) may have been inspired in part by the Hindu *tilak* (see Chapter 1, n. 46). The emphasis on anointing *(mañosatra)* in the service to reconstruct the menaty also suggests that the tsintsoraka and forms of anointing may have developed in the course of responding to, yet remaining different from, Christian practices.

Raison-Jourde (1983, plates 7, 8) suggests that Indian women's saris, nose ornaments, pendant earrings, and filigree bracelets have influenced the dress and adornment of local women in northwest Madagascar.

5. This line usually went: "Bevaoko rules." "[The] Man/Men rule(s)" *(Lehilahy manjaka)* was a recurrent line in some Zafinimena praise songs.

6. Each group of questions and answers is often repeated, as is the whole song.

7. Royal followers attributed the rarity with which the Great-Grandfather and Grandfather possessed their mediums in the meeting house at the Mahabo, that is, in the company of many people, to their extreme 'ferocity' *(siaka)*. In contrast, they often 'possess their mediums in the forest' *(mianjaka anatiala)*. Because of their ferocity, they possessed very few people compared to the Father and the Brother. Their much greater meanness compared to the Father and Brother, who were more convivial and who 'married' many mediums, was directly related to their seniority in age and death.

8. Poirier (1926:19–21) cites correspondence from 1925 indicating that Bemihisatra followers expected the ampanjaka to help them in everyday matters, for example, in conflicts with Muslim traders. This was not a

prominent aspect of what the ampanjaka did in the 1970s.

9. The rice field in each royal administrative district was donated by a different person each year, but all the members of the communities within the district were expected to work on it. These fields undoubtedly varied in size. One in the Ambolobozo Peninsula, which I saw sown, took five gunny sacks of seed. Two cattle were killed on that occasion to feed the crowd, one in the morning and the second in the afternoon. Several people commented on the fact that the ampanjaka ate hardly any of the rice she received. She gave it to her royal officials and to the Sambarivo.

10. Correspondence cited in Poirier (1926:11–12), together with the archival material, cited in Chapter 3 on Tondroko's predecessors, indicates that writing had always been a regular part of the administration of the Southern Bemihisatra monarchy. Tondroko's predecessors corresponded in Arabic. The Grandfather once wrote to the Commandant in Nosy Be, telling him to write only in Arabic, since no one there could read French. The Commandant's letters were in French, Arabic, and occasionally in Malagasy (correspondence of Temboula ben Sultan to the Commandant de Nossi-Be, 1854–1856, CAOM MAD 4 Z 5; correspondence of

A'gnonou to the Commandant de Nossi-Be, 1865–1891, CAOM MAD 4 Z 8).

11. *Fehy* is the root of a series of words with overlapping semantic fields, ranging from 'tying/binding/knotting' to 'guiding/controlling/governing,' which are contrasted with such terms as *mivavatra,* 'loosening/untying/opening'. The contrast is often made in the context of speaking, for example *mifehy vava,* 'to tie shut the mouth of a corpse', and *mamavatra kabary,* which one speaker explained as 'to open the mouth of the [formal] speech' *(mampibiaña ny vavan' ny kabary).* *Mifehy* also contrasts with *afaka,* 'unlocked/untied/separated/emptied' and 'freed,' in the case of slaves.

12. As indicated in Chapter 3, this arrangement probably dates back to the beginning of the colonial period, when French administrators appointed royal officials as their own district heads.

13. At the Northern Bemihisatra mahabo of Tsiomeko, the manantany was chosen from the Maromavo group of Sambarivo in the northern half of the settlement and the door-keeper from the Bahary to the west. Baré mentions no other Sambarivo besides these two and the Bemongo, the "Sambarivo of the Sakalava Mañoroñaomby," who are one of the groups of Ancestor People common to both places (Baré 1980:351, 352, 361).

14. The first of the female rulers in Imerina, Ranavalona I who ruled from 1828 to 1861, called her new palace "Ruling in Peace" (Manjakamiàdana). Given the importance of tree cores and stone in Sakalava royal architecture, it is notable that the palace, completed by Ranavalona's Réunionaise master-builder Jean Laborde in 1839, was constructed entirely of wood around a central tree-trunk, one hundred and thirty feet high. Five thousand men are said to have hauled it from a forest on the east coast to Antananarivo. In 1868–1869, her successor Ranavalona II, commissioned the Scottish weaver, James Cameron, to enclose the wooden palace in stone.

15. See Launois, ca. 1938. Launois commented that the house "mixed ancestral customs with more modern methods."

16. In the early 1970s, the Bemihisatra were in the process of constructing another house for the ampanjaka in Antognibe, where many of her father's followers still lived. It had palm-stalk walls *(riba ketikety),* like the houses around it, but it was built on a cement foundation and would be finished with a iron roof.

17. People always said they 'go up to a village' *(manonga an-tanana)* from the countryside. But, as one of Soazara's followers put it, 'Whenever people ask for goodness, they move upwards!' *(Olo mangataka tsara boka, manonga!).*

18. When royal spirits possessed mediums, they seated themselves along the east wall from north to south in order of seniority by generation and age, like living people. The royal ancestors buried in the Mahabo were likewise placed with their heads to the east, ordered north to south in the order in which they died, which reproduced their seniority by generation, except for the premature death of Ambilahikely, Tondroko's son.

19. The living ruler's children were allowed to live in the royal compound at the post because it was not seen as the real doany, since there was no ancestors' house there. Even so, they were not allowed to stay in the compound overnight if the ampanjaka was not there. If she was traveling, they had to stay with Sambarivo or royal followers outside the fenced compound.

20. Zomba means house in the royal vocabulary, derived from Swahili *jumba,* 'large house'. Most of the other structures were also designated by terms from the royal vocabulary, a topic to be discussed elsewhere. Most of the structures that were prohibited have French names, reflecting their colonial origins: windows *(lafenêtra)* and verandas *(lavaraña)* in general, and fenced yards *(lakoro)* for the guardians. The fenced courtyards that have long been the prerogative of royalty are known by Malagasy names.

21. Mañary is a kind of rosewood with a very hard, reddish colored wood. Male mañary (mañarilahy), darker than the female kind (mañarivavy), were preferred. Bemihisatra said that in the precolonial period, all the royal buildings at the Doany and the Mahabo were roofed, gabled, and walled with kirovaka—the stalk of the maivenaty palm, cut into planks. Commoners were prohibited from using teza (hardwood cores) or kirovaka, or raising their houses on posts like the ancestors' house. When Launois was stationed in Analalava during the mid-thirties, the royal buildings at the Doany in Analalava were made of the same materials that Sakalava used to build their own houses (see Launois, ca. 1938)—the stalks and leaves of palm trees as described below.

In the early seventies, the royal buildings at the two royal cemeteries on Nosy Lava were still constructed entirely of kirovaka. The buildings at the Doany Miadana were constructed of the materials that commoners used to build their own houses. The walls were made of panels of palm ribs (ketikety, maivenaty, or falafa), supported by wooden timbers raised on posts. The roofs, supported by two end poles and one center pole, were made of palm leaves (satrana, ravinala) or, rarely, bundles of grass (bozaka). Kirovaka

was occasionally used to build temporary structures or kitchens. Many people in farming villages and at the post built houses raised on posts or cement foundations to keep the house and its contents from rotting during the rainy season.

22. According to Launois (ca. 1938), the door of the Sambarivo was also called 'the door of the Tsimaniha' (varavara Tsimaniha), the collective name for the groups of Sambarivo in the southern half of the community. In fact, only the groups in the southeastern quarter were allowed to serve the ancestors.

23. The valamena was made of untrimmed posts, lashed to two tiers of horizontally placed poles. It was constructed only after the ancestors' house was finished.

24. According to Launois, it was called 'the door of blessing' (varavara mitahy), but I never heard it called by any specific name.

25. Poirier (1939c:43–44) states that a famous spirit-medium Tsimijotso constructed a valamena with a pair of royal drums to honor his spirit (probably in 1914–1918, when Poirier served as chef de province d'Analalava). Southern Bemihisatra confirmed this, saying that Tondroko had given him special permission to do this, since his spirit's place of origin—the doany at Mahajanga—was so far away.

26. The Sambarivo door led to

the reception room, because only certain Sambarivo were allowed into the bedroom. According to Launois (ca. 1938), commoners were forbidden to put doors in their houses in any of those three places. Like the prohibition against raised houses, prohibitions on doors were no longer widely followed in the seventies.

27. Launois, ca. 1938.

28. The ruler's house, kitchen, and bathhouse were built as they had been in Launois's (ca. 1938) time, except that the kitchen door was then in the center of the east wall and is now in the east end of the north wall. The ruler bathed with water drawn from a stream east of the Doany where everyone else also bathed, but no one else had urinal/bathhouses, which were common at the post and becoming more common in farming villages.

29. One royal guardian said that the prohibition against looking over the fence dated to the colonial period, when French people— prohibited from entering the enclosure because they were wearing trousers—watched royal services from outside. Several series of photos of the ampanjaka and her followers were taken during the mid-thirties from inside the tsirangôty (see Plate 6).

30. Noël described the fence around Tsiomeko's doany—the 'Golden Enclosure'—as being fortified with this kind of door

(Noël 1844:394–95, see Chapter 2). The Northern Bemihisatra ampanjaka Binao's first tomb on Nosy Komba had such a door in the late 1920s (Poirier 1939d:108, 109, planche 17). Decary (1958b: 42, 44, 62, 64–65) describes doors of this sort in the fences that Betsimisaraka in northeastern Madagascar and Bara in the southern highlands built around their homesteads. He compares the Betsimisaraka door to the doors in the fences around Sakalava royal compounds that he may have seen in the late 1920s, when he was stationed in the northwest. Since the early colonial period, when several lumber mills were founded in Analalava region, sturdy doors have been made of planks, nailed together, hinged at the side, and sometimes fitted with locks, a style described as "carpentered" (saripatiay) (see Decary 1958a:53). Temporary doors were made of handy materials like bundles of straw and old wall-panels.

31. Most of the prohibitions associated with life at the Doany and the Mahabo were common knowledge throughout the region. We were instructed on proper behavior before we went to either place and also within minutes after arriving. At the Doany Andriamisara in Majunga during the colonial period, the prohibitions were listed in a 'Notice' (Avis), posted at the entrance to the royal compound (Rakoto 1947–1948:110).

32. See Feeley-Harnik 1980.

33. See Bakhtin 1981:84–258.

34. Commoners' houses could not be built too large or too well in the precolonial period because they had to be destroyed after a death, since Sakalava rulers were prohibited from entering houses in which deaths had occurred. They also had to be destroyed when fleeing from enemies, for example the Hova, who were pursuing the Sakalava during the late nineteenth century. The "microscopic" size of Sakalava houses observed by Jully (1898:905) in the Narinda Bay area during Toquenne's pacification probably derived from such considerations rather than the "laziness" which is Jully's explanation. "Bordering Narinda Bay and particularly in all this region which formerly served as refuge to 'Marofelana' [bands of men alleged to be bandits], the houses are very carefully made and, I stress this point, are microscopic: we recall having with great difficulty been able to put up a portable bed inside, from which, like Schaunard's garret, the sleeper's legs still emerged."

35. The prohibitions concerning sleeping were especially important because of the parallel seen between sleep and death. To attempt to assume the powers of living, waking rulers was sorcery, but to attempt to assume the powers of the royal ancestors was infinitely

worse. Richardson (1885:606) cites a provincial proverb: "Sleep is the beloved child (or very image) [actually, first born] of death" *(Talan'olo ny faty ny torimaso)*.

36. The ampanjaka could wear shoes. Commenting that "Hova were joined with vazaha, Sakalava didn't count, a different government" *(Hova kambana am'vazaha, Sakalava tsy mikonty, fanjakana hafa)*, one guardian at the Doany said that hats with brims were prohibited because Hova and Vazaha used them—"Those are enemies, they can't enter." Then he added that *kofia mena* (the brimless tarboosh and skull caps of Silamo) were not prohibited. In keeping with the involvement of Silamo in the monarchy, as essential middlemen, if not followers, pork was prohibited, and Silamo were appointed to sacrifice cattle so the meat would be properly clean *(lintaigny)*.

37. The body wraps *(salovaña)* that women wore every day were usually sewn together at the ends to form a closed tube, which was then wrapped more tightly around the body.

38. People who had recently had sexual intercourse, menstruating women, or babies whose clothing might have urine or excrement on it were prohibited from entering the enclosure.

39. The words for carrying royal objects or supporting royalty in

general *(miloha, miloloha)* (for
example, in the praise song in
Chapter 1) always referred to
carrying on the head, like a
woman, in contrast to carrying on
shoulder poles, like a man. Men did
carry royal objects on their
shoulders.

40. There were no stated
prohibitions concerning the use of
left and right hands, because
throughout the region, the left hand
was prohibited for everything
except handling or cleaning bodily
'filth.' MamanDjoma, who had
been left-handed as a child, said
that her parents had beaten her left
hand with a stick until she had
finally learned to use her right
properly.

41. Lunar eclipses every seven
years, when the moon glowed red
behind the shadow of the earth,
were described and handled in the
same way.

42. Decary 1951b:263.

43. Richardson 1885:183.

44. This might explain Guillain's
observation (1845:86) that when
Andriantsoly had the Hova build
him a new doany in his place of
exile at Marovoay, he brought
jambs "to which he and his family
attached great value, as coming
from houses in which their glorious
ancestors had lived." Perhaps these
were special doors (see Chapter 2).

45. In contrast to the ambiguity
surrounding the door in the menaty
at the Southern Bemihisatra

Mahabo, the Northern Bemihisatra
menaty of Binao on Nosy Komba
had a wooden door with two
panels, "sculpted in indian style,"
locked with a padlock (Poirier
1939d:108, 109, written in 1929).

46. One guardian said that
children had to stay down 'below'
because they are 'dirty' *(maloto)*.
Likewise, menstruating women
(mañangy misy fotoaña) had to stay
below. "If a medium has her time,
they *(zareo)* don't possess her. They
don't like it, they don't like dirt.
They wait until the medium has
washed, then they come to rule on
her."

47. Guillain (1845:47–50) dates
fighting between the Bemihisatra
and Bemazava to around 1812–
1814. See also Chapter 2.

48. As indicated in Chapter 1,
Sakalava followers emphasize that
they do not exhume their dead to
rebury them in another tomb like
the Merina and other highland
peoples. Where they are buried is
where they stay. The medium of
the first and eldest spirit buried in
the southern Mahabo is prohibited
from leaving the Mahabo to
accompany services like the menaty
service precisely because he is the
"master" or "owner" of the
southern Mahabo and therefore
cannot leave it (see Chapter 8).
Nevertheless, a major controversy
among the Northern Bemihisatra
during the colonial period, between
the deceased ampanjaka Binao and

her half-brother and successor, Amada, concerning precisely this issue, was finally resolved by moving her body from the tomb where he had first buried her to a new tomb (see Baré 1980).

49. Creuse's account (1955), written when he was chef de district in Analalava, also mentions this.

50. Saha Barimaso said they were so-called because they had been bought in exchange for iron pots. Apart from implicitly acceding to the difficulty of forcing local people into this kind of work, this arrangement may have been beneficial to royalty because such strangers with no local ties to kin or friends were less able to profit from their intimate knowledge of the rulers they served.

51. Northern Bemihisatra recognized just four groups of Sambarivo around royalty, but these were also grouped in pairs according to north (Antavarabe), including Maromavo and Antavarabe, and south (Tsimania), including Bahary and Tsimania (see Baré 1980:300).

52. See Decary 1951b:221–222, 1954b, based in part on historical material. The L.M.S. missionary, William Ellis, in his *Madagascar Revisited* (1867:479), commented on the intense aversion of people in Imerina for "all even numbers," which extended even to words sounding similar to the words by

which they were called. "The number eight in any measurement is not allowed, as Mr. Cameron [the weaver who covered Ranavalona I's wooden palace in stone, see note 14] informed me, because the word *valo* denoting that number, resembles, or rather rhymes with, the word for enemy, *fahavalo*. No measurement of six or eight has been permitted in the structure of the present palace."

53. The order of the pens at the Mahabo had become somewhat skewed because sharp drops in the land prevented residents from expanding to the west and south of the original settlement.

54. Molet (1959:165), writing about the neighboring Tsimihety, known for resisting the Sakalava monarchy, argues that fanompoaña means not only corvée labor, but also, by a play on words, "what one does for nothing, what one does in vain" (fan*ao*m*p*oana). Tsimihety could also have been referring to the forced labor of the colonial period.

55. See Poirier 1939c:112, who mentions Northern Bemihisatra services at the Mahabo led by the ampanjaka, and also Baré 1980. For the Bemazava, see Ndremahefa and Feeley-Harnik 1975.

56. One of the Sambarivo at the Doany married a man who subsequently became possessed by the Brother at the Mahabo. Once he had been legitimated, he had to

live at the Mahabo part of the year. They lived there together during the dry season, when the new year's ceremony was held, in the northern pen corresponding to hers at the Doany. He said they would have lived in the south, in keeping with the fact that he was possessed by the descendant of the Great-Grandfather and Grandfather, but there was no room there. They lived in his farming village south of Analalava during the growing season. She returned to her northern pen at the Doany to do her part in royal services there, and he always joined the southern pens in gatherings at the Mahabo.

57. The name, usually referring to cattle given in compensation for wrongs, may have been an allusion to compensation for the ruler's death, which—not happening 'naturally'—had to be the result of sorcery. Such issues could not be discussed.

58. Sambarivo at the Doany were not faced with the same problems. They had their own rice land around the Doany, which they did not have to share with mediums. The ampanjaka also redistributed tribute rice to Sambarivo, but I do not know what they received or the proportions given to those at the Doany and those at the Mahabo.

59. Hiring prisoners was common practice at the Mahabo, as it was elsewhere in the region.

Antimahabo who lived there through the year had tried for some time to get the community to work together to dig a deeper well, lined with stones, so their water would not dry up during the dry season. Those who cultivated on the mainland consistently refused to cooperate; and those who remained were too few to do it themselves. Finally, in the late sixties, the ones who remained raised money among themselves to hire prisoners to do the work.

60. Some Antimahabo men said that it was prohibited to form liaisons with spirit-mediums because they were considered to be kin. Others said they could marry, but preferred not to because mediums, and thus those closely associated with them, had to observe prohibitions on food and sexual behavior that were too difficult to keep. As one man explained it, "if you step out with another woman, you have to wash *everywhere and everything* before you can sleep with your wife again. Otherwise one of you will get sick, and you will have to go and pay your respects to the royal ancestors." Some people attributed the chronic illnesses of men from the Antibe pen who were closest to the royal ancestors to their marriages with mediums. Local people in the region had similar concerns about the dangers of close relationships with Sambarivo at the

Mahabo and the Doany. The prisoners were said to become involved with the women at the Mahabo because they had no choice.

61. They did not think of themselves as lesser. Matombo from Tsinjorano (Fig. 9, F22), who was descended from one of the female guardians at the Mahabo, said that she worked "with all the many others of them. They are all heads *(kapobe)* together, all Antimahabo. There is no one greater than the others. The ampangataka just has more work."

62. In 1936, Ralaimongo Jean, a Betsileo schoolteacher with ties to the Communist Party in Madagascar, came to Analalava to petition French authorities to allow the ampanjaka Soazara, then ten years old, to leave Analalava and return to Antognibe, where her father had lived before his exile to Manongarivo. Ralaimongo may have learned about her situation when he himself was in *résidence fixe* in Port Bergé in 1930–1935, as punishment for agitating against French labor and land legislation in ways that were said to compromise public security (CAOM MAD c. 354, d. 957; MAD 6(2) D 121). Knowing her influence, he may have hoped to rally the support of Sakalava followers in the northwest. Instead, Soazara's guardians, describing Ralaimongo as a highlander *(ambaniandro),*

petitioned French authorities to protect her from what they saw as an effort to kidnap her, and Ralaimongo was turned away (Randrianja 1983:297–303; I am grateful to Françoise Raison-Jourde for bringing this thesis to my attention). Ralaimongo is currently recognized as one of Madagascar's earliest nationalist leaders, but most royal followers in the Analalava region still remember him as a would-be kidnapper (see frontispiece and Feeley-Harnik 1988:78 for some further details).

63. *Mangery*—from *hery,* 'strength/power/weight'—is the direct word for 'moving the bowels,' in contrast to the common euphemism *miboaka* (to go out).

64. This may explain why, of all the pens of Sambarivo at the Doany, it is the Bahary (*be* and *bitiky,* 'big' and 'little' or 'senior' and 'junior', the commonest way of subdividing a growing group) who are missing altogether. They were the Sambarivo dedicated to cooking and washing for the ampanjaka.

65. Royal followers related *mitregny,* usually referring to the bellowing of cattle, to *misaontsy,* the royal word for a ruler's formal speech to his or her followers. *Zaka,* besides referring like *kaka* to unusual or monstrous things, is also the root of *mizaka,* 'to speak at length.' The praise songs evoke the image of royal ancestors speaking

from their hidden places through living rulers the way they speak through mediums (see also Carol 1898:418–419).

66. Whether these were Sambarivo who had formally been Bahary belonging to the western pens at the current Doany or the doany of her father, I do not know.

67. Levelt's (1990) comprehensive review of research on *Speaking: From Intention to Articulation* examines speech not simply in terms of cognitive models of mental processes, but as a wholly embodied phenomenon, "man's most complex motor skill."

Chapter 7, Filthy Land, notes to pp. 367–400.

1. Malaza said that Ndramamahaña died at 8:00 a.m., a strikingly 'complete' time in the context of Southern Bemihisatra royal practice. Poirier, in his account written in 1926, but published in 1939, states that he died at 7:00 p.m. (Poirier 1939c:103), but Malaza would be confirmed in the fact that Poirier (1926), in his report of the succession controversy, cites Philibert's report indicating that Tondroko's partisans came to his office to announce the death between 1:00 and 2:00 p.m. that afternoon (1926:37).

2. Similar words were also prohibited and replaced with substitutes, for example *tondro*

(forefinger) with *rantsan-tañana* (branch of the hand).

3. Poirier 1926:37, 59, 70.

4. See Poirier 1939c. His "Note on the Funeral of Tondroko II," dated December 27, 1926, appeared at the end, pp. 103–104, but Poirier also included texts from the "prohibited songs" and the "voluptuous, insulting, and injurious songs" of the funeral in his account of the succession battle, pp. 68–76. Neither the songs nor the note were included in the report he sent to the Governor-General's office in 1926.

5. Poirier (1939c:103) describes sobaiya as "cotonnade," but according to Southern Bemihisatra, it is an Arabian silk.

6. Savaly is derived from the French word *chevalet*, familiar from the operations of the several lumbering companies established during the colonial period, which employed local people as workers. The common term for a sawhorse or comparable kind of frame is *laika*. The animal (horse) is called *savaly kaka,* combining the French term *(cheval)* with the Malagasy *kaka* meaning beast or monster.

7. Poirier 1939c:104, 68. The drums, which Poirier calls *hazolahy* [male wood, another name for the pair of royal mañandria drums, which can only be played by men], may have been played, as they are in current royal services, at sunup and sundown, when the door to the

royal tomb is opened and then closed on good days. I do not know whether such distinctions were effaced in the course of the burial or not. Poirier's own comments concerning the days on which royal corpses could be moved suggests that they were not.

8. Ibid.

9. Ibid.:68.

10. Ibid.:68–69.

11. See Poirier 1926:8; 1939c:49, 61. Sakalava followers in Menabe say that the gold coins in the mouths of dead royalty account for why the royal ancestors can speak out in possessing people, while commoners' ancestors cannot (Rabedimy 1979:177–178). In fact, the words for speech *(vola/ña)* and money *(vola)* are related (see Feeley-Harnik 1989).

12. Poirier 1939c:104; Mellis 1938:67. Mellis states that Malagasy *"never talk of these things* [the mahabo, royal ritual, and the like] with a stranger, especially if he sees in him *a chef who does not observe his customs"* (1938:59, his emphasis); and "Under the appearance of frankness and bonhomie, the Malagasy dissimulates, deceives . . ." (p. 7). He supports the authenticity of his own report by saying that he has lived since late 1899 in the same region, having traveled all around it in every sense, often on foot, and always modestly equipped, "a recommended means of penetrating the Malagasy soul"

(ibid.). But he does not indicate where he was or whether he was still living there in 1938 when the book was published.

13. Poirier ibid.; Mellis ibid.

14. Mellis 1938:67, 62. Richardson (1885:515) defines *riana* as "water flowing over and on to rocks; a cascade, a cataract"; *riambato* are "rocks over which water flows"; the phrase *Efa an-doharian' ny aina,* literally 'the breath is already at the head [source] of the spring,' is "used of a person on the point of death." Riaka also refers to water, but without the association to rocks. People throughout the Analalava region used riaka to refer to waves and to the sea in general. According to Richardson (1885:515), it refers to "small streams of water running here and there after rains and running into rivers; the little streams of water after a wave; fig. the sea"; *anivon' ny riaka,* literally 'in the midst of the waters or waves' expresses "the whole island of Madagascar."

15. See Richardson 1885:515; Heseltine 1971:68.

16. Mellis 1938:67.

17. Poirier 1939c:104 says December 15, 1925 in his account of Tondroko's death, but notes in his earlier account of the succession battle that the funeral was curtailed "under administrative pressure" (see Chapter 3, note 97).

18. Poirier 1939c:104.

19. Philibert cited in Poirier

1939c:67; Dandouau 1911:169; Poirier 1939c:104.

20. Poirier 1939c:69.

21. Ibid.:70.

22. Ibid.:69, 70. Poirier says *conscience,* perhaps meaning to suggest 'conscience' as well as 'consciousness.' See Huntington (1973) for an alternative explanation of comparable behavior in Bara funerals.

23. This was not always done as the royal ancestor wanted. The ampanjaka Amada (died 1968), the younger brother and successor of Binao who died in 1923, buried her on Nosy Komba against her will. Only after dreams and orders through her mediums, did he finally agree to build her a new tomb in the middle of Nosy Be, not far from Tsiomeko's tomb. It was begun in 1938 and completed in 1941 (see Baré 1973:139–46; 1980:37, 296–304).

24. Mellis 1938:62. On page 67, Mellis says that "One of the particularities of the cultural ceremony of the burial of an Ampanjaka Bemihisatra, is that the coffin does not enter by the door of the first enclosure." Here, he attributes the back and forth movements of the procession to the spirit's desire to "rejoin his ancestors in God and that of his faithful, who want to keep him near them."

25. Dandouau 1911:171–172; Poirier 1939c:104; Mellis 1938:61,

photographs, 67, 62. But Poirier, speaking of Binao's first tomb on Nosy Komba, notes that the Northern Bemihisatra ampanjaka is not allowed to go to the Mahabo for a year after the reconstruction of the innermost fence—menaty— has been completed. Once the year is up, the ampanjaka comes to pay his respects and ask for the ancestors' blessings (1939d:112).

26. One person said that the man came from a village in the Ambolobozo Peninsula north of Analalava.

27. The earliest correspondence after Tondroko's death, dated September 26, 1925, confirms this (cited in Poirier 1926:59). *Tsimahasenga,* literally 'does not cure', also means 'not a royal body,' because *mahasenga* (cures) is the name for the ruler's body in the royal vocabulary.

28. Mellis 1938:62.

29. I heard mamahaña used mainly to refer to feeding or fattening people or animals or to putting up a resistance and standing fast, 'holding on when someone is trying to pull you away,' as one person explained it. Richardson (1885:147) cites the "provincial" expression, *Mamahana ny didin' ny Mpanjaka,* "to resist the laws of the sovereign," which might have been how Ndramamahaña's followers saw his relationship to French authorities, though no one volunteered this. The form of the

praise name places the emphasis on the relationship between rulers and followers, how he supported the 'thousands' who were his followers, not how he resisted thousands who were his enemies. Most of the people I asked about Ndramamahaña's praise name explained it in terms of his generosity, for example: "He likes to care for *(mitarimy)* many people—he was good-natured, eager to give food." Only Ndremahazo Jean-Pierre once included the other meaning as well, saying, "When they took him to the Mahabo, he didn't want to go, so it took them a long time."

30. See Feeley-Harnik 1989.

31. Mellis 1938:59.

32. *Mirôtso* (past tense, nirotso), ordinarily referring to becoming 'ruined' *(robaka),* was used in the royal vocabulary as meaning 'to sleep' in reference to the living ruler; 'to decay, become ruined' in reference to royal buildings; and 'to die.'

33. See Poirier 1926:67–68 for the original Malagasy text. The manantany and fahatelo in charge of the service wrote to Amada the same day, also asking for his help in extending the funeral and in getting Ndramamahaña's child recognized as heir to his office and to his goods, which French authorities otherwise intended to keep, claiming the estate was vacant; adding, "the newborn child

is a girl" (ibid.:65–67). In fact the funeral was terminated the next day, as a Silamo minister informed Amada by telegram that same day (ibid.:70–71).

34. The council house *(fantsina)* and the storage house *(tsizoizoy)* inside the fiaroaomby of Binao's first tomb on Nosy Komba was already covered with corrugated iron in 1929, but the menaty was still made of teza (Poirier 1929:107, 108, 111).

35. Perhaps it is not surprising that Malaza spoke so strongly, since he, like other descendants of Sambarivo who stayed south when the French moved Tondroko's doany north, had already put a distance between himself and the Doany, even though he still served there. Judging from the fact that the sheet metal for the roofs was bought, and negotiations were underway for the cement, his views were shared far more widely.

36. I do not know whether the disagreements about the cement and metal roofing came before or after the Southern Bemihisatra were denied permission to do the service.

37. See Chapter 3, note 126.

38. See Althabe 1980 and Covell 1987:45–56 for fuller accounts of these events.

39. I did not learn enough about the social organization of the Zafinifotsy doany to know what motivated the decisions of Bevaoko and Ampela Be.

40. Malaza emphasized to the two Sambarivo from the Mahabo the importance of keeping everyone in their right places by giving them examples of how things had gone wrong in the preceding menaty service. So, for example, when it came time for the ox's blood to be brushed on the door—"'Where's the person for this, where!' They thought it should be a Jingo [Ancestor Person]. But they were wrong, the Sakalava Mañoroñaomby [head of the Ancestor People] should have been in charge" *(Misy talen' ny Marovavy, Fihitry, sy Sambarivo ambalaka sy avaratra. Samby am place. Irô tsy mety miharo).*

41. Sambarivo described the Maromainty as 'strong people' *(olo mahery, fatatra)* and also as 'bad' *(ratsy).* In the precolonial period, they were ordered after thieves of royal property, people who had disregarded royal orders, and people who had not paid their tribute.

42. Given enough space, this is decided by whether they live north or south of the Mahabo. Some people at the Mahabo, who should live in the south, live north of the fantsina because the south has long been too crowded.

43. See Feeley-Harnik 1988:74.

44. The Sakalava group of Ancestor People are also associated with the Bemongo among the Northern Bemihisatra. These Bemongo are considered the 'people' or 'slaves' of the Sakalava (Baré 1973:171). Among the Southern Bemihisatra, the Bemongo are their people at the Mahabo, but the Tsimazava, in charge of the ancestors' house at the Doany, are their people at the Doany.

45. Their most important work, in this respect, was to transport the royal corpse from the Doany to the Mahabo at the time of the 'hot service' or royal funeral.

46. Shakespeare, *Richard III,* II, ii, 96–139 [1964:81–83].

47. Ibid.

Chapter 8, Serving in the Forest, notes to pp. 401–440.

1. *Ny zavatra ilaina dia ilaina amin' izy io dia: Voalohany: Ny avy ao amin' ny mpanjaka manoro dia ireto avy: Tsy maintsy manendry Manantany sy Fahatelo, Mpanjaka tompon' ny lamban-tànana (jadò) io no voalohany, Rangitra ampanjaka, Marovavy, Fihitra, ary Razan'olona ka ireto avy ireo Razan'olona ireo: JINGO, ANTANKOALA ary SAKALAVA.*

Ny zavatra tsy maintsy miaraka amin' izy ireo dia ireto avy: Famaky, Angady, Mesobe, ary Tomainty na Damozany iray aza. Ireo rehetra voalaza eo ambony ireo dia afantoka ao Doanibe mialoha. Ka rehefa voafantoka tsara ireo, dia mivavatra amin' izay ho any Ankaliava (Mahabo).

The word *manoro* (to sacrifice, direct, give joy), used to refer to the living ruler, is an example of words from Sakalava royal vocabulary that were kept in the text, which was otherwise composed according to Merina grammatical patterns, using Merina vocabulary even where Sakalava variants existed. The phrase "master of the cupped hands" refers to the living ruler's role as head of services honoring the royal ancestors. A petitioner bends down on both knees or sits cross-legged, cups hands *(mandamban-tàñana),* raises them up to the face and usually brushes them over the top of his or her bowed head, when making an offering and at the same time asking for the blessing of the royal ancestors. Guardians at the Mahabo explained *Aliava* or *Ankaliava* (At the Aliava) as meaning "land where royal spirits dwell" *(tany pitrahan' zanahary).* Bemazava in the Maromandia area also used these words interchangeably. Except where indicated, the data on which this chapter is based, was provided by royal officials and guardians of the Doany and the Mahabo and by other workers in the service. I was present during the time the service was first at the Mahabo, but not during the times it was at the Doany and work camp, and when it was finally completed six years later.

2. The *Customs Concerning the Menaty Service* . . . specifies the participation of three groups of Ancestor People: Jingo, Antankoala, and Sakalava [Mañoroaomby]. In other contexts, Southern Bemihisatra included a fourth: the Ndrarameva, who were paired with the Sakalava Mañoroaomby, as the Jingo were paired with the Antankoala. One guardian at the Mahabo explained why they were not mentioned in the *Customs* . . . by saying: "Ah, but they are there! The Sakalava [Mañoroaomby] there are mixed in with the Ndrarameva; they are there. They have one work; Sakalava and Ndrarameva, they work together. The Ndrarameva are not entered there, but they are all in the book. They have the same work after all." As I have already indicated, Saha Barimaso stated that of the Sakalava Mañoroaomby and the Sakalava Ndrarameva, only the latter could go to the Mahabo.

3. See also Poirier 1926:70. Jado probably derives from *jadona,* the root of various forms that Richardson (1885:297) defines as referring to things that are fixed firmly upright, straight or stiff, like "soldiers hidden away in reserve," or a spear. He cites the phrase, *manao jàdon' ny Mpanjaka* as meaning, "to issue a command from which no one is exempt, or which must be fully carried out."

The jadô was clearly intended to guard that the menaty service was performed correctly. Later, armed

with the jambia, he sat on top of
the tomb to protect it from
sorcerers. But his junior status and
youth meant that royal officials
were the ones who actually directed
the workers.

4. In principle, these were all
junior lines, ineligible to rule.
Nevertheless, in the first days of
October 1925, scarcely two weeks
after Tondroko's death, some of his
followers went to the chef de
district to declare Hanina, a woman
about sixty-five years old from the
Zafinimena group at Anjiajia as
Tondroko's heir by virtue of being
his "aunt" *(tante)*. The chef de
district later reported that he
refused with the support of the chef
de province. He claimed that she
fell from favor shortly afterwards
for wanting to prohibit alcohol to
former and new royal subjects,
since this had been the cause of the
deaths of Tondroko and his son
barely a year apart (cited in Poirier
1926:37–38). It is evident from
Poirier's own report that the
ampanjaka Hanina went to Philibert
after having recognized Soazara as
Tondroko's child, and that she
continued to serve as a kind of
regent, organizing the effort to get
Soazara recognized by French
authorities, paying the lawyers, and
so on, perhaps precisely because she
was ineligible to rule.

5. The tools for the two earlier
menaty services were forged by a
blacksmith from the Antifañaigny

ancestry, in a village south of
Andampy, who was succeeded by
his son (Fig. 16). This time, they
were purchased from Indian
merchants in Analalava, using
tribute money from the Doany.

6. See Raison-Jourde (1983,
plates 4–5) for photographs of
Bemazava rulers carrying jambia at
their waists.

7. The drums were never
covered. The offering dish, the
kaolin, and the dancing costumes
were kept clean by wrapping them
separately in pieces of white cotton
cloth *(bafota malandy)*. New red and
white cloth were bought for the
shoulder belts and body wraps
worn by the lead dancers who play
royalty. They took one pair of
dance-hats from the storage house
at the Mahabo, leaving two pairs
behind (see Feeley-Harnik 1988).

8. The man who served as the
Great-Grandfather's medium lived
at the Mahabo during the dry
season but lived near his rice fields
on the mainland during the rainy
season. The three women who
served as mediums for the other
spirits were among the eight or ten
mediums who lived at the southern
Mahabo all year. Some of them are
simply fulfilling the year's residence
required of a legitimate medium.
Once that was finished, they would
go back to the villages where they
cultivated during the rainy season
and return to the Mahabo only
during the dry season.

9. Toquenne 1897a:973.

10. Cited in Poirier 1926:15–17.

11. Ibid.:17–18.

12. Any part of the reconstruction that cannot be completed in the single day allotted to it must wait until the next menaty service.

13. The practice of drawing up lists of people appointed to particular royal services dates at least to the colonial period as indicated in the letter of a local official to the ampanjaka Amada in Nosy Be, listing the names, and in some cases their positions as royal workers (ranitry, marovavy, etc.) in response to his request for people to serve at his daughter's wedding (cited in Poirier 1926:52).

14. Antidoany said that if they could not have used a *lakafiara,* then they would have used either a *lakajilo,* a larger kind of outrigger canoe with a prow, or a dhow, because they also have 'heads' in contrast to the *lakarakisy* and *lakadrao,* which are like 'round things' in having no head or foot. Lakafiara were used all along the west coast (see Smith 1896:12 for a photograph of a laka-piaro in the Tsiribihina River area). Richardson (1885:369, 183) defines fiara as a provincial word meaning "a moveable platform," specifically, "an open palanquin adorned with scarlet in which the sovereign is carried" or "a ship"; missionaries took over the term to refer to "the sacred ark of Scripture."

Some Antidoany said that 'formerly' the Silamo would have served without payment, like the Antandrano. Now that they are no longer economically dependent on the monarchy, they have to be paid.

15. The singing and dancing in the night with which the first good day begins is called *tsimandrimandry,* 'not dozing' (see Feeley-Harnik 1988).

16. Antibe at the Mahabo had asked us to make them a copy of the guide to use during the service, but they had not brought it with them. Knowing that we had brought our copy, one of the brothers asked us the night before the workers were to leave if we would make a copy of the section concerning the order the procession was to take. During the time they were working inside the storage house, he left the burial compound to get the paper in his house, so he could be sure that the order would be right. Turning something over, around, inside out or upside down *(mivadiky)* was associated with betrayal, as indicated earlier in discussing social relations at the post. Reversing royal orders was a form of insubordination equivalent to sorcery.

17. They removed their head cloths and tied them around their chests; let down their braids; washed their hands as people do in preparing for royal service and in

preparation for becoming possessed by royal spirits. They lined up from north to south. The equipment was put on the head of the southernmost woman and shifted north from head to head with both hands, until it reached the head of the northernmost person. When it was carried, it was also held with both hands, in contrast to ordinary burdens held with one hand, if at all.

18. As the women were lining up, the supplicator and his brothers dressed the Jado and the Ancestor People in shoulder belts made of new white cotton cloth bought especially for this purpose and stored in the house inside the burial compound. The shoulder belts were wrapped over the right shoulder and around the waist, the ends spread out like the tails of a loin cloth in the front and back. Antidoany and Antimahabo said this was how men dressed for war in the precolonial period (see Feeley-Harnik 1988:78). The leaders of the service were dressed to protect the royal ancestors, just as the Jado was later armed with the jambia before climbing up onto the top of the tomb.

Savôko is the royal word for shoulder belt, otherwise known as *sàndoka*. The common term may derive from *sàndy* (proper, elegant), but possibly also sàndoka, a 'fraud' or 'forgery,' based on deceptive appearances. In putting on white shoulder belts, like those worn by royalty, the Ancestor People do assimilate themselves to royalty. Though participants in the menaty service did not express the relationship of the Ancestor People to royalty in these terms, Richardson (1885:550) cites a derivative of sàndoka that might be relevant: "*manando-drazana* . . . to pretend to be of another family, etc.," literally to take on the appearance of another's ancestry.

19. Instead of walking west, the way petitioners leave the area in front of the door to the tomb, the procession headed north, filing out between the western wall of the outermost fence and the open-air meeting house, which is an area restricted to royal officials and Sambarivo.

20. Some Antimahabo said that in the past when there were many more participants from the Mahabo than now, those who were not involved with the spirit-mediums would help with the trees.

21. Abinal and Malzac (1970:223, 224) define the reduplicative form of this root—usually a diminutive—as a seldom used word meaning "clean," or as a more commonly used word meaning "perfidious flattery, irony," with transitive verb forms *(mangasohaso, manasohaso)* meaning to make "very white, spotless" and "to praise" or "to mock." Richardson (1885:237) defines *manasohaso* without the

irony as meaning "to speak of or to in a very appreciative manner."

The *Customs* . . . states: *Eto dia tsy maintsy ho tsarovina tsara fa ireo kakazo rehetra ireo dia tsy maintsy hasoinina aloha (c'est-à-dire tous les bois doivent être s'écorcés ou rabotés par Antidoany).*

22. The major Kongo service was done toward the end of the rainy season, in the tenth month of the lunar year (around April), in preparation for the new year's services two months later (the mead for that service was made in the eleventh month and allowed to ferment during the last 'dead' month). A shorter cleaning service was done at the beginning of the new year's service, one of the main purposes of which is to clean the ancestors with the mead. As with some other words from the royal vocabulary—for example *hena (viande), ny pilasiny (à leur place)*—the written *Customs* . . . clarify *hanompo Kongo* in French: *"pour nettoyer de tous ou enlever les feuilles des arbres."* The author of the guide goes on to say that there is not much to explain about the Kongo service, because "we [the selective we, that is, Antimahabo] already know it—but in case you cutters do not really understand it, I will recount here below how the Kongo service is done inside the real aliava [that is, the actual burial compound, as opposed to the settlement known as the Mahabo]."

23. The six gourds are consistent with the six francs (30 FMG, about 13 cents) that people normally pay as a door fee, in addition to their gift, when they address petitions to the royal ancestors at the Doany or Mahabo. Perhaps the Ancestors' People give eight five-franc coins because there are four kinds of them. One man explained the difference characteristically by saying "Each to his customs" *(Samby am fombany).*

24. The Sakalava-Ndrarameva conducts the service, while the Antankoala and Jingo do the actual work. The work is always divided between northern and southern halves, allotted to the Antankoala and Jingo respectively. Thus they are always distinguished. The lead position could be associated with the east-west coordinate, but the only time such an opposition is made is when the Ancestor People as a whole work on the east side or head of the tomb, in contrast to the Bemihisatra as a whole, who complete the western end or foot. Perhaps this is why the Ndrarameva were assimilated to the Sakalava, rather than distinguished like the Antankoala and Jingo, because the Sakalava-Ndrarameva served as one head, while the Antankoala and Jingo served as his pair of subordinates.

25. Poirier 1939a:18.

26. Various words were used to describe this work: *mampiboaka* and

mamoaka, 'to put out,' and *mandrorona,* 'to put down in a lower place, to make something descend.' According to Richardson (1885:530), mandrorona has social implications in Imerina: "to marry or have criminal connection with one of an inferior rank."

27. There were no special prohibitions on the eight women, except that having a clean body meant that they could not be menstruating. The *Customs . . .* stipulated that the women should be Ancestor People, but participants said they were Antidoany (Sambarivo). In fact, all the Ancestor People in the service were men. The Sambarivo from the Doany, men and women alike, seemed to serve as their attendants, just like the Sambarivo from the Mahabo attended the spirit-mediums.

28. Residents of the Northern Bemihisatra mahabo on Nosy Komba, where the ampanjaka Binao was formerly buried, were also prohibited from using old posts from the menaty for firewood (Poirier 1939d).

29. Participants used the word *mampizoana* from the royal vocabulary to refer to the process of putting up the new menaty, in addition to the common words *manangana* and *mañorigny,* which were used in referring to the actual work. Manangana referred to setting something upright,

including a memorial stone for one's own ancestor; mañorigny referred to construction. I did not hear mampizoana used in any other context.

30. When Sambarivo from the Doany reconstructed the ancestors' house there, they also rebuilt it somewhat south as well as east of its former location, 'because the royal ancestors constantly desire to return to their southern ancestral home.'

31. The term *mampilomanosina* for 'washing' is used in almost every context in which the royal ancestors—in the royal regalia or in the tomb—are cleansed with mead, including the annual new year's services. The word is probably compounded from the verbs *milona* (to wet, soak, steep, or bathe) and *manosina* (to besmear), thus meaning to wash by smearing with mead. The dust is cleaned off with the serviettes, then the mead is poured at the base. The serviettes are returned to the storage house afterwards, and later washed and distributed to the guardians at the Mahabo.

32. This division of labor is characteristic of other royal services, and might have been characteristic of the organization of fighting in the precolonial period (see, for example, Guillain 1845:59).

33. The author of the *Customs . . .* was careful to explain that the term mañidina is a Sakalava

word: "It does not mean to fly like a bird, as it does in Merina; it means to scatter or strew about, whether you are actually scattering something or simply spreading out what is already there."

34. Dandouau (1911:170–171) reports that the area between the menaty and the fiaroaomby is covered with sand, but according to Antimahabo in the 1970s, the area outside the menaty was left as it was after weeding. Even so, it was not called dirt (fòtaka). As indicated earlier, all the earth in the burial compound, including the area 'at the door,' is called 'oil' (famonty).

35. People in the area had different ways of talking about shutting doors, depending on how tightly: 'shut' (manakatona), '[walled] shut' (mandriba), or 'locked' (migadra, manidy).

36. Cattle are singly and collectively known as omby, which I have translated in singular form as 'cow.' Additional words qualify omby as 'male' (lahy) or 'female' (vavy), 'one' (araiky) or 'many' (maro) and so on.

37. Dandouau 1911; Decary 1962:213–256.

Chapter 9, Rooting Ancestors, notes to pp. 441–467.

1. Natolotr' ireo Dadilahy ireo no an' ny Taranaka, Doria, mba tsy handiso ny Fanompoana hatao.

2. Richardson (1885:643–644) notes several relevant examples, including mateza aina, 'enduring in breath,' namely 'long-lived' or 'very persistent in work'; mateza ditra, 'very persistent . . . used as a characteristic of the English'; mateza dinihina, 'used of anything whose nature or beauty is only seen after close examination'; miandry teza ho lava [to wait for a teza to fall], "to wait for a good opportunity for paying a person out; lit. to wait for the death of a patron."

3. 'Hot trees' (Hazo mafana, Diospyros spp.) were also prohibited because their name associated them with sickness and death. But as Jaotogny and Saha Fiara from the Mahabo commented, "They may be prohibited, but there aren't any around here anyway." Some hardwood trees are prohibited for reasons I do not know: kitàta, hazomena (Weinmannia rutenbergii Engler), and mañary (palisandra).

Among Southern Sakalava at the turn of the century, royalty alone could use katrafay to build their houses (lapa, donaka) and the enclosures around their tombs (valamasy). People ennobled by royalty were permitted to use it in making memorial posts dedicated to their ancestors (hazomanga) in circumcision ceremonies. Trees that grew over neighboring trees, thus killing them, were prohibited as "sorcerers of trees." The mañary tree was associated with death (Rey 1913:52–54).

4. The lumber companies of the colonial and later periods cut

mainly hardwood trees, including
those left standing by fires.
Participants in the menaty service
said they would tell the ampanjaka
if they were unable to find enough
dry hardwoods of the right kinds.
She would appeal to the royal
ancestors for permission to use wet
trees, because it was prohibited to
take trees for a menaty from any
other place except the one
originally chosen.

5. Participants said that
Antsantsarafa (sometimes
Antsandrarafa) had no other
referent and that its component
parts were meaningless, perhaps
because they never described
exactly what happened to the royal
corpse at that place. Based on
Richardson (1885:169, 487, 683) and
local usage, I think the term means
'at the drying bed' (locative *an-*
+ *tsantsana,* 'very dry thing' or
'something dried up in the
sun' + *rafa,* 'bed', a word that also
refers to the structure where a
corpse is prepared for burial).
Estrade (1977:62) mentions
"Tsianjarafa" [*Tsi,* 'not'
+ Antsa[ntsa]rafa?] as being the
grand plaza, shaded by mango
trees, where people gathered to
dance the rebiky war dance
honoring Sakalava royal ancestors
in Majunga.

6. For example, Bloch 1971;
Gueunier 1977; Kottak 1980;
Rajaonarimanana 1979.

7. See Molet's (1956)

comparative study of the 'royal
bath' in precolonial Madagascar.

8. The fiaroaomby is made
primarily of 'dead-living'
(matambelona) trees, which owe
their name to the fact that they root
and grow from a bare stalk stuck in
the ground. Because of its ability to
regenerate itself from a bare stalk,
matambelona is also an important
ingredient in medicines, as
mentioned earlier. I do not know
whether the term refers to a quality
shared by several different kinds of
trees and shrubs or to one kind in
particular.

9. *Vataña* (body/trunk), *sandry*
(arms/branches), and *faka* (root,
slang for penis) are used in referring
to trees and people alike. (*Voto* is
the ordinary word for 'penis'; *doany*
is the formal word for royal
genitals, regardless of gender, in the
Sakalava royal vocabulary.)

The *teza,* at the core of a
hardwood tree trunk, has its own
core or pith—*votoaty (voto,* 'penis,
growing tip of plant' + *aty,*
'inside')—surrounded by an outer
layer of 'flesh' *(nofo). Votoaty* is also
used to describe the heart of any
matter. Soft, fleshy materials are
usually associated with women, but
male genderedness may also be
implicit in the 'whiteness'
(tafotsiny), or sapwood surrounding
the teza, which is also called
kotofotsy (koto + *fotsy,* 'white').
Koto (or *Boto,* cognate of *voto*) is a
common boy's nickname,

comparable to *Bozy* ('little') for girls.

According to a "Sakalava" folktale about the origin of death, people die like trees because they are made of their wood (see also Renel 1920–1921:33). The graves of both royalty and commoners, in southern and northern Sakalava domains, are usually surrounded by trees (see also Rey 1913:68, Abadie 1947–1948).

In Rakoto's account of royal services honoring the royal ancestors at the Doany Andriamisara at Miarinarivo near Mahajanga during Hova rule, pilgrims to Miarinarivo, identified with the royal ancestors at the doany from which they have come, speak in similar terms. The host of a Sakalava doany, where pilgrims from the doany Mahabo near Marovoay have stopped en route to Miarinarivo, asks his guests how they are. They, representing Ndramandisoarivo who is one of the founders of the monarchy, respond that they are well and ask after the well-being of their hosts who respond: "As long as you, Roots and Trunk, are well, we the Branches and Twigs, we are well also" (Rakoto 1947–1948:111).

10. Most examples of tamberono referred to its use in replenishing lost blood. One man explained it as a means of getting "sleeping" blood to move again, thus restoring "force" to a person who has suffered a great blow or shock. He,

too, compared tamberono to wine. He said: "A person goes in an automobile and has an accident. He is struck with a strong shock *(vaodono, voa shock mafy)*. The blood sleeps, the blood does not break out, it is left inside *(Mandrindio, lio tsy vaky, tavela anatiny)*. He drinks tamberono, the blood inside is loosened *(ravana ley lio anatiny)*. Like the way Vazaha use wine—to restore, to create force *(manampodipody, mampisipisy force)*. It is given to a person struck by a strong shock!"

11. Kottak 1980.

12. Bloch 1971.

13. Bloch 1986:175, 193; see also 1982.

14. Covell (n.d. [ca. 1978]), based on fieldwork in the highland town of Fianarantsoa in 1969–1970, argues that relations between national and local politics were then mediated mainly through patron-client relationships in Malagasy government bureaucracy. She concludes her assessment of these as "linkage or line of defense?" by saying: ". . . the system persists *because* [my emphasis] the bulk of the population is only partially incorporated in it. The general population of a country like Madagascar enjoyed a brief period of political relevance at the time of the pre-independence elections and before the consolidation of a one-party or military regime. Since then the system has shrunk, as has the number of people whose opinions

must be taken into account by the political elite. It is within this group that reliable channels of communication are necessary; for the partially integrated, partial channels suffice" (ibid.:32).

The system was attacked shortly afterwards in the 'commotion' (rotaka) of May 1972, leading to radical changes in the organization of government. Nevertheless, questions concerning reciprocity and autonomy in relations between international, national, and local authorities, especially under increasingly difficult economic conditions, continue to be matters of intense concern throughout Madagascar.

15. Burke 1937, vol. 2, p. 70.

16. See Neil Smith 1984:75–76.

17. For further discussion of the work of economic geographers like Manuel Castells and Henri Lefebvre, see Smith (1984:90–92, 136–137).

18. Lévi-Strauss 1965:204.

19. See Bourdieu 1977. Foucault (1979:195–228), entitled in French *Surveiller et Punir: Naissance de la prison*. Foucault does this even though he wonders (ibid.:203) whether Bentham's prototype was Le Vaux's menagerie at Versailles, the first menagerie in which the objects under scrutiny were not mixed together in a park. He sees in both the logic of a "naturalist," with a mechanistic bent, even suggesting: "The Panopticon is a royal menagerie; the animal is

replaced by man, individual distribution by specific grouping and the king by the machinery of a furtive power. With this exception, the Panopticon also does the work of a naturalist" (ibid.). He mentions in passing that the only room at the center of Le Vaux's menagerie was the king's salon, but he does not consider the possibility that the visual logic for the menagerie might have its own prototype in the reception halls, corridors, and bedrooms of Versailles itself, where royal followers also learned "the art of observing people" (see Elias 1983:104–106).

20. Elias notes that the successors to artists of observation at Versailles, like Saint-Simon, La Bruyère, and La Rochefoucauld were writers observing the "French 'good society'" which succeeded court life, in short stories and novels. He mentions Balzac, Flaubert, de Maupassant, and Proust (1983:106, n. 36). By the same token, the anthropologists, historians, and other scholars of space should be seen together with writers like Stendhal, Balzac, and Proust. Both Bakhtin (1981:246–247) and Knapp (1985:xiv) single out Balzac for his "[extraordinary] ability to 'see' time in space," as Bakhtin describes it (ibid.:247, his emphasis).

21. Foucault 1979; Rose 1977.

22. Foucault 1979:141–169.

23. O'Brien 1982; Nye 1984.

24. Sykes 1958.

25. Sykes 1958:40–62.
26. Coser 1974:21–63.
27. See Tambiah 1989. All three of Tambiah's "scenarios" (ibid.:345–347) are relevant in different ways to Malagasy history and contemporary social-cultural organization.
28. Haeringer 1980:290, cited in Chapter 5, p. 234.
29. The total population was then about four million. Most of those who died were noncombatants, who had fled into the forests to escape the fighting and who died there from hunger or exposure. Trials and executions were still being held in 1954. Government controls were not lifted in many parts of the east coast until 1956. The sentences of three leading MDRM *(Mouvement de la Rénovation Malgache)* party members, commuted from death or life imprisonment to exile, were not lifted until independence in 1960 (see Covell 1987:7, 26–28; Thompson and Adloff 1965:54–69; Tronchon 1974:73–74).
30. Decary 1951b:278.
31. See, for example, Bloch n.d.; Decary 1957:39–41; Gueunier 1977; Rajaonarimanana 1979, figs. 1–4; Rey 1913:67–68; Renel 1920–1921:118–127. Hardyman's (1938) notice of stories about the "man-eating tree" of Madagascar, appearing in scholarly and popular publications in Madagascar, England, France, Germany, Australia, and the United States

between 1881 and 1924, and possibly originating in India in 1894, warrants further attention in this context. Ozouf (1988) analyzes the liberty trees of the French Revolution (see Chapter 5, note 7).
32. Gluckman (1945) summarizes Richard's (1939) account of *Land, Labour and Diet in Northern Rhodesia,* by saying "The Bemba live in, with, and by, their trees" (1945:22). In *The Forest of Symbols,* Turner (1967) argues that all of the "dominant symbols" (ibid.:30–31, 50–52) of Ndembu religion are trees, associated with specific colors, and healing properties. Banzie, "Angels," practitioners of the Fang religious movement known as Bwiti, describe Bwiti as a "path of trees" (Fernandez 1982:651, note 4). Fernandez summarizes Bwiti as "a religion of trees" (ibid.:472), and comments about the introductory words of a Bwiti sermon, "Fang are Forest (or of the Forest)": "That identification of one of the central social subjects of Bwiti with trees or a forest of trees is recurrent and basic" (ibid.:544). Fox's (1971) analysis of Rotinese ideas and practices about "sister's child as plant," and mother's brother as "trunk," concludes with a brief discussion of the prevalence of such imagery in Southeast Asia and Melanesia.

Wood (1982) interprets *The Golden Bough* (Frazer 1913–1915) as a torch of knowledge to illuminate the underworld of "primitive" thought, with which Frazer also exposed the fragile underpinnings of positivism. Besides the studies of francophone Africa cited in Chapter 5 (Pélissier et al. 1980), European case studies are included in Cosgrove and Daniels (1988) and Green (1990). Pollan (1990) discusses changes in the political imagery of trees in the United States since colonial times, while Faber (1990) provides a contemporary example.

33. Schabecoff 1989, E3.

34. Salmond 1982:81, 84.

35. See Casey 1987, who explores the strangely neglected bodily and spatial dimensions of memory (they would be "cow paths" in Burke's [1937, vol. 2, p. 70] sense) in predominantly temporal theories of memory in Western philosophy. See also Fernandez's (1979) discussion of metaphors of stasis and movement embedded in Western social theory.

36. See, for example, Beidelman (1980, 1986), Fernandez (1979, 1982), Needham (1978).

37. Wolf 1982.

38. Forster 1921, title page, pp. 186–187, 208.

Appendix 2, notes to pp. 473–480.

1. Ambilahikely died in 1924, when the Sambarivo appointed as guardians of the Mahabo were still required to live in Andronjona, where French authorities had relocated them in 1916 (see Chapter 3). Beloha, who probably became possessed by the spirit of Ambilehikely in the 1920s, is likely to have lived in Andronjona part of the year. Nevertheless, guardians and spirit-mediums were not permitted to reoccupy the Mahabo until some years later, as early as 1927, but possibly as late as 1956.

2. The official term for this arrangement is *sesi-tany* (forced off land), a kind of banishment or exile. In late nineteenth-century usage, *sesy* (driven or dwindling out/off/down) could also mean 'degenerated, lowered, become a slave' (Richardson 1885:567–568). As Sefo explained it, the Antimoro was a 'prisoner' *(gadra)* who did sesi-tany in Tsinjorano; he was released from prison but still not allowed to return home. There were different 'kinds'; the Antaimoro's sesi-tany was five years. The prisoner had a notebook (carnet) and had to report to the police every three months to get it stamped, but he was able to chose the place where he wanted to farm.

3. The third son, then living in (29), was in the process of building a larger house (31) south of his parents, leaving (29) to his younger brother, then living in his rice-field house.

Glossary

ampangataka—'supplicator'; a royal official at the Doany (a Sambarivo from the Mosohery 'pen') and at the Mahabo (a Sambarivo from the Antibe 'pen'), whose principal work is to speak for suppliants to the royal ancestors.

ampanjaka or 'mpanjaka—ruler, literally 'burdener', from the verb *manjaka*, 'to impose/exert/burden', whence *fanjakaña*, referring to all forms of government; people descended from royalty or ennobled may call themselves or be called ampanjaka; the sovereign ruler is distinguished as the 'great ruler' *(ampanjaka be)*.

ampanompo—royal servitor, from the verb *manompo*, to serve, whence *fanompoaña*, royal service.

anadoany—people descended from nonruling royal lines, from which royal substitutes *(jado)* are chosen; perhaps a shortened form of *anaka doany*, 'children of the doany'.

andevo—slave; also used in speaking of royal servitors *(ampanompo)*, and royal followers *(mpanaraka)* in general, where the term is interpreted to mean 'person/people who agree to serve the ruler' *(olo mañeky manompo ny ampanjaka)*, in contrast to the common association of 'enslaving people' *(magnindevo olo)* with force and money.

anjara—a person's fate, share, lot in life or in any activity involving other people.

Antidoany—royal guardian (Sambarivo) at the Doany; *ant(i)* is a locative prefix commonly used to identify person(s) by place.

591

Antimahabo—royal guardian (Sambarivo) at the Mahabo.

Antsandrarafa—'At The Drying Bed,' the place along the shore below the Mahabo, where the royal corpse is dried to bone in preparation for burial, and where the leaves, branches, and bark are removed from the tree trunks cut during the *menaty* service, exposing the *teza*, the heartwood of trees, from which the new menaty fence will be made.

Arabo—descendant of an ancestor (invariably male) born in one of the countries bordering the southern Arabian Peninsula and Persian Gulf, who came to Madagascar as a trader and settled there in the last three to four generations; three large 'networks' *(fehiny)* of kin are distinguished as Arabo among the Silamo (Muslims) in the Analalava region.

avak'aomby—'cow/cattle separated from the herd'; Sambarivo sent with the corpse of a deceased ruler from the *doany* to the *mahabo* to be his or her guardians; in principle, at least one is selected from each 'pen' *(vala)* of Sambarivo at the *doany*.

doany—royal compound, extended to include the village of guardians surrounding it on all sides; in the Analalava region, the doany includes the living ruler's house as well as the royal ancestors' house (inside its own fence); in the Mahajanga area, the doany includes only the royal ancestors' house; the word in the royal vocabulary for 'royal genitals.'

fahatelo—'third'; the third ranking person in the administration of the living ruler after the *ampanjaka* (1) and the *manantany* (2); in charge of internal affairs at the *doany*. The position does not exist at the *mahabo*, although the *ampangataka* there is sometimes called *fahatelo* because he has similar duties.

fanjakaña—'government'; also used to refer to royal spirits possessing mediums, individually or as a group.

fanompoaña—'royal service'; any act in the service of living or ancestral royalty; the royal funeral is distinguished from all other kinds of service as the 'hot service' *(fanompoaña mafana)*.

fehitany—a royal follower appointed as head of a *fehezina*, a group of two to five villages, which constitutes the smallest administrative unit in a royal domain.

fiaroaomby—the outermost of the two fences surrounding the tomb of the royal ancestors at the *mahabo*; made of quickset branches.

firazaña—'ancestry'.

havana—kin, friend(s).

jambia—curved fighting knife carried by the royal substitute *(jado)* during the *menaty* service.

karazana—kind(s).

mahabo—'to elevate'; the royal burial compound, extended to include the village of guardians and spirit-mediums surrounding it on the north, south, and west sides; usually located on an island.

manantany—'(person) having land'; the second most important person in the administration of the living ruler after the ruler; concerned with work in the 'ruler's land' *(tany ny ampanjaka)* as a whole.

menaty—'red inside'; a palisade immediately surrounding the royal tomb, with an unopenable 'door' called *menalio* (red blood), marked by two sharpened posts in the middle of the west side.

mikapa—'to cut/clear land', 'to weed'.

ontso velo—'living cleanser', from *manontsana* (to wash/clean by rinsing, usually with water) and *velona* (living); an uncooked mixture of honey and water used to cleanse people, especially spirit-mediums, and things of dirt, especially body fluids, connections with death, and wrong-doing.

raha sarotra—'difficult/precious things', the commonest name in the Analalava region for royal ancestors in relics or entombed.

rañitry—'sharp'; name of the royal cattle mark; men who serve to represent ancestries of royal followers at the *doany*.

Razan'olo—'Ancestor Person/People'; ancestries of people, including named groups—Sakalava Mañoromaomby, Sakalava Ndrarameva, Antankoala, Jingo—charged with burying the royal corpse and rebuilding the *menaty* fence around the royal tomb.

saha—'conduit'; medium of an important royal ancestor, one of the founding ancestors of the Zafinimena (Maroseraña) dynasty or one of the rulers buried in the immediate area.

Sambarivo—'Every One A Thousand'; royal guardians meant to be permanent residents at the *doany* and the *mahabo,* charged with the daily care and guardianship of living and ancestral royalty; the Sambarivo are divided into sixteen named groups known as 'pens' *(vala),* located in specific places around the royal compounds at the *doany* and the *mahabo* according to the nature of their work.

Silamo—'Muslim'; sometimes opposed to *kiSilamo,* 'Silamolike (person)', '(person) adopting Silamo ways', a Malagasy convert to Islam (usually referring to a woman who has married a Silamo man) in contrast to a person descended through men from earlier generations of Silamo ancestors.

takitaky—offering(s) from the living ruler at the *doany* to the royal ancestors at the *mahabo.*

teza—the core of a hardwood tree, referring as in the English term heartwood, to the hard, nonliving wood at the center of the tree, in contrast to the soft, outer sapwood between the heartwood and the bark; the heartwood serves to keep the tree upright, in contrast to the sapwood, which serves to conduct the sap from which the tree grows; the heartwood is darker in color than the sapwood, increasingly impervious to air and water, and consequently more durable toward the center; as the tree grows older and bigger, the heartwood increases in size; teza form the core of royal coffins and most royal houses and fences in the Analalava region.

togny—'calm, peaceful'; a tree 'stood up' or 'cultivated' as a 'means of remembering' *(fahatsiarovaña)* ancestors, those of 'simple people' or royalty, connecting people to the land from which they live as 'masters of the land' or as 'strangers.'

tô mainty—'blackness'; mead made from cooked honey and water fermented with bark from the *Katrafay* tree, drunk at the royal new year's celebration in the first month *(fanjava mitsaka)* of the lunar new year, around July; also used to cleanse persons and things of dirt, especially dirt associated with death and wrong-doing (see *ontso velo*).

tompon'tany—'master of the land'; first settler or descendant thereof.

tompon'tanana—'master of the village'; resident.

tromba—a medium of a nonlocal royal ancestor; the royal spirit may also be called a tromba.

vady—spouse, one of a pair.

vahiny—'stranger', 'visitor', 'guest'; later settler; 'person who has just come' *(olo vao navy)*.

vala—'fence', 'enclosure', referring to fences or enclosures of any kind—around people's houses, gardens, animals—and to the positions of named groups of royal guardians (Sambarivo) around the royal compounds at the Doany and the Mahabo, which are not marked off by fences.

valamena—'red fence'; the palisade around the royal ancestors' house at the *doany*.

varavara menalio—'red-blood door'; the 'door' made from two adjacent posts in the middle of the west side of the *menaty* fence around the royal tomb, distinguished from the others by their sharpened 'heads.'

Vy Lava—'Long Iron', short for 'Long Iron That Rules Alone' *(Vy Lava Manjaka Tokana),* a knife with an iron blade and wooden handle, an embodiment of Sakalava royal ancestry, which Southern Bemihisatra consider comparable to the ancestral relics of Boina and Menabe kept at Sakalava *doany* in Mahajanga and Belo-sur-Tsiribihina; kept in the royal ancestors' house *(zomba)* at the Doany in the Analalava region.

Zafinifotsy—'Grandchildren of the White', a short form of *Zafimbolafotsy*, 'Grandchildren of the Silver', royalty in the northern Sakalava domains of Boina who have no currently living descendants because they drowned themselves in the Loza River north of Analalava rather than submit to the Hova who were pursuing them; they form the junior partner of a pair with *Zafinimena* royalty, associated with water as opposed to land, uplands *(antety)* as opposed to the coast *(andrano)*, indigenous rulers as opposed to foreign conquerors, 'Tsimihety' as opposed to 'Sakalava,' and—as argued in Chapters 4 and 6—'children of women' as opposed to 'children of men.'

Zafinimena—'Grandchildren of the Red', a short form of *Zafimbolamena*, 'Grandchildren of the Gold', a name given to the ruling line of Sakalava royalty in the northern domains of Boina, especially in contrast to the *Zafinifotsy* (see above); the ruling line from which the current ruler of the Southern Bemihisatra branch of Sakalava royalty, is descended.

zomba—'royal house', the royal equivalent of *trano* (house) among 'simple people' *(olo tsotra)*; zomba—the house of the living ruler at the Doany; *zomba be, zomban-drazaña, zomba mitahy*—the royal ancestors' house at the Doany; *zomba vinta*—the house inside the burial compound where ancestors' things are kept at the Mahabo; *zomba bekiviro*—the house just outside the burial compound at the Mahabo, where the royal drums are kept.

References Cited

Archival Documents

Archives Nationales, Repoblika Demokratika Malagasy, Antananarivo (ANRDM)

    Série D (10, 55) Cabinet Civil (Travaux publics)

    Série D (438, 439) Affaires Politiques, Provinces

Centre des Archives d'Outre-Mer, Aix-en-Provence (CAOM). Cartons formerly at the Archives Nationales, Section Outre-mer, Paris, now at CAOM (MAD = Madagascar; c. = carton; d. = dossier):

    MAD c. 1, d. 5 [Esclavage—Nossi-Bé, 1844–1847]

    MAD c. 14, d. 28 [Carte générale de la partie occidentale de Madagascar 1843]

    MAD c. 146, d. 203 [Notes sur les affaires de Nossi-Bé, Mars 1851]

    MAD c. 293, d. 726 [Budget—Nossi-Bé, 1841, 1842, 1843]

    MAD c. 295, d. 737 [Correspondance générale—Nossi-Bé, 1839–1843]

    MAD c. 296, d. 738 [Correspondance générale—Nossi-Bé, 1844]

    MAD c. 296, d. 739 [Correspondance générale—Nossi-Bé, 1847–1849]

    MAD c. 296, d. 740 [Affaires politiques et adminstratives—Nossi-Bé, 1793–1853]

    MAD c. 354, d. 957 [Affaire Ralaimongo]

CAOM, Madagascar, Series D: Politique et administration générale, 1870–1959.

    MAD 2D [Rapports périodiques des circonscriptions (politiques—économiques—financiers—main d'oeuvre)]

MAD 3D [Missions d'inspection des colonies (1903–1946)]

MAD 6D [Dossiers divers de la direction des affaires politiques et de l'administration générale, 1870–1958]

CAOM, Madagascar, Series Z: Diverse public and private papers concerning Madagascar prior to 1896

MAD 1Z [Ste. Marie (1785–1889) including Conventions et instructions relatives à la répression de l'esclavage, 1841–1859, dossiers 338–348]

MAD 2Z [Consulat de France et Résidence générale de France à Tananarive (1830–1898) including documents on the suppression of slavery, 1859–1896]

MAD 4Z [Pièces diverses concernant Nosy Be, Mayotte, et la côte Nord-Ouest de Madagascar (1841–1897)]

Archives of the London Missionary Society, School of Oriental and African Studies, London (LMS)

Madagascar Odds Series: private letters, manuscripts, newspaper clippings, etc.

Official Periodicals

Bibliothèque universitaire, Antananarivo, Madagascar.

Guide Annuaire de Madagascar et Dépendances à l'usage des colons planteurs, commerçants, industriels, fonctionnaires et voyageurs. République Française. Imprimerie Officielle, Tananarive.

Journal Officiel de Madagascar et Dépendances. République Française. Imprimerie Officielle, Tananarive.

Other Manuscripts and Publications

Abadie, C.

1947–1948   Note sur une tombe sakalava au Sud du Mangoky. *Bulletin de l'Académie Malgache* (n.s.) 28:21–23.

Abinal, F.G., and V. Malzac

1970   *Dictionnaire malgache-français.* [First edition 1888.] Paris: Editions Maritimes et d'Outre-mer.

Althabe, Gérard

1969   *Oppression et libération dans l'imaginaire: Les Communautés villageoises de la côte orientale de Madagascar.* Paris: Maspero.

1980   Les Luttes sociales à Tananarive en 1972. *Cahiers d'Études Africaines* 20:407–447.

André, E.C.

1899   *De l'Esclavage à Madagascar.* Paris: Librairie Nouvelle de Droit et de Jurisprudence.

599   **References Cited**

Anonymous

ca. 1908a   Tantaran' ny Andrian' Sakalava. Manuscript notebook,
Académie Malgache, no. 2238/1. Antananarivo.

ca. 1908b   Niandohan' ny Fivavahan' ny Sakalava. Manuscript
notebook, Académie Malgache, no. 2238/2. Antananarivo.

ca. 1908c   Tromba sy Razana. Manuscript notebook, Académie
Malgache, no. 2238/3. Antananarivo.

Armstrong, James C.

1982   St. Augustine's Bay and the Madagascar Slave Trade in the
Seventeenth Century. Manuscript on file with author.

1983–1984   Madagascar and the Slave Trade in the Seventeenth
Century. *Omaly sy Anio* 17–20:211–233.

Asiwaju, A.I.

1976   Political Motivation and Oral Historical Traditions in Africa: The
Case of Yoruba Crowns, 1900–1960. *Africa* 46:113–127.

Association des Géographes de Madagascar

1969–1970   *Atlas de Madagascar.* Antananarivo: Le Bureau pour le
Développement de la Production Agricole et le Centre de l'Institut
Géographique National à Madagascar.

Atkins, K.E.

1988   'Kafir Time': Preindustrial Temporal Concepts and Labor
Discipline in Nineteenth-Century Colonial Natal. *Journal of African
History* 29:229–244.

Augagneur, Victor

1927   *Erreurs et brutalités coloniales.* Paris: Éditions Montaigne.

Bakhtin, Mikhail M.

1981   *The Dialogic Imagination: Four Essays by M.M. Bakhtin,* edited by
M. Holquist. Austin: University of Texas Press.

Baré, J.-F.

1973   *Conflits et résolution des conflits dans les monarchies Sakalava du Nord
actuelles.* Travaux et documents du Musée d'Art et d'Archéologie de
l'Université de Madagascar, XII, publication provisoire.

1974   La Terminologie de parenté Sakalava du Nord (Madagascar).
L'Homme 14:5–41.

1977   *Pouvoir des vivants, langage des morts. Idéo-logiques Sakalava.* Paris:
Maspero.

1980   *Sable rouge. Une Monarchie du nord-ouest malgache dans l'histoire.*
Paris: L'Harmattan.

1986   L'Organisation sociale Sakalava du Nord: Une Récapitulation. In
Madagascar: Society and History, edited by C.P. Kottak, J.-A.

Rakotoarisoa, A. Southall, and P. Vérin, pp. 353–392. Durham, N.C.: Carolina Academic Press.

Barthes, Roland
1957   Grammaire africaine. In *Mythologies*, pp. 155–161. Paris: Éditions du Seuil.

Basso, Keith
1983   "Stalking with Stories": Names, Places and Moral Narrative among the Western Apache. In *Text, Play and Story: The Construction and Reconstruction of Self and Society*, edited by S. Plattner, pp. 19–55. Seattle, Wa.: American Ethnological Society.

Beidelman, T.O.
1980   The Moral Imagination of the Kaguru: Some Thoughts on Tricksters, Translation and Comparative Analysis. *American Ethnologist* 7:27–42.
1986   *Moral Imagination in Kaguru Modes of Thought.*Bloomington: Indiana University Press.

Belrose-Huyghues, Vincent
1983   Structure et symbolique de l'espace royal en Imerina. In *Les Souverains de Madagascar: L'Histoire royale et ses résurgences contemporaines*, edited by F. Raison-Jourde, pp. 125–151. Paris: Karthala.

Bénévent, Charles
1897   Étude sur le Boueni. *Notes, Reconnaissances, et Explorations* 1:355–379, 2:49–77.

Bernard
n.d.   Notice sur le *Vy Lava*. Manuscript du Bibliothèque Poirier, Document 623. Antananarivo: Bibliothèque Universitaire.

Berg, Gerald M.
1980   Some Words About Merina Historical Texts. In *The African Past Speaks: Essays on Oral Tradition and History*, edited by J.C. Miller, pp. 221–239. London: Dawson.
1985   The Sacred Musket: Tactics, Technology, and Power in Eighteenth-Century Madagascar. *Comparative Studies in Society and History* 27:261–279.
1986   Royal Authority and the Protector System in Nineteenth-Century Imerina. In *Madagascar: Society and History*, edited by C.P. Kottak, J.-A. Rakotoarisoa, A. Southall, and P. Vérin, pp. 175–192. Durham, N.C.: Carolina Academic Press.

Bloch, Maurice
1971   *Placing the Dead: Tombs, Ancestral Villages, and Kinship Organization in Madagascar*. London: Seminar.

1973   The Long Term and the Short Term: The Economic and Political Significance of the Morality of Kinship. In *The Character of Kinship,* edited by J. Goody, pp. 75–87. Cambridge: Cambridge University Press.

1978   Marriage among Equals: An Analysis of the Marriage Ceremony of the Merina of Madagascar. *Man* (n.s.) 13:21–33.

1982   Death, Women, and Power. In *Death and the Regeneration of Life,* edited by M. Bloch and J. Parry, pp. 211–230. Cambridge: Cambridge University Press.

1986   *From Blessing to Violence: History and Ideology in the Circumcision Ritual of the Merina of Madagascar.* Cambridge: Cambridge University Press.

n.d.   The Resurrection of the House. Manuscript on file with author.

Boiteau, Pierre

1948   La Situation matérielle et morale des travailleurs malgaches. *Esprit* (February):240–256.

Boudou, R.P.

1941   Querelles de roitelets antankarana et sakalava: 1865–1875. *Bulletin de l'Académie Malgache* (n.s.) 24:171–180.

Bouillon, Antoine

1981   *Madagascar: Le Colonisé et son "âme." Essai sur le discours psychologique colonial.* Paris: L'Harmattan.

Bourdieu, Pierre

1977   *Outline of a Theory of Practice.* Cambridge: Cambridge University Press.

Brain, J.L.

1973   Ancestors as Elders in Africa—Further Thoughts. *Africa* 43:122–133.

Brown, Elizabeth A.R.

1978   The Ceremonial of Royal Succession in Capetian France: The Double Funeral of Louis X. *Traditio* 34:227–271.

1980   The Ceremonial of Royal Succesion in Capetian France: The Funeral of Philip V. *Speculum* 55:266–293.

1985   Burying and Unburying the Kings of France. In *Persons in Groups,* edited by Richard C. Trexler, pp. 241–266. Binghamton: SUNY Press.

Burke, Kenneth

1937   *Attitudes Toward History.* 2 vols. New York: The New Republic.

Cahuzac, Albert

1900   *Essai sur les institutions et le droit malgaches.* Tome I. Paris: A. Chevalier-Marescq.

Callet, R.P.

1974 *Histoire des Rois/Tantaran' ny Andriana.* 4 vols. Antananarivo: Éditions de la Librairie de Madagascar. [Original published in 1908.]

Cagnat, R.-L.

1941 Tombeaux royaux et *mahabo* du nord-ouest. *Revue de Madagascar* 30:83–90.

Calhoun, C.J.

1980 The Authority of Ancestors: A Sociological Reconsideration of Fortes's Tallensi in Response to Fortes's Critiques. *Man* (n.s.) 15:304–319.

1981 Correspondence. *Man* (n.s.) 16:137–138.

Campbell, Gwyn

1988 Slavery and Fanompoana: The Structure of Forced Labour in Imerina (Madagascar): 1790–1861. *Journal of African History* 29:463–486.

Camy, Lieut.

1905 Au Pays des Sakalava du nord-ouest Madagascar sur le cercle d'Analalava. Manuscript, 174 pp., Bibliothèque Grandidier, Institut de la Recherche Scientifique Malgache, Antananarivo.

Carol, Jean

1898 *Chez les Hova (au pays rouge).* Paris: Pavanne.

Casey, Edward S.

1987 *Remembering: A Phenomenological Study.* Bloomington: Indiana University Press.

Charsley, S.R.

1976 The *Silika:* A Co-operative Labour Institution. *Africa* 46:34–47.

Chazan-Gillig, Suzanne

1983 Le *Fitampoha* de 1968 ou l'efficacité du mythe de la royauté sakalava dans l'actualité politique et économique malgache. In *Les Souverains de Madagascar: L'Histoire royale et ses résurgences contemporaines,* edited by F. Raison-Jourde, pp. 451–476. Paris: Karthala.

Cherrier, R.

1932 *La Législation concernant le travail indigène à Madagascar.* Paris: Édition Domat-Montchretien, F. Leviton.

Chevalier, Louis

1952 *Madagascar: Populations et ressources.* Paris: Presses Universitaires de France.

Cohen, D.W., and E.S. Atieno Odhiambo

1989 *Siaya. The Historical Anthropology of an African Landscape.* London: James Currey.

Cohen, R., J. Copans, and P.C.W. Gutkind

1978   Introduction. In *African Labor History,* edited by P.C.W. Gutkind, R. Cohen, and J. Copans, pp. 7–30. Beverly Hills, Calif.: Sage.

Comaroff, Jean
1985   *Body of Power, Spirit of Resistance: The Culture and History of a South African People.* Chicago: University of Chicago Press.

Condominas, Georges
1961   *Fokon'olona et collectivités rurales en Imerina.* Paris: Berger Levrault.
1968   Introduction à une étude sur l'émigration greque à Madagascar. In *Contributions to Mediterranean Sociology,* pp. 215–234. The Hague: Mouton.

Cooper, Frederick
1977   *Plantation Slavery on the East Coast of Africa.* New Haven, Conn.: Yale University Press.
1980   *From Slaves to Squatters: Plantation Labor and Agriculture in Zanzibar and Coastal Kenya, 1890–1925.* New Haven, Conn.: Yale University Press.

Coser, Lewis A.
1974   *Greedy Institutions: Patterns of Undivided Commitment.* New York: Free Press.

Cosgrove, Denis, and Stephen Daniels (editors)
1988   *The Iconography of Landscape: Essays on the Symbolic Representation, Design and Use of Past Environments.* Cambridge: Cambridge University Press.

Covell, Maureen
1987   *Madagascar: Politics, Economics and Society.* London: Frances Pinter.
n.d.   Linkage or Line of Defense? Patron-Client Relationships in the Malagasy Bureaucracy. Manuscript on file with author [ca. 1978].

Creuse
1955   Naissance d'un prince (ou d'une princesse) sakalava. *Revue de Madagascar* 49:49–52.

Dandouau, André
1908a   La Facilité des moeurs malgaches. *La Revue* (15 February):401–405.
1908b   Le *Fatidra* (serment du sang) (région d'Analalava). *Bulletin de l'Académie Malgache* 6:73–80.
ca. 1911   Rites Funéraires. Manuscript on file, M. and Mme. G. Pain, Antananarivo.
1911   Coutumes funéraires dans le nord-ouest de Madagascar. *Bulletin de l'Académie Malgache* 9:157–172.
1922   *Contes populaires des Sakalava et des Tsimihety de la région d'Analalava.* Algeria: Jules Carbonel.

Debray, M., H. Jacquemin, and R. Razafindrambao
1971   Contribution à l'inventaire des plantes médicinales de Madagascar. Travaux et Documents de l'ORSTOM, 8. Paris: ORSTOM.

Decary, Raymond
1951a   Groupements de travail collectifs. Encyclopédie Mensuelle d'Outre-Mer 13:252–254.
1951b   Moeurs et coutumes des malgaches. Paris: Payot.
1954a   Contribution à l'histoire de la France à Madagascar. Bulletin de l'Académie Malgache (n.s.) 31:49–58.
1954b   La Puissance mystique du nombre 7 chez les malgaches. Revue de Madagascar 21:40–48.
1956   La Notion du travail chez les Malgaches. Encyclopédie Mensuelle d'Outre-mer 71–72:303–305.
1957   L'Habitation chez quelques tribus malgaches. Mémoires de l'Institut scientifique de Madagascar (Série C), 4:1–34.
1958a   Contribution à l'étude de l'habitation à Madagascar. Pau: Marrimpouey Jeune.
1958b   L'habitat à Madagascar. Pau: Marrimpouey Jeune.
1960   L'Île Nosy Bé de Madagascar. Histoire d'une Colonisation. Paris: Éditions Maritimes et d'Outre-Mer.
1962   La Mort et les coutumes funéraires à Madagascar. Paris: G.-P. Maisonneuve et Larose.
1964   Contes et légendes du sud-ouest de Madagascar. Paris: Maisonneuve et Larose.

Decary, Raymond, and Rémy Castel
1941   Modalités et conséquences des migrations intérieures récentes de population à Madagascar. Tananarive: Imprimerie Officielle.

Decraene, Philippe
1964   Madagascar, An VII de la République. Le Monde, May 20–23.

Delelée-Desloges
1931   Madagascar et dépendances. Exposition Coloniale Internationale de Paris, Commissariat Général. Paris: Société d'Éditions Géographiques, Maritimes et Coloniales.

Delivré, Alain
1974   L'Histoire des rois d'Imerina: Interprétation d'une Tradition orale. Paris: Klincksieck.

Demortière
1905–1906   Note au sujet des "Jiny" (reliques royales) des rois du Fiherenana (province de Tuléar). Bulletin de l'Académie Malgache 4:138–139.

Deschamps, Henri

1959   *Les Migrations intérieures à Madagascar.* Paris: Berger-Levrault.

Dez, J.

1956   Le Retournement des morts chez les Betsileo. *Société d'Ethnographie de Paris* 51:115–122.

Donque, Gerald

1972   The Climatology of Madagascar. In *Biogeography and Ecology of Madagascar,* edited by R. Battistini and G. Richard-Vindard, pp. 87–144. The Hague: Dr. W. Junk B.V.

Elias, Norbert

1983   *The Court Society.* Translated by Edmund Jephcott. New York: Pantheon.

Ellis, Stephen

1985   *The Rising of the Red Shawls: A Revolt in Madagascar, 1895–1899.* Cambridge: Cambridge University Press.

Ellis, William

1838   *History of Madagascar.* 2 vols. London: Fisher.

1867   *Madagascar Revisited, Describing the Events of a New Reign, and the Revolution Which Followed.* London: John Murray.

Esoavelomandroso, Faranirana V.

1975   Les Sadiavahe: Essai d'Interprétation d'une révolte dans le Sud (1915–1917). *Omaly sy Anio* 1–2:139–171.

1976   Langue, culture et colonisation à Madagascar: Malgache et français dans l'enseignement officiel (1916–1940). *Omaly sy Anio* 3–4:105–165.

Estrade, J.-M.

1977   *Un Culte de possession à Madagascar: Le Tromba.* Paris: Éditions Anthropos.

Evans-Pritchard, E.E.

1940   *The Nuer: A Description of the Modes of Livelihood and Political Institutions of a Nilotic People.* Oxford: Clarendon.

Faber, Harold

1990   New York's Historical Trees Honored with New Registry. *New York Times,* August 6, p. B2.

Fanony, Fulgence, and Noël J. Gueunier

1980   Le Mouvement de conversion à l'Islam et le rôle des confréries musulmanes dans le nord de Madagascar. *Asie du Sud-Est et Monde Insulindien* 11:151–168.

Faroux, Emmanuel

1980   Les Rapports de production sakalava et leur évolution sous l'influence coloniale (région de Morondava). In *Changements sociaux dans l'ouest malgache,* edited by G. Sautter et al., pp. 81–107. Collection Mémoires, 90. Paris: ORSTOM.

Feeley-Harnik, Gillian

1978   Divine Kingship and the Meaning of History among the Sakalava (Madagascar). *Man* (n.s.) 13:402–417.

1980   The Sakalava House. *Anthropos* 75:559–585.

1982   The King's Men in Madagascar: Slavery, Citizenship, and Sakalava Monarchy. *Africa* 52:31–50.

1985   Issues in Divine Kingship. *Annual Review of Anthropology* 14:273–313.

1988   Dancing Battles: Representations of Conflict in Sakalava Royal Service. *Anthropos* 83:65–85.

1989   Cloth and the Creation of Ancestors in Madagascar. In *Cloth and Human Experience,* edited by J. Schneider and A.B. Weiner. Washington, D.C.: Smithsonian Institution Press.

Fernandez, James W.

1979   On the Notion of Religious Movement. *Social Research* 46:36–62.

1982   *Bwiti: An Ethnography of the Religious Imagination in Africa.* Princeton, N.J.: Princeton University Press.

Ferrand, Gabriel

1891, 1893, 1902   *Les Musulmans à Madagascar et aux îles Comores.* 3 vols. Paris: E. Leroux.

1908   Note sur le calendrier malgache et le *fandruana.* (Extract of 33 pages from the *Revue des Études ethnographiques et sociologiques,* April–May, 1908.) Paris: Librarie Paul Geuthner.

Filliot, J.M.

1974   *La Traite des esclaves vers les Mascareignes au XVIIIe siècle.* Mémoires, 72. Paris: ORSTOM.

Fischer, David Hackett

1976   The Braided Narrative: Substance and Form in Social History. In *The Literature of Fact,* edited by Angus Fletcher, pp. 109–133. New York: Columbia University Press.

Forster, E.M.

1921   *Howard's End.* New York: Knopf.

Fortes, Meyer

1961   Piètas in Ancestor Worship. *Journal of the Royal Anthropological Institute* 91:166–191.

1965   Some Reflections on Ancestor Worship in Africa. In *African Systems of Thought,* edited by M. Fortes and G. Dieterlen, pp. 122–144. Oxford: Oxford University Press for the International African Institute.

1976 An Introductory Commentary. In *Ancestors,* edited by William H. Newell, pp. 1–16. The Hague: Mouton.

1981 Correspondence. *Man* (n.s.) 16:300–302.

Fox, James J.

1971 Sister's Child as Plant: Metaphors in an Idiom of Consanguinity. In *Rethinking Kinship and Marriage,* edited by R. Needham, pp. 219–252. London: Tavistock.

1979 'Standing' in Time and Place: The Structure of Rotinese Historical Narratives. In *Perceptions of the Past in Southeast Asia,* edited by A. Reid and D. Marr, pp. 10–25. Singapore: Heinemann Educational Books.

Foucault, Michel

1979 *Discipline and Punish: The Birth of the Prison.* New York: Vintage.

Frank, Joseph

1945 Spatial Form in Modern Literature: An Essay in Three Parts. *Swanee Review* 53:221–240, 433–456, 643–653.

François, Edmond

1937 Plantes de Madagascar. *Mémoires de l'Académie Malgache* 24:1–75.

Frazer, James G.

1911–1915 *The Golden Bough.* London: Macmillan.

Fremigacci, Jean

1975 Mise en valeur coloniale et travail forcé: La Construction du chemin de fer Tananarive-Antsirabe (1911–1923). *Omaly sy Anio* 1–2:75–137.

Galliéni, J.S.

1908 *Neuf ans à Madagascar.* Paris: Hachette.

Gardenier, William J.G.

1976 *Witchcraft and Sorcery in a Pastoral Society: The Central Sakalava of West Madagascar.* Ann Arbor, Mich.: University Microfilms International.

Gevrey, A.

1972 *Essai sur les Comores.* Reproduction de l'édition de 1870 Pondichéry: Saligny. Travaux et Documents, X. Antananarivo: Musée d'Art et d'Archéologie de l'Université de Madagascar.

Gibson, Thomas

1986 *Sacrifice and Sharing in the Philippine Highlands: Religion and Society among the Buid of Mindoro.* London: Athlone.

Giesey, R.E.

1960 *The Royal Funeral Ceremony in Renaissance France.* Geneva: E. Droz.

1985 Models of Rulership in French Royal Ceremonial. In *Rites of Power: Symbolism, Ritual, and Politics since the Middle Ages,* edited by S. Wilentz, pp. 41–64. Philadelphia: University of Pennsylvania Press.

Glazier, Jack
1984   Mbeere Ancestors and the Domestication of Death. *Man* (n.s.) 19:133–148.

Gouvernement Générale de Madagascar
1899   *Rapport d'ensemble sur la pacification, l'organisation et la colonisation de Madagascar (octobre 1896 à mars 1899).* 13 March 1899. Tananarive: Imprimerie Officielle.

Gow, Bonar A.
1979   *Madagascar and the Protestant Impact: The Work of the British Missions, 1818–95.* New York: Africana.

Grandidier, A., and G. Grandidier (editors)
1903–1920   *Collection des ouvrages anciens concernant Madagascar.* 9 vols. Paris: Comité de Madagascar.

Green, Nicholas
1990   *The Spectacle of Nature: Landscape and Bourgeois Culture in Nineteenth-Century France.* Manchester: Manchester University Press.

Guédès, L'Administrateur-adjoint
1898   Les Tournées exécutées récemment par M. Guédès dans le secteur d'Antonibé et dans la région d'Antsohihy. . . . *Journal officiel de Madagascar* 298:2384–2386.

Gueunier, Noël J.
1977   *Les Monuments funéraires et commémoratifs de bois sculpté betsileo.* Série Recherche no. 1. Toliara: Publications du Centre Universitaire Régional.

Guillain, Charles
1845   *Documents sur l'histoire, la géographie, et le commerce de la partie occidentale de Madagascar.* Paris: Imprimerie Royale.

Guyer, Jane
1980   Head Tax, Social Structure and Rural Incomes in Cameroun, 1922–1937. *Cahiers d'études Africaines 20:305–329.*
1984   Naturalism in African Models of Production. *Man* (n.s.) 19:371–388.

Haeringer, Philippe
1980   L'Arbre dans la ville. Lecture sociale en quatre tableaux du couvert végétal dans la ville africaine. In *L'Arbre en Afrique tropicale: La Fonction et le signe,* edited by Paul Pélissier et al., pp. 289–308. Cahiers ORSTOM, Série Sciences Humaines, XVII (3/4).

Hallam, Elizabeth M.
1982   Royal Burial and the Cult of Kingship in France and England, 1060–1330. *Journal of Medieval History* 8:359–380.

Hanley, Sarah

1983   *The Lit de Justice of the Kings of France: Constitutional Ideology in Legend, Ritual, and Discourse.* Princeton, N.J.: Princeton University Press.

1989   Engendering the State: Family Formation and State Building in Early Modern France. *French Historical Studies* 16:4–27.

Harding, Susan

1987   'Convicted by the Holy Spirit': The Rhetoric of Fundamental Baptist Conversion. *American Ethnologist* 14:167–181.

Hardyman, J. Trenchard

1938   Madagascar and the Man-Eating Tree. *Notes and Queries* (9 April):264.

Harvey, David

1985   *Consciousness and the Urban Experience: Studies in the History and Theory of Capitalist Urbanization.* Baltimore: Johns Hopkins University Press.

Hastie, James

1918–1919   Journal de M. Hastie d'après son manuscrit conservé aux archives coloniales de Maurice. Partie I (du 14 Nov. 1817 au 26 Mai 1818), Partie II (du 26 Mai 1824 au 2 Nov. 1824) [edited by Jean Valette]. *Bulletin de l'Académie Malgache* (n.s.) 4:147–197.

1968   Le 'Journal' d'Hastie du 14 Novembre 1824 au 7 Mai 1825 [edited by Jean Valette]. *Bulletin de l'Académie Malgache* (n.s.) 46:111–122.

Hayden, Dolores

1976   *Seven American Utopias: The Architecture of Communitarian Socialism, 1790–1975.* Cambridge: M.I.T. Press.

Heseltine, Nigel

1971   *Madagascar.* New York: Praeger.

Hocart, Arthur M.

1927   *Kingship.* Oxford: Oxford University Press.

1937   Kinship Systems. *Anthropos* 32:345–351.

1970   *Kings and Councillors: An Essay in the Comparative Anatomy of Human Society,* edited with an introduction by R. Needham. Chicago: Chicago University Press.

Horton, Robin

1971   Stateless Societies in the History of West Africa. In *History of West Africa,* vol. 1, edited by J.F.A. Ajayi, M. Crowder, pp. 78–119. London: Longman.

Huntington, W.R.

1973   Death and the Social Order: Bara Funeral Customs (Madagascar). *African Studies* 32:65–84.

1978   Bara Endogamy and Incest Prohibition. *Bijdragen tot de Taal-, Land-, en Volkenkunde* 134:30–62.
1988   *Gender and Social Structure in Madagascar.* Bloomington: Indiana University Press.
Hurvitz, David Jay
1980   *A Record of Anjoaty History in Vohemar, Madagascar.* Ann Arbor, Mich.: University Microfilms International.
Isnard, Hildebert
1950   La Vie rurale à Madagascar. *Les Cahiers d'Outre-mer* 12:301–318.
1964   *Madagascar.* Paris: A. Colin.
Jacquier, L.
1904   La Main-d'oeuvre locale à Madagascar. Paris: Henri Jouve.
Johnstone, Frederick
1976   *Class, Race, and Gold: A Study of Class Relations and Racial Discrimination in South Africa.* London: Routledge and Kegan Paul.
Jully, André
1898   L'Habitation à Madagascar. *Notes, Reconnaissance et Explorations* 4:899–910.
1907   La Politique des races à Madagascar. *Revue de Madagascar* 9:3–17.
Kantorowicz, Ernst H.
1957   *The King's Two Bodies: A Study in Medieval Political Theology.* Princeton, N.J.: Princeton University Press.
Karp, Ivan
1987   Beer Drinking and Social Experience in an African Society: An Essay in Formal Sociology. In *Explorations in African Systems of Thought,* edited by I. Karp and C.S. Bird, pp. 83–119. [Reprint with new preface by I. Karp.] Washington, D.C.: Smithsonian Institution Press.
Keenan, Elinor
1974   Norm-Makers, Norm-Breakers: Uses of Speech by Men and Women in a Malagasy Community. In *Explorations in the Ethnography of Speaking,* edited by R. Bauman and J. Sherzer, pp. 125–143. Cambridge: Cambridge University Press.
Kent, Raymond K.
1970   *Early Kingdoms in Madagascar, 1500–1700.* New York: Holt, Rinehart and Winston.
Kipp, Rita Smith
1986   Terms of Endearment: Karo Batak Lovers as Siblings. *American Ethnologist* 13:632–645.
Kloosterboer, Wilhelmina
1960   *Involuntary Labour since the Abolition of Slavery: A Survey of Compulsory Labour Throughout the World.* Leiden: E.J. Brill.

Knapp, Bettina L.
1985   *Archetype, Architecture, and the Writer.* Bloomington: Indiana University Press.

Koechlin, Jean
1972   Flora and Vegetation of Madagascar. In *Biogeography and Ecology in Madagascar,* edited by R. Battistini and G. Richard-Vindard, pp. 149–190. The Hague: Dr. W. Junk B.V.

Kopytoff, Igor
1971   Ancestors as Elders in Africa. *Africa* 41:129–142.
1981   Correspondence. *Man* (n.s.) 16:135–137.

Kottak, Conrad P.
1980   *The Past in the Present: History, Ecology and Cultural Variation in Highland Madagascar.* Ann Arbor: University of Michigan Press.
1986   Kinship Modeling: Adaptation, Fosterage, and Fictive Kinship among the Betsileo. In *Madagascar: Society and History,* edited by C.P. Kottak, J.-A. Rakotoarisoa, A. Southall, and P. Vérin, pp. 277–298. Durham, N.C.: Carolina Academic Press.

Krapf, Ludwig
1964   *A Dictionary of the Swahili Language.* Ridgewood, N.Y.: Gregg Press. [Original published in 1882.]

Kuechler, Susanne
1987   *Malangan:* Art and Memory in a Melanesian Society. *Man* (n.s.) 22:238–255.

Kuipers, Joel C.
1984   Place, Names, and Authority in Weyéwa Ritual Speech. *Language and Society* 13:455–466.

Lambek, Michael
1981   *Human Spirits: A Cultural Account of Trance in Mayotte.* Cambridge: Cambridge University Press.

Lan, David
1985   *Guns and Rain: Guerrillas and Spirit Mediums in Zimbabwe.* Berkeley: University of California Press.

Last, J.T.
1895   Notes on Western Madagascar and the Antinosi Country. *The Geographical Journal* 3:227–252.

Launois, P.
1938   Enquête no. 2 sur l'habitation des indigènes: L'Habitation sakalava. Unpaged typescript bound with other documents from 1938.

Lemolle, Le Chef de bataillon
1899   Rapport sur les opérations auxquelles a donné lieu le mouvement

insurrectionnel du nord-ouest. *Journal officiel de Madagascar* 393:3272–
3274; 395:3284–3287.

Lestringant, Frank

1982 Rabelais et le récit toponymique. *Poétique* 50:207–225.

Levelt, Willem J.M.

1990 *Speaking: From Intention to Articulation.* Cambridge, Mass.: M.I.T.
Press.

Lévi-Strauss, Claude

1961 *Tristes Tropiques.* New York: Atheneum.

Lombard, Jacques

1973a *La Royauté sakalava. Formation, développement et effondrement du
XVIIe au XXe siècle. Essai d'analyse d'un système politique.* Tananarive:
ORSTOM.

1973b Les Sakalava-Menabe de la côte Ouest—La société et l'art
funéraire. In *Malgache qui es-tu?* pp. 89–99. Neuchâtel: Musée
d'Ethnographie de Neuchâtel.

1976 Le Royaume Sakalava-Menabe: Résultat d'une enquête et
présentation d'un corpus de traditions et de littérature orales. *Cahiers
ORSTOM,* série Sciences humaines, 13:173–202.

Macdonald, Ronald R.

1987 *The Burial-Places of Memory: Epic Underworlds in Vergil, Dante, and
Milton.* Amherst: University of Massachusetts Press.

Mack, John

1986 *Madagascar: Island of the Ancestors.* London: British Museum
Publications.

Malinowski, Bronislaw

1961 *Argonauts of the Western Pacific.* New York: Dutton.

Mantaux, Christian G.

1969 Note sur Anorotsangana: Fort Merina en pays sakalava. *Bulletin de
l'Académie Malgache* 47:147–155.

Marks, Shula, and Richard Rathbone (editors)

1982 *Industrialization and Social Change in South Africa: African Class
Formation, Culture and Consciousness, 1870–1930.* London: Longman.

Marshall, Mac

1981 Introduction: Approaches to Siblingship in Oceania. In *Siblingship
in Oceania: Studies in the Meaning of Kin Relations,* edited by M.
Marshall, pp. 1–15. Ann Arbor: University of Michigan Press.

Mayer, Adrian C.

1985 The King's Two Thrones. *Man* (n.s.) 20:205–221.

McCrate, Elaine

1989 Discrimination, Returns to Education and Teenage Childbearing.

Paper presented at Middlebury College Conference on Discrimination Policies and Research in the Post-Reagan Era, April 6–8, 1989.

McMahon, E.O.

   1892   The Sakalava and Their Customs. *Antananarivo Annual* 16:385–393.

Mellis, J.V.

   1938   *Nord et nord-ouest de Madagascar. Volamena et volafotsy, suivi d'un vocabulaire du nord-ouest expliqué, commenté et comparé au Merina.* Tananarive: Imprimerie moderne de l'Emyrne.

Mettam, Roger

   1989   *Power and Faction in Louis XIV's France.* Oxford: Blackwell.

Middleton, Karen

   1990   *Marriages and Funerals: Some Aspects of Karembola Political Symbolism (South Madagascar).* Oxford: Oxford University Press.

Mintz, Sidney W.

   1977   The So-called World System: Local Initiative and Local Response. *Dialectical Anthropology* 2:253–270.

   1978   Was the Plantation Slave a Proletarian? *Review* 2:81–98.

Molet, Louis

   1956   *Le Bain royal à Madagascar. Explication de la fête malgache du fandroana par la coutumes disparue de la manducation des morts.* Tananarive: Imprimerie Luthérienne.

   1959   L'Expansion Tsimihety. *Mémoires de l'IRSM,* série C, t.5, pp.1–196.

Ndremahefa, Claude, and Gillian Feeley-Harnik

   1975   Fomba sy Tataran-drazan' ny Ampanjaka Bemazava (Maromandia). Typescript, 325 pp., in authors' possession.

Needham, Rodney

   1978   *Primordial Characters.* Charlottesville: University Press of Virginia.

Neville, Gwen Kennedy

   1987   *Kinship and Pilgrimage: Rituals of Reunion in American Protestant Culture.* New York: Oxford University Press.

Nérine-Botokeky, E.

   1983   Le *Fitampoha* en royaume de Menabe. In *Les Souverains de Madagascar: L'Histoire royale et ses résurgences contemporaines,* edited by F. Raison-Jourde, pp. 211–220. Paris: Karthala.

Noël, Vincent

   1843–1844   Recherches sur les Sakalava. *Bulletin de la Société géographique,* série 2 [1843], 19:275–95; 20:40–64, 285–306; série 3 [1844], 1:385–416.

Nye, Robert A.
1984 *Crime, Madness and Politics in Modern France: The Medical Concept of National Decline.* Princeton, N.J.: Princeton University Press.

O'Brien, Patricia
1982 *The Promise of Punishment: Prisons in Nineteenth-Century France.* Princeton, N.J.: Princeton University Press.

Ottino, Paul
1964 La Crise du système familial et matrimonial des Sakalava de Nosy-Be. *Civilisation malgache* 1:225–248.

Ozouf, Mona
1988 *Festivals and the French Revolution.* Translated by Alan Sheridan. Cambridge: Harvard University Press.

Pavageau, Jean
1981 *Jeunes paysans sans terres: l'exemple malgache. Une communauté villageoise en période révolutionnaire.* Paris: L'Harmattan.

Poirier, Charles
1939a Les *"Dady," "Fibaby"* ou *"Ampagnito Be"* des anciens rois sakalava du Menabé septentrional. *Mémoires de l'Académie malgache* 28:13–18.
1939b Le *"Zomba"* d'Ambararatakely. Le *"Dady"* de la mpanjaka sakalava Vololona. *Mémoires de l'Académie malgache* 28:31–34.
1939c Notes d'ethnographie et d'histoire malgaches: Les Royaumes Sakalava Bemihisatra de la côte nord-ouest de Madagascar. *Mémoires de l'Académie Malgache* 28:41–104.
1939d Les Mahabo de Nosy Be et de Nosy Komba. *Mémoires de l'Académie Malgache* 28:105–114.

Pollan, Michael
1990 Putting Down Roots. *The New York Times Magazine,* May 6, pp. 38–40, 44, 82.

Rabedimy, Jean-François
1979 Essai sur l'idéologie de la mort à Madagascar. In *Les Hommes et la mort: Rituels funéraires à travers le monde,* edited by Jean Guiart, pp. 171–179. Paris: le Sycomore-Objets et Mondes.
1983 Contribution de l'*ombiasa* à la formation du royaume Menabe: Le Toñy. In *Les Souverains de Madagascar: L'Histoire royale et ses résurgences contemporaines,* edited by F. Raison-Jourde, pp. 177–192. Paris: Karthala.

Rabedimy, Jean-François, and Ramanankevitra
1987 Tromba chez les Masikoro. Paper presented at a colloqium sur "Représentations du monde dans la société malgache," 7–11 December.

Raharijaona, Suzanne, and Jean Valette
1959   Les Grandes fêtes rituelles des Sakalava du Menabé ou 'Fitampoha.' *Bulletin de Madagascar* 155:1–33, annexes.

Raison-Jourde, Françoise
1984   Le Travail et l'échange dans les discours d'Andrianampoinimerina (Madagascar-XVIIIe siècle). In *Le Travail et ses représentations,* edited by Michel Cartier, pp. 223–273. Paris: Éditions des Archives Contemporaines.

Raison-Jourde, Françoise (editor)
1983   *Les Souverains de Madagascar: L'Histoire royale et ses résurgences contemporaines.* Paris: Karthala.

Rajaonarimanana, Narivelo
1979   Achèvement des funérailles et offrande de linceuls: Rites funéraires et commémoratifs des Betsileo du Manandriana. In *Les Hommes et la mort: Rituels funéraires à travers le monde,* edited by Jean Guiart, pp. 171–179. Paris: le Sycomore—Objets et Mondes.
1986   Quelques traits de l'organisation sociale des Betsileo du Manandriana. In *Madagascar: Society and History,* edited by C.P. Kottak, J.-A. Rakotoarisoa, A. Southall, and P. Vérin, pp. 245–262. Durham, N.C.: Carolina Academic Press.

Rakoto, Alexis
1947–1948   Le Culte d'Andriamosara. *Bulletin de l'Académie malgache* (n.s.) 28:108–114.

Randrianja, Solofo
1983   *Le Parti communiste de la région de Madagascar (1936–1939). Genèse, développement, caractéritiques et décomposition.* Thèse de troisième cycle, Université de Paris VII.

Rasoamiaramanana, Micheline
1983–1984   Pouvoir merina et esclavage dans le Boina dans la second moitié du XIX siècle (1862–1883). *Omaly sy Anio* 17–20:323–335.

Renel, Charles
1920–1921   Ancêtres et dieux. *Bulletin de l'Académie malgache* (n.s.) 5:1–261.

Rey, H.
1913   Le Folk-lore menabé (April–May 1912). *Bulletin de l'Académie malgache* 12:50–74.

Richards, Audrey I.
1941   A Problem of Anthropological Approach. *Bantu Studies* 15:45–52.
1961   *Land, Labour and Diet in Northern Rhodesia: An Economic Study of*

the Bemba Tribe. 2nd edition. London: Oxford University Press for the International African Institute.

Richardson, J.
1885   *A New Malagasy-English Dictionary.* Antananarivo: The London Missionary Society.

R-N-J-S
1872   Razan' Andrian' ny Sakalava. *Teny Soa* (September):45–50.

Rose, Willie Lee
1977   The Domestication of Domestic Slavery. In *Slavery and Freedom,* edited by W.W. Freehling, pp. 18–36. Oxford: Oxford University Press.

Sabatier, F.
1903   *Le Problème de la main-d'oeuvre à Madagascar depuis la supression de l'èsclavage.* Toulon: Librairie Maritime.

Salmond, Anne
1982   Theoretical Landscapes: On Cross-Cultural Conceptions of Knowledge. In *Semantic Anthropology,* edited by D. Parkin, pp. 65–87. London: Academic Press.

Şaul, Mahir
1983   Work Parties, Wages and Accumulation in a Voltaic Village. *American Ethnologist* 10:77–96.

Schabecoff, Philip
1989 Where the Planet Is Loosing Its Life Forms. *New York Times,* July 30, p. E3.

Schneider, David M.
1981   Conclusions. In *Siblingship in Oceania: Studies in the Meaning of Kin Relations,* edited by M. Marshall, pp. 389–404. Ann Arbor: University of Michigan Press.

Schomerus-Gernböck, Lotte
1981   *Die Mahafaly: Eine Ethnische Gruppe im Süd-Westen Madagaskars.* Berlin: Dietrich Reimer.

Serre-Ratsimandisa, G.
1978   Théorie et pratique de *"Fokonolona"* moderne à Madagascar. *Canadian Journal of African Studies* 12:37–58.

Shakespeare, William
1964   *The Tragedy of Richard the Third,* edited by Mark Eccles. New York and London: New American Library and New English Library, Ltd.

Sibree, James
1897   The Malagasy Custom of 'Brotherhood by Blood.' *Antananarivo Annual* 21:1–6.

Simmel, Georg
1965   The Ruin [1911]. In *Essays on Sociology, Philosophy and Aesthetics by George Simmel et al.*, edited by Kurt H. Wolff, pp. 259–266. New York: Harper and Row.
Smith, George Herbert
1896   *Among the Menabe; or, Thirteen Months on the West Coast of Madagascar.* London: Society for Promoting Christian Knowledge.
Smith, Neil
1984   *Uneven Development: Nature, Capital and the Production of Space.* Oxford: Blackwell.
Southall, Aidan
1986   Common Themes in Malagasy Culture. In *Madagascar: Society and History*, edited by. C.P. Kottak, J.-A. Rakotoarisoa, A.Southall, and P. Vérin, pp. 411–438. Durham, N.C.: Carolina Academic Press.
Southall, Aidan (subeditor)
1971   Kinship, Descent, and Residence in Madagascar. *American Anthropologist* 73:144–208.
Stack, Carol B.
1974   *All Our Kin: Strategies for Survival in a Black Community.* New York: Harper.
Stevens, Wallace
1982   *The Collected Poems of Wallace Stevens.* New York: Vintage.
Stoler, Ann L.
1989   Making Empire Respectable: The Politics of Race and Sexual Morality in Twentieth-Century Colonial Cultures. *American Ethnologist* 16:634–660.
Sykes, Gresham M.
1958   *The Society of Captives: A Study of a Maximum Security Prison.* Princeton, N.J.: Princeton University Press.
Tambiah, Stanley J.
1989   Ethnic Conflict in the World Today. *American Ethnologist* 16:335–349.
Thomas, Keith
1983   *Man and the Natural World: A History of the Modern Sensibility.* New York: Pantheon.
Thomas-Fattier, Dominique
1982   *Le Dialecte sakalava du nord-ouest de Madagascar: phonologie—grammaire—lexique.* Langues, Cultures et Sociétés de l'Océan Indien (CeDRASEMI), no. 10. Paris: Selaf.
Thomassin, Lieut.
1900   Notes sur le royaume de Mahabo. *Notes, Reconnaissances, et Explorations* 6:395–413.

Thompson, Edward P.

1967   Time, Work-Discipline and Industrial Capitalism. *Past and Present* 38:56–97.

Thompson, Virginia, and Richard Adloff

1965   *The Malagasy Republic: Madagascar Today*. Stanford, Calif.: University Press.

Toquenne, Capitaine

1897a   Territoires civils: Province d'Analalava. *Journal officiel de Madagascar* (25 September):971–973; (28 September):979–980.

1897b   Territoires civils: Analalava. *Journal officiel de Madagascar* (25 November):1121–1122.

Tronchon, Jacques

1974   *L'Insurrection malgache de 1947: essai d'interprétation historique*. Paris: Maspero.

Tsien Tche-Hao

1961   La vie sociale des Chinois à Madagascar. *Comparative Studies in Society and History* 3:170–181.

Turner, Victor

1967   *The Forest of Symbols: Aspects of Ndembu Ritual*. Ithaca, N.Y.: Cornell University Press.

van Onselen, Charles

1976   *Chibaro: African Mine Labour in Southern Rhodesia, 1900–1933*. London: Pluto.

1982   *Studies in the Social and Economic History of the Witwatersrand, 1886–1914*. vol. 1. *New Babylon;* vol. 2. *New Nineveh*. London: Longman.

Vérin, Pierre

1972   Histoire ancienne du nord-ouest de Madagascar. *Taloha* 5:1–174.

1986   *The History of Civilization in North Madagascar*. Rotterdam: Balkema.

Vinogradov, Amal

1974   French Colonialism as Reflected in the Male-Female Interaction in Morocco. *Transactions of the New York Academy of Sciences* 36 (Series II, no. 2):192–199.

Waast, Roland

1980   Les Concubins de Soalala. In *Changements sociaux dans l'ouest malgache,* edited by G. Sautter et al., pp. 153–188. Collection Mémoires, 90. Paris: ORSTOM.

Weiner, Annette B.

1980   Reproduction: A Replacement for Reciprocity. *American Ethnologist* 7:71–85.

White, Luise

1987   Prostitution, Differentiation and the World Economy: Nairobi 1899–1939. In *Connecting Spheres: Women in the Western World, 1500 to the Present,* edited by M.J. Boxer and J.H. Quataert, pp. 223–231. New York: Oxford University Press.

Wilson, Peter

1967   Tsimihety Kinship and Descent. *Africa* 35:133–154.

Wolf, Eric R.

1982   *Europe and the People Without History.* Berkeley: University of California Press.

Wood, Geoffrey

1982   Frazer's Magic Wand of Anthropology: Interpreting "The Golden Bough." *Archives Européennes de Sociologie* 23:73–91.

Wylie, Lawrence

1974   *Village in the Vaucluse.* 3rd edition. New York: Harper and Row.

Yates, Frances A.

1966   *The Art of Memory.* London: Routledge and Kegan Paul.

Yates, JoAnne

1989   *Control Through Communication: The Rise of System in American Management.* Baltimore: Johns Hopkins University Press.

You, A., and G. Gayet

1931   *Madagascar: Colonie française, 1896–1930.* Paris: Société d'Éditions Géographiques, Maritimes, et Coloniales.

Index